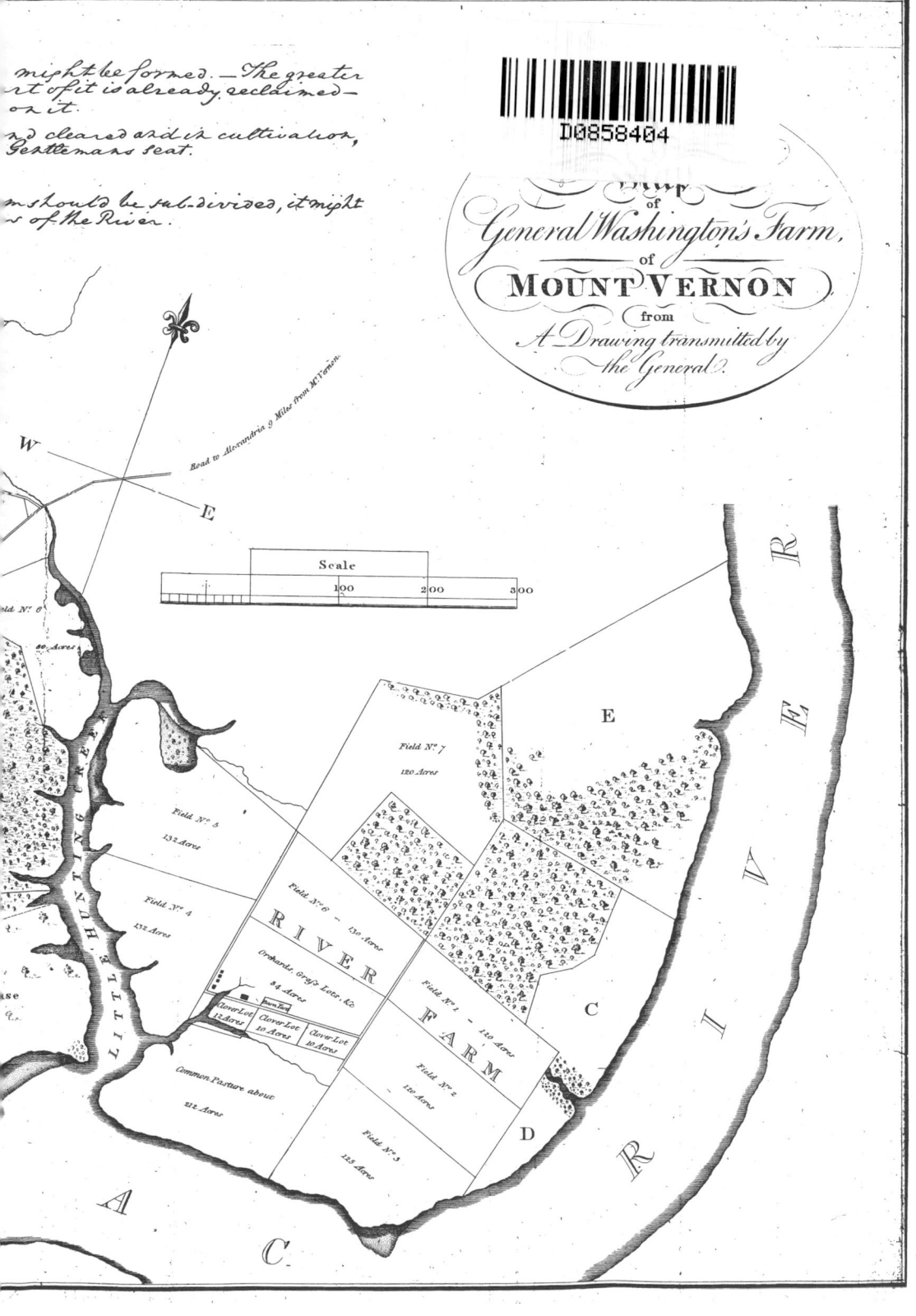

might be formed. — The greater
rt of it is already reclaimed —
on it.

nd cleared and in cultivation,
Gentlemans seat.

m should be sub-divided, it might
s of the River.

MAP
of
General Washington's Farm,
of
MOUNT VERNON
from
A Drawing transmitted by
the General.

W

E

Road to Alexandria 9 Miles from McVernon.

Scale

100   200   300

Field Nº 6
80 Acres

E

Field Nº 7
120 Acres

Field Nº 5
132 Acres

Field Nº 4
132 Acres

Field Nº 6 — 130 Acres

R I V E R

C

Orchards, Grass Lots. &c.
84 Acres

Field Nº 1 — 120 Acres

Clover Lot
12 Acres

Clover Lot
10 Acres

Clover Lot
10 Acres

Field Nº 2
120 Acres

D

Common Pasture about
212 Acres

Field Nº 3
122 Acres

R I V E R

A

C.

LITTLE HUNTING CREEK

R I V E R F A R M

The Papers of
George Washington

Frontispiece: Portrait of George Washington by Edward Savage, 1793. (National Portrait Gallery, Smithsonian Institution.)

The Papers of
George Washington

Theodore J. Crackel, *Editor in Chief*

Philander D. Chase, *Senior Editor*

David R. Hoth, Edward G. Lengel, Christine Sternberg Patrick,
and Beverly H. Runge

Associate Editors

William M. Ferraro and Jennifer E. Stertzer
Assistant Editors

Presidential Series

15

1 January–30 April 1794

Christine Sternberg Patrick, *Editor*

UNIVERSITY OF VIRGINIA PRESS

CHARLOTTESVILLE AND LONDON

This edition has been prepared by the staff of
The Papers of George Washington sponsored by The Mount Vernon Ladies'
Association of the Union and the University of Virginia with the support of
the National Endowment for the Humanities and the National Historical
Publications and Records Commission.

The preparation of this volume has been made possible by
gifts from the Elis Olsson Memorial Foundation of West Point, Va.,
Stephen and Ann West of Bernardsville, N.J., and
Philip G. and Michelle LeDuc of Seattle, Wash.

The publication of this volume has been supported by a grant from the
National Historical Publications and Records Commission.

UNIVERSITY OF VIRGINIA PRESS
© 2009 by the Rector and Visitors of the University of Virginia
All rights reserved

First published 2009

The paper used in this publication meets the minimum requirements of
ANSI/NISO Z39.48–1992 (R 1997) (Permanence of Paper).

Library of Congress Cataloging-in-Publication Data
Washington, George, 1732–1799.
    The papers of George Washington, Theodore J. Crackel, ed.
    Presidential series vol. 15 edited by Christine Sternberg
Patrick.
    Includes bibliographical references and indexes.
    Contents: v. 1. September 1788–March 1789—
[etc.]—v. 15. 1 January 1794–30 April 1794
        1. United States—Politics and government—1789–1797.
2. Washington, George, 1732–1799—Correspondence.
3. Presidents—United States—Correspondence. I. Crackel,
Theodore J.; Patrick, Christine Sternberg II. Presidential
series. III. Title.
E312.72 1987b 973.4'1'092 87-410017
ISBN 0-8139-1103-6 (v. 1)
ISBN 978-0-8139-2846-3 (v. 15)

Front endpapers: "A map of General Washington's farm of Mount Vernon from a drawing transmitted by the General," in *Letters from His Excellency General Washington, to Arthur Young, Esq., F.R.S., containing An Account of His Husbandry, with a Map of His Farm; His Opinions on Various Questions in Agriculture; and Many Particulars of the Rural Economy of the United States* (London, 1801). [This illustration was based on a sketch enclosed in GW to Young, 12 Dec. 1793.] Library of Congress, Geography and Map Division.

Back endpapers: [L'Enfant] Plan of the City of Washington in the Territory of Columbia . . . [as drawn by Andrew Ellicott and engraved by Samuel Hill of Boston in 1792]. Library of Congress, Geography and Map Division.

Administrative Board

John T. Casteen III   Boyce Lineberger Ansley
                    Penelope Kaiserlian

Editorial Board

Stuart W. Bruchey   Jean B. Lee
Emory G. Evans   Peter S. Onuf
Jack P. Greene   Jacob M. Price
Peter R. Henriques   Bruce A. Ragsdale
Warren R. Hofstra   James C. Rees
Richard H. Kohn   Norman K. Risjord
                    Thad W. Tate

Editorial Staff

Erik B. Alexander   Stephanye A. Hunter
Philander D. Chase   Jeffrey Katra
Ronda Chollock   Edward G. Lengel
Theodore J. Crackel   Alexis D. Luckey
Caitlin M. Dallas   Kelly McConnell
Stacy Diggs-Allen   Erica Mitchell
Thomas E. Dulan   Sean Nalty
Jason Farr   Christine Sternberg Patrick
William M. Ferraro   C. Rebecca Rine
Pamela J. Grizzard   Beverly H. Runge
Gabriel Haley   Dana J. Stefanelli
Lawrence Hatter   Jennifer E. Stertzer
David R. Hoth   R. S. Taylor Stoermer
                    Samuel A. Turner

Cartographer

Rick Britton

Contents

NOTE: Volume numbers refer to the *Presidential Series*.

Contents

Illustrations

Maps

Introduction

In the period covered in this volume, 1 Jan. through 30 April 1794, Washington continued to focus his efforts as president on preventing the United States from becoming entangled in the continuing war between France and Great Britain. Of particular concern was French and British interference with American shipping, despite U.S. claims of neutral rights. In an attempt to address this problem temporarily, Congress declared a thirty-day embargo on all ships and vessels in American ports. Washington and members of his cabinet quickly set out to enforce this resolution (Cabinet Opinion on Enforcing the Embargo, 26 March).

The administration also continued its efforts to implement the rules and regulations established by a series of earlier decisions regarding the presence of foreign privateers and their prizes in American ports, including those set forth in the two cabinet opinions reached on 3 Aug. 1793 (*Presidential Series,* 13). Particularly troublesome was the case of the *Aimée Marguerite,* a former British sloop seized by the French and converted to a privateer, and the ownership of a chest containing gold and silver taken by this privateer from a Spanish brig. The privateer and the stolen money were subsequently seized and held at Wilmington, N.C., while a resolution was reached (Richard Dobbs Spaight's first two letters to GW of 8 Feb.).

The threat of U.S. involvement in the European war led Congress to pass legislation designed to increase the military strength of the United States. As a result, Washington and Secretary of War Henry Knox directed the construction of coastal fortifications, the creation of an American navy, and the establishment of federal arsenals and magazines (Henry Knox to GW, 10 April). The war also produced an exodus of refugees to the United States from the French colony of Saint Domingue and a subsequent federal program of monetary relief, which the administration oversaw (Edmund Randolph's first letter to GW of 27 Feb.).

Problems in the diplomatic sphere persisted during this time period. Although the United States already had requested the recall of Edmond Genet, the French minister plenipotentiary, in August 1793 (Cabinet Opinion on the Recall of Edmond Genet, 23 Aug., *Presidential Series,* 13), Washington debated whether Genet's current activities warranted an immediate revocation of his diplomatic privileges (Alexander Hamilton's Proposed Presidential Message to Congress, 6–13 January). News of Genet's recall by the French government, however, made this move unnecessary, and in late February, Washington officially received credentials from Genet's replacement, Jean-Antoine-Joseph Fauchet (Randolph to GW, 22 Feb.). French complaints about Gouverneur Morris, the U.S. minister to France, prompted Washington to begin a search for the proper person to replace him (GW to John Jay, 29 April).

The question of neutral rights, the threat of an Indian war in the Northwest Territory, British retention of military posts in American territory, and a desire for a favorable trade agreement prompted Washington to appoint John Jay as envoy extraordinary to Great Britain in order to resolve these issues (GW's first letter to the U.S. Senate of 16 April). At the same time, other U.S. diplomats continued their efforts to reach an understanding with Spain over the right of free navigation of the Mississippi River by Americans, Indian unrest in the Southwest Territory, and the boundary between Georgia and Florida, as well as the attainment of a commercial treaty between the two nations (Randolph to GW, 7 Jan.).

Washington maintained his oversight of the development of the Federal City in the District of Columbia through his correspondence with the commissioners for the district. To his dismay, two of the three original commissioners had sent him their intentions to resign. Although he persuaded them to remain for a few more months, he started a search for suitable replacements (GW to David Stuart, 20 Jan.). He also made arrangements to purchase additional lots in the new Federal City (GW to the Commissioners for the District of Columbia, 14 March).

As was common throughout his presidency, Washington received personal appeals for various types of assistance from strangers in the United States and overseas, including a series of letters concerning a scam being perpetrated in several German towns by someone claiming to be a representative from the United States (Johann Benjamin Erhard to GW, 27 Jan.). Washington unsuccessfully made his own personal appeal for a favor on 15 Jan. when he wrote King Frederick William II of Prussia asking for the release of the Marquis de Lafayette from prison.

In an effort to manage his Mount Vernon farms while residing in Philadelphia, Washington regularly sent detailed instructions to William Pearce, his newly hired estate manager. Of particular concern was the implementation of a five-year plan of crop rotation designed by Washington in 1793 and the acquisition of a sufficient supply of buckwheat and other   seed for spring planting (GW to Pearce, 12 Jan.).

Washington continued to be a benefactor for his extended family, particularly his sister, Betty Washington Lewis, and his orphaned niece, Harriot Washington, promising a mule to the former and sending money and clothing to the latter (GW to Pearce, 30 March; Harriot Washington to GW, 9 February). He also directed the refurbishment of his house in Alexandria, Va., for Frances Bassett Washington, the widow of his nephew, George Augustine Washington (GW to Pearce, 12 Jan.).

Editorial Apparatus

Transcription of the documents in the volumes of *The Papers of George Washington* has remained as close to a literal reproduction of the manuscript as possible. Punctuation, capitalization, and spelling of all words are retained as they appear in the original document, except as noted below; only for documents printed in annotations is paragraphing ever modified. Dashes used as punctuation have been retained, except when a dash and another mark of punctuation appear together. The appropriate marks of punctuation have always been added at the end of a paragraph. When a tilde (~) is used in the manuscript to indicate a double letter, the letter has been doubled. Washington and some of his correspondents occasionally used a tilde above an incorrectly spelled word to indicate an error in orthography. When this device is used the editors have corrected the word.

In cases where a tilde has been inserted above an abbreviation or contraction, usually in letter-book copies, the word has been expanded. Otherwise, contractions and abbreviations have been retained as written, except that a period has been inserted after an abbreviation when needed. If the meaning of an abbreviation or contraction is not obvious, it has been expanded in square brackets: "H[is] M[ajest]y." Editorial insertions or corrections in the text also appear in square brackets. Angle brackets 〈 〉 are used to indicate illegible or mutilated material. When there is a basis for doing so, conjectural text is supplied within the brackets. Footnotes or source note will indicate if the text is taken from another version of the document. A space left blank in a manuscript by the writer is indicated by a square-bracketed gap in the text [   ].

Material deleted by the author of a manuscript is ignored unless it contains substantive material, and then it appears in a footnote. If the intended location of marginal notations is clear from the text, they are inserted without comment; otherwise, they are recorded in the notes. The ampersand has been retained, and the thorn(Þ in Old English, but by Washington's day essentially indistinguishable from the letter Y) is transcribed as "th." Superscripts have been lowered. The symbol for per (℀) is used when it appears in the manuscript. The dateline has been placed at the head of a document, regardless of where it occurs in the manuscript.

Where multiple versions of a document are available, the document closest to the one actually received by the addressee is printed. The other versions have been collated with the selected text, and significant variations are presented in the annotation.

Since GW read no language other than English, incoming letters written to him in foreign languages were generally translated for his information. Where this contemporary translation has survived, it has been used as the text of the document. If there is no contemporary translation, the document in its original language has been used as the text.

All of the documents printed in this volume, any documents omitted or not printed in full, the original foreign language documents (where otherwise not provided), and a number of ancillary materials ultimately will be available in a digital edition of the Washington Papers. The reports of Washington's farm managers at Mount Vernon, some of which have been printed in previous volumes of the *Presidential Series*, from now on will appear only in the electronic edition. To learn more about the electronic edition, visit the website of The Papers of George Washington (www.gwpapers.virginia.edu) or of Rotunda, the digital imprint of the University of Virginia Press (http:// rotunda.upress.virginia.edu).

During both of Washington's administrations, he was besieged with applications for public office. Many of the applicants continued to seek appointment or promotion. The editors usually have printed only one of these letters in full and cited other letters, both from the applicant and in support of his application, in notes to the initial letter. When Washington replied to these requests at all, the replies were generally pro forma reiterations of his policy of noncommitment until the appointment to a post was made. In such cases, his replies have been included in the notes to the original application and do not appear in their chronological sequence. These and other letters to or from Washington that, in whole or in part, are printed out of their chronological sequence are listed in the table of contents, with an indication of where they may be found in the volumes.

Individuals mentioned in the text usually are identified at their first substantive mention in each series. The index to each volume indicates where identifications appear in earlier volumes of the *Presidential Series*. Also in the index, main entries are alphabetized letter-by-letter, with alphabetization interrupted only by either a comma or a parenthesis. Any other punctuation is ignored, as is a letter space. Minor words such as articles, prepositions, and conjunctions are ignored as the first word in an entry, but as interior words they are considered in the alphabetization. Names beginning with Mc or Mac are alphabetized as they appear; however, any name beginning with a variation of saint (St., Ste., Sainte) is alphabetized as though spelled out as "Saint."

In subentries, personal names are alphabetized by surname, even though presented in a first-name-last-name format.

For his secretarial services in late 1793, Washington depended primarily on Bartholomew Dandridge, Jr., and Howell Lewis. Dandridge had entered the president's employment in 1791, and Lewis began in 1792. Most drafts not written by Washington were written by Dandridge, and for the most part only he communicated in writing directly with cabinet members or others in the name of the president. In some instances, the drafts contain emendations by Washington.

For most of the correspondence found in Record Group 59, State Department Miscellaneous Letters, in the National Archives, there are also letter-book copies in the Washington Papers collection at the Library of Congress. Some of the letters for this period probably were copied into the letter books close to the time they were written, but others obviously were entered much later. When the receiver's copy of a letter from Washington has not been found, the editors generally have assumed that the copy in Miscellaneous Letters was made from the receiver's copy or the draft and have used it as the text rather than the letter-book copy, and they have described the document either as a copy or a draft, depending on the appearance of the manuscript.

Washington never used the term *cabinet* when referring as a group to the attorney general and the heads of the State, War, and Treasury departments. However, for the sake of clarity, the editors have used this term to indicate corporate meetings by these individuals, both with and without Washington, and to describe documents issued as a result of these meetings.

Symbols Designating Documents

AD	Autograph Document: a document in the handwriting of the author
ADS	Autograph Document Signed: a document in the handwriting of, and signed by, the author
ADf	Autograph Draft: a draft in the handwriting of the author
ADfS	Autograph Draft Signed: a draft in the handwriting of, and signed by, the author
AL	Autograph Letter: a letter in the handwriting of the author
ALS	Autograph Letter Signed: a letter in the handwriting of, and signed by, the author
D	Document: a document (not a letter) neither signed by, nor in the handwriting of, the author

DS   Document Signed: a document (not a letter) signed by the
     author, but not in the author's handwriting
Df   Draft: a draft in the handwriting of someone other than
     the author
DfS   Draft Signed: a draft of a letter or document signed by the
     author, but not in the author's handwriting
L   Letter: a letter neither signed by, nor in the handwriting
     of, the author
LS   Letter Signed: a letter signed by the author, but not in the
     author's handwriting
LB   Letters copied into a bound letter-book
[S]   Replaces S when author's signature has been cut from the
     original manuscript
Copy   A contemporaneous handwritten representation made of
     any version of a letter or document
Tran-   A non-contemporaneous, handwritten representation
scripts   made of a letter or other document (generally not used
     or cited unless no other version is available, except in
     the case of a Sprague transcript)
Sprague Handwritten transcripts made in the 1820s by William B.
tran-   Sprague to replace documents that he removed from
scripts   GW's papers

Repository Symbols and Abbreviations

CSmH Huntington Library, Art Collections and Botanical
     Gardens, San Marino, Calif.
CtHi   Connecticut Historical Society, Hartford, Conn.
DLC   U.S. Library of Congress, Washington, D.C.
DLC:GW U.S. Library of Congress, George Washington Papers,
     Washington, D.C.
DNA   U.S. National Archives and Records Administration,
     Washington, D.C.
DSoC   Society of the Cincinnati, Washington, D.C.
FrPMAE Ministère des affaires étrangères, Archives, Paris,
     France (photocopies at Library of Congress)
G-Ar   Georgia State Department of Archives and History,
     Atlanta, Ga.
ICHi   Chicago Historical Society, Chicago, Ill.
KyLoF   Filson Club, Louisville, Ky.
MdAA   Maryland Hall of Records Commission, Annapolis, Md.
MdAN   U.S. Naval Academy, Annapolis, Md.

MdHi	Maryland Historical Society, Baltimore, Md.
MeHi	Maine Historical Society, Portland, Me.
MH	Harvard University, Cambridge, Mass.
MHi	Massachusetts Historical Society, Boston, Mass.
MiU-C	University of Michigan, William L. Clements Library, Ann Arbor, Mich.
MWiW	Williams College, Williamstown, Mass.
NbO	Omaha Public Library, Omaha, Neb.
Nc-Ar	North Carolina Office of Archives and History, Raleigh, N.C.
NcU	University of North Carolina, Chapel Hill, N.C.
NHi	New-York Historical Society, New York, N.Y.
NIC	Cornell University, Ithaca, N.Y.
NjMoHP	Morristown National Historical Park, Morristown, N.J.
NjP	Princeton University, Princeton, N.J.
NN	New York Public Library, New York, N.Y.
NNC	Columbia University, New York, N.Y.
NNGL	Gilder-Lehrman Collection, on deposit at the New-York Historical Society, New York, N.Y.
NNPM	Pierpont Morgan Library, New York, N.Y.
NSchU	Union College, Schenectady, N.Y.
PHarH	Pennsylvania Historical and Museum Commission, Harrisburg, Pa.
PHi	Historical Society of Pennsylvania, Philadelphia, Pa.
PPAmP	American Philosophical Society, Philadelphia, Pa.
PPRF	Rosenbach Museum and Library, Philadelphia, Pa.
PWacD	David Library of the American Revolution, Washington Crossing, Pa.
R-Ar	Rhode Island State Archives, Providence, R.I.
RiNA	Newport, Rhode Island, Artillery Company, Newport, R.I.
RPJCB	John Carter Brown Library, Providence, R.I.
ScC	Charleston Library Society, Charleston, S.C.
ScCoAH	South Carolina Department of Archives and History, Columbia, S.C.
Vi	Library of Virginia, Richmond, Va.
ViFfCh	Fairfax County Courthouse, Fairfax, Va.
ViMtvL	Mount Vernon Ladies' Association of the Union, Mount Vernon, Va.

Short Title List

Annals of Congress.   Joseph Gales, Sr., comp. *The Debates and Proceedings in the Congress of the United States; with an Appendix, Containing Important State Papers and Public Documents, and All the Laws of a Public Nature.* 42 vols. Washington, D.C., 1834–56.

ASP.   Walter Lowrie et al., eds. *American State Papers: Documents, Legislative and Executive, of the Congress of the United States.* 38 vols. Washington, D.C., 1832–61.

Baldwin, *Whiskey Rebels.*   Leland D. Baldwin. *Whiskey Rebels: The Story of a Frontier Uprising.* 1939. Reprint. Pittsburgh, Pa., 1968.

Baltimore Directory, 1796.   William Thompson and James Walker. *The Baltimore Town and Fell's Point Directory. . . .* Baltimore, Md., 1796.

Bayley, *National Loans.*   Rafael A. Bayley. *The National Loans of the United States, from July 4, 1776, to June 30, 1880.* 1881. Reprint. New York, 1970.

Bee, *Reports of Cases.*   Thomas Bee. *Reports of Cases Adjudged in the District Court of South Carolina.* Philadelphia, 1810.

Boyd, *Elias Boudinot.*   George Adams Boyd. *Elias Boudinot, Patriot and Statesman, 1740–1821.* Princeton, N.J., 1952.

Brigham, *American Newspapers.*   Clarence S. Brigham. *History and Bibliography of American Newspapers, 1690–1820.* 2 vols. Worcester, Mass., 1947.

Brockett, *Lodge of Washington.*   Franklin London Brockett. *The Lodge of Washington. A History of the Alexandria Washington Lodge, No. 22, A.F. and A.M. of Alexandria, Va., 1783–1876.* Alexandria, Va., 1876.

Bryan, *National Capital.*   Wilhelmus Bogart Bryan. *A History of the National Capital: From Its Foundations through the Period of the Adoption of the Organic Act.* 2 vols. New York, 1914–16.

Calendar of Virginia State Papers.   William P. Palmer et al., eds. *Calendar of Virginia State Papers and Other Manuscripts.* 11 vols. Richmond, Va., 1875–93.

Carter, *Territorial Papers.*   Clarence Edwin Carter et al., eds. *The Territorial Papers of the United States.* 27 vols. Washington, D.C., 1934–69.

Claghorn, *Naval Officers of the American Revolution.*   Charles E. Claghorn. *Naval Officers of the American Revolution: A Concise Biographical Dictionary.* Metuchen, N.J., 1988.

Clark, *American Militia.*   Murtie June Clark. *American Militia in the Frontier Wars, 1790–1796.* Baltimore, Md., 1990.

Clark, *Greenleaf and Law.*   Allen Culling Clark. *Greenleaf and Law in the Federal City.* Washington, D.C., 1901.

Coldham, *American Loyalist Claims.* Peter Wilson Coldham. *American Loyalist Claims.* Washington, D.C., 1980.

Counter Case. *The Counter Case of Great Britain as Laid before the Tribunal of Arbitration, convened at Geneva. . . .* Washington, D.C., 1872.

Cruikshank, *Simcoe Papers.* E. A. Cruikshank, ed. *The Correspondence of Lieut. Governor John Graves Simcoe, with Allied Documents Relating to His Administration of the Government of Upper Canada.* 5 vols. Toronto, 1923–31.

Diaries. Donald Jackson and Dorothy Twohig, eds. *The Diaries of George Washington.* 6 vols. Charlottesville, Va., 1976–79.

Documentary History of the Supreme Court. Maeva Marcus et al., eds. *Documentary History of the Supreme Court of the United States, 1789–1800.* 8 vols. New York, 1985–2007.

Dorr, *Historical Account of Christ Church, Philadelphia.* Benjamin Dorr. *A Historical Account of Christ Church, Philadelphia: from its Foundation, A.D. 1695, to A.D. 1841; and of St. Peter's and St. James's, until the Separation of the Churches.* New York, 1841.

Elias and Finch, *Digges Letters.* Robert H. Elias and Eugene D. Finch, eds. *Letters of Thomas Attwood Digges (1742–1821).* Columbia, S.C., 1982.

Felder, *Fielding Lewis.* Paula S. Felder. *Fielding Lewis and the Washington Family.* Fredericksburg, Va., 1998.

Fields, *Papers of Martha Washington.* Joseph E. Fields, ed. *"Worthy Partner": The Papers of Martha Washington.* Westport, Conn., and London, 1994.

Ford, *Writings.* Worthington Chauncey Ford, ed. *The Writings of George Washington.* 14 vols. New York, 1889–93.

Fothergill and Naugle, *Virginia Tax Payers.* Augusta B. Fothergill and John Mark Naugle. *Virginia Tax Payers 1782–87 Other than Those Published by the United States Census Bureau.* 1940. Reprint. Baltimore, 1974.

Franklin Papers. William B. Willcox et al., eds. *The Papers of Benjamin Franklin.* 37 vols. to date. New Haven, Conn., 1959—.

Greene Papers. Richard K. Showman et al., eds. *The Papers of General Nathanael Greene.* 13 vols. Chapel Hill, N.C., 1976–2005.

Griffin, *Catalogue of the Washington Collection.* Appleton P.C. Griffin, comp. *A Catalogue of the Washington Collection in the Boston Athenæum.* Cambridge, Mass., 1897.

Hamilton Papers. Harold C. Syrett et al., eds. *The Papers of Alexander Hamilton.* 27 vols. New York, 1961–87.

Harris, *William Thornton Papers.* C. M. Harris, ed. *The Papers of William Thornton.* Charlottesville, Va., 1995.

Heads of Families (Maryland). *Heads of Families at the First Census of the United States Taken in the Year 1790: Maryland.* 1907. Reprint. Baltimore, 1965.

Heads of Families (North Carolina). *Heads of Families at the First Census of the United States Taken in the Year 1790: North Carolina.* 1908. Reprint, Baltimore, 1966.

Heitman, *Historical Register.* Francis B. Heitman. *Historical Register of Officers of the Continental Army during the War of the Revolution, April, 1775, to December, 1783.* 1893. Rev. ed. Washington, D.C., 1914.

Hogan, *Philadelphia Directory, 1795.* Edmund Hogan. *The Prospect of Philadelphia, and Check on the Next Directory.* Philadelphia, 1795.

Household Accounts. Presidential Household Accounts, 4 March 1793–25 March 1797. Manuscript ledger on deposit at Historical Society of Pennsylvania, Philadelphia.

Humphreys, *Life and Times of David Humphreys.* Francis Landon Humphreys. *Life and Times of David Humphreys, soldier—statesman—poet, "belov'd of Washington".* 2 vols. New York and London, 1917.

JCC. Worthington C. Ford et al., eds. *Journals of the Continental Congress.* 34 vols. Washington, D.C., 1904–37.

Jefferson Papers. Julian P. Boyd et al., eds. *The Papers of Thomas Jefferson.* 34 vols. to date. Princeton, N.J., 1950—.

Jennings and Fenton, *Iroquois Indians.* Francis Jennings and William Fenton, eds. *Iroquois Indians: A Documentary History of the Diplomacy of the Six Nations and Their League.* Woodbridge, Conn., 1985. Microfilm. 50 reels.

JPP. Dorothy Twohig, ed. *Journal of the Proceedings of the President, 1793–1797.* Charlottesville, Va., 1981.

Kappler, *Indian Treaties.* Charles Joseph Kappler, ed. *Indian Affairs: Laws and Treaties.* 5 vols. Washington, D.C., 1903–41.

Kelsay, *Brant.* Isabel Thompson Kelsay. *Joseph Brant, 1743–1807: Man of Two Worlds.* Syracuse, N.Y., 1984.

King, *Life and Correspondence of Rufus King.* Charles R. King, ed. *The Life and Correspondence of Rufus King.* 6 vols. New York, 1894–1900.

Knopf, *Wayne.* Richard C. Knopf, ed. *Anthony Wayne, a Name in Arms: Soldier, Diplomat, Defender of Expansion Westward of a Nation; The Wayne-Knox-Pickering-McHenry Correspondence.* Pittsburgh, Pa., 1960.

Ledger B. Manuscript Ledger Book 2, 1772–93, in George Washington Papers, Library of Congress.

Ledger C. Manuscript Ledger in Morristown National Historical Park, Morristown, N.J.

Madison Papers. William T. Hutchinson et al., eds. *The Papers of James Madison* [Congressional Series]. 17 vols. Chicago and Charlottesville, Va., 1962–91.

Madison Papers, Presidential Series.   Robert A. Rutland et al., eds. *Papers of James Madison, Presidential Series.* 6 vols. to date. Charlottesville, Va., 1984—.

Md. Laws 1793.   *Laws of Maryland, Made and Passed at a Session of Assembly, Begun and held at the city of Annapolis on Monday the fourth of November, in the year of our Lord one thousand seven hundred and ninety-three.* Annapolis, 1793.

Miller, *Treaties.*   Hunter Miller, ed. *Treaties and Other International Acts of the United States of America.* Vol. 2, 1776–1818. Washington, D.C., 1931.

Moore, *International Adjudications.*   John Bassett Moore, ed. *International Adjudications: Ancient and Modern, History and Documents, Together with Mediatorial Reports, Advisory Opinions, and the Decisions of Domestic Commissions, on International Claims.* Modern Series, Vol. 4. New York, 1931.

Mount Vernon Farm Manager's Accounts, 1794–97.   Mount Vernon Farm Manager William Pearce's Accounts, 6 Jan. 1794–19 Jan. 1797. Library of Congress, George Washington Papers.

MVHR.   *Mississippi Valley Historical Review.* 50 vols. 1914–64.

Naval Documents.   William Bell Clark et al., eds. *Naval Documents of the American Revolution.* 11 vols. to date. Washington, D.C., 1964—.

N.C. House Journal 1793.   *Journal of the House of Commons. North-Carolina. At a General Assembly, begun and held at Fayetteville, on the second day of December, in the year of our Lord one thousand seven hundred and ninety-three and of the independence of the United States of America the eighteenth: it being the first session of this Assembly.* Halifax, N.C., 1794.

N.C. Senate Journal 1793.   *Journal of the Senate. North-Carolina. At a General Assembly begun and held at Fayetteville, on the second day of December, in the year of our Lord one thousand seven hundred and ninety-three, and of the independence of the United States of America the eighteenth: it being the first session of this Assembly.* Halifax, N.C., 1794.

New-York Directory, 1794.   William Duncan. *The New-York Directory, and Register, for the year 1794.* New York, 1794.

Norris, *Lower Shenandoah Valley.*   J. E. Norris, ed. *History of the Lower Shenandoah Valley.* 1890. Reprint. Berryville, Va., 1972.

Pa. Archives.   Samuel Hazard et al., eds. *Pennsylvania Archives.* 9 ser., 138 vols. Philadelphia, 1852–1949.

Papers, Confederation Series.   W. W. Abbot et al., eds. *The Papers of George Washington, Confederation Series.* 6 vols. Charlottesville, Va., 1992–97.

Papers, Retirement Series.   W. W. Abbot et al., eds. *The Papers of George Washington, Retirement Series.* 4 vols. Charlottesville, Va., 1998–99.

Papers, Revolutionary War Series.   W. W. Abbot et al., eds. *The Papers of George Washington, Revolutionary War Series.* 18 vols. to date. Charlottesville, Va., 1985–.

Parker, *Uncle Sam in Barbary.*   Richard Bordeaux Parker. *Uncle Sam in Barbary: A Diplomatic History.* Gainesville, Fla., 2004.

Parliamentary History of England.   *The Parliamentary History of England from the Earliest Period to the Year 1803.* . . . 36 vols. London, 1806–1920.

Parry, *Consolidated Treaty Series.*   Clive Parry, ed. *The Consolidated Treaty Series.* 231 vols. Dobbs Ferry, N.Y., 1969–1981.

Pease, *Laws of the Northwest Territory.*   Theodore Calvin Pease, ed. *The Laws of the Northwest Territory, 1788–1800.* Collections of the Illinois State Historical Library, 17. Springfield, Ill., 1925.

Philadelphia Directory, 1793.   James Hardie. *The Philadelphia Directory and Register.* Philadelphia, 1793.

Philadelphia Directory, 1794.   James Hardie. *The Philadelphia Directory and Register.* Philadelphia, 1794.

Philadelphia Directory, 1796.   Thomas Stephens. *Stephen's Philadelphia Directory, for 1796.* Philadelphia, 1796.

Powell, *General Washington and the Jack Ass.*   J. H. Powell. *General Washington and the Jack Ass and Other American Characters, in Portrait.* South Brunswick, N.J., 1969.

Prussing, *Estate of George Washington.*   Eugene E. Prussing. *The Estate of George Washington, Deceased.* Boston, 1927.

Rice and Brown, *American Campaigns of Rochambeau's Army.*   Howard C. Rice, Jr., and Anne S. K. Brown, eds. *The American Campaigns of Rochambeau's Army, 1780, 1781, 1782, 1783.* 2 vols. Princeton, N.J., 1972.

Roberts, *Historic Forts.*   Robert B. Roberts. *Encyclopedia of Historic Forts: The Military, Pioneer, and Trading Posts of the United States.* New York, 1988.

Scharf, *Chronicles of Baltimore.*   John Thomas Scharf. *The Chronicles of Baltimore: Being a Complete History of "Baltimore Town" and Baltimore City from the Earliest Period to the Present Time.* Baltimore, Md., 1874.

"Selections from the Draper Collection."   "Selections from the Draper Collection in the Possession of the State Historical Society of Wisconsin, to Elucidate the Proposed French Expedition under George Rogers Clark Against Louisiana, in the Years 1793–94." *Annual Report of the American Historical Association for the Year 1896* 1 (1897):930-1107.

Slaughter, *Whiskey Rebellion.*   Thomas P. Slaughter. *The Whiskey Rebellion: Frontier Epilogue to the American Revolution.* New York, 1986.

Stat.   Richard Peters, George Minot et al., eds. *United States Statutes at Large: Containing the Laws and Concurrent Resolutions . . . and*

Reorganization Plan, Amendment to the Constitution, and Proclamations. Washington, 1789–.

Turner, *Correspondence of the French Ministers.*   Frederick J. Turner, ed. *Correspondence of the French Ministers to the United States, 1791–1797.* 2 vols. Annual Report of the American Historical Association for the Year 1903. Washington, D.C., 1904.

U.S. House Journal.   Martin P. Claussen, ed. *The Journal of the House of Representatives: George Washington Administration 1789–1797.* 9 vols. Wilmington, Del., 1977.

U.S. Senate Executive Journal.   *Journal of the Executive Proceedings of the Senate of the United States of America.* 147 vols. to date. Washington, D.C., 1828—.

Va. Statutes.   William Waller Hening, ed. *The Statutes at Large; Being a Collection of All the Laws of Virginia from the First Session of the Legislature, in the Year 1619.* 13 vols. 1819–23. Reprint. Charlottesville, Va., 1969.

Va. Statutes, 1792–1806.   Samuel Shepherd, ed. *The Statutes at Large of Virginia, from October Session 1792, to December Session, 1806, Inclusive.* n.s. 3 vols. Richmond, Va., 1835–36.

Whitaker, *Spanish-American Frontier.*   Arthur Preston Whitaker. *The Spanish-American Frontier: 1783–1795.* Boston and New York, 1927.

WMQ.   *William and Mary Quarterly: A Magazine of Early American History.* Williamsburg, Va., 1944–.

The Papers of George Washington
Presidential Series
Volume 15
1 January–30 April 1794

To Thomas Jefferson

Dear Sir,   Philadelphia January 1st 1794

I yesterday received with sincere regret your resignation of the office of Secretary of State.[1] Since it has been impossible to prevail upon you, to forego any longer the indulgence of your desire for private life; the event, however anxious I am to avert it, must be submitted to.

But I cannot suffer you to leave your Station, without assuring you, that the opinion, which I had formed, of your integrity & talents, and which dictated your original nomination, has been confirmed by the fullest experience; and that both have been eminently displayed in the discharge of your duties.

Let a conviction of my most earnest prayers for your happiness accompany you in your retirement; and while I accept with the warmest thanks your solicitude for my welfare, I beg you to believe, that I always am Dear Sir Your Sincere friend and Affecte Hble Servant

Go: Washington

ALS, DLC: Jefferson Papers; ALS (retained copy), DNA: RG 59, Miscellaneous Letters; LB, DLC:GW.

1. Jefferson formally resigned as secretary of state in his second letter to GW of 31 Dec. 1793. On his desire to resign much earlier and GW's efforts to prevent this, see Jefferson's second letter to GW of 31 July 1793, and notes 2 and 3.

To Henry Knox

Sir   United States January 1. 1794.

I enclose you a resolve of the Senate of the United States of the 31. Ultimo, and request you would state what measures have been taken relative to the subject alluded to.[1]

Go. W——

Df, DLC:GW; LB, DLC:GW. After the draft was written by a clerk in the War Department, Knox enclosed it for GW's approval in his letter of 4 Jan. to Bartholomew Dandridge, Jr.

1. The Senate resolved "That the Senate will, on Tuesday next, resume the consideration of the treaty made with the Illinois and Wabash tribes of

Indians, on 27th September, 1792" (*U.S. Senate Executive Journal,* 1:144). On this treaty, see GW to U.S. Senate, 13 Feb. 1793, and notes. For Knox's reply, see his letter to GW of 2 Jan. 1794.

From Howell Lewis

Dear Uncle,   Mount Vernon January 1st 1794
   I recd Mr Dandridg's letters of the 18th & 23d of last Month.[1] There directions I shall attend to. I will if you think proper, deliver all the receipts for money paid by me, to Mr Pearce, and when I return to Philadelphia will bring you an accurate Accot of the whole Sum. I shall deliver the Plans of the several Farms to him[2]—Mr Pearce has not yet arrived, & I cant learn any thing of him. Mr Butler leaves Mount Vernon this day, and has applied to me to settle his accot with you, but not having recd any directions from you, I declined having any thing to do with it, until I heard from you, I gave him 10 Dollars till then—There is but 85 dollars in the house & Mr Stuart not paid yet—Mr Davenport had £22.4.10 & the rest I have paid for the use of the Farms & Mansion house.[3]
   The weather was so severe the last week as to Block up the River so Close, as to suffer People to walk a cross at Alexandria, at this Place it was frozen a cross, & as low dow[n] the River as I could see; It is now breaking up, & if Mr Pearce, does not take the advantage of the present situation of the Rive[r], I question whether he gets here at all this winter by water—I perceive that this Freezing & thawing weather has injured your wheat considerably, from the frost spewing it up, & the Sun thawing the earth from the roots & leaves them bare.
   We are all well here, & I must conclude with my compliments to my Aunt & the Family & those of the new year & I am your Affecte Nephew
                                        Howl. Lewis

ALS, DLC:GW.
   1. The letters of 18 and 23 Dec. 1793 from Bartholomew Dandridge, Jr., which have not been identified, covered GW's letters to William Pearce of 18 and 23 Dec. 1793. Pearce, however, had not yet arrived at Mount Vernon to assume his duties as estate manager. Lewis, therefore, continued to serve in this position temporarily until Pearce's arrival later this month (see GW to

William Stuart, Hiland Crow, and Henry McCoy, 14 July 1793; GW to Pearce, 19 Jan. 1794).

2. On the plans for the farms, see the "Crop Rotations for Mount Vernon Farms," enclosed in GW to Pearce, 18 Dec. 1793.

3. James Butler and William Stuart were the respective overseers of the Mansion House and River farms. Joseph Davenport was the miller. Butler received £13.16.4 on 7 Jan. 1794 for "his wages in full for the year 93" (Mount Vernon Accounts, 1794–97). On the eventual payment of Stuart's past wages, see n.9 of GW to Pearce, 9 Feb. 1794.

To the United States Senate

Gentlemen of the Senate,   United States Jany 1st 1794.
    I nominate Edmund Randolph, to be Secretary of State for the United States; vice Thomas Jefferson, who has resigned.[1]
                                        Go: Washington

LS, DNA: RG 46, Third Congress, 1793–95, Senate Records of Executive Proceedings, President's Messages—Executive Nominations; LB, DLC:GW.

1. The Senate approved Randolph's nomination on 2 Jan. (*U.S. Senate Executive Journal*, 1:144). For Jefferson's resignation, see his second letter to GW of 31 Dec. 1793.

From William White

Honoured & dear Sir,   Jany 1. 1794.
    It appears to me, that the Way in which your benevolent Purpose expressed in your Note of Yesterday, may best be answered, is, by lodging the intended Donation in the Hands of the Treasurer of the Overseers of the poor—Mr Wm Millar in Front Street;[1] with an Intimation, that it is expected, the Money will be distributed, according to the private Discretion of the Gentlemen, to the more deserving poor; & in Addition to the stated Allowance. My Reason for recommending this Provision, is, that the Overseers have occasionally under their Notice Families, for whom their Feelings must incline them to do more, than the legal Execution of their Trust would warrant.[2]
    I would cheerfully, Sir, offer my personal Attention, to the Distribution of what you intend to bestow: But being by an annual Duty, engaged at the present Season, in Connection with our

Church-Warden, in the distributing of sundry Charities among the poor Members of our Church, my Knowlege of the poor is proportionably greatest in that particular Line; which would occasion a partial Division, of what I presume to be intended in Favor of the poor of the City, generally. I can think of no Plan that promises so much Impartiality, as that which I have taken the Liberty to recommend.[3]

In writing to Mr Ogden, Sir, I shall pay Attention to what you desire me to express to him. That Gentleman has frequently endeavoured to interest me in Matters, in which I could not interfere with Decency, or to any useful Purpose: But I little expected, that he would have brought them before the President of the United States.[4]

Wishing you, Sir, an happy New Year; & many, very many Returns of this annual Day, I have the Honour to subscribe myself, Your most respectful & affectionate humble Servant

Wm: White

ALS, DLC:GW.

1. For the possibility of a previous gift from GW to the "Guardians of the Poor in the City of Philadelphia," as the overseers were formally titled, see White to Tobias Lear, 3 Jan. 1793.

William Miller probably is the merchant listed at 104 South Front Street in the 1793 Philadelphia directory. White wrote GW later this day to inform him that "William Sansom, in Second Street, near and below Arch Street," was the correct name of the treasurer and that if "the Plan which has been suggested should meet the Presidents Approbation, Dr White, if wished to do so by the President, would undertake to communicate the Charge to Mr Sansom, with whatever Intimations may be thought proper, in regard to Secresy or to any other Effect" (DLC:GW). William Sansom (1763–1840), a Quaker merchant and real estate developer, was located at 67 North Second Street, but at some point later in 1794 he moved his place of business to 43 North Front Street (*Philadelphia Directory, 1793*, 125; *Philadelphia Directory, 1794*, 134).

2. On the incorporation of the overseers on 27 March 1789, see William Clinton Heffner, *History of Poor Relief Legislation in Pennsylvania, 1682–1913* [Cleona, Pa., c.1913], 95–118.

3. Despite White's suggestion, GW enclosed his donation in his letter to White of this same date. In addition to being a bishop of the Episcopal Church, William White currently served as rector of the united parishes of Christ Church and St. Peter's Church in Philadelphia. Merchant John Wilcocks and shopkeeper Thomas Cumpston were the church wardens, 1793–94 (Dorr, *Historical Account of Christ Church, Philadelphia*, 299; *Philadelphia Directory, 1793*).

4. On the Rev. John Cosens Ogden's complaints about the treatment of the Episcopal Church by local and state governments in New England, see his

letters to GW of 9 Jan. 1791 and 24 Nov. 1792. GW's request of White regarding a letter to Ogden may have been given during a personal conversation. Whatever White wrote, it did not stop Ogden from airing his grievances to GW (see Ogden to GW, 7 Feb., 16 March 1794).

To William White

Dr Sir,   Phila. Jan. 1st 1794
  I have been favoured with two notes from yo⟨u⟩ of this date—the last, in time to prevent the mistake which the first would have led me into.[1]
  The mode which you have suggested for imparting the small pittance my resources will enable me to contribute towards the comfort of the needy in this City appears to be a very eligable one, and as you have been so obliging as to offer to place it in proper hands, for this purpose, I take the liberty of enclosing 250 dollars.[2]
  I have no desire that my name should be mentioned; if so small a sum can effect any good purpose my object will be answered, and all my wishes respecting it gratified.
  I offer you the compliments of the season⟨—the⟩ happy return of many of them—and the sincere respects & regard of Yr Affecte Hble Servt

                                                       Go: W——n

ADfS, DLC:GW; LB, DLC:GW. The text in angle brackets is from the letter-book copy.
  1. For the second letter of 1 January from White and the correction it contained, see n.1 of White's first letter to GW of that date.
  2. GW's donation of $250 was noted in his financial records for 28 Jan. 1794 (Household Accounts; see also Account Book, 2 Sept. 1793–4 April 1794, DLC:GW).

From William White

                                    [Philadelphia] Jany 1. 1794.
  Dr White presents his most respectful Compts to the President; & will, with great Pleasure, call on Mr Sansom with the Presidents generous Donation of two hundred & fifty Dollars, just now received.[1]

In Order to prevent the Supposition of Dr Whites having given the whole or a Part of the Money, he would wish if the President has no Objection, to mention his Name to Mr Sansom, but not to be handed to the Board. Dr White, if he does not hear again, will presume, that he may go as far as this.[2]

AL, DLC:GW.

1. See GW to White, this date.

2. GW's reply on "Thursday Morning," 2 Jan., reads: "The President presents his respectful regards to Doctor White. The benefit to be derived, and not the merit of bestowing it, is the only motive which has governed in the case wch has been the subject of this corrispondence—of course, to know from whence it flowed ought not to be an object of enquiry, and as to conjectures they are very immaterial; however, as Doctr White has a delicacy on the subject the P—— did not intend nor would by any means wound it—he therefore leaves it to him (knowing the motives) to accompany the contribution with such explanations as he shall think proper" (ADf, DLC:GW; LB, DLC:GW).

From Henry Knox

Sir,   War Department, Jan. 2d 1794

Most of the principal Chiefs of the Wabash Indians who visited this City having died with the smallpox, it would have been improper & nugatory to have attempted with the remainder any explanation of the fourth article of the treaty of Post Vincennes the 7th day of Septr 1792.[1]

It was presumed that at the intended treaty to be held with the North Western Indians that the Wabash tribes would have been represented. With a view therefore to this subject generally the following article was inserted in the instructions of the Commissioners.[2]

"You will in all your negotiations carefully guard the general rights of preemption of the United States to the Indian Country against all other nations of individuals, as established by the treaty of 1783 with Great Britain. But in describing these rights to the Indians, you will impress them with the idea that we concede to them fully the right and possession of the soil as long as they desire to occupy the same; but when they choose to sell any portion of the Country, it must be sold only to the United States who will protect the Indians against all imposition."

But the expectation of the treaty having been frustrated, nothing has been effected upon the subject.[3] I have the honor to be with the greatest respect Your Obedt Servant

H. Knox Secy of War.

LB, DLC:GW; copy, DNA: RG 46, Third Congress, 1793–95, Senate Records of Executive Proceedings, President's Messages—Indian Relations. Knox wrote this letter in response to one from GW of 1 Jan. and enclosed it in his letter to GW of 4 January. A copy of this letter was enclosed in GW's letter of 6 Jan. to the U.S. Senate.

1. At the conclusion of the peace treaty of 27 Sept. 1792 with the Wabash and Illinois Indians, which Rufus Putnam negotiated at Post Vincennes in the Northwest Territory, a delegation of fifteen men and three women was escorted to Philadelphia to meet with GW and other government officials. During the first month of their visit, two of the men died of smallpox and five died from being inoculated against the disease, while at least one more died of pleurisy (Knox to GW, 7 Nov. 1792, and notes 1 and 2; Knox to Tobias Lear, 25 Dec. 1792; *Independent Chronicle and the Universal Advertiser* [Boston], 24 Jan. 1793; *National Gazette* [Philadelphia], 12 Jan. 1793). For the submission of this treaty to the Senate and the Senate's objections to the controversial fourth article, which guaranteed the Indians a right to their land, see GW to U.S. Senate, 13 Feb. 1793, and notes. For the text of the entire treaty, see *ASP, Indian Affairs,* 1:338.

2. Indian commissioners Benjamin Lincoln, Timothy Pickering, and Beverley Randolph had been charged with negotiating a peace treaty with the hostile Indians of the Northwest Territory. For their instructions, see *ASP, Indian Affairs,* 1:340–42.

3. On the failure of the negotiations, see Indian Commissioners to Knox, 21 Aug. 1793, in *ASP, Indian Affairs,* 1:359.

From Edmund Randolph

Sir   Philadelphia January 2. 179[4][1]

I do myself the honor of inclosing to you a certificate from Judge Wilson, of my having qualified, as secretary of state. A duplicate is deposited among the files of the office.[2]

I must intreat you, sir, to receive my very affectionate acknowledgments, for the various instances of your confidence; and to be assured, that, let the consequence be, what it may, in this perilous office, no consideration of party shall ever influence me; nothing shall relax my attention or warp my probity; and it shall be my unremitted study to become an accurate master of this new and important business.

At the commencement of my duties, I have thought it advise-able to write to the Secretaries of the Treasury and of war,[3] and to the President of the bank of the U.S. the letters of which the inclosed are copies.[4] I have the honor, sir, to be with sincere respect and attachment yr mo. ob. serv.

Edm: Randolph.

ALS, DNA: RG 59, Miscellaneous Letters; LB, DLC:GW; LB, DNA: RG 59, GW's Correspondence with His Secretaries of State; LB, DNA: RG 59, Domestic Letters.

1. Randolph erroneously wrote 1793 on the ALS.

2. For GW's recent nomination of Randolph as secretary of state, see GW to U.S. Senate, 1 January. Prior to this, Randolph had served as attorney general. For the certificate, see the following enclosure.

3. In his letter to Alexander Hamilton and Henry Knox of this date, Randolph wrote: "I have just taken the Oath of Office, which reminds me that I am brought into a nearer relation to your department than hitherto. While official men are under no less an obligation than others, to live in harmony; there are too many opportunities for misconception and misrepresentation to interrupt it. I have therefore prescribed this rule for myself: that if any thing, supposed to be done in the other departments, shall create dissatisfaction in my mind, I will check any opinion, until I can obtain an explanation, which I will ask without reserve. By these means I shall avoid the uneasiness of suspicion; and I take the liberty of requesting, that the same line of conduct may be pursued with respect to myself.

"I trust, that under these principles, whatsoever difference of sentiments may at any time exist between us, it will be the difference of men, who equally pursue the objects of their appointment, and that the public good will thereby be promoted, rather than injured" (DNA: RG 59, Miscellaneous Letters).

4. Randolph wrote to Thomas Willing that according to a memorandum from Thomas Jefferson (see *Jefferson Papers*, 27:649–52), "the monies, allotted to the foreign fund of this department, are generally deposited in the bank of the U.S. I beg the favor of you, (in order to prevent mistakes) to give an instruction to your officers, to apply no checks, drawn by me, to that fund, unless they be subscribed by me, as Secretary of State" (DNA: RG 59, Miscellaneous Letters).

Enclosure
Affidavit from James Wilson

United States to wit: [Philadelphia, 2 Jan. 1794]

I James Wilson one of the associate Justices of the Supreme Court of the United States do hereby certify that I have this day administered to Edmund Randolph in pursuance of an act entituled "An act to regulate the time and manner of administering certain oaths," an oath, that he will support the constitution of the United States;[1] and that I have also at the same time administered to the same Edmund Randolph in pursuance of the act intituled "An act for establishing an executive department to be denominated the department of foreign Affairs," an oath well and faithfully to execute the trust committed to him in the office of Secretary of State for the United States.[2]

Given under my hand and Seal at the City of Philadelphia this second day of January 1794.

James Wilson

LB, DNA: RG 59, Domestic Letters.
  1. For this act of 1 June 1789, see *Stat.* 1:23–24.
  2. For this act of 27 July 1789, see *Stat.* 1:28–29.

To the United States Senate

Gentlemen of the Senate,   United States 2d January 1794.

I nominate Philip Burr Bradley of Connecticut, to be Marshal of and for the Connecticut district, continued, the legal term of his former appointment having expired.[1]

Go: Washington

LS, DNA: RG 46, Third Congress, 1793–95, Senate Records of Executive Proceedings, President's Messages—Executive Nominations; LB, DLC:GW.
  1. For Bradley's original nomination to this position, see GW to U.S. Senate, 24 Sept. 1789. Section 27 of "An Act to establish the Judicial Courts of the United States," 24 Sept. 1789, specifies that federal marshals shall be appointed "for the term of four years" (*Stat.* 1:87). GW had first submitted Bradley's reappointment in his letter to the Senate of 27 Dec. 1793, but an error in Bradley's name necessitated another nomination letter. The Senate confirmed Bradley's reappointment on 2 Jan. (*U.S. Senate Executive Journal,* 1:143–45).

From J. W. Böeleker

Altona[1] Jany 3d 1794.

Once more I make bold to impl⟨o⟩re Your Excellency's Concern for graciously seconding the Petition of the Widow, Mrs Hinrichsen of this place concerning an Estate of her brother's, the late Lieutenant Wrisberg, who departed this Life in the Year 1774 at Morrishoop, in the State of New Jersey, which Estate she claims lawfully.[2]

It would afford much Satisfaction, if Your Excellency might please to condescend to have Information given to us by one of Your Secretaries, whether certain Documents relative to the Succession aforementioned, which were transmitted one year and a half ago purporting the Legitimation of the Claimant have been duly received and whether any Prospect to recover that Estate appear at all or not.

We shall be satisfied with the Interests leaving the Capital to the Disposition of the constituted Administrators of the State.

A short Answer might dissipate so painful an Uncertainty, so on our part, persuaded of Your Excellency's gracious Disposition, we cannot but expect, the favour will be granted we must humbly pray for. The Supplicant being a Widow of indigent Circumstances, Your Excellency will largely contribute towards Charity by Supporting that cause.[3] I beg Leave to remain with the highest Respect and Veneration Your Excellency's most humble & devoted srvt

J.W. Böeleker

Grand Bailiff to His Majy the King of Denmark.[4]

L (translation), DNA: RG 59, Miscellaneous Letters; ALS (in German), DNA: RG 59 Miscellaneous Letters.

1. Altona, now incorporated within the westernmost district of Hamburg, Germany, was at this time in the Duchy of Holstein, which was ruled by the Danish monarch.

2. For earlier correspondence from Böeleker and his client, Johanna Lucia Henrietta Hinrichsen, concerning property owned in New Jersey and New York State by the late Conrad Daniel Wrisberg, see Thomas Jefferson to GW, 16 Nov. 1792, and notes, and Böeleker to GW, 31 Jan. 1793. Hinrichsen's petition of 21 Aug. 1792 and other statements regarding this estate are in DNA: RG 59, Miscellaneous Letters.

3. No reply to either Böeleker or Hinrichsen has been identified.

4. Christian VII (1749–1808) was the king of Denmark, but from 1784 until his death, Frederick VI (1768–1839) ruled as regent in his father's name.

From Cormeille, Sr.

New York le 3. janvier 1794
l'an 3e de la republique française une et indivisible

L'amie de la vertu à Washington

Si Galbaud était coupable voudrait-il paraître devant ses juges? cette reflection peut-elle échaper a l'homme juste. Galbaud a

écrit le 23 xbre 1793. à monsieur genet, malheureusement ministre de la republique française, pour lui demande⟨r⟩ son passage
pour france.[1] il s'est, de suite, rendu chès monsieur hauterive,
malheureusement consul de la republique française, pour y con-
stater sa demande; il y est allé avec Son épous⟨e⟩, Son aide-de-
camp, le citoyen courré et Son épouse, les citoyens dunij, leber-
ton et tarrin toutes personnes connües et recommandables; et
il S'en est suivis une dénonciation! dénonciation aussi absurde
que criminélle, faite par Monsieur hauterive, chès le maire de
new-york, tendante à obtenir un ordre d'arestation pour tous ces
citoyens, qui cependant, n'a eu lieu que contre l'aide-de-camp,
jeune homme de 20 ans, qu'il accuse d'avoir montré un pisto-
let, fausseté insigne, et qui en éffet n'est coupable à ses yeux
que d'avoir Su Souffrir tous les maux, braver tous les danger⟨s⟩
plutôt que d'abandonner la vertu persecutée, comme l'ont fait
six autres personnes attachées au général galbaud, gangnées
avec de l'argent et des promesses par monsieur cambis, monsieur hauterive, et monsieur genet, ces êtres païtris de la boue
infernale. depuis cette demande, de fausses dénonciations, se
font journellement chès le maire, il est clair que ces monstres
monstrueux, ces Sélérats illimités ont soif du sang de ces dignes
citoyens, ont faim de ces coeurs sanctuaires de la vertu et de la
vérité qu'ils voudraient anéantir à jamais.[2]

Galbaud, pour se mettre a l'abri des complots, des machinations, des trâmes ourdies dans l'antre du crime, des piéges ten-
dus par les forfaits, a demendé a être constitu⟨er⟩ prisonnier,
afin que le geolier repondit de ses actions—puis quil ni avait
pas d'autre moyen pour Sa Sureté: chose inoüie! tout, jusqu'aux
cachots, tout est fermé à l'innocence poursuivie par le coupable audacieux. qui peut donc arreter tous ces maux? toi. à qui
l'humanité impose t-elle cette Sainte obligation? à tous les hom-
mes mais particulierement à toi; parce que tes mains sont les plus
pures et tes moïens les plus puissants. dans la position où Sont
les choses, comme allié de la france tu lui dois galbaud, innocent
où coupable; Sans égard à Genet, ce fauteur de tous les articles
de la constitution 1re. qu'un batiment fort Secretement disposé
pour cette famille, l'arrache a ses boureaux et la transporte en
france: la france tiendra compte des avances et témoignera Sa
reconnaisance pour cet important Service. un refus! Serait un
acte de ferocité politique que ton coeur, oui, que ton coeur

désavoüerait. ah! Si tes yeux pouvaient pénétrer jusques dans le galetas qu'habite cette respectable famille, ce ne serait pas en vain que tu les verrais sans vetement d'hiver, couchés sur le plancher; éxposés tantôt au vent tantôt a la pluïe, malade de misère n'ayant pour tout Secours qu'un dolars, chacun par Semaine que leur donne le comité americain. fixe un moment tes regards sur ce tableu: toi! *docteur ⟨d⟩ès droits de la nature, des gens et de la Société civile.* laisse, laisse agir ton coeur: ces mouvemens sont trop délicieux pour ne pas cèder a leur douce impulsion![3]

Si je reclâme sans Succès auprès de toi, et que par une suite des criminelles intrigues, cette famille, que je m'occupe à consoler, Soit au pouvoir de ces êtres de fange, de vices et de crimes, je te déclare que j'aurai le courage de les Soustraires aux Suplices multipliés que leurs préparations leurs vils et infâmes ennemis; je poignarde le pere, la mere, les enfans: je suis capale de cet éffort parce quils en sont dignes. j'éxpedie par touts les voïes possibles ces mots a mon païs. je voulais te Sauver tes plus zèlés diffenseurs, plains moi, mes pouvoirs sont impuissant⟨s⟩.

j'ai cherché partout Washington, et ne l'ai point trouvé! . . . je me rends chès toi, où j'expire à tes yeux en te reprochant les crimes que j'aurai eu l'humanité de commettre.

adieu, grand homme, te bénir! ou mourir! mais en mourant je ne peux encore me deffendre de t'aimer et de t'admirer, ces Sentimens, que tu justifies, sont devenus des *modes dêtre* de mon coeur qui ne peut plus changer.[4]

Cormeille ainée
republicaine

reponce! reponce! mon adresse, Citoienne Cormeille aimée *poste restante.* je veux que ces malheureux ignorent ma demande.

ALS (in French), DNA: RG 59, Miscellaneous Letters.

1. In this letter, Cormeille expresses his indignation at the treatment of François Thomas Galbaud du Fort, the governor general of Saint Domingue, who fled to the United States in the summer of 1793 (Millet to GW, 20 Aug. 1793, and n.8). Shortly after Galbaud's arrival, Edmond Genet, the French minister to the United States, made an unsuccessful attempt to place Galbaud and members of his entourage under arrest for their opposition to the commissioners of Saint Domingue and their role in that island's civil war (George Clinton to GW, 2 Sept. 1793, notes 1 and 5, and enclosures). After fleeing briefly to Canada, Galbaud wrote a letter of 23 Dec. 1793 to Genet, in which he sought permission to board the *St. Honore* for passage to France,

where he could plead his case before a French tribunal. For an English version of this letter, see *Independent Gazetteer* (Philadelphia), 4 Jan. 1794.

2. According to Cormeille, Galbaud also wanted passage for his wife, the former Marie Alexie Tobin de Saint-Aubin; André Conscience, his aide-de-camp; colonist Courré and his wife; colonist Duny; Jean-Marie le Breton de Mardin de Villandry, a major general in the National Guard at Port-au-Prince; and colonist Tarrin. Cormeille also criticizes the failure of Hauterive, the French consul at New York City, to assist Galbaud (see also Duny's public letter on Galbaud's encounter with Hauterive on 23 Dec. 1793 and a rebuttal of Duny's account by Genet's supporters that were printed in the *Daily Advertiser* [New York], 26 Dec. 1793, 1 Jan. 1794). Hauterive attempted to obtain an arrest warrant for Galbaud and his associates from the mayor of New York City, Richard Varick, but only one was issued, that for Conscience, who was accused of threatening Hauterive with a pistol. According to Cormeille, six other unnamed associates of Galbaud had abandoned their allegiance to Galbaud, having been won over by money and promises given by Admiral Joseph Cambis, Hauterive, and Genet.

3. Cormeille suggests that the French nation would be very grateful if GW would approve a plan to put a ship secretly at the disposal of Galbaud. In the meantime, Galbaud's family lives in a drafty garret, where they lack winter clothes, sleep on the floor, and survive on the dollar per week given them by an American relief committee for French refugees.

4. Despite the problems mentioned in this letter, Galbaud returned to France later this year and in 1795 resumed his military career.

From Henry Knox

Sir,   War department January 3d 1794
    I have the honor to submit to your consideration letters just received from General Wayne.[1] I have the honor to be with greatest respect Your obedient Servant

H. Knox

LS, DLC:GW; LB, DLC:GW.
    1. After receiving notice of the failure of Indian commissioners Benjamin Lincoln, Timothy Pickering, and Beverley Randolph to achieve a peace treaty with the hostile Indians of the Northwest Territory, Gen. Anthony Wayne began preparations to move his army from its headquarters at Hobson's Choice, near Fort Washington, and closer to the villages of the Miami Indians on the Auglaize River (see notes 1 of Knox to GW, 16, 30 Nov. 1793). By 10 Oct., Wayne had established new headquarters on a branch of the Miami River now known as Greenville Creek, and approximately six miles from Fort Jefferson (Wayne to Knox, 23 Oct. 1793, Knopf, *Wayne*, 278). During the remainder of 1793 and into 1794, Wayne would oversee the construction of Fort Greene Ville at this site, from which the two enclosed letters were written. In his first

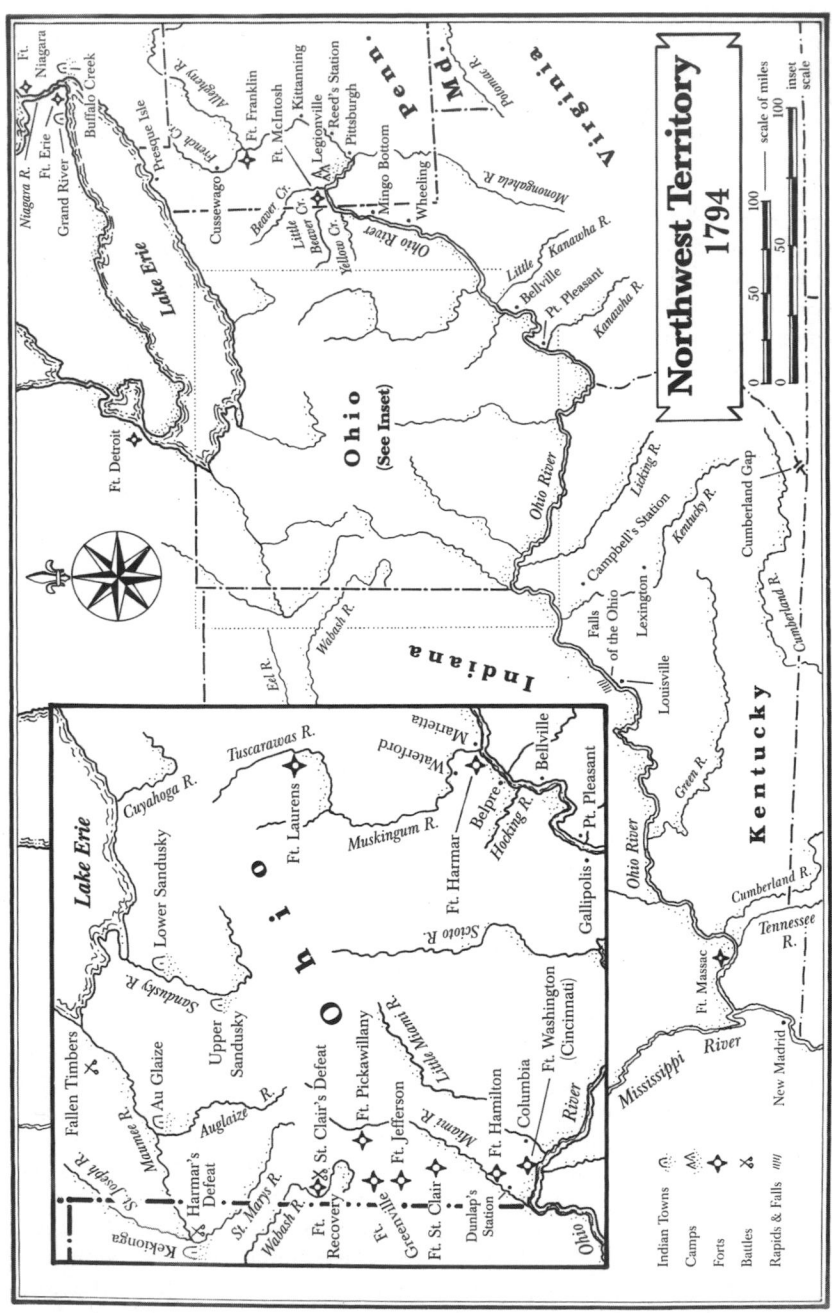

Map 1: *Northwest Territory, 1794. (Illustrated by Rick Britton. Copyright Rick Britton 2008.)*

letter to Knox of 15 Nov. 1793, Wayne wrote that it was the opinion of the general officers that the army stop its advance at this point, which was "within striking distance" of the principle Miami villages and from which the army could "cover the frontiers & our heavy convoys from depredations & insults of the Savages. . . ."

Wayne reported that the "Mounted Volunteers of Kentucky," under Maj. Gen. Charles Scott, had returned home. He also expressed his exasperation with the failure of army contractors to provide supplies in a timely manner and was especially anxious that a convoy with clothing should arrive soon, as "the greater part of the troops are nearly naked" (Knopf, *Wayne,* 281–84; see also *JPP,* 276).

A second letter from Wayne to Knox of 15 Nov., which was marked private, also was enclosed. In this letter, Wayne wrote about problems within the officers corps. "The rights of man, has been held up as a Criterian, even of Military Government. Attempts have frequently been made to evade & disobey Orders, under various & unworthy pretexts & idle quibles . . . It has been advanced as a Cardinal principle, & Officers have been advised to say 'Sir I have owed my Country service—& I have done it—I still owe allegiance, & that in return for a Granted right—of going, & coming, *when I please'* & to such a pitch was this doctrine carried (at a crises when we have scarcely a Guard & reliefs) that when some young Gentlemen were refused a furlough, they offered their resignations & prepared to depart without any further Cerimony, saying they were advised, to do so, by *experienced* Officers!" Wayne promised to make an example of the instigator of this behavior, when identified. Wayne then complained about the neglectful behavior of army contractors, warning that from "present appearances, it most certainly was *expected,* that I shou'd be compeled to retreat, for want of supplies: this was only intended to Operate against me but principally against Government: The Honor & dignity of which shall never be Committed by any Conduct of mine. I mention those facts & circumstances in confidence—which will probably be openly demonstrated in a little time; as they have failed in causing me to retreat—probably their next attempt will be to default my Advance." In a postscript, Wayne noted that James Wilkinson, having been ill, has only recently returned to active duty (NNGL: Knox Papers). GW returned both these letters to Knox on 4 Jan. (*JPP,* 276).

From Edmund Randolph

Sir   Philadelphia January 3. 1794

I had the honor of observing to you this morning, that the commissioners ought not, in my opinion, nor indeed in the opinion of Mr Jefferson and Mr Madison, to abandon the legal title to the lots sold.[1]

The facility, which occurred to me, was, that the commissioners might by a power of attorney authorize Mr Pinckney[2] or any other of our ministers residing at places abroad, where Mr Greenleaf might sell lots, to convey the legal title to any purchasers, whom he may designate, upon receiving the purchase money for public use. It is true, that some of the lots may be worth more, than the average-price stipulated, and that sales may be made of the choicest. Still I should think, that the personal obligation of Messrs Greenleaf and Morris, added to the hold on the remaining lots, would sufficiently secure the U.S. against the inconvenience of picking the lots; that is, would always secure the payment of the remainder.

I have mentioned nothing of lots, which Mr Greenleaf may sell here; because the legal title of them may be at any moment adjusted. I have the honor, sir, to be, with the highest respect, yr mo. ob. serv.

Edm: Randolph.

ALS, DNA: RG 59, Miscellaneous Letters; LB, DLC:GW; LB, DNA: RG 59, GW's Correspondence with His Secretaries of State; LB, DNA: RG 59, Domestic Letters.

1. The commissioners for the District of Columbia had signed an agreement on 23 Sept. 1793 to sell James Greenleaf 3,000 lots (GW to D.C. Commissioners, 20 Aug. 1793, n.3). This arrangement was superceded in December when the commissioners signed another agreement with James Greenleaf and his partner Robert Morris. This new contract raised the number of lots to 6,000 and modified some of the conditions. The commissioners enclosed this agreement in a letter to GW of 23 Dec. 1793. For a copy of this later contract, dated 24 Dec. 1793, see DNA: RG 42, Records of the Commissioners for the District of Columbia, Proceedings, 1791–1802. GW apparently then sent the December agreement to Randolph for his legal opinion. If there were any written opinions from Thomas Jefferson and James Madison, they have not been identified.

2. Thomas Pinckney was the U.S. minister plenipotentiary to Great Britain.

From Alexander Hamilton

Treasury Department Jany 4. 1794

The Secretary of the Treasury, to whom was referred, by the President of the United States a Letter from the Minister of the French Republic to the Secretary of State, dated the 21st instant,[1] respectfully makes the following, Report.

The Minister observes, that it results from the report of the Secretary of the Treasy that upon an accidental error, the interests of the French republic and the character of it's representative were compromitted by a refusal to accept drafts, delivered to the agents by whom they were supplied, for sums due to the republic;[2] adding to this observation, the further one, that it seems to him that a like measure meritted the most serious attention, and that he knows not by what name to call the negligence which was committed i[n] this respect.

This asperity of remark might, it would seem, have been prevented by a due attention to circumstances and facts. It was stated, in the report to which the Minister refers, that the error in question was the mere mistake of the Clerk charged with registering his drafts, as they were presented at the Treasury. It will not be alleged that this was not the proper business of a Clerk, and all that could be expected from the head of the Department, or the officer having in his place the principal direction, is, that there should have been due care in selecting the person to whose immediate agency the duty was entrusted. To this point there was no want of attention. The clerk selected had been long tried in public business and has a well established reputation for fidelity and accuracy. This officer is himself persuaded, that in the instance, which occasioned the demur, no error was committed; and firmly believes, that the convenience of parties had produced an alteration in the bill, after it was noted by him. But this surmise of his has been rejected, and it has been taken for granted & admitted, that there was a mistake on his part; though, as no mark was set upon any bill presented and noted, that admission was founded on considerations, in which candour & delicacy governed. No palliation of the mistake will be attempted to be derived from topics connected with any derangement of the course of business resulting from the late calamitous condition of the City of Philadelphia, nor from the absence of the Secretary of the Treasury from the seat of Government for the recovery of his health, when the incident deemed so exceptionable took place.[3]

The hesitation about the registering of the bills, which appeared to have been overdrawn, was a mere consequence of the first mistake.

The main object of the registry of the bills, was to ascertain for the satisfaction of holders, that there were funds in the treasury, subject to the payment of them, and to secure to those holders a priority, *in the event of there being an overdrawing.* It was therefore a matter of course that the registry should cease, as soon as itself shewed that the amount of the bills presented equalled the amount of the fund destined for satisfying them. Being the proper and regular guide to the officers of the Treasury, they could not but be expected to follow it.

All that could be asked (if a mistake happened) was, that the consequences of it should be corrected as soon as the mistake was discovered—and this was in fact done. Nor did more than a week elapse before the drafts, which had been suspended on account of the mistake, were recognized & admitted.

But it is suggested by the Minister, that tho' the error was rectified, the injury which it occasioned, has not been cured. That event, it is asserted, has furnished to the ill disposed, and to the enemies of the French republic, a powerful mean of hurting it's cause, by alarming the merchants & ruining the credit of it's agents.

If this assertion were better founded than it is, it would only afford room to regret the consequence of an involuntary error. But whatever injury the credit of France in this Country or of her agents may have sustained, it is to be traced to other sources. More adequate causes can be assigned for it. The assertion which has been made calls for a specification of those causes.

The first of them was, the disappointment of our Citizens in not receiving payment of bills to a large amount furnished to them by the administration of St Domingo, with assurances of being paid here by the agents of France; at the same time that it was known, that these agents had obtained from the Government of the United States, funds adequate to such payment, which had been applied to other objects. In mentioning this circumstance it is only intended to note the fact, and it's effect—not to question the propriety of the application which was made of the funds.[4]

Another, and a far more powerful cause, was, the refusal of the present minister to pay certain bills, which had had the positive sanction of his predecessor; diverting from that destination funds which were understood to have been appropriated to it—and this too in contravention of his own arrangement with the Treasury.[5]

These bills had, like those first mentioned, been drawn by the administration of St Domingo. But they had in addition been virtually accepted by the late Consul of France, in concert with it's then minister & in conformity with an understanding between the latter & this Government.[6]

The arrival of the present minister devolved upon him the disposal of the unfurnished residue of the funds which had been promised to his predecessor. An early opportunity was taken to intimate to him the reliance of the Government, that the bills accepted as above, and unpaid would be satisfied by him out of that residue. He gave, without hesitation, a correspondent assurance, & on the 3d of June last addressed to the Secy of the Treasury, a letter in the following terms (viz:). "I pray you to put hereafter in the disposition of Citizen Bournonville, Secretary of Legation of the Republic, the funds destined to the acquittal of the drafts of the Colony of St Domingo, according to the order of payment settled between you & my predecessor."[7]

A part of these funds was accordingly put into the hands of Mr Bournonville, in expectation that they would be applied as had been agreed. And upon the enquiries of some of the holders of the bills at the Treasury, in whom apprehensions had been excited, they were assured that they need not entertain any, as it was the known intention of the present Minister to fulfill the engagements of his predecessor; and that funds had been furnished to him for taking up the bills which were falling due.

The Minister afterwards deemed it necessary to change the destination of these funds, as he announced in his letter of the 18. of June to the Secretary of State, and in fact refused payment of the bills.[8]

This measure, of a nature destructive to credit, had the effect, which was to have been anticipated.

The very expedient of registering at the Treasury the drafts of the minister, was rendered necessary by a pre-existing bad state of credit. It engaged the treasury to nothing more than to secure to those, who presented bills, a preferrence against others, to whom subsequent drafts might be given overrunning the fund for payment; and was devised to facilitate to the Minister an auxiliary mean of credit, of which he stood in need.

These unquestionable truths demonstrate, that there is no room to impute to the consequences of the mistake, which was committed, any deficiency of credit which may have embarrassed the operations of the minister.

But it is a further truth, that if his credit has suffered by the refusal of the treasury to admit his drafts, it is chiefly to be referred to the draft for 20,000 Dollars predicated upon the fund to be at the disposal of France in January; which was *finally* refused, because not authorised by any previous arrangement between the Government and the Minister.[9]

The temporary demur about other bills speedily abandoned and explained, could not have had an influence, bearing any proportion to that of the ultimate refusal of the above mentioned bill.

As far as this refusal may have had a prejudicial operation, 'tis imputable wholly to the irregularity of having drawn the bill, not only without the consent of the Government, but even contrary to an intimation from it; in a case too in which it was free to refuse.

That it was with the consent of the Government, will not be pretended. The Letter from the Secretary of the Treasury to the Minister, of the 24 of July, accompanying his former report on the subject, excludes all plea of constructive or implied consent.

That it was contrary to an intimation from the Government, results from the following facts.

The Minister, by a letter of the 14 of June to the Secretary of State, communicated the intention of giving to those, who should furnish him with Supplies, "delegations," or assignments of the debt to France in payment; desiring, as a pre-requisite to this operation, that the Treasury should be instructed to come to a speedy adjustment with him, of the account of the debt from the United States to France.[10]

To this suggestion the Secretary of State, by a letter of the 19 of June, (after assuring him that instructions would be given for the settlement of the account) replied as follows—"In the mean time, what is further to be done, will doubtless be the subject of further reflection and enquiry with you, & particularly the operation proposed in your letter will be viewed under all its aspects. Among these, we think it will present itself as a measure too questionable both in principle & practicability, too deeply interesting to the credit of the United States, & too unpromising in its result to France to be found eligible to yourself. *Finally we rest secure that what is of mutual concern will not be done but with mutual concert.*[11]

Without mutual concert, without even an intervening consultation for that purpose, the Minister thought proper to issue his "delegations" or drafts upon a fund not embraced by any previous arrangement: and he now makes it matter of complaint that these "delegations" were not registered. Was it to have been expected that the treasury should become the passive instrument of a measure so irregular—so unwarranted?

But the Minister in justification of the stop, makes two observations.

1.   That as the 300,000 livres due the first of January are the interest of the Loan of [6000000][12] made by France to the United States in 1783, *the reimbursements of which are not [to] commence 'till 1797,* he can see no motive, that could arrest the payment of the interest of that sum at the epoch stipulated, as long as there was due to France an equivalent.[13]

2d.   That supposing the payments, which have been made by the Treasury, to exceed the amount of the sums due, he has always been firmly convinced that these advances (to which the urgent wants of France had forced a recourse) would be applied to the extinction of the debt taken in totality; a measure perfectly agreeing with the clause inserted in the different contracts, which expresses that the United States might, if they judged proper, liberate themselves sooner than the epochs fixed by those Contracts.

These observations admit of obvious answers. 'Tis affirmed on our part, and the Minister seems himself to be sensible of its truth, that our payments hitherto exceed the sums demandable by the terms of our Contracts. It may be taken for granted, that this is the case beyond the amount of the interest of the [6000000] accruing in January. The United States are at liberty to consider the excess as an anticipation of the capital of the Loans; but they are not bound to do so. They have an option to do that, or to set it off against the interest accruing on the unpaid residue of the debt. The universal course of business will justify them in the latter and their contracts say nothing to the contrary. Not having declared a different option, they were free to pursue that alternative, and consequently, as has been said, to refuse the drafts of the Minister, predicated upon the January interest.

The circumstance which he notices, of the *reimbursements of the [6000000] loan not commencing 'till 1797,* cannot affect this conclusion. These reimbursements so postponed relate to the *Capital* of the debt; & that postponement of course cannot bring into question the propriety of setting off against the *interest,* annually payable, sums advanced beyond those which were antecedently due.

The conviction of the minister, that the advances, which might have been made would be deferred towards the final extinction of the debt, could be no rule to the treasury, as long as it had not been authorised by any assurance from the Government; or when it was recollected, that the propriety of a mutual previous concert, about whatever was not a matter of course, was indicated to him, no only by the reason of the timing, but by unequivocal declarations.

In fact, whether the course on which he declares himself to have relied could have been pursued or not depended on circumstances; that is, on the means which should exist of making intermediate payments and postponing the advances to an ulterior arrangement; a point at this moment unascertained, from causes which have heretofore been disclosed.

But the Minister not only hazarded his credit, by drawing without a previous arrangement the bill for 20,000 dollars, payable out of the January interest—he hazarded it likewise by *actually* overdrawing the funds placed at his disposal in September & November last; so that if no mistake had occurred at the treasury, he might have been exposed by his own conduct to consequences which in that respect happened by accident.

The Secretary now proceeds to the demands contained in the Memorial of the Minister—these are

1.   That the state of the account of the United States with France be presented with the least possible delay.

2.   That the sums, which may have been advanced to France, beyond those which were demandable on the terms of the Contracts, be applied to the extinction of the debt taken in totallity.

3.   That, provisionally, and until the state of the account can be determined, the Secretary of the Treasury be autho-

rised to register the "Delegations" or drafts, which the Minister shall have occasion to issue, to the extent of Five millions Tournois.

With regard to the first point—the account is now in a course of adjustment between the Comptroller, on the part of the Treasury, & Mr Bournonville on the part of the Minister. There are some points which require a mutual adjustment before they can be fixed definitively.[14] A correct view of the account cannot be presented 'till these points are settled. That done, it shall be immediately laid before the President.

With regard to the second point, the Secretary is of opinion that a determination concerning it cannot now be made. The adoption of the Minister's proposition would amount to an agreement to pay the accruing instalments at the periods stipulated in the Contracts, though the advances which have been made should exceed them. But such an agreement cannot safely be entered into, because it is now problematical whether the Executive will be possessed in time of funds which can be applied to that purpose, without neglecting objects of positive obligation and essential to our credit—as has been already explained & communicated.

With regard to the third point—the answer to the second is an answer to this also. If rightly understood this proposition depends upon the second. It appears necessary first to ascertain what is to be paid & when it is to be paid, before any sanction can safely be given to the proposed "delegations" or drafts. This pre-supposes a settlement of accounts & a further view of our pecuniary prospects. All which is respectfully submitted.[15]

Alexander Hamilton
Secy of the Treasury

LB, DLC:GW; LB, DNA: RG 59, Domestic Letters; copy, FrPMAE: Correspondance Politique, Etats-Unis, Supplement Volume 20. The text in angle brackets is taken from the LB, DNA: RG 59.

1. A note in the right margin of the letter-book at DLC:GW reads, "say Decr last." Hamilton is referring to Edmond Genet's first letter of 21 Dec. 1793 to Thomas Jefferson (see *Jefferson Papers*, 27:601–3).

2. For the report under discussion, see Hamilton to GW, 2 Dec. 1793. See also Hamilton to GW, 23 Nov. 1793.

3. Philadelphia residents suffered from a yellow fever epidemic during the late summer and fall of 1793. Hamilton and his wife, Elizabeth Schuyler

Hamilton, contracted the disease in early September (GW to Hamilton, 6 Sept. 1793). Following his recovery, Hamilton took his family to Albany, N.Y., to stay with his father-in-law, Philip Schuyler. He did not return to the Philadelphia area until 23 Oct. (Hamilton to GW, 24 Oct. 1793).

4. On the allocation of a portion of the American debt payment to France for the purchase of provisions for the French colony of Saint Domingue, see Hamilton to GW, 19 Nov. 1792. On subsequent problems with this arrangement, see George Latimer to Hamilton, 2 Jan. 1793, and source note, in *Hamilton Papers*, 13:443–47.

5. For the agreement made with Ternant and for Genet's acceptance of this agreement, see Tobias Lear to Thomas Jefferson, 14 Jan. 1793, and n.1 to that document; and Hamilton to Ternant, 13 Jan. 1793, and to Genet, 25 May and 4 June 1793 (*Hamilton Papers*, 13:478–79; 14:482–83, 517).

6. On the role of Antoine-René-Charles Mathurin de La Forest, the French consul general, in acquiring provisions for Saint Domingue, see Hamilton to GW, 19 Nov. 1792, and n.4 to that document.

7. Genet's letter to Hamilton of 3 June 1793, concerning Charles-François Bournonville's authorization, has not been identified.

8. In his letter to Jefferson of 18 June 1793, Genet wrote that he would no longer use advances on the American debt to pay for provisions shipped directly from the United States to Saint Domingue (*Jefferson Papers*, 26:308–11; translation, *ASP, Foreign Relations*, 1:158). For a list of merchants holding unpaid bills of exchange from Saint Domingue officials, totaling $93,533.20, which were discharged by the Treasury Department from 3 Sept. through 20 Dec. 1793 out of funds allocated to the French debt, see *Hamilton Papers*, 17:537–38. On this payment, see Hamilton's conversation with Genet, 27 June, and Hamilton to Genet, 24 July 1793 (*Hamilton Papers*, 15:29–30, 124–25).

9. On this refusal, see Hamilton to GW, 2 Dec. 1793.

10. For Genet's letter to Jefferson of 14 June 1793, see *Jefferson Papers*, 26:283–84 (translation, *ASP, Foreign Relations*, 1:156–7).

11. See Jefferson to Genet, 19 June 1793 (*Jefferson Papers*, 26:320). On Jefferson's submission of this letter to GW for approval, see *JPP*, 183.

12. At this point and throughout the remainder of this letter, the clerk erroneously wrote "600,000."

13. On the 1783 loan from France of 6 million livres, see Bayley, *National Loans*, 14.

14. On the negotiations conducted by Oliver Wolcott, Jr., and Bournonville, see Hamilton to Genet, 26 Nov.; Genet to Hamilton, 20 Nov.; and Hamilton to Bournonville, 10 Dec. 1793 (*Hamilton Papers*, 15:411, 423, 453).

15. Edmund Randolph enclosed this report with his letter to Genet of 8 Jan. 1794, which reads: "I do myself the honor of inclosing to you the report of the Secretary of the Treasury, upon your letter of the 21st ultimo to the Secretary of State. It was referred to the former, as being within his department" (FrPMAE: Correspondance Politique, Etats-Unis, Supplement Volume 20).

Henry Knox to Bartholomew Dandridge, Jr.

Dear Sir   War department January 4th 1794

Will you be so good as to present to the President the enclosed draft of a letter to me on the subject of the resolve of Congress of the 31st Ultimo, and also my answer thereto.[1] I am Dear Sir Your obedt Servant

                                                        H. Knox

LS, DLC:GW; LB, DLC:GW.

1. The draft was of GW's letter to Knox of 1 January. For the enclosed answer, see Knox to GW, 2 January.

From Henry Knox

Sir,   War department January 4th 1794

I suggest to your consideration the propriety of creating by law, an Office of Commissary of Stores, the person who should be appointed thereto to have the superintendence and accountability of receiving, safekeeping and issuing all the public Stores under such regulations as the wisdom of Congress may devise.[1]

An Office similar to this existed and was found indespensible during the late War, but which was abolished by a resolve of Congress of the 20. July 1785.[2]

It is however conceived necessary and proper that under the prospect of augmenting the means of our defence that this branch of public service should be placed under the direction of a responsible Officer.[3] I have the honor to be with the greatest respect sir Your obedient Servant.

L, DLC:GW; LB, DLC:GW.

1. In their respective outlines to GW of November 1793 and circa 28 Nov. 1793, in which they suggested topics for GW's fifth annual address to Congress, both Alexander Hamilton and Edmund Randolph suggested the creation of this office.

2. For the abolishment of this office in 1785, see *JCC* 29: 561.

3. The letter-book copy has "office." GW recommended the establishment of this office in a letter of 7 Jan. 1794 to the U.S. Senate and House of Representatives.

From Edmund Randolph

Sir   Philadelphia January 4. 1794.

I must beg the favor of you to cast your eye over the list of business, which remains to be acted on in this office.[1] My object in making this request is, that, if any part of it should deserve a priority, different from that, which I shall pursue in executing it, you would be pleased to suggest it. The order, in which I mean to take the subjects up, is according to the numbers 1. 2. 3. 4. 5. The lesser matters will be occasionally laid before you, as leisure from the greater will permit. I have the honor, sir, to be with the highest respect yr mo. ob. serv.

                                                        Edm: Randolph.

ALS, DNA: RG 59, Miscellaneous Letters; LB, DLC:GW; LB, DNA: RG 59, GW's Correspondence with His Secretaries of State; LB, DNA: RG 59, Domestic Letters.

1. The enclosed list has not been identified.

From Edmund Randolph

Sir   Philadelphia January 4. 1794.

I have examined the journal of the proceedings of the Executive in the territory North West of the Ohio. It is very little more, than a history of bickerings and discontents, which do not require the attention of the President. I shall therefore forbear to send it to you, unless you should call for it.[1]

The laws of that territory are now under transcription, that they may be forwarded to Congress. It was for some time doubted, whether they were to be laid before that body, without a special order for that purpose. But the doubt is now removed, by a conversation with Colo. Sargent.[2] I have the honor, sir, to be with the highest respect yr mo. ob. serv.

                                                        Edm: Randolph.

ALS, DNA: RG 59, Miscellaneous Letters; LB, DLC:GW; LB, DNA: RG 59, GW's Correspondence with His Secretaries of State; LB, DNA: RG 59, Domestic Letters.

1. On 12 Aug. 1793, Tobias Lear sent the "Copy from the Journal of proceedings in the Executive Department of Government, Territory of the United States Northwest of the River Ohio, commencing January the 1st. 1793 and ending upon the 30th. of June in the same year By Winthrop Sargent Secre-

tary" to former secretary of state Thomas Jefferson for examination, asking him to report "anything that may be found therein requiring the agency of the President." For this journal, see DNA: RG 59, Territorial Papers, Territory Northwest of the River Ohio; see also Carter, *Territorial Papers*, 3:390–411.

2. The transcriptions were being made from "A Copy of Laws passed in the Territory of the United States Northwest of the River Ohio from July to Decr 1792 inclusive," which Sargent had prepared earlier (DNA: RG 59, Territorial Papers, Territory Northwest of the River Ohio; printed in Pease, *Laws of the Northwest Territory*, 57–119; see also Lear to Jefferson, 26 Feb. 1793). According to "An Ordinance for the government of the territory of the United States North west of the river Ohio," 13 July 1787, the "governor, and judges or a majority of them shall adopt and publish in the district such laws of the original states criminal and civil as may be necessary and best suited to the circumstances of the district and report them to Congress from time to time, which laws shall be in force in the district until the organization of the general assembly therein, unless disapproved of by Congress" (Carter, *Territorial Papers*, 2:42–43). For GW's submission of these laws, see GW to U.S. Senate and House of Representatives, 21 Jan. 1794.

From George Read

Sir   New Castle [Del.] 4th Janry 1794.

As the two fugitive Ladies from St Domingo who addressed those two letters to you which I now return in this inclosure[1] lived very retired from their coming into this place I had heard nothing more respecting them than from the report of three of the Inhabitants acting as a Committee to inquire into the situation and wants of the French strangers that had temporary residence among us—That they appeared to be well bred women who spoke of possessing real property in the district of Jeremie[2] and had for some time expected the arrival of a considerable quantity of Coffee, part of it's produce which had been nearly ready for shipping when they left the Island—that they expressed a desire to obtain a Loan or advance of monies on the credit of their property but declined to make known their particular wants or to accept any part of the provision made here for distressed French Fugitives who might come among us. As I do not speak their language I had not made them any personal visit until after I received your Favour of the 26th Ulto and making every inquiry within my reach then of their character situation and circumstances, the result of which is that I am induced to believe they are such persons as they represent themselves in their inclosed Letters and further that their family Connections have been among the most respectable of that Island. Under this Impression I delivered your Letter addressed to them with its particular contents and they expressed much satisfaction at receiving it. I have hopes that the legislature of the State who will be in Session in the next Week will provide further relief than what can be obtained from the private contributions of a few—there are several other wanting persons (fugitives) in our Town and the burthen of supply is borne by a few.[3]

It wou'd Afford me pleasure at all times to carry into Execution your wishes and more particularly so on Occasions similar to the present one. with the utmost Esteem and respect I am Sir Your most Obedient and very humble Servt

Geo: Read.

ALS, PHi: Sprague Collection.

1. GW had enclosed the two letters from Laurent de Saxÿ and Laurent de Verneüil of 6 and 10 Dec. 1793 in his letter to Read of 26 Dec. 1793. He also had enclosed his reply of 26 Dec. to the two women and $25, both of which Read was instructed to deliver if the recipients seemed deserving of GW's assistance.

2. The district of Jérémie, and its port city of the same name, was located on the Jacmel Peninsula of present-day southwest Haiti.

3. The Delaware General Assembly that met from 7 Jan. until 8 Feb. 1794 did not pass any laws to provide additional relief for the French refugees within the state (*Laws of the state of Delaware, passed at a session of the General Assembly, which was begun and held at Dover on Tuesday, the seventh day of January, and ended on Saturday, the eighth day of February, in the year of our Lord, one thousand, seven hundred and ninety-four, and of the independence of America, the eighteenth. Published by authority* [Wilmington, Del., 1794]).

From Louis Busque

A Son Excéllence Washington, président du congrés des Etats unis de l'amérique

Général,   A Baltimore Le 6 janvier 1794

Ecrire au Réstaurateur de La Liberté américaine! Ecrire a ce Républicain! on dévine aisément que c'est a Washington, qu'on parle: Lui Rappéllerons nous qu'il a degagé son pays des préjugés qui Le dégradoint, qu'il a terrassé Le déspotisme en Rappellant Le peuple américan a Sa grandeur! et qu'il a donné ce ton mâle d'Enérgie á l'homme pour Lui faire connoître ce qu'il est ⟨a⟩ nous Sa modéstie me Le défend, et Sa délicatesse me dispense de cét Eloge. Essayons de Lui éxposèr nôtre Situation avec une plume Simple, La Seule qui puisse Lui convenir.

je mêtts Sous Les yeux de Son Excèllence que jai été victime des criminalistes qui ont pérdu nôtre colonie, et que j'ai été En Butte a La faction des Emissaires de L'ancien gouvernement pour avoir manifesté de patriotisme, et fait des Efforts pour Sauver St domingue; ces vértus dans un chéf de La garde nationale, ont été considerées comme des crimes aux yeux des Ennémis implacables de La République française, qui avoint Résolu d'anéantir un pays jadis aussi fortuné. a ces traits d'horreur on Recconnoît Bien Les commissaires nationaux civils, qui ont massacrés incendiés, ambarqués, et proscrits Le Restes des français Le plus Réccommandables, dévoués entiérement a La constitution Républicaine, et tout ce qu'ils poccédoint a tombé au pouvoir de Leurs Ravisseurs. á péine Suis-je Echappé au couteau de Ses assassins, que je Rétrouve dans La pérsonne du ministre Génét, un 3me commissaire, qui n'a pas moins de cruauté que Les polverél et Sonthonax, de Laisser périr de misére et de faim Les français, qui Lui demandent sécours et assistance; ainsi général, mourir d'une maniére ou d'autre c'est toujours mourir, et cétte Barbarie Remplit Entiérement Le plan de nos Ennèmis conjuré et pour Rendre nôtre position plus amére, ce ministre infidélle Répend avéc profusion hor de La République a Ses ennemis, en abusant une infinité des français qui ne Savent ou donnér de La tête.[1] Le coeur me saigne Républicaine général, de voir une partie des français Répendus dans vôtre continent faire des voeux pour La pérte de Leur mére patrie, et non Se joindre a ceux des véritables français, qui ne céssent d'en faire pour La Réütssitte de Ses armes contre toute L'europe. mais Le tems approche? Les ennemis commencent a Se confondre. cet Espoir me Rédonne La vie! et tout Séra compensé. á Se tableau Washington Sensible, Recconnoîtra Lâme franche d'un colon français, qui a eu L'honneur de combattre dans Les grénadiéres de gatinois, pour accélérér la Reduction d'York; et faire mêttre Bas Les armes a Ses Ennémis et attend de Sa Bonté facile des Sécours de Son Excéllence, qui n'a peu obténir du Répresentant de Sa Nation
  Salut,

Busque

Chef du 1er Bataillon de La

garde nationale du port au prince

a Son Excéllence Washington   addrésse poste Réstante

ALS, DNA: RG 59, Miscellaneous Letters. The docket on this letter identifies the writer as Louis Busque. He was one of many refugees who fled to the United States in 1793 to escape the ravages of a civil war in the French colony of Saint Domingue. According to his letter, Busque was the commander of the national guard battalion stationed at the colony's capital of Port-au-Prince. During the Revolutionary War, he served as a grenadier in the Gâtinais regiment. This regiment, Busque reminds GW, was responsible for the seizure of Redoubt No. 9 at Yorktown on 14 Oct. 1781 (see Rice and Brown, *American Campaigns of Rochambeau's Army*, 1:138–42, 150).

1. Busque praises the republican virtues of GW before expressing bitter complaints about the conduct of colonial commissioners Etienne Polverel and Léger Félicité Sonthonax. After criticizing Edmond Genet, the French minister to the United States, for his failure to offer aid to those who had asked for help, Busque asks GW to provide assistance for the French refugees. No reply from GW has been found. On the aid program established by the federal government, see Edmund Randolph to GW, 27 Feb. 1794 (first letter).

From J. Des Moulins

Most worthy Sir   Philadelphia January 6th 1794

I humbly presume to remind your Excellency, of, at present, a very unfortunate Man, who did himself the Honor of troubling You with a long Letter from Wilmington on the 1st of last Novr, taking the Liberty in it, of explaining the very unlucky Chances it has been my Lot to experience in my warm Endeavours to settle myself advantageously in your Country.[1]

The very material Concerns that must at present Engross your Excellencys Attention, leaves little Reason for an humble Individual like myself, to entertain my Surprise that my Letter may have been overlooked, notwithstanding I am so fully aware of your Excellency's truly great and Philanthropick Mind.

I have been in this City, since the 8th Octr, but it has pleased the supreme Disposer of all Events, to continue upon me a very severe Cold I caught on Board, and to inflict me with a Deafness ever since I have been here, which has prevented my Exertions to establish myself in a Situation—The October Packet being still due, I have not received a Remitance I expected, and am in the greatest Distress. In the Course of the Spring my Circumstances and Health, will be, I trust in a very different State and if your Excellency's generous Heart induces You to afford me some temporary Assistance, your Goodness will ever be acknowledged by me with the warmest Sense of Gratitude.

That I am no Impostor, I can refer your Excellency for Proof, to Genl Proctor, who I have had the Honor and Happiness of knowing since I have been here, and other respectable Persons, who are acquainted with the Truth of my unfortunate Situation.[2] I am about to form a Connection with some Gentleman of the Law, from the very good Prospects I have of bringing over considerable Agency Business from Europe, and mean as soon as possible, to enroll myself a Citizen of your State.[3] I have the Honor to be most faithfully, Sir, your very respectfull, most obedient, and very humble Servant

J: Des Moulins

ALS, DNA: RG 59, Miscellaneous Letters.

1. The letter to GW of 1 Nov. 1793, probably from Wilmington, Del., has not been found.

2. Thomas Proctor was currently a brigadier general in the Pennsylvania militia.

3. There is no Moulins or Des Moulins listed in the Philadelphia directory for 1795 (Hogan, *Philadelphia Directory, 1795*).

From William DuVal

Sir   Richmond [Va.] January 6th 1794
I beg leave to introduce to your Notice Mr Ast a Merchant in this City and a Gentleman of respectibility. He lived several Years in the Family of the late Thomas Barclay Esqr. when they were in Europe. He will offer Sir to your Consideration Three Schemes or plans which I am told, may be, if adopted benefial, of that Sir, you'll be the most competent Judge, and if they merit your approbation their Utility will induce you to afford Mr Ast your Countenance and patronage.[1] I am Sir, with the highest Respect, Your mo. obt Servant.

William DuVal.

ALS, DNA: RG 59, Miscellaneous Letters.

William DuVal (1748–1842) was a lawyer, businessman, and veteran of the Revolutionary War. He married Lucy Ann Pope (1753–1795) in 1772 and after her death, Susan Brown Christian. He served in the Virginia House of Delegates, 1782, and was the mayor of Richmond, 1805–6 (Bessie Berry Grabowski, *The Du Val Family of Virginia, 1701; Descendants of Daniel Du Val, Huguenot, and Allied Families*, [Richmond, 1931], 187–93). On 7 Jan., DuVal wrote a second letter to GW recommending William Frederick Ast; while not identical to this one, its wording is very similar (DLC:GW).

1. William Frederick Ast (c.1767–1807) emigrated first to France from his native Germany. By 1787 he was serving as secretary to Thomas Barclay, the U.S. consul general to France. Ast arrived in Norfolk, Va., in early 1793 and established the mercantile firm of Ast, Bingham & Company with stores in Norfolk, Petersburg, and Richmond, where he settled. On 6 Nov. 1793, Ast solicited Thomas Jefferson's assistance in forwarding to Congress his petition concerning a plan to provide insurance on a much less expensive scale than that offered by British companies (*Jefferson Papers*, 27:306–8). He had three different plans that would cover, respectively, losses on buildings, ships, and goods at sea. Although Ast did not receive the desired support from Congress, his fire insurance plan for buildings was chartered by the Virginia General Assembly on 22 Dec. 1794 as the Mutual Assurance Society, against Fire on Buildings of the State of Virginia (see John B. Danforth and Herbert A. Claiborne, *Historical Sketch of the Mutual Association of Virginia, Richmond, Va., from its organization in 1794 to 1879*, [Richmond, 1879]). Ast attempted, unsuccessfully, to solicit GW's participation in a letter of 7 Oct. 1795, in which he enclosed a broadside explaining the terms and conditions of this insurance company and a list of its current subscribers (ALS, DLC:GW).

Alexander Hamilton's Proposed Presidential Message to Congress

[Philadelphia, 6–13 Jan. 1794]

Since the application, which was made to the Government of France, for the Recall of its present Minister,[1] that Minister has furnished new and material causes of dissatisfaction with his Conduct. But these occasions of offence have hitherto passed without particular notice; in the hope that it would not be long before the arrival of an order of Recall would terminate the embarrassment—and in the desire, inspired by sentiments of friendship and respect for his Nation, to avoid as long as possible an Act of extremity towards its Agent. But a case has occurred, which is conceived to render further forbearance inconsistent with the dignity and perhaps the safety of the United States. It is proved, as will be seen by papers now transmitted for the information of Congress, that this foreign Agent has proceeded to the extraordinary length of issuing commissions in the name of the French Republic to several of our citizens, for the purpose of raising, within the two Carolinas and Georgia, a large military force with the declared design of employing them, in concert with such Indians as could be engaged on the Enterprize, in an expedition against the colonies, in our neighbourhood, of a Nation with whom the U. States are at peace.[2]

It would seem, likewise, from information contained in other papers, herewith also communicated, that a similar attempt has been going on in another quarter, namely the State of Kentucke; though the fact is not yet ascertained with the requisite authenticity.[3]

Proceedings so unwarrantable, so derogatory to the sovereignty of the U. States, so dangerous in precedent and tendency, appear to render it improper that the person chargeable with them should longer continue to exercise the functions and enjoy the privileges of a diplomatic character.

The supersedure of the exercise of those functions, nevertheless, being a measure of great delicacy and magnitude, I have concluded not to come to an ultimate determination, without first placing the subject under the eye of Congress.

But unless the one or the other House shall in the mean time signify to me an opinion that is it not adviseable so to do, I shall consider it as my duty to adopt that measure after the expiration of [   ] days from this communication.[4]

ADf, DLC:GW; copy, DLC: Hamilton Papers.

1. On the administration's request that the French government recall its minister plenipotentiary to the United States, see Cabinet Opinion on the Recall of Edmond Genet, 23 Aug. 1793. Despite this earlier request, GW and the cabinet discussed in early January whether Genet's recent activities warranted an immediate revocation of his diplomatic privileges (GW to John Adams, 8 Jan. 1794; King, *Life and Correspondence of Rufus King,* 1:479–80).

2. On Genet's attempt to recruit Americans from the Carolinas and Georgia for service in an expedition against the Spanish colonies of East and West Florida, see William Moultrie to GW, 7 Dec. 1793, and enclosures.

3. On an attempt to recruit residents of Kentucky to serve in an expedition against the Spanish in Louisiana, see Genet's conversation with Thomas Jefferson, 5 July; José Ignacio de Viar and José de Jaudenes to Thomas Jefferson, 27 Aug., and enclosure; and Jefferson to Isaac Shelby, 29 Aug. 1793, *Jefferson Papers,* 26:438–39, 771–74, 785–86.

4. GW did not use Hamilton's proposed message. According to Rufus King's notes of February 1794, "Hamilton conferred with me, and I think with [Oliver] Ellsworth, and some others" upon submitting this message to Congress. King, however, opposed this idea "on the ground that it was throwing the Apple of Discord into Congress, and would inevitably produce a violent struggle and convulsion." After Hamilton's proposal was dropped from consideration, GW "announced to the heads of the Departments that he had

well weighed the question and had come to a decision—that he possessed
the Right to dismiss, that the occasion would justify dismission and that the
Duties of his station required of him the exercise of this power in the immediate dismission of Mr. Genet. Orders were therefore given to make the
requisite preparation to communicate this Resolution to Congress" (King,
Life and Correspondence of Rufus King, 1:479–80). When reports indicating
that the French government had issued Genet's recall arrived from France in
mid-January, GW abandoned this option and made no mention of revoking
Genet's diplomatic privileges in his message to the U.S. Senate and House
of Representatives of 15 Jan. (Gouverneur Morris to GW, 19 Oct. 1793, and
n.1 to that document; Washington's Note Concerning the Recall of Edmond
Genet, c.16 Jan. 1794). For the official notice of Genet's recall, see Provisional
Executive Council of France to GW, 15 Nov. 1793.

Letter not found: from Howell Lewis, 6 Jan. 1794. GW wrote William
Pearce on 12 Jan. acknowledging receipt of "Mr Lewis's of the 6th
enclosing the Weekly reports."

To Howell Lewis or William Pearce

Mr Lewis—or Mr Pearce[1]   Philadelphia Jan. 6th 1794
     The Reports of the 28th of December have been received,
and Mr Butlers acct therewith—As I have no Acct against him,
and Mr Whiting only kept memorandums, instead of regular
Accounts, he must be paid according to his own statement. for
this, and other purposes, I send two bank notes for one hundred
dollars each.[2]
     It is very unlucky that the late spell of freezing weather should
be suffered to pass away without filling the Ice house. do not let
this happen again; but embrace the first freezing that happens[3]
to accomplish this work.
     Let me know what quantity of Oats have been threshed at the
Mansion house, and what has been done with them? By the time
employed in getting them out there ought to be a good many
of them. I wish to know also what quantity Stuart has? These
two parcels, together with those at Dogue Run I directed to be
reserved for Seed—& when the whole quantity contained at the
different places are known I shall be abl⟨e⟩ to decide how much
more to provide—or what further to do in the case.[4]
     There was Oats raised from a few grains of a particular sort
which I sent to my Gardener last Spring—get these from him,

and make the most of them, by sowing them in drills the coming Spring.[5] By Mr Jefferson, I sent a Bundle of Poccon or Illinois nut and desired them to be left at the Post Office in Alexandria. When they are recd desire the Gardener to plant them in a nursery.[6] I shall send more by the first Vessel, or other proper conveyence wch shall offer. I also gave the Gardener a few Seed of East India hemp to raise from, enquire for the seed which has been saved, and make the most of it at the proper Season for Sowing.

What is the present appearance of the growing Wheat? I am in a hurry and shall only add, that as soon as I hear of Mr Pearce's being settled at Mount Vernon—I shall write more fully on some other matters. I am &ca

Go: Washington

P.S. Recollecting since writing the fore going, that Mr Whitings Memo. Book was here I have desired Mr Dandridge to take a copy from it of the charges against Butler; which he has done, and it is now enclosed[7]—By this you will settle with him.

ALS, ViMtvL; ALS (letterpress copy), DLC:GW. The docket, written by Pearce, reads "Letter No. 2 from the president Jany 6 1794."

1. By this date Pearce had arrived at Mount Vernon, where he assumed the duties of estate manager that Lewis had been handling temporarily (Mount Vernon Accounts, 1794–97).

2. The farm reports dated 28 Dec., the carpenters' reports of 29 Dec., and James Butler's financial account probably were enclosed in Lewis's letter to GW of 1 January. The enclosed account has not been identified, but Butler received £13.16.4 on 7 Jan. 1794 for "his wages in full for the year 93" (Mount Vernon Accounts, 1794–97). The farm and carpenters' reports are at DLC:GW.

3. At this point, GW struck out the word "again" on the receiver's copy but not on the letterpress copy.

4. Butler, William Stuart, and Henry McCoy were the respective overseers of the Mansion House, River, and Dogue Run farms.

5. GW had sent "English Oats" the previous Spring to head gardener John Christian Ehlers "for the purpose of raising" seed (GW to Lewis, 25 Aug. 1793).

6. The pecan, *Carya illinoinensis*, is a species of hickory and is native to North America. Thomas Jefferson arrived at Monticello, his home near Charlottesville, Va., on 15 Jan. (Jefferson to Archibald Stuart, 26 Jan. 1794, *Jefferson Papers*, 28:11).

7. Neither Anthony Whitting's memorandum book nor the enclosed copy of Butler's account has been identified. Butler did not leave GW's service until late August 1794 (GW to Pearce, 7 Sept. 1794, ALS, ViMtvL; ALS [letterpress copy], DLC:GW).

From Garret Rapalje

New York Jany 6th 1794

The Memorial of Garret Rapalje of the City of New York Merchant—Humbly Sheweth,[1]

That your Memorialist, has resided upwards of five Years at New Orleans in West Florida in the Spanish Dominion that he is well acquainted with the Situation Politicks and Commerce of that Country—That the Trade from the Interior Parts of the Continent in the United States down the Misissipi is very great and extensive.

That the Inhabitants of the United States suffer much from a Want of a proper Person in the Character of a Consul to represent the Interests of the Traders to the Spanish Government to prevent any Grevances which daily happen from the Want of such a Person to interfere in their Behalf.

That your Memorialist is well known to Mr Elias Boudinot of the House of Representaives in Congress from the State of New Jersey.[2]

That your Memorialist hopes your Excellency will consider the Necessity of such an appointment—that he has a numerous Family to support that he has been a great Sufferer during the lat[e] War between America and Great Britain that it is the best Service he can render himself and his Country—that a small Salary to enable him to maintain his Family with his Knowledge and experience in Trade and Commerce will make the Situation more eligable to him than any other Person.[3]

That your memorialist hopes your Excellency will take into Consideration the Prayer of this your Memorialists humble Petition and your memorialist will ever Pray &c.

Garret Rapalje

ALS, DNA: RG 59, Miscellaneous Letters.

1. Merchant and land speculator Garret Rapalje (1730–c.1795) was of Dutch ancestry and resided in New York City prior to the Revolutionary War. By 1777, however, he had settled at Squire's Point in Sussex County, N.J., where he owned the Brooklyn (Brookland) forge. During the war his loyalty to the American cause was questioned on several occasions, eventually leading to periods of brief incarceration in 1777 and 1778. In addition to his trade in iron, he also speculated in land in British West Florida, where he received a grant for 25,000 acres in 1774. With the profit received from the division and sale of this land, Rapalje purchased a plantation near Baton

Rouge, in present-day Louisiana, but he did not move there until after the Revolutionary War had ended. Rapalje's ventures in Louisiana proved unsuccessful, and he returned to New York City sometime before his death. See Charles Shimer Boyer, *Early Forges and Furnaces in New Jersey* (Philadelphia, 1931), 46–47, 218–19; Christopher Morris, *Becoming Southern: The Evolution of a Way of Life, Warren County and Vicksburg, Mississippi, 1770-1860* (New York, 1995); and real estate advertisement, *Pennsylvania Gazette* (Philadelphia), 17 June 1778.

2. In 1777, Elias Boudinot made arrangements with Rapalje to harbor his wife, Hannah Stockton Boudinot, should British troops threaten their home (Boyd, *Elias Boudinot,* 42).

3. On behalf of GW, Edmund Randolph wrote Rapalje on 7 Feb. that "circumstances have hitherto prevented the establishment of such an office" in New Orleans and "continue to prevent it" (DNA: RG 59, Domestic Letters).

From Augustin Regnaud

Général   Philadelphie Le 6 janvier 1794
    Avocat au Parlement de Paris et cy-devant Conseiller au Conseil Superieur du Cap, je suis arrivé Sans ressources dans ce Continent: reduit à la derniere extremité et creancier de La Republique francoise d'une Somme assez considerable, je me Suis adressé au Ministre françois pour lui demander du Secours; ignorant à quel titre il en distribue, il a rejetté ma petition. Veuillez, Général, agreant mes foibles travaux, disposer de moi, et considerant, quant à present, mes besoins, Daignez m'arbitrer à titre de prêt, une Somme quelconque, pour Sureté de la quelle j'offre de deposer une reconnoissance de 9,000 [livres tournois] jusqu'à ce que des circonstances plus heureuses me mettent à même de la retirer et de Satisfaire, avec interets, à une dette contracteé Sous vos auspices.[1] Salut en la prosperité de vos jours et Le bonheur de vos Etats

                                    A. Regnaud
                        2e Rue Nord No 227. chez Mr Antony[2]

ALS (in French), DNA: RG 59, Miscellaneous Letters.
    Augustin Regnaud (born c.1768) was listed as a grocer at 227 North Third Street in the *Philadelphia Directory, 1796*. He continued for many years as a merchant and broker and was a member in 1802 of the Freemasons Loge Française l'Amenité in Philadelphia (*Tableau des ff. composant la T.R. Loge Française l'Amenité, No. 73 réqulièrement constituée à l'O. de Philadelphie par le T.R. Grand Orient de Pennsylvanie* [Philadelphia, 1802], 9).
    1. Regnaud was among the many refugees who came to the United States

in 1793 to escape the devastation wrought by a civil war in the French colony of Saint Domingue. Since Edmond Genet, the French minister to the United States, had denied his request for assistance, Regnaud now asked GW for a loan.

GW's secretary, Bartholomew Dandridge, Jr., replied to Regnaud on 9 Jan.: "The President of the United States has received a letter from you dated the 6 instant: In answer to it the President directs me to inform you, that, however desirous he is at all times to releive distress, and to give aid to the succourless, yet so multiplied are the calls upon his benevolence, that his resources are far short of enabling him to satisfy them. The President regrets his inability to afford you the relief asked for, and presumes, under the circumstances above stated, you will see the propriety of his declining to comply with your request" (DLC:GW).

2. In the *Philadelphia Directory, 1794,* Jacob Anthony, Sr. (c.1736–1804), a turner and maker of musical instruments, is listed at 227 North Second Street.

From Richard Dobbs Spaight

Sir   No. Carolina Fayetteville 6th Jan: 1794

I do myself the honor to enclose to you a copy of the proceedings of the General Assembly respecting our frontiers,[1] in conformity to the request of the legislature expressed in those proceedings I have given orders to Col: D. Vance of Buncomb county to call into service the Scouts or patroles agreable to the instructions contained in the Secretary of Wars letter of the 19th Decem: 1792.[2]

I have likewise given the necessary orders for having the militia of the districts of Salisbury and Morgan, divided into four classes, with orders to the first class to hold themselves in readiness to act whenever occasion may require at the same time I have directed the officers to act on the defensive only.[3]

The Indians have committed depredations on the property of the Citize⟨ns⟩ of this State by stealing their horses, but they have not as yet killed any person within our limits. By accts lately received from thence it appears that they have killed three persons just without the line of this state.[4] I have the honor to be &c.

R.D. Spaight

LB, Nc-Ar: Governors' Letterbooks.

1. The enclosed copy has not been identified.

2. On 19 Dec. 1792, Henry Knox had written Anthony Martin, Spaight's

predecessor as governor, concerning defensive measures for North Carolina's frontiers (Nc-Ar: Governors' Letterbooks). According to Spaight's address to the state's General Assembly on 9 Dec. 1793, Knox's letter gave "me the power of calling into service or not calling into service, as the necessity of the case might require, a certain number of scouts or patroles, not exceeding six or eight for a frontier of twelve miles extent." In this same address, Spaight mentioned that a letter from Col. David Vance of Buncombe County reported that the Indians "have become lately very troublesome, and have committed very considerable depredations on the property of the citizens of this state, and that it is probable that they may make an attack on our frontier" (*N.C. House Journal 1793,* 9).

In his letter to Spaight of 22 Nov. 1793, Vance wrote about the "hostile appearance of our neighbours the Cherokees. . . . For several months past there has scarcely one week past, but the Indians have stolen horses from us, more or less, and it appears to me (without a stop is put to their conduct) that in a little time our County will be entirely stripped of horses. They have not murdered any person yet in our county. but about forty miles below us in the [Southwest] territory they are frequently murdering, and I know not how soon it may be the unhappy fate of some of ourselves." Vance then speculated that it would not be long before residents would retaliate against the Indians. He had already heard reports of the murder of two Indians, and he reported that a group of men from Buncombe County planned to join a party of men from the territory on 30 Nov. for an expedition against nearby Indian towns. While he would try to prevent the expedition, he doubted that he would succeed (Nc-Ar: Governors' Letterbooks).

Col. David Vance (1745–1813) moved from Frederick County, Va., to North Carolina around 1774. After serving first in the Continental army and then in the state militia during the Revolutionary War, Vance moved his family near present-day Asheville. He served several terms in the state's General Assembly, was clerk of the court for Buncombe County, and was the commander of the county militia. For the orders given to Vance, see n.3 of Spaight's third letter to GW of 8 Feb. 1794.

3. For administrative purposes, North Carolina's counties were grouped into several judicial and militia districts. In January 1794, the Salisbury and Morgan districts covered the western portion of the state. The Morgan District included Lincoln, Rutherford, Burke, Buncombe, and Wilkes counties. The Salisbury District included Rockingham, Guilford, Montgomery, Stokes, Surry, Iredell, Rowan, Cabarrus, and Mecklenburg counties. For the orders given to the commanding officers of Burke, Lincoln, and Wilkes counties, see Spaight to Col. J. McDowell, 1 Jan. 1794 (Nc-Ar: Governors' Letterbooks).

In his address to the state assembly of 9 Dec. 1793, Spaight requested approval of his plan to call the scouts into service in Buncombe County and said that he would "at the same time issue instructions to the commanding officer of the district of Morgan to have the militia of that district classed into three or four divisions, as the case might require; with instructions to the first class to hold themselves in readiness to march at a moment's warning to such part of the frontier as may be attacked by the Indians" (*N.C. House Journal 1793*, 9). In its 18 Dec. response to Spaight's address, the assembly noted that the inhabitants of the state's westernmost counties "are much exposed to the attacks and depredations of the Indian savages, which ought to entitle them to the attention of the General Government, who ought to provide for their protection and defence." It then approved Spaight's plan to call up the militia, in accordance with Knox's earlier letter. At the same time, it resolved that the militia officer and residents of these counties "be directed to confine themselves to act on the defensive only, until such times as the laws of the United States, ⟨or⟩ the orders of the President, shall authorize offensive measures against the Savages" (*N.C. Senate Journal 1793*, 16.)

4. Under GW's direction, Bartholomew Dandridge, Jr., sent Spaight's letter and its enclosures with his second letter to Knox of 20 January. "The President," Dandridge wrote, "desires you will report to him what steps you think ought to be taken in consequence thereof" (DLC:GW). For Knox's subsequent reply to Spaight, see n.1 of Knox to GW, 21 January.

From Richard Dobbs Spaight

Sir. No. Carolina Fayetteville January 6th 1794

Agreeable to the request of the legislature I do myself the honor to transmit to you, a copy of the petition of Thomas Person and others proprietors of lands in the Territory South of the Ohio And a copy of the petition of the Trustees of the University of North Carolina, together with sundry resolutions of the General Assembly on that subject.[1]

I have to request that you will be pleased to recommend the subject matter of the said petitions to the early consideration of Congress and to urge them to do speedy and ample justice to the petitioners.[2] I have the honor to be sir Your Most obedt Servant

Richd: Dobbs Spaight

ALS, DNA: RG 59, Miscellaneous Letters; LB, Nc-Ar: Governors' Letterbooks.

1. Thomas Person (1733–1800), although born in Virginia, spent most of his life in North Carolina at his estate in Goshen, Granville (now Warren) County. After first accumulating land and money as a surveyor, he served in a number of public offices. He was a county sheriff, a justice of the peace, and a member of the General Assembly beginning in 1764 and serving almost continuously for thirty years. He helped to secure a charter for the University

of North Carolina in 1789 and was a member of its first board of trustees, 1789–95.

Person, John Rutledge, Hugh Williamson, William Polk, and Robert Irwin presented a petition to the North Carolina General Assembly on 21 Dec. 1793, asking for compensation on behalf of themselves and others for land granted them as bounties for their military service during the Revolutionary War or purchased for speculation. North Carolina, however, subsequently surrendered these western lands to the United States. The U.S. government ceded these same lands to the Chickasaw and Cherokee Indians in the respective treaties of Hopewell (1786) and Holston (1791), thus voiding the state grants. On 26 Dec. 1793, William R. Davie presented a petition on behalf of the trustees of the university, asking for compensation for the 20,000 acres granted to the university that also lay within the ceded territory. In its resolutions, the North Carolina General Assembly declared that the U.S. Congress was "bound by every principle of justice and equity, to grant complete and ample redress to the petitioners." It called on Spaight to solicit the president "that he will be pleased to recommend" the petitions to Congress for consideration and will "urge them to do speedy and ample justice to the petitioners" (Petitions of the University and Others to the Legislature Relative to Western Land Claims, 21 Dec. 1793, in Connor, R.D.W., *Documentary History of the University of North Carolina, 1776–1799*, 2 vols. [Chapel Hill, 1953], 1:279–86). The enclosed copies have not been identified.

2. Under GW's direction, Bartholomew Dandridge, Jr., enclosed Spaight's letter and its enclosures in a letter to Edmund Randolph of 20 Jan., in which he wrote: "The President wishes the Secy to report such measures as may seem to him proper to be taken relatively thereto" (DNA: RG 59, Miscellaneous Letters). GW subsequently complied with Spaight's request with a letter to the U.S. House of Representatives of 30 Jan., which reads: "I lay before you, the copy of a letter from the Governor of the State of North Carolina; together with two petitions, to which it refers, and which I am requested by the Legislature of that State, and himself, to transmit to Congress" (LB, DNA: RG 233, Third Congress, 1793–95, House Records of Legislative Proceedings, Journals; LB, DLC:GW).

From David Stuart

Dear Sir, Hope-Park [Va.][1] 6th Jany 1794

Time and longer experience having fully confirmed me in the sentiments I formerly expressed on the subject of my continuance in the office of Commissioner, I have to beg, you will consider my place as vacant after the first of March next[2]—It was my expectation, when I last conversed with you on this subject, that I should have been able to have resigned with propriety at the expiration of the late year: but the continuance of the lottery, begun under our auspices; seems to make it necessary, that we should keep together 'till it's termination[3]—It gives me great pleasure, when taking this step, to reflect that the object entrusted to our care, seems now by the tide of public opinion turning in its favor, to be secured beyond the reach of accident. I am with the greatest respect Your Affecte Servt

Dd: Stuart.

ALS, DLC:GW.

1. Stuart's home of Hope Park was located west of Alexandria near the road to Centreville and about five miles from that town.

2. Stuart continued to serve as a commissioner for the District of Columbia until July 1794 (4–6, 27–31 July 1794 minutes, DNA: RG 42, Records of the Commissioners for the District of Columbia, Proceedings, 1791–1802).

3. On the lottery administered by Samuel Blodget, Jr., in his capacity as superintendent of the District of Columbia and his delay in selecting and paying the winners of this lottery, see Thomas Johnson to GW, 23 Dec. 1793, and n.2 to that document.

To the United States Senate

Gentlemen of the Senate,   United States 6. January 1794.

I herewith transmit the copy of a Letter from The Secretary of War, stating the circumstances which have hitherto prevented any explanation of the fourth article of the Treaty with the Wabash Indians.[1]

Go: Washington

LS, DNA: RG 46, Third Congress, 1793–95, Senate Records of Executive Proceedings, President's Messages—Indian Relations; LB, DLC:GW.

1. For the enclosed letter, see Henry Knox to GW, 2 January. The Senate refused to ratify this treaty on 9 Jan. by a vote of 21 to 4 (*U.S. Senate Executive Journal*, 1:146).

From William Washington

Sir   Sandy-Hill [S.C.] Jany 6th 1794

Some time in April last I had the honor of addressing a Letter to you giving a particular account of the situation of Royal

Gift, together with Mr Freazer's account of his covering, which left a balance in your favor, of six hundred & seventy eight Dollars & 64/100, after deducting James Allen's charge, which was enclos'd in a Bill drawn by Prestman & Calhoun of Charleston upon Wm Bell of Philadelphia.[1] Some weeks thereafter I forwarded a duplicate with the second Bill: as I have not receiv'd an answer to either of those Letters it leaves me in doubt whether both have not miscarried.[2] In the Letters to which I have alluded I inform'd you that Royal Gift had been affected with a stiffness in his joints & a periodical lameness ever since his arrival in this Country which I believed to be the effects of his Journey, & am now sorry to add that his situation at present is not better & am apprehensive that it never will. Upon minute enquiry I have only been informed of two Foals which were produced from forty odd Mares & Jennies which were sent to him the Season before last. Under these circumstances I thought it prudent to lower the Terms of covering, but it did not answer the desired effect, only fifteen or sixteen Mares & Jennies were sent to him, all the property of those Gentlemen who had been disappointed the Season before.[3] The Money has not yet been paid & I now submit to you the propriety of demanding it except for those which shall eventually prove in foal.

If you think proper to let Royal-Gift remain in this Country I shall with pleasure take charge of him & consult your interest in the management of him, but am confident that it will be useless to advertise him for covering again in this Country, even at a very reduced price unless a great alteration takes place in his situation. If you think proper to have him sent to Virginia he must be conveyed by Water as I am certain that he cannot travel thither by land.[4] I am Sir with the greatest Respect & Regard Yr Very Obedt Serv.

W. Washington

ALS, PPRF; ALS (photocopy), DLC:GW.

1. For William Washington's letter and its enclosures concerning GW's jackass Royal Gift, see his letter to GW of 20 April 1793 and n.1. The bill probably was drawn on Philadelphia merchant William Bell of 217 High Street. (*Philadelphia Directory, 1794*, 10).

2. The duplicate letter from William Washington has not been found. GW's reply to the letter of 20 April 1793 and its duplicate has not been found (see GW to William Washington, 9 Feb. 1794).

3. The original cost for Royal Gift's services was six guineas for a jenny and five guineas for a mare (William Washington to George Augustine Washington, 15 Oct. 1792, in n.1 of GW to William Washington, 30 Jan. 1793).

4. For GW's reply, see GW to William Washington, 9 February.

Letter not found: from William Pearce, 7 Jan. 1794. GW wrote Pearce on 12 Jan. acknowledging receipt of "yours of the 7th Instt."

From Edmund Randolph

Philadelphia January 7. 1794.

The Secretary of State, after reviewing the letters from our Ministers, unanswered, has the honor to report to the President as follows:

Three of those letters are from Messrs Carmichael and Short jointly of June 6th Aug. 15th and Sep. 29th in the last year. The first, which is the only important one, pressed for new instructions, adapted to the new relations, which had sprung up between the different powers of Europe, as well as to the unpromising appearance of the negotiation. But as Mr Blake, the messenger to Madrid was to sail by direction in October, so as to be here about the middle of the last month, and the intelligence by him must essentially govern the conduct of our government, it is submitted to the President, whether it may not be better to postpone further, any decisive measures.[1]

The same observations, apply to the postponement of an answer to Mr Short's separate letters of June 7. July 1. and Augt 20. 1793. They relate entirely to his associated mission, except where they convey information, to which no answer was expected.[2]

No other letter from Mr Morris is now to be acted upon, but that of June 25. 1793; and no part even of it requires a reply, except the Decree of France, which has been so often made and revoked, and at length comprehends the Ship Laurens of South Carolina. But the dispatches, hourly expected from france, cannot but give the tone to our animadversions.[3]

Mr Pinckney's letters are dated July 8. Augt 1. 15. 27. & 28. and Sept. 25. & 27. 1793. That of aug. 15. being in cypher, appears to have been decyphered; but the solution is either mislaid or in the hands of Congress. Nothing can yet be answered, except the receipt of the copper. For the piracy on an American vessel by a french frigate—Philip Wilson's case—and that of the Marquis la Fayette, will become distinct subjects for the consideration of the President. Congress are occupied with the Severities of the British Government, which constitute the weightier parts of Mr Pinckney's correspondence; and the infraction of neutral rights, and the contest for the security of our Seamen will doubtless come into view.[4]

Altho' Mr Humphreys' letters are more numerous being of Aug. 4. 15. & 25. Sep. 1. 3. 13. 16. 17. & 26 Oct. 3. 6. 7 & 8. 1793. none of them are pressing; being letters of intelligence principally.[5]

As to Mr Dumas, even if he can be called a diplomatic character, his letters of may 1. June 22. July 13, and August 14. are only effusions of the pen. But it appears from a memorandum of Mr Jefferson, that Mr Dumas a considerable time ago suggested the propriety of selling the Hôtel at the Hague, which perhaps cannot be too soon attended to.[6]

It is designed, therefore, at present, to prepare for Mr Pinckney, Mr Morris, Messrs Carmichael and Short, and Mr Short, letters to be laid before the President;[7] acknowledging the receipt of theirs, notifying the change of the officer in the department of State,[8] and containing such other matters as may relate to them particularly, and any intelligence founded upon public documents in the United States.

Edm: Randolph.

LS, DNA: RG 59, Miscellaneous Letters; LB, DLC:GW; LB, DNA: RG 59, GW's Correspondence with His Secretaries of State; LB, DNA: RG 59, Reports of the Secretary of State to the President and Congress.

1. William Carmichael and William Short served as commissioners plenipotentiary to Spain. They were charged with obtaining the right to free navigation on the Mississippi River, a settlement of the disputed boundary between Georgia and Florida, and a commercial treaty with Spain. Additional instructions stressed the need to end Spanish encouragement of Indian hostilities in the Southwest Territory and to arrange the mutual exchange of fugitives and escaped slaves, (Jefferson to Carmichael and Short, 18 March, 24 April, and 14 Oct. 1792, *Jefferson Papers*, 23:292–93, 453–54; 24:479–80). The letters from Carmichael and Short to Thomas Jefferson of 6 June, 15 Aug., and 29 Sept. 1793 are in *Jefferson Papers*, 26:206–12, 668–671; 27:161–63. On the departure of James Blake for Spain and the dispatches he carried for Carmichael and Short, see Jefferson's first memorandum to GW of c.11 July 1793, and n.1.

2. For Short's letters to Jefferson of 7 June, 1 July, and 20 Aug. 1793, see

Jefferson Papers, 26:222–28, 428–30, 732. His associated mission was to gather intelligence for the United States.

3. The French decree of 9 May 1793 authorized the seizure of neutral vessels carrying provisions "destined for an enemy's port, or with merchandises belonging to an enemy," while that of 23 May exempted U.S. ships. According to Gouverneur Morris's letter to Jefferson of 25 June 1793, the National Convention had provisionally repealed the U.S. exemption on 28 May (*Jefferson Papers,* 26:363–69; *ASP, Foreign Relations,* 1:365, 377–78). On the capture of the ship Laurens (Lawrence), commanded by Capt. Thomas White, see Delamotte to Jefferson, 2 June, and Thomas Pinckney to Jefferson, 27 Sept. 1793, *Jefferson Papers,* 26:166–67; 27:158; and Jefferson to GW, 30 Nov. 1793, and n.2 to that document. The dispatches from France had been entrusted to William Culver, who commanded the sloop *Hannah* (Morris to GW, 19 Oct. 1793). This ship arrived at Philadelphia in mid-January 1794 (*Gazette of the United States and Evening Advertiser* [Philadelphia], 14 Jan. 1794).

4. For the letters from Thomas Pinckney, U.S. minister to Great Britain, to Jefferson of 8 July, 1, 15, 27 and 28 Aug., and 25 (two letters) and 27 Sept. 1793, see *Jefferson Papers,* 26:454–55, 598–99, 673–65, 770–71, 776–82; 27:149–52, 158. Pinckney had been charged with purchasing copper for the U.S. Mint (Jefferson to GW, 28 Nov. 1792). In his first letter of 25 Sept., Pinckney wrote that a portion of the copper was on board the *Pigou,* which had already set sail for the United States, and that the remainder would accompany this letter. In his letter of 8 July, Pinckney asked for instructions on handling the case of the American brig *Maria,* which had been seized and plundered on 19 May 1793 by the French frigate *Medie* and then captured by the English privateer *Ned.*

Jefferson had recommended the case of Philip Wilson to Pinckney's attention in a letter of 11 June 1792 (*Jefferson Papers,* 24:59–64). Wilson's ship, the *Mentor,* had been driven ashore and destroyed by H.M.S. *Centurion* and H.M.S. *Vulture* on 1 April 1783. Wilson then sought restitution from the British government and, as Pinckney reported in his letter of 27 Aug. 1793, was still waiting for a favorable outcome to his claim. On GW's interest in obtaining the release of the Marquis de Lafayette from his imprisonment by Prussia, see GW to Frederick William II, 15 Jan. 1794. For other initiatives concerning the plight of Lafayette and his family, see Pinckney's second letter of 25 Sept. and Jefferson to GW, 30 Dec. 1793. Jefferson noted in his Memorandum on State Department Business of 31 Dec. 1793 that both Wilson's claim and Lafayette's situation probably should be referred to Congress (*Jefferson Papers,* 27:649–52).

GW mentioned continuing difficulties in settling unresolved issues pertaining to the 1783 peace treaty with Great Britain, the problems of maintaining American neutrality and neutral rights for U.S. shipping during the current European wars, and other foreign policy issues for consideration by Congress in his previous messages to the U.S. Senate and House of Representatives of 3, 5, 16 (two messages), 23, and 30 (first message) Dec. 1793.

5. For the letters from David Humphreys, minister plenipotentiary to Al-

giers, to Jefferson of 4, 15, 25 Aug., 1, 3, 13, 16, 17, 26 Sept., and 3, 6, 7, 8 Oct. 1793, see *Jefferson Papers,* 26:613–14, 673, 755–56; 27:4–5, 24–25, 106–7, 125–26, 152–53, 187, 196–200, 222–23.

6. For two letters from Charles William Frederick Dumas to Jefferson of 1 May 1793, see *Jefferson Papers,* 25:631–32. The letters of 22 June, 13 July, and 14 Aug. 1793 have not been identified. Dumas, an unofficial agent for the United States at The Hague, had suggested in a letter to Jefferson of 21 Feb. 1792 that the U.S. embassy at The Hague be sold, given the high cost of maintaining it. Jefferson mentioned the proposed sale in his Memorandum on State Department Business of 31 Dec. 1793 (*Jefferson Papers,* 23:128; 27:649–52).

7. Letter-book copies of Randolph's letters of 10 Jan. to Pinckney, Morris, Carmichael and Short, Short, and Humphreys are in DNA: RG 59, Diplomatic and Consular Instructions, 1791–1801. Randolph submitted these replies to GW for approval on 10 Jan. (*JPP,* 277).

8. Randolph assumed the duties of secretary of state on 2 Jan. (GW to U.S. Senate, 1 Jan. 1794, Affidavit from James Wilson, 2 Jan. 1794, enclosed in Randolph to GW, 2 Jan. 1794).

To the United States Senate
and House of Representatives

United States January 7. 1794.
Gentlemen of the Senate, and of the House of Representatives.

I lay before you an Official statement of the expenditure to the end of the year 1793, from the sum of Ten thousand dollars, granted to defray the contingent expences of Government, by an Act passed on the 26th of March 1790.[1]

Go: Washington

LS, DNA: RG 46, Third Congress, 1793–95, Senate Records of Legislative Proceedings, President's Messages; LB, DNA: RG 233, Third Congress, 1793–95, House Records of Legislative Proceedings, Journals.

1. Section 3 of "An Act making appropriations for the support of government for the year one thousand seven hundred and ninety," 26 March 1790, authorized the president to draw up to $10,000 from the treasury to defray contingent expenses of the government and required him to submit to Congress "a regular statement and account of such expenditures . . . at the end of the year" (*Stat.* 1:105).

According to the enclosed statement, prepared at the Register's Office of the Treasury Department on 31 Dec. 1793, $8 was paid on 26 Feb. 1793 to "Warrant No. 2496 in favour of William Laurance Attorney for Lewis R. Morris, Marshall for the District of Vermont being for so much paid by the Marshall to James Bowtell for making and engraving a Seal for the said District as ℔ Account of the said Bowtell filed in the Registers Office and which the President of the United States has directed to be paid out of the ten thousand Dollars Appropriated agreeably to a Resolution of Congress of the 2nd August 1790." On 6 June 1793, $140 was paid to "Warrant No. 2823 in favour of James Seagrove being for his Expences whilst on Public Business by Order of the President of the United States to the Spanish Government of East Florida."

As of 31 Dec. 1793, the remaining balance in this account was $8,154.50 (DNA: RG 46, Third Congress, 1793–95, Senate Records of Legislative Proceedings, Committee Reports and Papers). The seal made by Vermont artisan James Bowtell, of Charlestown, Vt., was for the use of the District Court in that state (Alexander Hamilton to Tobias Lear, 26 Feb. 1793). On James Seagrove's mission and GW's authorization to pay his expenses, see Hamilton to Lear, 25 May 1793, notes 1 and 2; and *JPP,* 155.

To the United States Senate and House of Representatives

United States January 7. 1794.
Gentlemen of the Senate, and of the House of Representatives.

Experience has shewn that it would be useful to have an Officer particularly charged, under the direction of the Department of War, with the duties of receiving, safe keeping and distributing the public supplies, in all cases in which the Laws and the course of service do not devolve them upon other officers; and also with that of superintending in all cases, the issues in detail of supplies, with power, for that purpose, to bring to account all persons entrusted[1] to make such issues, in relation thereto. An establishment of this nature, by securing a regular and punctual accountability for the issues of public supplies, would be a great guard against abuse, would tend to ensure their due application, and to give public satisfaction on that point.[2]

I therefore recommend to the consideration of Congress, the expediency of an establishment of this nature under such regulations as shall appear to them adviseable.[3]

Go: Washington

LS, DNA: RG 46, Third Congress, 1793–95, Senate Records of Legislative Proceedings—President's Messages; LB, DLC:GW; LB (fragment), DNA: RG 233, Third Congress, 1793–95, House Records of Legislative Proceedings, Journals.

1. The letter-book copy at DNA: RG 233 ends at this point.

2. Henry Knox, Alexander Hamilton, and Edmund Randolph previously had recommended to GW that this position should be created (Knox to GW, 4 Jan. 1794, and n.1 to that document).

3. Section 3 of "An Act to provide for the erecting and repairing of Arsenals and Magazines, and for other purposes," 2 April 1794, established this position. This officer would receive a salary of $125 per month, be appointed by the president, and work under the direction of the secretary of war (*Stat.* 1:352). GW nominated Tench Francis, Jr., as the first "Purveyor of Public Supplies" on 24 Feb. 1794, and the Senate approved the nomination on the following date (*U.S. Senate Executive Journal*, 1:173–74). Francis (1730–1800) was a Philadelphia merchant and the first cashier of the Bank of North America. Previous to this appointment, he also served as an agent for purchasing supplies for the War Department (see Report on an Account of Receipts and Expenditures of the United States for the Year 1793, 26 Dec. 1794, *Hamilton Papers*, 17:520).

From Harriot Washington

Culpeper [Va.] January [7, 1794]

I hope My dear Uncle will excuse my troubling him so soon again, but as he is the only Freind, on earth that I can apply to, for any thing I am induced to think that my necesity will apologize for me. I have spent the winter in Culpeper with Cousin Carter, in a very retired manner, we have scarcely seen a person since we came up, and as I am just a going to return to Fredericksburg, I shall be thousand time's oblieged to My dear Uncle, if he will give me as much money as will get me a silk jacket and a pair of shoes to wear to the birth night as that will be the first Ball I shall have been to this winter.[1]

Cousin Carter join's me in love to you and Aunt Washington. I am My dear Uncle Your affectionate Neice

Harriot Washington

ALS, ViMtvL. GW's docket reads "From Miss Harrt Washington Jan. 7—1794."

1. Although Harriot had lived at Mount Vernon for some years, she was sent in late 1792 to live in Fredericksburg, Va., with GW's sister, Betty Washington Lewis (GW to Betty Washington Lewis, 7 Oct. 1792). In November of 1793, Harriot accepted the invitation of her cousin, Betty Lewis Carter, to spend the winter at Western View, the Carters' home near Stevensburg in Culpeper County, Va. (Harriot Washington to GW, 16 Nov. 1793). Harriot was planning to attend a ball held in Fredericksburg to honor GW's birthday

on 22 Feb., just as she had done the previous year when she made a similar request (Harriot Washington to GW, 5 Jan. 1793, and n.2).

To John Adams

Dear Sir,   Wednesday 8th Jany 1794.

I would thank you for giving the papers herewith sent a perusal—and for the result of it.[1]

I am now deliberating on the measure proper & necessary to be taken with respect to Mr G——t and wish for aid in so doing; the critical state of things making me more than usually anxious to decide right in the present case.[2]

None but the heads of departments are privy to these papers, which I pray may be returned this evening or in the morning. With very sincere esteem & regard I am always Your obedt & Affect. Servant

Go: Washington

ALS, MHi: Adams Papers; ADfS, Ia-HA; LB, DLC:GW.

1. The papers sent Adams pertained to French minister Edmond Genet's attempts at recruiting Americans from the Carolinas and Georgia for service in expeditions against Spanish colonies in North America. The papers probably included South Carolina governor William Moultrie's letter to GW of 7 Dec. 1793 and the enclosed resolves and affidavits sent the governor by the South Carolina legislature, as well as Moultrie's proclamation of 9 Dec. 1793 against Genet's efforts. It also may have included a copy of Genet's letter to Thomas Jefferson of 25 Dec. 1793, in which Genet denied authorizing the formation of any expeditionary force within U.S. territory, although he admitted that he had been authorized by the French government to deliver military commissions to willing volunteers (*Jefferson Papers*, 27:619–20; translation, *ASP, Foreign Relations*, 1:311). GW submitted these documents to the U.S. Senate and House on 15 Jan. 1794.

2. For the various options discussed by GW and the cabinet and GW's ultimate decision, see Alexander Hamilton's Proposed Presidential Message to Congress, 6–13 Jan. 1794, and notes 1 and 4.

Henry Knox to Bartholomew Dandridge, Jr.

Dear Sir   January 8. 1794

Please to submit, the enclosed letters from Governor Blount, to the President.[1] I am Dear Sir Yours &c.

H. Knox

LS, DLC:GW; LB, DLC:GW.

1. The letters to Knox of 4, 9, 13, and 17 Dec. 1793 from William Blount, the governor of the Southwest Territory, have not been identified. GW returned these letters to Knox later this same date (*JPP*, 277).

From Gautier de la Pecoutiere

Baltimore [Md.] le 8 janvier 1794
Au Grand General Waginton des etats unis du Continant de lamerique

Le Citoyen Gautier de la pecoutiere habitant de la plainne du Cap français, lieutenant des volontaire Destain à savanna ayant Recue trois Blessures au dit siége, le General d'estain lui á envoyé le Ruban et laigle de la ⟨s⟩o⟨c⟩iation de ⟨sinsinnatus⟩ et son Brevet par ordre du Grand General Waginton pour Recompences davoir Bien servie le Continant.[1]

Le Citoyen Gautier ayant été incendier deux fois pas peu Rien sauver que sa femme qui á Recue quatres Coups de sabre qui est estropier et prete daccouchée; nous sommes á Baltimore Grand General dans une detresse des plus Grande notre seule Resources est en vous nous vous prions de nous envoyer quelque choses pour les Besoin les plus urgent si vous navés egard a notre situation nous allon perir de Chagrin et de miseres, si javais eu les moyen de passer à votre hautel vous faire le tablau de vive voix de Ce qui mest arivée depuis trois ans vous verrier que Cela est digne de compasion.[2]

si je peu etre utile Grand General pour les etats unie je vous prie de menployer je suis pret á sacrifier mes jours pour votre services, en Cas que le continant serait ataqué j'ai des Connaisence pour etablir des forts ou Baterie.

mon epouses et moi nous elevons nos ⟨y⟩eux au Ciel pour la Conservation de vos jours.

Salut Gautier de la pecoutiere

ALS (in French), DNA: RG 59, Miscellaneous Letters.

1. Gautier de la Pecoutiere, a refugee from the French colony of Saint Domingue, had served in the Revolutionary War as a lieutenant in a volunteer corps under Admiral d'Estaing (Charles-Hector, comte de Estaing) during the October 1779 siege of Savannah, Georgia. He was wounded three times during this battle and later, by order of GW, received the ribbon and eagle of the Society of the Cincinnati.

2. Both Gautier and his wife were injured during the fighting and subsequent fire that destroyed Cap Français in June 1793. Having escaped to the United States, they were now living in Baltimore in a state of great poverty. Seeking some assistance from GW, Gautier volunteers to help defend the United States from invasion, explaining that he is competent in the construction of forts and batteries. No reply from GW has been found. Gautier appears to have continued living in Baltimore until at least 1796, when two individuals by that name are listed in the *Baltimore Town Directory* for that year.

From the Citizens of Savannah, Ga.

Sir,   [8 Jany 1794][1]
    The Citizens of Savannah, strongly impressed with the danger and mischeifs, to which the United States have been exposed, by the possibility of their being involved in the War existing between those European Nations, with whom we are most intimately united in Amity, and connected by Commerce; beg leave to take this method of expressing to you, the sincere and cordial sentiments of approbation and applause, with which the measures you have adopted, in this very interesting situation, have inspired them.
    The Services performed by you for our common Country, on so many, such various, and important occasions, in the exercise of the highest civil and military authority, were such as not to have rendered necessary the public declaration of our sentiments, concerning this last instance of the paternal Zeal, with which you have incessantly watched over the public happiness— But when some of our Citizens have spared us pains to inflame the public mind, and to stimulate individuals to actions contrary to their duty as citizens, and distructive of the most important interests of the United States—And when such individuals have not only been publicly countenanced and encouraged by the French Minister, but that he has *dared* to distribute Commissions, and instructions for enlisting soldiers in the name of the French Republic, within the Jurisdiction, and without the approbation or knowledge of our Government;[2] We think it right thus publicly to declare, that in our opinion the timely notice given by your proclamation of the Neutrality of the United States— Your instructions for preventing the fitting out of armed vessels

in our ports—The sentiments contained in your Speech to Congress, and your letter concerning the conduct of the person employed in America as the Minister of the French Republic, are agreeable to the principles of our excellent Constitution;[3] and wisely calculated to ensure a continuance of Peace—promote the public prosperity—And preserve the Dignity of the American Nation. To the wisdom of these measures, and the good Sense, and manly firmness of the great bulk of the American People, it is owing, that we have not yet experienced the horrid carnage, and devastation of an unnecessary War—And We rejoice that Congress have so cordially expressed their approbation and concurrence in the measures you have adopted for the preservation of Peace to our Country.[4]

Accept, Sir, the tender of our gratefull acknowledgements, for your past services, and the sincere profession of that *perfect confidence* with which such an uniform series of great and good actions have inspired us, with respect to your future conduct.[5]

Signed by order of a public meeting of the citizens of Savannah.

Nathl: Pendleton
Chairman[6]

DS, DLC:GW; LB, DLC:GW. This address was enclosed with a brief cover letter of the same date from Nathaniel Pendleton, judge of the U.S. district court in Georgia (DLC:GW). Pendleton mistakenly wrote the year of his letter as 1793.

1. The date in brackets is from the docket on the DS. The DS does not have an original date on it, although two different and later hands added the erroneous date of 1793 on both the first and last pages. The LB is dated "Jany 8. 1794." This letter appears in the 16 Jan. 1794 issue of the *Georgia Gazette* (Savannah), which indicates that this letter was approved at a meeting held on "Wednesday the 8th day of January."

2. On the attempt by Edmond Genet to recruit Americans from Georgia and the Carolinas for service in expeditions against Spanish territory in North America, see GW to John Adams, this date, and n.1 to that document.

3. See Neutrality Proclamation, 22 April 1793; Cabinet Opinion on the Rules of Neutrality, 3 Aug. 1793; and GW to U.S. Senate and House of Representatives, 3 and 5 Dec. 1793.

4. See U.S. House of Representatives to GW, 7 Dec. 1793, and U.S. Senate to GW, 9 Dec. 1793.

5. GW replied to Pendleton on 3 March: "The sentiments, expressed by the Citizens of Savannah, are a very acceptable addition to the testimonies of public approbation, already given to my late conduct, with respect to the belligerent powers of Europe.

"The favorable views, in which you have placed my past endeavors receive my warm acknowledgments, and I request you to convey them to the citizens whom, on this occasion, you represent" (LS, NHi: Correspondence of Alexander Hamilton and Aaron Burr; LB, DLC:GW).

6. This word is in the same handwriting as the body of the address.

From Edmund Randolph

January 8th 1794

The Secretary of State has the honor of informing the President of the United States, that he examined Mr Rittenhouse on the third instant, as to the state of the mint and received from him the inclosed answer.[1]

LB, DLC:GW; LB, DNA: RG 59, GW's Correspondence with His Secretaries of State.

1. The enclosed answer from David Rittenhouse has not been identified.

To James Madison

Dear Sir,   Friday 10th Jany 1794.

Herewith you will receive Sundry Pamphlets &ca under the patronage of Sir John Sinclair. I send you his letters to me also, that the design may be better understood.[1]

From all these, you will be able to decide, whether a plan of enquiry similar to the one set on foot in G. Britn, would be likely to meet legislative or other encouragement, and of what kind, in this Country.[2]

These, or any other ideas which may result from the perusal of the papers, I would thank you for, as the letters remain unacknowledged, and the writer of them will expect this if nothing more.[3]

AL[S], PWacD: Feinstone Collection; ADfS, DLC:GW; LB, DLC:GW.

1. For the enclosed letters and pamphlets from British agriculturist John Sinclair, see his letters to GW of 15 June and 15 Aug. 1793.

2. The United States did not have any official agency similar to the British Board of Agriculture and Internal Improvement, which Sinclair helped to establish in 1793, until the creation of the U.S. Department of Agriculture in 1862.

3. Madison did not find the time to evaluate the information in Sinclair's letters and pamphlets (Madison to GW, 8 Feb. 1794). GW did not acknowledge Sinclair's letters and pamphlets until his reply of 20 July.

Bartholomew Dandridge, Jr., to Henry Knox

11 January 1794.
B. Dandridge has the honor by the Presidents order, to send the enclosed Proceedings of the Senate, on the subject of the Treaty with the Wabash & Illinois Indians, to the Secretary of War for his information.[1]

AL, DLC:GW; LB, DLC:GW.

1. The enclosure has not been identified, but it contained a copy of the resolution passed on 9 Jan., in which the Senate refused, by a vote of 21 to 4, to give its consent to the treaty that Rufus Putnam negotiated with the Wabash and Illinois Indians in September 1792 (*U.S. Senate Executive Journal*, 1:146; GW to U.S. Senate, 13 Feb. 1793).

From Edmund Randolph

Sir   Philadelphia January 11. 1794
Mr Jefferson has noted among the papers, which accompany the Algerine communications, that "there is no fund, out of which the hire of the Swedish vessel can be paid."[1] I beg leave therefore to submit, to your consideration, Whether you will order payment of Mr Church's bill, to the amount of one hundred and fifty pounds sterling, out of the contingent fund in your disposal.[2] I have the honor, sir, to be with the greatest respect yr mo. ob. serv.

Edm: Randolph

ALS, DNA: RG 59, Miscellaneous Letters; LB, DLC:GW; LB, DNA: RG 59, GW's Correspondence with His Secretaries of State; LB, DNA: RG 59, Domestic Letters.

1. Randolph is referring to Thomas Jefferson's report of 14 Dec. 1793 on U.S. relations with Morocco and Algiers. This report and its accompanying papers were enclosed in GW's letter to the U.S. Senate and House of Representatives of 16 Dec. 1793. Near the end of this report, Jefferson wrote that the U.S. consul at Lisbon, Edward Church, "have thought instantaneous warning to our commerce to be on it's guard, of sufficient importance to jus-

tify the hiring a Swedish vessel to come here express with the intelligence," and noted the lack of funds to pay for such a ship. For Church's hiring of the Swedish snow *Maria,* see his letter to Jefferson of 12 Oct. 1793 (*Jefferson Papers,* 27:230–35; see also *JPP,* 266). For the payment of this expense, despite Jefferson's misgivings, see Alexander Hamilton to John Lamb, 16 Dec. 1793 (*Hamilton Papers,* 15:460).

2. Bartholomew Dandridge, Jr., wrote Randolph later this same date: "By the President's direction B. Dandridge has the honor to inform the Secry of State that the President thinks some arrangemt for the paymt of Mr Church's draft was made between Mr Jefferson & the Secy of the Treasury. If upon enquiry this should not have been the case, the President will direct it to be paid out of the Contgt Fund" (DNA: RG 59, Miscellaneous Letters). For the payment on 11 Feb. 1794, out of the contingency funds, of Church's draft for £150 sterling, see *Hamilton Papers,* 16:452. On the creation of a contingency fund for use by the president, see section 3 of "An Act making appropriations for the support of government for the year one thousand seven hundred and ninety," 26 March 1790 (*Stat.* 1:105).

From Edmund Randolph

Sir   Philadelphia January 11. 1794.

I saw Mr Bourne and Mr Bradford together yesterday. The former is disinclined to the office of district attorney, saying, among many other things by way of objection, that nothing would tempt him to bring down upon him the fire of both parties.[1] They agreed in the superiority of Howell as to talents; but as he never read the law, until he began to practise, I cannot conceive, that he possesses any depth of law-knowledge. In other respects, they did not speak with much ardor in his behalf.[2] Barnes is but moderate in skill, a new-comer, and would be liable to more exception, than his competitor[3] But they were decided in thinking, that Green was equal in abilities to the office; of fair and amiable character; universally beloved; and that the people would not only take an interest in any thing, which gratified him; but that his appointment would also content the parties. They seemed to me to go, as far as delicacy would permit, in pronouncing, that it would be an advantageous circumstance, if you were to fix on him.[4]

Did you hear, sir, the report, which was circulating yesterday, that Mr Genet intended to return to France immediately, and that he had taken a farewell dinner with the democratic society two days ago? The report came to me, without farther authenticity, than that Mr Wadsworth, and Mr Hunter, owner of my lodgings, told me of its general circulation. Indeed Mr Wadsworth added, that his recal had been debated in the national convention, and no result had transpired.[5] I have the honor, sir, to be with sincere & respectful attachment yr mo. ob. Serv.

Edm: Randolph

ALS, DLC:GW.

1. Benjamin Bourne and William Bradford represented Rhode Island, respectively, in the U.S. House of Representatives and Senate. Randolph apparently had discussed the current vacancy in the office of U.S. district attorney for Rhode Island. On political divisions within that state, see Arthur Fenner to GW, 7 Oct. 1793, and Issac Senter to GW, 24 Jan. 1794, and n.4 to that document.

2. On David Howell's legal expertise, see John Brown et al. to GW, 2 Oct. 1793, and Issac Senter to GW, 24 Jan. 1794.

3. For a letter recommending attorney David Leonard Barnes, see Arthur Fenner to GW, 7 Oct. 1793.

4. Ray Greene (1765–1849), who was born in Warwick, R.I., graduated from Yale in 1784, studied law, and then practiced in Providence, Rhode Island. He was the eldest child of former Rhode Island governor William Greene and his wife Catharine Ray. At this time he was the state attorney general. He later served in the U.S. Senate, 1797–1801. For other recommendations, see Henry Marchant to Alexander Hamilton, 9 Dec., and William Ellery to Hamilton, 16 Dec. 1793, *Hamilton Papers*, 15:447–48, 458–59. For Greene's nomination as district attorney, see GW to U.S. Senate, 24 January.

5. On the U.S. request that the French government recall its minister to the United States, see Cabinet Opinion on the Recall of Edmond Genet, 23 Aug. 1793. Genet may have attended the meeting of the Democratic Society of Philadelphia that met on 9 January. During this meeting the society passed a resolution supporting "agents of foreign powers" and protested attempts "to vilify a foreign minister" (*General Advertiser* [Philadelphia], 11 Jan. 1794). On the recent reports from France concerning official action on the request for Genet's removal, see n.4 to Alexander Hamilton's Proposed Presidential Message to Congress, 6–13 Jan. 1794. Genet did not return to France, but instead he settled permanently in New York State.

Jeremiah Wadsworth represented Connecticut in the House of Representatives. William Hunter (1756–1814) had emigrated from Scotland to Philadelphia in 1774 with other members of his family, and by 1794 he owned the largest coach factory in Philadelphia. Randolph was among the many prominent customers, both in the United States and Saint Domingue, who purchased a coach from Hunter. During the 1780s, Hunter speculated in Philadelphia land with his brother, George Hunter (1755–1823), a partner in the coach factory until 1792. Together the brothers built a series of three-story brick townhouses on the north side of High Street, now Market Street, between Eighth and Ninth streets, including the one at 319 High Street that Randolph rented from 1794 until late 1795 (Richard E. Powell, Jr., "Coach-making in Philadelphia: George and William Hunter's Factory of the Early Federal Period," *Winterthur Portfolio* 28 [1993], 247–77; Lu Ann De Cunzo, "An Historical Interpretation of William Birch's Print 'High Street, from Ninth Street, Philadelphia,'" *Pennsylvania History* 50 [1983], 109–47).

From William Stephens Smith

Philadelphia Jany 11th 1794.
To the President of the United States–

When I had the honor of addressing a Letter to The President, last, it was dictated by the necessity I was then under of retiring from public employment—in which I took the liberty of observing, that I should not discover a disposition to return to it, under the *then* administration.

without entering into a detail of the Circumstances which produced that decission, on my part, I shall observe, that the late change in administration, removes all my personal objections to public stations.[1]

Considering the present unpleasing situation of my Country relative to European Powers, and the position of some of its internal affairs, and that for myself I have during my attention to private business, acquired a sufficiency to justify me, in offering my service, without injury to my family.[2] I have the pleasure to inform The President, that I am ready to return to public employment, should it be supposed that I am capable of rendering service, either in the present, or expected situation of affairs. In making this communication, I gratify my own feelings on public Subjects, and flatter myself it will be pleasing to The President to learn, that I have no personal accommodation in view on this subject.

It may not be improper to remark, that tho' I am untainted with party Zeal, I am firmly attached to the Constitution and Government of my Country, that it is my lott to stand alone, free from personal commitment, that, in general I am rather attached to measures than under the influence of Individuals—and that I shall always study to carry with me a proper Zeal for my Country's welfare, directed by that integrity and aided by that small weight of personal Character, which supported by the flattering opinions of my friends, have bouyed me thus far thro' Life.

If with such dispositions and thus situated, I should be considered as capable of rendering service, I shall always consider myself complemented by The Presidents notice.[3] I have the honor to be The Presidents most Oblidged & very Humble Servant

W. S. Smith

ALS, DLC:GW.

1. In resigning from his position as the supervisor of the revenue for the District of New York, Smith offered no specific reasons. Instead, he wrote: "I am induced to take this step from some existing causes, which it would be unpleasant for me to detail" and that he would now "turn my attention to such private pursuits as may guard my own feelings from further unpleasant exercise" (Smith to GW, 7 Feb. 1792, in GW to Smith, 10 Feb. 1792, n.1). The "late change" probably refers to the resignation of Thomas Jefferson as secretary of state (Jefferson to GW, 31 Dec. 1793 [second letter]).

2. In 1786 Smith had married Abigail Amelia Adams, the daughter of Vice President John Adams and his wife, Abigail. The Smiths had two children at this time: William Steuben (1787–1850) and John Adams (1788–1854).

3. GW did not appoint Smith to any federal position.

From Joseph Caverly

Dear Sir   West River [Maryland] 12th Jany 1794
I under stand that their are A Number of Ships of war to Be Built. I Should Be Glad if it would not Be to troblesom to you for you to Assist me In Arecting A Yard In this state[1] and if you should not think me capelable of that Business I could Git A Recommendation from comedore Nickelson of New York to whome I have Rote on the Subject their is A Near Neighbour By Name Richard Spriggs that has A Very Larg Quanety of timber Both pine and Oak and of a Good Quallity in Diferen[t] parts of this State if Youl Be so Kind as to Assest me in this Business I shall take it A Very Great favour also to send the Inclosed Letters to Commedore Nickelson.[2] I am with Respect Your Obet Svt

Jos: Caverly

ALS, DNA: RG 59, Miscellaneous Letters.

1. Apparently, Joseph Caverly recently had decided to move his shipbuilding business from Alexandria, Va., to Maryland. By 1796 he had formed a partnership with Jeremiah Yellott of Baltimore. The *USS Baltimore,* a sloop of war, was built at Caverly's shipyard in 1798 as the merchant ship *Adriana* before its acquisition by the Navy later that year (*Federal Gazette & Baltimore Daily Advertiser,* 27 July 1796, 11 Aug. 1798; *Dictionary of American Naval Fighting Ships* [Washington, D.C., 1959], 1:88).

2. Caverly's letter to James Nicholson, a resident of New York City, has not been identified. His neighbor may have been Richard Sprigg, Jr., whose estate of Strawberry Hill overlooked Annapolis, Maryland. No reply from GW has been found.

To William Pearce

Mr Pearce,   Philadelphia Jany 12th 1794
    Taking it for granted that you have arrived at Mount Vernon, before this, I shall direct this letter to you at that place, & shall mention such things as have occurred to me, proper for your notice & government.[1]
    From a review of the plan of rotation which has been already communicated to you,[2] it appears (if it can be carried into affect this year) that you will want the following seeds, and at the following farms, &ca viz.

	Oats bushls	B. Wht bushls	Potato bushls	Clover lbs.	Timothy pint	Orchd grass pints
Mansion house	10		64	80		40
Union farm	120	75	40	100		
D: Run farm	150	73	120	800	250	
Muddy hole Farm	60	95	40			
River farm		120				
Total	340	363	284[3]	980	250	40

I have put none of these articles down to the River farm except Buck Wheat, because I do not know what you may find necessary to put into the ground between No. 6 at that place and the lane by the Barn; nor in any of the lots in front the latter; where, possibly, the Clover may be worn out and wanting to be renewed; Consequently if Oats, Potatoes, Clover or other grass seeds are required at this farm they will be in addition to the quantities of each, mentioned on the other side.
    To explain the uses of the foregoing articles at each place, it is necessary to observe if it has not been done so already, (in some former letters) that the ground at Mansion house (which was in Potatoes last year) I want to sow with Oats (thin) and clover, mixed with Orchard grass or Timothy this year; the size of the

inclosure I guess to be about 10 Acres—and it is my wish to plant Potatoes in the other enclosure, (at the same place) which was in Oats last year; provided it shall, upon examination, be found to be too thinly taken with clover, with which it was sown last Spring. The part allotted for Clover at Union farm, has already been marked in the sketch which accompanied my letter of the 23d of December, numbered 1 & 2.[4] The Potatoes (if any are planted there; the propriety of which you may be the judge) may be in the upper Meadow, adjoining to; but above the lane leading from the Mill road to the Barn where Corn grew as part of it wants cultivation to reclaim & fit it for the reception of grass. At Dogue run farm—the 5 acre lot by the New Barn[5] will require about 40 B: of Pots., and the Corn ground in No. 4, every other row with Potatoes, will take as I calculate, about 80 Bushels more (allowing two Potatoes to a hill)—The field No. 4, for these two Crops, is to be prepared, and listed as if for Corn only; four feet a part each way; but, to be planted alternately through the whole of it with each; letting the Rows run No. and South, or as nearly so as the back fence near the Swamp does. No. 3d at this place will receive clover alone, & about eight pints to an Acre; the other Corn ground there will be sown with clover & timothy mixed, at the rate of about five pints each to the Acre, which will take according to my calculation, the quantity before mentioned, that is—800 lbs. or pints of the first, and 250 pints of the latter. To plant the South west lot of grass at Muddy hole, will require about 40 bushels of Potatoes, there being five acres of it. I have said nothing respecting the disposal of the Oats & Buck Wheat at the different farms, at this time, because it is mentioned in the Plans of rotation. But that I may know how to provide for your want of ⟨any⟩ of these articles, it is necessary for one to be informed, with precision, ⟨the⟩ quantity on hand of each, & without delay.[6]

From a Gentleman at Leesburg (Colo. Ball) you are to look for Buck wht; and he has assured me I shall not be disappointed. It is to be sent to Mount Vernon as soon as the roads will permit.[7] On yourself, I hope you may depend nearly, if not altogether, for Oats: It will be hard I think if the ⟨Stack⟩ at Dogue run does not yield 1⟨5⟩0 bushels—Stuart,[8] If I recollect rightly, told me he had ⟨got out⟩ 30; but what to expect from the M⟨a⟩nsion house I know not. By the Weekly reports, already come to my hands, there had been 53 days spent in threshing them out ⟨of⟩ the straw;[9] but I shall confess I am not able to form any conclusive ideas of ⟨*illegible*⟩ from hence, as my people will take a week to do what others would accomplish in a day or two, & Butler had not spirit, or authority enough to effect a change of this conduct.[10] I am anxious therefore to know what quantity has come out of the stack at the Mansion house, and what quantity Stuart has; those at Dog. run can only be guessed at from the size of the Stack, & the ground on which they grew. The quantity of Clover seed, Timothy seed, & Orchard grass seed on hand you can ascertain exactly, and I ought to be informed of it immediately, that the dificiency may be got & sent round by the first vessel, as opportunities of doing it may not present at the moment of sowing.[11] The Meadows at Union farm or that at Dogue run, should be well examined (as mentioned in a former letter) to see whether any, and what quantity of Seed may be required to make good the defects of the last sowing which was done greatly too late in the Season, and if more than I have enumerated is wanting for purposes which may occur to you though it has escaped me, let me know it and it shall be sent. Of Potatoes I presume (if care be taken to overhaul and keep them from injury) there will be a sufficiency as, by the report to me,[12] there were 418½ Bushels put into the Cellar.

If, after taking a full view of the several farms—the situation they are thrown into by the insufferable management of my Overseers, and considering the advanced season compared with the plowings necessary for my rotations, & the means to effect it, you should be of opinion that it cannot be adopted this year; suggest, as soon as you are able to make up your mind upon the Subject, some other plan for the present; keeping in mind what my ⟨intentions⟩ are—namely—to pursue the rotat⟨ion plan⟩ laid down as soon as possible, as my great object is to recover, & preserve my fields in good condition. At any rate howevr the plan for Dogue run farm, must be strictly adhered to this year, although it is accomplished at the expence of the other farms.

Although I have called several times on Mr Lewis for the exact quantity of Corn made at the different farms, & how it has been disposed of; yet to this moment, I remain in ignorance, unless the reports, which in some weeks says so much has been measured, in others none, and added altogether make but 576 barrls, forms the sum total, which, surely, cannot be the whole produce of 666 Acres; which (at the different places) I had in Corn last year. If, however, this is all the Overseers mean to account for, I shall, in the first place, have very little doubt of their villainy; because, from the most reasonable Calculation I could make, after the fodder was gathered, and after repeated examinations of the respective fields, I had no doubt of making between one thousand & 1200 barrls at the least; and in the next place, because it will fall far short of my consumption of this article; which, as you will perceive by my calculations already forwarded to you, 1008 Bar⟨ls⟩ (including what the Mill will receive) is required for my annual supplies. If the case be, as I have here stated it, it will be necessary for you to substitute every article you can by way of help; & to ease me, as much as possible from the purchase of so much Corn. And this may be accomplished, in a degree at least, by the cultivation (at each farm) of Potatoes, Pease, Pumpkins, and such like things in the fields that were intended for Oats & Buckwheat, which will not interfere with the rotation System another year.

You will perceive by the articles of agreement entered into with Thomas Green the quantity of Meat he is entitled to: let him have that, and no more. He will draw, if permitted, double that quantity, & when you come to settle with him either deny having ordered it, or dispute the price. and, as from appearances, I shall be obliged to buy Corn myself, let none of the Overseers have more of this article than they are entitled to by their agreements.[13]

As you have not your family with you, and will now eat my provisions, let there be as much Cooked every day as will serve the Gardeners &ca, after you have done with it, as the case used to be when I was at home.[14]

Let there be a piece of ground prepared in what is called the Vineyard Inclosure for about 40 lbs. of French furse seed (for hedging) which I shall send you by the first vessel from this place to Alexandria[15]—And I would have the thorn berries, Cedar berries, honey locust seed and such other things as may be intended for hedges raised first in nurseries, that, when transplanted they may receive due ⟨culti⟩vation. As the case has been, they are sowed, or planted along the ditches and for want of attention afterwards are smothered & entirely destroyed by the Weeds. Do not neglect planting cuttings of the Willow & Lombardy poplars however, along these ditches, at such times as the Gardener may think best; especially on the ditches across the Mill swamp—But let the ground be well prepared by the Spade, or hoe, before the cuttings are put in. In a word, let whatever you do, be well done. Much labour & much time is saved by this means. both of which has been lost in the manner this business has been conducted: that is by putting in the plants, the cuttings or the Seeds and thinking no more of them afterwards.

I would recommend it to you to read my letters & instructions over often, that you may understand & have them impressed upon your mind. I give this advice because I expect to have them complied with, or reasons assigned for not doing it; and here, as in your agreement, I leave you at full liberty at all times, to propose plans of your own⟨,⟩ or alterations in mine, which in your own judgment, on a nearer view of matters before you than I have, you may think is for the best; for you will in all things find me open to conviction.

The Advertisements herewi⟨th⟩ enclosed, I found necessary some years ago to set up. It may be so still, and for that reason I send the remaining of what I happened to have by me, that they may be used, or not, as occasion shall require.[16]

Since I began this letter, yours of the 7th Instt and Mr Lewis's of the 6th enclosing the Weekly reports have been recd.[17]

The man who supplies Butlers place ought to be stout, active & spirited, yet cool & steady; for I expect there will be some difficulty to encounter before my people can be brought into good habits, & a regular discharge of their duty; so long is it since they have been under any controul in my absence.[18]

With respect to the Seins, I wd have you, immediately upon the receipt of this letter, send for the man who usually does this work for me, to see if he will, at the accustomed prices, agree positively, to nett them in time. If so, let him chuse his twine (if it is to be had in Alexandria) & set about them immediately. If he will not do this, or if the twine (of good quality) is not to be had there, let me know it, that I may see in time what can be done here, in this matter. When he is at Mount Vernon let him examine the Seins thoroughly, and see how far they are capable of repairs—parts of them to the best of my recollection were new last Spring, if so there must have been abominable mismanagement of them to be unfit for use now—but this indeed I do not wonder at—for less care of things I believe was never used on any estate, than has been on mine of late years.[19]

I beg your particular attention to the Porke, and making it into Bacon; as, ever since I left home ⟨much⟩ ⟨*illegible*⟩ has been sustained in it; some ⟨sayg⟩ because it was not sufficiently salted; and others because fires instead of smoak was made under the Bacon. Send me a list of the numbers & weight ⟨of your Hogs from⟩ each farm, ⟨&⟩ from the list⟨, how many⟩ have been disposed off.[20]

Having Wheat to ⟨gather at⟩ this time (by horses) is among ⟨*illegible*⟩serable conduct of my Overseers ⟨espe⟩cially as the horses were not ⟨employed⟩ in plowing as I had ordered. When you look into these things you may be able to discover the causes—At this distance I am unable to do it upon any ground that does not merit punishm⟨en⟩t.

Let me know what remains to be done to the New Barn & sheds at Dogue run. The conduct of that Rascal Green is beyond all forbearance, and it is my repeated request, that if he does not proceed in such a manner as to give you satisfaction, that he may be discarded without hesitation or ceremony.[21] I wish you to examine the flax that was ⟨made⟩ at Dogue run; knowing when it was put out to rot, & comparing it with the time it was taken up, I should conceive that it is entirely ruined; if so, I will make McKoy pay for it; because I not only charged him myself to wat⟨ch⟩ it, but wrote about it once or twice after I ⟨left home⟩ to see that it did not re⟨main⟩ out too long.[22]

The house in Alexandria must be repaired, & in order for Mrs Washington to go into in April, as I have promised this. When it is got in order, & made perfectly clean, I shall send paper from hence for the rooms.[23]

Charlotte at the Mansion house has been reported sick for several weeks—Mrs Washington desires you will examine her case, and if it appears necessary to request Doctor Craik to attend, & prescribe for her.[24] A fellow Sam also, who under prete⟨nse⟩ (for I believe this is the greatest part of his complaint) of an Asthmatical complaint never could be got to work more than half his time, has not done a days work since I left Mount Vernon in

October. examine his case also, but not by the Doctor, for he has had Doctors enough already, of all colours & sexes, and to no effect. Laziness Is I believe his principal ailment.[25]

I am in hope & expectation that after you have had time to examine & pry well into matters you will be able to give me your opinion fully upon the state of things. In the meanwhile let me know how the Wheat, which was too thin in the beginning, stands these open frosts; & see that there ⟨are⟩ ⟨*illegible*⟩ furrows to prevent injury from ⟨*illegible*⟩ standing on it.[26] I am Your friend & Servant

Go: Washington

ALS (letterpress copy), DLC:GW.

1. Pearce's financial records indicate that he arrived at Mount Vernon no later than 6 Jan. (Mount Vernon Accounts, 1794–97).

2. For GW's plan of rotation, see GW to Pearce, 18 Dec. 1793, and enclosure.

3. The correct total is 264.

4. The sketch has not been identified.

5. On the barn recently constructed on Dogue Run farm, see GW to Anthony Whitting, 28 Oct. 1792, and enclosure.

6. GW added the previous three words to the letterpress copy and presumably to the letter sent.

7. On Burgess Ball's promise to acquire buckwheat seed for GW, see Ball to GW, 17 Dec. 1793. On the receipt of this seed, which arrived at Mount Vernon in several shipments that extended from late January until early April, see Pearce to GW, 4 Feb.; Ball to GW, 13 Feb. and 5 April; and GW to Ball, 23 March.

8. William Stuart was the overseer of the River farm.

9. For the previous extant farm reports, sent by temporary manager Howell Lewis, see those for 22–28 Dec. 1793 (DLC:GW). No farm reports for September through early December 1793 have been found.

10. James Butler was the overseer of the Mansion House farm.

11. On the shipment of clover seed to Mount Vernon, see GW to Pearce, 16–17, 23 March.

12. This report has not been found.

13. According to GW's agreement of 25 Oct. 1793 with Thomas Green, the overseer of carpenters, Green was entitled to receive "four hundred pounds of Fresh pork & one hundred pounds of fresh beef at killing time" (ViMtvL). According to an agreement that Henry McCoy, the overseer of Dogue Run farm, made with Anthony Whitting, the former manager of Mount Vernon, on 17 Dec. 1792, he received 300 lbs. of pork and 200 lbs. of beef (GW to Whitting, 9 Dec. 1792, n.9). An earlier agreement made by former manager George Augustine Washington with Hiland Crow, the overseer of Union farm, provided Crow with 400 lbs. of pork and 100 lbs. of beef (Articles of Agreement, 15 Sept. 1790, DLC:GW). Written agreements with Stuart and

Butler have not been found, nor has any been found for the dower slave Davy, the overseer of Muddy Hole farm.

14. John Christian Ehlers was assisted by John Gottleib Richler in attending to GW's gardens. Ehlers' wife, Catherine, helped to supervise the spinners at Mount Vernon.

15. The vineyard enclosure consisted of four acres and was located south of the stables. It was used as an orchard and a garden nursery, where new plants were nurtured before being transplanted to other portions of the estate. For the shipment of the French furze seed, see GW to Pearce, 16–17 March.

16. The enclosed advertisements have not been identified.

17. The letter of 7 Jan. from Pearce and that of 6 Jan. from Howell Lewis and its enclosure have not been found.

18. GW notified Butler in late August 1794 that his contract would not be renewed (GW to Pearce, 17 and 24 Aug. 1794, ALS, ViMtvL; ALS [letterpress copy], DLC:GW). Near the end of the year, Pearce engaged John Allison (Allistone) to replace Butler as overseer of the Mansion House farm (GW to Pearce, 14 Dec. 1794, ALS, ViMtvL; ALS [letterpress copy], DLC:GW).

19. On the cost of hiring Lawrence McGinnis to repair fishing nets in the spring of 1793, see Whitting to GW, 27 March 1793, and n.3 to that document. On 3 Feb. 1794, Pearce paid £22.15.00 to Alexandria merchant Robert Hamilton for 182 lbs of "Seine Twine @ 2/6 ℔ lb.," and on 1 April he paid McGinnis £13.09.04 for "kniting A new Seine & puting a piece in the Old Shad Seine" (Mount Vernon Accounts, 1794–97).

20. No such list has been identified.

21. Thomas Green left GW's service in September (GW to Pearce, 21 Sept. 1794, ALS, ViMtvL; ALS [letterpress copy], DLC:GW).

22. The only extant letter written to Henry McCoy prior to this date and after GW departed Mount Vernon on 28 Oct. 1793 is that of 23 Dec. 1793, but it does not mention flax.

23. On plans for Frances Bassett Washington to live in GW's townhouse at the corner of Pitt and Cameron streets in Alexandria, Va., see her letter to GW of 22 Nov. 1793. According to GW's Household Accounts for 28 May, he paid $22 for "paper hangings" sent to Virginia.

24. The dower slave Charlotte, who was a seamstress on the Mansion House farm, was listed as sick for six days on the spinners report of 28 Dec. 1793 (DLC:GW). Physician James Craik, Sr., often attended to seriously ill slaves and overseers at Mount Vernon, as well as to members of the Washington family.

25. Sam, who was owned by GW, was listed as a laborer in 1786 and as a cook on the Mansion House farm in 1799. At 40 years of age in 1799, he was judged "Passed Labour." He was married to Al[i]ce, another of GW's slaves, who was 38 years old in 1799 and worked as a laborer at Muddy Hole farm in 1786 and 1799 (*Diaries*, 4:278, 282; Washington's Slave List, June 1799). Sam was listed as sick for six days on the farm report for 22–28 Dec. 1793 (DLC:GW).

26. Pearce's reply has not been found.

From Juris Peritus

Sir   13. Jany 1794.

The promotion of Mr Randolph to the office of Secretary of State having left his place vacant, the public mind is considerably interested in conjecturing who will be his successor[1]—Aware of your zeal for the public welfare & persuaded that you regard your power of nominating to office as a trust for the benefit of the people; the universal sentiment is, that in order to fix on the most suitable character for any office, in the genl govt it is only requisite that such a character should be presented to your view.

Under these impressions a citizen who cannot communicate his sentiments to you personally, avails himself of the present mode of introducing to your attention a character which in *every point of view,* is consider'd as the most suitable one for the place to be filled; of perhaps any within the United States.

The qualifications of an Attorney General of the U.S. it is presumed, should in substance be the following.
1.   Eminence as a counsellor at law
2.   A fair moral character
3.   That he should possess the entire confidence of the people of the State from which he is taken
4.   That he should be a known friend to the Genl Governt
5.   To the knowlege of the principles & practice of the law he should add, a general acquaintance with science in other words, he should be a *scholar*
6.   That his manners should be agreeable to you personally—in other words he should be a *gentleman*

These are qualities not *commonly* united in *one man* but if the general Sentiment of Pennsylvania be right, they *all* meet in that of *William Bradford.* Introduced into public life under the enlighten'd administration of the late Governor Reed, & at the early age of 27. appointed Attorney General of Pennsylva. he has continued in that place until his late promotion to the office of Judge of the Supreme Court, (a period of above 14 years,) with distinguish'd honor to himself & advantage to the State— At the Bar he was ev⟨er⟩ consider'd as one of its brightest ornaments, & on the Bench he is considerd as inferior to neither of his Bretheren—His political sentiments are known to be decisively favourable to the Governt of the U. States—while no one stands higher in the opinion of the people of this State His late publication on the subject of the penal Code of Pennsylvania, proves his talents in Composition, & his humane dispositon—a publication which seems to have arrested the attention of the legislatures of the different States & promises to produce the happiest effects.[2]

In private life *no* character can be fairer—his benevolency is diffusive & his charities unremitting.

His delicacy would revolt at the present measure, had he any intimation of it—but though it is foreign from his nature to request in the most indirect way, the place now contemplated, yet were it *offerd* him, it would not probably meet a refusal.

Mr Bradford from his abilities & charater, cannot but prove an acquisition to any governt in whose service he may be engaged—& his nomination to the post of Attorney Genl of the U. States would add to the many civic honors you have already acquired in calling forth modest merit & in filling the first stations under the Genl Governt with men of talents & integrity.[3]

This State also, has perhaps a claim to this place—for altho one of the 3. first, her citizens have not shared more of the first offices of the Genl Governt than some of the smallest of the United States.[4] With the sincerest wishes for your personal welfare, that of the governt over which you preside with so much glory—I remain Sir Yours most humbly.

Juris peritus[5]

ALS, DLC:GW.

1. Edmund Randolph assumed the duties of secretary of state on 2 Jan. 1794 (Affidavit from James Wilson, 2 Jan., enclosed in Randolph to GW, 2 Jan. 1794). Previous to this date, he served as the administration's first attorney general.

2. William Bradford, Jr. (1755–1795) was a native of Pennsylvania and a graduate of the College of New Jersey, 1772. After service in the Continental army during the Revolutionary War, 1776–1779, he returned to civilian life and the practice of law, settling in Yorktown, Pennsylvania. Joseph Reed (1741–1785), who served as the state's governor from 1778 to 1781, selected the young lawyer to be the state's attorney general in 1780, a position he held for the next eleven years until Gov. Thomas Mifflin appointed him a justice on the state's supreme court in 1791. Bradford's *An enquiry how far the punishment of death is necessary in Pennsylvania. With notes and illustrations* (Philadelphia, 1793) led to a revision in 1794 of Pennsylvania's penal code, whereby

the death penalty was removed from all capital crimes except for murder in the first degree.

3. GW submitted Bradford's nomination as attorney general in his first letter to the U.S. Senate of 24 Jan. 1794.

4. Pennsylvania was one of the first three states to ratify the U.S. Constitution, in 1787: Delaware on 7 Dec., Pennsylvania on 12 Dec., and New Jersey on 18 December. Of the members of GW's cabinet and the Supreme Court, Justice James Wilson was from Pennsylvania.

5. This Latin phrase means "one learned in the law."

From Edmund Randolph

Monday P.M. [13 Jan. 1794][1]

E. Randolph has the honor of sending to the President the inclosed letter, which came from the Post-office. E.R. cannot ascertain, whether it came by the mail, or some vessel recently arrived here. E.R. will thank the President to direct Mr Dandridge to inclose it, after he has read it.[2]

AL, DNA: RG 59, Miscellaneous Letters; LB, DLC:GW; LB, DNA: RG 59, GW's Correspondence with His Secretaries of State.

1. The docket on the AL reads "13 Jan. 1794," which was a Monday.
2. The enclosed letter has not been identified.

Bartholomew Dandridge, Jr., to William Shotwell & Co.

Gentlemen,   Philadelphia 13 January 1794

The President of the United States is desirous of obtaining about 10 bushels of the best Clover seed Some timothy d[itt]o to send to his Farms in Virginia—& as you have heretofore furnished him with seed, he has now directed me to ask of you the *lowest* prices at which the best Clover & Timothy seed is to be had with you. As the time approaches when it will be wanted, & as the President will depend on your answer to know whether the seed can be most advantageously procured at New York or at this place—he will thank you for the information as soon as possible. In case the seed should be bought of you, could a ready conveyance be had for it from New York to Alexandria? so as to have it there at any rate by the middle of february.[1] I am &c.

Bw: Dandridge

LB, DLC:GW.

1. For a purchase of 442 lbs. of clover seed from the New York City firm of William Shotwell & Co. in 1793, see n.12 of GW to Anthony Whitting, 5 May 1793. No reply from Shotwell has been found. On 19 March 1794, GW paid $126.67 to C. Roberts for clover seed that was shipped from Philadelphia that same week. Ice on the Delaware River and the lack of an available vessel had prevented its earlier shipment (Household Accounts; GW to William Pearce, 16–17, 23 March).

Cabinet Opinion on a Letter to the King of Prussia

[Philadelphia, 14 Jan. 1794]

At a meeting of the heads of departments at the President's, on the fourteenth day of January 1794.

It was propounded by the President, whether in consideration of the eminent services of M. de la Fayette, to the U.S. and his present sufferings, it be not adviseable for the President, in a *private*, and *unofficial* character, to address to the King of Prussia a letter, requesting his release on parole, founded on motives of personal friendship only. The opinion is, that such a letter is proper to be written.[1]

H. Knox
Alexandr Hamilton
Edm: Randolph

DS (in Edmund Randolph's handwriting), DLC:GW. GW's docket reads, "Opinions of the heads of Depart. on the propriety of Addressing (in a private manner) the King of Prussia in behalf of the Marquis de la Fayette 14th Jany 1794."

1. While fleeing France in August 1792, the Marquis de Lafayette was arrested by Austrian forces near the French border, but he was soon transferred to Prussian custody. After receiving this cabinet opinion, GW wrote Frederick William II of Prussia on 15 January. Lafayette, however, was returned to Austrian custody in May 1794 and imprisoned at Olmütz, where he remained until his release in September 1797. For other prisons in which Lafayette was held, see n.7 of Marquise de Lafayette to GW, 12 March 1793.

Letter not found: from William Pearce, 14 Jan. 1794. In a letter to Pearce of 19 Jan., GW acknowledged receipt of "Your letter of the 14th instt."

From John Taylor

SIR, [Philadelphia, c.14 January 1794][1]

IN the spirit of truth, and not of adulation, does the following performance solicit your attention. Nor is its hope of acquiring some share of your countenance diminished, by the circumstance of your not having in an official character withheld your signature, from several of the measures investigated.[2]

A responsibility in the chief magistrate, for the effects of every legislative act—an avowal, that unforeseen consequences, however mischievous, ought to be submitted to, for the sake of consistency in error—that experiment in search of truth, is to be rejected; are positions to which a liberal and enlightened mind will never accede.

Your general assent to laws ought to be ascribed to republican principles, and not to an indiscriminate approbation of their contents. To yourself therefore, as well as to every other citizen, remains intire the invaluable birth-right of freedom in the re-examination of public measures. For surely the right and duties of a citizen cannot be absorbed by official functions.

Whilst, under the influence of republicanism, you have cautiously checked the will of the people, you have also reserved your negative power, to be exerted on great and momentous occasions, for the preservation of their rights. Such an occasion occured in a *direct* attempt upon the principles of representation,[3] the defeat of which sufficiently evinces, that you cannot approve of the *indirect* means by which these principles have been so much more deeply wounded, than that attempt contemplated. Can it then be delusion to cherish a hope, that assaults directed against the vital organ of popular government, are destined to be defeated by the same laudable vigilance?

THE AUTHOR.

Printed, [John Taylor], *An Enquiry into the Principles and Tendency of Certain Public Measures* (Philadelphia, 1794), pp. iii–iv. John Taylor (1753–1824), of Caroline County, Va., was at this time representing Virginia in the U.S. Senate. By May 1793 he had written a long essay on the Bank of the United States, which circulated in manuscript during that year (*Madison Papers*, 15:13–14, 17, 34–35, 52–53, 89–91, 104, 111, 121, 123). When the essay finally was published in January 1794, this letter served as a preface to the pamphlet. *An Enquiry*, according to one reviewer, constituted "a very bold attack on the Bank" using "a great variety of facts and arguments.... The work... comprehends a review of the whole range of American politics. The author tells his countryman their faults and their errors, or at least what he considers to be so" (*Philadelphia Gazette and Universal Daily Advertiser,* 4 Feb.).

1. This letter was reprinted in the *Philadelphia Gazette and Universal Daily Advertiser,* 15 Jan., which noted that the pamphlet to which it was "prefixed" was "just published."

2. In addition to "An Act to incorporate the subscribers to the Bank of the United States," approved on 25 Feb. 1791 (*Stat.* 1:191–96), Taylor took issue with "An Act making provision for the [payment of the] Debt of the United States," approved 4 Aug. 1790 (*Stat.* 1:138–44). For GW's consideration of the constitutional issues raised by the Bank of the United States, see Edmund Randolph to GW, 12 Feb. 1791, and enclosures; Thomas Jefferson to GW, 15 Feb. 1791; GW to Alexander Hamilton, 16 Feb. 1791; James Madison to GW, 21 Feb. 1791; and Hamilton to GW, 23 Feb. 1791, and enclosure.

3. Taylor was referring to GW's veto on 5 April 1792 of "An Act for an apportionment of Representatives among the several States according to the first enumeration" (see The First Presidential Veto, 3–5 April 1792).

From Frantz Joachim von Aken

Sir!   Orebro in Sweden the 15th January 1794.

The 1st instant I humbly took the liberty to wait on the Congress or states of America with my Discovery of extinguishing fires;[1] but fearing that either have I not rightly adressed the Letter or could there be some hindering accidents for it's arrival, occasioned by our actual wars in Europe: I hope Sir! that You'll graciously excuse my repeated writting to the American People, adressing my discovery [to] It's noble Chief and humbly solliciting Him to order that it may be strictly examined and speedily published amongst His dear Countrymen. May it please You Sir, to see this done as soon as possible in order that no European surprizes your generous nation with noveltys of the Kind, as I sent to all Governments of Europe my discovery the very same day as to America, and it is possible that Luck-seekers from our Quarter might otherwise turn their ungenerous plans to your Country, after having got hold of the true extinguishing art. I beg leave to mention the reason of my suspicion: at the last great experiment I exhibited before the Royal family of this Country and all foreign ambassadors with many thousand other spectators, some ill-minded persons provided them selves with the extinguishing matter, and being informed that the late King as well as the Regent had promised me a sum of money, they made their best to prevent this and got so far in their success as to deprive me even of payment for all those expensif experiments which I by his Majesty's the late King's and the Regent's commands made at Stockholm and Drottningholm[2]—This being done the Nation began to collect a sum in order to prevent my ruin, every one, almost, being sensibel of my unjust sufferings and at the same time thankfull for the discovery I allready in the year 1790 published.[3] But then my Ennemys made known how farr they had succeeded in analysing my *matter* and recommended a man in NorrKoping as a fine discoverer of an art equal to mine. and tho', very unfortunately for them, the analysis proved quite misscarried, they succeeded however in dividing the People's opinions; wherefore after all I took the party to act as I have now done, giving up the secrecy to all Kings and Governments, only depending upon their generosity after a true and fair examination into the discovery; which examination also is the only favour I have required for to convince myself if it be possible that any better discovery of the Kind ever was mad[e].

Sir! the great Dr Franklin is no more, but General Washington lives admired and beloved of the whole world. What my discovered art of extinguishing fires looses in its reputation, for want of the former's approbation: I certainly shall gain my self as the discoverer, if not ⟨r⟩efused your protection or totally deprived of the honour to be called usefull even to the free and generous Nation, whos Chief You are. May Heaven bless You Sir! and your country! and may America by the art of preventing and extinguishing fires hasten the more to the Power You have prepared H⟨er⟩, of making at last tremble all those nations, who ⟨e⟩ver dare to be Her enemys. The above-said art shall better be explained in the work which soon will be printed and which I beg leave to Know where to deposit.[4] The last of my humble desires is that You'll graciously pardon my way of expressing my self, being so little acquainted with the American language and I remain with the utmost Respect Sir Your most obed⟨ient⟩ serva⟨nt⟩

　　　　　　　　　　　　　　　　　　Frantz Joachim von Aken

LS, DNA: RG 59, Miscellaneous Letters. The docket reads "recd. May 22."

Swedish chemist Frantz Joachim von Aken (1738–1798) gained valuable experience at Hjorten, the pharmacy company of his father, Frans Mikael von Aken, in Örebro, before working and studying in England, 1761–62. In 1772 he took over the management of Hjorten, where he developed a chemical compound that could be used to extinguish fires and prevent their spread to nearby surfaces. Called *Akenska eldsläckningsämnet,* this compound was made out of potassium aluminum sulfate, iron oxide, iron sulfate, and clay. Aken demonstrated its use in Stockholm before the royal family in 1791 and 1792. On 15 Jan. 1793, he received permission to manufacture this product for public sale ("von Aken," *Svenskt Biografiskt Lexikon,* 32 vols. to date [Stockholm, Sweden, 1918—], 1:342–44).

1. Aken's letter to Congress of 1 Jan., which has not been identified, was laid before both the House and Senate on 2 June. It stated "the particulars of his discovery of an Art, described in the Swedish language, for extinguishing fires and preventing conflagrations, whether in war or peace, on board vessels, or in houses on fire" (*Annals of Congress,* 3d Cong., 116, 746).

2. King Gustav III (b. 1746) was assassinated in March 1792; his brother Karl (Charles; 1748–1818), duke of Södermanland, acted as regent until 1796, when Gustav IV Adolf (1778–1837) came of age. The royal family had palaces in Stockholm and the nearby village of Drottningholm.

3. In 1790, Aken's research appeared in an article entitled "Om eld-släckning; uti bref til Kungliga patriotiska sällskapets förste sekreterare" in the 16 Aug. issue of *Inrikes Tidningar* (Stockholm).

4. Secretary of State Edmund Randolph replied to Aken on 26 June: "The President of the United States of America has requested me to inform you, that he will be very happy to see the art of extinguishing fires, carried to the perfection, which you suppose to have been discovered by you, and that the work, which you purpose to send to him, explanatory of this art, will be safely forwarded to him, thro' the channel of Mr Pinckney, our Minister plenipotentiary in London" (DNA: RG 59, Diplomatic and Consular Instructions).

In 1794, Aken published an English version of his research as *The Dreadful and Calamitous Effects of Fire, in many cases totally prevented, in all . . . checked and . . . subdued, with much less expense than by any other method known* (London). GW had Aken's *Korrt Afhandling om det bästa Eldsläcknings sätt med Därtil lämpad Brand-Redskap och nödig Brand-Ordning* (Stockholm, 1797) in his library at the time of his death (Griffin, *Catalogue of the Washington Collection,* 5).

To Frederick William II of Prussia

Sire,   Philadelphia Jany 15th 1794.

However unusual it may be for your Majesty to receive an address from a person, who, at the very moment of making it, disclaims the exercise of any public function, and acts as a private individual; yet it is believed from your illustrious character, that the Motives, which lead me to the Measure, will serve as an ample apology.[1]

I cannot longer resist the impulse of friendship, to lay before you, who know so well, how to appreciate its force, my personal and affectionate anxiety for the welfare of M. de la Fayette. Report informs us, that he is under confinement in the dominions of Prussia, and therefore at your disposal.[2]

At an early period of his life—at a season, and on an occasion, far remote from the time and causes, which have subjected him to his present condition, he pursued his military career, with so much benefit to my country, and honor to himself, that he acquired a most endearing place in my affections.[3] A sincere attachment then commenced was strengthened by an intercourse which continued after the return of peace had seperated us until more active and interesting scenes served to interrupt it. Upon the events, which succeeded, I shall be silent; only entreating your Majesty to be persuaded, that as I seperate myself, in this letter, from my official station, to render a tribute to your liberality; so I beg to be understood as intending to observe that delicacy, which becomes every man, whose country has, with perfect sincerity, cherished peace and impartiality towards the whole world.

Permit me then to ask and obtain from your Majesty, a favor, in which the most lively sensibility of my fellow-citizens is engaged—the release of M. de la Fayette on his parole—If his word should not be deemed a sufficient pledge, I shall regret, that your Majesty does not entertain the same conviction of fidility, as a full experience has impressed upon myself. But I can never be persuaded of the possibility of his departing from that innocence of conduct, which is always to be expected from a prisoner of war.

This request, unsolicited by, and unknown to him asks the patronage of your Majesty's sensibility; and is dictated by a confidence, that he could not be in the power of any sovereign, who would more delight in indulging a friendship, which cannot acquit itself, without thus endeavouring to deliver him, under your benevolent auspices.[4] I pray God to preserve your Majesty in his holy keeping

Go: Washington

ALS, NNPM.

1. GW sought the approval of the cabinet before writing this letter (Cabinet Opinion, 14 Jan. 1794).

2. In January 1794 the Marquis de Lafayette was held by Prussia in the fortress at Neisse in Silesia, but in May he was transferred to Austrian custody and imprisoned at Olmütz, where he remained until set free in 1797.

3. Lafayette was the highest-ranking foreign officer in the Continental army during the American Revolution. On his arrival in the United States

in 1777 and the beginning of his friendship with GW, see n.1 of GW to Silas Deane, 13 Aug. 1777.

4. This letter apparently was sent to Thomas Pinckney, the U.S. minister to Great Britain, who then entrusted it to James Markham Marshall (1764–1848), a Virginia lawyer then living overseas, for delivery to Frederick William II. Upon his return to London, Marshall reported on his efforts in a letter of June 1794 to Pinckney: "I deliverd your letter to Prince Henry of Prussia [1726–1802] on the 28th of April and at the same time declared to him my intention of following implicitly his advice in the business which had been entrusted with me—he appeard highly gratified by the confidence which was placed in him, and express'd himself in terms of the warmest admiration of our President, & friendship for M. de la Fayette. Whilst I remain'd with him he wrote a letter to the King his Nephew—informing him of the letter with which I was charged, and urgin⟨g⟩ a compliance with the request which it contained

"On my departure from Rheinsbg—his Royal highness gave me a letter to the Minister of State on the same subject who immediately inform'd me that nothing could be done for M. de la Fayette, as an agreement had actually taken place by which he was to be deliver'd up to the Austrians and he added that probably the agreement was already executed. he spoke favorably of M. de la Fayette & lamented that it was not in the power of Prussia to comply with the request of his friends[.] As the only chance which remain'd, I endeavor'd to discover if it were possible to prevail on the ministry to favor the escape of Fayette from the fortress where he was confined. [Philipp Karl] Alvensleben [1745–1802] the Minister of State to whom I made the proposal, acknowledged his wish that it could be done but declared to me that it was too late[.] I could not press the subject further but as the Minister had not said that M de la Fayette was actually in the hands of the Austrians, I wrote requesting permission to se⟨e⟩ him before that event took place, intending if my request was grantd to renew my proposal. I enclose you the answer of Alvensleben, my business with him was at an end. I wrote, as I had promis'd, to give Prince Henry an account of my want of success, & to enquire if he could point out any step by which I could yet be of service to M. de la Fayette[.] the answer by the Baron [Karl Friedrich Hieronymus] Münchausen [Münchhausen; 1720–1797] I enclose you, I can not very well understand it, but I clearly perceiv'd that Prince Henry could do nothing for Fayette, and as I did not wish to be obliged to converse with him, on what our government might possibly yet do to procure his enlargement, I declined the invitation to Rheinsburg" (DLC: Pinckney Family Papers). The date of this letter is taken from the first docket; a second docket reads: "Copy forwarded to the Secretary of State 21st June 1794. by Mr Francis Duplicate 27th June 1794."

From James Hendricks

Sr   Wilkes County Georgia 15th Jany 1794

By the death of my worthy friend that good man Majr Forsyth the office of Marshal for this State has become Vacant[1] I have presum'd to offer myself to your Excellency for the Vacancy, I need not say any thing of my abilities to Exercise the duty incident thereto, shall only observe that being cast on this climate and not finding the discription of the country answer'd to my wishes, the compliance with my request will help to Smooth the declining years of a family always devoted to your Service—I need not attempt to give your Excellency the news of our Country as no doubt you have it Officially, I Shall only observe the disquietude I am under to see a parcell of Blockheads around us with Cockades in their Hats said to be in the Service of Mr Genet and ready to embroil us in a contest with the Spanierds our neighbours who appear to wish to live in Harmony & friendship with the United States,[2] every indirect method seems to have been used by these adventurers and others of the Same Stamp to provoke the Creek Indians to Hostilities but I hope their artifices will prove fruitless, as I am decidedly of opinion these People is not inclin'd to war if treated with decency, This opinion is the result of an attentive observation since my first Settling in Georgia.[3] beleive me with much respect Your Excellency's Obedt Hble Servt

James Hendricks

ALS, DLC:GW. Postal inscriptions on the cover read "Alex 12 Febry" and "Free."

James Hendricks, formerly a merchant in Alexandria, Va., moved to Georgia in 1789 or 1790.

1. Robert Forsyth was shot and killed on 11 Jan. 1794 while attempting to serve papers on Beverly Allen, a former Methodist minister from South Carolina, and his brother William Allen. For a contemporary account of this incident, see *Georgia. The Augusta Chronicle and Gazette of the State*, 18 Jan. 1794.

2. On the efforts of Edmond Genet, the French minister to the United States, to recruit Georgia residents for an expeditionary force against Spanish colonies, see William Moultrie to GW, 7 Dec. 1793, and enclosures.

3. Hendricks sent a second, and very similar, letter of application to GW on 22 Jan. because "the water being up the Port will be Stopp'd for two weeks, this I Send by way of Augusta" (DLC:GW; postal stamps read "BALT FEB 16" and "FREE."). He also sent a third letter, dated 1 Feb., in which he wrote: "I am Solicited by the Widow & the Sweet little Orphan Boys of my departed friend to be thus importunate, as their estate will be much embarrass'd by the untimely death of the Majr it is conceived that a Successor to the office who is their friend might be much to their advantage, as the greatest part of the suits in the Federal court is nearly at Issue after which the Marshal wou'd have had his fees and he has done the greatest part of the drudgery on his own expence, and I think it highly reasonable the

family ought to have the result of his labours especially as they will need it much" (DLC:GW). Robert Forsyth and his wife, Fanny Johnston Houston, had two sons, Robert Moriah (1778–1797) and John (1780–1841). Mrs. Forsyth had at least one child from a previous marriage, a daughter named Sarah (Alvin L. Duckett, *John Forsyth: Political Tactician* [Athens, Ga.: University of Georgia Press, 1962], 2–8). According to "An Act to make provision for the widow and orphan children of Robert Forsyth," 7 June 1794, Congress granted $2,000 to Mrs. Forsyth "for the use of herself and the children" (*Stat.* 6:17). GW was not swayed by Hendrick's three letters, and he nominated Josiah Tattnall as the next federal marshal for Georgia (GW to U.S. Senate, 5 March 1794).

Letter not found: from Charles Simms, 15 Jan. 1794. GW wrote Simms on 28 Jan., acknowledging receipt of "Your letter of the 15th instant."

To the United States Senate and House of Representatives

United States 15. January 1794.
Gentlemen of the Senate, and of the House of Representatives.

I lay before you, as being connected with the correspondence, already in your possession, between the Secretary of State and the Minister plenipotentiary of the French Republic, the copy of a Letter from that Minister of the 25th of December 1793; and a copy of the proceedings of the Legislature of the State of South Carolina.[1]

Go: Washington

LS, DNA: RG 46, Third Congress, 1793–95, Senate Records of Legislative Proceedings, President's Messages; LB, DNA: RG 233, Third Congress, 1793–95, House Records of Legislative Proceedings, Journals; Df (in Edmund Randolph's writing), DLC:GW; LB, DLC:GW. The draft appears on the last page of Randolph's proposed letter to Edmond Genet of 13 Jan. 1794.

1. For the previous submission of correspondence between Thomas Jefferson, the former secretary of state, and Edmond Genet, see GW to U.S. Senate and House of Representatives, 5 Dec. 1793. GW's current letter was prompted by the efforts of Genet to recruit residents of the Carolinas and Georgia for an expeditionary force against Spanish colonies. In his letter to Jefferson of 25 Dec. 1793, Genet denied having any authorization to raise such a force, but admitted granting commissions to several citizens of South Carolina who were willing to serve in this capacity (*Jefferson Papers*, 27:619–20; translation, *ASP, Foreign Affairs,* 1:311). For the enclosed proceedings of the S.C. legislature, see William Moultrie to GW, 7 Dec. 1793, and enclosure.

From John Berrien

Sir, Savannah [Ga.] Jany 16th 1794

By the unfortunate death of Major Forsyth, the Office of Federal Marshall of this State has become vacant—I beg leave to offer myself a Candidate for that appointment.[1] I am Sir, with profound veneration & respect Your Most Obt huml. Servant

John Berrien

ALS, DLC:GW.

1. On the death of Robert Forsyth, see n.1 of James Hendricks to GW, 15 January. Berrien, the current surveyor of customs at Savannah, Ga., did not receive the appointment (GW to U.S. Senate, 5 March).

From the Commissioners of the Sinking Fund

16. Jan. 1794.

Resolution of the Trustees of the Sinking Fund

At a Meeting of the Vice President & President of the Senate,[1] the Secretary of State, the Secretary of the Treasury Philadelphia Jan: 16. 1794.[2]

Resolved, That the two last dividends of Interest on the several species of Stock standing on the books of the Treasury to the credit of the Trustees of the Sinking fund, and of Saml Meredith in trust for the United States, be applied to the purchase of the public debt within the limits of the last resolution of the board, and according to the Act in that behalf That Samuel Meredith, Treasurer, be the Agent, and Philadelphia the place of purchase.[3] Signed in behalf of the board

John Adams.

Approved Jan. 16. 1794. Go. Washington.

LB, DLC:GW.

1. According to Article I, section 3, of the U.S. Constitution, the vice president of the United States also served as president of the Senate.

2. On the function of the sinking fund and the responsibilities of its commissioners, see "An Act making Provision for the Reduction of the Public Debt," 12 Aug. 1790, *Stat.* 1:186–87. Other commissioners were the attorney general and the chief justice of the Supreme Court.

3. The limits imposed by the resolutions of 20 Aug. 1793 were "to apply the last quarter's interest arising from the purchased Stock, to the purchase of other stock" and "to apply 50,000 Dollars to the purchase of the Public Debt

of that kind which should be cheapest" (*JPP*, 225). For purchases made by Meredith during the current year, see the report from the Commissioners of the Sinking Fund to the U.S. Senate of 19 Nov. 1794 in *ASP, Finance,* 1:302–16.

To the United States Senate
and House of Representatives

United States 16. Jany 1794
Gentlemen of the Senate, and of the House of Representatives.

I transmit for your information certain intelligence lately received from Europe, as it relates to the subject of my past communications.[1]

Go: Washington

LS, DNA: RG 46, Third Congress, 1793–95, Senate Records of Legislative Proceedings, President's Messages; LB, DNA: RG 233, Third Congress, 1793–95, House Records of Legislative Proceedings, Journals; LB, DLC:GW; LB, DNA: RG 59, Reports of the Secretary of State to the President and Congress.

1. The enclosed documents included an extract of Gouverneur Morris's second letter to Thomas Jefferson of 10 Oct. 1793, in which the U.S. minister to France wrote that he was "very anxious that Consuls & vice Consuls should be appointed in all the ports. My Countrymen are incessantly applying to me from every quarter about property taken from them. I am desired from abroad to claim such property. I have decidedly refused to lend my name on such occasions, because I am certain that I should be thereupon represented as a party interested, and of course my representations against the proceedings, which are but too frequent, would be disregarded." To illustrate his point, Morris summarized what happened when "a deputation of four ship Captains, chosen by their bretheren of Bordeaux," called on Morris "with a representation of the injustice they experienced in being prevented from sailing with their cargoes &c." (DNA: RG 46, Third Congress, 1793–95, Senate Records of Legislative Proceedings, President's Messages; the entire letter is in *ASP, Foreign Relations,* 1:373).

Also enclosed were translations of Morris's letters to François Louis Michel Chemin Deforgues, France's minister of foreign affairs, of 1 and 12 Oct. 1793. In the first, Morris enclosed "copies of two Judgments rendered with regard to the American vessel the George. . . . Captain Richard Stevens of the American vessel the Hope, also complains very bitterly of a sentence rendered lately against a part of the cargo of this vessel which is incontestably American property." Morris continued, "I request you, Sir, to pardon an observation which regards the particular interests of France. The circumstances of the moment prevent the fitting out of Privateers—consequently it would cost it nothing to cause the treaty to be observed with the greatest exactitude. Then the contrast which the Americans would make between the conduct of France and that of its enemies could not but be favorable." In the second,

Morris enclosed "the Copy of a letter which has been addressed to me, by citizen Postic, a Lawyer residing at Morlaix. It appears that in the proceedings of which he has given an account, there are extraordinary irregularities, and I think it my duty to inform you of them" (both, DNA: RG 46, Third Congress, 1793–95, Senate Records of Legislative Proceedings, President's Messages; *ASP, Foreign Relations,* 1:374, 376).

The fourth enclosure was an extract of a translation of Deforgues' reply to Morris of 14 Oct., in which he defended France's policies toward American vessels (DNA: RG 46, Third Congress, 1793–95, Senate Records of Legislative Proceedings, President's Messages; a copy of the complete translation, plus the enclosed copy of the French decree of 9 May 1793, which was not sent with the extract, is in *ASP, Foreign Relations,* 1:376–77).

The fifth enclosure was a translation of Morris's letter to Deforgues of 19 Oct., in which Morris writes: "I have examined with respectful care, the Decree of the ninth of May emanating from the conduct of your enemies, and supported by some reasons to which you have given their greatest lustre. It is possible, sir, that the difference of our position leads us to see the same object in a different manner." Morris concluded this letter by writing: "You will agree, Sir, that it is hard for my fellow Citizens not to have the advantage either of the Treaty or of the law of nations—to lose their merchandises by the Treaty, and not to be able to compensate themselves for it, under the protection of this same Treaty, by the freight of enemy-merchandises. In comparing the facts of the same epoch, you will be amazed on seeing what passed at Paris and at Philadelphia. Your good sense will lead you to anticipate the claims of our merchants, and the insinuations of our enemies" (DNA: RG 46, Third Congress, 1793–95, Senate Records of Legislative Proceedings, President's Messages; *ASP, Foreign Relations,* 1:378). For previous mention of problems caused by France's policies on neutral shipping, see GW to U.S. Senate and House of Representatives, 5 Dec. 1793.

GW's Note Concerning
the Recall of Edmond Genet

[c.16] Jany 1794

Whilst the measure, which gave a rise to these papers, was under consideration—advice was recd from our Minister at Paris, that Mr Genet wd be immediately recalled which arrested the business in this stage of it.[1]

AD, DLC:GW. This note is on the back of the cover for an unidentified letter to GW. The postal stamp on the cover reads "N. YORK Jan 15." A handwritten notation on the cover indicates that this letter was sent per "Woolwich Capt. Stimson." According to newspaper accounts, the ship Woolwich, under Capt. John Stimson, had arrived in New York City's port from Cork, Ireland, by Wednesday, 15 Jan. (*Greenleaf's New York Journal and Patriotic Register,* 15, 22 Jan. 1794).

1. The exact papers to which GW refers are not known, but they probably included Alexander Hamilton's Proposed Presidential Message to Congress of 6–13 Jan. 1794. For the news from Gouverneur Morris that the French government would recall Edmond Genet, its minister to the United States, see his letter to GW of 19 Oct. 1793, and n.1.

From Edmund Randolph

Sir   Philadelphia January 17. 1794.
    Since I had the honor of seeing you this morning, I met with Colo. Nicholas Lutz, of the town of Reading. He has requested me to inform you, that he shall be obliged to you to nominate him to be the inspector of the excise for that district. His son stands recommended to you; but he wishes to take his place. Mr Lutz says, that he is known to you, and is a member of the legislature of Pennsylvania,[1] and that Mr Forrest and Mr Nichols do not live in the district.[2] I have the honor, sir, to be with the highest respect yr. mo. ob. serv.

                                                          Edm: Randolph

ALS, DLC:GW.
    1. Nicholas Lutz (Lotz; 1740–1807) emigrated from the German Palatinate as a young man and by 1775 was settled in Reading, Pennsylvania. In 1776, Lt. Col. Lutz commanded the Berks County regiment of flying camp troops at the Battle of Long Island, N.Y., during which British forces captured him. Freed in a prisoner exchange in 1779, he served as commissioner of forage for Berks County from 1780 until the end of the war. He represented Berks County in the Pennsylvania state legislature, 1783–85 and 1789–94, and served as an associate judge of Berks County, 1795–1806. Exactly which of his seven sons (Philip, Nicholas, Jacob, John, Henry, Michael [b. 1764], and William) he wished to replace as a candidate is not known.
    Berks County was included in the second survey of the district of Pennsylvania along with Luzerne, Northampton, and Northumberland counties (Executive Order, 15 March 1791). On the vacancy created in the office of inspector of the revenue for this survey by the incompetency of James Collins, see Alexander Hamilton to GW, 23 Dec. 1793. Jacob Morgan wrote a letter to GW of 25 Jan., in which he recommended Lutz as "a person in my opinion very capable of doing the duties of that Office—he has been frequently employed in the service of the public, & always found to be punctual & industrious, particularly in purchasing supplies for the Army in the State of Pennsyla. during the late War; first under my Superintendance; next under Col. [Samuel] Miles, & then under Mr Robert Morris when he became financier; & has always given general satisfaction which Mr Morris will testify—Being a prisoner to the British during the late war, he was obliged to sell the most valuable Mill in Berks County to support himself & family, this

with other losses make it an object of some consequence his obtaining the post for which he has applied" (DLC:GW).

2. Mr. Forrest and Mr. Nichols, who have not been identified, did not receive the appointment, nor did Lutz or one of his sons (see GW to U.S. Senate, 29 Jan. 1794).

To William Pearce

Mr. Pearce,   Philadelphia 19th Jany 1794

Your letter of the 14th instt came to my hands to day, when the Post ought to have been in yesterday.[1]

Having been very full in my late letters to you, I shall have less to say in this—The condition you describe my stock to be in at Union farm, and at Dogue run, & want of shelter for them at those places, is a fresh instance of the misconduct of Crow & McKoy; and of the neccessity of watching their ways well. As you have taken Butler again, you must make the most you can of him.[2] The man means well, but he wants activity & Spirit to fit him for the Overlooker of Negroes. You will find him useful though in raising hedges, &ca—& particularly so in cultivating the French furze. It was he that induced me to send for the seed of it, wch will be sent to you by the first Vessel to Alexandria—about 40 lbs. of it.[3]

Let the most that can, be made of the pint of Oats which the Gardener raised last year, and of the Hemp seed; but more especially of the St foin seed which I desired him to be particularly choice of; as I wish much to get into a stock of it. The latter must not be sown where Hares can get to it, or they will cut it down as fast as it springs.[4]

When McKoy is getting out the Oats at Dogue run, have a strict eye to him. He told me he expected 150 Bushls from the stack, & if all the Oats which grew in what was called the New ground, went into it, there ought to be 200 at least—but what by waste, mismanagement, or something worse, I have, of late, got very little from any of my Overseers; what becomes of it is more difficult to determine.

If you should have another freezing spell, do not by any means omit to fill the Ice house with Ice, as the advantage of it for keeping fresh meat &ca is indiscribable; but before you begin to put a weight on the floor let both it & the Joice (or Sleepers) be well examined, lest, by being rotten they may give way & destroy those who may be below pounding the Ice as it is thrown in. If the floor is found unsafe take it away altogether—I do not know but that the Ice will keep as well without, as with it.

If on account of the springiness of the ground you cannot proceed in digging the Mill race, which is a thing to be regretted, you might employ the Ditchers on the fence from the Millers, leading upwards, for the purpose of securing the meadow lots if nothing *more* pressing calls for their labour.[5] Opening the Visto is not a work of neccessity; & it never was intended to be extended beyond Muddy hole swamp; to which I think it ought to have got before this time.

You may keep Isaac and the boy Joe, constantly employed about the Carts, Plows, Harrows &ca until they are in order.[6] Let stuff, however, be always in the Barn that the other Carpenters may work upon, when the weather will not permit them to be out. What are Mrs Fanny Washington's Carpenters employed about, that they should (altho' hired by me) be withdrawn from mine so long. All I know they had to do, was, out of the materials of an old Tobacco house, to make a shed for her plow horses—Ask Tayler what more than this they have done, and by whose authority?[7]

The Midlings and ship stuff may be sold whenever you find the market good; & the money applied to such uses as are proper. If twine (for the Seins) is to be had in Alexandria, it will be better to get it there than to depend upon having it sent from thence.[8] And you have my full consent to give the Cattle as much Salt as you judge necessary, preventing waste.

I perceive by the Report from River farm that Stuart is plowing in No. 7 (a field that was in Wheat last year, & by the rotation which I have transmitted to you, was intended to remain in pasture this year)—What is the meaning of this? No. 1 by the copy I have by me is intended for Buck Wheat as a manure, and No. 3 for Corn, but I do not recollect that any direction has ever been given for plowing No. 7.[9] If the case be otherwise I have forgot it; and the design must be for Oats & Buck wheat for Crops; & of course, if accomplished, will require 120 bushls of the first, and 60 of the latter more than I had calculated to seed the field; the contents being 120 acres. Let me know how this matter really stands.[10] How much of the field is already plowed. and whether you will be able to prepare the residue of it; and at the sametime execute your other plowing well, & in season, with your present force of horses, aided by Oxen; which, in the Eastern states is almost the only teams they plow with. I am your friend

Go: Washington

ALS, ViMtvL; ALS (letterpress copy), DLC:GW.

1. Pearce's letter to GW of 14 Jan. has not been found. According to the postal schedule, a letter sent to the postmaster at Alexandria, Va., on Wednesday, 15 Jan., should have arrived at Philadelphia on Saturday, 18 Jan. (GW to Anthony Whitting, 2 Dec. 1792).

2. Hiland Crow and Henry McCoy were the respective overseers of Union and Dogue Run farms. On GW's previous assumption that Pearce would find a replacement for James Butler, the overseer of the Mansion House farm, see his letter to Pearce of 12 Jan. 1794.

3. For the shipment of the French furze seed, see GW to Pearce, 16–17 March.

4. John Christian Ehlers was the head gardener at Mount Vernon. Sainfoin, *Onobrychis viciaefolia,* is a Eurasian perennial leguminous herb that is grown for forage.

5. For GW's previous instructions regarding the construction of a race for the gristmill and a fence leading from Joseph Davenport's house on Dogue Run farm, see GW to Pearce, 23 Dec. 1793, and n.13.

6. The boy Joe is probably the same dower slave identified in 1799 as a carpenter who was married to Dolshy, a spinner and dower slave also assigned to the Mansion House farm. For the names of slaves listed in 1786 and 1799 as carpenters at Mount Vernon, including Isaac, see *Diaries,* 4:278, and Washington's Slave List, June 1799, in *Papers, Retirement Series,* 4:527–37. For the names of current slaves employed as carpenters, see the Farm Reports of 27 Jan.–2 Feb. 1794.

7. GW leased the services of carpenters Reuben and Gabriel, slaves belonging to Frances Bassett Washington (GW to Whitting, 3 March 1793, and n.5 to that document). Tayler was the overseer of her estate, which was on Clifton's Neck and adjoining Mount Vernon.

8. On 3 Feb., Pearce paid £22.15.00 to Robert Hamilton, a merchant in Alexandria, Va., for 182 lbs. of "Seine Twine @ 2/6 ℔ lb.," and on 1 April he paid Lawrence McGinnis £13.09.04 for "kniting A new Seine & puting a piece in the Old Shad Seine" (Mount Vernon Accounts, 1794–97).

9. For GW's plan of rotation, which GW expected William Stuart to follow, see GW to Pearce, 18 Dec. 1793, and enclosure.

10. Pearce's immediate reply to this question has not been found, but he returned to this topic in a letter to GW of 4 Feb. 1794.

From Daniel Gaines

Dear Sir,   Georgia, Washington, Jany the 20th 1794

The office of Marshal for the district of Georgia, being vacant, by the death of Major Forsyth,[1] I am a candidate for it—But being wholly unknown to you, I have solicited several of my friends, who are now in Philadelphia, to inform you what is my general character, both as to integrity, and abilities to perform the duties of the office.

I have wrote on that subject to the Secretary of State, the Attorney General, and several members of Congress from Georgia, as well as from my native state—Virginia.[2]

I endeavoured to procure a letter from Governor Matthews, but previous to my hearing the news of Major Forsyth's death, he had started on a tour thr⟨o⟩ugh the frontiers;[3] and the several water courses he had to pass, being uncommonly high, prevented him (I suppose) from punctual attendance on the appointed ⟨*mutilated*⟩ at the respective posts; so that my messenger could not find him.

I hope Sir you will excuse the freedom of my enclosing a copy of a letter from myself to Colonel Taliaferro (now President of the Senate of Georgia) and his answer thereto. A few words in it have puzzled me. Those are "one excepted, which at our first interview shall be explained." Colonel Taliaferro and myself have differed in a few political points, the only points in which we ever did differ; so that I am obliged to conclude those are what he alludes to; and if my conjecture is right, I expect it cannot operate against me in my present application; for mere speculative opinions can never bias a man possessed of the sentiments of honor in the execution of any office he undertakes.[4] Whether I am possessed of those sentiments, you will judge by the credentials adduced to you, and the information of Gentlemen acquainted with me in Virginia and Georgia.[5] I am, with due respect, Sir, Your most obedient, and very hble servant

Dan: Gaines

ALS, DLC:GW.

Virginia native Daniel Gaines moved to Georgia after the Revolutionary War, where the Commissioners of Confiscated Estates granted him 500 acres on the south side of the Broad River at the mouth of Chickasaw Creek in 1783 or early 1784. In 1791, he purchased lot #18 in the town of Washington, in Wilkes County. See Grace Gillam Davidson, *Early Records of Georgia: Wilkes County*, (1933. Reprint ed., Vidalia, Ga., 1968), 2:118–19, 229.

1. On the death of Robert Forsyth, see n.1 of James Hendricks to GW, 15 January.

2. For extant letters written by Gaines to various federal officials asking for letters of recommendation, see the notes to Randolph's letter to GW of 17 February. Georgia congressman Francis Willis, also a native of Virginia

and a resident of Wilkes County, described Gaines in a letter to GW of 17 Jan. as a man who "is greatly reduced in fortune but has an independant and intrepid mind and can give (I beleive) both in this State and Virginia sufficient security, Colo. Gaines foreseeing his declining circumstances studied Law and is licenced to plead but the bar is so crouded he can not expect to support a numerous family of children, in addition to his qualifying himself for the practice of the Law he acted as a justice of the peace twenty years in the state of Virginia, which added to a good natural understanding and a general acquisition of knowledge, places him beyond all doubt in a state not to be rejected for want of capability" (DLC:GW).

3. Virginia native George Mathews (1739–1812) was an officer in the Continental army during the Revolutionary War, including a year's service in Gen. Nathanael Greene's southern army. Shortly after the war's end, he moved with his family to Georgia, where he settled on lands granted him in Wilkes County by the Georgia legislature. He served as a justice of the peace, 1785–90, and in the state assembly, 1787–89 and 1793. He was elected governor of Georgia for 1787 and later to a term in the U.S. House of Representatives, 1789–91. He then served as a justice of the Inferior Court of Wilkes County, 1792–93, until his election in November 1793 to a second term as governor.

4. In his letter to Benjamin Taliaferro of 15 Jan., Gaines asked for a letter of recommendation, "being entirely unacquainted with the President of the United States." He requested it with "confidence from the long and intimate acquaintance that has been between us" (DLC:GW). Taliaferro (1750–1821), who was the current president of the Georgia state senate, was a Virginia native. He saw active duty in Georgia during his military service in the Continental army during the Revolutionary War and was captured by the British in 1780. In 1785 he settled in Wilkes County, and he represented Georgia in the U.S. House of Representatives, 1799–1802. In the enclosed letter to Gaines of c.16 Jan. 1794, he wrote: "From my acquaintance with you, I cannot doubt, either your abilities, or your determination to acquit yourself with propriety in the Office of Federal Marshal, but satisfied as I am on this head, I cannot flatter myself, or be persuaded into a belief, that the recommendation which you request, will avail you any thing in procuring it; on the contrary, I believe it would have an ill affect; as the President would naturally, and in my oppinion, very properly conclude I had presumed too highly on a very slight acquaintance. He would consider it as an improper attempt in me (unacquainted as I am) to influence his determinations, all which would only tend to lessen me in his estimation, without effecting any thing favourable to your claim. I am persuaded that the best plan you can persue, to ensure success, will be, to obtain recommendatory letters from Gentlemen having influence with our Representatives in Congress, for I doubt not but they will be the first, and perhaps, the only persons applied to by the President: Perhaps a letter from Governor Mathews, as he has had a personal, and recent, acquaintance with him, might have some weight. I sincerely wish it were in my power to serve you in this business, for I repeat that from my knowledge of your Character, I believe you in every way qualified for the Office, one excepted, which at our first interview shall be explained, I hope my reasons will

be satisfactory, if they are not, I conclude with one other. I am always afraid to weigh my Consequence in the Political scale, for fear it be found wanting" (DLC:GW).

5. GW nominated Josiah Tattnall to be the next federal marshal for Georgia (GW to U.S. Senate, 5 March 1794).

From Alexander Hamilton

Sir,   Treasury Dept. Jan: 20. 1794.

I have the honor to send herewith a letter to me from the Commissioner of the Revenues of the 17 of August 1793; relating to the then state of execution of the laws laying a duty on spirits distilled within the United States, and on Stills, which was directed with the ultimate view of laying before you the information which it contains.[1]

You will perceive that upon the whole the execution of the law has been progressive, though the obstacles to it are yet far from being entirely vanquished, and that supplementary provisions by the Legislature are necessary.[2]

I beg leave to submit to your consideration the expediency of calling the attention of the Legislature to the subject by a message.[3] With perfect respect and the truest attachment, I have the honor to be &c.

Alexr Hamilton

LB, DLC:GW.

1. The letter from Tench Coxe to Hamilton of 17 Aug. 1793 has not been identified. For the relevant laws, see "An Act repealing, after the last day of June next, the duties heretofore laid upon Distilled Spirits imported from abroad, and laying others in their stead; and also upon Spirits distilled within the United States, and for appropriating the same," 3 March 1791, and "An Act concerning the Duties on Spirits distilled within the United States, 8 May 1792 (*Stat.* 1:199–214, 267–71).

2. On the need for further legislative action on the collection of the federal excise tax on whiskey, including the extension of the tax to the Northwest and Southwest territories and the creation of a separate revenue district for the state of Kentucky, which was currently included in the Virginia District, see Coxe to Hamilton, 11 Dec. 1792 (*Hamilton Papers*, 13:305–14).

3. See GW's message to the U.S. Senate and House of Representatives of 21 January.

Henry Knox to Bartholomew Dandridge, Jr.

Dear Sir   War department January 20. 1794.

Please to submit to the President of the United States the enclosed letters from James Seagrove, Major Gaither and Constant Freeman, all of which have just been received.[1] I am Dear Sir Your obedt Servant

H. Knox secy of war

LS, DLC:GW; LB, DLC:GW.

1. According to GW's executive journal, Knox submitted four letters this day (*JPP*, 278). The first was from James Seagrove to Knox of 30 Nov. 1793, in which the Indian agent described his journey to the Creek villages of Cussetah and Tuckaubatchie and his subsequent conversations with the Indians at these locations. "After sitting in council two days and nights" at Tuckaubatchie, he wrote, "it was unanimously determined on, that all acts of hostilities or depredations should, from that moment, cease between the United States and the Creek nations." As a condition of peace Seagrove asked for the return of all white prisoners, slaves, cattle, and horses taken by the Indians and the punishment of those Indians responsible for recent murders within Georgia's borders. In a second letter of 30 Nov., Seagrove informed George Mathews that "peace and good understanding is again re-established" with the Creeks and asked the Georgia governor to promulgate this information in order "to prevent any outrage being offered to such Indians as may appear on your frontier" (*ASP, Indian Affairs*, 1:471–72). The two letters of 14 Dec. 1793 from Maj. Henry Gaither and Indian agent Constant Freeman, Jr., both to Knox, have not been identified, but presumably they also concerned U.S. relations with the Creeks and other southern Indians.

"By the President's direction," Dandridge returned the letters to Knox later this day, with a request "to enquire what, or whether anything is thought necessary to be done in consequence of the information contained in them" (DLC:GW). For Knox's suggestion, see his letter to GW of 21 January.

From the Non-Commissioned Officers and Privates of the New-York Line

SIR,   [New York City, c.20 Jan. 1794]

THE non-commissioned officers and privates of the New-York line, in the late American army, beg leave most respectfully to address you, and to present to you the services we rendered to our country during the late glorious struggle with the armies of the King of Great-Britain, and the mode in which we have been paid.

That at the conclusion of the war we retired to private life, with assurances of compensation for our hard but approved of services.

That for reasons unknown to us, we were paid (not in specie) agreeably to contract, but in certificates, which we were compelled through extreme distress and poverty, to sell for two ⟨and⟩ sixpence for every twenty shillings, after g⟨e⟩tting to our respective homes or to such places a⟨s coul⟩d be found as an asylum from fatigue, and which were after some time funded and paid to holders at the rate of sixteen shillings in the pound.

That there at present remains a ballance of four shillings for every twenty shillings due to us in the hands of government, which we conceive ought in honor of the country, to be paid to those who earn't it, or to their representatives, and which can be done without interfering with any system heretofore established.

That in the last and former sessions of Congress, we were well pleased to hear that Mr. James Madison, with several other of the members of the House of Representatives of the United States, stept forward in our defence and proposed a mode of payment of the certificates so issued, in our favor; but to our unhappy situations add the failure of their good intentions.

That a recital of our past services so well known to you, Sir, we conceive to be useless, but beg leave to say that for want of the ballance due, justly due us from our country, we are obliged to seek relief from the cold hand of charity, even from those who enjoy affluence through our earnings and the destruction of our families.

We therefore relying on your wisdom, humbly implore your assistance and influence at the present session of Congress, to obtain for us the ballance due on the said certificates.

And subscribe as well for ourse⟨l⟩ves as in behalf of the said line. Your most obedient humble servants.

To be presented by Serjeant John Clark, on behalf of the said line.[1]

JOHN CLARK, late Serjt. 2d New-York Regt.

L, *Daily Advertiser* [New York], 13 Feb. 1794; *Greenleaf's New York Journal*, 15 Feb. 1794. The text in angle brackets is from the 15 Feb. printing.

1. On the complaints contained in this letter, see the notes to a similar letter of 30 Aug. 1793 that was sent by the same veterans of the Revolutionary War. Apparently, after receiving no response from GW to the earlier letter, Clark wrote this later version and delivered it personally to GW's house in

Philadelphia. GW's response is contained in Clark's report to the veterans, which accompanied the publication of this letter: "ON the 21st of January last I delivered your petition to the Secretary of the President [Bartholomew Dandridge, Jr.], who promised me he would present it to him the moment he was at leisure. On the 25th following I had a private conference with the President—he informed me that he was not the proper person to be applied to, that it was Congress we should apply to, 'tho it was his opinion, if we did, we should not meet with success—I answered that it was the opinion of many, and I acquiesced that he was the proper person—for two reasons. 1st. That the commissioned officers had applied repeatedly to Congress, and never received any redress. 2d. That he had promised the army, that he would before they quitted the service, see that full and ample compensation should be made to them, and that their hard and approved service should not go unregarded—he answered that he had done every thing he could: I replied I never heard of your stepping forward in any respect, and further, that while in Congress there were speculators, and enemies to a republican government, the veteran need not or may not expect justice.

"President—I never bought nor sold a note to either officer or private.

"Clark—I never said you did, or know whether you did or did not.

"President—If Congress is applied to, and they think proper to compensate the late army, whatever they do, I should gladly augment, was it in my power, rather than diminish.

"Clark—I wish you may live to see a pure Congress, and perform your promise."

From Edmund Randolph

Monday afternoon. [20 Jan. 1794]

E. Randolph has the honor of informing the President, that the message of to-day, appears to have given general satisfaction. Mr M-d———n in particular thinks, that it will have a good effect. He asked me, whether an extract could not have been given from Mr Morris's letter; and upon my answering, that there were some things interwoven with the main subject, which ought not to be promulged, he admitted, that the discretion of the President was always to be the guide.[1]

I have received a letter from Galbaud; insisting that he should be brought to trial upon the accusation of Genet, that he was concerned in a conspiracy in the U.S. The mail, which brought his letter, brought a paper, in which it was published.[2]

I am told, that a message is to be sent to the President, for a letter, which has been omitted from the correspondence between Mr Genet and Mr Jefferson.[3]

Hauterive, the french Consul, at N. York, has written to Mr Jefferson, to know, whether it was with his permission, that Bache's paper assigned the cause of his resignation to be, that he was compelled to sign dispatches, which he disapproved: and particularly to ask, whether a particular letter, which related to himself, was among the number of things, disapproved by him.[4]

AL, DLC:GW.

1. For the message, see GW to the U.S. Senate and House of Representatives, this date. The specific letter from Gouverneur Morris, U.S. minister to France, to which Virginia congressman James Madison referred, may be his first letter to Thomas Jefferson of 10 Oct. 1793, in which Morris wrote that the French government had agreed to recall Edmond Genet "immediately" as its minister to the United States. A letter to Jefferson of 19 Oct. 1793, however, offered more details on Genet's recall and the assignment of his successor (*ASP, Foreign Relations,* 1:372, 374–75).

2. On former French minister Edmond Genet's charges against Galbaud, the former governor-general of the French colony of Saint Domingue, see Cormeille, Sr., to GW, 3 Jan. 1794. On Genet's denouncement, his attempts to have Galbaud arrested by New York officials, and the administration's response, see n.2 of Jefferson to GW, 15–16 Sept. 1793. Galbaud's letter to Randolph of 17 Jan., which has not been identified, was written at New York City. In the published, English version, Galbaud wrote: "I am publicly accused, by MR. GENET, of having intended to disturb the tranquility of the United States, in devising a complot which would compromit the good understanding which subsists between them and *France.* Such a conduct would be a crime against your laws; the accusation is too serious to be overlooked. Since MR. GENET offers to prove this accusation to the people of *America,* I demand then to be made a prisoner, that a process be instituted, and I may be judged by the tribunals of the United States, in which a decision shall be had of the crime" (*Universal Daily Advertiser* [Philadelphia], 21 Jan. 1794). Genet made public his accusation by publishing, in English, his letter to Thomas Jefferson of 6 Sept. 1793 (*Daily Advertiser* [New York], 16 Jan. 1794; see also *Jefferson Papers,* 27:41–43, and translation, *ASP, Foreign Relations,* 1:77). After acknowledging receipt of Galbaud's 17 Jan. letter in a reply of 7 Feb., Randolph wrote: "No order can be given by the President on this occasion. Any person within the United States, who wishes voluntarily to surrender himself for examination or trial, must apply to the magistrates within the State" (DNA: RG 59, Domestic Letters).

On 10 Feb., Galbaud wrote Randolph, in French and from Philadelphia, that he intended to leave shortly for France from New York City upon the *St. Honoré* and that he needed a letter stating that he had broken no American laws. He believed that having such a letter upon his return to France would help clear his name with officials there (DNA: RG 59, Miscellaneous Letters). Randolph replied on 11 Feb.: "I had written to you on the 7th instant . . . and as it is probable, that you were on the road, when my letter was on its way, I do myself the honor of now enclosing to you a copy. This morning

I laid before the President of the United States your letter, dated yesterday. He cannot interfere in the business, in which you seem to be so much interested, farther than the rules of duty permit, and those rules will not suffer him to go beyond what is said in my letter of the 7th instant" (DNA: RG 59, Domestic Letters).

3. Copies of correspondence between Jefferson and Genet were submitted with GW's letter to the U.S. Senate and House of Representatives of 5 Dec. 1793. For those enclosures, see *ASP, Foreign Relations,* 1:142–246. Any written request to GW for additional Genet correspondence has not been found, but a request was made for copy of a letter from Jefferson to British minister George Hammond (U.S. House of Representatives to GW, 20 Jan. 1794).

4. French consul Hauterive inquired about Jefferson's resignation as secretary of state in his letter to him of 15 Jan. 1794 (*Jefferson Papers,* 28:7–8). The editorial commentary about the cause of Jefferson's resignation appeared in the 6 Jan. issue of Benjamin Franklin Bache's *General Advertiser* (Philadelphia). The letter that Hauterive suspected Jefferson disapproved may have been the circular letter written to the French consuls and vice-consuls of 7 Sept. 1793 (see Cabinet Opinion on Relations with France and Great Britain, 7 Sept. 1793, and n.1 to that document; *Jefferson Papers,* 27:51). For Jefferson's response to these speculations, see his letter to Randolph of 3 Feb. (*Jefferson Papers,* 28:15–16).

From George Barlow Smith

Sir   Tregony Cornwall 20th Jany 1794

I suppose you will be surprised to receive a letter from a person who you never saw or likely never heard of but from what I have been told by my Father I have reason to suppose that you are nearly related to me My Grandmother was born at Dorcester in Yorkshire whoes maiden name was Washington & I am Informed was a sister to you.[1] I am at present a Lieut. of the British Navy on half pay but having a family my Pay is rather scanty for their Maintainance If you can recollect the relationship & woud Assist me it woud be doing a peice of Charity I have a sister at Philadelphia Married to Mr Alexander James Dallas who I understand is secretary to the state of Pensilvania whom I dare say you may have heard of—My Father was a Captain in the Army & latterly resided at Jamaica as Leit. Governor of Fort Charles—but died about ten years Since—& left four Children you may say Orphans[2]—I shoud thank you to consider wether what I have wrote is not True & excuse the Liberty I have taken.[3] & I remain with respect Your Obedient Humble Servt

Geo. B. Smith

ALS, DLC:GW. George Barlow Smith (d. 1799) was commissioned a lieuten-ant in the Royal Navy in 1783.

1. GW's only sister to survive infancy was Betty Washington Lewis, and like her brother, she was born in Virginia.

2. Alexander J. Dallas, secretary of the Commonwealth of Pennsylvania, was a native of the British colony of Jamaica, but he spent much of his youth in England, where he married Arabella Maria Smith (c.1764–1837) on 4 Sept. 1780. Her father, Maj. George Smith (died c.1782), was stationed in Jamaica at the time of their marriage.

3. No response from GW has been found.

To David Stuart

Dear Sir,   Philadelphia 20th Jany 1794
Your letter of the 6th instant came duly to hand. As you appear to have taken a final determination, I can say nothing more on the subject of its disclosure than that it would have been pleas-ing to me if it had been convenient to yourselves, that those who began shd have compleated the work; and not to have left the harvest to your labours to be reaped by others.[1]

As you are better acquainted than I am with characters in the vicinity of the federal City, and with those not so remote as to make an attendance therein inconvenient: Know also the con-nections of individuals in point of interest with the same, & how far those connections ought to disqualify them for Commission-ers, I would thank you for the names, of such as in your judg-ment are most likely to subserve the public purposes. Wishing as I do to make a good choice of successors, every aid I can derive towards the accomplishment of it would be gratefully received.[2]

Well qualified men might perhaps be had in George Town, or among the Proprietors;[3] but how far their local, & perhaps jar-ring interests and views might render them unfit for the trust, being questionable, your opinion thereon would be agreeable to Dear Sir Your Obedt & Affecte Servt

Go: Washington

ALS, NbO; ALS (letterpress copy), DLC:GW; LB, DLC:GW.

1. On Stuart's appointment as one of the three original commissioners for the District of Columbia, see Commission, 22 Jan. 1791. For his intention to resign this commission as of 1 March, see his letter to GW of 6 January. Stuart, however, did not terminate his service until July (4–6, 27–31 July 1794 minutes, DNA: RG 42, Records of the Commissioners for the District of Co-lumbia, Proceedings, 1791–1802).

2. For the individuals suggested by Stuart, see his letter to GW of 6 February. In August and September 1794, GW appointed, respectively, Gustavus Scott and William Thornton to replace Stuart and Thomas Johnson, who also resigned from the D.C. Commission this year (GW to Tobias Lear, 28 Aug. 1794, DLC:GW; Harris, *William Thornton Papers,* 1:287).

3. On the proprietors of the Federal District, see source note to Agreement of the Proprietors of the Federal District, 30 March 1791.

From the United States House of Representatives

Monday the 20th of January 1794
In the House of Representatives of the United States.

Resolved, that the President be requested to direct the Secretary of State, to examine whether, among the papers relative to Great Britain, by him laid before the house, a letter from Mr Jefferson to Mr Hammond, of the 5th of Decr 1791. has not been omitted, and if so, to cause the same, or so much thereof as he shall think proper, to be laid before the House:[1]

Ordered, that Mr Cadwalader & Mr Holten, be a Committee to wait on the President, with the foregoing resolution.[2]

Extract from the Journal
William Lambert[3] for John Beckley, Clerk.

D (written and signed by William Lambert), DNA: RG 59, Miscellaneous Letter; LB, DLC:GW.

1. The missing letter from Jefferson to George Hammond of 5 Dec. 1791 should have accompanied GW's address to the U.S. Senate and House of Representatives of 5 Dec. 1793. For this letter, which concerns the possibility of negotiating a treaty of commerce with Great Britain, see *Jefferson Papers,* 22:378–79. Following instructions from GW, Bartholomew Dandridge, Jr., sent a copy of this resolution to Edmund Randolph, the current secretary of state, on 21 Jan. and requested that he "furnish the letter therein required, if in his possession" (DNA: RG 59, Miscellaneous Letters).

2. New Jersey native Lambert Cadwalader (1742–1823) was a graduate of the College of Philadelphia in 1760, an officer in the Continental army during the Revolutionary War, and a delegate to the Continental Congress, 1785–87. He represented New Jersey in the U.S. House of Representatives, 1789–91 and 1793–95.

Dr. Samuel Holten (1738–1816) was a native of Massachusetts, where he served several terms in the state legislature and on the Governor's Council. He was a delegate to the Continental Congress, 1778–80, 1783–85, and 1787. He served in the U.S. House of Representatives, 1793–95, and then as a judge of the probate court for Essex County, Mass., 1796–1815.

3. William Lambert (d. 1834) was a native of Virginia. He served as a clerk in the State Department under Thomas Jefferson, 1790–92, and later in the House of Representatives as the principle assistant to John Beckley (Lambert to Jefferson, 8 June 1793, *Jefferson Papers*, 26:234–35).

To the United States Senate and House of Representatives

United States January 20th 1794.
Gentlemen of the Senate, and of the House of Representatives.

Having already laid before you a Letter of the 16th of August 1793, from the Secretary of State to our Minister at Paris; stating the conduct and urging the recal, of the Minister plenipotentiary of the Republic of France;[1] I now communicate to you, that his conduct has been unequivocally disapproved; and that the strongest assurances have been given, that his recal should be expedited without delay.[2]

Go: Washington

LS, DNA: RG 46, Third Congress, 1793–95, Senate Records of Legislative Proceedings, President's Messages; DS (in Edmund Randolph's writing), DNA: RG 59, Miscellaneous Letters; LB, DNA: RG 233, Third Congress, 1793–95, House Records of Legislative Proceedings, Journals; LB, DLC:GW. The cover of the draft is addressed to "Colo. Hamilton & General Knox," with instructions that "The bearer will take the letter from the one to the other gentleman." Alexander Hamilton's initials and Henry Knox's signature appear on the draft under the word "approved," which Hamilton added beneath the text of the message. Randolph then enclosed the draft with a brief cover letter to GW of 19 Jan. that reads: "E. Randolph has the honor of inclosing to the President, a message, concurred in by all the gentlemen" (DNA: RG 59, Miscellaneous Letters).

1. On the administration's decision to ask for the recall of Edmond Genet, see Cabinet Opinion, 23 Aug. 1793. Thomas Jefferson's letter to Gouverneur Morris of 16 Aug. was submitted along with GW's message to the U.S. Senate and House of Representatives of 5 Dec. 1793. For Jefferson's letter to Morris, see *Jefferson Papers*, 26:697–715.

2. Morris's first letter of 10 Oct. and that of 19 Oct. 1793 to former secretary of state Thomas Jefferson revealed that the French government had agreed to recall Genet (*ASP, Foreign Relations*, 1:372, 374–75). William Culver, who commanded the sloop *Hannah*, arrived at Philadelphia with these dispatches in mid-January (*Gazette of the United States and Evening Advertiser* [Philadelphia], 14 Jan. 1794). For the official notice of Genet's recall, see Provisional Executive Council of France to GW, 15 Nov. 1793.

From Josef Yznardi, Sr.

Rota [Spain] 20th January 1794.
Very Honorable and respectable Sir, of my particular esteem:

Having present to my mind the obligations that a Father contracts when favors are bestowed on his Children, because the latter ought to be imitators of their originals in good actions, I cannot do less than make known my acknowledgements for the multiplied favors which Joseph Yznardy Joven (who is my Son) has received from Your Excellency, and more especially, for the very great one of having given him the appointment of Consul of your Republic in the Port of Cadiz and its dependencies. That he may not forfeit the good opinion that he has deserved from the Senate and Congress, I shall give him on my part all the necessary assistance in this respect;[1] as in effect, I shall relinquish the conveniences of my House; and the satisfaction that my fortune and family afford me, for two years, to place myself at his side, and with serious reflections, and my advice direct his conduct and proceedings in the discharge of his Duty. His Youth may be the cause of some emulation in him;[2] besides it will be a great satisfaction to me to direct his conduct. Your Excellency will deign to believe that the advice and necessary aid requisite for the protection of the Commerce of those States shall not be wanting as long as my said Son shall continue in the Office, to whom I pray, Your Excellency, to continue your favor and Protection, assuring you that my actions will correspond with my offers. I have the honor of tendering my services to Your Excellency with all respect, praying God to lengthen your important Life for many years. Most Excellent Sir I Kiss Your Excellency's hands, Your humble Servant

Joseph Yznardi[3]

L (translation), DLC:GW; LS (in Spanish), DLC:GW.

1. For the appointment of Joseph Yznardi, Jr., see GW to U.S. Senate, 19 Feb. 1793. The translator failed to render "Joven" into "junior." The U.S. Senate confirmed the appointment on 20 Feb. 1793 (*U.S. Senate Executive Journal*, 1:130–31).

2. A better rendering of the phrase "puedan ser causa de alguna emulacion" would be: "could be the cause of some envy."

3. The signature on the LS reads: "Josef Yznardi."

From Burgess Ball

Dear sir,   Leesburg [Va.] 21st Jany 179[4].[1]

I wrote you on the 17th ult: which I hope you recd—We have been obliged to Inoculate our family, White & Black, all of whom, (except one old woman not much less than 100 Years, who died) thank God, are at length over it.[2] I mention this as some appology for my not havg yet totally finished gettg the Buck wheat.

None is yet gone to Mt Vernon, but tomorrow I intended commencg that Bussiness—I have got abt 425 Bush: & expect to get the Ballance this Week—To make sure, I have taken it all from the places where I bot it, and deposited it in my mill, from whence I shall haul it with my own waggons.[3] The Post from hence goes only every other Tuesday, which keeps us here much in the Dark for News.

A rain havg fallen last night, wch it seems has made the road very bad, I fear we can't haul for some days. Wishg you & yours all happiness Im Dr sir, with the highest Esteem yr mo: obt st

B. Ball

ALS, DLC:GW.
    1. Ball mistakenly wrote "1793."
    2. Ball evidently had his family and slaves inoculated against smallpox since writing his letter of 17 Dec. 1793.
    3. William Pearce wrote GW on 4 Feb. that Ball had already sent 60 bushels of buckwheat to Mount Vernon and intended to continue sending it until a total of 500 bushels had been delivered.

From Benjamin Hawkins

Senate Chamber 21st Jany 1794

The gentleman who wrote the inclosed I have long known his character is unexceptionable, he is a brother of the late Colo. Richd Henderson, who purchased Kentuckey, one of the Royal Judges of North Carolina: He resides in the interior part of the State and is a native of it.[1]

I have no other intimation of the intention of Mr Thomas than this from Mr Henderson.[2] With the most respectful attacmnent I have the honor to be sir, yr most obedient servt

Benjamin Hawkins

ALS, DLC:GW.

1. In his letter of 17 Dec. to Hawkins, a senator from North Carolina, Thomas Henderson (1752–1821) wrote: "I have received information from John Skinner esqr. Marshal of this State, that he intends very shortly to resign that office, Our early and long Acquaintance will I hope be a sufficient apology for soliciting your influence and Interest in procuring for me that appointment" (DLC:GW; a post office notation reads, "Guilford C. House Decemr the 20th 1793"). Henderson, a former merchant at Guilford Court House, held a variety of appointed and elected positions in North Carolina, including clerk of court for Guilford and then Rockingham counties, clerk of the Council of State in 1789, and member of the Council of State in 1795. He served two terms between 1792 and 1795 as a delegate from Rockingham County to the state House of Commons, and in 1796 he served one term in the state Senate. His brother Richard Henderson (1735–1785), who was born in Virginia, was a lawyer and land speculator. Colonial governor William Tryon appointed him an associate justice on the colony's Superior Court in 1768, and he served as such until 1773. In 1774 he formed the Louisa Company, and the following year this association negotiated a treaty with the Cherokee Indians that granted the company title to a large tract consisting of present-day Kentucky and part of Tennessee. Although this venture eventually failed to gain either state or national legitimacy, Henderson continued his speculation in western lands and founded present-day Nashville, Tennessee. He represented Granville County in the North Carolina state legislature in 1781 and served on the Council of State, 1782–83.

2. Hawkins probably means Mr. Skinner's intention to resign. GW appointed Michael Payne to replace John Skinner as marshal of North Carolina (GW to U.S. Senate, 10 Dec. 1794, LS, DNA: RG 46, Third Congress, 1793–95, Senate Records of Executive Proceedings, President's Messages—Executive Nominations; LB, DLC:GW).

From Henry Knox

Sir   War department January 21st 1794

I have the honor to submit to you a draft of a letter to the Governor of North Carolina in answer to his of the 8. instant.[1]

I also submit to you the propriety of my transmitting by your order to both houses of Congress such parts of Mr Seagrove's letter as may be necessary to give a complete idea of the result of his mission, but not to communicate any of the corrosive parts relative to Georgia or individuals, or the Spanish Treaty with the Southern Indians.[2] I have the honor to be with the highest respect Your obedient Servant

H. Knox

LS, DLC:GW; LB, DLC:GW.

1. Knox's letter to Richard Dobbs Spaight of 21 Jan. acknowledged the receipt of Spaight's first letter to GW of 6 Jan. and its enclosure. Knox continued: "As the measures which you have been pleased to direct are in pursuance of my letter written by order of the President on the 19th of Decem. 1792 he cannot but approve them at the same time he hopes and expects that the state of the Frontiers will render unnecessary the continuance of those scouts in service for any length of time. For authentic information has been received that Mr [James] Seagrove has tranquillized the creeks, and reestablished peace with them, and that it is to be expected that Governor [William] Blount may be able to restore peace with the Cherokees. In this latter event any patroles on the frontiers of No. Caro[lin]a would not be required. An accuracy in mustering the patroles at their entrance during their continuance and at the expiration of their services, will be essential to their payment. The rolls supported by the musters will be required to be authenticated by Coll [David] Vance whom you have authorized to call the Scouts into Service" (Nc-Ar: Governors' Letterbooks). Under GW's direction, Bartholomew Dandridge, Jr., wrote Knox later this day, returning the draft and announcing that it had been "approved by the President" (DLC:GW).

2. In a brief letter to Dandridge of 20 Dec. 1793, Knox enclosed for GW's consideration a letter to Knox from James Seagrove of 30 Nov. and Seagrove's letter to Georgia governor George Mathews, also of 30 Nov. 1793. GW's subsequent instructions, as written by Dandridge in a letter to Knox of this date, were that it was "proper that such parts of Mr Seagrove's letter as the Se[c]retary suggested should be laid before Congress" (DLC:GW). Although Knox is referring here only to portions of Seagrove's letter to him, he submitted both letters to the U.S. Senate on 22 Jan., along with a brief cover letter. For the text of the letters submitted to the Senate, see *ASP, Indian Affairs,* 1:471–72.

From Edmund Randolph

January 21. 1794.

The Secretary of State has the honor of informing the President, that he has caused two copies to be made of the laws of the North Western territory, and now incloses them.[1] It was long doubted, whether it was the duty of the Executive to lay them before congress. But upon a closer examination of the ordinance, the propriety of the step flows from the right, reserved to congress, to disapprove these laws.[2] For how are congress to get official possession of them, but by an official communication from the executive files, among which they are lodged? The form of a message is not sent; because it is apprehended, that the President may choose to connect these laws with some other information, and one message may cover both.[3]

AL, DNA: RG 59, Miscellaneous Letters; LB, DLC:GW; LB, DNA: RG 59, GW's Correspondence with His Secretaries of State; LB, DNA: RG 59, Domestic Letters.

1. The transcriptions were being made from "A Copy of Laws passed in the Territory of the United States Northwest of the River Ohio from July to Decr 1792 inclusive," which Winthrop Sargent, the secretary for the territory, had prepared earlier (DNA: RG 59, State Department, Territorial Papers, Northwest, 1787–1801; printed in Pease, *Laws of the Northwest Territory*, 57–119; see also Tobias Lear to Thomas Jefferson, 26 Feb. 1793, and Randolph to GW, 4 Jan. 1794 [second letter]).

2. According to "An Ordinance for the government of the territory of the United States North west of the river Ohio," 13 July 1787, the "governor, and judges or a majority of them shall adopt and publish in the district such laws of the original states criminal and civil as may be necessary and best suited to the circumstances of the district and report them to Congress from time to time, which laws shall be in force in the district until the organization of the general assembly therein, unless disapproved of by Congress" (Carter, *Territorial Papers*, 2:42–43).

3. For GW's submission of these laws, see GW to U.S. Senate and House of Representatives, 21 Jan. 1794. For the rejection by Congress of all but one of these laws, see *ASP, Miscellaneous*, 1:82.

To the United States Senate and House of Representatives

United States January 21st 1794.
Gentlemen of the Senate, and of the House of Representatives.

It is with satisfaction I announce to you, that the alterations which have been made by law in the original plan for raising a duty on spirits distilled within the United States, and on Stills, cooperating with better information, have had a considerable influence in obviating the difficulties, which have embarrassed that branch of the public revenue. But the obstacles, which have been experienced, though lessened, are not yet entirely surmounted; and it would seem that some further legislative provisions, may usefully be superadded; which leads me to recall the attention of Congress to the subject. Among the matters, which may demand regulation, is the effect, in point of organization, produced by the separation of Kentucky from the State of Virginia; and the situation, with regard to the law, of the Territories North west and South west of the Ohio.[1]

The laws respecting Lighthouse establishments require as a condition of their permanent maintenance, at the expence of the United States, a complete cession of soil and jurisdiction. The cessions of different States having been qualified with a reservation of the right of serving legal process within the ceded jurisdiction, are understood to be inconclusive, as annexing a qualification not consonant with the terms of the law. I present this circumstance to the view of Congress, that they may judge whether any alteration ought to be made.[2]

As it appears to be conformable with the intention of the "ordinance For the Government of the territory of the United States, northwest of the river ohio," although it is not expressly directed, that the laws of that territory should be laid before Congress, I now transmit to you a copy of such, as have been passed from July to December 1792, inclusive; being the last which have been received by the Secretary of State.[3]

Go: Washington

LS, DNA: RG 46, Third Congress, 1793–95, Senate Records of Legislative Proceedings, President's Messages; LB, DNA: RG 233, Third Congress, 1793–95, House Records of Legislative Proceedings, Journals; LB, DLC:GW.

1. For the current laws regulating the federal excise tax on whiskey and the need for additional legislation, see Alexander Hamilton to GW, 20 Jan., and notes. Kentucky became the 15th state on 1 June 1792.

2. On the need for clarification of U.S. jurisdiction over lighthouses, see Hamilton's Outline for Washington's Fifth Annual Address to Congress, November 1793, and n.2.

3. On the need for congressional review of laws passed by the territorial government of the Northwest Territory, see Edmund Randolph to GW, 4 Jan. (second letter) and this date.

Letter not found: from William Pearce, 22 Jan. 1794. GW wrote Pearce on 26 Jan. that his "letter of the 22d and the Reports, came duly to hand."

To Charles Cotesworth Pinckney

(Confidential)
My dear Sir,   Philadelphia Jany 22d 1794
Although I am not encouraged by the joint letter which I had the honor to receive from you, and our friend Mr E. Rutledge (under date of the 12th of June 1791); yet, in a measure to which I am strongly prompted both by judgment and inclination, I am

unable to restrain myself from making a second application to you, similar to the former one.[1]

I have cause to believe that, the private concerns of the Gentleman who is now at the head of the department of War, will occasion his resignation of that Office unless imperious circumstances (which heaven avert) should force us into a war with any of the Belligerent Powers; and, under such circumstances, he should hold it dishonorable to retreat from his post.[2]

Towards, or at, the close of the present Session of Congress (which is hardly to be expected before April, if then) this event, if it takes place, is likely to happen.[3]

Will you, upon this hypothesis, allow me to endulge a hope that you would fill his place? It is not for the meer detail duties of the Office I am in pursuit of a character; these, might be well executed by a less important one than yours: But, as the officer who is at the head of that department is a branch of the Executive, and called to its councils upon interesting questions of National importance; he ought to be a man not only of competent skill in the Science of War, but possessing a general knowledge of political subjects; of known attachment to the government we have chosen; and of proved integrity. To whom then can I turn my eyes with more propriety than on you? I mean not to compliment, but to express the real sentiments and wishes of my heart.

The intention of writing this letter, and the purport of it, is unknown to any one but myself; the result may be equally so, since it is placed upon a hypothetical base, and declared to be confidential. No more therefore than you chuse need be disclosed until the event, which has given rise to the application, shall have taken place; although it is essential I should know in the mean while on what ground I rest; without which inconveniencies might result from the vacancy of the Office.[4] With much truth & sincerity I am Dear Sir Your Affecte Servt

Go: Washington

ALS, ScC; ADfS, DLC:GW; LB, DLC:GW. The postal stamps on the cover read "22 JA" and "FREE."

1. In their joint reply to GW of 12 June 1791, Pinckney and Edward Rutledge declined GW's suggestion, contained in his letter to them of 24 May 1791, that one of them accept an appointment to the U.S. Supreme Court.

2. Henry Knox's resignation as secretary of war became effective on 31 Dec. 1794 (Knox to GW, 28 Dec. 1794, DLC:GW).

3. The first session of the Third Congress ended on 9 June 1794 (*Annals of Congress*, 3d Cong., 784).

4. For Pinckney's refusal, see his letter to GW of 24 February.

From Edmund Randolph

Wednesday 12 o'clock. [22 Jan. 1794]

E. Randolph has the honor of inclosing to the President a copy of the abstract from Mr Short's letter.[1]

Mr Strong,[2] of the Senate, called upon E.R. about half an hour ago, and desired me to mention in his name to the President, that Mr Bradford would be extremely acceptable to many persons, as the Atty General.[3]

There is a load of English papers, down to the middle of October, just come to hand; but without a letter. If the President wishes to see them, they shall be sent to him.

AL, DNA: RG 59, Miscellaneous Letters; LB, DLC:GW; LB, DNA: RG 59, GW's Correspondence with His Secretaries of State. The docket reads "From the Secy of State 22d Jan: 1794."

1. It is not clear which letter Randolph abstracted. For letter-book copies of official dispatches received from William Short, see RG 59, Despatches from U.S. Ministers to Spain.

2. "Short" has been erroneously substituted for "Strong" in the letter books. Caleb Strong (1745–1819) graduated from Harvard in 1764, studied law, and then began his legal practice in Northampton, Mass., in 1772. He served several terms in the state legislature, 1776–78 and 1780–88. Elected to the U.S. Senate in 1789 for an initial four-year term, he was re-elected for a full six years in 1793, but he resigned on 1 June 1796. He was governor of Massachusetts, 1800–1807 and 1812–16.

3. For GW's nomination of William Bradford, Jr., of Pennsylvania as attorney general, see his letter to the U.S. Senate of 24 January.

From William Thompson

sir, District of Georgia, Savannah, 22nd Jany 1794.

The unfortunate Death and melancholy fate of Major Forsyth which have doubtless reached you ere this, embolden me to venture in the present application,[1] I have acted in the capicity of Deputy Marshal for these last eighteen months, and was continued as such by the late Marshal's Commission to me directed, a Copy of which I take the liberty of enclosing under Notary seal.[2]

The necessity of filling up the vacancy appearing obvious, I am induced from the Vouchers I forward, to address my self to the President's notice for that appointment, and must with diffidence and submission suggest that probably the Title of an old Continental Officer of the ninth Pennsylvania Regiment, who served with some reputation from it's formation in 1776, to it's dissolution in 1781, as may appear by the certificates of Genls Moyland & Butler to Genl Knox in 1785, (which I have requested Genl Irvin to present you) may have some weight in the present decision,[3] and should you, Sir, from these short truths think me worthy of the appointment in preference to other applications, as partiality is a stranger to your Actions, on the Following principles only I beg leave to ask it; as the merit and worth of Major Forsyth were known to all his friends and acquaintances when alive, that esteem which was then his share must in part be transferred to his family, and as probably they are in distress, I propose & happily submit to allow one half of all the Commissions from Marshals Sales in this district for the term often specified in his last Commission as Marshal.[4]

The incompatibility of holding two Offices, will make me resign the appointment of Collector of Hardwicke if chosen to the place of Marshal;[5] I have the Honor to be, most respectfully, Your obedient Servt

Wm: Thompson

ALS, DLC:GW.

William Thompson (1754–1830), originally from Northumberland County, Pa., served in the 9th Pennsylvania Regiment during the Revolutionary War, 1776–81. At some point after the war he moved to Georgia. Besides serving currently as a deputy federal marshal for Georgia, he was also the collector of revenue at the port of Hardwick, Ga. (GW to U.S. Senate, 4 March 1793).

1. On the death of Robert Forsyth, the U.S. marshal for Georgia, see n.1 of James Hendricks to GW, 15 January.

2. The commission from Forsyth was dated 1 Dec. 1793 and signed at Augusta, Georgia. The enclosed copy was notarized at Savannah, Ga., on 24 Jan. 1794 by Justus H. Scheuber, notary public and justice of the peace (DLC:GW).

3. The certificates from Revolutionary War generals Stephen Moylan and Richard Butler to Henry Knox have not been identified. William Irvine of Pennsylvania recently had been elected to his first and only term in the U.S.

House of Representatives, 1793–95, which was currently in session at Philadelphia. Thompson also may have enclosed the certificate of 23 Jan. from Nathaniel Pendleton, judge of the U.S. district court in Georgia, in which Pendleton wrote that Thompson's conduct as deputy marshal "has been upright and fair, and the duties of it performed with diligence and attention," and "satisfactory" to Forsyth's expectations (DLC:GW).

A letter of recommendation also came from Georgia attorneys Matthew McAllister, John Glen (1744–1799), Thomas Gibbons (1757–1826), John Young Noel (1762–1817), and Jacob Waldburger (d. 1797). In their letter to GW of 22 Jan., they wrote that Thompson, in his role as deputy marshal, had "acted with propriety & Official integrity" (LS, DLC:GW).

4. On fees and compensations granted to a U.S. marshal, see "An Act for regulating Processes in the Courts of the United States, and providing Compensations for Officers of the said Courts, and for Jurors and Witnesses," 8 May 1792 (*Stat.* 1:275–79). On Forsyth's family and provisions made for its support, see n.3 of James Hendricks to GW, 15 January.

5. GW did not appoint Thompson (see GW to U.S. Senate, 5 March).

To the United States Senate and House of Representatives

United States 22d January 1794.
Gentlemen of the Senate, and of the House of Representatives.

I forward to you extracts from the last advices from our Minister in London;[1] as being connected with communications already made.[2]

Go: Washington

LS, DNA: RG 46, Third Congress, 1793–95, Senate Records of Legislative Proceedings, President's Messages; LB, DLC:GW.

1. On 21 Jan., Edmund Randolph sent GW two letters from Thomas Pinckney addressed to the Secretary of State. The first, which Pinckney erroneously dated 12 Aug. 1793, enclosed a copy of a decree of 3 Sept. from the British Court of Admiralty, and the second letter was that of 11 Nov. 1793 (*JPP*, 278–79). The extract sent to Congress from the letter dated 12 Aug. described Pinckney's recent discussions with Lord Grenville (William Wyndham Grenville; 1759–1834), the British foreign secretary, on the subject of neutral shipping and the enclosed decree clarified British regulations concerning compensation for the seizure of neutral American ships and cargoes. The extract from the 11 Nov. letter reported that Tuscany and Genoa had "been obliged to abandon" their neutrality by the "commanders of a combined Spanish and British fleet" and that a recent proclamation required "our vessels from Pennsylvania Jersey and Delaware to perform a quarantine of fourteen days" (DNA: RG 46, Third Congress, 1793–95, Senate Records of Legislative Proceedings, President's Messages). Both extracts and the decree are printed in

ASP, Foreign Relations, 1:315. The original letters and decree received by Randolph are in RG 59, Despatches from U.S. Ministers to Great Britain.

2. See GW to U.S. Senate and House of Representatives, 5 Dec. 1793, and n.6.

To Thomas Johnson

Dear Sir   Philadelphia Jany 23d 1794.

Your letter of the 23d Ulto came duly to hand. With regret I perceive your determination to with draw from the Commission under which you have acted—for executing the plan of the federal City.[1] My wish was, and still is, if it could be made to comport with your convenience and inclination, that it should be changed; or at least suspended: for I should be sorry to see others (coming in at the eleventh hour, as it were) reap the fruits of your difficult labours; but if this cannot be, I would thank you for naming (which may be in confidence) such persons as you shall think best qualified to succeed you in this interesting and important business. My limited acquaintance with *convenient* characters does not enable me to do it, to my own satisfaction; and even among those which might happen to present themselves to my view, there might be local circumstances in the way, unknown to me, which would render them ineligible in the opinion of the public, for the impartial execution of the trust reposed. Were it not for this, I presume proper characters might be had in George town, or among the proprietors of the City; but how far their connections with, or jarring interests therein, may be a let to such appointments, is worthy of that consideration which you can so well appreciate, for my information.[2]

With respect to Mr Blodget, I have not hesitated on former occasions to declare—and I think to the Commissioners themselves—from the moment his conduct began to unfold itself, that his appointment did not, in my judgment, answer the end which had been contemplated. At first I was at a loss how to account for a conduct so distant from any ideas I had entertained of the duties of a superintendant; but it appears evidently enough now, that speculation has been his primary object from the beginning. My letters (if not to the Commissioners, to an individual member I am sure) when compared with the conduct of Mr Blodget, will shew that he has in no wise answered my expectations as a

Superintendant, for my ideas of these (in the exercise of a competent character, always on the spot with sufficient powers, & fully instructed) were, that it would render a meeting of the Commissioners oftener than quarterly, or half yearly, unnecessary in the ordinary course of the business; cases it is true might occur requiring occasional ones; but these, after the stated meetings were sufficiently promulgated, woud very rarely happen. According to these ideas, fixing on a plan, giving the out lines of it, receiving the reports, inspecting the proceedings, examining the accounts, revising the instructions or furnishing new ones at the periodical meetings, is all that appeared to me necessary for the Commissioners to do; leaving to the Superintendant, who ought to be competent thereto & responsible, the execution in detail.[3]

I wish you may have yet seen the worst features in Mr Blodgets conduct. Finding that he was determined to proceed in his second lottery, notwithstanding the admonition that had been given him by the Commissioners; that he had actually sold tickets in it—and for Georgia land;[4] I directed the Secretary of State to inform him in explicit terms, that if he did not instantly suspend all further proceeding therein until the sanction of the Commissioners should be unequivocally obtained, I would cause the unauthorised mode in which he was acting to be announced to the public, to guard it against imposition—In consequence, he has set out, it is said, to wait upon them—if this be true the result you must know.[5] Little confidence, I fear, is placed in Mr Blodget—& least where he is best known. With much truth, I remain Dear Sir Your Affecte Servant

Go: Washington

ALS, CSmH; LB, DLC:GW.

1. On Johnson's appointment as one of the three original commissioners for the District of Columbia, see Commission, 22 Jan. 1791.

2. For Johnson's inability to suggest suitable candidates, see his letter to GW of 6 Feb. 1794. In August and September, GW appointed, respectively, Gustavus Scott and William Thornton to replace Johnson and David Stuart, who also resigned from the D.C. Commission this year (GW to Lear, 28 Aug. 1794, ALS, DLC:GW; Harris, *William Thornton Papers*, 1:287).

3. For GW's thoughts on the usefulness of a superintendent for the Federal City and on the appointment of Samuel Blodget, Jr., to that position, see GW to D.C. Commissioners, 13 Nov. 1792, and to Benjamin Stoddert, 14 Nov. 1792. On the proprietors, see source note to Agreement of the Proprietors of the Federal District, 30 March 1791.

4. Shortly after his appointment, Blodget received permission from the D.C. commissioners to establish a lottery in which the winner would receive ownership of a hotel to be constructed in the Federal City (D.C Commissioners to GW, 9 April 1793). Other, monetary, prizes would be paid one month after the drawing, which originally was set to begin on 9 Sept. 1793. Failure to conduct the drawing on time and repeated delays in awarding prizes raised suspicions of mismanagement and corruption (*Gazette of the United States* [Philadelphia], 23 Jan., 14 Sept., and 20 Dec. 1793). When Blodget proceeded with a second lottery, the commissioners withdrew their support (D.C. Commissioners to GW, 23 Dec. 1793).

5. At GW's direction, Edmund Randolph met with Blodget in early January to inform him of GW's opposition to the second lottery. Randolph's account of this meeting, GW's instructions to the commissioners to "prevent the progress of this second scheme," and notice of Blodget's departure on 17 Jan. for the Federal City are contained in Randolph's letter to the D.C. Commissioners of 19 Jan. 1794 (see D.C. Commissioners to GW, 23 Dec. 1793, source note and n.7). Following GW's instruction, the commissioners decided to publicly disavow any association with Blodget's second lottery (18 May 1794 minutes, DNA: RG 42, Records of the Commissioners for the District of Columbia, Proceedings, 1791–1802; *Maryland Journal and Baltimore Advertiser,* 23 May 1794). For the prizes offered in the second lottery, which Blodget continued on his own, see the advertisement placed in the 3 Sept. 1794 issue of the *Gazette of the United States and Daily Evening Advertiser* (Philadelphia).

Henry Knox to Bartholomew Dandridge, Jr.

Sir.   January 24. 1794.

Please to submit to the President of the United States, the enclosed letters from Mr Dallas;[1] and the proposed answer thereto to the Governor[2]—The answer is according to the principles adopted.[3] Yours sincerely

H. Knox

LS, DLC:GW; LB, DLC:GW.

1. The enclosed letter of 24 Jan. from Alexander J. Dallas, the secretary of Pennsylvania, reads: "The Governor has directed me to transmit to you the inclosed copy of a letter from Mr Harrison, a Ship builder of this City; in which it is stated, that an application has been made to him, to open five portholes on each side of the French vessel, called the Citizen of Marseilles. Whether, under the circumstance of this case, the proposed alteration can be deemed an augmentation of her military equipments, is a matter in doubt with Governor, on which he wishes to receive the Opinion of the Executive of the United States." John Harrison's letter to Gov. Thomas Mifflin of 24 Jan. reported that the portholes were for "mounting Guns which are now on board. . . . The guns were all on board, at the time of her coming into the

harbour; and she had before that ports in the same places, which had been shut up, in order to turn her more conveniently into a packet" (both letters, PHarH: Executive Correspondence, 1790–99).

2. Knox's reply to Mifflin of 25 Jan. acknowledged receipt of Dallas's letter before continuing: "This letter, Sir, has been submitted to the President of the United States who has directed me to inform you that the said port Holes having been closed previously to the arrival of the said vessel in this port that the opening of them in order to mount Cannon therein would in his judgment be as much an augmentation of the force of the said vessel as if the port Holes were now to be cut for the first time, and that the measure therefore is to be prevented. It is to be remembered that the same principles operated in the decision of the President in July last relatively to the British Letter of Marque Ship Jane whose force was reduced to the same situation it was at the time of her arrival, by closing her new port Holes, dismounting the additional Cannon, and Destroying or relanding her new Gun Carriages, before she was permitted to leave the port" (PHarH: Executive Correspondence). On the issues surrounding the presence of the *Jane* in Philadelphia waters, see Mifflin's letter to GW of 27 July 1793, and Thomas Jefferson's notes on the 29 July cabinet meeting in *Jefferson Papers*, 26:579–80.

During a meeting on 30 July, the cabinet decided that "all new Carriages, port holes, Guns &c. which had been added to the Jane since she came into the Port was contrary to treaty & not to be suffered." After Philadelphia officials examined the *Jane* once again and found an increase in her armaments and crew, a request was made to British minister George Hammond "to have her reduced to the state in which she entered the Port" (*JPP*, 211–12; see also Jefferson to Edmond Genet, 4 Aug. 1793, *Jefferson Papers*, 26:611).

3. See Cabinet Opinion on the Rules of Neutrality, 3 Aug. 1793.

From Isaac Senter

Sir,   Newport State of Rhode Island, Jany 24th 1794

By the Death of my worthy friend & fellow Citizen, William Channing Esqr. the office of District Attorney for this Department, some time since, became vacant, & as I have been lately informed Still continues so.[1]

There have been two gentlemen, I am told, residing in Providence, recommended to fill that vacancy.[2]

It is Sir, with great deference that I presume to address you on a Subject of this kind—and were I much more advantageously known to the President, than I can boast of being, it would never be my expectation, or desire, to influence his Judgement in matters of this nature—but only to give that kind of honest information, which perhaps in Some instances may be indulgantly considered as a Duty to my country, as well as to its first magistrate.

David Howell Esqr. L.L.D. one of the gentlemen in nomination, by some of the Citizens of Providence,[3] was one of the patriots of this State as early as the year, 1775 & to my Knowledge has unremittingly continued So through the revolution—He adds to the most extensive *Erudition,* a legal knowledge, Second to no one Among us—He has been formerly a member of the Continental Congress & has Sustained Several important officces in this State—Among which was that of Judge of the Superior Court, at a period when iniquity was established by Law—By his extensive Law Knowledge, firmness & perseverance, he was the greate cause on the bench, of preventing the extensive and ruinous application of the penal Law of this State, which made it a Crime to refuse a tender of paper bills at par, at a time when they could be purchased with gold & silver, of the framers of this law, at *Six for one*[4]—Had it not been for this & I may add some other able & honest exertions of Dr Howell in the various State offices he has held, the names of Some who are *now* high in Office, in this Government, would have been Seen, Among those of the other Gentlemen who recommend him to the President to fill the office of District Attorney for this District.

May I be permitted to add, that it is my opinion as relative to the two candidates in question, that it would be agreeable to the greate body of freemen of this State, as well to the Generality of the Bar, that Dr Howell, should fill that vancancy.[5] Sir, I have the honor to be your most obedt & devoted Servant

Isaac Senter

ALS, DLC:GW. Newport doctor Isaac Senter (1755–1799) was president of the Rhode Island Society of the Cincinnati.

1. William Channing died on 21 Sept. 1793 (Theodore Foster to GW, 3 Oct. 1793).

2. Besides David Howell, whom Senter recommends, the other candidate from Providence was David Leonard Barnes. For letters to GW recommending his appointment, see the 7 Oct. 1793 letters from Arthur Fenner and Jeremiah Olney. On the dissension surrounding the selection of a suitable candidate and for letters critical of Howell and favorable to Barnes and other candidates, see Olney to Alexander Hamilton, 7 Oct.; Hamilton to unknown, 20 Nov.; Henry Marchant to Hamilton, 9 Dec.; and William Ellery to Hamilton, 16 Dec. 1793 (*Hamilton Papers,* 15:357–58, 402, 447–48, 458–59).

3. For earlier letters recommending Howell, see John Brown et al. to GW, 2 Oct., and source note; Theodore Foster to GW, 3 Oct.; and Moses Brown to GW, 7 Oct. 1793. Howell wrote a letter of application to GW on 4 Oct. 1793.

4. The Rhode Island legislature's creation of a paper-currency system and passage of penal laws to enforce its use was successfully challenged in the fall of 1786 by the state's superior court of judicature, of which Howell was a member. On the relevant legislation, the unanimous decision against the state, and Howell's assertion of judicial review before the state legislature, see James Mitchell Varnum, *The case, Trevett against Weeden: on information and complaint, for refusing paper bills in payment for butcher's meat, in market, at par with specie. Tried before the Honourable Superior Court, in the county of Newport, September term, 1786. Also, the case of the judges of said court, before the Honourable General Assembly, at Providence, October session, 1786, on citation, for dismissing said complaint. Wherein the rights of the people to trial by jury, &c. are stated and maintained, and the legislative, judiciary and executive powers of government examined and defined* (Providence, 1787).

5. GW nominated Ray Greene to the position of district attorney (GW to U.S. Senate, 24 Jan. 1794).

To the United States Senate

Gentlemen of the Senate,   United States, 24th Jany 1794.

I nominate William Bradford, of Pennsylvania, to be Attorney General for the United States; vice Edmund Randolph appointed Secretary of State.[1] and, Ray Greene, of Rhode Island, to be Attorney for the United States in the District of Rhode Island; vice William Channing, deceased.[2]

Go: Washington

LS, DNA: RG 46, Third Congress, 1793–95, Senate Records of Executive Proceedings, President's Messages—Executive Nominations; LB, DLC:GW.

1. For a letter extolling Bradford's qualifications for this position, see Juris Peritus to GW, 13 January. For Randolph's appointment as secretary of state, see GW to U.S. Senate, 1 January.

2. For letters recommending Greene, see Edmund Randolph to GW, 11 Jan. (second letter), and n.4. Channing died on 21 Sept. 1793 (Theodore Foster to GW, 3 Oct. 1793). The Senate approved both nominations on 27 Jan. (*U.S. Senate Executive Journal*, 1:147).

From the United States Senate

Congress of the United States.   In Senate January 24. 1794.

The Senate resumed the consideration of the motion made the 17th instant, together with the amendment proposed on the 23d respecting the correspondences which have been had between the Minister of the United States, at the republic of France, and said republic:[1]

And on motion to agree to the resolution amended as follows:

Resolved, that the President of the Ud States be requested to lay before the Senate the correspondences which have been had between the Minister of the United States at the republic of France, and said republic; and between said Minister and the Office of Secretary of State.

It passed in the affirmative { Yeas 13.
{ Nays 11.

The yeas and nays being required by one fifth of the Senators present—those who voted in the affirmative are,

Mr [Stephen R.] Bradley [Vermont],
 " [John] Brown [Kentucky]
 " [Aaron] Burr [New York]
 " [Pierce] Butler [South Carolina]
 " [John] Edwards [Kentucky]
 " [Albert] Gallatin [Pennsylvania],
 " [Benjamin] Hawkins [North Carolina],

Mr [James] Jackson [Georgia],
 " [John] Langdon [New Hampshire],
 " [Alexander] Martin [North Carolina],
 " [James] Monroe [Virginia],
 " [Moses] Robinson [Vermont]
        and
 " [John] Taylor [Virginia]

Those who voted in the negative are—

Mr [William] Bradford [Rhode Island],
 " [George] Cabot [Massachusetts],
 " [Oliver] Ellsworth [Connecticut],
 " [Theodore] Foster [Rhode Island],
 " [Frederick] Frelinghuysen [New Jersey],
 " [Ralph] Izard [South Carolina],

Mr [Samuel] Livermore [New Hampshire]
 " [Stephen M.] Mitchel[l Connecticut],
 " [Robert] Morris [Pennsylvania],
 " [Caleb] Strong [Massachusetts],
        and
 " [John] Vining [Delaware].

Ordered, that the Secretary lay this resolution before the President of the U. States.

Attest Sam. A. Otis—Secretary.

LB, DLC:GW.

1. The original motion of 17 Jan. was that the secretary of state "be directed" to lay the desired correspondence before the Senate, while the amendment proposed on 23 Jan., and adopted the next day, "requested" the president to submit Gouverneur Morris's official correspondence (*Annals of Congress*, 3d Cong., 34, 38).

Letter not found: from John Gwinn, 25 Jan. 1794. GW wrote Gwinn on 10 March that he "was favoured with your letter of the 25th of Jany."

From Edmund Randolph

Sir   Philadelphia January 25. 1794
    I had the honor of calling at your house, when Colo. Hamilton was with you, this morning. We have had two conversations upon the subject of the resolution, which, I understand, is not to be sent to you before monday.[1]
    I am in possession of all Mr Morris's letters; and was proceeding on them, when my servant brought me word, that my youngest son lies dangerously ill at German Town[2]—This compels me to go thither; from whence I shall endeavour to return to morrow morning. If, however, I should not; I shall go on with the letters, and perhaps with less interruption there, than here. I believe, that nothing has occurred to-day, or been received, which would require my attendance on you to-day.[3] I have the honor, sir, to be with the highest respect yr mo. ob. serv.
                                                        Edm: Randolph

ALS, DLC:GW.
    1. The resolution under discussion asked GW to provide the U.S. Senate with copies of Gouverneur Morris's official correspondence as the U.S. minister to France (U.S. Senate to GW, 24 Jan. 1794).
    2. Randolph had four children who lived to adulthood: Peyton (d. 1828), Susan Beverley (b. 1782), Edmonia Madison (b. 1787), and Lucy Nelson (b. 1789). The younger son mentioned here has not been identified and presumably died young, as did another son, John Jennings (1785–1786). After the 1793 yellow fever epidemic in Philadelphia, Randolph maintained a residence for his wife and children in the nearby village of Germantown (Thomas Jefferson to Martha Jefferson Randolph, 1 Dec. 1793, *Jefferson Papers,* 27:467–68).
    3. After his return to Philadelphia on 26 Jan., Randolph wrote two letters to GW that day concerning the recent Senate request.

From Tobias Lear

My dear Sir,   London, January 26th[–30] 1794
    Presuming on the wish which you had the goodness to express when I left you last, that you might sometimes hear from me after my arrival in Europe, I have ventured to write you one letter from Glasgow, and now improve the opportunity offered by the Ship Delaware, Capt. Truxon, to write to you again.[1]
    I was between 3 & 4 weeks in Scotland, during which time I improved every occasion (and many offered) of making myself

acquainted with the manufactures and other important objects in that Country. Altho' my sailing for Scotland was a matter determined upon so short a time before I left America as to prevent my taking so many letters for that part of the Kingdom as I should otherwise have obtained; yet I found civilities and attentions heaped upon me in the most unbounded manner. An unreserved communication respecting the manufactures, commerce & agriculture of Scotland, as far as I had an opportunity of making enquiries, was a circumstance peculiarly pleasing.[2]

On my way from Edinburgh to London, I visited Dryburgh Abbey (about 30 miles from Edinbg) and deliverd to Lord Buchan the letter which you had the goodness to give me for him. Altho' I had determined to spend but one day at this place; yet I found it impossible to carry that determination into effect; for so pressing were the entreaties of Lord & Lady Buchan that I should prolong my stay there, and such was the undisguised hospitality—and I may say affectionate treatment which I received from them, that at the end of three days I was obliged to say in strong terms that I *must* pursue my journy. Finding that I could stay no longer at Drybugh Abbey without inconvenience to my business—Lord & Lady Buchan put into my hands letters to some of their best friends in London & earnestly pressed me to make use of them to encrease the number of my useful or agreeable acquaintances in this City—And no resistance on my part could prevent his Lordship from taking me on for the distance of twenty miles in his Carriage to the town of Coldstream, and as little could my entreaties avail to prevent his going with me. As we were to set out at six o'clock in the morning (which at that season is nearly two hours before day light in Scotland)—I concluded that we should take breakfast at the first stage of ten miles; but when I came down at half past five, I was surprized and distressed to find Lady Buchan already up and breakfast provided. I expressed my concern; but in vain: the reply was—we love General Washington so dearly that we wish to conduct towards one who has been long a member of his family and is esteemed by him, as we would towards our own child if we were so happy as to have one.

Lady Buchan wrote the enclosed note to Mrs Washington, begging her acceptance of the Earl's likeness, in pa⟨s⟩te, taken by the famous Tassie, from whom I received it in London, and have transmitted it herewith.[3]

I have ventured, my dear Sir, to give the preceding detail because I felt myself most delightfully impressed in receiving such
peculiar marks of kindness, in consequence of the letter which
you gave me, as it discovered the veneration and affection with
which you are considered in this part of the world. And altho' I
have had an opportunity of seeing & feeling it more peculiarly
in this instance than in any others; yet I have every where met
with enthusiastic expressions of admiration & affection for your
character.

Sir John Sinclair had left Scotland for this City before I got to
Edinburgh, which is his place & residence in Scotland. I have
had the pleasure of seing him here, and put into his hands the
letter with which you honored me for him; he has been very
particular in his attentions to me, and being possessed of a large
fund of useful knowledge and very happy and ready in his communication of it, I expect much benefit from his Acquaintance.
He is of one of the first families in Scotland—possesses a very
large estate there—is a member of Parliament—President of the
national board of Agriculture—and considered by all parties a
useful & most valuable member of Society—He is a friend of
the present ministry and said to be much in the confidence of
Mr Pitt. He is above 35 years of age; but his appearance bespeaks
him younger, his dress plain & his manners perfectly easy & free
from formality.[4]

Mr Young came in town a few days ago, to attend a meeting
of the national Society for promoting Agriculture, of which he
is Secretary, with a salary of 500£ per year. He soon found me
out, and I have been much with him since. He is a man whose
appearance does not charge him with being more than 45 years
old, which is less than his real age some 7 or 8 years, as I am
informed;[5] he is about 5 feet 10 inches high—rather thin—an
interesting countenance, aquiline nose & good eye; his conversation is animated and he handles his subject with dexterity;
but many who know him well consider him rather as a theorist
on the subject of farming—and even say that he never made
half the experiments of which he has published the result—and
his own farm is said to be one of the most slovenly in the part
of the Country where he lives: It is however acknowledged by
All, that he has done very great good to the cause of agriculture, by his writings and perseverence.[6] In his political opinions

it is said there has been a change since the commencement
of the war with France—and some are so ill-natured as to impute it to the 500£ which he receives as Secy to the Board of
Agriculture—Certain it is that he is now as high a monarchist as
any in Britain.

I have given this personal description of those persons with
whom you are in the habits of correspondence; because I know
one feels desireous of knowing something more of persons with
whom they converse by letter, but have never seen, than what
they can collect from a general account.

Of the Earl of Buchan I should say something also. His Lordship is about the middle size, rather thin—his manner & conversation full of vivacity, the portrait which accompanies this
resembles him; but I think it must have been a better likeness
of him 8 or 10 years ago—he now appears to be about 55. He
has been married to his present and only lady about 23 years.
They have no issue[7]—and the title will go to his Brother Henry
Erskine—who is at present at the head of the Scotch Bar—and
what is remarkable, his Lordship's Youngest Brother, the Honble
Thomas Erskine, is considered at the head of the English Bar.
We have often heard of this gentleman, from the conspicuous
figure he has made in most of the important causes which have
come before this Court for several years past.[8] Had it not been
the Earls misfortune to have been born a Lord, he would in
all probability have made as conspicuous a figure in the law or
some other literary pursuit as his Brothers have done; for he has
been assiduous in the acquisition of knowledge—and is considered as possessing very considerable talents; his moderate disposition has however helped him from pressing himself forward
in the political world in the manner that his rank & abilities
would have given him a right to do. He has rather chosen to
enjoy domestic life, and attend to the improvemt of his Estate, as
well as to promoting the interest of agriculture & manufactures
in general. In the former I understand he has been successful,
and from being ranked as a poor nobleman 15 years ago, he has
become the reverse—and what is much to his honor, all the tenants in his Estates have grown rich as well as himself.

Mr Anderson, Professor of Mathematics & natural Philosophy
in the University of Glasgow, informed me that he had written to
you some months ago on the subject of an improvement which

he had made in Artillery—and had also sent some publications which he had made therein. This Gentleman seems to be an enthusiastic admirer of America & her Government and is very anxious that our Country should derive an advantage from his improvements. The French, it is said, have received vast advantage from Mr Anderson's Artillery; it being carried over there by himself in 1789, after the improvement was rejected by the Duke of Richmond, or rather after the proposal to let him have the improvement was rejected; for Mr A. tells me that he never deigned to make any enquiry into it. The most important point is his having found a method of destroying the recoil of the Cannon without moving or injuring the carriage. This Mr A. shewed to me very fully & clearly—and gave me every information on the subject of it. Its simplicity is as astonishing as its effects. Besides his improvement of Artillery, Mr Anderson has introduced many very useful & important inventions & improvements for their Manufacturing machines of various descriptions in Scotland, and having communicated them gratis & without reserve to the manufacturers he is much venerated & beloved by them. If we should carry into effect the intention of establishing a national University in Washington City, Mr A. would be a great acquisition to it, provided he could be drawn over there. He is spoken of whereever he is know[n] as a man of great talents as a natural Philosopher & Mathematician; but his liberality of opinion in politics gives great offence to the high government folks here.[9]

Before this reaches you, I trust you will have received a letter which I had the honor of writing to you from Glasgow, together with a Box containing a few Articles which I took the liberty of putting up for yourself & Mrs Washington, as Specimens of the manufactures of the Country. These I left to be sent to America by the first vessel sailing from Glasgow for that place, and they will either go to Norfolk in the Ship Alnomac or to New York, in the Brigantine John & Jane; these being the first Vessels to sail for America: and in whatsoever vessel they go, they will be forwarded to Philadelphia. I enclose a duplicate of the Invoice of the Articles.[10]

The watch for Mrs Washington is preparing; but cannot be got ready to go by this Vessel. It will be sent in the next that sails, which will be in about ten days. The man who is finishing the watch, wishes it to be a very good one, altho plain, and therefore choses rather to finish one on purpose than to send any one which he had ready, altho, he considered them as good—He is spoken of as one of the most honesst among the most eminent in his way. The white thorn plants will be ready for the next vessel also.[11]

In the Box from Glasgow there is some furze seed; which I sent under an impression that it might answer for hedges with you, as it was used for that purpose about Glasgow, and looked well; but I was afterwards informed, that the hedges of it were not secure against swine—and that when it once got root in the ground it spread over every part & became a troublesome weed.

When I came to this Country I determined, as much as possible, to avoid all conversation on political subjects, knowing that any opinion of mine on those points could be of no use to any one, and that possibly they might be detrimental to me: Altho' I have adhered pretty well to this resolution, yet it has not prevented me from hearing opinions expressed, of such a nature, and with so much openness as astonished me, when I knew the excess of punishment which the Government had inflicted on some individuals who had openly avowed their sentiments. An Idea not uncommon in Scotland, and the northern parts of England through which I have passed, is, that it is now folly to talk of a reform in Government—nothing short of a revolution can be thought of—men of moderation who espoused the cause of a reform havg been run down & put out of countenance, they lay by to see the event of measures which they know to be disagreeable to the Country at large—and leave to the more violent to push matters with a high hand, which would not have been necessary if the voice of reason and moderation had not been violently suppressed in its early stages. The Government beleive, because these moderate & respectable Characters rest in silence at present, that they approve their measures; but the reverse of this is true. They cannot approve, and they do not venture to express their disapprobation openly, because the cry of "*Mad Dog*" against them would cause them to be hunted down by the Underlings of party, and make their lives very uneasy; they therefore chuse to let the matter work in the only way in which it now can work, fully convinced that no great length of time can elapse before the storm will burst upon those who seem to have taken peculiar pains in preparing materials for it.

Altho', as I observed before, I have avoided as much as possible entering into any political conversations; yet persons who would not openly express their sentiments to others, subjects of this Country, have spoken to me in a style which I have thought imprudent for them to use even tho' they knew I should never use it to their disadvantage—and some of them have been persons of no inconsiderable standing here.

After giving this detail of what I have observed respecting the sentiments of many here; it may, notwithstanding, be proper to remark, that so large is the majority in Parlament for supporting the present ministry and for prosecuting the war, no doubt can remain but that it will be pursued, and especially as it is said that Mr Pitt can command in loan any sums he may want, and upon better terms than he could make last year. The want of employment at the manufacturies gives a great number of men to the Army & navy. But the truth is, a strong spirit of discontent prevails more or less in every part of the Kingdom—the causes which first excited it not only still exist, but increase every day— Those who are discontented are not by any means altogether of the lower order of people—many of distinguished property— many of distinguished talents—and some of distinguished rank are among them.

The Speech of the President on opening the Session of Congress arrived here the day before the Parliament met. It was universally approved & admired—at least so far as I could hear of any expressions respecting it—and very honorable mention was made of it as well as of America in general in some of the speeches on the day that Parliament met. Mr Fox in particular dwelt with enthusiastic energy on the—virtues—the talents— and the peculiar good fortune of General Washington. He drew, with much warmth, a lively comparison between the conduct of the American Governmt and that of this Country—much to the disadvantage of the latter. In an animated voice he cried—"All the Kings of Europe when compared with the great & the good Washington appear—small—and I had almost said contemptable"; but says he, in a lower voice, "I *must* except our own King." The public papers, you will observe, have noticed this part of Mr Fox's speech in the debates; but they have not given a just statement of it. I was present and felt his words strike my very soul—I wished to have embraced him for them.[12]

On your goodness, my dear Sir, do I rely to pardon me for the trouble of this tedious letter—I have written it for the purpose of giving you some idea of things here as they really are—and shall feel peculiarly happy if you find a moment's amusement or one thing that is acceptable as information through the whole of it.

Everything respecting my own affairs is a[s] favorable as I could expect, considering the prospect of a continuance of the war, which is always more or less detrimental to a regular system of mercantile business. I have found every disposition in the great manufactures and merchants with whom I have been particularly conversant, to promote my views in business; but I have done nothing yet decisive in business, as we shall not be ready 'till mid-summer to pursue our plan fully at the City of Washington.[13] Generally speaking I find a strong affection towards the americans in the manufacturing part of the Community—it is less in the mercantile—and still less I beleive in another class.

I take the liberty to enclose some papers from the opening of parliament to the present date, by which you will see something of what may be expected from the complexion of the debates.[14]

For Mrs Washington my best and grateful respects I beg may be made acceptable and to my young friends Nelly & Washington I send my love.[15] And that they and yourself may enjoy all the health and happiness that this life can afford is the earnest prayer of my dear Sir, Your affectionate friend & grateful & obliged Servant

Tobias Lear.

P.S. Jany 30: 1794 Captn Truxon not sailing so soon as he expected has given time for finishing the watch for Mrs Washington, which I have committed to the special care of Capt. Truxon, together with the likeness of Lord Buchan. The watch, as you will see by the enclosed Bill has a little exceeded the sum which you put into my hands for the purchase of it. But this being a horizontal Watch (which are decidedly the best) and made with very particular care by one of the first hands in London, I thought I might venture to go a triffle beyond the mark, rather than send one which could not be so well warranted.[16]

I have engaged 5000 of the white Thorn plants which will be put on board the Ship Peggy bound to George Town, She will sail by or before the 10th of next month, and is addressed to Colo. Deakins.[17]

Having mixed very much in almost all ranks of people since I have been here, and heard with attention all sentiments on public matters: Besides which I have been sought for and have had communications pressed upon me from quarters where the best knowledge of the views of this Governmt are to be found— Summing up in my mind all circumstances & communication I hesitate not to say to you, my dear Sir, that I am clearly impressed with a beleif, that it is the wish & view of the present Governmt of this Country to quarrel with the U.S.—and that their object is to make the U.S. appear to be the first open Aggressors, then endeavour to persuade the people that on the part of Britain it is a war of defence. Sure I am however that this excuse will never be accepted by the people of this Country—and that if the present ministry should be mad enough to plunge the nation in a War with the U.S. it will only *hasten* their own ruin. Their ruin & a terrible crush in this Kingdom, I cannot help looking upon as inevitable and at no great distance. It is impossible for me to communicate to you at this time the grounds upon wh. this opinion is founded—And I should hardly venture to say as much as I have done; but that I shall deliver this letter into Capt. Truxon's hands and rely upon his special care of it.[18]

The eyes of the people here are beginning to open with respect to France—It is openly said here & in Almost every part of the Kingdom that it is folly to contend longer with that Nation—which is now considerd as the most powerful & energetic at this moment in Europe. The great successes of France can no longer be hid from the people—and the reports of their internal divisions are no longer beleived—as all operations & the Accounts of impartial men coming from that Country give the lie therto.

ALS, DLC:GW.

1. Lear's previous letter to GW was dated 25 Dec. 1793 and written at Glasgow, Scotland. On its receipt by GW, see note 10. The *Delaware*, Capt. Thomas Truxtun, arrived at Philadelphia in late April (*Philadelphia Gazette and Universal Daily Advertiser,* 22 April 1794). On the purpose of Lear's journey and his departure for Scotland, see his letter to GW of 3 Nov. 1793.

2. On 1 Sept., GW wrote letters of introduction for Lear to Gouverneur Morris, Thomas Pinckney, William Short, Nicholas Van Staphorst, and Arthur Young. He wrote two additional letters, on 8 Nov., to the Earl of Buchan and John Sinclair. Lear probably had a few letters from "some respectable merchants" to their business correspondents (Lear to GW, 3 Nov. 1793).

3. In a brief letter to Martha Washington of 8 Jan., Lady Buchan wrote that she was sending a "Medallion Paste" of Lord Buchan's portrait "as a Mark of the Interest she takes in the House & Family of Mount-Vernon & in the happiness of Mrs Washington" (ViMtvL). Artist James Tassie (1735–1799) was born near Glasgow, Scotland. His neo-classical portrait medallions brought him international fame and customers from the upper echelons of British and European society. Work on Buchan's portrait may have begun in late 1791, when Tassie was modeling his portraits in Edinburgh and Glasgow. The model, usually a profile of the subject's head and shoulders, was made from red wax, while the cameo itself was created from a vitreous paste. This medallion may be that identified as "1 Profile in plaister," listed in the 1810 inventory of Mount Vernon as being in the study (Prussing, *Estate of George Washington Deceased*, 417).

4. John Sinclair, who was born on 10 May 1754, often supported the policies of William Pitt the Younger, who served as prime minister of Great Britain, 1783–1801 and 1804–6.

5. English agriculturist Arthur Young was born on 11 Sept. 1741. He was appointed secretary of the Board of Agriculture in 1793.

6. GW had 31 volumes of Young's *Annals of Agriculture,* as well as other works by Young, in his library (Griffin, *Catalogue of the Washington Collection,* 95, 230–32, 273, 548).

7. Buchan married his cousin Margaret Fraser (d. 1819) on 15 Oct. 1771. While Buchan and his wife had no children together, he did have a son, David Erskine (1772–1837), who was brought up in their household. During his tenure as a professor at the Royal Military College, Sandhurst, he became a well-known writer of historical fiction and drama. Upon his father's death in 1829, he inherited Dryburgh Abbey, and he received a knighthood in 1830.

8. Henry Erskine (1746–1817), a lawyer and politician, was Buchan's youngest brother. Henry's eldest son, Henry David, succeeded as twelfth earl of Buchan upon the death of his uncle. Thomas Erskine, first Baron Erskine (1750–1823), was also a lawyer and politician, and later in life he was lord chancellor, 1806–7.

9. For John Anderson's improvements in artillery, the rejection of his inventions by Charles Lennox, the third duke of Richmond, the adoption of his inventions by the French army, the publications he sent GW, and GW's interest in bringing Anderson to the United States, see Anderson's letter to GW of 26 Aug. 1793 and the enclosed memorial of 20 August.

10. Lear's letter of 25 Dec. 1793 and the accompanying box of articles were placed on the brigantine *John and Jane,* which did not set sail until 13 Feb. and which arrived in New York City in May (James Greenleaf to GW, 19 May 1794).

The enclosed invoice (DLC:GW), written at Glasgow on 24 Dec. 1793, reads:

Invoice of Articles sent from Glasgow to America
for George Washington, by Tobias Lear
Packed in a Box marked G. Washington—Mt Vernon or Philada

Three dozn Tumblers—Cut with Crest &c.	@ 15/	2. 5. 0
One p. Cotton Shirting contg 25 yds	@ 3/8	4.11. 8
Three 9/8 fine muslin Hkfs	@ 6/9	1. 0. 3

Three do do Book do	@ 7/	1. 1. 0
One p. sewed muslin contg 10 yds	@ 13/	6.10. 0
One p. Cotton Cambrick 8 yds	@ 4/9	1.18. 0
Furze & Kail seeds		0. 3. 0

Sterling   £17. 8.11

Errors Excepted

Tobias Lear.

11. For GW's instructions on purchasing a watch, see his letter to Lear of 25 Sept. 1793. Lear sent five thousand white thorn plants along with his letter to GW of 4 Feb. 1794. According to the farm reports for 25–31 May, these plants were retrieved from Georgetown, D.C., and planted at Mount Vernon on 31 May 1794 (DLC:GW).

12. For GW's annual address, see GW to U.S. Senate and House of Representatives, 3 Dec. 1793. The 17th British Parliament opened its fourth session on 21 Jan. 1794. Charles James Fox was the leader of a Whig faction that opposed both the domestic and foreign policies of the Whig and Tory coalition under the leadership of Prime Minister Pitt, and especially the current war against France. Fox's speech begins: "I cannot help alluding to the president of the United States general Washington, a character whose conduct has been so different from that which has been pursued by the ministers of this country. How infinitely wiser must appear the spirit and principles manifested in his late address to the congress than the policy of modern European courts! Illustrious man, deriving honour less from the splendor of his station than from the dignity of his mind, before whom all borrowed greatness sinks into insignificance, and all the potentates of Europe (excepting the members of our own royal family) become little and contemptible!" For the entire speech, see *Parliamentary History of England*, 30:1274–76.

13. On Lear's plans to establish a mercantile business in the Federal City, see GW to D.C. Commissioners, 13 June 1793, and n.1 to that document.

14. The enclosed British newspapers have not been identified.

15. Eleanor Parke "Nelly" Custis and George Washington Parke Custis, two of Martha Washington's grandchildren, lived with the Washingtons.

16. Lear originally received $120 in bank notes from GW to cover the cost of the watch and chain. According to GW's financial records, Lear paid £32 sterling (GW to Lear, 25 Sept. 1793; Ledger C, 4).

17. The ship *Peggy* was under the command of Capt. Lunt (Lear to GW, 4 Feb., n.4). William Deakins, Jr., was a Georgetown merchant.

18. For GW's receipt of this letter, see his letter to William Pearce of 20 April.

To William Pearce

Mr Pearce,   Philadelphia Jany 26th 1794.

Your letter of the 22d and the Reports, came duly to hand by yesterdays Post.[1]

You will perceive by my rotation plan (with which you have been furnished[2]—or rather by the notes annexed thereto) that if the fields allotted for Corn at the several farms were deemed inadequate to the consumption of this article, that such parts of the fields as were designed for Buck Wheat, *as a Crop,* might be converted to this purpose, and I repeat it again here; leaving the proportion thereof to your own judgment, with a proviso, however, that there be Buck Wheat enough sown to raise a sufficiency of Seed for all the purposes of my rotation system another year; as it is certainly a reflection upon a farmer to have his Seeds to buy. The reason why I prefered increasing the quantity of Corn ground in these fields, is, that nothing might interrupt the manurings of *one field,* at each farm, every year with green manure; whilst the Cowpens, & dung from the farm yards, would do the like to the *poor parts* of a second field, annually. By this means, and a judicious rotation, I am not without hope of bringing my land, in time, into a profitable state of cultivation; and unless some such practice as this prevails, my fields will be growing worse and worse every year, until the Crops will not defray the expence of the culture of them.

By the report of the week before last, it appeared that Stuart was plowing in No. 7;[3] but as that field, according to the rotation which I have by me, was to remain this year in Pasture I could not account for it, otherwise than as a mistake in him, or a direction of mine which I had forgotten; the reason however of my mentioning the matter again, in this letter, is, that if that field is designed for Oats and Buck Wheat, the part, or such proportion thereof (as you like) which was designed for the latter, may go into Corn in like manner as is allowed at the other farms; but if it has not been touched, nor intended to be touched this year, (and I again desire that you will not undertake more than you can execute well) then such part of No. 1. as you may deem proper may be put into Corn: or you may do what Stuart suggested to me before I left home[4]—namely—to plant *all* the *good* ground in both No. 1 & No. 3 with Corn & Sow all the broken & poor parts of them with Buck Wheat for manure; the same might be done at the other farms; remembering always, that these fields are to be sown with Wheat in the months of August & September next agreeably to the plan of Rotation, which you have.

I will send by the first vessel going round to Alexandria 14 bushls of Clover Seed, as I fear what you have (except of your own growth) is bad; and because I would not be sparing of Seed, either to the ground you have to sow, or that which has been sown, and is now missing.[5] Of Timothy Seed I shall send more, as 10 bushels is sufficient I conceive to answer all your purposes; but it is to be feared that the Timothy & Orchard grass seeds have got mixed (as they are very much alike) for I am sure there was Orchard grass seed saved, & Butler and old Jack ought to know what was done with it.[6] That you may know what dependence to place on the Clover seed which went from hence last year, & put into the Store mix it well together, & then promiscuously take out a certain (precise) number of seeds & see what proportion of them will come up. The Gardener can ascertain this, or by putting them under a brick on the ground, in a warm place, you can do it yourself. I shrewdly suspect that that seed was bad, even last year, otherwise the clover lot at the Mansion, and the Meadows at Union & Dogue run farms, would not be so dificient now (the latter after twice sowing in some parts).[7]

Speaking of these Seeds, I must give you a hint of what I also very strongly suspect; and that is—that my Negro Seedsmen takes a considerable toll from every thing that goes into their hands—for this reason, make it an invariable rule before it is delivered to them, to mix in a bushel of Sand or well dried earth, as many pints of seed as you allow to an Acre, and let it be sown in this manner. Two valuable purposes are answered thereby—1st in this State, the Seed is rendered unsaleable; and 2dly a person not skilled in sowing small seeds, will do it more regularly when thus mixed; for being accustomed to sow a bushel of Wheat to the Acre, the same cast, & fill of the hand, does for the small Seed when so mixed; in doing of which pains is to be taken that the mixture is perfect; otherwise one part of the Acre will have more sand & less seed than the other, & so vice, versa.

Give what manure you can to the lot at Mansion house which is to be sown with Oats and grass seeds; or to the one which is to be planted with Potatoes, as circumstances and your own judgment shall direct: for both, I do not presume there is dung enough. It is better to do one well than both by halves.

The Ground between No. 6 at River farm, and the Barn lane, you may apply to the purposes mentioned in your letter of the 22d, & let it remain under the fence which incloses No. 6 until a division fence can be run. It my be worth some consideration whether Potatoes (if some part of the Clover lot in front of the Barn does not require to be broke up) ought not to be planted in part of it.

You may continue to eat of my meat, as the white people will take it after it goes from your table, until your family arrives, and afterwards also if it shall be found more convenient than to keep seperate stocks, as I believe it will. I perceive Thomas Green draws fine flour from the Mill when the Miller & others are content with Midlings; and which I am sure is good enough for him. Does his agreement in this respect differ from the others?[8]

The thorn berries should be buried a year before they are sown, in order that they may pass through a state of fermentation; unless they do this they will not come up. Butler ought to be acquainted with the process, if he is the practical farmer he pretends to be—The Ceder berries should have all the casing of the Seed rubbed of[f] before they are sown, or they will not come up.[9]

Mr Dulany is right in his application, but when you pay him the hundred dollars (which is herein sent you) take his receipt for £150 pounds on Acct of the Rent due to Mrs French for the year 1793; and give him a receipt for £120 for the Rent he owes me, for the same year.[10]

There is part of the Wages for 1793 due to the Estate of Mr Anthony Whiting; but how much I am unable at this moment to say presisely. They commenced the first of Jany and he died about the middle of June, but how much of my money which was in his hands he may have applied to his own use I cannot, without some investigation, decide. If the Administrators have any thing which leads to this, obtain it from them, that the Acct may be closed; as I do not want to keep them out of what is due, a day.[11] I remain Your friend &ca

Go: Washington

ALS, ViMtvL; ALS (letterpress copy), DLC:GW.

1. Pearce's letter to GW of 22 Jan. has not been found. Of the enclosed farm reports, only the spinners report of 21 Jan. has been found (DLC:GW).

2. For the plan of crop rotation, see GW to Pearce, 18 Dec. 1793, and enclosure.

3. These farm reports have not been found. William Stuart was the overseer of the River farm.

4. Fleeing the yellow fever epidemic in Philadelphia, GW and Martha Washington returned to Mount Vernon the previous fall for an extended stay, arriving there by 14 September. GW remained at Mount Vernon until 28 Oct. and Martha until December (*JPP*, 239, 241; Household Accounts, 4, 11 Dec. 1793).

5. On the shipment of clover seed to Mount Vernon, see GW to Pearce, 16–17 and 23 March.

6. James Butler was the overseer of the Mansion House farm. On Old Jack's responsibilities at the Mansion House farm, see n.4 of Howell Lewis to GW, 6 Aug. 1793.

7. For the 442 lbs. of clover seed purchased and sent to Mount Vernon in the summer of 1793, see GW to Anthony Whitting, 2 June, n.5, and 9 June 1793, n.10. John Christian Ehlers was assisted by John Gottlieb Richler in attending to the gardens at Mount Vernon.

8. According to their contracts with GW, Thomas Green, the overseer of the carpenters, and the overseers of the various farms at Mount Vernon received middlings, or common flour, as part of their wages, as apparently GW expected the miller Joseph Davenport to do also (Indenture with Thomas Green, 9 Nov. 1790–14 Dec. 1791, and n.2 to that document; GW to Whitting, 9 Dec. 1792, n.9; Articles of Agreement with Hiland Crow, 15 Sept. 1790, DLC:GW).

9. For GW's previous instructions on collecting thorn and cedar berries in order to cultivate hedgerows at Mount Vernon, see his letter to Pearce of 23 Dec. 1793.

10. On GW's purchase in 1786 of the 543-acre French-Dulany tract near Mount Vernon, see the source note for George Clinton to GW, 27 Feb. 1784; GW to Charles Lee, 20 Feb. 1785, and n.1 to that document; and *Diaries*, 4:84–85. For a map of this purchase, see *Diaries*, 1:240. As part of this purchase, GW was obliged to pay an annual fee to Mrs. Penelope French, Benjamin Tasker Dulany's mother-in-law. Dulany, in turn, rented from GW a 376-acre tract on Hunting Creek known as the Dow tract. On 30 Jan. 1794, Pearce recorded receipt of GW's enclosed bank note for $100, or £30, and on 6 Feb., he noted paying £30 to Dulany "for Mrs Penelope French" (Mount Vernon Accounts, 1794–97).

11. An entry in GW's accounts for 25 Dec. 1792 indicates that Anthony Whitting, GW's former estate manager, who died on 21 June 1793, received £84 for "one years service from the 25 Decr 91. to the present date at 60 Gui[nea]s ℗ yr" (Ledger B, 310; Tobias Lear to GW, 24 June 1793). For the final settlement of Whitting's account, see GW to Pearce, 20 April 1794, and n.3 to that document.

From Edmund Randolph

Sir   Philadelphia January 26. 1794.
I have examined all Mr Morris's ministerial correspondence; and after the impression, which I had received from others, whom I supposed to be conversant with it, I am really astonished to find so little of what is exceptionable, and so much of what the most violent would call patriotic.[1] The parts to be witheld,[2] will probably be of these denominations: 1. What relates to Mr G——t;[3] 2. some harsh expressions on the conduct of the rulers in France, which, if returned to that country, might expose him to danger; 3. the authors of some interesting information, who, if known, would be infallibly denounced. He speaks indeed of *his court;* a phrase, which he might as well have let alone. I shall do myself the honor of waiting on you in the morning; and I write now, only to give you an outline of the true state of the business.[4] I have the honor, sir, to be with the highest respect yr mo. ob. serv.

                                                  Edm: Randolph

ALS, DLC:GW.
    1. A recent Senate resolution asking for the official correspondence of Gouverneur Morris, the U.S. minister to France, prompted Randolph's examination (U.S. Senate to GW, 24 Jan.; see also Randolph to GW, 25 Jan.).
    2. Randolph substituted this word for "suppressed."
    3. The administration had decided in August to ask the French government to recall Edmond Genet, its minister to the United States (Cabinet Opinion, 23 Aug. 1793).
    4. After receiving a reply from GW, which has not been found, Randolph wrote a second letter to GW later this day concerning Morris's correspondence.

Letter not found: to Edmund Randolph, 26 Jan. 1794. In his second letter to GW of this date, Randolph wrote that he "has just had the honor of receiving the President's letter."

From Edmund Randolph

                                        Sunday Evening [26 Jan. 1794]
Mr Randolph has just had the honor of receiving the President's letter, which came, while he was dining out.[1]
Mr R. writes this note for the consideration of the President.

If the resolution was made in the *executive* character of the Senate; then a resistance *in toto* seems at present the true path; because they are *executive,* only on *nominations* or *Treaties;* and can call for papers relative to those subjects, only when the one or the other is propounded to them by the President.[2]

On the other hand, as a branch of the *legislature,* the Senate have a greater latitude of power. They may call for papers, al- tho' they do not relate to a business, actually depending before them. They may call for them, with a view to originate business. But then, the President interposes his discretion, so as to give to them no more, than, in his judgment, is fit to be given.

So that a very important question seems to be, whether the vote be a legislative or executive vote. It now stands on the legis- lative journal.[3]

Mr R. thanks the President for his kind enquiry, after his son, who is much better.[4]

AL, DLC:GW. This letter is filed at DLC under February 1794.

1. GW's letter to Randolph of this date, which has not been found, was written in response to Randolph's first letter of this date.

2. The Senate's resolution requested GW to provide it copies of the offi- cial correspondence of Gouverneur Morris, the U.S. minister to France (U.S. Senate to GW, 24 Jan. 1794). For the legislative powers of the U.S. Senate, see Article I of the U.S. Constitution. For its executive powers, as defined by Randolph, see Article II, section 2. For Randolph's further clarification of the distinction between the legislative and executive powers of the U.S. Senate, see his letter to GW of 2 February.

3. See *Annals of Congress,* 3d Cong., 38.

4. On the illness of Randolph's son, see Randolph to GW, 25 January.

From Johann Benjamin Erhard

translation   Muenchen [Munich, Germany] Jan. 27th 1794

It is to the full Confidence in Your Excellency's general Be- nevolence to Mankind, which cannot but constitute one of the chief Ornaments of a Character destined by Providence to break the fetters of a World, That I owe the Resolution humbly to ad- dress to Your Excellency the present Relation of the most unfor- tunate Event of an Imposture, that involves a number of honest Persons in Europe, while abusing the Authority of the United States. In vain Delicacy urges the Apprehension of being taxed an Intruder for the particular Complexion of my case and the flattering hope of obtaining some Redress from the Generosity of United States suppress every hesitation arising from that principle of Decency ever so powerful with liberal minds. In order to form a proper series of those Events which, Tho in an indirect manner operated my falling a Sacrifice to the late sad Event, I beg Leave, Shortly to premise an Account of the principal Transactions of my former Life, which will also implici⟨tl⟩y serve to state what little Abilities I may pretend to possess. I am a Native of Nueremberg. My father, a wire manufacturer by procuring me a liberal Education succeeded in his View, to instill Sound republican sentiments in my mind. Accordingly I was at a pretty early Period of my life undeceived as to the true Conception of what they in Europe call honour & grandeur, & resolved to follow the business of my father. Ever since that time I cherished a preponderating Inclination to live in America. My Spare-hours were spent in studying Mathematics which led me to theoretical part of Physic without having any Intention in the least, to embrace that Profession. However I happened in the year 1786 to meet with the Acquaintance of Counsellor Siebold one of the most celebrated Surgeons in this Country, who finding me so well prepared persuaded me, wholly to devote me to the study of Physic, while that Gentleman found means to procure a proper Opportunity of obtaining the practical part of that Science by employing me in the great Hospital at Wuerzburg under his Direction.[1] From Thence I repaired to several places calculated to improve physical Knowledge, when in the year 1792 I was created Doctor in Phc & fixed my Domicile at Nurembergh again resolved to acquire if possible a Reputation by publishing some eminent litterary Performance in that Line, yet still attentive to my favourite plan to spend the Rest of my life in America.[2]

Being so disposed in the month of Octr last past a seemingly Favorable Opportunity of accomplishing so fond a wish offered, which alas! proved a source of the most sad Reverse on my Part, to wit: I became acquainted with a person called William who came to see me furnished with Letters of Recommendation from ⟨my⟩ friends at Wuerzburgh, but afterwards, when I entered into more unreserved Conversation with him, he professed to be an American and proved by producing a number of letters and Documents his proper Name was William Pearce and his Capacity a

Colonel & Commander of a newly raised Regiment of Infantry and a member of the Order of The Cincinnati. Then he produced to me as well as to my father and father in Law a written power of Attorney bearing Date June 1793 signed: Washington & Jefferson and sealed with the seal of the Union, that is vested in him a discretionary Power[3] (the Original says, illimited power) to engage for the service of the United States Six Captains and eight Lieutenants, the power of Attorney to be in force for the Space of nine months from the Date thereof. By his Assertions there was a first surgeon & an Auditor to be comprehended among the six officers of Captn's Rank. I myself in the first Emotions of so advantageous an Offer accommodated him at my own Dwelling house, where he further told me, he had fought thro' all the American war on Your Excellency's side as Adjutant mentioning several Events and the particulars thereof with a Degree of Accuracy and Probability, that suppressed with me even the remotest Thought of Imposition. Amongst many other Things past he related to have resided at Copenhagen in the fall of the Year 1791 filling the place of an Envoy from the United States. That being exactly the time when I left that City, (where I resided some time to reap Advantage of those excellent Institutions of Surgery and Midwifery established There) I made different Inquiries about some Characters & found all, what he advanced conformable to a Nicety. He without any apparent Design produced Letters and Cards of respectable Officers of The Danish Court. Blinded by so many concluding Circumstances I neglected to write for more authentic Information from Baron Shimmelmann, Minister of Finances, who honours me with his Confidence.[4] From Copenhagen The Impostor according to his own Relation departed for Sweden & Stettin.[5] He showed me a letter from the Commander of the latter place, in which he is requested to grant a Commission to that Gentleman's Nephew. Having on his way appointed several Officers whose names escaped my memory (except one Swiss gentleman, called, de Eckhard he said) returned to Philadelphia. He had in his possession Documents, as to Their external Appearance fully authentic, authorizing him to engage Officers in the Swiss Canton of Basel[6]—also Powers of Attorney to recover Estates & Legacies within the United States, and obligatory notes or Receipts for Sums advanced drawn by Those Officers appointed by him. That Concurrence of facts so palpable & apparently incontrovertible could not but prevail on a liberal temper naturally not suspicious. Therefore I readily accepted his Proposals and he executed in my behalf a Brevet in which he appoints me first surgeon, of which I take the Liberty here to subjoin a Copy certified by a Notary public.[7] I do not deny I received that Brevet with Rapture of Joy thinking myself fortunate for having obtained that long wished for Object, being at the same time persuaded, That allways [I] should be able honorably to acquit myself of The whole Province of Duties annexed to That Commission. A spirit of Patriotism began to animate me in such a Degree as to use every means in my power towards contributing to an exquisite choice of Those subjects he wanted to engage in the service of the Union, in which I unfortunately but too well Succeeded by persuading a certain Fick of Anspach[8] a young man of promising talents, who, being acquainted with the English and French language, instantly resigned his place and now bewails his misfortune with an interesting family—In that first Emotion I even carried matters so far, as to persuade my father in Law Mr Golling to purchase Bills of Exchange drawn on Robert Hardy, London, sd Colo. wanted to dispose of being out of cash.[9] Then I accompanied him in a second Excursion in quest of subjects to engage, when I left him at Salzburg with my chariot, having agreed to meet again at Muenchen. On my Arrival at this place he was not to be found, but I found, in the contrary letters from my father in Law informing me, that the Letters of Exchange had been returned protested, whereupon he to undeceive Us had opened a letter directed to the pretended Colo., which had been re-expedited and Thereby was convinced of his being an Impostor—It is impossible to describe Those poignant desolating feelings like mine were at That moment, I only mention, what greatly heightens my misery I mean the sarcastic strictures of narrowminded persons, who are ever ready to add Injury to Affliction, when it befalls any Man, who does not idolize Their own Prejudices. How far any Relief can or may be granted to me I dare not to imagine but I implore Your Excellency's Interposition to That End with all the Anguish of a person, that owes only to Religion's Support to have been able to survive so complicated a Disappointment and Distress, for the dreadful conscious Thought to have plunged in Desolation & Ruin all what is dear to me on Earth, my father, wife, & her own father preys vulturelike on my soul. Some Answer, I flatter myself, I may expect from Your Excellency, as it is still something to clear up the uncertain Prospects of an unfortunate, who might be rendered useful again to Society by changing Imposture in Truth. In that peculiar state of woeful Anxiety I have the honor to remain with unexpressible Respect Your Excellency's most humble devoted servant

John Benjamin Erhard. Med. Dr

P.S. I have put every thing in motion to have the Villain apprehended, Then I shall also lay before You his fictitious power of Atty.[10] He gave himself for 32 years asserting his father was governor in America, his uncle Earl of Pearce & his father Lord Pce he is of middling size, fair complexion, has black curled hairs, is wounded on each thigh. He had about him printed Brevets in German, Latin & french, for Distribution.

L (translation), DNA: RG 59, Miscellaneous Letters. This letter was enclosed in Johann Paul Golling to GW, 4 February. For a somewhat variant text in German, evidently taken from Erhard's retained copy, see Karl Auguste Varnagen von Ense, *Denkwürdigkeiten des Philosophen und Arztes Johann Benjamin Erhard* (Stuttgart and Tübingen, 1830), 378–85).

Physician and philosopher Johann Benjamin Erhard (1766–1827) studied at Würzburg and Jena before establishing his medical practice in Nuremberg. In 1795, he published *Über das Recht des Volkes zu einer Revolution* (Jena & Leipzig).

1. Erhard's father was Jacob Reinhard Erhard. Karl Kaspar von Siebold (1736–1807) taught anatomy, surgery, and obstetrics at the University of Würzburg.

2. Erhard's 1792 dissertation was entitled *Dissertatio Inauguralis Medica Exhibens Ideam Organi Medici*. . . .

3. The person using the assumed name William Pearce had no authority to recruit officers for the U.S. Army. On Erhard's father-in-law, see Johann Paul Golling to GW, 4 February.

4. Count Ernst Heinrich Schimmelmann (1747–1831) was the finance minister of Denmark, 1784–1814.

5. Stettin, now Szczecin, Poland, was at this time the capital of the Prussian province of Pomerania.

6. The canton of Basel in northern Switzerland borders both France and Germany.

7. The enclosed copy, which was translated into English, reads: "I William Pearce Colonel and Commander of a Regiment levied for the Service of the United States Member of the Order of the Cincinnati

"Do make known by these Presents: that Mr Benjamin Erhard Doctor in Physic the Bearer hereof hath on this day been appointed a first Surgeon in my Regiment with yearly Salary of Sixteen hundred Spanish milled Dollars. the Expences of his Passage to America to be defrayed by the United States.

"I therefore request His Excellency General Washington President of Congress of the Unitd States to be pleased to acknowledge Said Mr Erhard in his Said Capacity and to order the lawful All[ow]ances for Equipment usually granted to foreign Officers to be furnished to the same. Given at Nurembergh Octr 14. 1793." This certificate was attested by notary public J. C. Haselbroek at Munich on 30 Jan. 1794 (DNA: RG 59, Miscellaneous Letters).

8. For Johann Fick's account of this scam, see his letter to GW of this date; see also Karl August Freiherr von Wangenheim to GW, 10 February. Ansbach, or Anspach, is a city approximately twenty-five miles southwest of Nuremberg.

9. Sir Robert Herries and Co. was a London bankinghouse. For letters from this firm denying any knowledge of Pearce, see n.1 of Wangenheim to GW, 10 February.

10. The enclosed power of attorney has not been identified. For GW's opinion on the impropriety of replying to this type of letter, see n.3 of Wangenheim to GW, 10 February.

From Johann Georg Christian Fick

Sir,   Erlangen[1] January the 27th 1794.

From another part of the globe I find myself induced, by reverence to You and Your great merits to Your Country, whose freedom and happiness You have been the founder of, to tell You an history, which I believe, shall be worthy of Your and Your country's notice. A quarter of a year past there arrived, three hours from hence, at Nuremberg, a Gentleman who pretended to be an Englishman, and who did give himself the name of Williams; some time after he shewed Diplomes and letters and declared himself for a Colonel in the Service of the United States of North-America; these Diplomes had the seals and arms of the North-American States, had to their subscription Your own name; and he pretended, that it had been committed to his care, to make suit for Officers to a new raising Regiment in Your Country's service. One of my friends at Nuremberg recommended myself to him,[2] and he promised me the place of an Auditor in this Regiment. Other persons here and at Nuremberg he promised also places and did bid us, to prepare ourselves to the journey. Now he went to Munchen with the declaration, to get there more Officers, and from thence he would send us our Patents. I began the preparation for the journey, anounced my place here at the University and squandered all my little stock of cash to the preparation of the journey. How happy did I dream myself to be so near in fulfilling my long concealed wishes, viz. to serve a Country, whose whole Governmnt did simpathize so much with my political sentiments; but, alas! at last we found ourselves deceived, he had imposed upon a Merchant at Nurem- berg with some thousand Florens, and he was gone off from Munchen, after having played there also, for some days, the same trick, having worn there the North-American Regimentals, with the letters P.W. at the girdle before the breast, having payed in this quality to the Elector of Bavarie some visits and having de- ceived also Merchants and other young people.[3] I am assured, Sir! this bad history will be very displeasant to You, the more, because the same trick has been played a Year ago in the North- ern Germany, and by which Your great Name has also been put to this wrong use. I believe, Sir, the best method for preventing it in the future, might be, to publish some declaration in ger- man and perhaps french news papers, and for this I wait Your kind command. How many misfortunes can such wretches oth- erwise commit in our Germany, because many thousands be- come transported at seeing Your name, and believe all, what is said to them! I know this by myself: some electrical strokc I did feel at looking at Your name, and therefore I threw myself and my great family in the greatest troubles; for now I am without a settlement, and know not, how to maintain my wife and five children. With these, it was my parting wish, to go to a coun- try, which has great Washington at its head! Already I did make many schemes, how I would serve my new country with my few parts, without my office! Perhaps, Sir, this betrayer should only be the mean of recommending myself to Your favour and per- haps this letter procures me a settlement in a country, to whose service my great family should be educated; perhaps I could be- come a real Auditor, or some teacher at a publick school or at the new establishing University at Philadelphia. Dare I wish, Sir, to see from You some lines in answer of this? they should be my greatest treasure. A Merchant, who lives here, has two broth- ers, likewise merchants, at New York, named Jacob Mark and Compy.[4] by these You will have these bold lines, and by these You can bless with an answer. Sir Your most humble devoted Servant

John Christian Fick,
late Professor at the University of Erlangen

ALS, DLC:GW.

The writer of this letter was Johann Georg Christian Fick (1763–1821), who wrote *Praktishce Englische Sprachlehre für Deutsche beyderley Geschlechts* (Graz, 1793).

1. The city of Erlangen is situated at the confluence of the Schwabach and Regnitz rivers in present-day southwest Germany and is approximately ten miles north-northwest of Nuremberg. It was the site of the Friedrich-Alexander University.

2. Fick's friend was Johann Benjamin Erhard, who wrote about this scam in a letter to GW of this same date; see also Karl August Freiherr von Wangenheim to GW, 10 February.

3. Karl Theodor (Charles Theodore; 1724–1799), who resided in Munich, was the Elector and Duke of Bavaria from 1777 until his death.

4. The New York City mercantile firm of Jacob Mark & Co. was at 99 Market Street (*New-York Directory, 1794*, 124). On Jacob's brother and former partner, Philip Mark, see Edmund Randolph to GW, 9 April (second letter), and n.1 to that document. No reply from GW has been found.

Letter not found: from John Jay and Rufus King, 27 Jan. 1794. In his letter to Henry Knox of 15 Feb., GW referred to "the subject of Mr Jay and Mr King's letter to me, of the 27th of last month."

From Henry Knox

Sir,   War department January 27th 1794

It is with great pain that I submit you the enclosed letters, giving an account of an infamous violation of the peace with the Creeks by some of the violent frontier people of Georgia.[1] I have the honor to be with the greatest respect Your obedient Servant

H. Knox

LS, DLC:GW; LB, DLC:GW.

1. In a letter to Knox of 1–2 Jan. 1794, Indian agent Constant Freeman described an unprovoked attack on 28 Dec. 1793 by white residents of Georgia upon a small hunting party of Creek Indians, which resulted in the deaths of two Creek men. The documents enclosed in Freeman's letter included his letter to Georgia governor George Mathews of 1–2 Jan.; an affidavit of 2 Jan. by Bartlet Walker identifying one of the white participants; and U.S. Army captain Richard Brooke Roberts's letters to Knox and to Mathews, both of 2 Jan., which also described the attack and echoed Freeman's concerns about the probability of escalating violence unless the state government intervened. All these documents were written at Fort Fidius, Ga., located on the north bank of the Oconee River and approximately six miles south of present-day Milledgeville (*ASP, Indian Affairs*, 1:472–74).

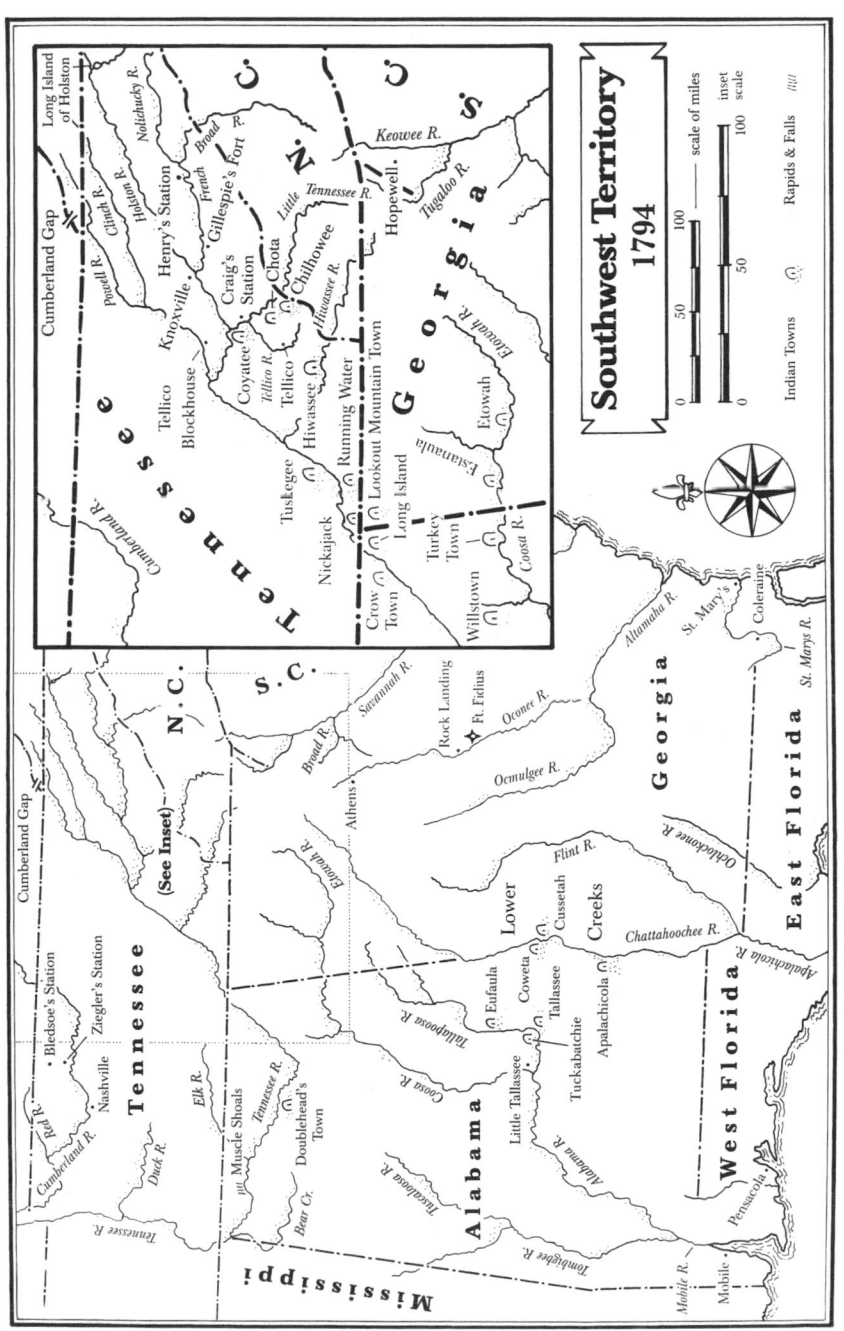

Map 2: *Southwest Territory, 1794. (Illustrated by Rick Britton. Copyright Rick Britton. 2008.)*

In addition, Knox enclosed two letters from Indian agent James Seagrove of 8 and 9 Dec. 1793. Seagrove wrote both letters to Knox from the Creek village of Tuckabatchie, where he was having some difficulty in getting the Creeks to relinquish their prisoners. Seagrove, however, was confident that the chiefs would agree to visit Philadelphia, which would help to counter hostile interference from Spanish agents. Knox also enclosed Seagrove's letter of 5 Dec. 1793 to William Blount, governor of the Southwest Territory, and "Notes taken at a treaty held between the Spaniards & Indians at the Walnut hills in Octobr. 1793." None of these additional enclosures has been identified (*JPP*, 279). Walnut Hills was the American name for the location of Fort Nogales in present-day Vicksburg, Mississippi. Spanish promises of support for the Choctaw, Chickasaw, Cherokee, and Creek Indians were formalized in the Treaty of Nogales, 28 Oct. 1793 (Parry, *Consolidated Treaty Series*, 52:175–78; Whitaker, *Spanish-American Frontier*, 167–69).

After reading all these letters, GW returned them to Knox, "with a request that he would give an opinion of what shou'd be done" (*JPP*, 280). For Knox's response, see his letter to GW of 28 January.

From Hudson Muse

Sir⟨e⟩   Virginia. Port Tappa. Jany 27 1794

I have been imprudent in giving Gentlemen Credit at the Office, for duties, and made myself liable by my returns, in expectation that the Money would be ready When Call'd for;[1] by which, I am not at present prepared to take up draughts forward'd last week by Messrs Lovell & Urquahart for five Thousand dollars, in Consequence of which presume they will be returned, as they have Signified they could not wait any time.[2] I can not pretend to Say any thing in Justification of myself for Such Conduct, but if I may be excused for not being pointed to my duty in this Instance, I flatter myself You Will do me the favour to Speak to the Secretary of Treasury on the Occasion, to grant me a Small indulgence, and he may rest Assured that the money Shall be ready for his order in less than two months from this date, and I will take care for the future never to be in the like Situation.[3] I am Your Excellencies Most Obt Hble Servt

Hudson Muse Colon[el]

ALS, DNA: RG 59, Miscellaneous Letters.

1. Hudson Muse was the customs collector for the District of Tappahannock, Va., and inspector of the port of Tappahannock on the Rappahannock River (GW to U.S. Senate, 3 Aug. 1789 and 6 March 1792 [third letter]).

2. William Lovell and Charles Urquhart were merchants in Fredericksburg, Va. (*Virginia Herald and Fredericksburg Advertiser*, 11 April 1793).

3. GW sent this letter to Alexander Hamilton for review shortly after its receipt (Hamilton to GW, 10 Feb.). Muse wrote GW on 16 Feb. that of the drafts presented at his office for $5,000, "only three thousand were returned, the other two, being retained, have since been provided for" (DLC:GW). Despite this second letter's attempt to present a more positive impression of Muse's performance, he was removed from office in early March (GW to U.S. Senate, 5 March).

Cabinet Opinion on a Resolution
of the U.S. Senate

January 28. 1794.
At a meeting of the heads of departments

Upon consideration of the resolution of the Senate, of January 24. 1794, calling for the correspondences, therein mentioned:[1]

General Knox is of opinion, that no part of the correspondences should be sent to the Senate.

Colo. Hamilton, that the correct mode of proceeding is to do, what General Knox advises; but that the principle is safe, by excepting such parts as the President may choose to withhold:

Mr Randolph, that all the correspondence, proper from its nature to be communicated to the Senate, should be sent; but that what the President thinks improper, should not be sent.

In either form messages are recommended to be prepared.[2]

H. Knox
Alexandr Hamilton
Edm: Randolph.

LS (in Edmund Randolph's handwriting), DLC:GW. GW's docket reads: "Opinions of the heads of Departs. respectg the resolve of the Senate requesting the corrispondence with the Minisr of the U.S. in France."

1. For the resolution asking for the diplomatic correspondence of Gouverneur Morris, the U.S. minister to France, see U.S. Senate to GW, 24 January.

2. For the reply sent, see GW to the U.S. Senate, 26 February.

From the Commissioners
for the District of Columbia

Sir, City of Washington January 28. 1794

Major Ellicotts return in November, after being absent great part of the Summer, and soon after we had employed his Brother

Joseph, was so plainly calculated to be heavy on the Funds, that we could not submit to it, and discharged him at our last Meeting:[1] we flattered ourselves, that we should have more expedition and Quiet too with his Brothers, but he has continued here, and has, we believe, worked like so much Levin in the Surveying Department; for the paultry press in this Town, has constantly since teemed with lies and abuse, in which the young men have been Instruments or Volunteers—Nothing of Consequence has been done in the Field, in the fine weather past, and the Idea seems to be, that little is to be done till the Spring but to count the time—We have on the whole, done now, what perhaps had better been done long ago—discharged the whole for there is evidently a want of Industry, and there are so many Instances of a total absence of probity and Honor, that we can no longer bear with the Corps.[2] As to the meer laying out the City we do not fear any difficulty. But the levelling the City and marking out the proper Drains, approach so quick, that a Man of real abilities in that Line, will be soon wanted, and perhaps the Time is not very distant, when it will be proper to have a real Enginier here in the public service. Unless you have some Gentleman in contemplation whose abilities recommend him to your Confidence, we think of inviting Mr Rivardi[3] hither—when he came as a Companion to Dr Thornton, he made a strong impression on each of us, in the two or three Days he staid with us; we should not presume to lead his expectations farther, than to the levelling part, and a general view of the Surveying Department, which we think might both be attended to by him; as each must be done, if well done, on the same intimate knowledge of the Ground, and Design of the City.[4]

Mr Rivardi is not a Shewy man, but he seems to us one of those Characters, who maintains the Ground he has gained; we wish him to be introduced to you—It is said, that Mr Rittenhouse is well acquainted with him.[5] We are sir very respectfully Your mo. obedt Servts

Th. Johnson
Dd: Stuart
Danl. Carroll

LS, DLC:GW; LB, DNA: RG 42, Records of the Commissioners for the District of Columbia, Letters Sent, 1791–1867.

1. On the dismissal of chief surveyor Andrew Ellicott in December 1793, see D.C. Commissioners to GW, 23 Dec. 1793, and n.8.

2. The commissioners met at Georgetown, D.C., from 24 to 31 January. During these deliberations they settled their financial accounts with surveyors Andrew, Benjamin, and Joseph Ellicott (DNA: RG 42, Records of the Commissioners for the District of Columbia, Proceedings, 1791–1802). They also wrote a letter of termination on 28 Jan. to Benjamin and Joseph Ellicott, asking them to relinquish all official papers in the surveyor's office (DNA: RG 42, Records of the Commissioners for the District of Columbia, Letters Sent, 1791–1802).

3. An "R" has been written over an "L" at both mentions of this name; the letter book has retained the original but incorrect spelling at both places.

4. John Jacob Ulrich Rivardi (d. 1808) was a Swiss engineer. He served in the Russian Army prior to 1790, when, accompanied by William Thornton, he went to the West Indies island of Tortola to convalesce (Harris, *William Thornton Papers*, xlvi, 1:124–26). Rivardi may have accompanied Thornton when the latter met with the D.C. Commissioners in April 1793 to discuss the design and construction of the Capitol (D.C. Commissioners to GW, 9 April 1793 [first letter]). Rivardi's first employment by the federal government was not by the D.C. commissioners, but rather by the War Department as an engineer for new coastal fortifications proposed at Alexandria and Norfolk, Va., and at Baltimore (GW to D.C. Commissioners, 11 April 1794). In 1795, GW appointed Rivardi a major in the U.S. Army's Corps of Artillerists and Engineers (GW to U.S. Senate, 25 Feb. 1795, LS, DNA: RG 46, Third Congress, 1793–95, Senate Records of Executive Proceedings, President's Messages—Executive Nominations; LB, DLC:GW).

5. David Rittenhouse was director of the U.S. Mint.

From Elizabeth Barbara Embry

28 Jan. 1794. Writes from Cork County, Ireland: "The Protector of the distressed, the Arbiter of differences will He disdain the Sufferings of an individual. penetrated with esteem of your Excellent qualities, and hoping relief from a beneficence so extensive, and an understanding So piercing as that of your Excellency's, for which you are not more famed than for a moderation, which makes you ⟨*illegible*⟩ all your great and astonishing talents with a Meakness as admirable, as surprizing, I am incouraged to address you." Gives a detailed account of her son who "early distinguished Himself in His literary pursuits, and not less for a probity, and love of truth, that made him respectable. . . . At seventeen His ardour for distinguishing himself became almost ungovernable. . . . At the age of Eighteen, He had passed through all our College Courses," and sets out on a tour of Europe, because a "certain ease, and Manner, was wanting to him, that is seldom possessed without mixing in the World—He had been

wholly taken up with forming himself on the great examples
he met with in Story. He was unsuspecting, modest, preferring
others to him self, Brave by Nature, warm, ambitious, but it was
the ambition of meriting distinction. It took the place of other
Youthful passions, never did I see a Being more free from sin,
or more truly religious, without any tincture of Fanaticism." His
traveling companion, however, was acquainted "with every vice
of which the human heart is capable, it was A World of Wonders
for My Son, of which till this moment He had been ignorant."
As a result, "His mind no longer preserved its steadiness. Something puting a Stop to their travells together, My Son returned
to me directly, all his plans broken, his Spirits extremely hurt. . . .
All my efforts were ineffectual, his Spirits were fled, and at last
his health became a prey to disappointment, and indolence." By
this time he had "become of age," and was responsible for an estate in Ireland, which had fallen into ruin. "He was cheated, and
hated a World in which He found so much fraud, and injustice.
He sequestred Himself from it, he began to consider it as a Duty
to manage his little patrimony to the best advantage, but the
accomplishment of this did not satisfy Him it was too bounded,
his education had been extensive. he had endeavoured to form
Him self for matters of ⟨extent⟩, of universal good, He sunk in
the mention of little things. . . . I find Him pale, languid, and
tho' not thirty Years of age, His fine person stooped as if he were
Seventy, his appetite gone, His Strength wasted. . . . He is convinced that neither his present employment, nor the air of this
place agrees with him, Yet afraid to change for fear of worse. I
know not what to do with him, or how to quit him for a moment.
I have pressed his trying the air of a little Villa, I have near Dublin, His answer is, he must be Employed, or nothing is done. I
alledge his Health must first be attended to, he answers Employment is as necessary as any thing else to the establishment of his
health. if it is ever to be restablished.

"His admiration of you Sir, is great as Your qualities deserve
He looks up to you as the first of Men, A word from Your Excellency might be the Means with the Blessing of Heaven of saving
this inestimable Young Man and of making the widowed heart
to sing for joy. Will this induce You Sir, to relieve me by Your
Advice or if that is too much to hope, at least May I flatter My

self You will pardon My taking up time so precious to the World with my cares and Miserys. . . . If Your Excellency shoud honor me with a line My address is Mrs Embry Inchannappa Wicklow Ireland."[1]

ALS, DNA: RG 59, Miscellaneous Letters.

1. Inchanappa is a country house in the parish of Inch, Arklow Barony of Wicklow County.

On 27 June, Secretary of State Edmund Randolph wrote Embry at GW's request, acknowledging this letter and expressing his sympathy before continuing: "it being impossible to promise to him the kind of employment in the United States, which he seems to wish, it is incumbent on my candor to say this to you explicitly. At the same time I may assure you, that our country abounds in liberty and hospitality" (DNA: RG 59, Diplomatic and Consular Instructions).

From Henry Knox

Sir   War department January 28. 1794

Having communicated to the Secretaries of State and the Treasury the purport of the recent communications from the frontiers of Georgia,[1] We unite in opinion that it would be proper that the papers should be laid before Congress accompanied by a special message from the President, stating the importance of Congress taking into their immediate consideration the measures requisite to prevent a repetition of, and to provide adequate punishments for, such atrocious offences.[2] I have the honor to be with perfect respect Your obedient Servant

H. Knox

LS, DLC:GW; LB, DLC:GW.

1. For recent correspondence received from Georgia, see n.1 of Knox to GW, 27 January.

2. For the papers and message sent to Congress, see GW to U.S. Senate and House of Representatives, 30 January.

To John Hamilton Moore

Sir,   Philadelphia Jany 28th 1794.

I have received, and pray you to accept my last thanks for "The New practical Navigator," which you had the goodness to send

me, and also for my share of the honor of your address on it.[1] I
am—Sir Your Most Obedient & Very Hble Servant

                                                        Go: Washington

ADfS, owned by Mr. Augustus P. Loring, Boston, Mass., 1985; LB, DLC:GW.
GW's docket on the draft reads: "To Mr Jno. Hamilton Moore—Tower Hill
London 28th Jan. 1794."

    1. British hydrographer John Hamilton Moore's *The New Practical Naviga-
tor; Being An Epitome of Navigation, Rendered Easy to Any Common Capacity: Containing All the Requisite Tables for Determining the Latitude and Longitude, and
Keeping A Complete Reckoning at Sea* (London, 1793) was his latest version of a
book that he originally published in 1772 as *The Practical Navigator and Seaman's New Daily Assistant.* For other works by Moore in GW's library, see Griffin, *Catalogue of the Washington Collection,* 546, 561. Any accompanying cover
letter from Moore has not been found.

Letter not found: from William Pearce, 28 Jan. 1794. GW wrote Pearce
on 9 Feb. acknowledging receipt of "your letter of the 28th of last
month."

To Richard Peters

Dear Sir,   28th January 1794.
    I thank you for keeping in mind my request concerning
Oats. For seed I want them. The purchase depends upon three
things—yea four. 1 the quality. 2 the time they could be delivered
in this City. and 3 the certainty of a passage to the Potomac. 4th
not having heard yet from my Manager, how much he requires,
I cannot be precise myself as to the quantity.[1]
    All therefore I would further request of you, *at this time,* is,
to continue your enquiries, where I could be supplied, if under
these uncertainties I should, hereafter, ask your assistance in
procuring them.[2] Yours—affectionately

                                                        Go: Washington

ALS (photocopy), ViMtvL; ADf, DLC:GW; LB, DLC:GW.
    1. For GW's estimate that he needed 340 bushels of oat seed for planting
on the five farms at Mount Vernon, see his letter to William Pearce, his estate
manager, of 12 January. At this time, GW was unsure how much seed was
already at Mount Vernon.
    2. On GW's acquisition of oat seed, see GW to Pearce, 16–17 March, and
Frederick Freylinghuysen to GW, 26 March.

Bartholomew Dandridge, Jr.,
to Auguste de Grasse

Sir,   Philada Jany 29. 1794

The President of the United States has been made acquainted, by a letter from you, with the situation in which you &, your family are at Charleston.[1] Such representations are daily made to him from various parts of the United States, by your Countrymen, in the same unfortunate predicament with yourself. No man feels more for your distresses than the President, nor is any one more willing to contribute to their alleviation, than he is. In fact, he has done this as far or perhaps further, than the resources of which he is possessed wou'd strictly justify—having no public fund which he is authorised to apply to these objects, his private purse is inadequate to satisfy the deplorable cases which are brought before him by letters and otherwise, for relief.[2] The subject has been laid before the Legislature of the U.S. now in Session here; & it is expected they will appropriate a sum for the immediate relief, in some degree, of the necessities of the unfortunate fugitives from St Domingo. Shou'd an Act be passed to this effect, it is hoped that your case, among others, will be embraced thereby.[3] The President directs me to assure you, Sir, that it is not from a want of inclination to serve you, or of sympathy for your accumulated distresses, that he gives you this answer, but from his real inability to afford you relief. I am Sir &c.

                                          Bw: Dandridge. S.P. U. States.

LB, DLC:GW.

1. The letter referenced may be de Grasse's letter to GW of 28 Dec. 1793, or it may be the one de Grasse wrote GW from Charleston, S.C., on 24 Aug. 1793.

2. Although GW declined to give de Grasse financial aid, he did make an occasional exception. In July 1793 he gave $250 to a committee established by Philadelphia citizens for the relief of refugees from Saint Domingue, and in January 1794 he gave $25 to two French women who had asked for his personal support (GW to De Saxÿ and De Verneüil, 26 Dec. 1793, and notes).

3. See "An Act providing for the relief of such of the inhabitants of Saint Domingo, resident within the United States, as may be found in want of support," 12 Feb. 1794, in which an amount not exceeding $15,000 was appropriated for this purpose (*Stat.* 6:13).

To James Keith

Dear Sir,   Philadelphia Jany 29th 1794.

The enclosed came to my hands a few days ago[1]—the means are also enclosed to discharge Colo. Simms account, and to receive his acquittal. I would thank you to get from, and forward to me, Mr Lees charge also; that my Administration of the Estate of Colo. Colvill may be finally closed, and the balance deposited some where for the benefit of the residuary legatees.[2]

That I may be better able to decide upon the latter point, I would thank you for an extract of that part of Colo. Thoms Colvills Will (or the Will itself, as I presume it is no longer of any use to you.) which makes this devise; and for *all* the claims, proofs, &ca which have been handed to his Executors in consequence thereof, and which were deposited (to the best of my recollection) with you, along with the other papers.[3] I am—Dear Sir Your Obedt Hble Servt

Go: Washington

P.S. are there not some parts of Colo. Simms charge which ought to be paid, or at least repaid by the defendants?[4]

ALS (letterpress copy), NN: Washington Papers; LB, DLC:GW.

1. The enclosed letter, which has not been found, was from Charles Simms to GW of 15 January.

2. GW also enclosed "bank notes & half a guinea" in this letter (GW to Simms, 24 Feb.). GW employed James Keith, who practiced law at Alexandria, Va., to assist in settling the tangled estates of brothers John and Col. Thomas Colvill. Simms and Charles Lee, also attorneys at Alexandria, were occasionally employed to settle suits involving the estate (Keith to GW, 15 July 1793). On this estate, of which GW was an executor, see Thomas Montgomerie to GW, 24 Oct. 1788, source note. A final settlement was not achieved until 1796 (Ledger C, 15).

3. Thomas Colvill's will, probated in 1767, is in Fairfax County Will Book, B–1, 424–32, Vi Microfilm.

4. On the failure of both Keith and Simms to reply to GW's letters, see GW to Simms, 24 February. GW enclosed this letter to Keith in a letter to Simms, which was dated 28 Jan. and which reads: "Your Letter of the 15th instant came duly to hand. The enclosed will furnish Mr Keith with means to pay your account. I pray you to deliver, or cause it to be delivered by a safe hand" (LB, DLC:GW).

Henry Knox to Bartholomew Dandridge, Jr.

Dear Sir   War department January 29. 1794

Please to submit the papers herein enclosed to the President of the United States—Those marked with red Ink have been copied to be presented to Congress with the message to morrow[1]—The letter to General Pickens being a private letter seems upon further consideration not proper to be submitted[2]—Governor Blounts letter of the 27. December and the enclosures have not been copied they being considered as irrelative to the subject of the recent offences of our own people.[3] I am Dear Sir Your obedient Servant

H. Knox

LS, DLC:GW; LB, DLC:GW.

1. For the documents submitted to Congress, see n.2 of GW to U.S. Senate and House of Representatives, 30 January.

2. The letter to Andrew Pickens has not been identified.

3. William Blount's letter to Knox of 27 Dec. and its enclosures have not been identified.

From Edward Pemberton

London at Mr Pridden's No. 100 Fleet street[1]

May it please Your Excellency   Jany 29th 1794

As I heretofore took the liberty of an address to Your Excellency, and of adding thereto a small Poetical Composition, which so far won Your approbation, as to gain from Your Excellency a letter of Notice in return; I again presume to rely upon your generous Candour to forgive another address to Your Excellency tho at a long interval of time from the first.[2] herein I have no claim whatever to Your Excellency's attention. in Obedience to the call of Friendship I step forth in behalf of a Young Man, whom I much Value and esteem. Your Excellency has honourd me much in one instance already, and I venture again to break in upon those most precious Moments, which are dedicated solely to the Good of Your Country, and of Mankind. A Glorious Cause it is; and has supereminently flourishd under Your auspicious Exertions.

Loth I am to exceed the bounds of that Modesty, which I am conscious I ought upon this occasion to observe. if Friendship excites me to go beyond them, it is the best plea that I can bring. May it weigh with Your Excellency. May You deign to look upon an humble Suitor—a deserving and Spirited Young Man who with a Young Wife, and Children in her Arms, is about to brave the Billows of the Atlantic, in quest of a distant Country, which he finds Motives to prefer to his Own; and where, in these turbulent times Security and Peace promise most to be found. could this Young Man succeed to a small degree of favour from Your Excellency happy would he be. tho humble, with Merit he may plead with the Great. the truly Great will over look no One. My Friend has been bred up in the Mechanical line, but with some others of his Countrymen, who are to accompany him to the States where Your Excellency Presides, he is desirous if he can to embark in Agriculture. By his talents indeed, he may be adapted to different Occupations. his Name is Patrick, a friend and Neighbour of mine; a Native of Suffolk, an inhabitant of Long Melford near Sudbury in that County where he exercised the trade of a Watch maker, and a Silversmith. he Seeks for favour only by his Industry and Merit.[3] May he prosper in a foreign Clime. The Eyes of the Lord are over All. And may Heaven long preserve Your Excellency as a Pattern of what ever is good and great. this is the devout Prayer of Your Excellencys devoted and most Obedient Servant

Edwd: Pemberton

ALS, DLC:GW.

1. John Pridden, Sr. (1728–1807) was a bookseller at 100 Fleet Street in London. See Patrick Boyle, *The General London Guide; or, Tradesman's Directory for the Year 1794* (London, 1793), 24.

2. Pemberton enclosed poems in two previous letters. GW replied on 20 June 1788 to the letter of 21 March 1788, but no reply has been found to that of 11 July 1789.

3. No reply from GW to this letter has been found.

From Edmund Randolph

Wednesday morning [29 Jan. 1794]

E. Randolph has the honor of informing the President, that he saw Judge Wilson yesterday, and Mr Madison last evening. The former, to whom E.R. took an occasion of bringing up the subject of the resolution of the senate in a *general* Shape, said, that what they might have, he thought, ought to be sent; and what they ought not to have, ought not to be sent.[1]

The latter expressed himself thus: "I told Colo. Monroe,[2] as far as delicacy would permit, that there must be many things, which the President cannot communicate with propriety: that if he was to select such as he thought proper, and transmit them; and the senate were to make an opposition, the people would go with the President against the Senate". Mr M[a]d[iso]n—then dilated upon the other view of the case; the witholding of papers altogether. This he conceived to be utterly inadmissible; whether the principle, or the particular suspicion, which some persons entertain of the diplomatic character, be considered. The consequence, he did suppose would be, as has been already suggested to the President, that instead of a dispute with the Senate, the house of representatives would make common cause.[3]

AL, DLC:GW. GW's docket reads "29th Jan. 1794," which was a Wednesday.

1. The Senate resolution, which Randolph discussed with Supreme Court justice James Wilson and congressman James Madison, requested copies of Gouverneur Morris's official correspondence as U.S. minister plenipotentiary to France (U.S. Senate to GW, 24 Jan. 1794).

2. James Monroe currently was one of the senators from Virginia.

3. For Randolph's own opinion on the Senate resolution, see his letters to GW of 26 Jan. (second letter) and 2 February.

From Edmund Randolph

Wednesday [29 Jan. 1794]

E. Randolph has the honor of inclosing to the President a memorandum from Mr Taylor, accounting for the delay in the commissions, sent to him this morning.[1]

AL, DNA: RG 59, Miscellaneous Letters; LB, DLC:GW; LB, DNA: RG 59, GW's Correspondence with His Secretaries of State.

1. The enclosed memorandum of this date from George Taylor, Jr., the chief clerk at the State Department, reads: "The Commissions sent to the President to day have been delayed in consequence of the urgent Business of the office, and upon a presumption that no injury would result to the public, the whole of the persons having been commissioned in the recess—except one" (DNA: RG 59, Miscellaneous Letters). For a list of the commissions, dated 28 Jan., which GW subsequently signed on 30 Jan., see *JPP*, 280–81. For GW's nomination and the Senate's approval of these individuals, see GW to U.S. Senate, 27 Dec. 1793 and 2 Jan. 1794, and *U.S. Senate Executive Journal*, 1:143–44.

To the United States Senate

Gentlemen of the Senate,   United States 29. Jany 1794.

I nominate John Boyd, of Northumberland, to be Inspector of the Revenue for Survey No. 2 in the District of Pennsylvania; vice James Collins:[1] and

John Driver, of Virginia, to be Surveyor for the Port of Suffolk; and Inspector of the Revenue for the same port; vice Samuel Riddick; resigned.[2]

Go: Washington

LS, DNA: RG 46, Third Congress, 1793–95, Senate Records of Executive Proceedings, President's Messages—Executive Nominations; LB, DLC:GW.

1. John Boyd (1750–1832) was a veteran of the Revolutionary War and a member of the Society of the Cincinnati. After the war he returned to Northumberland County, where he married Rebecca Bull in 1794. Active in Pennsylvania politics prior to this appointment, Boyd was a member of the Supreme Executive Council, 1783–86; the state ratification convention, 1787; and the state legislature, 1790–92. He later served as register and recorder for Northumberland County, 1805–9.

2. John Driver (died c.1797) was a merchant in the town of Suffolk. Riddick's correct first name is Lemuel (Josiah Parker to GW, 19 Dec. 1791, n.2). The U.S. Senate approved both appointments on 30 Jan. (*U.S. Senate Executive Journal*, 1:148).

From Henry Knox

Sir,   War department January 30th 1794

I submit to your Consideration a letter proposed to be written to the Governor of South Carolina in consequence of a private letter received by Mr John Ross of this Town of which the enclosed is an extract.[1]

The Secretaries of State and Treasury approved the draft now submitted.[2] I have the honor to be with perfect respect Your obedient Servant

H. Knox

LS, DLC:GW; LB, DLC:GW.

1. Knox's letter to William Moultrie of this date, which has not been identified, was "on the subject of fitting armed vessels & enlisting men" in South Carolina (*JPP*, 282). Neither the letter sent to Philadelphia merchant John Ross nor its extract has been identified.

2. GW approved the draft and returned it to Knox on this same date (*JPP*, 282).

From William Patterson et al.

Sir   Baltimore 30th Jany 1794

A Memorial in behalf of the distressed Emigrants from the Island of St Domingo now in this Town having been presented to
Congress early in the Session and some Member's of that Body
doubting their Powers to grant them relief, We beg leave to call
the Attention of the Executive to these unhappy Sufferers, Who
without some Aid from the United States must soon perish in
the Streets of Baltimore, every source of assistance here being
so entirely exhausted as to render all hope of future Contributions from our Citizens not only unreasonable but vain[.][1] These
People to the number of upwards of three thousand including
the fleet which brought them here driven from St Domingo by
the Savage Barbarity of the People of Colour arrived in this
Town in July last destitute of every Necessary of Life and of the
means to procure them[.] Tho' so great and Sudden an Accession of numbers to this place immediately affected our Markets
to a great degree the Citizens of Baltimore subscribed and paid
more than Twelve thousand Dollars in Money for the Relief of
these Unhappy Sufferers beside making large Contributions
in Cloaths and other specific Articles[.][2] The People from the
Country contributed upwards of Five thousand Dollars, And at
their last Session the Legislature of this State granted them a
further Aid of Four thousand five hundred Dollars as a Temporary relief till Congress could take order in the business[.] These
several Funds tho' distributed with the strictest Oeconomy are
exhausted and there are now between four and five hundred
of the distressed Emigrants from St Domingo consisting of Old
Men Women and Children most of them a few Months since
in the highest Affluence who are destitute of every necessary
of Life and who must in a very few Days become the Victims of
Cold and Hunger unless Aid can be had from the Congress or
the Executive: Such Scenes in a Country overflowing with Plenty
appear to us too disgraceful to Humanity, to Christian Charity
and to the National Character to be permitted to be realized
within the Limits of the United States.

We claim no Merit for the little we have done but sincerely
Lament that our Powers will permit us to do no more, else Congress and the Executive would have been saved the trouble of
this Application[.] No longer able to avert a Calamity disgrace-

ful to Humanity we conceive ourselves bound to lay before the President of the United States the dreadful Scenes about to take place that the Power's of Gover'nment may be exerted to prevent them,[3] and that we may be hereafter saved the painful Sensations of having been Silent Spectators of Scenes of Misery which timely Exertions on our parts might have been prevented.[4] We are with great Respect Sir Your Most Obedt Servts

Wm Patterson	Gusts Scott
Samuel Sterett	James Buchanan
Jas Calhoun	W: Smith
Robert Oliver	David Harris
David Stewart	Rd Smith
Robt Gilmor	Z. Hollingsworth
Archd. Campbell	David McMechen
John Hollins	Samuel Chase
John Smith Junr	Wm. Paca
James Somerville	O.H. Williams
Her[cule]s Courtenay	Heny Nicols

LS, DNA: RG 59, Miscellaneous Letters.

1. In November 1793, the Maryland legislature appointed a committee, consisting of William Patterson, Samuel Sterett, and Gustavus Scott, that was authorized to make a weekly drawing of $500 from 1 Dec. 1793 until 2 Feb. 1794, "for the subsistence of the distressed French citizens now in this state, from Saint-Domingo (*Md. Laws 1793*, resolutions). On 1 Jan., a memorial from this same committee was presented to the House of Representatives "and read, stating that their funds are nearly exhausted, and praying the relief and aid of Congress in the premises." Subsequent debate on this memorial took place in the House on 10 Jan., after which the report was sent to committee (*Annals of Congress*, 3d Cong., 153, 169–73).

2. On the establishment of a Baltimore relief committee in the summer of 1793, see Scharf, *Chronicles of Baltimore*, 266.

3. "An Act providing for the relief of such of the inhabitants of Saint Domingo, resident within the United States, as may be found in want of support," 12 Feb. 1794, provided "a sum not exceeding fifteen thousand dollars," to be distributed, "under the direction of the President," to those states affected by the surge of refugees who fled to the United States in 1793 to escape the civil war in this French colony (*Stat.* 6:13). On the distribution of these federal funds, see Edmund Randolph to GW, 27 Feb. (first and second letters).

4. This letter to GW was enclosed in a signed letter of this date from Patterson, Scott, and Sterett that was addressed to "The Representatives of Maryland In Congress" and that reads: "We beg leave to thank you for your Public Exertions in behalf of the distressed French Emigrants here[.] Enclosed is a Letter in their behalf meant to be laid before the Executive[.] What success it may have we are at a loss to say but if no Relief is obtained we think exhausted

as this Town may be by the unequal Burthens laid upon it we shall yet be able to raise a sufficient sum to transport the distressed French to the City of Philadelphia where we hope the Scenes of Distress so long exhibited here and so often in vain represented to the General Government will execute their Compassion more Strongly than we have been able to do" (DNA: RG 59, Miscellaneous Letters).

From Robert Taylor

Dear Sir   Norfolk [Va.] January 30th 1794

I was favoured with two letters from you under date of the 10th and 17th December containing information necessary for the Trade of this Town to be acquainted with.[1] I have delayed replying to them till I had something new to communicate or untill some matter came before Congress in which we were particularly interested. In the Debates of Congress on a Petition from Baltimore relative to the ill fated French that have found refuge amongst us we note the part you have taken respecting those at Norfolk and for which allow me to return you the thanks of the Inhabitan⟨ts⟩ of this Town and in which be pleased to include mine.[2]

It has been insinuated by a Member that as no Application has been made from this Place that he concludes that the relief afforded by the Assembly of Virginia must by supposed sufficient for the purpose, without wishing to combat with this Argument, I take leave to inform you that an Application was made from this Town for Cloathing during the Winter and for a support for these unfortunate People till the first of April only,[3] by which time we supposed the French Government would do something for their support or that they themselves by getting acquainted with the Language, & with modes of acquiring subsistance be enabled to do without the aid of the Country[.] this estimate as well as every other Paper relative to it if you think it necessary I will take care to forward to you, but you will first let me here observe that the Commissioners in estimating the sum necessary for their support included six hundred pounds expected from some of the Counties of Virginia exclusive of the Publick Bounty, this sum has not as yet come forward and I greatly fear from the supposition of its not being necessary will not. tho' I am still in hopes the sum the County has so liberally Voted for their relief will be sufficient to carry them forward to the first of April after which I am totally at a loss to know how they are to subsist for it cannot be supposed that this Town is equal to the support of two hundred and fifty five Poor exclusive of the Parish Poor[4]—all those that have arrived here from Cape Francois or elsewhere that had any property went to Baltimore and consequently only those that were really Poor and not able to go any further were left with us[.] of this truth I became a melancholly Eye witness[.] to enable the Commissioneres here to send forward to the Assembly such a statement as required it became necessary to see every individual[.] I had therefore the disagreable task to visit the Houses and to question these truly distressed respecting their Age, Situation, and Abillity of providing for themselves and I can therefore with confidence say if Childhood, Old Age, Infirmity, Poverty, and the heart rending thought of what they were and what they now are form Objects of Charity and commiseration I hope Congress nor no other Public Body will ever again have it in their power to exert their Benevolence and Compassion to a set of People so deserving of it all, While I am writing it may be perhaps not unnecessary to remind you that by our Act of Assembly no Master of a Ship or other Person can bring any pauper or Persons lyable to be burthensome to the Parish, without either giving security for their maintenance or be subject to a Penalty of twenty pounds for every person so landed or brought into the Parish and that although this Law has not been put in execution against the Masters of the French Ships, yet as it cannot be denied that the Ships belonging to the Republic of France brought them in distressed Citizens and landed them here without taking the necessary steps for their support[5] I should conceive that in Justice as well as Law that Nation ought out of the funds they have in the hands of Congress at least pay a small sum to this purpose. I hint this to you, it is in good hands who I know will make the most of it.[6]

The French Ships, Normand, and Ambuscade, are lying here as well as the British Ship Dædalus, and I am happy to say that we have as yet experienced no inconveniency from either, and I trust will not as the Officers of all seem desirous to keep the Peace, on the Water; and it is our Interest to make them if we had the power so to do on Land.[7] I am respectfully Dear Sir

Robert Taylor

ALS, DNA: RG 59, Miscellaneous Letters.

1. The letters of 10 and 17 Dec. 1793 from GW to Robert Taylor, the current mayor of Norfolk, have not been found.

2. On the memorial from Maryland, the debate in Congress respecting the granting of federal assistance to French refugees within the United States, and the relief act passed by Congress in February, see William Patterson et al. to GW, this date, and notes 1 and 3 to that document.

3. In "An ACT for the relief of the emigrants from Saint Domingo," 8 Nov. 1793, the Virginia assembly authorized the governor to "draw out of the public treasury a sum of money not exceeding two thousand pounds" (*Va. Statutes, 1792–1806,* 1:273–74). For an earlier grant of $2,000 specifically for the refugees in Norfolk, see Taylor's letter to Virginia governor Henry Lee of 13 July 1793. The application for winter clothing has not been found, but on 17 Jan. 1794, Taylor wrote Lee to acknowledge receipt in December of the $2,000 grant. He informed the governor that this sum was "exhausted" and that there was a "need" for "any further sum" that could be obtained (*Calendar of Virginia State Papers,* 6:447, 7:12–13).

4. Lists of approximately 250 French refugees at Norfolk can be found in DNA: RG 59, Miscellaneous Letters, filed at the end of 1794.

5. Taylor may be referring to section 9 of "An ACT reducing into one, the several acts for unlading ballast, and burial of dead bodies from on board ships; and prohibiting the putting sick or disabled seamen and servants on shore, without providing for their maintenance, 23 Dec. 1792 (*Va. Statutes, 1792–1806,* 1:145–47). On the arrival in Norfolk of large numbers of refugees from the French colony of Saint Domingue in July 1793, see Thomas Newton, Jr., to Lee, 6 July 1793 (*Calendar of Virginia State Papers,* 6:437).

6. This reference probably is to the administration's earlier decision to allocate a portion of the U.S. payment on its debt to France for use by French officials to purchase provisions for the French colony of Saint Domingue (Hamilton to GW, 19 Nov. 1792).

7. The French ships *Embuscade,* a privateer, and *Normande,* an East Indiaman, left Norfolk in February (*Daily Advertiser* [New York], 8 March 1794; Taylor to Lee, 10 Feb. 1794, *Calendar of Virginia State Papers,* 7:28–29). The British frigate *Dædalus,* under Sir Charles Henry Knowles (1754–1831) and armed with "32 guns," left Norfolk in May (Taylor to Lee, 23 March, *Calendar of Virginia State Papers,* 7:75; *Mirrour* [Concord, N.H.], 16 June 1794).

To the United States Senate
and House of Representatives

United States. Jany 30. 1794.

Gentlemen of the Senate, and of the House of Representatives

Communications have been made to Congress, during the present Session, with the intention of affording a full view of the posture of affairs on the south western frontiers. By the information, which has lately been laid before Congress, it appeared, that the difficulties with the Creeks had been amicably and happily terminated.[1] But it will be perceived, with regret, by the papers herewith transmitted, that the tranquility has unfortunately been of short duration, owing to the murder of several friendly Indians by some lawless white men.[2]

The condition of things, in that quarter, requires the serious & immediate consideration of Congress; and the adoption of such wise and vigorous laws, as will be competent to the preservation of the national character, and of the peace, made under the authority of the United States, with the several Indian tribes. Experience demonstrates that the existing legal provisions are entirely inadequate to those great objects.[3]

Go: Washington.

LB, DNA: RG 233, Third Congress, 1793–95, House Records of Legislative Proceedings, Journals; LB, DLC:GW.

1. For previous correspondence submitted to the first session of the Third Congress, see the enclosures to Knox's letters to the U.S. Senate of 16 and 18 Dec. 1793 and 22 Jan. 1794 (*ASP, Indian Affairs*, 1:361–472).

2. For the several papers enclosed with this message, which recounted recent unwarranted attacks on Cherokee and Creek Indians, see *ASP, Indian Affairs*, 1:472–75.

3. Existing legislation consisted of "An Act to regulate Trade and Intercourse with the Indian Tribes," 1 March 1793. Congress did not establish additional federal regulations until passage of "An Act for establishing Trading Houses with the Indian Tribes," 18 April 1796, and "An Act to regulate Trade and Intercourse with the Indian Tribes, and to preserve Peace on the Frontiers," 19 May 1796 (*Stat.* 1:329–32, 452–53, 469–74).

From David Humphreys

(Secret & Confidential)

My Dear Sir.   Lisbon Janry 31st 1794

Immediately after my return from Spain, I asked an audience of Mr Pinto the Secretary of State for foreign affairs for the purpose of learning decisively, whether the Truce between Portugal & Algiers was likely to be improved into a Peace, or not.[1] Yesterday I waited upon him, and, with as much delicacy as I was master of endeavoured to give an opening for him to explain himself on the subject, which he did nearly to the following effect.

He began by saying, that, with the candour he had always professed to me, he had no difficulty in explaining the whole rise & progress of the transactions between Portugal and Algiers to this time. That, although Portugal is not engaged at all in the war with France, yet it is obliged by Treaty to furnish Contingents to England & Spain on the occasion of their being attacked[2]— this event having happened, Portugal found it convenient to be disembarrassed of her Enemy in the Mediterranean in order to withdraw her fleet from Gibralter & employ her ⟨m⟩arine force elsewhere, without augmenting the expences of Government; that therefore through the British Minister at this Court[3] the British Consul at Algiers had been desired to sound the Regency on the subject of a Peace; that a consequent report having been made from Algiers that the Dey demanded four or five millions of Cruzadoes for a Peace (which being entirely contrary to the system of Portugal) the affair was given up; but that a short time afterwards, without any previous informations or instructions the said British Consul concluded a Truce on the part of Portugal for one year, even without the knowledge & contrary to the wishes of this Court; that, the affair being thus situated, different communications have been made, and that this Court has lately insisted upon a catagorical answer to the Alternative, either, that the Truce shall be annulled, or a Peace take Place upon perfectly equal terms, according to the original system of Portugal.

Mr Pinto mentioned, that the following in substance are a part of the conditions peremptorily insisted upon by Portugal, viz., no money whatever shall be paid to the Government of Algiers for a Peace by way of tribute or presents; and, in case of a Peace, three months shall be allowed for Portugal to give information of it to all commercial nations with which it is connected before the fleet of Algiers shall be permitted to come into the Atlantic. Besides this, no vessels coming to or going from Portugal, or others within a certain limited distance from its coasts, shall ever be captured by the Corsairs: or in case of capture, shall be restored; the Captors paying the damages of detention.

The Dey has also been informed, that until these terms shall be agreed upon, the Portuguese Government will use means to protect all vessels trading to that Kingdom.

No one can hesitate to conclude that these terms (which are entirely comformable to what the same minister had formerly declared to me) will be rejected by the Dey. In which case, the Minister of State observed, it will be necessary for Portugal to maintain even a larger force than usual at Gibralter: because the Algerines being piqued at the conduct of Portugal would undoubtedly endeavour to seek revenge by force or surprize and possibly to find their way into the Atlantic at all events. He added that this would occasion a heavy expence to be borne by Portugal alone, while other nations (particularly the U.S. of America) were likely to benefit equally by it: since it would not only be to protect their commerce to Portugal, but even to some parts of Spain. At the same time he intimated, it would apparently be but just, that those nations which were benefitted by the measure, should by subsidy or in some way or another bear a part of the burden, as the Hanse Towns seemed well disposed to do. I replied, that I could say nothing, from authority, but that perhaps the events which had recently happened might tend to accelerate the period at which something of a marine must be created by the U.S.,[4] in which case the U.S. would doubtless be glad to co-operate with any Powers which might have the same enemy to combat, & the same objects in view; but that, in my judgment, the U.S. were rather in a natural state to be subsidized than to subsidy others, having more materials & men, than Money. He rejoined that, dropping the ideas of subsidy, it would undoubtedly be desirable for any Nations having a common enemy to act in concert. He expressed his opinion very unequivocally that the Truce would be broken off, though the Dey had hinted with much finesse, that the original demands would be greatly abated, and that he was seriously disposed to give a preference to Portugal over Holland & the U.S. of A.—both of which had at that moment proffered him immensely large sums of money for a Peace.[5] Mr Pinto however finished by assuring me that Portugal would give no money at all (except for the redemption of its Subjects now Slaves in Algiers). He promised also that he would let me know the result as soon as the Messenger last dispatched to Algiers shall return.

I thought it my duty to acquaint you with the substance of the conversation on the part of Mr Pinto, as nearly as I could comprehend & recollect it. You will perceive thereby that my original conjectures were not ill founded.

I had already (while in Madrid) endeavored to sound some of the Ministers of the neutral Powers, which have been menaced by a rupture with Algiers; but I found them not ripe for any thing. I took likewise the Liberty (as private person merely) of submitting the enclosed three Quæries to the Minister of Genoa in Madrid. To the first & second he did not hesitate to answer in the affirmative. To the third he found himself incompetent to give any opinion, but said that he would take measures for gaining information.[6]

Having no time to lose before the sailing of the vessel which is to carry this letter,[7] I hasten to subscribe myself, with offering my affectionate remembrances to all around you, My dear most respected Sir, Your most affectionate & most devoted Servant

D. Humphreys.

ALS, DLC:GW.

1. On the purpose of Humphreys' recent visit to Spain, see his letter to GW of 23 Nov. 1793. Humphreys met with Luís Pinto de Sousa Coutinho, viscount of Balsemão. Because the British government was eager to solicit the assistance of the Portuguese navy in its war with France, it attempted to procure a truce between Portugal and Algiers. To this end, the British consul at Algiers, Charles Logie, informed the dey of Algiers that Portugal was willing to pay a large tribute, and on 12 Sept. 1793, the dey consented to a twelve-month truce. This truce, however, was contrary to American interests because Portugal's previous naval blockade of the Straits of Gibraltar, which was designed to protect Portugal's commerce with its colony of Brazil, also protected America's merchant ships from Algerine attacks. Portugal later concluded that the cost was excessive, and it repudiated the truce and reestablished the blockade (Parker, *Uncle Sam in Barbary*, 75–79, 227–29).

2. France declared war against Great Britain on 1 Feb. 1793 and against Spain on 7 March 1793. Portugal signed a Provisional Convention with Spain on 15 July and a Treaty of Alliance and Reciprocal Assistance with Great Britain on 26 Sept. 1793 (Parry, *Consolidated Treaty Series*, 52:97–106, 147–56).

3. Robert Walpole (1736–1810) served as envoy extraordinary and minister plenipotentiary to Portugal from 1772 to 1800.

4. For the creation of an American navy, starting with four ships of forty-four guns and two ships of thirty-six guns, see "An Act to provide a Naval Armament," 27 March 1794 (*Stat.* 1:350).

5. On the willingness of the United States to pay $40,000 for the release of the American captives held in Algiers and a $25,000 annuity to Algiers if a peace treaty was accepted by that nation, see GW to U.S. Senate, 8 May

1792 (third letter), and n.2 to that document. See also the detailed diplomatic instructions given by Thomas Jefferson to John Paul Jones in a letter of 1 June 1792 (*Jefferson Papers*, 24:3–10). For Senate approval of this proposed expenditure, see *ASP, Foreign Relations*, 1:290. In the Treaty of Peace, Friendship and Commerce with Algiers of 5 Sept. 1795, the United States agreed to pay the value of $21,600 in "Maritime Stores" to the dey of Algiers (Parry, *Consolidated Treaty Series*, 52:461–68).

6. Pietro Paolo Celesia (1731–1806) served as Genoa's minister plenipotentiary to Spain from 1784 until 1797. The enclosed list of questions, labeled "secret & Confidential," reads: "1st In case the U.S. should send an armed force to the Mediterranean, may they rely upon its being received with friendship & hospitality at Genoa? 2nd Will Genoa combine any naval force, & what, with any Powers that might be disposed to act in concert, in repelling the hostile attacks of Algiers? 3d Whether, in case Genoa shall find it difficult or inconvenient to encrease its Marine, of sudden sufficiently to protect its Trade completely against the Algerines, it would take into its pay Ships of the U.S. or give a subsidy for enabling them to block the Corsairs in their harbours, & to what amount?" (DLC:GW).

7. Contrary to Humphreys' expectation, the ship did not sail on this date. For its departure and GW's receipt of this letter in early April, see Humphreys to GW, 3 February, and n.1 to that document.

Samuel A. Otis, Sr.,
to Bartholomew Dandridge, Jr.

Sir   In Senate of the United States. Jany 31st 1794.

There is a standing order of Senate that I lay before the President of the United States, from time to time, a copy of their records, when acting in their Executive capacity. This I have done to the close of the last session, and left the book in which the proceedings are copied with the President of the U. States, which if you will procure to be returned by the bearer, I will continue the copy.[1] I am Sir your most humble Sert

Sam. A. Otis Secy

LS, DNA: RG 59, Miscellaneous Letters.

1. The second session of the Second Congress, 1791–93, ended on 2 March 1793, but the Senate convened for a special one-day session on 4 March. For a printed version of the records kept by Otis, see *U.S. Senate Executive Journal*, Vol. 1.

From Edmund Randolph

sir, Philadelphia January 31. 1794.

I do myself the honor of informing you, that the executive proceedings of the territory South of the river Ohio, from the 1st of march 1793 to the 15. of June 1793, contain nothing of any importance.[1] I have the honor to be with sentiments of the highest respect, Sir, your most obedient & very humble servant

Edm: Randolph.

LS, DNA: RG 59, Miscellaneous Letters; LB, DLC:GW; LB, DNA: RG 59, GW's Correspondence with His Secretaries of State; LB, DNA: RG 59, Domestic Letters.

1. The "Journal of the Proceedings of William Blount Governor in and over the territory of the United States of America south of the river Ohio, in his executive department," 1 March–15 June 1793, is printed in Carter, *Territorial Papers*, 4:453–57.

From Richard Dobbs Spaight

Sir North Carolina New Bern 31st Jan: 1794

Since I wrote to you on the 19th Decem: last application having been made to me by Capt: James Robertson the former master of the Sloop Providence of Montego bay (now called L'amee Margueritte) which was captured in June last by the Vanqueur de Bastille to cause the said sloop to be restored to him upon a principle of her having been captured within the distance of three miles from the coast and being at the same time informed that she then lay at Wilmington.[1] I issued orders on the 3rd inst. to Colo. Thomas Wright to seize her and detain her untill such time as the necessary testimony should be taken to ascertain the facts and that he should order out a militia guard to secure her,[2] at the same time I wrote to Mr Hill the Attorney of the United States for this district to notify him of the orders I had given, and requesting him to proceed to the examination of the Witnesses in this case, to have them taken in writing properly authenticated and forwarded to me and for his information enclosed him a copy of the Secretary of Wars letter to me on that subject.[3]

I have since received letters from Colo. Wright informing me that he had seized and secured the sloop on the 10th instant and also that on the 24th no examination of Witnesses had taken place I have had no reply from the attorney to my letter.[4]

By the last Southern post I received a letter dated the 19th Decem. from the British vice Consul at Charleston respecting the said Sloop claiming her as the property of the Subjects of his Britannic Majesty upon the principle of her having been taken by a proscribed vessel subsequent to the 7th June last and requesting that I should take measures to have her secured in order to be restored to her former owners. a copy of this letter I enclose you.[5]

In consequence of the above letter I shall cause the vessel to be securely kept till I receive your decision thereon; the fact of the L'amee Margueritte & the Sloop Providence being the same and of her having been captured after the 7th day of June last by the Vanqueur de Bastille is not in the least doubted, the agent for the French Consul at Wilmington and the party who took her acknowledging it.[6]

On this subject my letter of the 19th Dec: was principally written as there was a difference of two months between the period fixed by Mr Knoxs letter of august and that of novem: last.[7] To my letter I have not as yet received any answer.[8] I have the honor to be &c.

R. D. Spaight

LB, Nc-Ar: Governors' Letterbooks.

1. On the capture of the British sloop *Providence,* of Montego Bay, Jamaica, and its subsequent outfitting as the French privateer *Aimée Marguerite,* see Spaight to GW, 24 June 1793.

2. Thomas Wright was the sheriff of New Hanover County, in which the port city of Wilmington is located. The orders from Spaight to Wright of 3 Jan. to use the local militia to seize and secure the *Aimée Marguerite* were prompted by an "Application having been made to me to restore the sloop providence . . . to her former owners, upon allegation that the said Sloop was taken within three miles of the coast of the United States and consequently within their protection." The sloop was to be held "untill such time as the fact respecting her being captured within the protection of the United States shall be fully investigated and reported to me and a decision had thereon" (Nc-Ar: Governors' Letterbooks).

3. In a letter of 3 Jan., Spaight notified William Henry Hill, the current U.S. district attorney for North Carolina, of the orders given to Wright. He also informed Hill that "the president considers the examination" of witnesses to the capture of the *Aimée Marguerite* "as a duty which at present ought to be performed by you." Spaight instructed Hill "so soon as Major Wright shall have secured the vessel, to give proper and sufficient notice to the par-

ties and to proceed and take the testimony offered by both of the parties in support of their respective claims." Such testimony "must be reduced to writing sworn to and properly authenticated and then forwarded to me" (Nc-Ar: Governors' Letterbooks). The enclosure was Knox's letter to Spaight of 12 Nov. 1793 (see n.1 of Spaight to GW, 19 Dec. 1793).

4. Wright reported in a letter to Spaight of 11 Jan. that he had successfully seized control of the *Aimée Marguerite*. In a letter of 24 Jan., Wright wrote that he had approached Hill with Spaight's request to gather testimony "without delay." From Hill's answer, however, "it appears the decision is either by arbiters appointed by the parties concerned or the President of the United States, therefore have to request further information from your Excellency on the subject" (both letters, Nc-Ar: Governors' Letterbooks).

5. James Shoolbred (c.1766–1847) was the British vice-consul for North Carolina, South Carolina, and Georgia. He wrote to Spaight from Charleston, S.C., on 19 Dec. 1793 to protest the capture of the *Aimée Marguerite*, noting that its captor, the *Vainqueur de la Bastille*, was "specially proscribed" in Alexander Hamilton's circular letter of 4 Aug. 1793 to the collectors of customs as a vessel " 'to whom as originally fitted out in a port of the United States no asylum henceforth should be given in any district of them.' " He added that George Hammond, the British minister to the United States, had "authorized me to assure all interested, that the Government of America had engaged to restore all prizes captured subsequently to the 7th June by any privateer fitted out in a port of the United States." Shoolbred then requested "that such measures as your Excellency may deem expedient may be forthwith adopted to restore her to her rightfull owners" (Nc-Ar: Governors' Letterbooks). For Hamilton's circular letter, see *Hamilton Papers*, 15:178–81. On the U.S. policy excluding the *Vainqueur de la Bastille* and other privateers armed in the United States from American ports, see the cabinet opinions on French privateers of 1 June and 3 and 5 Aug. 1793.

6. J. B. Brouard was the vice-consul at Wilmington, and François-Henri Hervieux was captain of the *Vainqueur de la Bastille*.

7. For Knox's circular letter of 16 Aug. to the governors of the maritime states, see n.1 of Knox to Tobias Lear, 17 Aug. 1793. On the discrepancy between the letters of 16 Aug. and 12 Nov. that bothered Spaight, see Spaight to GW, 19 Dec. 1793, and n.7.

8. Spaight acknowledged receipt of Henry Knox's reply of 13 Jan., which was written at GW's direction, in his second letter to GW of 8 February. GW sent Spaight's letter of this date to Knox on 17 Feb., instructing him "to take such steps in the case as might appear proper" (*JPP*, 285). Knox subsequently sent further instructions to Spaight in a letter of 22 Feb. (Knox to Bartholomew Dandridge, Jr., 22 Feb., and n.1 to that document).

From Jeremiah Wadsworth

Sir   [Philadelphia] Jan. 31 1794
  I am requested by several of my friends to name the Revd Daniel Storey as Chaplin to the Army[1]—Col. Meigs by a letter says he is a Man of real learning & Religion has been the Minister at Marietta for a long time That since the Indian War they have not been able to give any reward for his labor. Col. Meigs is a Man of real piety and would not r[e]commend Mr Storey if he was not so.[2] I have the honor to be with great respect Your Excellencys most obt Hum. Serv.

                                                  Jere. Wadsworth

ALS, DLC:GW.
  1. Connecticut congressman Jeremiah Wadsworth was in Philadelphia to attend the first session of the Third Congress. Daniel Story (Storey; 1756–1804), a native of Boston, Mass., graduated from Dartmouth College in 1780. After serving as pastor to several New England churches, he was hired in late 1788 by the Ohio Company to preach the gospel to residents of Marietta, Ohio, and nearby towns in the Northwest Territory. He arrived at Marietta in the Spring of 1789 and remained an employee of the company until 1796. He served as the minister of the newly organized Congregational Church at Marietta from 1798 until shortly before his death (Thomas Jefferson Summers, *History of Marietta* [Marietta, 1903], 198–202). For the resignation of John Hurt, the current chaplain for the U.S. troops in the Northwest Territory, see Hurt to GW, 12 April 1794. GW nominated David Jones to replace Hurt (GW to U.S. Senate, 12 May 1794).
  2. Col. Return Jonathan Meigs, Sr. (1740–1823) was a native of Middletown, Conn., and a veteran of the Revolutionary War. Receiving an appointment as a surveyor for the Ohio Company in 1787, he settled in Ohio the following year. He later served as an Indian agent to the Cherokee Indians, 1801–23. Meigs County, Tenn., is named for him. His letter to Wadsworth has not been identified.

From William Bradford

                                    [Philadelphia, January 1794]
  The Attorney General has the honour to report, That having considered the Resolve of the Senate of the 24th instant whereby the President of the United States is requested to lay before that body the correspondence which has been had between the minister of the United States at the French Republic and the said

Republic and between said Minister and the office of Secretary of State[1]—

He is of opinion, that it is the duty of the Executive to withhold such parts of the said correspondence as in the judgment of the Executive shall be deemed unsafe and improper to be disclosed. He also conceives that the *general* terms of the resolve do not exclude, in the construction of it, those just exceptions which the rights of the executive and the nature of foreign correspondences require. Every call of this nature, where the correspondence is secret and no specific object pointed at, must be presumed to proceed upon the idea, that the papers requested are proper to be communicated; & it could scarcely be supposed, even if the words were stronger, that the Senate intended to include any Letters, the disclosure of which might endanger national honour or individual safety.

The Attorney General is therefore of opinion, That it will be advisable for the President to communicate to the Senate such parts of the said Correspondence as upon examination he shall deem safe & proper to disclose: withholding all such, as any circumstances, may render improper to be communicated.[2]

Wm Bradford

ALS, DLC:GW. GW's docket reads: "Bradford's Opinion respecting the Resolve of the Senate requesting the President to lay before them the Correspondence betwn the Governmt of the U.S. and our Minister in France[.] no date."

1. For the resolution concerning the diplomatic correspondence of Gouverneur Morris, see U.S. Senate to GW, 24 January.

2. For GW's response to the Senate's request of 24 Jan., see GW to U.S. Senate, 26 February.

Notes on Spurrier's Rotation of Crops

[Philadelphia, circa January 1794][1]
Spurriers—Rotation of—Crops.

1st As soon as harvest is done, plow in the Stubble, & lay it up in one bout ridges, to remain in that rough state till the Spring following; then, as soon as the weather will permit, give it a good harrowing; in May obliquely plow it; the latter end of

June give it another good harrowing; then haul on the Manure, spread, & plow it in, Sow Turnip seed, broad cast, every day what is plowed. These Turnips to be fed off.

2d   The following spring, give th⟨i⟩s field two plowings, the first as shallow as possible, the secd obliquely deeper, which will turn up the Sheeps dung: Then harrow it as flat as possible, to lay it even, fit for mowing. Sow spring Barley pretty thick in drills, at a foot distance in the rows, 6 pecks to the acre; & clover broad cast 6 lbs., with 4 lbs. of trefoil to the acre, harrowed in at once, with light harrows. The grass that grows after harvest to be left, to keep the roots warm in winter. In the succeeding spring sow ashes, & roll the field. Take two crops of Hay.

3d   As soon as the last Crop of Hay is taken off, give one deep plowing, and sow wheat in drills, at one foot distance (one bushel of Seed to the acre)—The beginning of May following hoe with a running hoe, & pull the weeds out of the rows.

4th   Immediately after harvest plow in this Wheat stubble; and let it remain in a rough state the Winter. In the spring early, harrow it, give it a deep plowing, & sow Oats in broad cast (2 bushls to the Acre). In May weed them. This compleats the rotation, & the field is ready to begin with fallowing & manuring again; which will continually keep the land improving, instead of impoverishing; and as it is 5 years going through its regular succession the land under tillage, should be divided into 5 parts—for instance, there will be one fallowed every year, one under grass, one under Barley, one under Wheat, and one under Oats.[2] viz.

No. of the field	1794	1795	1796	1797	1798
1	Fallow with Turnips	Sprg Barl. & Clover	Clover	Wheat	Oats
2	Oats	Fallow with Turnips	Sprg Barl. & Clover	Clover	Wheat
3	Wheat	Oats	Fallow with Turnips	Sprg Barl. & Clover	Clover
4	Clover	Wheat	Oats	Fallow with Turnips	Sprg Bar. & Clover
5	Spr: Bar. & Clover	Clover	Wheat	Oats	Fallow with Clover

Culture for the above accordg to Mr Spurrier

		Fall 1793	Wintr	Mar.	Aprl	May	June	July	Augt	Sep.	Total
Fallow & Turnips 1794	Plowing stubble	100									100
	1 Bout ridges										50
	Spring—1st plow					75					75
	Summer						75				75
Barley & Clover 1795	1st Plowing			100							100
	2 Ditto				75						75
Clover 1796											
Wheat 1797	1 Plowing								100		100
Oats 1798	1st Ditto							100			100
	2 Do			100							100
		100		200	75	75	75	100	100		775

Probable (annual) produce of the foregoing Rotation of Crops

acres

75.	In fallow & Turnips, the latter uncertain				
75.	Barley—& Clover	@15 Bls	1125 B.	@3/6	£197. 7.6[3]
75.	Clover	uncertain			
75	Wheat	10	750	5/	187.10.0
75.	Oats	12½	937½	2/	93.15
					478:12.6

AD, DLC:GW.

1. GW's notes are based on John Spurrier, *The Practical Farmer: being a new and compendious system of husbandry, adapted to the different soils and climates of America. Containing the mechanical, chemical and philosophical elements of agriculture. With many other useful and interesting subjects* (Wilmington, Del., 1793). Although the book was advertised as "Just Published" in 1793, it was not until 7 Jan. 1794 that an advertisement announced that "The Subscribers' Books are ready to be delivered to them in boards at one dollar each, at the respective places where they subscribed their names" (*Dunlap's Daily American Advertiser* [Philadelphia], 24 Aug. 1793; *Philadelphia Gazette and Universal Daily Advertiser,* 7 Jan. 1794). GW's name is listed among the subscribers, and a copy was in his library (Spurrier, *Practical Farmer,* x; Griffin, *Catalogue of the Washington Collection,* 192).

2. These four paragraphs are based on text found on pages 94–99 of Spurrier's book.

3. This number should be £196.17.6, thus making the total £478.2.6.

From Laurence Muse

Sir   Virginia, Port Tappahannock February 1. 179[4]

Being under apprehensions of a new appointments taking place in the Collectors Office for this Port, I take the liberty of advising you that I am a candidate for that office.[1] I should have made personal application for that appointment but my engagements here will not admit of my absence.[2] I trust therefore that no objection will be made on that account. Ever since the establishment of the Offices, under the present Government, I have ⟨*mutilated*⟩ employed therein and have made it ⟨*mutilated*⟩ obtain a knowledge of the business ⟨*mutilated*⟩ myself that now I am enabled, not only ⟨*mutilated*⟩ Satisfaction to individuals but to attend ⟨*mutilated*⟩ interest of the public.—Give me leave to refer you to the Secretary of the Treasury for some information of my Capability—And if I am fortunate to get the appointment rely the trust reposed in me Shall not be abused.[3] I am Sir with much Respect Your very obt & Humle Servt

Laurence Muse

ALS, DLC:GW.

1. Laurence Muse presently was the deputy collector of customs for the District of Tappahannock. The current collector was his kinsman Hudson Muse, whose mismanagement led to his removal from office in March (Hudson Muse to GW, 27 Jan.). Laurence later served as the first secretary of the Tappahannock Jockey Club, which was established in 1796, and as justice of the peace for Essex County, Virginia. He was removed from the collector's office in 1811 (Vincent Bramham to James Madison, 28 Jan. 1811, and n.2 to that document, *Madison Papers, Presidential Series,* 3:136–37). For a list of Laurence Muse's extensive business and personal land holdings in Virginia and the Federal City, which were for sale in 1808, see his advertisement in the 19 Feb. 1808 issue of *The Enquirer* (Richmond, Va.).

2. For other letters of recommendation sent to GW on Laurence Muse's behalf, see Madison to GW, 12 Feb., and n.2; Richard Henry Lee to GW, 8 March; and GW to Alexander Spotswood, 15 March, and n.3 to that document. Fredericksburg, Va., merchants William Lovell and Charles Urquhart wrote a letter on 3 Feb. to James Monroe, currently a U.S. senator from Virginia, in which they asked Monroe to "mention to the President, Mr Laurance Muse, as a Gentleman well quallified," who "has been the Deputy ever since Mr [Hudson] Muse filld the office & has done all the Business with much credit to himself & pleasure To the merchants & owners of Vessels" (DLC:GW). Laurence Muse also wrote to Monroe for assistance on 22 Feb., enclosing a letter of 20 Feb. from George W. Smith, who noted the "esteem & respect which I entertain for this Gentleman" (both letters, DLC:GW). Monroe then forwarded these three letters to GW.

3. GW submitted Muse's nomination to the U.S. Senate on 5 March, and the Senate approved it the following day (*U.S. Senate Executive Journal,* 1:149).

From Edmund Randolph

Sunday evening [2 Feb. 1794][1]

E. Randolph has the honor of informing the President, that, as far as he has understood, it is not intended, that a *committee* should wait upon him, with the resolution; but that it should be *transmitted.* If this be the case, as it pretty certainly is, no immediate answer will be necessary.[2]

Supposing it to be otherwise; namely that a committee are to be the bearers of the resolution Still the answer, which the President has recited, seems to be proper in the first instance.[3] For time must be taken to consider the resolution, so as to determine how far it is to be complied with, or if at all. The President will be pleased to recollect, that a distinction was taken at the first interview, between the resolution, as an executive and a legislative act.[4] At least it was not meant by E.R. that if papers were asked for in a legislative capacity, altho' without qualification, what was proper for the public eye should not be sent. The only idea, which he contemplated, was, that what was required without qualification, should not be granted without qualification; but that what was improper should be witheld.

E.R. had asked himself, how the President was to know, whether the resolution was a legislative or executive act? For it is very probable, that it will not be specified. To this the answer appears to be, that if the President chooses to understand it, without more accurate information, to be executive; he may then oppose in toto. If he chooses to understand it, as a legislative act, for the sake of avoiding unnecessary contests; he may do so, without injury to the executive rights, and discriminate such parts of the correspondence, as are unfit to be communicated. Or if he should be of opinion, that he ought to observe a different line of conduct, according as the resolution may be executive or legislative; and will not undertake to decide, whether it be of an executive or legislative nature; he may, it is presumed, call for an explanation, as to the source, from which it proceeds.

Be this as it may; and even if a *committee,* contrary to what is now probable, should bring the resolution; the answer, mentioned by the President, remains perfectly apt and proper.

AL, DLC:GW.

1. GW's docket reads "2d Feby 1794," which was a Sunday.

2. The resolution under discussion requested GW to provide the Senate with copies of the official correspondence of Gouverneur Morris, the U.S. minister to France (U.S. Senate to GW, 24 Jan. 1794). The exact date that GW received this resolution is not known, but Randolph's letter to GW of 25 Jan. also indicates that both men knew its contents before its official delivery. This resolution first appeared in the Philadelphia newspapers on Friday, 31 Jan. (*Gazette of the United States*).

3. For GW's official response, see his letter to the Senate of 26 February.

4. For Randolph's previous thoughts on the distinction between the Senate's legislative and executive authority and its impact on GW's obligation to comply with the resolution, see his second letter to GW of 26 January.

To Burgess Ball

Dear Sir,   Philadelphia Feby 3d 1794

In due course of the Post I have received your letters of the 17th of December & 21st of the last month; and congratulate you on the birth of a Son—and the passage of your family through the Small Pox.[1]

As you had acknowledged the receipt of the needful for purchasing the Buck Wht, and had assured me that no disappointment should follow, I have not given you the trouble of a letter until now, since I wrote from German Town; and now principally to beg that the Buck Wheat may be got down in time for early sowing; the present frost being favorable for transportation.[2]

I have procured for you, and it shall be sent with my own by the first vessel to Alexandria, three bushels of Clover Seed which appears to be clean, & warranted fresh. It will cost delivered at Alexandria about eight dollars a bushel. It shall be directed to the care of Colo. Gilpin to whom my own things will be consigned; as the Captn is not at liberty to land any part of his Cargo before he arrives at the Port to which he is bound. No opportunity has offered since the first frost (in december) set in, or both yours & mine would have gone e'er this. To say now when they will go is more than I am able, as the Delaware is close[d], & navigation at an end until there comes a thaw.[3]

With this letter is enclosed a box containing bracelets &ca for Mrs Ball, wch I hope will get safe to hand, as I have directed them to the particular care of the Post master in Alexandria— Mrs Washington and the family, join me in every good wish for you, Mrs Ball & Miss Milly, if with you,[4] and with Affectionate regard I am Dr Sir Your Obedt Servt

Go: Washington

P.S. As soon as you have ascertained the amount of cost & charges of the Buck Wheat delivered at M. Vernn let me know it, & I will remit what may be due on the Acct[5]—The freight of the Clover Seed from hence to Alexandria, as well as the first cost of it will be paid here.

G.W.

ALS (photocopy), DLC: GW Ephemera—Burgess Ball Papers; ALS (letterpress copy), NN: Washington Papers; LB, DLC:GW.

1. Ball announced the birth of his son Charles Burgess Ball in his letter to GW of 17 Dec. 1793. He wrote about the successful inoculation of his family and slaves against smallpox in his letter to GW of 21 Jan. 1794.

2. In his letter to Ball of 24 Nov. 1793, GW enclosed a bank note for $200 to be used for the purchase of buckwheat seed. Contrary to GW's hopes, Ball sent the buckwheat seed in several shipments that extended from late January until early April (William Pearce to GW, 4 Feb.; Ball to GW, 13 Feb. and 5 April; and GW to Ball, 23 March).

3. On the shipment of the clover seed to the care of George Gilpin, and the cost of the three bushels intended for Ball, see GW's letter to Ball of 16 March.

4. Ball acknowledged receipt of the bracelets and other items intended for Frances Washington Ball, GW's niece, in his letter to GW of 13 February. Mildred Gregory Washington was the younger sister of Mrs. Ball and had been residing with the Ball family since the previous fall (Ball to GW, 16 Nov. 1793).

5. According to Ball's letter to GW of 27 May, the price of the buckwheat was 2/6 per bushel and the cost of transporting it was 1/ per bushel, for a total cost of £79.10.9 for the 454½ bushels delivered to Mount Vernon (DLC:GW).

From David Humphreys

My dear Sir.   Lisbon [Portugal] Febry. 3d 1794.

The Swedish vessel which was to have sailed with my last letters three days ago, has been unexpectedly detained until this time,[1] I therefore take the liberty of addressing you again, principally with the object of recommending Mr James Simpson of Gibralter to be appointed Consul of the U.S. for that Port. This I am the rather induced to do, because I think a Consul at that Place highly expedient & necessary; and because I know of no person there who appears to me, by any means, so suitable & worthy of the appointment as that Gentleman. He has not only faithfully accounted for the various matters committed to him by the late Mr Barclay, but he has spontaneously on many occasions given real assistance to the masters of our vessels when they were in need of his services. He has also a considerable correspondence in Barbary & knowledge of the affairs in that Country. He is a British Subject & a Merchant; but so far as I can judge, he has demonstated intelligence, fideli⟨t⟩y and attachment to the U.S. wheresoever their interests or that of their Citizens has come within the sphere of his action or interference.[2]

Without touching on Consular appointment, in general, I will just say in passing, that I think that of Mr Morphy at Malaga a very good one—he appears to be a very respectable Character.[3]

Mr Logie, late Consul of his Britannic Majesty at Algiers, arrived here the day before yesterday. Yesterday a Merchant of the British Factory came to invite me to dine with him in company with Mr Logie, who, he said, had expressed a wish of becoming acquainted with me. Whatever I might have felt, I could have wished a previous engagement had not prevented me from deriving all the intelligence possible from Logie. He is going to England by the Packet.[4]

Since my last, two English Captains, and a Dutch Captain, who lately made their escape from Prison at Brest, arrived here. They assert, that a fleet of eight sail of the Line with several frigates & armed vessels sailed on a secret expedition, on the 13th of last month: that twenty one or twenty two sail more were fit for Sea, riding at single anchor in that Port; that the People were much united & greatly animated by their late successes; and that Provisions were plenty & particularly that grain was in such abundance, that the Churches were obliged to be occupied as Store Houses for receiving it. This intelligence does not seem to be contraverted even by the Aristocrates.[5] With sentiments of perfect esteem & respect, I have the honour to be my dear Sir Yr affecte friend & devoted Servt

D. Humphreys

P.S. no Packet has yet arrived with the British King's speech.[6]

ALS, DLC:GW.

1. Other letters sent at this time included Humphreys' letters to the secretary of state of 7 and 25 Dec. 1793 and 30 Jan. 1794, all of which are docketed as received on 1 April 1794 (DNA: RG 59, Despatches from U.S. Ministers to Portugal; see also Humphreys, *Life and Times of David Humphreys*, 2:191–92, and *ASP, Foreign Relations*, 1:418–23). Edmund Randolph submitted these three letters to GW on 2 April (*JPP*, 296). Humphreys' previous letter to GW of 31 Jan. also was included with this packet of letters.

2. For James Simpson's nomination as the U.S. consul for the Spanish port of Gibraltar, see GW to U.S. Senate, 28 May. On the death of American diplomat Thomas Barclay at Lisbon in January 1793, see n.1 of Humphreys to GW, 23 Jan. 1793.

3. For the appointment of Michael Morphy as the U.S. consul for the Spanish port city of Málaga, see n.4 of Thomas Jefferson's memorandum to GW of 28 Feb. 1793 and GW to U.S. Senate, 1 March 1793 (first letter).

4. For a possible cause of Humphreys' apparently negative feelings about Charles Logie, see n.1 of Humphreys to GW, 31 January.

5. Brest is a port city located on an inlet of the Atlantic Ocean in northwest France. The Battle of Hondschoote, 6–8 Sept.; the Battle of Wat-

tignies, 15–16 Oct.; the removal of the Austrian Army from Alsace in December; and the retaking of Lyon on 9 Oct. and Toulon on 19 Dec. are some of the events that boosted the morale of the French nation in late 1793 and early 1794 as the French drove foreign armies out of France and subdued counter-revolutionary activity.

6. Humphreys is referring to the speech that King George III gave at the opening of the current session of Parliament on 21 January. After reviewing the progress of the war against France, the king urged continued British participation until a peace was achieved that provided for the "permanent safety" of British citizens and "the independence and security of Europe" (*Parliamentary History of England,* 30:1045–47). It was published in the *Times* (London) on 22 January.

To William Pearce

Mr Pearce,   Philadelphia Feby 3d 1794
    The Post which ought (in course) to have arrived here On Saturday last, will not be in, it seems, until tomorrow. When it arrives, I shall (if anything requires immediate notice) by the Post of Wednesday write to you—If not, I shall delay doing it until the usual time—that is, on Sunday next.[1]
    By the last Post I sent you a bank note for One hundred dollars, to pay Mr Dulany—I hope it got safe to hand.[2] I now enclose you Mr Lewis's draught on Mr Horatio Ross of Alexandria which when received place to my credit and advise me thereof that I may repay the amount here.[3] I am Your friend &ca
                                         Go: Washington

ALS, MWiW; ALS (letterpress copy), DLC:GW.
    1. For the schedule of mail service between Alexandria, Va., and Philadelphia, see GW to Anthony Whitting, 2 Dec. 1792. The letter that GW expected on Saturday, 1 Feb., was Pearce's letter to GW of 28 Jan., which has not been found. Apparently it did not require an immediate response, because GW waited until Sunday, 9 Feb., to reply.
    2. The bank note for Benjamin Tasker Dulany was enclosed in GW's letter to Pearce of 26 January. Pearce acknowledged its receipt in his letter to GW of 4 February.
    3. According to the 5 March entry in GW's Household Accounts, $93.33 from the "President's Accot." was paid Howell Lewis "in full for a draft on mister Ross of Alexa. in favr of Wm Pearce, & recd by him." Pearce acknowledged this instruction in a letter to GW of 11 February.

Letter not found: to Harriot Washington, 3 Feb. 1794. In her letter to GW of 9 Feb., Harriot acknowledged receipt of her "dear Uncle's letter" and the "bundle" that accompanied it. Betty Washington Lewis, in her letter to GW of 9 Feb., acknowledged the arrival of GW's letter of "the 3th of this Month" with its present for Harriot.

From Johann Paul Golling

Translation.

Sir.   Nueremberg [Germany] Febr. 4. 1794

At the pressing Instance of my Son-in-Law John Benjamin Erhard, Doctor of Physic I take the Liberty to forward to Your Excy's Address his Letter relating the melancholy Circumstances of a late unfortunate Event concerning him, that involved me in the deepest sorrow as also my Daughter his wife and his own father.[1] We are all honest people and every Thing, what he in his letter advances is pure Truth. I adjoin here the names of a number of gentlemen of Respectability who might give Information of his Character, in case Your Excellency do his petition think worth any Notice. I remain most respectfully Your Excellency's most humble & devotd Servant

John Paul Golling

Count Schimmelmann at Copenhagen.
Professor Baggerson at the same place.
Prof. Kant at Koenigsberg. Prof.
Reinhold at Kiel. Counsellor Wieland
at Weimar. Cr Siebold at Würzburg.[2]

L (translation), DNA: RG 59, Miscellaneous Letters.

1. See Johann Benjamin Erhard to GW, 27 Jan. 1794.

2. Count Ernst Heinrich Schimmelmann and Karl Kaspar von Siebold are mentioned also in Erhard's letter. Jens Immanuel Baggesen (1764–1826) was a Danish poet. Immanuel Kant (1724–1804), an eminent German philosopher, lectured at the University of Königsberg in East Prussia (present-day Kaliningrad, Russia), 1770–97. Karl Leonhard Reinhold (1757–1823) was a native of Vienna, Austria. A philosopher and follower of Kant, he lectured at the University of Jena, 1787–94, and then at the University of Kiel, 1794–1823. Christoph Martin Wieland (1733–1813) was a German poet, novelist, and translator who lived in the German city of Weimar, Thuringia, from 1772 until his death.

From Tobias Lear

My dear Sir,   London february 4th 1794.

I had the honor of writing a long letter to you on the 26th ul-timo by the Ship Delaware, Captain Truxon, to whose particular care I committed the Watch & chain for Mrs Washington, also a profile of the Earl of Buchan, by Tassie, which Lady Buchan committed to my charge with a note for Mrs. Washington.[1] Since which I have received a letter from the Earl with the enclosed packets for you which he requested me to forward by the first Oppy. These he tells me are curious Mss relative to the Fairfax family and he wishes to have them preserved in your hands.[2] You will find enclosed likewise a vest pattern of a new fabric which Sir John Sinclair pressed upon me to send to you, and in a way that I could not decline it, altho' I know full well your wishes to avoid anything, however trifling, coming to you in the shape of a present. This, Sir John, begs to send in order that you may judge of the perfection to which the wool of Scotland (of which this is made) is brought, as well as of the progress in manufactures of the finer kinds.

I have put on board the Ship Peggy of George Town, by which this letter goes, 5000 plants of the white thorn. These you will see by the enclosed Acct are 8/ pr M which is 2/ dearer than they would be at another season; the ground being at this time hard frozen makes it very difficult to take them up; but this is considered as the best season for sending them abroad.[3]

I have likewise taken the liberty, as the season and opportu-nity are so favorable, to send addressed to you a number of the best kinds of fruit trees & goosberry & Currant bushes. These I have taken for myself, as it will be one of my first objects, as soon as I fix myself in the City of Washington, to have a garden of good fruit. Not knowing how I could otherways have them taken care of, I have ventured, my dear Sir, to trespass so much on your goodness as to send them to you, beleiving that you will direct your gardener to plant them at Mount Vernon—and as these are intended for standard trees & bushes they will not only furnish me with as many scions or grafts as I may have occasion for my self hereafter; but will afford abundantly more for you or your friends.[4]

Mr Young tells me that in a letter which he has lately received from you, he is requested to send out a number of good farmers to go upon some of your lands, provided he can find such as are disposed to go—can be recommended—and will become tenants. He is very doubtful whether he shall be able to meet with such as are good for any thing who would be willing to become tenants; the great object with those who go out to America (at least if they have a little property to take with them, and such as have not are generally but indifferent folks) is to obtain a free hold; and so strongly are they possessed with this idea that they will hardly consent to become tenants, however advantageous the terms of a lease might be. But Mr Young is not without hopes of being able, in some measure, to comply with your wishes, as he knows of a considerable number of farmers who have it in contemplation to emigrate to America in the ensuing spring.[5]

In my letter by Captain Truxon I said so much on the subject of politicks that I shall add nothing on that score here further than to enclose a few of the latest papers.[6]

The pamphlet containing a few remarks which I made on the River Potomack &c. has had an astonishing effect here in producing more particular enquiries about that part of the Country[7]—and I flatter my self that not a few of those who emigrate this spring will turn their eyes to that quarter—And I think no great length of time will elapse before I shall have the pleasure of seeing a verification of the opinion with which I have always been impressed with respect to the federal City. I find some of my Countrymen here who are not well pleased with the eagerness of enquiry respecting the *Potomack*—and altho they do not venture to contradict a single fact contained in the Pamphlet; yet they cry up certain other parts of the U.S. as having infinitely greater advantages: But I find what I always beleived, to be true, that a reasonable & fair statement of facts will make a much deeper & more lasting impression on the public mind than any florid description which may, in the first moment, lead the imagination astray, but is most assuredly afterwards the destruction of the very point which it wished to establish.

I will intrude no longer on your precious time, my dear Sir, than to beg that my best & most cordial respects may be made acceptable to Mrs Washington—my love & best wishes given to my young friends Nelly & Washington as well as to Mr Dandridge

& Mr Lewis[8]—and to assure you that I am with the most perfect respect & inviolable attachment, Your affectionate friend & grateful Servt

Tobias Lear.

P.S. I heard a report last evening that the Portuguise would not adhere to the terms of the truce which had been made with the Algerines, and that the consequence would be that those depredators would be again shut up in their ports. This however is a mere report, and as such I give it. But it has been all along said that the truce between the Portuguise & Algerines was made by another power without the assent of the Portuguise Court.[9]

I am informed that the British Merchants trading to Am. have determined to petition Parliament for a Convoy to protect the Am. Ships from the Algerines!

T. Lear

Sir John Sinclair has committed to my care the enclosed letter and a packet containing the Reports made to the Society for Promoting Agriculture, which will go by the same vessel with this.[10]

ALS, DLC:GW.

1. For GW's receipt of Lear's letter of 26–30 Jan. and its accompanying packages, see GW to William Pearce, 20 April, and to Lear, 6 May.

2. The enclosed packets have not been identified. On the Earl of Buchan's kinship ties to Lord Thomas Fairfax, the sixth Baron Fairfax, see n.5 of Buchan to GW, 22 Oct. 1792.

3. On the receipt of the white thorn plants and their planting at Mount Vernon, see the farm reports for 25–31 May (DLC:GW). The enclosed account has not been found, but GW's financial records indicate that he paid £2.5.0 sterling for the plants (Ledger C, 4).

4. On Lear's purchase of land in the Federal City, see his letter to GW of 24 June 1793. Lear enclosed a "List of Fruit trees and bushes put on board the Ship Peggy, Capt. Lunt, bound to George Town." The trees and bushes, which were "packed up in matts and directed to G: Washington, Mount Vernon," consisted of twenty-four gooseberry and twenty-four currant bushes, plus six apple, twelve pear, twelve plum, twelve cherry, two almond, three apricot, and thirty nectarine trees (DLC:GW).

5. For GW's plan to lease the farms on his Mount Vernon estate, reserving the Mansion House farm for his own use, see his letter to Arthur Young of 12 Dec. 1793. On Young's inability to recruit tenant farmers, see his letter to GW, 2 June 1794.

6. The enclosed newspapers have not been identified.

7. See Lear's *Observations on the River Potomack, the Country Adjacent, and the City of Washington* (New York, 1793).

8. Eleanor Parke "Nelly" Custis and George Washington Parke Custis were Martha Washington's grandchildren. Bartholomew Dandridge, Jr., and Howell Lewis were GW's current secretaries.

9. Portugal's previous naval blockade of the Straits of Gibraltar, which was designed to protect commerce with its colony of Brazil, had also protected America's merchant ships from Algerine attacks since 1786. The British government was eager to solicit the assistance of the Portuguese navy in its war with France in 1793. Therefore, by assuring the dey of Algiers that Portugal was willing to pay a large tribute, Charles Logie, the British consul at Algiers, obtained on 12 Sept. 1793 the dey's consent to a twelve-month truce. By late November, however, Portugal concluded that the cost was excessive, repudiated the truce, and re-established the blockade (Parker, *Uncle Sam in Barbary*, 75–79, 227–29).

10. For Sinclair's letter and his description of the reports accompanying it, see his letter to GW of 6 February.

From William Pearce

Sir   Mountvernon Feby 4th 1794

I Receved your Letter of the 26 Janry and a bank note of 100 dollars—I took notice that you had put down in the notes in the plan of Rotation—that Corn might be planted in such parts of the fields that ware alloted for the Buck wheat—as would produce it[1]—If the feilds that ware alloted for Corn was not Likely to produce a Soficient Quantity To answear the Several demands that would be for that Article—and uppon Examening the Several Feilds I did not think they would do it—and that was the Reason I mentioned it In my letter[2]—I was looking over The Grass lot at River farm before the snow come And I find that the Clover is Very thin in it—& I think thare ought to be a part of It Broke up this spring—& put in Potatoes—I have Inquired of Mr Butler & old Jack about the orchard Grass Seed but they Can Give no acct of it, & say that thare was none Saved to thare knoledge—when the Clover Seed Comes I will Take Good Care that none [of] It shall be Stolen or Wasted and when it is to be sown will manage It as you have directed[3]—and Indeed I will Indeavour to do Every thing In my power according to the best of my Judgment—Col. Ball has Sent Sixty Bushels of Buck wheat & wrote that he Intended to keep hauling till he Sends 500 Bushels down—He wrote to have 3 shoats Sent him of the China Breed.[4]

I am Sorry to have to Inform you that the Stock of sheep at Both Union & Dogue Run farms are Some of them Dieing

Every week[5]—& a Great many of Them will be lost, let what will be done—Since I come I have had shelters made for them & Troughs to feed them In & to Give them salt—& have attended to them myself & was In hopes to have saved those that I found to be weak but they ware too far gone—and Several of the young Cattle at dogue Run was past all Recovery when I come & some have died already & Several more I am affraid might die before spring, they are so very poor & weak—The stock at River farm & Muddy hole I am In hopes will be Brought through the winter without much loss and I am in hopes that the Cattle at Union farm will be brought through the winter prety well Likewise some of the young ones are very thin & they have Lost one.

Mr Stewart Sais part of his last years wages are due & he is in want of money but as you had directed me not to pay any Acct without first Informing you—I shall not pay him Any till I receive orders from you[6]—the Ice house is Better than half filled with Ice—but the Ice was so thin It all melted be fore we Could Get Enough to fill It. I am Sir with the Greatest Respect Your Humble Servt

William Pearce

ALS, DLC:GW.

1. On the substitution of corn for buckwheat, see n.13 of the plan of crop rotation enclosed in GW to Pearce, 18 Dec. 1793.

2. This information probably was contained in Pearce's letter to GW of 22 Jan., which has not been found.

3. For the shipment of clover seed to Mount Vernon, see GW to Pearce, 16–17 and 23 March.

4. On Burgess Ball's promise to acquire buckwheat seed for GW, see Ball to GW, 17 Dec. 1793. For shipments of additional buckwheat seed from Ball, see Ball to GW, 13 Feb. and 5 April, and GW to Ball, 23 March. Ball's letter to Pearce asking for three young hogs of the Big China breed has not been identified.

5. Pearce's Farm Reports for 2–8 Feb. reported a loss of "6 Sheep & 1 Yearling" at Union farm and "2 sheep 1 yearling" at Dogue Run farm (DLC:GW).

6. For GW's orders regarding William Stuart's wages, see his letter to Pearce of 24 February.

From Robert Lewis

Hond Uncle,   Frederick County [Va.] February 5 [1794][1]
    Inclosed I send you the Deed which you re-acknowledged at Mount Vernon and a fair copy of the same which I will thank you

to sign. Thro' the neglect of Doctor Stuart & Colo. Ball who did not attend to prove your re-acknowledgment, the Deed is out of date, and the Court of Frederick will not admit it to record[2]—I therefore request you will be so obliging as to sign the new Deed (as the old one is in a very tattered condition) or reacknowledge the old one, either of which will do. I wish you to sign the Deed in presence of old Mr Rutherford & any others that may accompany him.[3]

I have just returned from among your tenants in Berkley and now on my way to Fauquier; from which place, I shall write you more fully & respecting to your business.[4] Present my affectionate regards to my Aunt & believe me with sincere respect your Affectionate Nephew

Robt Lewis.

ALS, ViMtvL.

1. GW's docket reads, "5th Feby 1794."

2. The enclosures have not been identified. David Stuart and Burgess Ball are the individuals criticized by Lewis.

3. Robert Rutherford was 65 years old at this time, and as a congressman from Virginia, he was in Philadelphia to attend the first session of the Third Congress.

4. If written, the promised letter has not been found. The next extant letter from Lewis to GW is that of 7 May (ViMtvL).

From Gouverneur Morris

Duplicate
My dear Sir,   Paris 5 Feby 1794.

In a New's Paper of this Day I find the Translation of your Message of the fifth of December to Congress, and observe that after stating the Violation of the Treaty by a Decree of the national Convention you tell them I have been instructed to make Representations on the Subject.[1] Now this my dear Sir is the first I hear and all I know of such Instructions. Indeed I have received no Letters New's paper or other Intelligence from America since those which Captain Culver brought.[2] I suppose this arises from the Difficulty of Communication but whatever be the Cause I feel the Effect. It would be of some Use if a Clerk in the Office of foreign Affairs had by Triplicates mention'd from Time to Time which of my Letters were receiv'd. Thus on the present Occasion, I should know whether my Correspondence with the Minister on the Subject of this obnoxious Decree was before you.[3] As it is, not being able to determine the nature of the Representations which you have desired me to make, I am oblig'd to be silent. And unless more than one Copy has been sent I may never receive your Orders, and at any Rate it will be at no early Day. I am sure it is superfluous to tell you how painful it is for a Person in my Situation to be totally ignorant of what passes in his own Country, and whether the Conduct which under Circumstances continually changing he finds it necessary to pursue does or does not consist with the Views of Government. Blaming a wrong Step would prevent a Repetition of it, but really at present I walk in the Dark or at best by the feeble Light of my own Conjectures. I know not whether my Brethren have the same Dearth of Intelligence. Mr Short complaind of it much when I last saw him and has since mentiond the same thing from Madrid so that I conclude the Evil to arise from the Negligence of those to whom Letters are entrusted.[4] Might it not be adviseable to send every Month a small Packet to Europe. They might come alternately to Havre and Lisbon and that which arrives at Lisbon come on thence to Havre that which arrives at Havre go from thence to Lisbon. In this way a regular correspondence would be kept up and seizing for unimportant Communications, the private Conveyances which offer full Intelligence would be given and receiv'd. Six packets would be amply sufficient for the Service and if, as I believe, small Schooners could be safely employd the prime Cost would not be above three thousand Pound Sterling and the annual Expense I should suppose not more than Half that Sum.

I beg your Pardon my dear Sir for troubling you with this groaning Scheeming Epistle. I will not say one word of news as in supposeable Circumstances it might prevent this Letter from reaching you. I adhere to the Opinions exprest in my last.[5] adieu I am very truly yours

Gouvr. Morris

P.S. I am sorry to see that your Love of Retirement struggles so strongly against a Continuance of public Life.[6] I am afraid the Devil (for it is from him you know that comes all Evil) will put it in your Head one Day to quit Outright which God in his Mercy forbid for I tell you, and you know me well enough to believe me, it will be a very sad Day for America. As to yourself I know that you will be more happy at Home and I judge from my own feelings how strong must be your Desire to get there. Apropos whenever you think the United States can gain any thing no matter how little by giving me a Successor let it be done.[7]

ALS (Duplicate), DLC:GW; ALS (fragment), DLC:GW; LB, DLC: Gouverneur Morris Papers.

1. On 9 May 1793 the French national convention approved a decree authorizing the seizure of "merchant vessels which are wholly or in part loaded with provisions, being neutral property, bound to an enemy's port, or having on board merchandise belonging to an enemy." This was interpreted by the United States as a violation of Article 16 of the 1778 Treaty of Amity and Commerce between the United States and France. After a protest from Morris, the French government issued a decree of 23 May "that the vessels of the United States are not comprised in the regulations of the 9th of May." A subsequent decree of 28 May, however, repealed that of 23 May (*ASP, Foreign Relations*, 1:244; Miller, *Treaties*, 2:14–15; Morris to Thomas Jefferson, 25 June 1793, *Jefferson Papers*, 26:363–69).

2. On the letters of late August 1793 entrusted to the care of William Culver, captain of the sloop *Hannah*, see Cabinet Opinion on the recall of Edmond Genet, 23 Aug., and notes 2 and 4.

3. The correspondence between Morris and the French foreign minister, first Lebrun and then his successor Deforgues, concerning restrictions on U.S. trade was presented to the U.S. Senate along with GW's address of 26 Feb. 1794 and is printed in *ASP, Foreign Affairs*, 1:358–78.

4. William Short was the current U.S. minister to The Hague in the Netherlands. In January 1792, however, he received the additional appointment of commissioner plenipotentiary to Spain and was thereby responsible for resolving several points in dispute with that nation. He arrived at Madrid in February 1793 (GW to Thomas Jefferson, 23 Aug. 1792, and n.2 to that document).

5. According to Morris's letter to GW of 12 March 1794, this was his letter of 18 Oct. 1793.

6. For GW's expression of his reluctance to serve a second term as president, see his letter to Morris of 25 March 1793.

7. For the nomination of James Monroe as Morris's successor, see GW to U.S. Senate, 27 May (LS, DNA: RG 46, entry 38).

From Samuel A. Otis, Sr., to Bartholomew Dandridge, Jr.

[Philadelphia] Feby 5th 1794.

Mr Otis's compliments to Mr Dandridge and sends him for the use of the President of the United States a Journal of Senate during the second Congress—Should more of the same kind be wanting, Mr Dandridge will be so good as to apply.[1]

Mr O. sends also the sheets of the present session as far as they are printed.[2]

L, DNA: RG 59, Miscellaneous Letters.

1. Otis sent GW the *Journal of the Senate of the United States of America; being the second session of the Second Congress, begun and held at the city of Philadelphia, November 5th, 1792, and in the seventeenth year of the sovereignty of the said United States* (Philadelphia, 1793).

2. The sheets eventually were incorporated into the *Journal of the Senate of the United States of America, being the first session of the Third Congress, begun and held at the city of Philadelphia, December 2d, 1793. And in the eighteenth year of the sovereignty of the said United States* (Philadelphia, 1794).

From Thomas Johnson

Sir.   Frederick [Md.] 6 February 1794.

Your Letter of the 23d of last Month came to Hand whilst I was attending on the Lottery Business at George Town:[1] I forbore to answer it immediately hoping that a little Delay might enable me to do it more to your Satisfaction, as well as my own for I could not think of any Gentleman of the Neighbourhd whom I could venture to recommend to you and the Proprietors, amongst whom there is the most Ability, have not lately gained in my Confidence—Reflection has not assisted me nor do I see a prospect of a favorable Change unless from an Accession of Strangers several of whom it is said will be at the City in the Spring and amongst them I hope such as will be proper for your Choice—In the Mean Time, with your Approbation I will continue to act for though I shd not Suffer much in seeing the little Credit I may have earned, transferred by common Opinion to a Successor, I should be very sorry a Change of Comrs should injure the Work I have very much at Heart.[2] I am sir, with the most Respect, Your affectionate Servant.

Th. Johnson

ALS, DLC:GW.

1. Johnson met with fellow D.C. commissioners David Stuart and Daniel Carroll (of Rock Creek, Md.) at Georgetown, D.C., from 24 to 31 Jan. (DNA: RG 42, Records of the Commissioners for the District of Columbia, Proceedings, 1791–1802). On problems with the lottery managed by former D.C. superintendent Samuel Blodget, Jr., see n.4 of GW to Johnson, 23 January.

2. On the proprietors, see source note to Agreement of the Proprietors of the Federal District, 30 March 1791. For persons suggested by David Stuart,

who also wished to resign as commissioner, see Stuart to GW, this date. For the men who replaced Johnson and Stuart on the commission later this year, see n.2 of GW to Johnson, 23 January.

From John Sinclair

Sir,   Whitehall [London]--6th Febry 1794
    I had the honour of receiving your Excellency's letter by Mr Lear, with whose appearance & conversation I am much pleased. He comes from a good school.[1] By this vessel I have the pleasure of sending copies of several of our Agricultural surveys, one or two of the best; it would be worth while to reprint, & circulate in america. The whole Kingdom will be completed in about 6 months from the commencement of the inquiry.[2] Excuse the shortness of this epistle, having such a mass of matter to attend to, & believe me, with sincere respect & esteem, your very faithful humble Servt

                                                    John Sinclair

N.B. We recognise the good sense and steady judgement of old England, in the conduct of her American descendants on a late trying occasion. I have perused with much pleasure Mr Jefferson's paper upon the subject. My best Compts to Mr Adams & him.[3]

ALS, PHi: Gratz Collection. GW's docket is erroneously dated "6th Feb. 1784."
    1. On Tobias Lear's trip to Great Britain and for the letter of recommendation that he presented to Sinclair, see GW to Sinclair, 8 Nov. 1793. For Lear's impression of Sinclair, see Lear to GW, 26–30 Jan. 1794.
    2. For a list of the agricultural surveys and essays published by Sinclair and the British Board of Agriculture and sent to GW over the next few years, see Griffin, *Catalogue of the Washington Collection*, 89–95. On Sinclair's plan to survey Great Britain, see his letter to GW of 15 Aug. 1793.
    3. The subject of Thomas Jefferson's paper has not been identified.

From David Stuart

Dear Sir   Hope-Park [Va.] 6th: Feby: 1794
    Your letter of the 20th Ultmo I recieved on my return home from Ge: town, where I have been for near ten days past. As you was informed of the result of the meeting, it is unnecessary to

observe, that it was one of the most unpleasant we have had—I hope the discharge of the Ellicotts (rendered unavoidable by their own conduct) will ensure not only peace, but honesty & industry too, to the surveying department in future.[1]

It gives me much pleasure, that my conduct has met with your approbation: my determination is certainly finally taken, and when I informed you of it, it was my wish to have complied with the request you signifyed to me in conversation last fall, of suggesting some characters to you, who might fill up the vacancy created by Mr Johnson's & my own resignation. But I could not at that time do it, to my satisfaction, nor can I now do it entirely so—My place may I think be easily supplied, but I know not where to look, for any one to supply Mr Johnson's—and here has been my difficulty. With respect to the Proprietors, perhaps my prejudices, may have some influence on my opinion: but it appears to me, that those among them who are best fitted for the office in point of talents, would be improper from the general sentiment entertained of them as to their cunning & design. Perhaps, if they were as free from this imputation as could reasonably be expected from their interests, the jealousy of those whose interests lie in a different quarter would still be troublesome. I think I speak on this head experimentally, from what is constantly suggested with respect to Mr Carroll; and in my opinion without foundation: if he who is interested in a very small degree any where, and certainly as much in Hamburg as Carrollsburg, has not been able to escape censure, how can it be expected from those who are more deeply so, and that in one part only?[2] I must therefore think upon the whole, that a proprietor to any extent would not be suitable. The only persons then, that I can think of, are Marsham Waring, & Major Ross of Bladensburg—the first of these, is a respectable sensible Merchant of Ge: town, who has never intermixed with any of the parties, and who has I believe no property in the City; the second you are acquainted with. Mr John Mason & a Mr Lowndes were spoke of, I understand by the People of Ge: town as fit persons— But from the connection of the latter with Mr Stoddert, and his being allso a very young man, and from Mr Mason's being so deeply interested opposite to Ge: town, I cannot think them so proper as the other two—As you are totally unacquainted I believe with Mr Waring, it may be necessary to say something more respecting him—he has been long an inhabitant of Ge: town, and some of his relations (I believe his brother) possessed large property in the city, but has sold out—he is universally well thought of, as a man of character, good temper and understanding[3]— Not knowing whether you might be able to fill up our places to your mind; by the first of March, we fixed on the third monday of that month for the next meeting; which will be an important one on account of the election of proper characters as Bank directors—Cashier &c.[4]—Mr Blodget contrary to our expectations, and many intimations we recieved, will not hesitate to recieve the salary fixed for his Agency; tho' he was seldom present, and rendered little or no service in that time—We are now quit of him, and I think it unfortunate that we ever had any connection with him in any way.[5] I am with the greatest respect Your Affecte: & Obt: Servant

Dd: Stuart.

ALS, DLC:GW.

1. Stuart met with fellow D.C. commissioners Thomas Johnson and Daniel Carroll (of Rock Creek, Md.) at Georgetown, D.C., from 24 to 31 January. On the dismissal of chief surveyor Andrew Ellicott in December 1793, see D.C. Commissioners to GW, 23 Dec. 1793, and n.8. For a recent report on their proceedings, including the dismissals of Benjamin and Joseph Ellicott, see D.C. Commissioners to GW, 28 Jan. 1794, and n.2 to that document.

2. The towns of Georgetown, Md., and Alexandria, Va., both established ports on the Potomac River, and the relatively undeveloped Maryland towns of Hamburg and Carrollsburg were situated on land that was incorporated into the District of Columbia in 1791. Commissioner Daniel Carroll (of Rock Creek) owned land near the northern portions of the district where Georgetown and Hamburg were located. He was a shareholder in the Potomac Company and co-owner of one of the Aquia Creek quarries that provided stone for the President's House and the Capitol. His nephew Daniel Carroll of Duddington and his brother-in-law Notley Young, moreover, had extensive land holdings in the southern portion of the district, near Carrollsburg (William C. di Giacomantonio, "All the President's Men: George Washington's Federal City Commissioners," *Washington History* 3 [1991], 59–61). For an example of the rivalry between the northern and southern proprietors of land within the district, see George Walker to GW, 8 Oct. 1792. On the acquisition of land within the federal district from its original landowners, see GW to Thomas Jefferson, 2 Jan. 1791, and Agreement of the Proprietors of the Federal District, 30 March 1791.

3. Georgetown merchant Marsham Waring (Warring) was one of the founders of the Bank of Columbia, the second bank established within the District of Columbia. GW had already appointed David Ross of Bladensburg,

Md., to audit the financial accounts of the D.C. commissioners (GW to the D.C. Commissioners, and GW to Ross and Robert Townsend Hooe, both 9 Sept. 1793). John Mason was an associate with the Georgetown mercantile firm of Fenwick, Mason & Company. On Benjamin Stoddert's economic interest in the District of Columbia, see William Deakins, Jr., and Benjamin Stoddert to GW, 9 Dec. 1790, and notes. Francis Lowndes (1751–1815), along with his brother Charles (1765–1846), was also a Georgetown merchant and one of the founders of the Bank of Columbia. As of late September 1793, Ross and Francis Lowndes served on a committee to manage the district's hotel lottery, which had been established by the district's former superintendent, Samuel Blodget, Jr. (*Bartgis's Maryland Gazette, and Federick-Town Weekly,* 25 Sept. 1793). None of the men suggested by Stuart received an appointment to the D.C. Commission. For the individuals who replaced Johnson and Stuart as commissioners, see n.2 of GW to Johnson, 23 January. John Waring sold the Jamaica tract, which included part of Florida Avenue, to a syndicate headed by Philip R. Fendall in 1791 (Scisco, "Site for Federal City," 146–47).

4. The commissioners met from Wednesday, 19 March, through Tuesday, 25 March. The Bank of Columbia received a charter from Maryland under "An ACT to establish a bank in the district of Columbia," 28 Dec. 1793 (*Md. Laws 1793,* chap. 29). Samuel Blodget, Jr., became its first president and John Mason its second. The individuals elected to the first board of directors have not been identified. The bank's charter permitted the D.C. commissioners to purchase 2,000 shares in the bank. They subsequently acquired 1,053 shares, thus ensuring a close connection between the interests of the new Federal City and the bank (Bryan, *National Capital,* 1:222–23).

5. On the dissatisfaction of both GW and the commissioners with Blodget's performance as D.C. superintendent, see D.C. Commissioners to GW, 23 Dec. 1793, and n.7, and GW to Thomas Johnson, 23 Jan. 1794, and n.4 to that document.

From Cyrus Griffin

Williamsburg [Va.] February 7th 1794

I hope, sir, you will pardon me for transgressing upon a Single moment of your very precious time; I avoid it to the utmost.

my Son John Griffin now in London and having Some years Studied the General and Common Law, is extremely anxious to be employed in Some inferior character abroad. he is twenty three years of age, of good Talents, of firm Integrity, a proper degree of Spirit, and I think of considerable Industry.[1]

I do not presume to ask any particular employment for him, indeed I am ignorant of any vacancy as Secretary to an Embassy or any other; neither Sir do I Send forward any recommendations in his favor, because I am not humble enough with Gentlemen to

ask those unwilling kindnesses; because I have long been convinced that the man who relies upon himself is the man who will
always best discharge the duties of his office, he has no pillar to
lean upon in his deficiency; and because I never made use of them
in my own Case either under the old or the present Government,
but only once in a letter to Mr Jefferson when it was Supposed he
would act as Secretary of State, from our former Intimacy & the
nature of his office I wrote him a request—if he Saw no impropriety in the Thing, to mention me to the President as a minister
to Some foreign Court, being the most Suited to my abilities
and general Course of reading and acting for Some years past.[2]

I offer this young Gentleman to you Sir if you should find it
convenient to notice him, at any future period, and I am Sure
his Gratitude to be employed under the present Administration
would be evinced by the acknowlegement and chearfulness of
his heart.

with lady Christina may I beg to present our best respects To
mrs Washington and yourself,[3] and permit me Sir to remain
with truest consideration Your most obedient Servant

Cyrus Griffin

ALS, DLC:GW.

1. Although John Griffin (1771–1849) did not receive an appointment
from GW, President John Adams appointed him one of the three judges of
the newly established Indiana Territory in 1800. Griffin remained in this
position until 1805, when Thomas Jefferson appointed him a judge of the
Michigan Territory. He retired in 1824 and settled in Philadelphia, where he
remained until his death ("Judge John Griffin," *Indiana Magazine of History*
[March 1924], 20:59–61).

2. Cyrus Griffin served as the U.S. district judge for Virginia from 1789
until his death in 1810 (Griffin to GW, 10 July 1789, and source note). In his
letter to Jefferson of 11 Dec. 1789, Griffin asked Jefferson to recommend
him to GW as Jefferson's replacement if Jefferson decided to relinquish his
position as the U.S. minister to France in order to become secretary of state
(*Jefferson Papers*, 16:14–15).

3. Lady Christina Stuart, of Scotland, was Griffin's wife and the eldest
daughter of John Stuart, the sixth earl of Traquair.

From John C. Ogden

Sir   Dartmouth College [Hanover, N.H.] Feby 7th 1794.
The enclosed was sent to the press, in obedience to the wishes
of many respectable characters, with an ardent hope, that it

would expedite the attainment of justice, which the necessities of The Church and sufferings of her Clergy require.[1]

Determined to be absolved in the eyes of The Church and of Posterity, and to do what humanity to my brethren, and duty to my own family require I circulate it into the hands of my civil & ecclesiastical rulers.

This measure perhaps will prevent the necessity of presenting the public with a full state of facts and the mens names, who have designedly and artfully taken the advantage of war to enrich themselves, and indulge party spleen, by spoiling the Church. That every felicity may be your portion, is Sir, the ardent prayer of Your devoted servant

John C. Ogden

ALS, DNA: RG 59, Miscellaneous Letters.

1. The enclosed newspaper clippings, addressed "For the Vermont Journal," contain an essay by Ogden that was published in two parts by *Spooners Vermont Journal* (Windsor, Vt.), 27 Jan. and 3 Feb. 1794. In this essay, Ogden expounded upon the dire consequences that may afflict the United States as a result of the mistreatment of the Episcopal Church by local and state governments in New England. The essay begins: "While the effects of war and pestilence, those means by which the Almighty Governor of the universe punishes the wicked, are yet visible, and their painful consequences have involved a large part of the American States in sorrow—while an enemy, savage and fierce, harrass our frontiers, and many wish to bring us into a share with the wars of Europe; it may not be amiss to call the public attention to a subject, which always has been followed with misery to the guilty individual or nation.

"The pillage of property devoted to pious uses during the late revolution, and since the peace, in the States from ⟨one⟩ end of ⟨the countr⟩y to the other, particularly in the States of New Hampshire and Vermont, has not been viewed in that serious manner, which becomes a nation professing godliness. The odious enormity of this sin of sacrilege, and a dread in the pious to hear it even mentioned—the share which many leading characters have had in spoiling religion of its support, have caused a silence, which no one has been sufficiently firm to interrupt, so as to gain restitution." Ogden then proceeded to give a summary of past misfortunes that followed similar acts of sacrilege, based on *The History and Fate of Sacrilege Discover'd by Examples of Scripture, of Heathens, and of Christians; from the Beginning of the World Continually to This Day* (London, 1698), by Sir Henry Spelman (1563/4–1641). For previous complaints from Ogden, see his letters to GW of 9 Jan. 1791 and 24 Nov. 1792.

To the United States Senate
and House of Representatives

United States February 7. 1794.
Gentlemen of the Senate and of the House of Representatives.

I transmit to you an act and three ordinances passed, by the Government of the territory of the United States south of the river ohio, on the 13th and 21st of March, and 7th of May 1793.[1] And also certain letters from the minister plenipotentiary of the French Republic to the Secretary of State, enclosing dispatches from the general and extraordinary Commission of Guadeloupe.[2]

Go: Washington

LS, DNA: RG 46, Third Congress, 1793–95, Senate Records of Legislative Proceedings, President's Messages; LB, DNA: RG 233, Third Congress, 1793–95, House Records of Legislative Proceedings, Journals; LB, DLC:GW. A later hand placed square brackets around the first part of this letter, beginning with "an act" and ending with "also," indicating that this section was to be omitted as "irrelevant." This probably was done in preparing this letter for publication in *ASP, Foreign Relations*, 1:323.

1. The enclosures included "An Act requiring p⟨e⟩rsons holding monies arising from fines and forfeitures imposed for the punishment of public offenders⟨, t⟩axes on proceedings in law and equity, on the pro⟨bate⟩ of deeds, on the registering of grants for land, and ⟨the is⟩suing marriage and ordinary licences, as directed ⟨by th⟩e laws of north Carolina, to account for and pay ⟨the s⟩ame," 13 March 1793; "An Ordinance forming the counties of Jefferson and Knox into a judicial district," 13 March 1793; "An Ordinance to amend the 'Ordinance for circumscribing the counties of Greene and Hawkins, and laying out two new counties,'" 21 March 1793; and "An Ordinance further to amend 'An Ordinance circumscribing the counties of Greene and Hawkins, and laying out two new counties,'" 7 May 1793 (all enclosed copies are in DNA: RG 46, Third Congress, 1793–95, Senate Records of Legislative Proceedings, President's Messages, except the ordinance of 13 March; see also DLC: RG 59, State Department Territorial Papers, Territory Southwest of the River Ohio, 1790–1795. The text in angle brackets is from the documents at DNA: RG 59. All these enclosures are in Carter, *Territorial Papers*, 4:242–43, 453–56).

2. The enclosures included both the French versions and English translations of: Edmond Genet's letters to Edmund Randolph of 30 Jan. and 4 Feb. 1794; the dispatch from the commissioners of Guadeloupe to Genet of 27 Oct. 1793; and the dispatch of the commissioners to the U.S. Congress of 6 Nov. 1793, in which the commissioners pledge friendship with the United States as a fellow republic and ask for provisions, ammunition, and men to resist British attacks on the colony (DNA: RG 46, Third Congress, 1793–95,

Senate Records of Legislative Proceedings, President's Messages; see also *ASP, Foreign Relations,* 1:323–26).

To James Madison

Dear Sir,   Saturday Morning [8 Feb. 1794]
   The Agricultural Society of Philadelphia, are preparing the "out lines of a Plan for establishing a state Society of Agriculture in Pennsylvania" to be laid before the Legislature.[1] Mr Peters—to whom sometime ago I mentioned the Pamphlets &ca which had been sent me by Sir John Sinclair; & who is appointed to prepare the business for the Legislature—wishes to have the perusal of those Pamphlets—as at this moment—they might be particularly serviceable to him.[2] I would, for this reason, thank you for them. They shall be returned to you, after he has availed himself of any information which is to be derived from them.[3] I am sincerely & Affectionately Yours

                                 Go: Washington

ALS (photocopy), DLC:GW, series 9.
   1. On 15 Feb. the Pennsylvania state legislature considered a petition "for promoting agriculture and rural æconomy," in which a request was made that "an Act may be passed for incorporating a State society, for the purposes mentioned in the plan submitted to the Legislature by the *Philadelphia* society" (*Journal of the first session of the fourth House of Representatives of the Commonwealth of Pennsylvania. which commenced at Philadelphia, on Tuesday, the third day of December, in the year of our Lord one thousand seven hundred and ninety-three* [Philadelphia, 1793–94], 193). The proposal, which never received legislative approval, was published by the Philadelphia Society for Promoting Agriculture as *Outlines of A Plan, for Establishing a State Society of Agriculture in Pennsylvania* (Philadelphia, 1794). According to this pamphlet, John Beale Bordley, George Clymer, Richard Peters, and Timothy Pickering comprised the committee charged with preparing the plan and the petition.
   2. On GW's loan to Madison of the pamphlets sent by John Sinclair, see GW to Madison, 10 January.
   3. Madison returned the pamphlets to GW along with a letter of this same date that reads: "J. Madison presents his apologies to the President for not sending the pamphlets &c. from Sir J. Sinclair, sooner for the use of Mr Peters, as was intimated when he last had the honor of seeing the President. He had hopes of being able prior to this to have looked a little into them, and have complied with the desire of the President expressed when the papers were put into J.M.'s hands. It has been impossible for him to do this hitherto. To day & tomorrow he had contemplated an effort for the purpose; but it will be even more convenient for him after Mr Peters shall have had the

requisite use of them" (DLC: Madison Papers). GW sent the pamphlets once more to Madison on 16 April along with a letter that reads: "Not 'till yesterday did I receive the Agricultural Pamphlets from Mr Peters. Knowing that you had not finished the perusal you intended to give them, I return them to you for that purpose. After you have examined them at your leizure I wd thank you for such remarks as shall have occurred to you on the occasion for I have yet to acknowledge Sir Jno. Sinclairs politeness in sending them" (ALS, MeHi). For GW's acknowledgment, see his letter to Sinclair of 20 July (ALS, UkLBM: Add MS 5757).

From Richard Dobbs Spaight

Sir   North Carolina New Bern 8th Feb: 1794

By the last Southern post I received Mr Hills letter dated the 25th January 1794 respecting the Sloop L'amee Margueritte, and enclosing me a copy of the instructions he had received from the Secretary of state. I find from them that he was directed in such cases in the first instance to call on the parties concerned to appoint by mutual consent arbiters to decide whether the capture was made within the jurisdiction of the United States—as no part of the instructions which I have received gave me any information of that mode of proceeding being adopted, had the present case now under enquiry been determined in that manner I should have felt myself much at a loss how to proceed, on receiving the reports of the arbiters. I certainly should not have thought myself at liberty to act by restoring the vessel to the former owner or by removing the arrest. as I had never been instructed so to do. I enclose you a copy of Mr Hills Letter of the 25th Jany also copies of my letters to him respecting the case now under consideration.[1]

I send you enclosed a copy of the memorial of James Robinson late master of the Sloop Providence, copy of a letter from J.B. Brouard agent to the French Consul at Wilmington together with a copy of the statement of the facts relative to the Sloop Providence received from the said Brouard. These papers will give you every information that is in my possession respecting the said Sloop.[2]

I have hitherto only sent you on copies of the papers in my possession, retaining the originals, so that if any accident should prevent the copy from reaching you another authenticated copy could be forwarded; or the original if required or thought necessary: If this proceeding does not meet with your approbation the original papers shall in future be sent on. I have the honor to be &c.

R. D. Spaight

LB, Nc-Ar: Governors' Letterbooks.

1. On Spaight's previous order for the seizure of the French privateer *Aimée Marguerite,* the former British sloop *Providence,* while at the port of Wilmington, N.C., and his instructions to U.S. District Attorney William H. Hill of 3 Jan. to take testimony from both parties in an effort to determine whether the vessel should be restored to its former owners, see Spaight to GW, 31 Jan., and notes 2 and 3.

In his reply to Spaight of 25 Jan., Hill reported: "I made application to the principal agents of the parties concerned and of the Consuls of the Nations interested for the purpose of ascertaining whether they would name arbiters to decide the question." Neither side, however, had complied with Hill's request. Hill continued: "You will find by the direction enclosed that I am to transmit to the *Executive* (which I understand the Executive of the United States) the deposition taken on the question which occasions the arrest." Hill wrote that the assumption that Spaight would decide the fate of the *Aimée Marguerite,* based on the depositions, did not coincide with the directions in Henry Knox's letter to Spaight of 12 Nov. 1793, which Spaight enclosed in his letter to Hill of 3 Jan., nor with those in the circular letter of 10 Nov. 1793 that former secretary of state Thomas Jefferson sent to the U.S. district attorneys. Hill concluded that the governor's "power to return to one or the other claimant is limitted to the decision to be had by arbiters" (Nc-Ar: Governors' Letterbooks). For Knox's letter of 12 Nov. 1793, see n.1 of Spaight to GW, 19 Dec. 1793; for Jefferson's circular letter, see *Jefferson Papers,* 27:338–40.

The enclosed letters to Hill were those of 3 Jan. and 3 Feb. 1794. In the latter, Spaight wrote: "As to your opinion of the authority that is delegated to me by the different instructions that I have received, it is utterly impossible that you can be a judge of it," and whether the depositions are "transmitted to me or to the President of the United States is a matter of great indifference to me. could the business be done wholly by the offices of the federal government without my interference, it would be perfectly agreable to me. I cannot however but differ from you in opinion, on the meaning and intentions of the Secretary of States instructions to you for certainly the Executive there meant must be the one which caused the vessel to be arrested." Spaight concluded: "You will please to proceed in the business in such manner as you may think proper, and agreable to your opinion of the instructions you have received" (Nc-Ar: Governors' Letterbooks).

2. The memorial of James Robertson has not been identified. The statement of facts, which has not been identified, was enclosed in a brief cover letter to Spaight of 11 Jan. from J. B. Brouard, the French agent at Wilmington, N.C. (Nc-Ar: Governors' Letterbooks). Brouard served under the guidance of Michel-Ange-Bernard de Mangourit, who was the French consul for North Carolina, South Carolina, and Georgia and was stationed at Charleston, South Carolina. Mangourit soon was replaced by Antoine-Louis Fonspertuis,

whose exequatur GW signed on 7 March (*Georgia. The Augusta Chronicle and Gazette of the State,* 20 Dec. 1794).

From Richard Dobbs Spaight

Sir   No. Carolina New Bern 8th Feb: 1794

On the 6th inst. I received the Secretary of Wars two letters of the 13th Jan: and his three letters of the 18th Jan: the latter directing me to restore the money papers and other property now in the custody of the Deputy Marshall, to the Agent of the Spanish Commissioners, I shall give the necessary orders for that purpose and send them on to Wilmington by the next Southern post which leaves this on Wednesday next.[1]

The papers which I informed you in my letter of the 19th Decem: last I had directed the marshal to send to me in order fully to establish the fact of the money having been taken from the Spanish Brig St Joseph. I recd whilst at Fayetteville but could not get them translated there[.] I brought them here with me and have employed a person well skilled in the Spanish language to translate them faithfully, and expected to have had them ready to send on to you by this post—but they are not quite finished.

As the Money is now ordered to be restored to the agent of the Spanish Commissioners, it may be unnecessary to proceed with the translation, but as it is in some forwardness & the person already engaged to do it⟨,⟩ I shall let it be finished and sent on to you. It is an extract from the cargo Book of the Brig St Joseph— specifying every article of the cargo shipped on board of her at Carthagena, and the names of the persons who shipped it—Also a paper in french appearing to be done by Capt: Hervieux & his Officers & crew agreeing to divide between them the money taken on board the Spanish brig. executed the 30th Sep: 1793:[2] I have the honor to be &C.

Rd. D. Spaight

LB, Nc-Ar: Governors' Letterbooks.

1. On the dispute over gold and silver taken from the Spanish brig *San Josef* at the time of its capture by the French privateer *Aimée Marguerite* and its subsequent impoundment by Capt. William Cooke of the U.S. revenue cutter *Diligence,* who then turned it over to U.S. deputy marshal John Blakely, see Spaight to GW, 21 Oct. and 19 Dec. 1793. In one of his letters to Spaight of 13 Jan., Henry Knox wrote: "The President of the United States

has directed me to acknowledge receipt and reply to your letters of the 26th Novem: and the 19th ulto. From the circumstances of not having possession of the papers upon the subject an error was committed in my letter dated at Germantown [Pa.] on the 19th Novem: last in saying that prizes taken of the fifth day of June by proscribed privateers and brought into our ports were to be secured for the purpose of being restored to their former owners. The date which such prizes were be restored is after the 5th day of August last.

"If the evidence in your possession establishes the fact that the money in possession of the marshall of North Carolina belonged to the Spanish brig it is to be delivered to such agents as his Catholic Majesty's ministers shall have empowered to receive it, or to the Captain or owner if they should make their appearance, An agent however it is understood has been appointed for this purpose.

"The expenses which have been or may be incurred in the prosecution of this business are to be defrayed by the general Government upon accounts which shall be authenticated by your Excellency and transmitted to the accountant of this office under cover to me.

"The principle established by the president of the United States and contained in my letter of the 16th of August last, prohibiting asylum to any armed vessels fitted originally in our ports as cruizers is considered as of the highest importance to be adhered to, unless such vessels will divest themselves entirely of all warlike equipments" (Nc-Ar, Governors' Letterbooks). For Knox's circular letter of 16 Aug. to the governors of the maritime states, see n.1 of Knox to Tobias Lear, 17 Aug. 1793. The other letter of 13 Jan. has not been identified.

Only one letter of 18 Jan. from Knox to Spaight has been identified. It reads: "His catholic Majestys commissioners being desirous that every obstacle may be removed to their agents receiving the money taken by the L Aimee Margueritte, an illicit french privateer from the Spanish brig St Joseph; and it appearing indisputable from the evidence received that the money in possession of the marshall of North Carolina was taken out of the said brig, Your Excellency will therefore please to cause it to be delivered to the agent who has been appointed by the Spanish commissioners for that purpose" (Nc-Ar: Governors' Letterbooks).

Spaight charged Blakely, the deputy marshal at Wilmington, and not marshal John Skinner, with responsibility for guarding the trunk filled with Spanish gold and silver (Spaight to Blakely, 31 Oct. 1793, Nc-Ar: Governors' Letterbooks). For the appointment by José Ignacio de Viar and José de Jaudenes of Edward Jones (1762–1841), a resident of Wilmington and the state's solicitor general, to act as their agent, see their letter to Thomas Jefferson, 23 Oct. 1793, *Jefferson Papers*, 27:268–69. For Spaight's orders to Blakely to restore the money and other confiscated items, see n.2 of Spaight to GW, 16 Feb., and n.2 of Spaight to GW, 15 March. The next scheduled southern post was Wednesday, 12 February.

2. Neither the original documents nor the translations enclosed in Spaight's letter to GW of 16 Feb. have been identified.

From Richard Dobbs Spaight

Sir　　　　　　　　　　No. Carola New Bern 8th Feby 1794

By the last post I received the Secretary of Wars letter of the 21st Jany 1794.[1]

At the time the legislature passed the resolutions which I did myself the honor to transmit you on the 6th July last[2] they had grounds to apprehend an attack on our frontiers by the Indians. they had from the representations made to me in novem: been in the habit during the Summer and fall of committing depredations on the property of the Citizens of this State,[3] and we had reason to think, after the attack made on the Indians by the Militia of the territory South of the Ohio under the command of general Sevier that they would have committed hostilities on our frontiers.

As soon as a peace is made with the Cherokees by Governor Blount and our frontier is in a state of safety the Scouts now in service can be discharged.[4]

I enclose you a copy of my orders to Colo. David Vance: you will perceive that they are conformable to the Secretary of Wars letter to me and the resolutions of the General Assembly.[5] I have the honor &c.

R.D.S.

LB, Nc-Ar: Governors' Letterbooks.

1. For Knox's letter to Spaight of 21 Jan., see n.1 of Knox to GW, 21 January.

2. Spaight is referring to the proceedings of the North Carolina legislature that he enclosed in his first letter to GW of 6 January.

3. For these representations about the Indians, see David Vance to Spaight, 22 Nov. 1793, in n.2 of Spaight to GW, 6 Jan. (first letter).

4. For an expedition in October 1793 against the Cherokee Indians by militia troops of the Southwest Territory under the command of Gen. John Sevier, and for William Blount's efforts to achieve peace with the Cherokee Indians, see Sevier to Blount, 25 Oct., and Blount to Knox, 28 Oct. 1793, *ASP, Indian Affairs*, 1:469–70.

5. In his letter to Vance of 1 Jan., Spaight instructed him to "proceed immediately to call into service seven Scouts or patroles of rangers consisting of eight men each, they must be composed of the most bold, active, & experienced hunters or woodsmen, and kept out on the frontiers, in order to discover signs or the approach of Indians, and give the necessary information to you to repel any attack that may be made on our people. Each patrole is to have as near as can be for its particular care, a frontier of twelve

miles in extent they must not by any means commit any hostilities on the Indians but merely observe their motions." Spaight ordered Vance to select fourteen men from Buncombe County, twenty-two from Burke, and twenty from Rutherford. "Each ranger or Scout will receive from the United States the sum of five sixths of a dollar ℔ day which is allowed in full of all expences whatever." After explaining the proper procedures for keeping records of actual time served and for submitting payrolls to the War Department, Spaight instructed Vance, as the commander, to divide the militia into four equal classes, the first of which should "hold themselves in readiness to be called into service whenever occasion may require it." The other classes are to be held in reserve. The rangers "must confine themselves to act on the defensive only" until further orders are sent (Nc-Ar: Governors' Letterbooks).

From Betty Washington Lewis

My Dear Brothe[r]   Febry 9th 1794
   your Letter of the 3th of this Month with your kind Present to Harriot Came safe to hand she values it more as it Comes from Philadelphia and Expects it is more fashonable[1]—things in this Town is Scarce and very dear she seems truly sensable of the many favours receiv'd and sayes that she will make it her hole study to deserve them, I Can assure you she is truly deserving of the favours receiv'd, a[nd] I am not acquainted with any One who takes more Cear of there things and turns them to greater advantage.
   My Dear Brother I wish you to give Howell some advice how to Proseed in regard to two Negroes that Runaway from me a few daye before Christmas two of the Principal hands on the Plantation[2] I Expect their intension is to get to Philadelphia as thay have a thought in geting there thay will be free,[3] the hole Crop I made the last year was thirty Barrils of Corn and a Hundred and tenn Bushels of Wheat, if I am so unfortunate as not to get them again, I have no Chance to make any thing the insuing year. I am Join'd by the Girls in Love and good wishes for you all,[4]
                                                          Betty Lewis

ALS, ViMtvL.
   1. The letter of 3 Feb. to Harriot Washington has not been found. On the probable contents of the package from GW, see Harriot Washington to GW, 7 January.
   2. No written advice about recovering runaway slaves from GW to his nephew Howell Lewis has been found. At this time, Betty Washington Lewis

lived in the Lewis family home, now known as Kenmore, on the edge of the then village of Fredericksburg, Virginia. According to the will of Fielding Lewis, Sr., her deceased husband, she was given lifetime use of the brick mansion and 661 acres from the original plantation (Felder, *Fielding Lewis,* 309, 317–18).

3. Anti-slavery sentiments in Pennsylvania had resulted in the passage of "An ACT for the gradual Abolition of Slavery" by the state legislature on 1 March 1780 (*Laws enacted in the second sitting of the fourth General Assembly, of the Commonwealth of Pennsylvania. Which commenced at Philadelphia, on Wednesday the 19th day of January, in the year of our Lord one thousand seven hundred and eighty* [Philadelphia, 1780], 296–99). On 29 March 1788, "An ACT to explain and amend an act, entitled, 'An act for the gradual abolition of slavery'" provided that residents of Pennsylvania could not remove slaves from the state "with the design and intention that the place of abode or residence of such slave or servant shall be thereby altered or changed" (*Laws enacted in the second sitting of the twelfth General Assembly of the Commonwealth of Pennsylvania, which commenced at Philadelphia, on Tuesday the nineteenth day of February, in the year of our Lord, one thousand seven hundred and eighty-seven,* [Philadelphia, 1788], 440–44). The existence of these two laws evidently was known among Southern slaves, although their understanding of the legal provisions contained within them may have been imperfect.

4. Betty Washington Lewis is referring not only to Harriot Washington but also to Ann Alexander "Nancy" Lewis and Catherine Dade Lewis, who resided with her at this time and who were the younger daughters of her impoverished son Fielding Lewis, Jr.

To William Pearce

Mr Pearce,   Philadelphia Feby 9th 1794

since writing you a few lines on the 3d instant, I have received your letter of the 28th of last month, and that of the third of the present.[1]

If you are satisfied with Mr Butlers conduct and exertions, I shall be so. He has always appeared to me as a well disposed man, obliging and sober one who has seen better days: and must have had a good deal of practical knowledge in husbandry. If you can make him active, & will support his authority, I do not see why he may not be more useful to you than a young man, who might have a greater propensity to be running about.[2]

With respect to the French furse, I shall leave it altogether to you and him, to manage it as you shall think best; for in truth I know nothing of the nature of the Plant. In the disposal of the Seed, howr, (where it is ultimately to remain) you cannot go amiss. The best guide perhaps is to sow it in Soil which is most congenial to it—and if this could be found around the enclosures at the Mansion house, I should give it a preference; but in this also, do as shall appear best.[3]

I am of opinion the Post & rail fence which runs from the Mill up to the tumbling dam, & so on, is too low and unsubstantial for an outr fence, against such neighbours as I have in that quarter; it was for this reason I proposed a more substantial one; especially, as the good posts & Rails in that fence would do very well for the inner & cross fences. I conceive also, that the out side ditch ought to be widened, & deepned. In a word, to make the whole of the exterior fence so formidable, & the Rails so close together, as to prevent trespass even from pigs; without this I shall never enjoy the sole benefit of my Inclosures, nor keep the meadows along the mill swamp from injury.

The out fence at the Mansion house I am sensible stands in great need of repair, and I shall be much pleased by your repairing it, & well; as soon as circumstances will permit. The idea of getting rails out of the dead, & decaying timber, I much approve; for the waste which has been committed on my timber & wood hitherto, has really been shameful. I have no doubt, if the trees which have been fallen in all parts of my land, & only a small part of them used, were corded for fire wood instead of lying to rot on the ground that they would sell for many hundreds of pounds. You will find it necessary, I presume, whenever you undertake the Mansion house (out) fence, to get the rails tolerably convenient, on acct of the Cartage. It has always been my intention to clear, in the same manner the ground now is, in front of the house, from the white gates as the road goes towards Alexandria, up to the little old field; & to extend the fence out to it; whenever a convenient moment should be found for the purpose. If there be, therefore, any stuff fit for Rails within that space, two purposes will be answered by using it; namely, fencing; and clearing the ground of its growth; but I fear there are but few trees that will answer for the first, that is for rails.

If you will examine the little sketch of the lots at Union farm, which was enclosed in one of my former letters, you can be at no loss in laying them off—a slipe of No. 2, from the fence of No. 1 to the fence of No. 3, of the breadth mentioned in that sketch, gives you the four lots; and dividing this slipe into four equal parts gives you the size of each lot. The two next to field

No. 1, are those which are to be sown with Clover on the wheat, because they have been cowpenned. The other two must remain to succeed, in order, as have been mentioned in former letters.[4]

If I do not confine myself as nearly as circumstances will permit to my rotation system, this year, I never shall get into it at all; for which reason, although I might find ground better adapted to Corn than what was intended for Buck Wheat (for a Crop) It is my desire that you will attend to, & pursue the course wch has been mentioned in my letter of the 26th of last Month; or in the Oat grd, if you shd want Seed Oats.

Let me know every now and then how the growing Wheat & Barley looks, as a week or two may change the appearance of them materially.

What, or how much is done to the new race of the Mill? and at which end did they begin? Is it got to its depth? and carried on a level, what has been done?

I have no chance to get honey locust seed this year; and as it is thought improper to sow the french furze for the purpose of transplanting, the ground prepared by the Gardener for these things will be useless; But as I have got about a quart, or a little more of what is called White bent Seed, which is given to me as a very valuable grass, I wish you would prepare about a quarter of an Acre of grd for it (I would not chuse to have the seed in more than that) in one of the New meadows at Dogue run or Union farm, and sow it at the time mentioned in the enclosed letter. If no opportunity offers of sending it by water with the Clover Seed &ca I will send it by Post.[5]

Let the Gardener know that the Seeds he wrote for[6] shall also be sent at the same time, with some others which will require his particular skill & attention. You have never informed me how much St foin and India Hemp seed he has saved.

If my Cattle & Sheep receive all the attention & care that is necessary, I can require no more, if they should die; but it shews how essenscial it is to pick, cull, & sell off before it is too late, & to provide well for the rest, & this I hope will be the case another year; and especially in attending to the breeding of them; both as it respects the choice of the Males (particularly) and the seasons proper for their going to the females.

In a letter which has just been received from Mrs Fanny Washington, she requests me, to desire you, to rent her fishing Landing at Taylers on the best terms you can obtain & make it a condition that the person so renting it, shall furnish for her own use two Barrels of Shad, and four of Herrings—and as many of the latter as hath usually been put up for the use of the negros under his (Taylers) care, of which he can inform you—It is my wish you should do this.[7]

Colo. Ball must have the three shoats he applies for—a boar & two sows.[8] I was in hopes the last spell of freezing weather wd have enabled you to fill the Ice house. It is very desirable it should be so, as the convenience on acct of fresh meat &ca in the summer is inconceivably great in the Country.

It appears by Mr Lewis's accounts that Mr Stuart has only recd £15.12. The difference between that Sum and his wages, is yet due to him; unless he has received money from Mr Whiting of which, if the fact is so, he unquestionably knows, and will tell.[9] Crows & McKoys wages are also due, & must be paid. If you have not money, nor a prospect of raising it from the midlings & Ship stuff in time for these purposes, let me know it, and I will send it from hence.[10]

I have nothing to add at present but to beg you will make my people (about the Mansion house) be careful of the fire, for it is no uncommon thing for them to be running from one house to another in cold windy nights with sparks of fire flying, & dropping as they go along, without paying the least attention to the consequences.

You will remember in time that my house in Alexandria is got in order for Mrs Fanny Washington; as I have promised to do this by the time mentioned to you in former letters.[11] If my Carpenters could be prevailed upon to go on with their work as they ought to do, I intended to build Daries both at Union and Dogue run farm; to see if the Milk at each could not be turned to some account; but the lower part I should build of Brick like that in the Neck, where Stuart lives.[12] I remain Your friend &ca

Go: Washington

P.S.[13] If upon tryal, the Clover Seed you have is found to be good, it would be well to sow what you have upon the first Snow that covers the ground after this letter reaches you. What I have here shall go by the first Vessel, for Alexandria; but when this may happen is impossible to say, as the Navigation of the Delaware is interrupted by Ice. Yrs &ca

G.W.

ALS, ViMtvL; ALS (letterpress copy), DLC:GW.

1. The letter from Pearce to GW of 28 Jan. has not been found. GW also is replying to Pearce's letter dated 4 Feb., not "the third."

2. On GW's previous assumption that James Butler would be replaced as the overseer of the Mansion House farm, see his letter to Pearce of 12 Jan. 1794.

3. For the shipment to Mount Vernon of French furze seed, from which GW hoped to produce hedgerows, see GW to Pearce, 16–17 March.

4. The sketch of Union farm that GW enclosed in his letter to Pearce of 23 Dec. 1793 has not been identified. For a map of the various farms and fields on the Mount Vernon estate, see "Washington's drawing of his farms at Mount Vernon, 1793," *Papers, Presidential Series*, 14:564–65.

5. The enclosed letter has not been identified. The white bent grass seed (*Agrostis stolonifera*) was sent by post along with GW's letter to Pearce of 16 February. On the shipment of clover seed to Mount Vernon, see GW to Pearce, 16–17 and 23 March.

6. The letter from head gardener John Christian Ehlers to GW has not been found.

7. The letter from Frances "Fanny" Bassett Washington probably was that of 26 Jan. to Martha Washington, which has not been found (Martha Washington to Frances Bassett Washington, 10 Feb. 1794, Fields, *Papers of Martha Washington*, 256). The fishing landing was part of Fanny's estate on Clifton's Neck, which adjoined Mount Vernon and was under the care of Mr. Tayler, her farm manager.

8. The letter from Burgess Ball to Pearce asking for three young hogs has not been identified (Pearce to GW, 4 Feb. 1794).

9. The accounts kept by GW's nephew Howell Lewis, who served as temporary manager of Mount Vernon from July 1793 until the arrival of Pearce in early January, have not been found. Former estate manager Anthony Whitting evidently had not paid William Stuart, the overseer of River farm, because, on 7 March, Stuart received £23.18.00 for "part of his wages Due for the year 93" (Mount Vernon Accounts, 1794–97).

10. Hiland Crow and Henry McCoy were the respective overseers of Union and Dogue Run farms. On 3 April, Pearce paid £12 to Crow for "part of his wages" and £3 to McCoy. On 1 March, Pearce recorded receiving £9 in cash "in Part payment for midlings & Ship Stuff," leaving a cash balance on 1 March of £40.07.06 (Mount Vernon Accounts, 1794–97).

11. For Fanny's plan to live in GW's house in Alexandria, Va., see her letter to GW of 22 Nov. 1793. For GW's instructions on preparing the house for her arrival "before the first of May," see GW to Pearce, 23 Dec. 1793, and 12 Jan. 1794.

12. The River farm was located on Clifton's Neck. The dairies, or cow sheds, at Union and Dogue Run farms were not completed until late 1795 or early 1796 (Farm Reports, 6–12 Dec. 1795, DLC:GW; "Terms on which the Farms at Mount Vernon may be obtained," 1 Feb. 1796, ADS, NIC; see also GW's advertisement, *Columbian Mirror and Alexandria Gazette* [Alexandria, Va.], 20 Feb. 1796).

13. Another hand wrote "No. 5" above the postscript on the ALS at ViMtvL.

From Harriot Washington

Fredericksburg [Va.] Febuary 9th 1794
I received my dear Uncle's letter the 9 of this month with the bundle and return him a thousand thank's for them beleive me my dear Uncle that I am very sensible of the many obligation's I am under to you and Aunt Washington and shall ever remember them with gratitude. I shall endeavour to let my conduct henceforward be such as to deserve them, the thing's that were sent are very pretty. I am much obleiged to you, for getting them there as there could not be any procured here as handsome.[1] We heard from Cousin Bob last week he has been so unfortunate as to lose his little boy. cousin Lewis and himself were very well.[2] Aunt Lewis join's me in love to you and Aunt Washington. if you please to give my love to Nelly Custis. I am my dear Uncle Your affectionate Neice

Harriot Washington

ALS, ViMtvL.
    1. GW's letter to Harriot of 3 Feb. has not been found (see Betty Washington Lewis to GW, 9 Feb.). In her letter to GW of 7 Jan., Harriot had requested a silk jacket and a pair of shoes, and these items may have been included in the bundle.
    2. William Burnett Lewis, the son of Robert Lewis and his wife, Judith Walker Browne Lewis, was born on 22 Nov. 1793 and died on 29 Nov. 1793.

To William Washington

Dear Sir,   Philadelphia Feb. 9th 1794.
    Your Letter of the 6th Ulto by way of New York, has been lately received; That you should be without any of my letters in answer to your former favors, is matter of extreme surprize to me, as the receipt of them had been regularly acknowledged.
    The Bill on Mr Bell of this City for six hundred and seventy eight dollars and 64/100 came safe to my hands, and was punctually paid. Of this I wrote you, altho' the letter has never it seems been received.[1]
    Previous thereto, I had informed you (about this time twelve month, if I recollect rightly) that as it was improper to travel the Jack in the winter season, and moreover, as he could not be got to Mount Vernon in *time* nor in *order* for covering the ensuing

spring, I requested you to keep him in So. Carolina and do for me in the case as if you were acting for yourself, until he could be removed more advantageously:[2] and now, in answer to your last letter of the 6th of Jany, requesting to know if those who have sent Mares a second time to Royal Gift with no better success than they met with the first time shou'd pay for those wch do not bring foal? I shall, under *my present view* of the subject answer No provided you are satisfied they have not cast them because in that case the failure is not in the Jack—But in this, as in every thing else which relates to the Jack—do (as I have before requested) the same for me as you would for yourself and I shall be perfectly satisfied.

His covering, while he stood at Mount Vernon was very sure; for no mare that went to him, scarcely ever missed; nor was he ever lame before he left that place; but from accounts which I have received from some Gentlemen in Virginia he was most abominably treated on the Journey by the man to whom he was entrusted; for instead of moving him slowly and steadily along as he ought, he was prancing (with the Jack) from one public meeting, or place to another in a gate which could not but prove injurious to an animal who had hardly ever been out of a walk before—and afterwards, I presume, (in order to recover lost time) pushed him beyond what he was able to bear all the remainder of the Journey—However, there is no remedy now for what has happened, but if he should get over his present disorder, and recover his flesh again, he may yet be a useful & valuable animal as he will not (if he live) be past his prime these fifteen or twenty years yet such is their longevity of this species of animal.[3] I was glad to hear from Mr Izard that he had got one very fine mule from two mares which he had sent to Royal Gift[4]—from thence I entertained a hope that he might be growing better—be this however as it may, I would thank you for giving me advice from time to time of his condition, that I may be enabled thereby to take measures accordingly. In the mean while, I entreat you to derive all the advantages you can from him to your own mares, without entertaining an idea of making compensation for it.[5]

Offer, if you please my best respects to Mrs Washington;[6] and be assured of the sincere esteem and regard with which I am— Dear Sir Yr affect. Hble Servt

G. W——n

ADfS, DLC:GW; LB, DLC:GW.

1. GW's letter in response to William Washington's letter of 20 April 1793, with the enclosed bill drawn on Philadelphia merchant William Bell, and a duplicate written "Some weeks thereafter" have not been found.

2. For these instructions, see GW to William Washington, 30 Jan. 1793.

3. On the journey of Royal Gift from Mount Vernon, see n.1 of GW to William Washington, 30 Jan. 1793. Royal Gift died in South Carolina in 1796 (William Washington to GW, 23 July 1796, PHi: Gratz Collection).

4. Ralph Izard was currently representing South Carolina in the U.S. Senate.

5. A later letter from William Washington to GW of 24 May 1795 reporting on the health of Royal Gift has not been found (GW to William Washington, 14 July 1795, ADfS, DLC:GW; LB, DLC:GW).

6. William Washington was married to Jane Reily Elliott Washington.

From Alexander Hamilton

Sir,   Treasury Departt 10 Feby 1794

The enclosed letter of the 27 of last month from the Collector of Tappahannock, relates to a subject equally delicate & disagreeable.[1] It is my duty to add, that bills have returned protested to the amount of 3000 Dollars.[2]

This conduct, though I trust proceeding from no ill motive in the Collector, is of a nature so fatal to the punctual collection of the revenue, and at the same time so vitally injurious to the public credit, that I cannot forbear to submit it as my opinion that the public good requires the superceding of the officer.[3] With perfect respect &c. &c.

                                        Alexander Hamilton.

LB, DLC:GW.

1. Hamilton is returning a letter that Hudson Muse wrote to GW on 27 Jan., in which the collector of customs confessed to a mismanagement of funds.

2. Muse confirmed Hamilton's information in a letter to GW of 16 Feb. (see n.3 of Muse to GW, 27 Jan.).

3. For GW's subsequent appointment of Laurence Muse to the collector's post at Tappahannock, Va., see GW to U.S. Senate, 5 March.

From Edmund Randolph

Sir   Philadelphia february 10. 1794

The bill, drawn by Edward Church on the Secretary of State and accepted by me, amounts to one hundred and fifty pounds sterling.[1] The Secretary of the Treasury is disinclined to pay it out of the monies in his hands. I must therefore request you to give an order for the payment, out of the contingent fund at your disposal.[2] The form of the Order may be somewhat in this shape. "The President of the U.S. desires the Secretary of the Treasury to cause a bill of exchange, drawn at Lisbon, on the 19th of October 1793 for one hundred and fifty pounds sterling, by Edward Church in favor of Jacob Dohrman & comp.; and accepted by the secretary of State in behalf of his department on the 10th of January 1794, to be adjusted and paid out of the contingent fund at his disposal. If the forms of the Treasury department require any further document from the President, he wishes it to be prepared and sent to him for his signature."[3] I have the honor, sir, to be with the highest respect yr mo. ob. serv.

Edm: Randolph

ALS, DNA: RG 59, Miscellaneous Letters; LB, DNA: RG 59, GW's Correspondence with His Secretaries of State; LB, DNA: RG 59, Domestic Letters.

1. Edward Church, the U.S. consul at the Portugese port of Lisbon, reported in his first letter to former secretary of state Thomas Jefferson of 22 Oct. 1793 that he had drawn a bill for £150 Sterling in favor of the mercantile firm of Jacob Dohrman and Company for the charter of a vessel to sail from Lisbon to New York City. This was done in order to procure a means for sending diplomatic dispatches to Jefferson (*Jefferson Papers*, 27:262–64). Jefferson submitted this letter and its enclosures to GW on 23 Dec. 1793 (*JPP*, 272).

2. Section 3 of "An Act making appropriations for the support of government for the year one thousand seven hundred and ninety," 26 March 1790, authorized the president "to draw from the treasury a sum not exceeding ten thousand dollars, for the purpose of defraying the contingent charges of government" (*Stat.* 1:105).

3. On this same date, GW directed Alexander Hamilton to pay this bill (*JPP*, 283).

From Karl August Freiherr von Wangenheim

Sir! Erlang[en, Germany] 10th February 1794.

To receive a letter from the other part of the world, and written by a youth, who has nothing yet done in the world to be known by, You, Sir! You will perhaps be very wonderd at. But I believe it is enough to be excused to send You a letter, being a man like You form'd by the same Creator and having the design to be usefull to You, Sir, and Your Country, and if it was possible to all mankind. Without preface, excepted this, that all, what

I'll make, is founded in the convictiveness, You are a great and very honourable man, I shall tell You, Sir! what is the design of this letter. Since some years it is a speculation of many betrayers, to give out themselves as Emissarys, sent by the united States of North-Amerika. They persuaded many peopel by very splendid conditions, to go with their littel fortune to Amerika. Commonly they bring them till Tuchland, and after this, it is known, that the pretended emissarys, partly rob'd them of the last reste of a very littel fortune, who did believe to be very near Amerika, and the end of their misfortunes, partly not content to have stolen, this poor men, did bring them yet in the hands of So⟨u⟩l-Sellers at Tuchland. You will know Yourself, Sir! how prejudicial such tricks can become for the good name of the united States and their politicks. It is very naturally, that by such trifly cases, likewise the true and usefull proposals, concerning good conditions for such persons, being willg, to till some yet uncultivated places of the united States, shall not be accepted, because every body fears to be betray'd. From this motive, I believe it will not be disagreeable to You, Sir! that I tell You with all particulars the history of such a trick in the paper adjoyned, if this matter, to discover the tricks of such raskels and to give to Your Emissarys or avertissements, more infallibel signs, which could not be obnoxious to errour, seems You worthy to take care of it.[1]

This, Sir! is the first and most uninterrested motive of this letter, but I have yet an other, what is not so without all interest for my own person.

You will read in the description of the trick of the pretended Colonel Pearce, that I myself would go in the service of the united States of North-Amerika. Now this Colonel is escaped, but my wishes to set out from Europe and to live in a free Country, has settled itself in my mind. If You, believe, Sir! that a good natured Youth, who has some parts and the best will to become usefull to the Republick, can receive the permission to go in the service of the united States, I offer You myself to such a one. I am not an adventurer, who is in need to leave his fathers Country; I am not without fortune, and without all views to become forward at Europe, no, Sir! I have many favourabel views for it; I have a father, who is in the service of a good prince; I am a noble-man (Gentilhomme. You do perhaps not know in Your happy country, this word) and this is at Germany a prerogative which procures many advantages, but all this my circumstances to my fortune at Europe, I despise. I can not be happy, if I do not become, what perhaps I would become once, by myself and my own few merits. Concerning my principles of Moral I can not sell my parts and my life to a prince, because I should do after this, not what I shall do by the laws of my reason, but what my prince did command me for. I know very well that no body should speak too much from himself, but now I am indeed in the case, to begin with speaking of myself because necessary I must be known by You, Sir! I am the eldest Son of Charles Wangenheim, who is Major in the service of the Duke of Saxe-Gotha. Three of my brothers are in the service of the King of Borussia.[2] I could likewise have a military place in the same service, but I did not like to fight against the French people, from whom I believe they are in the right. I prefer also the proposal of my father, to become a Lawyer. But, dearest Sir! the justice is blind at Europe, and I like very much to see with open eyes. Since half a Year, therefore I did more cultivate, the english and french languages, Mathematics and Philosophy, than the old Roman laws, which however I did not neglect. That are allready my bussiness at the University at Erlang near Nurnberg in Franconie, and I will yet stay a year longer. I can not pretend, that You, Sir! shall believe me upon my word, but certainly You do know some person at Germany, from whom You are persuaded, that he is a honourable man. Let me be put on the proof Sir! by such a one, and if he finds, that I could be usefull to You and the Republick, give me a place, and with it the happyness to live in a free State, and to have nothing other heads, than virtue and my duty. Procure me, Sir! the place of a Lieutnant, that I have some fixt views, tell me, what I should learn the first, and if You believe that it should be better, I remain yet, upon my own expences, a year at Europe, for learning all, what You believe usefull and necessary. Should You find after this, that I could be more usefull to the Republick in a other place than a military function, I shall surely all do, what You proved that it is the best.

If You can not procure me a settlement in the free State, at least be so kind to give me in a few words an answer, that You will not be offended by my good will.[3] With the esteem, I have every time for a virtuous man, I shall remain for ever Sir! Your's

　　　　　　　　　　　　　　　　　Charles Wangenheim

L, DLC:GW; L, DLC:GW. John Jay enclosed these documents in his letter to GW of 11 Aug. 1794.

Politician and philosopher Karl August Freiherr von Wangenheim (1773–1850) studied law in Jena and Erlangen. He had a successful political career under King Friedrich I of Württemberg (1754–1816). He published several books on political subjects, including *Die Idee der Staataverfassung in ihrer Anwendun auf Wirtembergs alte Landesverfassung und den Entwurf zu deren Erneuerung* (Frankfurt am Main, 1815), which dealt with the idea of constitutional reform in Württemberg.

1. The enclosed account reads: "John Williams, a pretended englishman, arrived with his wife and sister in law, from Wurtzburg, where he was since half a year, at Nurnberg in Franconie, Octob: the 14th 1793. At first he did give out himself for a man of letters, and in the following time he wished to give lessions in the english language. At least in the month of Decem: he told, that he was the best friend of John Williams Pearce, Colonel in the united States of North-Amerika. This Colonel, told he, was sent, by the united States, to Germany and Sueden for procuring Officers, 4 Captans, 8 Lieutnants, a Coppyman and a Physicien for a new Regiment at Philadelphia. Now as he, Mr Williams, to his own pretension, was very good known by Colonel Pearce, in the Amerikan war, this Colonel did beg him to procure himself some good natured gentlemen, because he did longer stay at Europe, than the Colonel himself. The constitution of Amerika is very well known and very much beloved at Germany, and therefore it is very easy, that Mr Williams, who pretended likewise, to have been General in the Amerikan war and after this an Embassedour, at Sueden and Danemark, could persuade some gentlemen to go in the service of the united States, chiefly he did makeselves them very splendid conditions, concerning the Salary, and the finest views to forward themselves in the following time. The first, who would make the journey to North-Amerika, was Mr [Johann Benjamin] Ehrhardt, a good Physicien and a yet better philosopher, who did like very much, to stay in a Country, where freedom and egality consist with reason. He was married with the daughter of a rich marchand, and Mr Williams was lodging in the house of this marchand. Before this old father in law of the young physicien would consent in the departure of his daughter, he did be naturally curious to see the Credidios of the Colonel. Now Mr Williams told him, that he was himself the Colonel Pearce, but having his reasons for it to be not known by this character at Nurnberg, he did beg him to say nothing to some body, concerning this discovery. After this he did shew him a Credidio, very fine written in english language, upon it setted the Seal of the united States of North-Amerika and signed by the President Washington and the Secretary of State. With this attestat the old marchand was content, and consented to the journey of his daughter[.] Being all ready, Colonel Pearce or Mr Williams presented to the Physicien a printed brevet, where nothing than the name of the Physicien was written by hand, and this brevet was likewise underwritten by President Washington and the States-Secretary. This brevet assured to Mr Ehrhardt the place of Physicien of the new Regiment Pensylvania, with 400£ Salary. From

this time the physicien received his salary and 200£ were promised him for the journey and his regimentals. This Somme should be him retracted in 6 years by and by. As this affair was settled, the physicien and Mr Williams did persuade Mr [Johann Georg Christian] Fick, Collaborator at the University Erlang near Nurnberg to accept the place of a Coppyman or Auditor, likewise with 400£ salary and the same conditions. He accepted this place with the greatest pleasure, because he has nearly to live and must entertain a wife and five childern. He did not receive the brevet in the same time, because he should not know, that Mr Williams and Mr Pearce, who was (as it was fancyd) at Munichen in Bavarie, did be only one person, and by this reason he should write a letter to him to Munichen. In the beginning of January 1794 Mr Williams set out with his new physicien to go likewise to the Colonel (they did fancy at least this reason) but before their departure, Mr Williams did give, to his housekeeper, the father in law of physicien, bills for 600£ addressed to Herries and Comp: at London. Concerning th⟨e⟩se bills, the old marchand, who is call'd [Johann Paul] Golling did lend to Mr Williams circa 200£ and let set out him to Munichen, because his son in law was likewise going with him. Before to set out, they promised yet to the Collaborator Fick the place of an Auditor, and charged him with procuring to them some gentlemen for Lieutnants. One of them was I myself, who accepted this occasion to see the world and to make so many experiences in it as possibel. In this moment Mr Fick was writing belonging myself and my resolution to take Services of the united states. After a few days, he received an answer favorable by Mr Ehrhardt, the physicien, that he should receive indeed the place of an Auditor, and myself the place of a Lieutnant, that they would return very soon to Nurnberg and bring with themselves our brevet. Now we did believe that all was in the right, and we were beginning to settle our family affairs, and to arrange all for so long a journey. A few weaks after we were extremely troubled in our happy dreams. A letter my Mr Williams written and signd with his own Seal, return'd from Vienna, because no body could find its man to whom the letter was written. The letter (no: 1.) came in the hands of Mrss Ehrhardt, and she was too much woman and also curious enough to read this letter, already open. By this letter it was known, Mr Williams or the pretended Colonel Pearce, was call'd Anton Simon, who told in this letter to his brother many things, concerning his life, having been Captain in french service the time of Amerikan war, and passed half a year having become General and having married a french Countesse (who shall have been indeed a publick whoor at Paris) he did not set out from Tuckland to Nurnberg, where he would stay and live quietly &c. &c. &c. This all can be seen in a coppy of this letter, which is written in very bad German language[.] A few days after having received this letter, another did arrive from London, which is written by the Banquier Herries that no money was lodged in his hand by some Mr Williams Pearce, and that very soon the bills should be return'd with Protest (No. 2). Now we did see very well, that all was a trick and old marchand set out in this moment to Munchen for catching this betrayer. But at his arrival at Munchen, he heard that his own Son in law did escape with

Mr. Anton Simon and his family. He has presented himself likewise there as Colonel Pearce in the service of the united states of North-Amerika, and has had in this character two Soldiers for Ordonances from the prince of this country.

"Till this moment nobody does know where they are, however all will be done for catching them. It seems very likely that Dr Ehrhardt has been betrayed by a Soul-Seller." Copies of the "letter written by the pretended Colonel Pearce" of 11 Nov. 1793 and the undated letter from the London bankinghouse of Sir Robert Herries and Co., which is in French, appear at the bottom of this account (DLC:GW). A later version of this account contains a postscript that reads: "After the newest accounts Mr Ehrhardt returned from the prosecution of this Anton Simon, who escaped him by a trick and is very set out for Constantinople. But before he betrayed Mr Ehrhardt, who lives now at Nuremberg with 6000 florins and a new carriage" (DLC:GW). For other letters about this scam, see Erhard to GW, 27 Jan.; Fick to GW, 27 Jan.; and Golling to GW, 4 February.

2. Ernest II (Ernst; 1745–1804) was the present ruler of the German principality of Saxe-Gotha-Altenburg. Borassia is another name for Prussia, which was currently ruled by Frederick William II.

3. In a letter to Jay of 1–4 Nov. 1794, GW wrote: "I write nothing in answer to the letter of Mr Wangenheim (enclosed by you to me)—Were I to enter into corrispondencies of that sort (admitting their was no impropriety in the measure) I should be unable to attend to my ordinary duties. I have established it as a maxim, neither to envite, nor to discourage emigrants. My opinion is, that they will come hither as fast as the true interest & policy of the United States will be benefited by foreign population. I believe many of these, as Mr Wangenheim relates, have been, and I fear will continue to be, imposed upon by Speculators in land, and other things. But I know of no prevention but caution—nor any remedy except the laws" (ALS, NNC: Jay Papers).

From Uriah Forrest

[Philadelphia] 11th Feb. 1794.

The only apology I have to offer for obtruding the within paper, is, that, the author has particularly requested me, to present it to you, in the hope & expectation it will be sanctioned, with your Signature.[1] I have the honor to be with all Possible respect, Your most obedient humble Servt

Uriah fforrest

ALS, DLC:GW.

1. The enclosure has not been identified. Uriah Forrest, a congressman from Maryland, was currently in Philadelphia to attend the first session of the Third Congress.

Henry Knox to Bartholomew Dandridge, Jr.

Sir.   War Department February 11th 1794
   Please to Submit the enclosed letters from Governor Shelby[1]
and Genl A. Campbell to the President of the United States.[2]
yours Sincerely

H. Knox

LS, DLC:GW; LB, DLC:GW.
   1. In a letter of 10 Jan., Kentucky governor Isaac Shelby wrote Knox in order "to call the Attention of the President of the United States to the defenceless situation of the frontiers of this state." In expectation of being "vigorously
attacked by the Indians early in the spring," Shelby sought "discretionary
powers" in order to call up and employ the state militia for use against the
Indians. He justified this request by noting that the federal army under Gen.
Anthony Wayne had provided to date "inadequate protection," was situated
too far away, and did not have enough familiarity with the different regions
within Kentucky to be effective (KyLoF: Isaac Shelby Papers).
   2. The letter from Arthur Campbell to Knox of 23 Jan. has not been found,
but according to GW's executive journal it was "on the subject of forming a
barrier between the US. & the southern Indians by introducing emigrants, &
forming a line of settlement." Both enclosures were submitted to GW on this
date and subsequently returned to Knox (*JPP*, 283).

Henry Knox to Bartholomew Dandridge, Jr.

Sir,   War Department, Feby: 11th 1794.
   Please to submit to the President of the United States, the
Letter from the Governor of Virginia and the proposed Answer
thereto[1]—The idea of the firing of the Dedalus has been communicated by the Secretary of State.[2] Yours sincerely

H. Knox

LS, DLC:GW; LB, DLC:GW.
   1. The enclosed letter from Henry Lee to Knox probably was that of
5 Feb., in which Lee expressed concern about the presence of "two french
and one british frigate" in the port of Norfolk. "A constant bickering," he
wrote, "prevails between them and unfortunately for the harmony and peace
of the town the discord between the hostile frigates I fear will be communicated to the inhabitants." Lee then assured Knox that "it will not require
much money to erect a fort and two or three batteries," that a garrison "can
be readily furnished" from the state militia, and that "sufficient Ordnance
belonging to the Commonwealth and the United States lay dismounted in
Norfolk and its vicinity." Lee also suggested: "It seems necessary that some

reasonable limits should be established respecting the time allowed to ships of War coming into our ports to refit. . . . The Dedalus a british frigate arrived in Norfolk about the 20th of November to repair some injuries received at sea and I am told did not commence her repair until the first of this month when a fortnight was all sufficient for the purpose. She is still there and probably may continue there for months" (Vi: Executive Letter Book).

Knox's reply of this date reads: "I have had the honor of receiving and submitting your letter of the 1. instant to the President of the United States. The subject of fortifying the principal Seaports of the United States, in which is included Norfolk, is now under the consideration of a Committee of the House of Representatives who it is expected will very shortly report their opinion thereon. From the prevailing sentiment little doubt seems to be entertained that a measure with which the peace safety and dignity of the United States is so intimately blended will be adopted. The subject of a long continuance in our ports of vessels of War belonging to the belligerent parties had been previously considered; the refute of which you will find in Mr. Jeffersons letter to Mr. Hammond the British Minister dated the 9 September last. It will appear that the Ships of War belonging to the belligerent powers, provided those at War with France do not bring prizes enjoy an equality in our ports: 1. In cases of urgent necessity. 2d. in cases of comfort and convenience and 3d. in the time they may chuse to continue. The case of the Ships of War on opposite sides being at Norfolk creates a delicate and dangerous situation for that Town which nothing can remedy so effectually as its being put in a state of respectable defence. Indeed some information has been received by which it would appear that the Dædalus had fired a shot in a very unjustiable manner. The President of the United States requests your Excellencys information upon this subject properly attested so that such measures may be taken thereon as shall appear proper" (Vi: Executive Papers; *Calendar of Virgina State Papers,* 7:30). For Jefferson's letter to George Hammond and F. P. Van Berckel of 9 Sept. 1793, see *Jefferson Papers,* 27:70–72.

2. According to a letter from Thomas Newton, Jr., to Henry Lee of 24 Feb., the "shot or shots fired" from the British frigate *Daedalus* while in the port of Norfolk, Va., occurred accidentally "or by means of some persons putting them into the Gun with a malicious intention, unknown to any officer on board the frigate." Newton reported that it appeared "that there was no intention of insult or injury" and that he found the British captain, Charles H. Knowles, "disposed to observe the strictest neutrality" (*Calendar of Virginia State Papers,* 7:39–40).

From Thomas Mifflin

Sir,   Philadelphia, 11th Feby 1794.

In order to enable me to carry into effect your instructions for preserving the peace and neutrality of the United States, within the jurisdiction of Pennsylvania, I was under the necessity of establishing a Fort at Mud-Island, agreeably to the intimation, which I gave you, in my letter of the Eighth day of July last.[1] and, as the object of that establishment still requires my attention, I have recommended it to the General Assembly, to make a legislative provision, not only with respect to what has been done, but with respect to what it may, in future, be necessary to do, in aid of those measures of the General Government, which are referred to the agency of the Executive Magistrate of the State.[2]

The exposed situation of the Western frontiers of Pennsylvania has, likewise, claimed the interposition of the Legislature; and, it is probable, that, as an auxilary to the force of the United States, three companies drafted from the militia will be stationed, during the ensuing summer, in the frontier counties for the purposes of protection and defence.[3]

I have thought it proper, Sir, to make this communication; as well for the general purpose of information⟨,⟩ as to obtain your sentiments on the subject. For, the Legislature in adopting, as well as I, in recommending, the proposed arrangments, certainly contemplate a re-imbursement of the expence which they occasion, from the Treasury of the Union: and on this, and on every official transaction connected with the General Government, it will give me sincere pleasure, to be honored with your concurrence and approbation.[4] I am, with perfect respect, Sir, Your most obed: hble serv:

Tho. Mifflin

ADfS, PHarH: Executive Correspondence; LB, PHarH: Governor's Letter Books.

1. On the instructions given Mifflin, the administration's approval of Mifflin's suggestion to build a fort on Mud Island, which lay in the Delaware River at Philadelphia, and for preliminary measures taken by Mifflin to fortify that island, see Cabinet Opinion, 8 July 1793, and n.7.

2. In his address to the Pennsylvania General Assembly of 5 Dec. 1793, Mifflin encouraged the legislature to extend provisions for fortifying Mud Island and to provide militia forces to defend the state's western borders against possible Indian attacks, and in a letter to the assembly of 7 Jan., he wrote to "remind" the legislators that "the fund heretofore appropriated by law" for the defenses at Mud Island "is exhausted, and that a further provision for this service, consequently, requires your immediate attention" (*Journal of the first session of the fourth House of Representatives of the Commonwealth of Pennsylvania, which commenced at Philadelphia, on Tuesday, the third day of December, in the year of our Lord one thousand seven hundred and ninety-three* [Philadelphia, 1793–94], 11, 86).

3. "An ACT for more effectually securing the trade, peace and safety of the port of Philadelphia, and defending the Western Frontiers of the commonwealth," 28 Feb. 1794, provided for an artillery company at Fort Mifflin on Mud Island and for the support of three infantry companies to be posted in the frontier counties of Westmoreland, Washington, and Allegheny (*Acts of the General Assembly of the Commonwealth of Pennsylvania, passed at a session, which was begun and held at the city of Philadelphia on Tuesday, the third day of December, in the year one thousand seven hundred and ninety-three* [Philadelphia, 1794], 463–65).

4. GW sent this letter to Henry Knox for his opinion (Bartholomew Dandridge, Jr., to Knox, 13 Feb. 1794).

From Edward Newenham

Dear Sir   Dublin [Ireland] 11th Feby 1794

It is, in my mind, an Age since I had the Honor and the real pleasure of a Letter from you—on my part, nothing shall interrupt a Correspondence, that I so highly esteem, but my Dissolution, or your deeming me unworthy of it.[1]

The situation we are, & have been, in, for these three last years, in this Kingdom has partly altered my Line of public Conduct, particularily as the People had obtained those Laws for which I Struggled many years—the Place—the Pension—& Responsibility Bills; I found a Faction here (without the walls of Parliament) ready to reduce us to a *Colony* of France, & hoping to devide both the Landed & Commercial Property among themselves; Adoring true Liberty, I voted for Every Measure tending to that blessing for 42 years in & out of Parliament, but the System adopted by that Faction of an Agrarian Law, I could not accede to; they had proceeded nearly to a Crisis—of the Sword being Drawn & the Scabbard thrown away—but the Existing Laws, at length exerting themselves, Stop'd their Career[2]—& to shew the Hypocrisy of Some of *these Men,* it need only be mention'd, that they were the bitterest Enemies to American Freedom; their Late audacious (though impotent) attempts in their public papers to traduce your Spirit & Memorable Proclamation,[3] & to Villify the Characters of Mr: Jay & Mr: Jefferson, prove the badness of their heart, & their fixd Enmity to those Virtues that adorn you & your Friends; was it possible, I should have deemed them Pensioners of Duplain & Genet—as well might a Regiment of the Roman Pontiffs Soldiers attempt to take Giberalter by Storm, as

That, Such Reptiles Should Succeed in attacking the Character of George Washington.[4]

According to present appearances the French are Every where Victorious—Toulon Evacuated—Alsace releived—Fort Louis blown up—The Toulon & Lyannois Armies gone to the Eastern Pyreneans must Subdue the Small force of the Spanish Dons—in the western Pyreneans they seem Victorious, & the Convention announce that Joudains Army is 3 Times as Strong as York's & Cobaugh—the Invasion of England is announced in all the Jacobin Speeches—the Plunder of Proud London's Bank is beheld, as a matter of Course by the San's Coulottes—they announce 170 sail of Transports ready to Bring over their Troopes; they declare that their fleet at Brest is 34 & our Channel Fleet, but 26 sail of the Line; that their fleet will, at least, prevent ours from disturbing the Invasion.[5]

All is Suspence in this Country 5 English mails due—my hopes rest on the Re-inforcements that may arrive to the Allied Armies before they risk a General Action—I think *Cobaugh,* like Sir Wm Howe, has made a *Chain of Posts* of greater Extent than from the Delaware to Statin Island—but I hope they have not a Washington to take another Trenton—if thcy had, Cobaugh would be *Burgoynd,* & the Duke of York's army forced to Embark or fly to Holland.[6]

our Parliament has been almost (5 members excepted) in Support of the present war—the best Freinds of Constitutional Liberty are of that Sentiment, but the Lower order of the People (in this as in every other Nation) wish for a Change, yet they being Papists abhor the Idea of the Destructions of Saints & Crosses—they wish for a Change, in order to get the *Landed* Property, & for this month past they have openly wished for the Landing of the French.

My Agent, for 20 years, Mr Napper Tandy, has been accused of Sedition & Conspiracy—he is fled this Country & *reported* to be now in Philadelphia or Boston, but I do not beleve it, as I do not see his Name announced in your Papers—his Co-partner Mr Hamilton Rowan was convicted of sedition, & instead of Transportation is sentenced to £500 fine & 2 years Imprisonment—had our Laws been exerted to their Extent—he would have been transported—he is a Gentleman that I have the highest respect for, but I do not Entirely agree with him in politics—It is said that

Mr Napper Tandy against whom Some Charges have been made on oath, is gone to America; he is an Intimate Freind of mine & my Estate Agent for many years; I have a great regard for him, but differ from him in the Line of Politics he now pursues.[7]

Every Question in our Parliament has hitherto gone unanimously, & it is probable there will be but one division of any Consequence during this Session & that on the Bill for the Reform of the Representation of the People; there are Errors in the present Representation, but at this Crisis, it would be imprudent to agitate a Question about which the best and most Virtuous & most Intelligent Men are devided.

our winter has been uncommonly fine, only 3 Days frost & Snow; the Sun in Great Splendor almost half the Last 2 months; Vegitation very forward; Scarse any of the Winter fodder has been used; a Great Stock of Hay remaining, so that, if we have a tolerable Spring, it will fall to a Lower Price than it has been these ten years; the wheat is very high above Grownd, & the fruit Trees pushing forward at least 20 or 25 Days Earlier than usual—Were we to have ten years Peace, we should rival many Nations in Wealth & prosperity, for the Land was improving to an amazing Degree, & our Manufactures getting forward & Trade encreasing.

I have this moment read the Fœderal News Paper; Mr Genets audacious publications, demands punishment, & the Conclusion of his Letter to the Attorney General, Evinces a Resolution to Stir up Troubles in the united States, but the good Sence of the Americans will never be warped from their own happiness & Interest by French Finesse[8]—After making Enquiries for near 3 Months, I find our worthy Freind, the Marquiss La Fayette is alive & well, but Still (most improperly) a Prisoner—My Letters, though sent open, are not allowed to be forwarded to him.[9]

It is reported, that the Duke of york is to return to England; in my mind, he was too young & too unexperinced to command Such an Army, & in *such a situation,* where Battles were *weekly* fought, & where long Experience only could secure Success; it is a matter of the last Importance to England, that the French should be Checqud in that Quarter, for if they defeat York & Cobough, they will overun Holland & Lower Germany; Jourdains Army is represented (as Double) to that of the Allies, besides the Reinforcements he Expects of 15000 Men from the Mozelle;

Jourdain has been a most Succesfull General, but he may Experience the fate of his Predecessors—The Jacobin Club may grow Jealous of him—denounce—Arrest—and Guilaitine him[10]—As to the Spaniards, they have fought very poorly this war, & though they have made some Progress into Rousillon,[11] I should imagine the Toulon Conquerers will *Burgoyne* them; with Every Sentiment of respect & Esteem, & most Sincere wishes for your health & Happiness I have to Remain My Dear Sir your most Faithfull & obliged Humble Sert

Edward Newenham

Lady Newenham, who is just recoved from a Severe Cold, joins me in best respects to Mrs Washington & your family.

ALS, DLC:GW.

1. The previous extant letter from GW to Newenham is that of 20 Oct. 1792. GW apparently did not write Newenham again until 6 Aug. 1797, when he wrote: "I am so much your debtor in the epistolary way, that it would upbraid me too severely was I to go into a particular acknowledgment of the receipt of all the letters with which you have honoured me in the course of the last two or three years" (*Papers, Retirement Series*, 1:290–91).

2. The Place Act of 1793 excluded pensioners and certain officeholders from the House of Commons. The Pensions Act of 1793 created a consolidated fund and a civil list, and it limited the pension list to £80,000 per year. The Responsibility Law refers to a unanimous adoption of a resolution to provide supplies for the British war effort against France. On these laws, agrarian discontent, and radicalism in Ireland, beginning in 1789 and encouraged by events in France, see T. W. Moody and W. E. Vaughan, eds., *A New History of Ireland* (9 vols., Oxford, England, 1976–2005), 4:200–201, 289–373.

3. This is a reference to GW's Neutrality Proclamation of 22 April 1793.

4. The references are to John Jay, the chief justice of the Supreme Court; Thomas Jefferson, the former secretary of state; Antoine Charbonnet Duplaine, the former French vice-consul at Boston; Edmond Genet, the former French minister to the United States; and the Papal States under Pope Pius VI (1717–1799).

5. A revolt in the French city of Lyons was defeated on 10 Oct. 1793; the French port of Toulon was retaken from the Royalists, who were assisted by British and Spanish forces, on 19 Dec. 1793; and in December 1793 the French drove the Austrians out of the province of Alsace. The Austrian army, which in November had captured Fort Louis, located on an island in the Rhine River and near the village of Rheinmünster in southwest Germany, evacuated that post and blew up its works on 17 Jan. 1794.

French general Jean-Baptiste Jourdan (1762–1833) led his army to victory over Austrian and Dutch troops commanded by Friedrich Josias, prince of Saxe-Coburg (1737–1815), at the battle of Fleurus, in Belgium, on 26 June 1794. As a British field commander, Frederick Augustus, Duke of York, had a series of victories over the French in early 1793, but he was defeated in the Battle of Hondschoote, near Dunkirk in northern France, 6–8 Sept. 1793. On 22 May 1794, he led British forces in cooperation with the Duke of Coburg to defeat the French at the Battle of Tournai, on the Belgium border.

The French fleet was defeated in a naval battle of 29 May–1 June 1794 (Ushant; First of June), thus eliminating the possibility of a French invasion of England at this time.

6. William Howe (1729–1814) served as commander in chief of the British army in North America from 10 Oct. 1775 to late May 1778. GW successfully led an American attack on 26 Dec. 1776 against the Hessian troops stationed at Trenton, New Jersey. British general John Burgoyne (1722–1792) surrendered his army to American forces at Saratoga on 17 Oct. 1777.

7. Dublin native James Napper Tandy (1737–1803) fled to England in March 1793 when faced with charges of treason for his radical political activities in Ireland. He remained in hiding for two years before joining other Irish exiles in Philadelphia in 1795. After two years, he left the United States for France, but in November 1798 he fell into British hands and was returned to England, where he was tried for treason. Escaping the death penalty, he was banished to France in 1802, where he remained until his death.

Archibald Hamilton Rowan (1751–1834), an Irish landowner, became increasingly involved in Irish radicalism during the 1790s. He was arrested on 21 Dec. 1792 for distributing an address entitled "Citizen Soldiers to Arms!" His subsequent prison sentence of two years commenced in January 1794, but he escaped in May and fled to France. Like Tandy, he emigrated to Philadelphia in 1795, but in 1800 he left for Hamburg, Germany. He was allowed to settle in England in 1803 and to return to Ireland in 1806.

8. The letters printed in the 27 Nov. 1793 issue of the *Federal Gazette, and Philadelphia Evening Post* were Genet's letter of 14 Aug. to Edmund Randolph, then the attorney general, and Randolph's reply of 19 November. Genet wrote to complain about a declaration of 12 Aug. 1793 that John Jay and Rufus King published in the *Diary; or Loudon's Register* (New York) on that same date. He asked Randolph to "take such steps, at the ensuing Federal Court, as the honour of your own country as well as of mine, exact upon such an occasion." For the text of the declaration by Jay and King, which Genet considered harmful to his own reputation and to the "cause of my country," see n.4 of Genet to GW, 13 Aug. 1793. In his reply, Randolph offered to meet with Genet to discuss the matter. No legal action against Jay and Rufus, however, was pursued by Randolph.

9. On the series of prisons in which the Marquis de Lafayette was held between August 1792 and May 1797, see n.7 of Marquise de Lafayette to GW, 12 March 1793.

10. The Jacobin Club was founded in 1789 and was the most radical of the French revolutionary clubs. It was responsible for the so-called Reign of Terror from September 1793 until late July 1794. The club itself was suppressed in November 1794. Despite his great victory at the Battle of Hondschoote in early September 1793, French general Jean-Nicholas Houchard (b. 1740) was sentenced to death on the guillotine in November 1793, having been

charged with cowardice for failing to take advantage of his great victory and subsequently suffering defeat at the Battle of Menin on 13 Sept. 1793.

   11. The province of Rousillon was situated on France's border with Spain.

From William Pearce

Sir   Mountvernon Feby 11th 1794

   I Recevd your letter of the 3rd Instant with Mr Howel Lewiss Draught on Mr Ross which he acknoledgs to pay within the time limmited.[1]

   I have paid Mr Dulany for Mrs French & Taken his Rece[i]p[t] as you directed me.[2]

   Mr Stewarts Daughter at River farm is Dead—she died Last thirsday night & that is the Reason he gave in no Report for last week.[3]

   The new barn is not yet done, but Green Sais that they will Git it done next week—but I doubt it—they go on Very Slow with thare business Green him Self has been Very ⟨u⟩nwell for some Time & Still Continues so—and I find him But a Very trifling person at best, and not fit to have the Charge of hands—but If he was Turned off I do not know whare to Git a Man to Soply his place & the negro Carpenters Could not Go on with the Business with out some person to durect them[4]—your House & stable In Alexandria wants a Good deal of Repairing & the fence is quite gone—And as your Carpenters have a Great deal of work to do on your farms—I thought I would Mention to you that I thought, prhaps it would be Better to hire Carpenters at town to do the work—and for this Reason, Green is fond of drink & So are all your Carpente[r]s—that I am affraid that as they would have it In their power to Git it often they would neglect thare work worse than do hire[.] you will please to direct what you think best in this matter—the Swamp at dogue Run is so full of water that thare Can be no work done in it, nor on the new Mill Race—I have got the Ditchers a Giting of post & Rails to make up the fence that Runs up from the mill.[5] I am Sir with the Greatest Respect Your Humbl. Servt

                                    William Pearce

ALS, DLC:GW.

   1. On this draft, see n.3 of GW to Pearce, 3 February.

2. On GW's instructions to obtain a receipt from Benjamin T. Dulany, and for GW's financial arrangements with Dulany and his mother-in-law, Penelope French, see GW to Pearce, 26 Jan., and n.10.

3. The daughter of overseer William Stuart died on Thursday, 6 February. The enclosed farm reports for 2–8 Feb. noted that the report from River farm was absent (DLC:GW).

4. According to the carpenters' report of 9 Feb., which Pearce included with the enclosed farm reports, overseer Thomas Green and the slave carpenters spent over half their working time the previous week on the new barn at Dogue Run farm (DLC:GW). On the design of this sixteen-sided treading barn, see GW to Anthony Whitting, 28 Oct. 1792, and enclosure.

5. Pearce had received instructions regarding the house in Alexandria, Va., in GW's letter of 12 Jan. and instructions concerning the race for the gristmill and the fence that ran from the mill in GW's letter of 19 January.

From Alexander Hamilton

[Philadelphia] Feby 12. 1794

The Secretary of the Treasury has the honor to transmit for the Inspection of the President the enclosed extract of a letter from the Supervisor of Virginia.[1]

LB, DLC:GW.

1. The enclosed letter from Edward Carrington, the supervisor of the revenue for Virginia, has not been identified.

From Tobias Lear

My dear Sir, London february 12th: 1794

Having had the honor of writing to you very fully by the Ship Delaware, Capt. Truxon (by whom I sent the watch for Mrs Washington)[1]—and a few days ago by the Ship Peggy of George Town, I shall at present take up no more of your precious time than to inform you that I have put on board the latter ship 5000 white thorn plants for you—and a packet containing Reports made to the Board of Agriculture of G.B. which were put into my hands by Sir John Sinclair, the President of the Board, to be forwarded to you. There are also on board said Ship a number of fruit trees which I have got for myself; but not knowing how they might fare if I did not commit them to the special care of some one who knew what should be done with them, I took the liberty to have them directed to you at Mt Vernon—And the letters in the Peggy will point out my wishes on that head.[2]

A Mr Bartrand, a famous Agriculturalist belonging to Flanders, put into my hands a few days ago several papers for Mr Jefferson on the subject of manures & vegetation, requesting that I would forward them to him by some vessel going to America, I could not decline it; but being uncertain whether Mr Jefferson is in Philada or Virginia, I have taken the liberty of putting them under cover to you.[3]

In the present critical state of Affairs here it is not prudent for me to say much on politicks; but if I recollect rightly, I had the honor of writing a letter to you some time in April last, when you was at Mount Vernon, in which I ventured certain predictions, and the opinion, which I then formed, I can now undertake to say, on better grounds, is just.[4]

My best respects & most grateful remembrance await Mrs Washington—My young friends, together with Mr Dandridge & Mr Lewis have my best regards.[5] With the purest respect & most affecte attachment I have the honor to be my dear Sir Your grateful & Obliged friend

Tobias Lear.

ALS, DLC:GW.

1. For this letter and a description of the various items placed aboard the *Delaware,* including the watch made for Martha Washington, see Lear to GW, 26–30 Jan., and n.10.

2. For this letter and information about the plants placed aboard the *Peggy,* see Lear to GW, 4 Feb., and n.4 to that document. On the packet of agricultural reports, see John Sinclair to GW, 6 February.

3. For papers sent by O. A. Bertrand, see his letter to Thomas Jefferson of 8 Feb. 1794 (*Jefferson Papers,* 28:16–19). *Questions sur l'agriculture et l'économie rural propres à donner une idée de la marche considérable qu'il y a encore à faire, pour porter l'agriculture & l'économie rurale à un certain point de perfection* (France, 1792) has been attributed to Bertrand. Jefferson, having submitted his letter of resignation to GW on 31 Dec. 1793, left Philadelphia on 5 Jan. and was now at Monticello, his home near Charlottesville, Virginia. Upon receipt of these papers in May, Jefferson decided that Bertrand's proposition for "an assignment of lands can only be answered by the government," and he forwarded these papers to Edmund Randolph, the current secretary of state (Jefferson to Horatio Gates, 3 Feb., and to Randolph, 14 May, *Jefferson Papers,* 28:14, 74).

4. For Lear's opinion on the state of British politics, see his letter to GW of 8 April 1793.

5. Bartholomew Dandridge, Jr., and Howell Lewis were currently serving as GW's secretaries.

From James Madison

Feby 12. 1794

Mr Madison presents his respectful compliments to the President, and begs leave to lay before him the inclosed letters, on behalf of a candidate for a vacancy in the Custom-House Department in Virginia. Mr M. being a perfect stranger to the candidate can add no information whatever of his own.[1] He knows Mr Maury well, and considers his recommendation as respectable.[2]

AL, DLC:GW.

1. On the reason for the vacancy in the position of customs collector for the District of Tappahannock, Va., see Hudson Muse to GW, 27 Jan., and n.3. The first of two enclosures sent by Madison was a brief letter from deputy collector Laurence Muse to Madison of 1 Feb. in which he asks for Madison's "interest with the President in my favor, in the appointment of a Collector." Muse points out that having "been imployed in that business from the Commencement of the Collection Law under the present Government ⟨I⟩ flatter myself I have now acquired a knowledge sufficient to do justice to the public, and individuals" (DLC:GW). See also Laurence Muse's letter of application to GW of 1 February.

2. Fredericksburg, Va., merchant Fontaine Maury wrote to Madison on 4 Feb.: "Having good reason to suppose that the Office of Collector at Tappahanock will soon be vacant, I have taken the Liberty to request you will do any thing which may be convenient to promote the Election of Mr Laurence Muse, who has long served with much reputation as a deputy in the above office, and is in all respects perfectly Qualified to do the Public every justice" (DLC:GW). On Laurence Muse's appointment, see GW to U.S. Senate, 5 March.

From James Muir

Sir   Alexandria [Va.] 12th February 1794

I am directed by the Trustees of the Alexandria academy to write you with respect to the donation which you give yearly for the education of a certain number of poor Children in this place.[1]

The Trustees have supplied the School where these Children are taught with Teachers during last year. We have been unfortunate. The sickness of one Teacher, Ill behaviour of another, and peculiar situation of a Third, have necessitated us to change the Teacher oftener than has been for the benifit of the

School. At present however we are happy in a Teacher who gives Satisfaction.

The number you design for education has not during the year, nor is it now complete. The deficiency is not more than Two or Three. None have been refused admission who appeared to the Trustees objects of this Charity.

It is the duty of the Trustees, to settle about this Time with the Teacher, or Teachers for their labours during the Past year. Your donation will enable us to do so which you will be pleased to order when and in what manner you shall think best. It would be a convenience to the Teacher were the donation given quarterly. Upon this point the Trustees wish to know your inclination.[2]

The Academy is not in so flourishing a state as we could wish, owing to various causes. these the Trustees are labouring to remove. a little time will discover how far their labours are successful. with great respect your H. Sert

James Muir

ALS, DLC:GW. The postal stamp reads "ALEX. Feb. 13."

1. On GW's pledge in 1785 to give an annual payment of £50 Virginia currency to this school, see GW to Trustees of the Alexandria Academy, 17 Dec. 1785, and *Diaries*, 4:251.

2. GW replied to Muir on 24 February.

From Burgess Ball

Dear sir, Leesburg [Va.]--13th Feby 94

I recd yours a few days past mentiong that you had procured the Clover Seed for me, and that it wd be forwarded as soon as the Ice wd permit.[1] As I have troubled you so far, I wd take the liberty of requesting you'll be so good as to procure & send me 2 or 3 Bush: of the Chocolate Shells such as we've frequently drank Chocolate of at Mt Vernon, as my Wife thinks it agreed with her better than any other Breakfast.[2] I hope you'll excuse my thus troubling you, as I know not how else we can procure it. We recd the Braceletts &c. for which Fanny is greatly obliged to Mrs Washington for her trouble in gettg made &c.[3] I have sent down but 13 Bush: of B: wheat, the Thaw havg come on just as I had set in to hauling. It shall all be down as soon as possible.[4] I am Dr sir Yr Affect. Hble servt

B. Ball

ALS, DLC:GW.

1. For this letter, see GW to Ball, 3 February.

2. In his letter to Ball of 24 Feb., GW promised to procure the desired chocolate, and on 24 Feb. he paid $2.20 for "2½ busls chocolate shels, and barl to send to Colo. Ball" (Household Accounts). On 16 March, GW wrote Ball that both the chocolate and clover seed were on board a vessel bound for Alexandria, Virginia. On Ball's receipt of these items, see his letter to GW of 5 April.

3. The bracelets for Ball's wife, Frances Washington Ball, were sent along with GW's letter of 3 February.

4. William Pearce, GW's farm manager, had received 131 bushels of buckwheat from Ball as of 18 March (GW to Ball, 23 March 1794).

Bartholomew Dandridge, Jr., to Henry Knox

U.S. 13. feb: 1794.

By the President's order Bw Dandridge has the honor to return to the Secretary of war the letters and enclosures from Gov. Blount which have been submitted to the Presidts perusal;[1] and to enclose, at the same time, a Letter from the Gov. of Pennsylvania to the President, with a request that the Secretary will report to the President his opinion on the subject thereof.[2]

Bw. Dandridge

ALS, DLC:GW; LB, DLC:GW.

1. On 12 Feb., Knox submitted letters from Gov. William Blount of 14 and 15 Jan., and their enclosures, for GW's consideration. According to GW's executive journal, these two letters, which have not been identified, "contain'd nothing of any particular importance; but mention that the Creeks generally are irritated against the Spaniards & wish for peace with UStates" (*JPP*, 283–84).

2. For the enclosed letter from the governor of Pennsylvania, see Thomas Mifflin to GW, 11 February. No written response from Knox to Mifflin's letter has been identified.

From Henry Lee

sir.   13th feby 94 Richmond [Va.].

This evenings post from Norfolk has brought information of the arival of a french fleet in Hampton Road with much european intelliga[n]ce.

My letr from Col. Newton I think proper to enclose (having not time to prepare a copy) that you may be possesd of the most accurate information on the subject, within.[1] I have the honor to be with unceasing affection & perfect respect your ob: st

Henry Lee

ALS, DNA: RG 59, Miscellaneous Letters.

1. The enclosed letter to Lee from Thomas Newton, Jr., which he wrote at Norfolk, Va., on 11 Feb. 1794, reads: "Yesterday arived in the bay several ships of War from France, some line of battle. They have brought an Ambasdour, and Consuls, to succeed those that are here, reports from them are, that Ostend is so closely beseiged & scarce of provissions that it must soon surrender, I have heard the garrisson had twice offer'd to capitulate but was refused, the conditions at discretion. They took a Brittish frigate from the East Indies loaded with the spoils of Pondicherry & the Colors, which they had taken & several other vessels on their passage, the officer landed here a few days ago, was Consul for Philadelphia; it is said that they have new consuls, for the differant States. that America stood well with France & that they wou'd have a fleet out in March of 60 sail of the Line, having 150 thousand marines ready to embark, many other matters are reported, but not worth relating & time must discover whether these are right, but in my opini⟨on⟩ the most of them are well founded and I have hopes will prove true." In a postscript, Newton added: "Much treasure is said to be brought in this fleet" (DNA: RG 59, Miscellaneous Letters).

On the arrival of Jean-Antoine-Joseph Fauchet, who replaced Edmond Genet as the French minister plenipotentiary to the United States, and other French diplomats, see James McHenry to GW, 18 Feb., and n.2; and Edmund Randolph to GW, 21 Feb., and n.1. The district of Pondicherry was once part of French India.

From Henry Lee

my dear sir   Richmond [Va.] febry 13th 94

Some time ago on a rumour that the collector for the rappahannock district was about to decline his office I took the liberty to bring to your view Mr Francis Brook as a gentleman extremely well qualified in my opinion for that office.[1]

I mentioned then the reasons which influenced my judgement & inclination, & will not now detain your time by a repetition of them.

Persuaded you will consult the public good entirely in the appointment, I am satisfied that Mr Brook will not escape your attention if on full enquiry you consider him most proper & on no other p[r]inciple do I commend him to your notice.

I had the honor to receive your letter in reply to mine just before your return to Philadelphia; & will when a fit occasion offers again trespass on your indulgence.[2]

Permit me to congratulate you on the return of your natal month & to wish you every happiness this world can afford. I have the honor to be sir with most affec: respect unalterably yours

Henry Lee

ALS, DLC:GW.

1. No previous written letter from Lee to GW recommending Francis T. Brooke for appointment as the collector of customs for the District of Tappahannock, Va., has been identified. On the creation of a vacancy in this post, see Hudson Muse to GW, 27 Jan., and n.3. For GW's subsequent appointment of Laurence Muse to this position, see GW to U.S. Senate, 5 March. For another letter recommending Brooke, see Alexander Spotswood to GW, 15 Sept. 1793.

2. For these letters, see Lee to GW, 7 Oct., and GW to Lee, 16 Oct. 1793. GW left Mount Vernon on 28 Oct., after an extended visit there due to the yellow fever epidemic in Philadelphia that fall, and on 1 Nov. he arrived at Germantown, a village outside Philadelphia where he took up temporary residence (*JPP*, 241).

From Tanguy

Sir,   Philadelphia, february 13--1794.

A Stranger in your Country, I desire to render myself useful to it, by publishing a French and English paper. I herewith send you one. Its success depends upon the protection You may afford it, by subscribing to this Undertaking.[1] I have the honour to be, Your most obedient Servant,

tanguy

DS (printed), DLC:GW. The day and month were added by hand to the printed document.

1. Beginning with an issue dated 1 Feb. 1794, Claude Corentin Tanguy de la Boissière, a refugee from Saint Domingue, published a tri-weekly newspaper in Philadelphia called the *American Star, or, Historical, Political, Critical, and Moral Journal*. Published in both English and French, it carried an alternative title of *L'Étoile Américaine, ou Journal Historique, Politique, Critique et Moral*. Publication was suspended after the 3 May 1794 issue (Brigham, *American Newspapers*, 2:890).

From Bushrod Washington

Dear Uncle   Richmond [Va.] Feby 13th 1794

It is with great unwillingness that I take the liberty of troubling you upon the business which is the subject of this letter, well knowing how little time you have to spare from public employments. It Was necessary to make you a party in the present suit, tho' only for forms sake. Indeed, I suppose you would wish for an opportunity of renouncing the character of Exectr of Mr Fairfax, which I am told you could not with convenience undertake.[1] I have taken the liberty to enclose you a rough draght of an answer to the only point necessary for you to notice, unless you should think proper to answer the whole or any other parts of the Bill.[2] this I did to prevent the inconvenience & expence of applying to Counsel. Should you approve of the one sent, or think proper to make any alterations in it, you will please sign, & enclose it together with the Bill to me—if convenient before, or as early in March as possible. It is usual to subjoin an affidavit, but in the present case we do not suppose it necessary, and it will save you trouble. The Copy of the Bill which accompanies it, is intended for your information in case you should incline to make any alterations or additions to the answer.

I am happy to inform you that my prospects here in business, are equal to my expectations; I wish they may not be superior to my merit, but I trust that my deficiencies will not be the result of inattention. Accept my most sincere wishes for your health and happiness. Mrs W. Joins me in love to Yourself & my Aunt & believe me to be Dear Uncle Your affectionate Nephew[3]

                                                    Bushd. Washington

ALS, ViMtvL.

1. The legal suit concerned the estate of George William Fairfax, who died in 1787. Although named an executor in Fairfax's will, GW had declined to serve as such (Samuel Athawes to GW, 20 July 1787; GW to Warner Washington, 9 Nov. 1787, and to Athawes, 8 Jan. 1788). For recent correspondence concerning this estate, see Hannah Fairfax Washington to GW, 2 Nov. 1793.

2. GW signed the answer that Bushrod prepared and enclosed it in his reply to Bushrod of 23 February. The enclosed bill of complaint has not been identified.

3. Bushrod had moved his law practice from Alexandria, Va., to Richmond in 1790. His wife was the former Julia Ann "Nancy" Blackburn.

From Henry Knox

Sir.   [Philadelphia] February 14. 1794.

I have the honor to submit a letter from major general Wayne of the 10th of last month with a number of enclosures which has been just received.[1] I have the honor to be Sir, with the greatest respect Your most obedt Servt:

H. Knox

LS, DLC:GW; LB,DLC:GW.

1. The correct date of the enclosed letter from Anthony Wayne to Knox is 8 January. In this letter, written from his headquarters at Greenville, Ohio, Wayne acknowledged the receipt of letters from Knox of 25 and 29 Nov. and 7 Dec. 1793 (for these letters, see Knopf, *Anthony Wayne*, 285–91). He then related the successful construction of Fort Recovery, which was located about 23 miles north of Fort Greene Ville. According to Wayne this new fort was "an object of consequence to our future Operations as well as to afford an additional security to the Western Frontier." To strengthen this fort's defenses, Wayne deemed it "proper to advance with a small reenforcement of Mounted Infantry, accompanied by the Officers mentioned in the Extract from the General Orders of the 28th of Decr." It also was "now furnished with a sufficient Garrison well provided with Ammunition Artillery & Provision." Wayne reported next on a skirmish between a small group of Indians and a party of soldiers sent "to reconnoitre a position between this place and Au Glaize preparatory to further operations" that resulted in one wounded and three dead Americans. A second party subsequently was dispatched to complete the mission (Knopf, *Anthony Wayne*, 297–98).

The enclosed copy of Wayne's letter to Kentucky governor Isaac Shelby of 6 Jan. 1794, offering help in suppressing an illegal expedition being planned against Spanish territory, is at PHi: Wayne Papers. The various returns and supply estimates that were also enclosed have not been identified. For a list of these enclosures, see *JPP*, 284.

From Richard Peters

Dear Sir   14 February 1794

I have returned, under a Hope of seeing them again when they have gone their rounds, the Papers you were so good as to lend me on Agriculture. I have not had sufficient Leisure to peruse them with the Attention they deserve. I have a great Desire to read them with Care.

I see no precise Object S[i]r J. has requiring more than a bare Acknowledgment of their reciept from you[1]—I have sent a Dozen of the Outlines for a State Plan of Agriculture; & on one of them have made the Remarks you will see there & for the Purpose I mentioned to you.[2] I am with my sincere Respect & Esteem your obed. Servt

Richard Peters

ALS, DLC:GW.

1. The papers that Peters was returning probably included some of those published by the British Board of Agriculture that John Sinclair enclosed in his letters to GW of 15 June, 15 Aug., and 11 Sept. 1793. For a list of the agricultural surveys and essays produced by this board that were in GW's library, see Griffin, *Catalogue of the Washington Collection,* 89–95. GW acknowledged receipt of the papers sent on 11 Sept. in a letter to Sinclair of 20 July 1794.

2. Peters enclosed a dozen copies of *Outlines of a Plan, for Establishing a State Society of Agriculture in Pennsylvania* (Philadelphia, 1794), which was published by the Philadelphia Society for Promoting Agriculture. On this proposal, see GW to James Madison, 8 Feb., and n.1 to that document.

To the United States Senate

Gentlemen of the Senate,   United States February 14. 1794.

I nominate Edwards St Loe Livermore, of New Hampshire, to be Attorney for the United States in the District of New Hampshire; vice Samuel Sherburne junr resigned.[1]

Go: Washington

LS, DNA: RG 46, Third Congress, 1793–95, Senate Records of Executive Proceedings, President's Messages—Executive Nominations; LB, DLC:GW.

1. For John Samuel Sherburne's resignation, see his letter to GW of 30 Aug. 1793. GW nominated him in 1789 as being "Saml Sherburne junior" (GW to U.S. Senate, 24 Sept. 1789). For Senate confirmation of Livermore's appointment, see *U.S. Senate Executive Journal,* 1:148.

To Henry Knox

(Private)
Dear Sir,   Phila. Feby 15th 1794.

You mentioned in the conversations, which I have lately had with you on the subject of Mr Jay and Mr King's letter to me, of the 27th of last month, and particularly in what passed between us on thursday, that they had repeatedly declared, that they never considered that letter, as an official one; that on the contrary they had intended it, as a mere private one; and that they did not in the most distant manner contemplate or design to give offence to me, or to wound my feelings, by the language or matter which it contains.[1] Thursday, after repeating the foregoing, you added that those gentlemen were desirous of having a personal interview with me concerning the letter. I should therefore be glad to know, in a line by the bearer, whether I am at liberty to act on the abovementioned communications, as being made by you to me with their knowledge & approbation?[2] Yours always & sincerely

Go. Washington

ALS, NNGL.

1. The letter that Knox and GW discussed on Thursday, 13 Feb., was one John Jay and Rufus King wrote to GW on 27 Jan., which has not been found. A draft of this letter was enclosed in Jay's letter to King of 25 Feb., on which King wrote a description of the enclosed draft that reads: "The paper inclosed was the draft of a Letter from Mr Jay & me, to the Pr. of the U.S.— dated 27. Jan. 1794, complaining of his conduct & that of the Secy of State and Atty Genl in respect to Genets requisition that we shd be prosecuted— and requesting from him an attested Copy of the Report of the Secy of State (with permission to publish it) stating that Dallas told him that Genet had said he wd appeal from the Pr. to the People—this Draft on Saturday 1 Mar. I delivered to the President—who told me that I should have the copy of the Report of the Secy of State on monday following [3 March]" (NHi: Jay Papers).

Jay and King had infuriated Edmond Genet, the French minister to the United States, by their public letter of 12 Aug. 1793, in which they asserted that Genet "had said he would Appeal to the People from certain decisions of the President" (*Diary; or Loudon's Register* [New York], 12 Aug. 1793; see also Genet to GW, 13 Aug. 1793, and n.4). On Genet's attempt to have Jay and King prosecuted for libel, see Thomas Jefferson to GW, 18 Dec. 1793, and n.1. For the report that Jay and King requested, which included a statement from Alexander J. Dallas about Genet's threatened appeal to the people, see Jefferson's Notes on a Conversation with Genet, 10 July 1793, enclosed in Jefferson's first memorandum to GW of 11 July 1793.

2. GW subsequently met first with Jay and then twice with King to discuss their differences. King, during his first meeting with GW, presented the draft of the offending letter to GW, who then "put into the fire" the draft, the letter received, and "a paper in the President's own handwriting justifying his conduct," which King was allowed to read beforehand. At a second meeting with King, GW provided a "certified extract from Jefferson's Report" (King, *Life and Correspondence of Rufus King*, 1:477–79). For the certified extract, see GW to John Jay and Rufus King, 3 March 1794.

Henry Knox to Bartholomew Dandridge, Jr.

Sir.   [Philadelphia] Feb: 15—1794.
  Please to submit to the President of the United States, the enclosed letter just received from the Governor of South Carolina,
dated the 23d of January, with the several papers accompanying
the same.[1] Yours sincerely

                                                   H. Knox

LS, DLC:GW; LB, DLC:GW.
  1. The letter from William Moultrie to Knox of 23 Jan. and its enclosures
have not been identified.

From Samuel Magaw

Sir,   [Philadelphia] Febry 15th 1794
  In venturing to lay before You the discourse herewith presented;[1] my diffidence is overruled, only by a Desire to pay some
Tribute of Duty and Respect, where much is owed. The instance,
indeed, is, of itself, quite inconsiderable: Yet, it appreciates in
my view, as under the immediate direction of those Gentlemen,
whose sentiments I can with greater safety rely upon, than on my
own. They have instructed me, on this occasion: and they allow
me the Honour of having this agreeable Communication with
them. I am, Sir, Your most obedient Servt

                                                  Sam. Magaw

ALS, DLC:GW.
  Samuel Magaw (1735–1812), a native of Pennsylvania, graduated from the
College of Philadelphia (later the University of Pennsylvania) in 1757. After
his 1767 ordination as a priest in the Anglican church, he served several
years in Dover, Del., as a missionary for the Society for the Propagation of the
Gospel. He was the rector of St. Paul's Church in Philadelphia, 1781–1804,
vice provost and professor of moral philosophy at the College of Philadelphia, 1782–91, and a member of the American Philosophical Society. He was
also one of the founders of the Academy of the Protestant Episcopal Church
in Philadelphia.
  1. The enclosure probably was Magaw's *Things Lovely and of good Report. A
Sermon, delivered in St. Paul's Church, Philadelphia. On the 27th of December, 1793:
being St. John the Evangelist's Day; in the the Presence of the Grand Lodge of Pennsylvania: to which is prefixed a Prayer, before the Sermon*, Philadelphia, 1794. This
sermon, as well as four other tracts by Magaw, were in GW's library. Added
to this collection after GW's death in 1799 was Magaw's *An Oration commemo-*

rative of the Virtues and Greatness of General Washington; pronounced in the German Lutheran Church, Philadelphia: before the Grand Lodge of Pennsylvania, on the twenty-second day of February, eighteen hundred, Philadelphia, 1800 (Griffin, Catalogue of the Washington Collection, 132–33, 176, 406).

Letter not found: from William Pearce, 15 Feb. 1794. GW wrote Pearce on 22 Feb. acknowledging "Your letter of the 15th instt."

From Edmund Randolph

[Philadelphia] Saturday ⟨15. February 1794⟩[1]

The Secretary of State has the honor of laying before the President the copy of a proclamation, put into his hands by Govr. St Clair for that purpose.[2]

AL, DNA: RG 59, Miscellaneous Letters; LB, DNA: RG 59, GW's Correspondence with His Secretaries of State.

1. The date, which is taken from the letter-book copy, did occur on a Saturday. The docket on the AL reads, "15. Feby 1794."

2. The enclosed copy of the proclamation of 8 Dec. 1793 by Arthur St. Clair, governor of the Northwest Territory, reads: "Whereas a War at present exists in Europe between France on the one part and certain other Powers on the other part, and although the United States are allied to France, yet they are not Parties to this War, but are at Peace with all the other Powers, and in particular with Spain, from which political situation results, by the Law of Nations, the Duty a strict neutrality and a Conduct perfectly equal and important towards all the belligerent Powers, the observation of which neutrality has been enjoined upon the Citizens of the united states by the President in his Proclamation bearing date the 22d day of April 1793; And it having been communicated to me thro the Secretary of War that Representations have been made to the President by the Representatives of Spain of the designs of certain Frenchmen by the Names of la Chaise, Charles Delpeau, Mathurin and Signoux to excite and engage as many as they could of our Citizens or others to undertake an Expedition against the spanish settlements within our Neighbourhood I have thought fit to issue this Proclamation enjoining all the Inhabitants of the Territory of the united States north west of the River Ohio to observe a strict neutrality towards Spain; and to abstain from every Act of hostility against the Subjects and Settlements of that Crown, and strictly forbidding all and every of the said Inhabitants to join themselves to the said la Chaise, Charles Depeau, Mathurin and Signoux or either of them in any attempt they may meditate or undertake against the spanish settlements on the Missisippi, or to aid and abett them in the same in any manner whatsoever: And all Persons who shall offend in the Premises may depend upon being prosecuted and punished with the utmost rigor of the Law: And I do hereby require and command all Officers civil and military

to use their utmost endeavours to prevent the said la Chaise &ca or either of them from making any levies of Men or other preparation for their intended Expedition within the Territory and to imprison them should they have the audacity to attempt it, and to restrain all and every of the Inhabitants from joining themselves to them or either of them.

"In testimony whereof I have caused the Seal of the Territory to be affixed to these Presents, and have signed the same with my Hand. Done at the City of Marietta in the County of Washington the 8th day of December 179[3] and of the Independance of the united States the seventeenth Year" (DNA: RG 59, Miscellaneous Letters). The docket on this copy reads "recd. feby 13. 94."

Auguste de la Chaise (d. 1803), a native of Louisiana and a former soldier stationed in Saint Domingue; Charles De Pauw (b. 1756), a Kentucky merchant of Huguenot ancestry who emigrated circa 1776 to the United States; Mathurin, a carpenter by trade; and Jean-Pierre Gignouse (Gignoux; Pisgignoux) were agents engaged by Edmond Genet, the French minister to the United States, to help raise military forces within Kentucky for an expedition against the Spanish colony of Louisiana ("Selections from the Draper Collection," 1002–7, 1047; see also Chaise to Democratic Society of Lexington, Ky., c.14 May 1794, *ASP, Miscellany*, 1:931). For the letters that apparently prompted the governor to issue this proclamation, see Thomas Jefferson to Isaac Shelby, 6 Nov. 1793, *Jefferson Papers*, 27:312–13, and Henry Knox to St. Clair, 9 Nov. 1793, *ASP, Foreign Relations*, 1:458. On the administration's concern about the activities of these and other French agents recruited by Genet, see GW to U.S. Senate and House of Representatives, 3 Dec. 1793; Cabinet Opinion, 10 March 1794; and GW's Proclamation of 24 March.

From Claude-Antoine
de La Morre de Ville aux Bois

15 Feb. 1794. Writes a lengthy letter in French while at Düsseldorf, a German city on the Rhine River. Starts with a brief synopsis of his military career, beginning with his 1774 enlistment in the Gâtinais regiment and his subsequent participation in the Revolutionary War, including the siege at Yorktown in 1781, after which his regiment was renamed the Royal Auvergne. Describes the causes of the French Revolution and the ensuing "Horreurs! Brigandages! Massacres" that forced him and other officers of the French army to emigrate to German principalities, where they joined the coalition armies in their fight against the French Republic. Summarizes military battles over the past two years, and then laments the fate of French emigrants if the republicans ultimately prove successful. Ponders the fate in store for himself and other refugees since they are unable to return to France, where their property has been sold or laid to waste. Closes with a plea for assistance from GW and announces his intention to set sail for the United States in six weeks.[1]

ALS (in French), DNA: RG 59, Miscellaneous Letters.

1. Whether La Morre (b. 1757) actually emigrated to the United States is not known, but he apparently returned to France after the restoration of the monarchy in 1814, residing first at Bar-sur-Aube in northeastern France and then at Paris in 1822.

To William Pearce

Mr Pearce,   Philadelphia 16th of Feby 1794

Your letter of the 11th instant, covering the reports of the preceeding week, came regularly to hand and gave me concern to hear of the death of Mr Stuarts daughter. What was her complaint?

My intention, with respect to the repairs of my house in Alexandria, and inclosing the lot, was, that every particle of the work, except putting it together, should be prepared at Mount Vernon, & carried thither by Water; for sure I am, if the whole was to be executed in Town that four faithful workmen would do more *there* in one week than any four of mine would do in a month. I expected that Green, or some one that was a judge of work, would examine critically what was to be done, that the whole might be carried on in the manner I have just mentioned.[1] This as far as the dwelling house is concerned, has been done already; but not I believe with the accuracy that is necessary to prevent mistakes. In truth, the man who lives in it, ought, by his agreement, to have kept the house &ca in perfect repair; for that is the only compensation he proposed (I believe) to make me for the use of it and when I saw him last, in October, he told me that he had made a new door, or doors, and some Sashes; and was going on with the work.[2] It might be well therefore, the first time you go to town, to examine minutely into the matter—see what he has done—what he talks of doing—on what terms—and how far he may be depended upon for what he engages; remembering always that the house must be in order by the time you have been informed of. Whether this man (that is the tenant) is a joiner or house Carpenter himself, or not, I am unable to say: If the former, and he is to be Depended upon, all you can get out of him, *in time*, by way of *compensation* for Rent, will be so much saved to me; but nothing that is essential to the two houses, must be left to uncertainties. Inclosing the lot in time is not quite so material; but let it be done in a very substantial manner when ever it is set about; with such Posts & Rails (close enough together) as will compleatly secure a garden, whenever it is converted to that use, and not easily pulled down for firing. You might—in order to know what the work can be accomplished for, by hiring—get a respectable workman of Alexandria to examine the two houses carefully, set down every thing wanting to them—and the lowest he will do it for. I could, after receiving this, with your opinion thereupon, be better able to decide whether to hire or employ my own people. This may also be done with respect to enclosing the lot; though I conceive there would be more propriety in doing the latter than the former, with my own Carpenters. If large & stout Cedar Posts, & chestnut or Cyprus Rails could be bought reasonably it would be better than to get them of Oak, from my own land, & let the estimate of the workman, you may consult, be made on the supposition of their being so—In wch case, it might be better to employ him: for otherwise they would, more than probably be to be brought from Alexandria to Mount Vernon & then to go back again, or my Carpenters must go there to dress—mortise—& tenant them; which, as I have observed before, I am sure would afford them the opportunity of being idle.

I am so well satisfied of Thomas Greens unfitness to look after my Carpenters, that nothing but the helpless situation in which you find his family, has prevailed on me to retain him 'till this time: but if you perceive more & more, as your opportunities encrease, that he is not to be entrusted, you had better be looking out in time to supply his place another year if there should not be cause to turn him sooner off.[3]

When he has compleated the New Barn at Dogue run, let it be well cleaned out, & a good lock put upon the lower door—the Key of which either keep yourself, or order McKoy never to let it be out of his own locked Chest. Then try how the treading floor will answer the purpose for which it was constructed.[4]

I perceive my Overseers are beginning to report the increase of Lambs this year as they did last; by which I never know what they lose. Let them know it is my expectation, that, every lamb that falls, and every one that dies in the week, and what are actually in being at the time, is to be precisely set down. It is from hence only I can form a judgment of their care and attention to them. According to their mode of rendering the Account, I may, if an hundred Lambs fall in a week, and fifty of them die, have an increase of 50 only in the report; and although this is true in fact, it is by no means a fair—or a satisfactory state of the case. The missing report of Mr Stuart ought yet to come forward, otherwise there will be a gap, or break in them.[5]

Whenever you shall have received the amount of Mr Lewis's order on Mr Ross, let me be informed of it; because I shall *then* pay the money here.[6]

Under cover with this letter you will receive, and I hope in good order, the White bent grass seeds mentioned in my last letter; half an ear of very early ripening corn; the Garden seeds written for by Ehler; and 4 kinds of seeds sent me by a Gentlemen in England; some (or I believe all) of which came from the East Indias.[7] In my last I gave directions concerning the Bent grass, and therefore shall say nothing about it here: If the Corn is not planted where it can be protected, it will all be eaten in its green state. The Gardener will see by the prices annexed to the Seeds he sent for, how necessary it is for him to save his own Seeds, which I hope he will do hereafter; and I desire he will take particular care of the other four sorts of foreign seeds; two of which he will perceive must be sown in moist ground, or kept moist after it is sown. Let him number the papers which contain these Seeds, and drive stakes with corrisponding numbers by each kind, when sown, that he may be at no loss to know them: Putting the papers as is usual, in a split stick by them, is apt to be lost; or so defaced by the weather as to become, after a while, unintelligable; and then the name will be forgotten: by the method I have proposed this cannot happen; On the papers too may be noted the places where they are sown. I remain Your friend &ca

Go: Washington

ALS, ViMtvL; ALS (letterpress copy), DLC:GW. The ALS at ViMtvL is docketed as letter "#11."

1. For GW's instructions to have his house and stable at the corner of Pitt and Cameron streets in Alexandria, Va., ready for occupancy in April by

Frances Bassett Washington, see his letter to Pearce of 12 January. Thomas Green was overseer of the slave carpenters at Mount Vernon.

2. On GW's tenant, a Mr. Jackson, see GW to John Fitzgerald, 3 Aug. 1793, and n.1 to that document. Fleeing the yellow fever epidemic in Philadelphia, GW and Martha Washington returned to Mount Vernon in September 1793. GW remained at Mount Vernon until 28 Oct. and Martha until December (*JPP*, 239, 241; Household Accounts, 4 and 11 Dec. 1793).

3. Despite an unfavorable opinion of Green, GW was reluctant to fire him because of sympathy for Green's wife, Sarah, who was the daughter of GW's former valet Thomas Bishop (see GW to Green, 31 March 1789, and source note). Green left GW's employment later this year (GW to Pearce, 21 Sept. 1794).

4. For the design of the new treading barn at Dogue Run farm, of which Henry McCoy was the overseer, see GW to Anthony Whitting, 28 Oct. 1792, and enclosure.

5. On the manner in which the overseers reported on the increase and decrease of lambs and other livestock, see Farm Reports, 2–8 Feb. 1794 (DLC: GW). A subsequent report for the River farm from William Stuart, which was not included with the weekly reports because of the death of his daughter, has not been found.

6. On the payment of Howell Lewis's draft on Horatio Ross, see n.3 of GW to Pearce, 3 February.

7. GW mentioned the white bent grass seeds in his letter to Pearce of 9 February. The seeds requested by John Christian Ehlers, in a letter to GW that has not been found, probably were those "sundry Garden seeds" whose purchase was posted on 24 Feb. 1794 in GW's Household Accounts as costing $4.87. For the seeds from Eastern Europe and Asia that Scottish agriculturalist James Anderson sent, see his letter to GW of 15 Aug. 1793.

From Richard Dobbs Spaight

Sir   North Carolina New Bern 16th Feb: 1794

I now do myself the honor to enclose to you the papers which I enformed you of in my last letter respecting the Spanish brig St Joseph.[1]

I likewise enclose you copy of a letter from Edwd Jones esqr. Atto. for the Spanish Commissioners demanding from me a reimbursement of the monies expended by him as Atto. for said Commissioners, in sending expresses, seeing lawyers &c. and also for me to repay a deduction of a 3 P. Ct which he says the Marshal is entitled to under the laws of the United States for safe keeping the money. As I did not conceive the instructions which I had received authorized me to pay any monies whatever, or that by them it was understood the General Government would pay any other expences than those which might have been incurred by the Marshall in guarding and securing the mony, I wrote to Mr Jones to that effect, a Copy of my letter is also enclosed.[2] I have the honor, &c.

R.D. Spaight

LB, Nc-Ar: Governors' Letterbooks.

1. For a description of the enclosed papers, which have not been identified, and for background on the legal questions concerning the Spanish request for restoration of the *San Josef* and its cargo, which included a trunk filled with gold and silver, see Spaight's second letter to GW of 8 February.

2. Edward Jones was hired by diplomats José Ignacio de Viar and José de Jaudenes to represent Spanish interests in the case of the *San Josef*. In his first letter of 8 Feb. to Spaight, written from Wilmington, N.C., he wrote that "the order for the restoration of the money empowers your Excellency also to discharge all incidentall expences incurred by the former owners recovering their property, that in consequence thereof as Attorney to the Commissioners from the Court of Spain I respectfully make a requisition of five hundred dollars being a part of the charges already incurred. . . . It may not be improper to inform your Excellency that the Marshal expects the three ℔ cent as by law established for the safe keeping" of the money. In a letter of 31 Oct. 1793, Spaight had charged U.S. deputy marshal John Blakely with the responsibility of guarding the confiscated gold and silver (both letters, Nc-Ar: Governors' Letterbooks). For the law regarding compensation for U.S. marshals and their deputies, see section 4 of "An Act for regulating Processes in the Courts of the United States, and providing Compensations for the Officers of the said Courts, and for Jurors and Witnesses," 8 May 1792 (*Stat.* 1:277). For the instructions sent Spaight to restore the money, see Henry Knox's letters to him of 13 and 18 Jan., in n.1 of Spaight to GW, 8 Feb. (second letter).

Spaight, in his reply to Jones of 11 Feb., wrote: "I have Sir agreable to the directions of the President to me given orders to Mr Blakely the Deputy Marshal at Wilmington to deliver to you as agent for the Spanish Commissioners the money papers and other property now in his possession taken from the Spanish brig St Joseph he taking the receipt for the same." He also wrote that he had no authority to pay the legal costs incurred by Jones, nor did he "conceive that the president contemplated anything of that kind in the decision which he has given." Spaight, however, promised to consult with GW about the correct procedure for paying Blakely for his services (Nc-Ar: Governors' Letterbooks). For GW's response, see Bartholomew Dandridge, Jr., to Henry Knox, 6 March.

Letter not found: from William Pearce, 17 Feb. 1794. GW wrote Pearce on 24 Feb. that "Your letter of the 17th instant came safe."

From Edmund Randolph

Philadelphia feby 17. 1794

The Secretary of State has the honor to inform the President of the United States, that he received this morning from Mr Daniel Gaines, of Georgia, two letters offering himself, as the successor of Major Forsyth, late marshal of that district.[1] Mr Gaines refers to the Secretary, as knowing his character; but he cannot call the gentleman to mind. The only thing, which occurs, is, that Mr Gaines is probably a son of old Colo. Harry Gaines, of Virginia, who was formerly known to the President.[2]

P.S. Since writing the above, the enclosed, recommending Mr Watts has been received.[3]

AL, DLC:GW; LB, DNA: RG 59, Domestic Letters. The docket on the AL reads, "Daniel Gaines Cover of Recommendns of Mr Watts & Mr Gaines to be marshl of Georgia."

1. On the death of Robert Forsyth, see James Hendricks to GW, 15 Jan., n.1. According to Gaines's letter to Randolph of 16 Jan., from Washington, Ga., "my exhausted finances requiring something to recruit them, I take the Liberty of requesting your friendly assistance in procuring me that post; a post which I know myself perfectly competent to the execution of, but which I can have no possible expectation of obtaining, without the intervention of my friends, as I am totally unacquainted with the President" (DLC:GW).

The second letter from Gaines to Randolph, also of 16 Jan., asked for Randolph's "friendly assistance" in obtaining the appointment as marshal. Gaines added: "If the post I solicit is bestowed on another, I will accept any that is suitable, and consonant to the dignity of a Gentleman. No matter in what state. My finances want recruiting and they *shall* be recruited honorably, or not at all" (DLC:GW). Gaines also sent a separate letter of application to GW of 20 January.

2. Harry Gaines (died c.1767) represented King William County, Va., in the House of Burgesses, 1758–61 and 1765–67. An entry in GW's diaries shows that GW lodged at his home on 21 April 1760 (*Diaries*, 1:270). Harry Gaines's relationship to Daniel Gaines has not been identified.

3. According to Virginia congressman Abraham Bedford Venable's letter to Randolph of this date, Edward Watts, now a resident of Georgia, "is a Virginian and from the part of the Country from which I come, he was brought up a merchant is well acquainted with business, and was an active man when I knew him, his connections are respectable, and some of them particularly meritorious for their exertions in the late revolution. I am not able to say from my own knoledge what his present situation is in that Country, or how he has conducted himself since his residence there, which has been about ten years, but I am told he is now Secretary to the Governour of that State this I think is sufficient to presume that he has conducted himself

well since he has lived in that State." Venable asked that his letter be given to GW along with the enclosed letter from Watts to Venable, written at Augusta, Ga., on 14 Jan., requesting a letter of recommendation from Venable (both letters, DLC:GW). Venable (1758–1811), a resident of Prince Edward County, was currently in Philadelphia to attend the first session of the Third Congress.

Randolph received a letter of recommendation from Virginia congressman Josiah Parker written at Philadelphia on this date. This, which Randolph presumably passed on to GW at some point, reads: "I have received letters from Mr Daniel Gaines & Mr Edward Watts both of Georgia formerly of Virginia Soliciting to be appointed Marshal of the District of Georgia vacant by the death of Mr Forsyth. The first served with me in the Militia and appeared to be a good man, he informs me he has a large family & is very poor. The other is a Brother of Captn [John] Watts late of the Cavalry of the United States is a well inform'd gentleman. I am told he is now a Secretary to the Governor of Georgia—my duty to them from a former acquaintance induces me to name them to you for the information of the President of the United States" (DLC: GW). Neither Gaines nor Watts received the desired appointment (see GW to U.S. Senate, 5 March 1794).

From Abraham Baldwin

Sir   Philadelphia 18th Feby 1794
    The office of Marshal in the district of Georgia being vacant by the death of Majr Forsyth, I have been requested to submit to your consideration the names of the following persons as candidates for that office.[1]

In Savannah and its vicinity
    John Berrien
    Richard Carnes
    Samuel Hammond

In Augusta and its vicinity
    Amasa Jackson
    Philip Clayton
    James Mason Simmons
    Daniel Gaines
    Nicholas Bugg
    George Hull

    The original letters on this subject I have not thought it necessary to transmit, and have only to add that the Candidates are all personally known to me,[2] and I shall be ready to give any information in my power respecting either of them, should other information not be sufficient to determine the President in the appointment.[3] with the most profound respect, I am sir, your obedient humble servant

Abr. Baldwin

ALS, DLC:GW.

1. Georgia congressman Abraham Baldwin was in Philadelphia to attend the first session of the Third Congress. On the death of Robert Forsyth, see n.1 of James Hendricks to GW, 15 January.

2. John Berrien currently was serving as surveyor of customs at the port of Savannah. Virginia native Samuel Hammond (1757–1842) was a veteran of the Continental army and settled in Savannah shortly after the end of the Revolutionary War. He was in the Georgia legislature, 1796–1800, and in the U.S. House of Representatives, 1803–5. After serving as governor of the Upper Louisiana Territory, 1805–24, he settled in South Carolina. He held a number of political positions in that state, including secretary of state, 1831–35. Revolutionary War veteran Amasa Jackson (1765–1824) was a Massachusetts native and currently a merchant in Augusta. For a letter of application from Daniel Gaines, see his letter to GW of 20 January.

3. Another list of potential candidates for consideration is at DLC:GW. This undated list reads:

"Persons Candidates for the Marshals Office District of Georgia

John Jenkins, bred in the Prothonotarys Office of Georgia under the British Government—took a Commission in the Georgia line at the commencement of the War & was active as an Aid of Genl Sumpter [Thomas Sumter] at its conclusion

Samuel Hammonds—An active Officer during the War, and Lt. Col. of a State Corps, which distinguished itself at Eaton [Eutaw Springs, S.C.]. Genl [Andrew] Pickens is well acquainted with this Gentleman.

Amasa Jackson An Officer in the Massachusets line during the War—& a Man of business

Thos E. Dorsey—An Officer of Maryland during the War in the Dragoon Service—bred to the law.

Richd Carnes—Father to the Representative in Congress [Thomas Petters Carnes] and a member of the Legislature of the State

Daniel Gaines—Formerly of Virginia, now a Resident of Washington in Georgia—Some of the Virginia members, must be well acquainted with him.

Jas M. Simmons—Formerly of Virginia, now of Augusta

Nicholas H. Bugg. Resident at Augusta

Chestly Bostick—   do

The above are all Men of Reputation & most if not all of them capable of the duties of the Office—they are all Inhabitants of Georgia at present" (DLC:GW).

None of the men on these two lists received the appointment (see GW to U.S. Senate, 5 March 1794).

From Daniel Carroll (of Rock Creek)

Sir, Geo: Town [Md.] feby 18th 1794

Mr Mathew Bourne of the State of New-York has sollicited me to give him a line of introduction, alledging that he has some private business with you—I know nothing of this person further, than that he has been here for some weeks past, and has found a connection in the City on a scheme of carrying on the Lumber trade to a considerable extent, and has left an application on that subject for the Commissioner⟨s⟩ at their next meeting.[1] I have the honor to be Sr with the greatest respect, Yr Mo. Obt & very Hble Servt

Danl Carroll

ALS, DNA: RG 59, Miscellaneous Letters.

1. Neither Matthew Bourne, the nature of his business with GW, nor his application to the commissioners for the District of Columbia has been identified. There is no mention of Bourne or his application in the minutes of the 19–25 March meeting of the commissioners (DNA: RG 42, Records of the Commissioners for the District of Columbia, Proceedings, 1791–1802).

From James McHenry

Sir. Fayetteville [Maryland] 18 Febry 1794

I have been requested by Dr Allison to mention to you Mr Robt McRea who removed some time ago from Alexandria to Wilks's County State of Georgia as a very worthy person and well qualified to discharge the office of Marshal which he understood was vacant by the death of Major Forsyth. It appears also by information I have received from other persons that Mr McRea is a good man who has experienced distress and has a large family to support, and that he is fully equal to such an office.[1]

The supposed successor of Mr Genet left Town early this morning for Philada under an escort of light horse which he requested. I understand that he carefully concealed his character and had no communication with the French consul. I hope M. Genet is not to be the cause of further trouble to Government: but some think he does not intend to return to France and that his Country will demand him from this.[2]

The extraordinary cares you have lately experienced have made a very proper impression upon the public mind in this quarter, in consequence of which the principal inhabitants will celebrate the 22 at Mr Grants; notwithstanding what was done on the 11th.[3]

I hope your hea[l]th enables you to meet the business you have to go through with some degree of satisfaction. I am sure no one wishes for it more sincerely than I do. Altho' it is some time since I recovered from my fever yet my health is by no means what it was before.

I beg you to present my sincere respects to Mrs Washington and to believe me Sir your most ob. st

James McHenry

The french merchantmen & other vessels of that Nation have received sailing orders or rather orders to be ready to sail on the first signal.

ALS, DLC:GW. The postal stamp on the cover reads, "BALT FEB 18."

1. Patrick Allison (1740–1802) served as pastor of the First Presbyterian Church in Baltimore from 1763 until shortly before his death. He graduated in 1760 from the College of Philadelphia (later the University of Pennsylvania), which granted him a doctor of divinity degree in 1782. Former Alexandria, Va., merchant Robert McCrea did not receive the desired appointment as the U.S. marshal for Georgia (see GW to U.S. Senate, 5 March 1794). On the death of Robert Forsyth, see n.1 of James Hendricks to GW, 15 January.

2. Jean-Antoine-Joseph Fauchet, who replaced Edmond Genet as the French minister plenipotentiary to the United States, presented his credentials to GW on 22 Feb., having arrived at Philadelphia on 21 Feb. (Provisional Executive Council of France to GW, 15 Nov. 1793; *JPP*, 286; *Gazette of the United States* [Philadelphia], 21 Feb. 1794). Genet did not return to France, but instead he settled permanently in New York State. Francis Moissonnier was the French vice-consul for Maryland.

3. GW's birthday according to the Julian calendar, which was abandoned by Great Britain and its colonies in 1752, was 11 February. Adoption of the Gregorian calendar moved the date to 22 Feb., but various municipalities continued to recognize the earlier date throughout GW's lifetime. A public dinner was held at Nathan Griffith's on 11 Feb. "on the celebration of the President's birth-day." Of the eleven toasts given on this occasion, the first was to "The President of the United States" (*Baltimore Daily Intelligencer*, 13 Feb. 1794). Griffith's newly established inn, Rights of Man, was located in Old Town, at 6 Bridge Street (*Baltimore Directory, 1796*, 32; *Baltimore Daily Intelligencer*, 10 Feb. 1794).

A second celebration was held by the citizens of Baltimore on 22 Feb. to demonstrate "another proof of the grateful remembrance in which they hold his many military and civil services, of their approbation of his principles and prudence, and reliance on his courage and skill to pilot with *dignity* and *safety,* through a difficult navigation and tempestuous sea, the vessel of state. On this occasion the several Baltimore companies of militia . . . appeared under arms, and went thro' a variety of well chosen evolutions and firings with great exactness and beauty: after which the merchants, joined by their fellow-citizens, dined at Mr. Grant's" (*Baltimore Daily Intelligencer,* 24 Feb. 1794). Daniel Grant's Fountain Inn, a frequent stopping point for GW, was located at 10 Light Street.

From the Supreme Court Justices

(Copy)
Sir, Philadelphia 18th Feby 1794.
   Impressed with an opinion, that the most proper method of conveying the enclosed representation to Congress, is through the President of the United States; we take the liberty of transmitting it to you, and to request that you will be pleased to lay it before them.[1] We have the honor to be, with perfect respect, Sir, Your most obedient, & most humble servants.

$$\text{Signed} \left\{ \begin{array}{l} \text{John Jay} \\ \text{Wm Cushing} \\ \text{James Wilson} \\ \text{John Blair} \\ \text{Wm Paterson.} \end{array} \right.$$

I certify the foregoing to be a true copy from the original.
                                        Bw. Dandridge
                         Secy to the Presidt of the U. States.

Copy, DNA: RG 46, Fourth Congress, 1795–97, Senate Records of Legislative Proceedings, President's Messages.
   1. See the following enclosure, a letter from the Supreme Court justices to the U.S. Senate and House of Representatives, c.18 Feb., which GW enclosed with a cover letter to the U.S. Senate and House of Representatives of 19 Feb. that reads: "I lay before you the copy of a letter which I have received from the chief Justice and associate Justices of the Supreme Court of the United States; and, at their desire, the representation, mentioned in the said letter, pointing out certain defects in the judiciary system" (LS, DNA: RG 46, Fourth Congress, 1795–97, Senate Records of Legislative Proceedings, President's Messages; LB, DNA: RG 233, Third Congress, 1793–95, House Records of Legislative Proceedings, Journals; LB, DLC:GW).

Enclosure
Supreme Court Justices to the United States
Senate and House of Representatives

[Philadelphia, c.18 Feb. 1794]

The Chief Justice and the Associate Justices of the Supreme Court of the United States, respectfully represent to the Congress of the United States,

That their Representation communicated, last year, thro' the President, to both Houses of Congress, and to which they refer; comprehended few other remarks than such as were suggested by the personal difficulties to which the Judges were subjected.[1]

They acknowledge, with Sensibility and Gratitude, that the Act which, thereupon, passed, and, whereby the attendance of one Judge only was made indispensible to the holding of a Circuit Court, afforded them great relief, and enabled them to pass more time at home and in studies made necessary by their official duties.[2]

They think it incumbent on them to submit to the Consideration of Congress, whether the sessions of the several Courts, comprehended in any of the three Circuits, ought to depend entirely on the Health of the Judge to whom either of them may be assigned; for, in Case, by accident or Illness his attendance should be prevented, the Inconveniencies and useless expences to all the parties would certainly be great as well as obvious.

It has already happened, in more than one Instance, that different Judges sitting at different times in the same Court but in similar Causes have decided in direct opposition to each other, and that in cases in which the parties could not, as the Law now stands, have the benefit of Writs of Error.[3] They, therefore, also submit to the Consideration of Congress, whether this Evil, naturally tending to render the Law unsettled and uncertain, and thereby to create apprehensions and diffidence in the public mind, does not require the Interposition of Congress.[4]

They fear it would not become them to take a minute View of the whole system, and to suggest the Alterations which to them appear requisite; and their Hesitation is increased by the reflexion, that some of those Alterations would, from the nature of them, be capable of being ascribed to personal Considerations.

John Jay
Wm Cushing
James Wilson
John Blair
Wm Paterson

DS, DNA: RG 46, Fourth Congress, 1795–97, Senate Records of Legislative Proceedings, President's Messages.

1. For the previous "Representation" sent to Congress that expounded on the difficulties associated with attending the various U.S. circuit courts, see n.1 of Supreme Court Justices to GW of 9 Aug. 1792. GW submitted this earlier representation with his second letter to the U.S. Senate and House of Representatives of 7 Nov. 1792.

2. For the response of Congress to the justices' previous complaint, see the Judiciary Act of 1793, which is titled "An Act to alter the times and places of holding the Circuit Courts, in the Eastern District, and in North Carolina, and for other purposes," 2 March 1793 (*Stat.* 1:335–36).

3. A writ of error is "a writ issued out of a court of appellate jurisdiction, directed to the judges of a court of record in which final judgment has been given, commanding them to send the record to the appellate court in order that some alleged error in the proceedings may be corrected" (*Documentary History of the Supreme Court,* 1:596).

4. For subsequent alterations in the circuit and district court systems, see "An Act further to authorize the Adjournment of Circuit Courts," 19 May 1794, and "An Act making certain alterations in the act for establishing the Judicial Courts, and altering the time and place of holding certain courts," 9 June 1794 (*Stat.* 1:369, 395–97).

From Henry Knox

Sir,   War department February 19th 1794

I have the honor to submit to your consideration the copy of a letter from the Secretary of the Treasury enclosing a letter from Mr Habersham Collector of Savannah in Georgia, and an Agent for the Treasury department in that State, relatively to the supply of Rations there on account of the United States.[1]

As the number of Militia in Georgia have very far exceeded the number permitted by you on the 30th of May last,[2] and as it does not appear by any information received to be under the contemplation of the Governor of Georgia to reduce them, it is hereby submitted whether a letter ought not to be written to

him in the name of the President of the United States directing him to reduce the number to be kept up at the expence of
the United States to the One hundred horse and One hundred
foot permitted on the said 30th of May last, and that the latter
number be retained no longer than circumstances shall render
indispensible.

That if a greater number be required the case must be stated
for the consideration and decision of the President of the United
States.

That these directions be considered as conformable to the
present state of things but that if an actual invasion should take
place the provisions contained in the constitution must govern.[3] I have the honor to be with perfect respect Your obedient
Servant

II. Knox.
secy of war

LS, DLC:GW; LB, DLC:GW.

1. For the letter from John Habersham to Alexander Hamilton of 16 Jan.
and Hamilton's letter to Knox of 12 Feb., both of which noted the large numbers of militia units called into active service by Georgia governor Edward Telfair and his successor, George Mathews, see *Hamilton Papers,* 15:643–44; 16:27.

2. In his letter to Telfair of 30 May 1793, Knox wrote that "from the circumstances of the late depredations on the frontiers of Georgia, it is thought
expedient to increase the force in that quarter for defensive purposes, The
President therefore authorizes your Excellency call into and keep in service,
in addition to the regular force stationed in Georgia, one hundred horse,
and one hundred Militia foot, to be employed under the orders of Lieut.
Colonel [Henry] Gaither in repelling inroads as circumstances shall require"
(DLC:GW; printed in *ASP, Indian Affairs,* 1:364).

3. According to GW's executive journal, he approved Knox's suggested
directions and instructed him "to write accordingly" (*JPP,* 285). Knox's subsequent letter to Mathews, c.19 Feb., has not been identified.

From Edmund Randolph

[Philadelphia] Wednesday morning Feby 19. 1794.
E. Randolph has the honor of inclosing to the President the
draught of a message upon the Representation of the judges—
Two copies are sent by the judges.[1]

He also forwards a letter from Mr Pinckney, received last
night. The cyphered part will be solved this morning; and

it is hoped, that it will explain something, which at present is unaccountable—E.R. has a duplicate.[2]

AL, DNA: RG 59, Miscellaneous Letters; LB, DNA: RG 59, GW's Correspondence with His Secretaries of State.

1. The letter composed by Randolph was GW's letter to the U.S. Senate and House of Representatives of 19 Feb. (see n.1 of Supreme Court Justices to GW, 18 Feb.). For the "Representation" of the Supreme Court justices, see their letter to the U.S. Senate and House of Representatives, c.18 Feb., which was enclosed in their letter to GW of 18 February.

2. The letter from Thomas Pinckney to the secretary of state of 25 Nov. 1793 reported on his meeting with Lord Grenville, the British foreign secretary, in which Pinckney outlined the "circumstances which were now particularly calamitous to the United States": Indian unrest in the Northwest Territory, "which I attributed to the detention of the posts"; "letting loose the Algerines upon us" by promoting a truce between Algiers and Portugal; and the "interruption to our commerce & neutral rights." The cipher of particular interest to Randolph probably concerned the British retention of military posts on American soil, contrary to the 1783 Treaty of Paris. When Pinckney asked if Great Britain would relinquish the posts if "we should comply with what they conceived to be the full execution of the treaty on our part," Grenville replied that after nine years of non-compliance by one party, "neither reason nor the law of nations would expect a strict compliance from the other party" (DNA: RG 59, Despatches from U.S. Ministers to Great Britain; an extract of this letter and the explication of the ciphers are in *ASP, Foreign Relations*, 1:327–28).

From Edmund Randolph

[Philadelphia] Wednesday evening feby 19. 1794.
E. Randolph has the honor to inform the President, that the subjects within the department of state for consultation, are

1. The form of a message, to accompany Mr Morris's letters.[1]

2. Whether Mr Pinckney's last dispatches are to be communicated to congress? and how, if at all?[2]

When E.R. came from the President's this afternoon, the office was shut; but he purposes to notify the gentlemen, as he was instructed by the President for tomorrow 12 o'clock.[3]

N.B. Perhaps a letter from Messrs Carmichael and Short, now under the decyphering clerk, may probably make a third article of deliberation.[4]

AL, DNA: RG 59, Miscellaneous Letters; LB, DNA: RG 59, GW's Correspondence with His Secretaries of State.

1. On the Senate request for the correspondence of Gouverneur Morris, the U.S. minister to France, see U.S. Senate to GW, 24 January. For GW's reply, see his letter to the U.S. Senate of 26 February.

2. For GW's submission of the correspondence of Thomas Pinckney, the U.S. minister to Great Britain, see GW to the U.S. Senate and House of Representatives, 24 February.

3. GW apparently had called for members of his cabinet to meet with him at noon on 20 Feb. to discuss the subjects mentioned in this letter.

4. William Carmichael and William Short currently were serving as joint commissioners plenipotentiary to Spain (see GW to U.S. Senate, 11 Jan. 1792). For GW's submission of their letter to the secretary of state of 22 Oct. 1793, see GW to U.S. Senate and House of Representatives, 24 February.

From Francis Corbin

Sir Virga. L⟨ane⟩ville[1] Feby 20th 1794

The office of Collector on this River—(Rappohannock) I am told, is vacant.[2] A desire to introduce to the public service a man of long tried worth is the best apology I can make to you, who are in the habit of rewarding merit, for my requesting your patronage of Mr George Turner. He is desirous to supply the vacancy—and he is competent, in Ev'ry way, to the discharge of his Duties should he be gratified with the appointment.

His fidelity and Integrity, during thirty years Service in our family, has Endeared him to the whole of it. His Virtues are notorious to the District in which he lives, and need not the panegyric of any Individual whatever.[3]

Permit me to add as a public Consideration, that all the Responsible part of my family will become his Securities—so that in case of a delinquency (which is almost impossible) the Secretary of the Treasury will have more property to Resort to than he could have under the appointment of any other person (who would solicit the office) on this River.[4] With Ev'ry Sentiment of Veneration and Esteem I am Sir Yr Mo. Obt Servt

Francis Corbin

ALS, DLC:GW.

1. Laneville was the Corbin family estate in King and Queen County.

2. On the vacancy in the office of collector of customs for the District of Tappahannock, on the Rappahannock River, see Hudson Muse to GW, 27 Jan., and n.3 to that document.

3. George Turner had begun his service as a steward at Laneville under Richard Corbin (c.1714–1790), the father of Francis Corbin (*Diaries*, 4:161).

4. Under section 52 of "An Act to provide more effectually for the collection of the duties imposed by law on goods, wares and merchandise imported into the United States, and on the tonnage of ships or vessels," 4 Aug. 1790, every collector must "give bond with one or more sufficient sureties, to be approved of by the comptroller of the treasury of the United States, and payable to the said United States, with condition for the true and faithful discharge of the duties of his office." The amount of the bond varied according to the location of the office. The bond expected from the collector of the Tappahannock district was $2,000 (*Stat.* 1:145, 171). For another letter recommending Turner, see Richard Bland Lee to Alexander Hamilton, 6 March (*Hamilton Papers*, 122–23). Mr. Turner did not receive this appointment (see GW to U.S. Senate, 5 March 1794).

From Henry Knox

Sir,   War department. February 20th 1794

Agreeably to the request of Major Thomas Cushing of the 3d Sub Legion, I submit to you his letter to me of the 4. of December 1793 and his correspondence relatively to his being arrested with Major General Wayne and his Aid de Camp and Brigadier General Posey.[1] I have the honor to be with the greatest respect Your obedient Servant

H. Knox
secy of war

LS, DLC:GW; LB, DLC:GW.

1. The letter from Thomas Humphrey Cushing to Knox of 4 Dec. 1793 and its enclosures, Cushing's correspondence with Anthony Wayne and Thomas Posey, have not been identified. According to GW's executive journal, this letter set "forth the injustice which has been done him & the contempt with which he has been treated before & during his arrest" (*JPP*, 285). At Cushing's court-martial, 11 Dec. 1793 to 8 Jan. 1794, he was tried for charges "exhibited against him by Captain Edward Butler, late acting adjutant general, on the 8th of November and 1⟨0⟩th of December 1793. 1st. For repeated neglect of duty, and disobedience of the general orders of the 27th of August 1792, in not having made reports of the Sub-Legion under his command to the acting adjutant general (and by reason of said neglect) . . . the provisions of the said Sub-Legion have been obtained at a late hour. 2d For neglect of duty as field officer of the day on the 2d and night of the 2d and 3d of November instant, in not having furnished the guard of the redoubts of the light corps (which furnished at least one half of the chain of sentinels) with the countersign, and for not having visited the guards and sentinels during the night, which conduct tends to eminent resque of the safety of the Legion. 3d. For neglect of duty, in not having furnished the acting adjutant general, with a

general return of the third Sub-Legion under your command when officially called on thereof on the 1st day of October last. 4th. For disobedience and contempt of the general order of the 6th day of November last—contempt of that order, in having on the morning of the 7th of November aforesaid signed a report & provision return for part of the third Sub Legion and afterward cut his signature therefrom, and sent them to me for my signature on the provision return.--2d. For disobedience of the said order, in having afterwards refused to sign any return, whereby part of the troops of the third Sub-Legion were kept long without provision." Cushing pleaded not guilty to all the charges and was acquitted on each count (*Centinel of the North-Western Territory* [Cincinnati], 25 Jan. 1794). Cushing may have been among those officers of whom Wayne complained to Knox in his second letter of 15 Nov. 1793 (see n.1 of Knox to GW, 3 Jan.).

Bartholomew Dandridge, Jr., to Edmund Randolph

[Philadelphia] 21st Feby 1794.
By the President's order Bw Dandridge transmits to the Secy of State, the draft of the Proclamation in order that it may be copied for the Presidents signature, after wch the President wishes the draft to be returned to him.[1]

AL, DNA: RG 59, Miscellaneous Letters; LB, DNA: RG 59, GW's Correspondence with His Secretaries of State.
1. The enclosed draft of GW's proclamation of 24 Feb. has not been found.

From Edmund Randolph

Friday 2 o'clock. 21st Feb. [1794]
E. Randolph has the honor of informing the President, that Fauchet, and Petrie have just this moment left him. They brought sealed credentials; but upon my informing them, that an open copy was necessary for me, they will send it instante⟨r⟩.[1] I am this instant at dinner; but shall wait upon you immediately after—They make the *demand;* but I told them, that the requisition must be in writing—They have a writing from the executive council to this effect—I this morning mentioned this subject again to the other gentlemen. But I have directed my messenger to receive orders from Mr Dandridge, whether he is to proceed

to summon the other gentlemen to your house immediately—If you approve of this, Mr Dandridge will only say to the Messenger to deliver the message Which I have given him for the other gentlemen.[2]

AL, DLC:GW.

1. Jean-Antoine-Joseph Fauchet had recently arrived in the United States to replace Edmond Genet as the French minister plenipotentiary (James McHenry to GW, 18 Feb., and n.2 to that document). Jean-Baptiste Petry, a former consul *ad interim* at Charleston, S.C., 1786–92, and vice-consul at Wilmington, N.C., 1783–86, was to become the new French consul at Philadelphia in place of François Dupont, who died in September 1793 during the yellow fever epidemic in Philadelphia. Both men presented their credentials to GW on 22 Feb., along with Antoine-René-Charles Mathurin de La Forest, who was to be consul general (*JPP*, 286). For additional preparations for this meeting, see Randolph to GW, 22 February. For Fauchet's credentials, see Provisional Executive Council of France to GW, 15 Nov. 1793. Other accompanying letters have not been identified.

2. Randolph's message for the other members of GW's cabinet has not been identified.

Henry Knox to Bartholomew Dandridge, Jr.

Dear sir   [Philadelphia] 22 Feby 1794

Be pleased to submit the enclosed drafts of letters to the Governors of North and south Carolina. probably the last paragraph but one, to the Governor of south Carolina may be a little differently shaped, but to remain the same in principle.[1] Yours sincerely

H. Knox

ALS, DLC:GW; LB, DLC:GW.

1. In his letter to North Carolina governor Richard Dobbs Spaight of this date, Knox acknowledged the receipt of Spaight's letter to GW of 31 Jan., and then wrote: "Under the circumstances of your having possessed yourself of the L'amee Margueritte formerly the sloop Providence it is to be regretted that my second letter of the 13th January should have been written as it is not improbable that in pursuance thereof you may have relinquished her, for from consideration of public importance, which have occurred since the writing of that letter it would have been desireable that the said vessel should have been restored to her former owners.

"If therefore she should still be in your actual possession it is the instruction of the President of the United States that upon a full ascertainment of her having been captured by the illicit privateer the Vanqueur de Bastille after the fifth day of June last that you cause her to be restored to her Master or owner at the time of her capture or to the agents of the British Government, who may apply duly authorized for that purpose.

"If however you should have relinquished the actual possession of her in pursuance of my said letter of the 13th January it is not desired or intended that you should now retake possession of her. But in this case it is to be explicitly understood that she is not to have asylum in our ports unless she divests [her]self of all warlike equipments" (Nc-Ar: Governors' Letterbooks). For two letters from Knox to Spaight of 13 January, see n.1 of Spaight's second letter to GW of 8 February.

Knox's letter to South Carolina governor William Moultrie has not been identified.

From the Newport, R.I., Artillery Company

[Newport, R.I., 22 February 1794]

The Artillery Company of the Town of Newport in the State of Rhode Island & Providence Plantations, assembled on this day to celebrate the birth of the chief magistrate of the United States, beg leave to present their congratulations and respect:

Associated by principles which effected a glorious revolution, and laid the basis of a free and permanent government, they contemplate with grateful emotions, the blessings which have resulted from a prudent and efficient administration.

Enjoying the inestimable priviledges of freemen, they commiserate the unhappy state of those who are in bondage, sympathize in the sufferings of those who are bravely struggling in the cause of freedom, and cordially rejoice with those, who are successful in regaining their rights: Equalized with their fellow citizens, they consider abilities and virtue, the only qualities which deserve public estimation, and give preeminence to a character; Influenced by these sentiments, they have presumed on this offering of congratulation and respect, as the purest testimony of their attachment for distinguished virtue; Humbly beseeching the Supreme Giver of all good gifts to continue your life and public usefulness, and that they with their fellow citizens, may still gratefully reciprocate the satisfaction resulting from a faithful discharge of important duties.

Signed in pursuance of the unanimous resolution of the Artillery Company of the Town of Newport February 22d 1794.

F. Malbone, Captain[1]

DS, DLC:GW; LB, DLC:GW.

1. Newport merchant Francis Malbone (1759–1809) represented Rhode Island in the U.S. House of Representatives, 1793–97, and in the U.S. Senate from 4 March 1809 until his death on 4 June 1809. He served as the captain of the Newport Artillery Company from its reorganization in 1792 until his death. He enclosed this letter with a brief cover letter that he wrote at Philadelphia on 17 March, which reads: "I have the pleasure to inclose an Address from the Artillery Company of the Town of Newport, which I received by the last Post" (DLC:GW). GW replied to the artillery company in a letter of c.18 March.

To William Pearce

⟨Mr. Pearce,   Philadelphia, 22d Feb. 1794.

Your letter of the 15th instt and the reports, have come to hand as usual.[1]

I was affraid the open weather we have had, with frost, would have injured the Wheat. A short crop of this article two years running, wod fall heavy upon me; as it seems to be the only thing, to any sort of amount, from which the means is derived, by which the various, and heavy expences of my estate, is borne. If the Wheat is thrown much out of the ground, and the roots exposed, try the roller thereon—repeatedly—as soon as the earth is a little settled, and the roller will pass over it without its sticking thereto; over the parts I mean (of the fields) that are injured. I tried this method one year with very good success; and it is a practice strongly recommended by all the Books on farming.[2] I have, myself, seen bunches of Wheat the roots of which have been *entirely* out of the ground, take again by the Roller's com⟩pressing them to the earth: and the chance of doing it is well worth the expence & time which is required by the roller, drawn with Oxe⟨n⟩.

Put such part of the field (intended to be enclosed) at the Mansion house, int⟨o⟩ Corn, or other things, as you shall judge best—regarding however, what I have repeatedly mentioned, that profit from any thing that can be raised there (at the Mansion house I mean) is not so much an object with me, as clearing the ground; beautifying it with trees; and laying it to grass. I had no ide⟨a⟩ of there being 70 Acres within the bounds you have described; nor do I perfectly comprehend your description of them; or rathe⟨r⟩ the length of each line is greater than I had any conception of—For in the first place, I had no idea of its measuring 80 perches[3] from the black gate (in the hollow) to the turn of the road by the corner of the clover lot; or, that from thence to the declivity of the hill, towards the Creek, could be 87 more. I do not mean that the fence from thence sh. descend the hill lower than merely to hide it from the house, & from the road going up to the house. To what part of the outer fence you propose to join the last mentioned course, I know not, & therefore can not judge so well of the distance.

I am a little at a loss for an answer to Mr Thos Ringgolds request, respecting the Jack. I should have no objection to letting one of my Jacks stand on the Eastern shore, if entire confidence could be placed in the person to whose care he was entrusted; but from the loose, and dissipated character of the abovenamed Gentleman so far as I have heard it spoken of I have doubts of the propriety of committing one of them to his management: and besides, it is almost, if not quite too late now, to negotiate this matter with him, or any other at a distance; as the Season would be too far advanced before the removal could be made, & sufficient notice thereof given.[4] A year or two ago I was offered by a Connecticut man (who could, & would have given good security for the performance of the agreement) Five hundred guineas for four (or five) years service (I am not certain which) of the Maltese Jack; although he would (for he went to Mount Vernon to see them) have preferred the one which I think is named *Compound*—And if I ever part with another, it shall be in that way; in order that I may know *certainly* what I am to receive. Letting one on shares I never will; for in that case expences are trumped up—one may be told of difficulties in collecting money—& many other things, when accounts come to be settled, with a view of staving off paymt which, if they do not breed disputes, are at least unpleasant things & ought to be avoided. The Connecticut man whom I have before mentioned, would have paid the money *down* and run the risk of the Jack's living. The advantage of which was very considerable; as it was the best security possible for his care of the Animal.[5]

If you, who ought to know Mr Ringgold as well as any body does, should be of opinion that he would pay five hundred guineas *down*, or give security for his doing it within a year; and should moreover th[in]k that his care of the Animal might be depended on, you might write him word that upon *these* conditions, he might have either of the Covering Jacks for four years; at the expiration of which he is to be returned in good condition, if living. As there is a young Jack from Royal Gift coming on, I believe it would be best to part with *Compound*, but it is not, to me, very material which of them is disposed of, on the terms beforementioned; as I do not know to which of their colts to give the preference from any knowledge I have of them—If you should write to Mr Ringgold, and he should accede to the terms here mentioned, the agreement must be drawn up in writing, by a professional man (that is by a lawyer, Mr Chs Lee for instance) and all the objects of it clearly expressed.[6]

Mr Pearse Bailey may be informed that I never lower my price of land; it is infinitely more likely that it will be encreased, than to stand even at what it has been offered for. This he might reasonably expect, as landed property is rising fast in value every where; from the number of emigrants, & others who are wanting to vest their money in that species of property.[7]

I am sorry my letter was so long getting to the hands of my Nephew Colo. Washington; for if I have not formed a very erroneous, and unjust opinion of the conduct of my Negro Carpenters—there is not to be found so idle a set of Rascals. In short it appears to me, that to make over a chicken coob, would employ all of them a week; buildings that are run up here in two or three days (with not more hands) employ them a month, or more.[8]

I will cause enquiry to be made here, into the price of Oznabrigs, but have little expectation that it can be bought on better terms in this City, than in Alexandria—for every thing is amazingly dear here.[9]

By the Trial, Captn Hand (I believe the Masters name is) I have shipped three bushels of Clover seed—two bushels of honey locust seed, and a keg of scaley bark hiccory nuts: the two last are in one Cask—the high price of clover Seed prevented me from sending more—what goes is fresh & good. Tell the Gardener he must plant the hiccory nuts in drills—as the Illinois nuts herewith sent, must also be—and they may be put near together in the drills, as they will be to be transplanted when they get to a proper size.[10]

Have your ground for the honey locust seed in readiness against the arrival of the Vessel, which will leave this it is said, tomorrow—or as soon the floating Ice in the river will permit her to go down. The sooner the locust seeds are in the ground the better. I do not care where you put them, so they are under a secure fence, at the Mansion house, or at any of the farms where they will be attended to will be equally convenient.[11] I am Your friend &ca

Go: Washington

ALS (letterpress copy, fragment), DLC:GW. The text in angle brackets is taken from Moncure Daniel Conway, *George Washington and Mount Vernon: A Collection of Washington's Unpublished Agricultural and Personal Letters* (Brooklyn, 1889), 163–67.

1. Pearce's letter of 15 Feb. and the enclosed farm reports have not been found.

2. For books and pamphlets on agriculture that were in GW's library, see Griffin, *Catalogue of the Washington Collection.*

3. A perch, or rod, is a unit of measure that is equivalent to 16.5 feet.

4. According to the 1790 federal census, there were three Thomas Ringgolds living on the Eastern Shore of Maryland, specifically in Queen Anne's County, any one of whom may have been interested in managing the stud services of one of GW's jacks and who was probably the same Ringgold who recommended Pearce as an estate manager for GW (*Heads of Families* [Maryland], 99, 101; GW to William Tilghman, 21 July 1793].

5. For the letter sent by Connecticut native Jeremiah Wadsworth containing a proposal to purchase the jack Compound, see Tobias Lear to GW, 15 May 1791, and n.6 to that document. For an offer to manage the services of one of GW's jacks, see Lear to Joseph Williams, 14 Jan. 1792. On Compound, Knight of Malta, Royal Gift, and other jacks at Mount Vernon, see George Augustine Washington to GW, 16 July 1790, n.4; and Powell, *General Washington and the Jack Ass,* 176–90.

6. On Pearce's acquaintance with Mr. Ringgold, see GW to William Tilghman, 21 July 1793, and n.8 to that document. Charles Lee practiced law in Alexandria, Va., and frequently provided legal services for GW.

7. A Peirce Bayly (Baily) is listed as a taxpayer on the 1782 tax rolls for Loudoun County, Va., and in 1768, while serving as sub-sheriff of Fairfax County, collected property taxes from GW (Fothergill and Naugle, *Virginia Tax Payers,* 8; *Diaries,* 2:86).

8. In the past year's correspondence with William Augustine Washington, GW first mentioned the need for carpenters in a letter of 3 March 1793. The previous extant letter on this subject from GW to his nephew is that of 21 Oct. 1793.

9. Oznabrig is a type of coarse linen originally made in Osnabrück, Germany.

10. The hickory nuts shipped by GW were from the scaly-bark or shagbark hickory, *Carya ovata.* "Illinois nuts" was an early American term for the nuts that come from a pecan tree native to the United States, *Carya illinoinensis.*

11. At this point the printed version adds "and agreeable to me."

From Edmund Randolph

[Philadelphia] Saturday 22d Feb. [1794]

E. Randolph has the honor of informing the President, that he will present Mr Fauchet certainly at 12 o'clock; at any rate rather before than after.[1]

Colo. H. could not go over the *whole;* but he has agreed to look at the parts, to which his attention may be arrested by my cross in the margin[.] To morrow he will do this.[2]

The message was advised, as it is now sent.[3]

As my carriage is not in town, and Mr Fauchet has not one of his own, I mean to borrow one; and to return his visit at 11 o'clock at the city-tavern. From thence, we will proceed to your house, at a quarter before twelve.[4]

The form, which is submitted is the following:

1.   to announce Mr Fauchet by name and description.

2.   He will present his sealed credentials with those observations, which the occasion may dictate.

3.   The President will open them; and may either deliver them to me to read, or say, that he is apprized of their contents.

4.   Will it not be proper for the President, then to say, "I receive you in the quality of minister plenipotentiary of the French Republic": and to add any complimentary matter.[5]

5.   This being interpreted to him, he will make a reply; which being communicated to you, if you choose to say nothing more, we will, after a convenient pause, retire.

It is probable, that he may return to visit you among others on this day.[6]

AL, DLC:GW.

1. During the meeting later this day, Jean-Antoine-Joseph Fauchet presented GW with the credentials from the French government that authorized him to succeed Edmond Genet as the French minister plenipotentiary to the United States (*JPP*, 286).

2. The material reviewed by Randolph and Alexander Hamilton may have included unsealed copies of Fauchet's credentials and other accompanying letters from the Provisional Executive Council of France (see Randolph to GW, 21 Feb., and n.1 to that document).

3. Randolph may have been referring to his letter to Fauchet of this date advising the minister of the proposed meeting with GW (DNA: RG 59, Domestic Letters).

4. The City Tavern, which was owned by Edward Moyston in 1794, was at

86 South Second Street. GW resided at 190 High Street (*Philadelphia Directory, 1794*, 110, 161).

5. Randolph acted as an interpreter for GW at this meeting. For an account of what GW reputedly said, see James Madison to Thomas Jefferson, 2 March 1794, *Jefferson Papers*, 28:26–28.

6. GW celebrated his 62nd birthday on this date. According to an account in the 25 Feb. issue of the Philadelphia *General Advertiser*, the "sound of cannon, bells and drums was heard throughout the day." A levee held at GW's home that afternoon "was very numerous. In the evening he and Mrs. Washington were present at a ball and supper given by the City Dancing Assembly, at which several of the foreign Ministers were also present." After supper, nine toasts were drunk, "the last after the President had retired." Another newspaper's account added that the supper and ball were attended by "a number of the members of Congress, the Secretaries of the treasury and of war, the Governors of the State [Thomas Mifflin] and of the Western Territory [Arthur St. Clair], and the most brilliant display of beauty, perhaps, ever exhibited in this city" (*Gazette of the United States* [Philadelphia], 24 Feb. 1794). The ball was held at Oellers's Hotel, which was owned by James Oellers and located on Chesnut Street between Sixth and Seventh streets (*General Advertiser* [Philadelphia], 18 Feb. 1794; *Philadelphia Directory, 1794*, 115).

To Thomas Johnson

Dear Sir,   Philadelphia Feby 23d 1794

Your letter of the 6th instant came Safe, but not until after it had lain many days in the Post Office in Frederick Town, by the mark thereon.[1]

Your consenting to remain longer in the Commission of the Federal District gave me much pleasure; for although I have no doubt with respect to the accomplishment of the law (establishing the permanent residence of Congress),[2] nor of the execution of the plan of the City; yet a great & sudden change of the Commissioners appointed to conduct this business is not likely, in my opinion, to produce good, but on the contrary, evil consequences. I am unwilling therefore to hazard any thing that can be avoided on this occasion; especially at a time when matters appear to be progressing fast to a favorable result.

Notwithstanding you have agreed to act longer under the Commission, than you had intended, there will, nevertheless, be a vacancy; occasioned by the resignation of Doctr Stuart; from whose last letters I have no expectation of his remaining in

Office after your next meeting.[3] With much esteem & regard I am—Dear Sir Your Affect. Servt

Go: Washington

ALS, NN: Emmet Collection; LB, DLC:GW.

1. The cover for Johnson's letter to GW of 6 Feb., with the date stamped on it by the Frederick, Md., post office, has not been identified.

2. For the laws establishing the District of Columbia, providing for the transfer of the federal government to the district on the first Monday in December 1800, and approving the district's location in a ten-mile square on the Potomac River, see "An Act for establishing the temporary and permanent seat of the Government of the United States," 16 July 1790, and "An Act to amend 'An act for establishing the temporary and permanent seat of the Government of the United States,'" 3 March 1791 (*Stat.* 1:130, 214).

3. David Stuart offered his resignation as D.C. commissioner, effective 1 March, in a letter to GW of 6 Jan., and in his next extant letter to GW, of 6 Feb., he suggested possible successors. Despite Stuart's intended resignation date, he continued to serve until July 1794. The next meeting of the D.C. commissioners was held on 19–25 March (DNA: RG 42, Records of the Commissioners for the District of Columbia, Proceedings, 1791–1802).

From Edmund Randolph

[Philadelphia] Sunday morning 23d feb. 94.

E. Randolph has the honor of informing the President, that Mr Hammond replied yesterday, that he had not received the definitive instructions, which he mentioned to Mr Jefferson[1]—E.R. begs the President to send by the messenger the decyphering of Mr Pinckney's last letter. The body of it has been copied; and the other part is wished for the same purpose; that it may be ready for congress tomorrow; together with copies of Mr Hammond's letter.[2]

AL, DNA: RG 59, Miscellaneous Letters; LB, DNA: RG 59, GW's Correspondence with His Secretaries of State.

1. The instructions desired by British minister George Hammond concerned anticipated negotiations between Great Britain and the United States on violations of the 1783 Treaty of Paris. Thomas Jefferson outlined various infractions and disagreements in a detailed letter to Hammond of 29 May 1792. Hammond acknowledged the lack of "such definitive instructions . . . as will enable me immediately to renew the discussions" on these issues in his fourth letter to Jefferson of 22 Nov. 1793 (*Jefferson Papers*, 26:551–613; 27:418).

Randolph wrote Hammond on 21 Feb. 1794: "From a review of your letter to my predecessor on the 22d day of November 1793, it appears, that you had not then received such definitive instructions, relative to his communication of the 29th of May 1792, as would enable you *immediately* to renew the discussions upon the subject of it. Suspended as this negotiation has been for so long a time, I have it in charge from the President of the United States to repeat the inquiry whether any instructions have yet been received by you for pursuing those discussions?" (DNA: RG 59, Domestic Letters; *ASP, Foreign Relations,* 1:328). Hammond's reply to Randolph of 21 Feb. stated that he had "not yet received the definitive instructions" (DNA: RG 59, Notes from Foreign Legations: Great Britain; *ASP, Foreign Relations,* 1:328).

2. For Thomas Pinckney's letter to the secretary of state of 25 Nov. 1793, see n.2 of Randolph's first letter to GW of 19 February. This letter and the Hammond-Randolph correspondence of 21 Feb. were enclosed with GW's letter to the U.S. Senate and House of Representatives of 24 February.

From Edmund Randolph

[Philadelphia] Feby 23. 1794.

E. Randolph has the honor of inclosing to the President the draught of a message for the letters of Mr Pinckney, and our commissioners in Spain.[1]

E.R. took occasion last evening, to introduce the President's invitation to the minister Fauchet, omitting the consul, with a view to ascertain the participation, which the latter may have in the functions of the former. It was quickly ascribed by them to the established etiquette; without any title being urged on the part of the consul, from the circumstance of having a diplomatic connection. But from the manner, in which they spoke; from Petry's running before Fauchet in very confidential discourse; and from a very animated contact between them, whether they had brought over a paper, which belonged to the ministerial character alone; I cannot doubt, that they are associated.[2]

Fauchet did not see Mr Morris before his departure; barely gave a tolerable account of his not doing so; was ignorant of the name of his residence; and almost of its position. He Said, that he understood it to be in the country. This leads me to suspect, that some thing is to come.[3]

When Fauchet speaks of Genet, he slips over the instructions, which have been published, as lightly as possible; saying, that whatever appearance of truth may be worn, he knows nothing of their truth.[4]

AL, DLC:GW.

1. The enclosed draft, which has not been found, was for GW's letter to the U.S. Senate and House of Representatives of 24 February. For Thomas Pinckney's letter to the secretary of state of 25 Nov. 1793, see n.2 of Randolph's first letter to GW of 19 February. For the letter from William Carmichael and William Short to the secretary of state of 22 Oct. 1793, see n.3 of GW's letter to U.S. Senate and House of Representatives of 24 February.

2. Unfortunately, Fauchet, the newly arrived French minister plenipotentiary, did not speak English and had no diplomatic experience. Randolph and others in the administration apparently suspected that the more experienced Petry, the new French consul at Philadelphia, had more influence and responsibility than was usually assigned to a consul.

3. Gouverneur Morris, the U.S. minister to France, purchased a home outside of Paris in 1793 in order to escape the often dangerous turmoil of the city during the French Revolution. The house was situated in the village of Seine-Port, approximately 27 miles from Paris (Morris to Thomas Jefferson, 13 Feb. 1793, *Jefferson Papers*, 25:193–94). Fauchet reputedly set sail from the French port of Brest on 18 Dec. 1793 (*General Advertiser* [Philadelphia], 25 Feb. 1794).

4. Printed translations of "Instructions to Citizen Genet, Minister Plenipotentiary from the French Republic to the United States, from the Executive Council, and Minister of Marine" were included in Genet's *Correspondence between Citizen Genet, Minister of the French Republic, to the United States of North America, and the Officers of the Federal Government; to Which Are Prefixed the Instructions from the Constituted Authorities of France to the Said Minister. All from Authentic Documents* (Philadelphia, 1793). On these instructions, see n.1 of Thomas Jefferson to GW, 28 Dec. 1793.

To Bushrod Washington

Dear Bushrod,   Philadelphia Feby 23d 1794

Your letter of the 13th instt with the enclosures, came duly to hand. I thank you for draughting the answer which I have put my signature to; and with the Bill, now return.[1]

If I mistake not, my renunciation of the Executorship of Colo. Fairfax's Will already stands on record in the Genl Court, on some former occasion; be this however as it may, I have always refused, & never intended—directly nor indirectly, to have any agency in the Administration of the affairs of that Estate.[2]

It gives me much pleasure to hear, through a variety of Channels, that you are becoming eminent, & respectable in the Law. In this, and every transaction of your life, let honor & probity be your polar star. Your Aunt & all here join me in best regards for you & Nancy & be assured of the Affecte regard & friendship of

Go: Washington

ALS, NjP: deCoppet Collection; ALS (letterpress copy), DLC:GW; LB, DLC: GW.

1. GW's answer of this date to the bill of complaint reads: "The answer of George Washington to the Bill of Complaint exhibited against him in the High Court of Chancery in the Commonwealth of Virginia by Wilson M. Cary only acting Exectr & Trustee in Virginia of Geo. William Fairfax decd.

"This defendt saving and reserving to himself all benefit of enception to the uncertainties and insufficiencies in the sd Bill contained for answer there unto or unto so much thereof as he is advised is material for him to answer unto saith that he admits that George Wm Fairfax may have departed this life about the time in the said Bill set forth, having first made & publish'd his last Will and Testament as in the Bill stated. He also admits that the Sd Geo. W. Fairfax in and by his said Will did appoint the said Complainant together with Geo. Nicholas and this defendant Executors & Trustees of his estates lying in Virginia and did make such bequests & dispositions as the Sd Bill States; but this defendant being too much engaged in public business as well as with his own private concerns to enter upon so considerable an undertaking as that confided to him by the will of the Sd Geo. W. Fairfax hath uniformly refused to Join in the burthen of executing the Said will, and still influenc'd by the same reasons must decline interfereing in the business of the Said estate as Executor & Trustee. He therefore hopes that no decree of this Honble Court will pass against him which can in any manner affect him, or bind him to undertake a Trust which for the reasons above mentioned he hath hitherto refused & denying all combination & confederacy he prays to be hence dismiss'd with his reasonable Costs in this behalf expended" (DS, ViFCtH; DS [photocopy], Vi).

2. On GW's refusal to serve as an executor for the estate of George William Fairfax, see GW's letters to Warner Washington, Sr., of 9 Nov. 1787 and to Samuel Athawes of 8 Jan. 1788.

To Burgess Ball

Dear Sir,   Philadelphia Feby 24th 1794

I am glad to find by your letter of the 13th instant that the bracelets were received, & pleased.

The chocolate shells which you request shall be procured and sent when the Clover Seed goes, which I hope will *now* soon happen, as the navigation is once more *just* opened; and because it is high time that both you and my Manager had received the latter; that is the clover Seed. No Vessel is yet up for Alexandria, but I am told two or three will soon Advertise for freight.[1]

We all join in best regards for Mrs Ball, yourself and Milly (if with you)[2] and with very great esteem I am—Dear Sir Your Affectionate

Go: Washington

ALS (photocopy), DLC: GW Ephemera—Burgess Ball Papers. The cover has postal stamps that read, "24 FE" and "FREE." GW addressed this letter to Ball at "Leesburgh," Virginia.

1. GW wrote Ball on 16 March that the chocolate and clover seed were on board a vessel bound for Alexandria, Virginia. GW's farm manager, William Pearce, forwarded these items to Ball, who received them on 4 April (Ball to GW, 5 April).

2. Mildred Gregory Washington, GW's niece, often stayed with her sister, Frances Washington Ball.

Bartholomew Dandridge, Jr., to Henry Knox

U.S. 24. feb: 1794.

By the President's order Bw Dandridge has the honor to transmit the letters herewith enclosed, from the Govr. of North Carolina to the President, to the ⟨Secry⟩ of War.[1] The President requests the Secry to inform him if, in his opinion, any thing is contained in them, that requires the President's particular attention; if not, to take such measures thereupon as to the Secry shall seem fit.[2]

Bw. Dandridge S.P.U.S.

ADfS, DLC:GW; LB, DLC:GW.

1. The enclosures were the three letters that Gov. Richard Dobbs Spaight wrote to GW on 8 Feb. (*JPP*, 286).

2. Any written reply from Knox to GW has not been found.

To James Muir

Sir,   Philadelphia 24th Feby 1794

I have received your letter of the 12th instant, and will direct my Manager Mr Pearce to pay my annual donation for the education of orphan children, or the children of indigent parents who are unable to be at the expence themselves.[1]

I had pleasure in appropriating this money to such uses—as I always shall in that of paying it. I confess, however, I should derive satisfaction from knowing what children have, heretofore, received the benefit of it; and who now are in the enjoyment thereof.

Never, since the commencement of this institution, have I ever received the least information (except in a single instance) on this head, although application for it to individuals has been frequently made.[2]

As you Sir, appear to be in the exercise of this trust—let me pray you to have the goodness to gratify this wish of mine.[3] with respect I am Reverend Sir Your most Obedt Servt

Go: Washington

ALS, ViMtvL; LB, DLC:GW.

1. GW wrote William Pearce on this date to arrange the payment of £50 Virginia currency to the Alexandria Academy.

2. For GW's previous receipt of a list of the charity scholars, see Muir and Samuel Hanson (of Samuel) to GW, 11 March 1791, and n.3 to that document.

3. Muir's reply of 3 March contained the desired information.

To William Pearce

Mr Pearce,   Philadelphia 24th Feby 1794

Your letter of the 17th instant came safe. Meeting your children at Baltimore is certainly necessary, and therefore I can have no objection to it.[1]

My last letter being full, respecting the repairs of my house in Alexandria, I shall add nothing on that subject in this;[2] and as Mr Stuart has not, according to his declaration, received any money from Mr Whiting, let him be paid with the deduction only of that which he has recd from Mr Lewis, or yourself.[3]

In my last, I omitted, through mistake, the Seed which is now sent: let it be given to the Gardener as part of that parcel; some early Colliflower Seed was sent to him by Mrs Washington (by a Gentleman of Alexandria of the name of Turner)—wch I hope you will have got.[4]

I hope the Posts & rails you are now getting, will not be so unsubstantial as to be blown down by every puff of wind as the last are; and I am sorry that the springeness of the ground, where you are digging the new race, does not admit that work to go on to advantage, as it is essential it should be compleated before the water begins to fail; but notwithstanding this, I would not have it proceed to a disadvantage, whilst the hands can be more benificially occupied in other things: more force must be employed when the ground is in order, and this will be between the *present* wet, and the drought which generally succeeds; & by which the soil binds, & becomes very hard. The Miller had the mode of sloping the race particularly explained to him both by the Gentleman who laid it off, and myself; his directions therefore in this case, is to be observed & followed.[5]

By the next Post, I will send you the copy of an Advertisement of the terms on which the Jacks and Stud horse are to cover. In the mean while, it may be said, the former will cover at Four pounds each; and the horse at 40/—Pasturage, Groom, &ca as usual.[6]

After culling my Sheep at Shearing time last year; and going over them a second time in the Summer; the loss at Union farm (near, or quite twenty since Autumn) seems to be very extraordinary; and I fear is too strong an evidence of Crows inattention to my Stock; as had been intimated to me before I left Mount Vernon in October.

I am very glad to hear that the Gardener has saved so much of the St foin seed, & that of the India Hemp. Make the most you can of both, by sowing them again in drills. Where to sow the first I am a little at a loss (as Hares are very destructive to it) but think, as the Lucern which was sown broad in the Inclosure by the Spring, has come to nothing; as the ground is good; and probably as free from Hares as any other place, it might as well be put there; as I am very desirous of getting into a full stock of seed as soon as possible. Let the ground be well prepared, and the Seed (St foin) be sown in April. The Hemp may be sown any where.

Enclosed you will find three Bank notes for one hundred dollars each; out of which pay the Revd Mr Muir of Alexandria Fifty pounds, & take his signature to the enclosed receipt; and Mr Hartshorne of the same place, £33.6.8—being the dividend of my five shares in the Potomack Company. Give me credit for these three hundred dollars, and cha: my Account with the above payments.[7]

Never Suffer a Mare to be taken from the Jacks, or Horse, where they are once admitted to Pasture, until the whole that is due for them be paid; for it has been found that after the Mares are gone, I have more trouble in collecting the money than it is worth. I am Your friend and well wisher

Go: Washington

ALS, ViMtvL; ALS (letterpress copy), DLC:GW.

1. Pearce's letter to GW of 17 Feb. has not been found. On Pearce's family, see Benjamin Chew, Jr., to GW, 16 Aug. 1793, and n.2 to that document.

2. Although GW's previous letter to Pearce was that of 22 Feb., the instructions regarding his house in Alexandria, Va., are in his letter to Pearce of 16 February. GW apparently sent his letter of Saturday, 22 Feb., and this current one of Monday, 24 Feb., by Monday's post. For the postal schedule between Philadelphia and Alexandria, Va., and GW's usual schedule for writing his managers at Mount Vernon, see GW to Anthony Whitting, 2 Dec. 1792.

3. On the request for past wages by William Stuart, the overseer of River farm, see Pearce to GW, 4 February. Any written declaration from Stuart concerning the failure of Anthony Whitting, the former manager of Mount Vernon, to pay him has not been identified. Howell Lewis served as temporary manager after Whitting's death in June 1793. On 7 March, Stuart received £23.18.00 for "part of his wages Due for the year 93" (Mount Vernon Accounts, 1794–97).

4. For the various seeds that GW intended for gardener John Christian Ehlers, see GW to Pearce, 16 Feb., and n.7 to that document.

5. GW sent Pearce instructions regarding the race for the gristmill and the fence that ran from the mill in a letter of 19 January. Joseph Davenport was the miller at Mount Vernon.

6. For the terms contained in the enclosed advertisement, see n.1 of Bartholomew Dandridge, Jr., to Angell & Sullivan and Samuel Hanson, 26 February.

7. On the payment of £50 Virginia currency to James Muir, see GW to Muir, this date, and n.1 to that document. Pearce recorded this payment and the £33.6.8 to Alexandria merchant William Hartshorne on 1 March, and on that same date he credited £90 as "cash Received from the president" (Mount Vernon Accounts, 1794–97).

From Charles Pettit

Sir   Philadelphia 24th February 1794

May I venture once more to approach Your Excellency, as disposer of public employments, in the character of an applicant? May I, without the imputation of impertinence, venture to suggest that my past services have given me some ground of claim to future confidence, especially when I can with truth say that altho' some of my public employments have been among those which were reputed lucrative, and altho' I have not squandered the emoluments of them in extravagance, I have not been enriched by them?[1] I have endeavoured to perform the duties to which I have been called, with fidelity & consciencious integrity; but I have shunned rather than courted that kind of popularity which usually excites public attention & eclat: I have sought no station that I did not feel myself equal to the duties of, nor endeavoured to supplant others in their possessions or just expectations. If I have been supplanted in either of these respects, I have not deserved it. I have been no man's enemy who was a friend to the common cause of the United States, nor joined in factions to disturb the order of society, or to impede the administration of Government. Have I been less assiduous than I ought to have been to obtain Your Excellency's favorable attention? It has happened from a desire to avoid intrusion, and not from a failure in respect for your character and station. Have I neglected to approach you through the application of friends? I did not suppose such aids necessary; and perhaps a tincture of pride may have had its influence. I have long since heard through a channel that claimed my belief, that my name was on the list of those who were considered as worthy of employment, and I would rather owe an appointment to the spontaneous choice of your Excellency than to the solicitation or even the suggestion of others.

But permit me, Sir, to suggest, that life is fast wearing away; that under an expectation which I had hoped was not wholly without foundation, I have brought myself to a situation in some degree dependant on public employment by devesting myself in a great measure of all engagements which might interfere with the exercise of it; and that at my time of life I cannot with facility again enter into pursuits for its support, which at an earlier period I abandoned at the public call. Had I been as fortunate as some others in establishing an independancy of labor by the means thus put in my power, the honor rather than the emolument, would have been the primary motive to a tender of farther service; but as I am now circumstanced, I will not pretend to conceal that the latter has become the stronger motive, tho' the former is not at all diminished by it.

Report has for some time past announced the probability that a vacancy will happen, by promotion, in the office of Post-Master General. The Duties of that office are far from being unknown to me, as well from some experience acquired in the early part of life, as from considerable attention paid to the conduct of it since the Revolution; and if I did not believe the business to be perfectly within the compass of my abilities, I would not offer myself a candidate for it.[2] But in a thorough confidence that I am equal to the execution of the Office to the satisfaction of your Excellency and the public, I venture to ask it, with that high degree of deference and respect with which I am, and always have been Your Excellency's most obedient and most humble servant

AL[S], DLC:GW.

1. On Pettit's previous, and unsuccessful, application for federal employment and for his military and public service career, see his letter to GW of 24 May 1789, and source note. In his later life, he served as president of the Insurance Company of North America, 1796–98 and 1799–1806.

2. Exactly what rumors Pettit had heard concerning Postmaster General Timothy Pickering is not clear, but Pickering did not leave his current position until 2 Jan. 1795, when he replaced Henry Knox as Secretary of War (*U.S. Senate Executive Journal,* 1:168–69). Pettit did not receive any federal appointment from GW.

From Charles Cotesworth Pinckney

My dear Sr: Charleston [S.C.] Feb. 24th. 1794
    I cannot find words to express the just sense I have of the many obligations I am under to you, nor how sensible I am of the very great honour you have conferred on me by your confidential Letter of the 22d: of last Month. Of all the public offices in our Country the one you mention to me is that which I should like best to fill; except in case of a general War, when if other matters would admit, I should prefer being in the field; and tho I am sensible I should appear to great disadvantage in an office which had been so ably filled by General Knox I should by close application and undeviating Integrity endeavour to apologize to my Country for your choice. Entertaining these sentiments, judge of my mortification when I am constrained to declare that circumstances not in my power to controul will prevent my accepting the offer your partiality for me has induced you to make. Your goodness to me,

and the many proofs I have received of your friendship require me to be explicit in my reasons. Soon after the conclusion of the War, Land & Negroes in this State, sold at a very high rate, far exceeding their real value. At that time tempted by the offer of a long credit, and mistaken in my Ideas with regard to the annual profit of such property, I became a considerable purchaser; and altho I have been assisted by a very lucrative profession in the practice of which I have been fortunate, I still remain very considerably in debt; so much so, that if I was to relax for some time to come in paying the closest attention to my private affairs, inevitable ruin would follow.[1] Mrs: Pinckney & her Brother & Sister have large demands on some persons in Georgia who are endeavouring to use every subterfuge to secrete their property & to avoid paying what they owe; her Brother is in Europe, and her Sister's Husband, Mr: Ralph Izard Junr:, is of so indolent a temper that the attending to this business of necessity devolves on me, and was I not to go to Georgia sometimes, particularly in April & November to watch over her affairs, her property there would be lost, and instead of protecting I should in fact sacrifice her interest. All the Children I have alive are females, it is therefore a duty I owe them to leave my affairs as little perplexed as possible; and from the best consideration I have been able to give these affairs, it will take me at least two years so to arrange them as to permitt me safely to be absent from them.[2] These reasons and a conviction that no man ought to be in high office whose affairs are entangled and embarrassed, tho his property if sold may be much more than sufficient to pay all he owes, compell me to decline the high honour you intended for me; at the same time permitt me to declare that if it was not for these circumstances, I would most readily avail myself of your friendship & partiality, and should you, when my affairs are in a more pleasing train, & I can with propriety dispense with an immediate attention to them, think fit to require my services in any way in which you may judge me qualified, I will most chearfully serve; for tho I am very fond of and prefer private life, & shall be forty Eight Years old tomorrow, I am too much flattered by your indulgent opinion not to wish to take a part in your administration.[3]

The purport of your Letter shall not be communicated by me, that the Gentleman who may be nominated for the Department may have the pleasure of thinking that he was early designated for the appointment.[4] With the sincerest gratitude I remain Your affectionate & devoted hble Servt

Charles Cotesworth Pinckney

Your Letter was not handed to me till last Thursday or it should have been sooner answered.[5]

ALS, DLC:GW.

1. Pinckney, who had been admitted to the South Carolina bar in 1770, resumed his law practice shortly after leaving military service at the end of the Revolutionary War.

2. Pinckney married his second wife, Mary Stead (d. 1812), on 23 July 1786. Her brother was Benjamin Stead. Her sister Elizabeth Stead (d. 1825) was married to South Carolina planter Ralph Izard, Jr. (died c.1812), who served several terms in the South Carolina General Assembly prior to 1790. At this time, Izard lived on Schieveling plantation in St. Andrew Parish. He also owned a townhouse in Charleston, S.C., and four rice plantations on the Pee Dee River: Weymouth, Hickory Hill, Milton, and White House. Charles C. Pinckney had four children with his first wife, Sarah Middleton (d. 1784): Maria Henrietta (1774–1836), Harriott (1776–1866), Charles Cotesworth (1780–1780), and Eliza Lucas (d. 1851).

3. In 1796, Pinckney would accept an appointment from GW to serve as U.S. minister plenipotentiary to France (*U.S. Senate Executive Journal*, 1:217).

4. Timothy Pickering replaced Henry Knox as secretary of war in January 1795, after the latter's resignation in December 1794 (Knox to GW, 28 Dec. 1794, DLC:GW; *U.S. Senate Executive Journal*, 1:168–69).

5. Pinckney received GW's letter on Thursday, 20 February.

Proclamation on Violent Opposition to the Excise Tax

[Philadelphia, 24 Feb. 1794]

By the PRESIDENT of the United States of America.

A Proclamation.

WHEREAS by information given upon oath, it appears that in the night time of the twenty second day of November, a number of armed men having their faces blackened and being otherwise disguised, violently broke open and entered the dwelling house of Benjamin Wells collector of the revenue arising from spirits distilled within the United States, in and for the counties of Westmoreland and Fayette in the district of Pennsylvania, and by assulting the said collector and putting him in fear and danger of his life, in his dwelling house aforesaid, in the said county of Fayette did compel him to deliver up to them his commission for collecting the said revenue, together with the books kept by him in the execution of his said duty, and did threaten to do further violence to the said collector, if he did not shortly thereafter publicly renounce the further execution of his said office:[1]

AND WHEREAS several of the perpetrators of the said offence are still unknown, and the safety and good order of society require that such daring offenders should be discovered and brought to justice so that infractions of the law may be prevented, obedience to them secured, and officers protected in the due execution of the trusts reposed in them, *therefore* I have thought proper to offer and hereby do offer a reward of TWO HUNDRED DOLLARS for each of the said offenders that shall be discovered and brought to justice for the said offence, to be paid to the person or persons who shall first discover and give information of the said offenders to any judge, justice of the peace, or other magistrate.

And I do hereby strictly charge and enjoin all officers and ministers of justice according as their respective duties may require, to use their best endeavors to cause the said offenders to be discovered apprehended and secured, so that they may be speedily brought to trial for the offence aforesaid.[2]

IN TESTIMONY WHEREOF I have caused the seal of the United States of America to be affixed to these presents, and signed the same with my hand. DONE at the city of Philadelphia the 24th day of February one thousand seven hundred and ninety four, and of the Independence of the United States of America, the eighteenth.

Go. WASHINGTON.

By the President
EDM: RANDOLPH.

D (printed), *Gazette of the United States and Evening Advertiser* (Philadelphia), 26 Feb. 1794.

1. At the time of this incident, Benjamin Wells (d. 1830) resided at Stewart's Crossing, on the western shore of the Youghiogheny River, in Fayette County. According to Wells' affidavit of 29 Jan. 1794, his six assailants, "two of them armed with pistols," were "all disguised by having their faces blackened and four of them had handkerchiefs tied over their mouths." Despite this disguise, he identified two of the individuals as "Robert Smilie son of

John Smilie Esquire" and "John McCulloch" (CtHi: Oliver Wolcott, Jr., Papers). For an earlier proclamation issued by GW in response to similar incidents of violence in western Pennsylvania in 1792, see the Proclamation of 15 Sept. 1792. On the opposition to the collection of the excise tax on whiskey in 1792, see Alexander Hamilton to GW, 1 Sept. 1792, and notes.

2. No one was ever charged with the assault on Wells (see Baldwin, *Whiskey Rebels*, 90–91; Slaughter, *Whiskey Rebellion*, 150–51, 158).

From Edmund Randolph

[Philadelphia] Feby 24. 1794.

E. Randolph has the honor of informing the President, that he last night received several bundles from Mr G. Morris; all of them duplicates, except one No. 35 of his letters. This number incloses so lengthy a correspondence between him and the Minister, *in French,* that it will be almost impossible to have it translated and copied to-day. The President will therefore determine, whether the papers prepared, shall wait for those last mentioned; or whether they shall go in, with an intimation of the others being in hand, to be forwarded, as soon as finished.[1]

La Foret and Le Blanc are arrived.[2]

Fauchet has delivered to Genet his letters of recal; and it is probable that Genet will this morning surrender all the official documents. He is calm and composed, and means to return to France to enter into the army.[3]

AL, DNA: RG 59, Miscellaneous Letters; LB, DNA: RG 59, GW's Correspondence with His Secretaries of State.

1. In accordance with a letter from the U.S. Senate to GW of 24 Jan., Randolph was preparing copies of the official correspondence of Gouverneur Morris, including that with François-Louis-Michel Chemin Deforgues, the new French minister of foreign affairs. Letter "No. 35" was that from Morris to Thomas Jefferson of 13 Aug. 1793. For this letter and its enclosures, see *ASP, Foreign Relations*, 1:368–72. GW sent copies of this letter and the other requested correspondence with his letter to the U.S. Senate of 26 February.

2. La Forest was the recently appointed French consul-general, and Georges-Pierre Le Blanc, a former chief of the Paris police department, was currently serving as secretary of the French legation. Together with Fauchet, the new French minister plenipotentiary, and Petry, the new consul at Philadelphia, these men formed a commission assigned to carry out the duties previously entrusted to Edmond Genet, the former minister to the United States.

3. Genet never returned to France but instead settled in New York State, where he married Cornelia Tappen Clinton (1774–1810), daughter of New York governor George Clinton, on 6 Nov. 1794.

To Charles Simms

Dear Sir,						Philadelphia 24th Feby 1794
    Near a month ago I wrote you to this effect, "that the letter
therein enclosed to Mr Keith furnished the means of discharging your claim upon me as Executor of Colvils Will—requesting
you to deliver, or send it by a safe hand, to him". The letter for
Mr Keith contained a request of some papers to be forwarded to
me which I then was, and still am in want of.[1]
    Since writing these letters I have heard from neither of you.
My letter to Mr Keith contained bank notes & half a guinea to
the *exact* a⟨m⟩ount of your Account. No accident has happened
to any of the Mails since that period; delay therefore cannot be
ascribed to *that* cause; & without it I am at a loss to acct for his silence & would thank you for information.[2] I am—Dear Sir Your
Obedt Servt

						Go: Washington

ALS (letterpress copy), ViMtvL; LB, DLC:GW. The text in angle brackets is
from the letter-book copy.
    1. The letter to Simms, which GW paraphrased, is that of 28 Jan., and the
letter to James Keith is that of 29 January.
    2. Simms replied to GW on 14 March, but no reply from Keith has been
found.

To the United States Senate
and House of Representatives

						United States 24th February 1794.
Gentlemen of the Senate, and of the House of Representatives.
    The extracts, which I now lay before you, from a letter of our
Minister at London, are supplementary to some of my past communications; and will appear to be of a confidential nature.[1]
    I also transmit to you copies of a letter from the Secretary of
State to the Minister plenipotentiary of his britannic majesty,
and of the answer thereto, upon the subject of the treaty between the United States and Great Britain;[2] together with the
copy of a letter from Messrs Carmichael and Short, relative to
our affairs with Spain; which letter is connected with a former
confidential message.[3]

						Go: Washington

LS, DNA: RG 46, Third Congress, 1793–95, Senate Records of Legislative Proceedings, President's Messages; LB, DNA: RG 233, Third Congress, 1793–95, House Records of Legislative Proceedings, Journals; LB, DLC:GW; copy, DNA: RG 59, Reports of the Secretary of State to the President and Congress. Edmund Randolph enclosed a draft of this letter, which has not been identified, with his second letter to GW of 23 February.

1. For Thomas Pinckney's letter to the secretary of state of 25 Nov. 1793, see n.2 of Randolph's first letter to GW of 19 February.

2. For the enclosed correspondence between Randolph and George Hammond, see n.1 of Randolph to GW, 23 Feb. (first letter).

3. The enclosed copy of the letter of 22 Oct. 1793 from U.S. commissioners William Carmichael and William Short to the secretary of state was marked "Triplicate," and the original, which has not been identified, was partially written in cypher. Short and Carmichael began this letter with a discourse on the difficulties of finding a safe means of transport, from Spain directly to the United States, for diplomatic dispatches and courier James Blake because of the presence of Algerine cruisers in the Atlantic Ocean. Therefore, this letter was being sent by means of a ship destined for Falmouth, England.

"The mode of conveying this letter prevents our going into detail, even by cypher. We think it, however, proper to mention to you, that on our communicating to [Diego Maria de] Gardoqui the subject of your dispatches, he gave us the strongest verbal assurance that it was not the intention of Spain to interfere, if war should take place between the U.S: and the Indians. He promised an immediate answer to that effect, to our letter of the first of this month, to him." Gardoqui, however, after delaying "in his way from day to day under the various pretexts of our letter being to be translated to present to the King &c.," informed the commissioners that the Spanish minister in charge of foreign affairs, Manuel Godoy Alvarez de Faria, Duque de la Alcudia (1767–1851), had determined that he would supply a written answer. "From experience," the commissioners wrote, "we do not think the verbal assurances [from] Gardoqui sufficient to affirm to you what a written answer will be—it will be the same, however, from the Duke, that it would have been from him. In the conversations which Mr Carmichael has had with him he has always found his sentiments consonant to the professions made by Gardoqui" (DNA: RG 46, Third Congress, 1793–95, Senate Records of Legislative Proceedings, President's Messages; *ASP, Foreign Relations,* 1:328).

From Christiana de Hanstein

Your Excellence, Unterstein[1] the 25th of Febr. 1794
    The Magnanimity of your Excellence encourageth me to write to You. My Father in the last American War being one of the Party of the Loyalistes divers times put out of the Possession of all that he had. Not only when he was taken Prisonner from his Enemys

under Captain Jerey Wolf he was deprived of A greate sum of Money: and at another time twenty Waggon Loden with Hemp was taken at the same time in Verginne, the whole sum that he had lost is at least two Thousand pounds Sterling.[2] The Parliament haveing concluded to pay all that the Loyalists have lost in the American War I do most humbly beg your Excellence to write to me as an assurance and to attest that all I deman is truly lost from my Father Stephen Wilkinson wich is now Dead.[3]

When Your Excellence will have the Gracious for me and reply what I beeg from Your Excellence I shall witho⟨ut⟩ any difficulty receive from the English Parliamant the payment of the sum my Father lost. You can be assurd for the benevolent favour. I am Your Excellence Most humble Servente

Christiana de Hanstein
born Wilkinson

L, DNA: RG 59, Miscellaneous Letters.

1. Unterstein probably is part of the current town of Arenshausen-Unterstein, which is located in the present-day district of Eichsfeld in the German state of Thuringia. Members of an extended Hanstein family resided here for several generations.

2. Her father probably was the Stephen Wilkinson who manufactured rope in New York City during the Revolutionary War (*New-York Gazette; and the Weekly Mercury,* 18 April 1774; Coldham, *American Loyalist Claims,* 501). The marriages, in New York State, of Christiana Wilkinson and John Hanstein on 16 Oct. 1783 and of Stephen Wilkinson and Christiana Flood on 20 April 1763 are recorded in Edmund B. O'Callaghan's *Names of Persons for whom MARRIAGE LICENSES Were issued by the Secretary of the Province of New York Previous to 1784* (Albany, N.Y., 1860), 169, 460.

3. Parliament established a commission in 1783 to review the claims of Loyalists who sought compensation for losses incurred during the Revolutionary War. No reply from GW has been found. Edmund Randolph, however, wrote to "Mrs. Wilkinson, Widow of Mr Stephen Wilkinson—New York" on 26 June regarding a letter, which has not been found, that John Hanstein wrote to GW, "requesting him to procure an attestation of the property lost by Mr Stephen Wilkinson during the last war. This being a business merely of a private nature which can be better executed by some person, specially employed for that purpose, cannot with propriety be attended to by the President. I have, however, caused the papers to be translated from the German language, and forward them to you inclosed, that you may have an opportunity of doing what Mr Hanstein desires" (DNA: RG 59, Domestic Letters).

Letter not found: from William Pearce, 25 Feb. 1794. GW wrote Pearce on 2 March that "Your letter of the 25th Ulto . . . came to hand this day."

From Richard Dobbs Spaight

Sir, No. Carolina 25th Feb: 1794

In the Year 1791 Francis Child the comptroller of the state, by order of the Governor and council lodged in the hands of William Skinner esquire commissioner of loans for the state of No. Carolina, certificates to the amount of 409,570. Dolls. 17/100 the property of the state in order to be funded, agreable to an act of Congress making provision for the debts of the United States.[1] in the same year and under the same act of congress certificates to the amt of 22,415. dolls. 10/100 were lodged in the hands of the said Commissioner by a certain Duncan McAusland and by him transferred to the State of North Carolina.[2] The Commissioner of loans has uniformly refused to allow the said certificates in the whole amounting to 413,985 dolls 27/100, to be funded, agreable to the aforesaid act.[3] The General Assembly being of opinion that in this transaction the State has not received that ample justice which she was entitled to under the act of Congress, have requested me to state the facts to you, and to require that justice be done in the premises.[4]

The legislature having been enformed at their last Session, that the Commissioner of loans had, agreable to instructions from the Treasury department of the United States, written his name or some other word on the face or back of the certificates lodged in his hands by this state, which might tend to deface them, directed John Craven esquire comptroller,[5] to call on Mr Skinner and examine them, and if he found them defaced or acted on in any manner by the said commissioner of loans, as might directly or ultimately affect the interest or convey an insult upon the right or dignity of the State to report the same to me as early as possible. Agreable to the directions of the legislature the comptroller has waited on the commissioner of loans and requested permission to examine these certificates which was possitively refused him by that officer. I think it my duty to remonstrate to you against the proceedings of the Commissioner of loans, in the present case for certainly the state has a right to be informed whether the certificates tendered by the Comptroller had been defaced or remained in the same situation as they were when lodged in his hands. I have further to request that you will be pleased to cause an enquirey to be made into the conduct of the treasury department respecting the certificates so that it may be fully ascertained, whether or not they have been defaced or acted upon in any manner that may tend to the injury of this State and if it shall appear to have been the case, that you will cause such reparation to be made as will be consistant with justice.

Of the interest which has acrued on the Balance of the 2,400,000 Dollars assumed by the state of North Carolina, but not subscribed under the act of Congress making provision for the debts of the United States, no part has ever been received by this State the General Assembly have therefore requested that I should demand payment of the amount of the interest which has acrued to the State upon the said balance.

I enclose you a copy of the resolutions of the general Assembly on this Subject, and a copy of the comptrollers letters to me informing me of the commissioner of loans having refused him permission to examine the certificates.[6] I have the honor to be &c.

R.D. Spaight

LB, Nc-Ar: Governors' Letterbooks.

1. Francis Child (d. 1792), a Revolutionary War officer, served as comptroller of North Carolina from 1784 until his death. On the issues discussed in this letter, see William Skinner's letters to Alexander Hamilton of 22 July, 11 and 29 Aug., and 15 Oct. 1791; Hamilton's letters to Skinner of 12 Aug. and 8 Sept. 1791; and Edmund Randolph to Hamilton, 9 Nov. 1791 (*Hamilton Papers*, 8:565–69; 9:27–28, 122–23, 190–92, 486). For the legislation providing for redemption of these certificates, see "An Act making provision for the [payment of the] Debt of the United States," 4 Aug. 1790 (*Stat.* 1:138–44).

2. Duncan MacAuslan was a Fayetteville, N.C., merchant.

3. According to a receipt of 30 Sept. 1791 that Skinner provided for certificates totaling $409,570.17, the certificates would remain in his office "subject to the Decision of the Secretary of the Treasury" (Skinner to Hamilton, 15 Oct. 1791, *Hamilton Papers*, 9:387–88). The correct total value of the certificates is $431,985, not $413,985.

4. Four resolutions adopted by the North Carolina assembly on 8 Jan. 1794 instructed Spaight to inform GW that the Treasury Department had refused to fund the certificates and "require that justice be done," to order the state comptroller to examine the certificates, to request that the federal government pay interest on the said certificates, and to transmit a copy of these resolutions and of correspondence on this subject to the state's representatives in Congress (*N.C. House Journal 1793*, 55).

5. John Craven (d. 1808) served as comptroller of North Carolina from 1792 until 1804.

6. In his letter to Spaight of 30 Jan. 1794, Craven wrote that Skinner "positively refused" to allow him to view the disputed certificates, but "observed at the same time that if the assembly, or your Excellency & the council thought proper to appoint some person to receive them & return the Receipts given

by him, he would at any time make that exchange & deliver them up" (Nc-Ar: Governor's Correspondence).

Under GW's direction, Bartholomew Dandridge, Jr., forwarded Spaight's "just received" letter and its enclosures to Alexander Hamilton with a brief cover letter of 20 March, in which he requested that Hamilton report to GW "in regard to the matter contained in the said letter & enclosures" (DLC:GW). For Hamilton's response, see his "Report to the Governor of North Carolina" of 31 July, in which Hamilton justified the denial of payment for the certificates and informed Spaight that North Carolina was not eligible for any interest payment. He wrote that the conduct of Skinner, "as suggested, in refusing an inspection of the Certificates, was unauthorized by this Department" (*Hamilton Papers*, 16:628–34). Edmund Randolph enclosed Hamilton's report with a brief cover letter to Spaight of 10 Aug. (DNA: RG 59, Domestic Letters).

Bartholomew Dandridge, Jr., to Angell & Sullivan and Samuel Hanson

Philada. 26th Feby: 1794

By direction of the President of the Ud States, I transmit you an advertisement of his Jacks & Stud-horse; with a request from him, that you will be so good as to insert it in your paper during four weeks—omitting it one week & inserting it another alternately.[1]

The cost attending the above will be paid, as soon as made known by you.[2] I am &c. &c.

Bw. Dandridge

LB, DLC:GW.

1. James Angell and Paul J. Sullivan published the *Maryland Journal and Baltimore Advertiser*, and Samuel Hanson published the *Columbian Chronicle* at Georgetown, D.C. The enclosed advertisement offered the stud services of Knight of Malta, a jack imported from the island of Malta, and of Compound, a jack "from a Jenny of the same Island, and got by the large Spanish Jack (*Royal Gift*), and is now five Years old. They will cover at *Mount Vernon*, the ensuing Spring, at *Four Pounds the Season* (estimating a Dollar at Six Shillings), and a *Half a Dollar* to the Groom." The services of Traveller, a "dark-bay Horse, in his prime, full fifteen Hands high, handsomely formed and marked, and more than the Quarters blooded, will cover, at *Forty Shillings* (Dollars as above), and *Half a Dollar* to the Groom. Very good Pastures are to be had at *Half a Dollar per Week,* for each Mare or Jenny. The Fences are good, and the whole within an exterior one of Post and Rail, which contributes much to their Security; but against Thefts or Escapes there will be no Warranty. No Accounts will be raised for the covering of these Animals; of course, the whole Cost must be paid at the Stand, before the Females are taken therefrom" (*Maryland Journal and Baltimore Advertiser*, 28 Feb. 1794).

2. About the cost, see James Angell to GW, 16 May 1797 (*Papers, Retirement Series*, 1:143).

To the United States Senate

Gentlemen of the Senate,   United States 26. February 1794.

I have caused the correspondence, which is the subject of your resolution of the 24th day of January last, to be laid before me.[1] After an examination of it, I directed copies and translations to be made; except in those particulars, which, in my judgment, for public considerations, ought not to be communicated.[2]

These copies and translations are now transmitted to the Senate; but the nature of them manifests the propriety of their being received as confidential.

Go: Washington

LS, DNA: RG 46, Third Congress, 1793–95, Senate Records of Legislative Proceedings, President's Messages; LB, DLC:GW. The two footnotes on the LS do not appear on the letter-book copy. They were apparently added when preparing this letter and its enclosures for publication in 1832 in *ASP, Foreign Relations,* 1:329–412.

1. The footnote indicated at this point reads: "See the Note."

2. The correspondence submitted was that of Gouverneur Morris, the U.S. minister plenipotentiary to France. The edited copies and translations, in which omissions are indicated by blank spaces and dashes, are in DNA: RG 46, Third Congress, 1793–95, Senate Records of Legislative Proceedings, President's Messages. For the discussions about whether and how to submit these documents, see Edmund Randolph to GW, 25 Jan., 26 Jan. (two letters), and 2 February.

The footnote indicated at this point reads: "Note. The paragraphs which were omitted in the papers communicated to the Senate are now suppled." This note is accompanied by an instruction that reads: "The Printer will insert this Note at the bottom of the page."

From Edmund Randolph

[Philadelphia] Feby 27. 1794.

The Secretary of State has the honor of submitting to the President of the United States the following observations on the act, providing for the relief of such of the inhabitants of St Domingo, resident in the United States, as may be found in want of support.[1]

As soon as the act had passed, a letter (marked A) was written to the Representatives of the several states in Congress.[2] Answers have been received from all, except the Representatives of Delaware and Jersey.[3] It is known with certainty, that in New Hampshire, Vermont and Kentucky, none of these unfortunate people have taken refuge; and in the other states, to wit, Georgia, South Carolina, North Carolina, Virginia, Maryland, Pennsylvania, New York, Connecticut, Rhode-Island, and Massachusetts, the numbers cannot be considered as authentic, altho' pains have been used, while the law was on its passage, to obtain an accurate account. From the present view, however, of the subject, the heads of the Departments concur in the following ideas:

1.   That the numbers in the ten last mentioned states be estimated according to the following conjecture.

Georgia	100
South Carolina	350
North Carolina	50
Virginia	290
Maryland	400
Pennsylvania	200
New York	350
Connecticut	10
Rhode Island	200
Massachusetts	50
Total	2000

2.   That for the present only 10,000 dollars be distributed; the remaining 5,000 being reserved to redress any inequalities, which may be found on a more precise knowledge of the numbers.

3.   That the proportions of the sum of 10,000 dollars will consequently be to each person five dollars, and to the ten states aforesaid as follows.

Georgia	500.
South Carolina	1750.
North Carolina	250
Virginia	1450
Maryland	2000
Pennsylvania	1000
New York	1750
Connecticut	50
Rhode Island	1000
Massachusetts	250
	10,000

4. That the rates of mere subsistance are exceedingly various in the different places in which the refugees are situated, and cannot be ascertained by any means so effectual, as by referring the distribution of these sums to the committees, which already exist for superintending their accommodation; or to other confidential persons, where committees have not yet been constituted.[4]

5. That letters be immediately written by the Secretary of State to these committees, or other confidential persons, requesting them to undertake the partition of this money; exhorting them to use œconomy; to keep accounts; to report their proceedings to the President; and to forward accurate intelligence.[5]

Edm: Randolph

LS, DNA: RG 59, Miscellaneous Letters; LB, DNA: RG 59, Reports of the Secretary of State to the President and Congress; LB, DNA: RG 59, GW's Correspondence with his Secretaries of State.

1. See "An Act providing for the relief of such of the inhabitants of Saint Domingo, resident within the United States, as may be found in want of support," 12 Feb. 1794, in which an amount not exceeding $15,000 was appropriated for this purpose (*Stat.* 6:13). Civil war in this French colony prompted hundreds of refugees to flee to the United States in the summer of 1793.

2. Randolph's copy of his circular letter to members of Congress, which was written on Friday, 14 Feb., reads: "The President of the United States is anxious to execute immediately the law, which has been lately passed, for the relief of the distressed fugitives from St Domingo. But without an actual or probable enumeration of them, according to the places of their dispersion the distribution to be made, of the money granted will be liable to great inequalities; particular places may absorb too much of it; and the time, for which the support of those unfortunate persons was contemplated by Congress may be abridged by the exhausting of the fund. I must therefore entreat you, altho' precision cannot be expected, to furnish me with the best information in your power of their total number, with a distinction of those who may not be desirous of receiving aid, the places of their residence within your State, and the lowest price for subsistence of Adults and Children at the spot. If you can prepare an estimate by monday next, it will hasten the succours to the indigent and lay me under a particular obligation" (DNA: RG 59, Miscellaneous Letters).

3. These answers, including any from New Jersey, have not been identified. For the number of refugees submitted by Delaware, see Randolph's second letter to GW of this date.

4. For some of the local and state relief efforts, see n.1 of Tobias Lear to Thomas Jefferson, 24 Aug. 1793; n.1 of GW to De Saxÿ and De Verneüil, 26 Dec. 1793; William Patterson et al. to GW, 30 Jan. 1794; and Robert Taylor to GW, 30 Jan. 1794.

5. The circular letter from Randolph of this date reads: "I do myself the honor of inclosing to you the copy of an Act, passed on the 12th instant by Congress, for the relief of certain inhabitants of St Domingo.

"As soon as it was approved by the President, measures were taken for ascertaining the number of those, who might be objects of the law in the different States. It being impossible to postpone the Succour, until an accurate estimate could be obtained from a distance, it was thought best to request a conjectural account from the Representatives who are on the spot. This has been in general furnished but still this procedure promises so little accuracy, that the President has resolved to distribute at present no more than Ten thousand dollars, and to reserve the remaining Five thousand for the purpose of redressing any inequalities in the partition.

"The quota allotted to the State of [   ] out of the 10,000 dollars, is [   ].

"This sum the President consigns to your care and management, relying, that the trust, reposed in you, will be accepted as a proof of his confidence in your philanthropy. But as it is not improbable, that you may wish to be aided by some other humane Citizens, he requests, that you will ask, in his name, the co-operation of such, as you may think proper to associate with yourself. If, however, a Committee has been already formed, for the purpose of superintending the accommodation of these unfortunate people, I must beg you to deliver the money and this letter over to them, who will be pleased to consider both, as addressed to them.

"The particulars of the law, most deserving your attention, will be found to be the following:

1.   The persons to be relieved are, thus described—Such of the inhabitants of St Domingo resident within the United States, as shall be found in want of support.

2.   The distribution is to be much for their relief, in such manner, and by the hands of such persons, as shall, in the opinion of the president, appear most conducive to the humane purposes of the act.

3.   A regular statement and account are to be kept of the monies expended, and to be lodged in the proper Office of the Treasury Department.

"In the execution therefore of this law, the President recommends, that the following mode be pursued, with any addition, which your prudence may suggest.

"1st. To give public notice in Newspapers or otherwise, that you are ready to make partition among all persons, coming within the foregoing description. But this is not to interfere with an immediate relief to those, who are immediately known to you; as you will reserve a sum for fresh applicants.

"2d. To observe perfect equality in the distribution; and to fix the dividend of each at the cheapest rate of subsistence.

"3d. To return to the Treasury Department a regular statement and account of your expenditures; to which it will be proper to add the vouchers, usually expected on public settlements.

"The 5,000 Dollars still left, being dependant upon the information, which may be hereafter received, I must entreat you to supply it as far as may be in your power. To this end the principal points to be established, are the number of persons in each State, entitled to relief, and the lowest sum, necessary for such relief, as the law contemplates. The necessity of an early answer appears indispensable; and I beg leave to solicit the most speedy reply on this head" (DNA: RG 59, Domestic Letters).

From Edmund Randolph

[Philadelphia] Feby 27. 1794.

The Secretary of State has the honor to inform the President, that it appears by a letter, just received from Mr Latimer, the representative of Delaware, that the numbers of distressed people from St Domingo in that State probably amount to about an hundred.[1] It is submitted to the President, whether it will not be better to give a sum to them out of the remaining five thousand dollars, rather than to disturb the distribution of the ten thousand, as already suggested.[2]

AL, DNA: RG 59, Miscellaneous Letters; LB, DNA: RG 59, GW's Letters to His Secretaries of State; LB, DNA: RG 59, Domestic Letters.

1. Henry Latimer's letter to Randolph of c.27 February has not been identified.

2. On the proposed distribution of $15,000 in federal funds designated to assist the refugees from Saint Domingue, see Randolph's first letter to GW of this date. On the actual disbursement of these funds as of 11 April, including $500 to Delaware, see n.1 of Cabinet Opinion, 22 April.

From Edmund Randolph

[Philadelphia] Feb: 27. 1794.

The secretary of State has the honor of reporting to the President on the letter of Mr Short from San Lorenzo, of Novr 6. 1793, as follows:

The first paragraph, and several others succeeding, relate to the causes of delay in the departure of Mr Blake.

The four marked thus (X) mention, that Spain has furnished a convoy to American vessels against the Algerines; that the answer, promised by the Duke de la Alcudia, is not yet given; and that there are some omens of a communication, being intended to be permitted between the citizens of the U.S. and New Orleans. These the Secretary proposes to be sent to congress.[1]

Most of the remaining parts of the letter are upon the European War and politics; but we have received later advices.

The last speaks of Colo. Humphries; and tho' it renders it certain, that he had not quitted Europe, leaves it uncertain in what part of Spain he was, at the date of the letter.[2]

Edm: Randolph

ALS, DNA: RG 59, Miscellaneous Letters; LB, DNA: RG 59, GW's Correspondence with His Secretaries of State.

1. The enclosed copy of William Short's letter to the secretary of state of 6 Nov. 1793, with its four marked passages, has not been found. A letter-book copy, however, is in DNA: RG 59, Despatches from U.S. Ministers to Spain, and an extract, containing the four marked passages, is in *ASP, Foreign Relations,* 1:413. For a previous report on the difficulty of finding a safe passage for American diplomatic dispatches and courier James Blake, see William Carmichael and Short to the Secretary of State, 22 Oct. 1793, in n.3 of GW to the U.S. Senate and House of Representatives, 24 Feb. 1794. The question presented to Godoy, Duque de la Alcudia, was whether Spain would interfere if war should take place between the United States and the Indians of the Southwest Territory. According to Carmichael and Short's letter of 22 Oct., Godoy had promised "an immediate answer." Part of Carmichael and Short's mission was to obtain from Spain the right to free navigation on the Mississippi River, with a right of deposit at or near the port of New Orleans for Americans ("Report on Negotiations with Spain," 18 March 1792, *Jefferson Papers,* 23:296–317).

2. David Humphreys' letters to the secretary of state of 5 and 9 Nov. 1793 were written at Alicante, a Spanish port on the Mediterranean Sea, where he had arrived on 1 Nov. in hopes of securing passage to Algiers (RG 59, Despatches from U.S. Ministers to Portugal). On Humphreys' commission to negotiate a treaty with Algiers and obtain the release of the Americans held captive there, see GW to the Dey of Algiers, 21 March 1793. On his failure to obtain a passport from Algiers at this time, see his letter to GW of 23 Nov. 1793.

From Edmund Randolph

[Philadelphia] Feby 27. 1794.

E. Randolph has the honor of transmitting to the President the extract of a letter, which Mr Brown, of the Senate, has just furnished. He thinks, that he cannot commit it to the public eye, nor would he wish, that it should be communicated to congress officially. He means it only for the private information of the President; tho' he does not object to its being spoken of, as intelligence, received from Kentucky.[1]

⟨Since writin⟩g the above, Mr Brown has shewn me a letter from ⟨the⟩ famous Dr O'Fallon to Capt. Herron, dated Oct: 18. 1793, It was intercepted; and he has permitted me to take the following extract.[2]

"This plan (an attack on Louisiana) was digested between General Clarke and me last Christmas. I framed the whole of the correspondence in the General's name; and corroborated it by a private letter of my own to Mr Thomas Pain, of the national assembly, with whom, during the late war I was very intimate. His reply reached me but a few days since, inclosed is the General's dispatches from the Ambassador."[3]

AL, DNA: RG 59, Miscellaneous Letters; LB, DNA: RG 59, GW's Correspondence with His Secretaries of State. The text in angle brackets is from the letter-book copy.

1. The extract sent by Senator John Brown of Kentucky concerned a proposed expedition by Kentucky residents against the Spanish colony of Louisiana. Revolutionary War general George Rogers Clark had been encouraged by Edmond Genet, the former French minister to the United States, to organize and lead this extralegal expedition. The enclosed extract is printed below.

2. James O'Fallon (1749–1794), a native of Ireland, studied medicine at the University of Edinburgh before emigrating to North Carolina in 1774. After serving in the Revolutionary War, he added the prefix to his original name of Fallon and moved to Charleston, S.C. He became an agent for the South Carolina Yazoo Company in 1790 and moved to Kentucky in order to promote the colonization of a tract near the mouth of the Yazoo River that the state of Georgia had granted to the company, despite this territory being under Spanish jurisdiction. In 1791, O'Fallon married Frances Eleanor Clark (1773–1825), the youngest sister of Gen. Clark. On the cause of O'Fallon's "fame," see Thomas Jefferson and Edmund Randolph to GW, 14 Feb. 1791, and source note, plus GW's Proclamation of 19 March 1791, which warned Americans against joining O'Fallon's efforts to acquire land. On O'Fallon's controversial activities after the Revolutionary War, see John Carl Parish, "The Intrigues of Doctor James O'Fallon," *MVHR* 17 (1930), 230–63. The original letter from O'Fallon to Capt. Herron has not been identified.

3. Thomas Paine, an English native and an immigrant to the United States in 1774, was a revolutionist and political writer famous at this time for *Common Sense* (1776) and the *Rights of Man* (1791–92). He went to Europe in 1787 and during the subsequent years alternated his time between France and England. In August 1792 he received French citizenship, and the following month he was elected to the French National Convention. When the French Revolution became more radical, Paine was stripped of his French citizenship

and imprisoned by the French government from 28 Dec. 1793 until November 1794. Paine eventually returned to the United States in 1802, where he remained until his death in 1809. O'Fallon's letter to Paine has not been identified, but for Paine's encouraging reply of 17 Feb. 1793, see Louis Phelps Kellogg, "Letter of Thomas Paine," *American Historical Review*, 29 (1924):501–5. The specific enclosed dispatches from Genet to Clark have not been identified, but for correspondence between them concerning the proposed expedition against Louisiana, see "Selections from the Draper Collection." Genet's letter to Clark of 12 July 1793, in which he designated Clark as commander in chief of the Independent and Revolutionary Army of the Mississippi, is printed there on p. 986.

Enclosure
Extract of A Letter from Kentucky

Lexington Jany 25th 1794.

I suppose the Voice of fame has apprized you of the attempts which are mediated by some of the Inhabitants of this Country against the Spanish Dominions in Louisiana. General Logan has, I am told, embarked in the enterprize as second in command, and will unless prevented by the *Federal Arm,* proceed down the River before the last of February, at the head of two thousand men. Clark it is said has resumed his sobriety, and attention, & yet promises to renew his fame.[1] Colo. Montgomery of Cumberland at the head of two hundred men has stationed himself at the mouth of Cumberland River with a view of interupting any Boats which might carry information to the Spainards of their designs.[2] When you hear that Logan is among the adventurers you will easily conceive that a number of very influential old Buffaloe Hunters are engaged in it.[3] Colo. Hall, Majr Lanier of Bourbon & some others of that County have nearly compleated the enlistment of a Regiment, & procure men with more ease than when the late Campaign was the object.[4] So popular is the undertaking here that I fear Government will want power, either to prevent it, or to punish the adventurers.[5] Besides an Attorney is wanted in the federal Court, & the Excise is so very odious that No Lawyer who has a reputation to loose will accept that Office. Perhaps H. Marshall, or W.C. might but what would be the consequence? They are fully as odious to the People as the Excise, & wou'd probably be mobb'd if the attempted to discharge the functions of that Office.[6] The Governor I am persuaded will

use his best efforts to put a Stop to so unlicenced an undertaking, but I fear his endeavours will only tend to render him
unpopular.[7]

Recd Feby 26th by J⟨o⟩: Brown

DS (in John Brown's handwriting), DNA: RG 59, Miscellaneous Letters.

1. Benjamin Logan, a delegate in the Kentucky House of Representatives
and a major general in the state militia, offered his services for the planned
expedition against Louisiana in a letter to George Rogers Clark of 31 Dec.
1793, in which he noted that he was "at liberty to go to any foreign country
I pleas" ("Selections from the Draper Collection," 1026). In order to ensure
his freedom to join Clark's expedition, Logan resigned his commission in
the Kentucky militia. See Charles Gano Talbert, *Benjamin Logan: Kentucky
Frontiersman* (Lexington, Ky., 1962), 274.

2. Virginia native John Montgomery (c.1748–1794) served under Clark
during the Revolutionary War. For Montgomery's solicitation of a position in
the Louisiana expedition and his subsequent preparations for advancing his
troops down the Mississippi River, see his letters to Clark of 26 Oct. 1793 and
12 Jan. 1794 ("Selections from the Draper Collection," 1018–19, 1034). .

3. Montgomery informed Clark in his letter of 26 Oct. 1793 that there
were "several old veteran officers" who were "very willing to Serve in your
Command under me provided you should think proper to leave it in my
power to favour them, they may be exceedingly Serviceable in raising and
Dessiplening troops." In an attempt to recruit troops, Clark, who identified himself as "Major General in the armies of *France,* and Commander in
Chief of the *French revolutionary Legions* on the Missisippi River," advertised
for "Volunteers for the reduction of the Spanish posts on the Missisippi, for
opening the trade of the said river, and giving freedom to its inhabitants
&c. All persons serving the expedition, to be entitled to one thousand acres
of Land—those that engage for one year, will be entitled to two thousand
acres, if they serve two years or during the present war with France, they
will have three thousand acres of any unappropriated Land that may be con-
quered—The officers in proportion pay &c. as other French troops.—All
lawful *Plunder* to be equally divided agreeable to the custom of *War.* All necessaries will be provided for the interpize, and every precaution taken to
cause the return of those who wish to quit the service, as comfortable as
possible, and a reasonable number of days allowed them to return; at the expiration of which time their pay will cease. All persons will be commissioned
agreeable to the number of men they bring into the field.—Those that serve
the expedition, will have their choice of receiving their Lands or one Dollar
per day" (*Centinel of the North-western Territory* [Cincinnati, Ohio], 25 January
1794).

4. Horatio Hall, while a major in Kentucky militia, had served in the ill-
fated expeditions of generals Josiah Harmar and Arthur St. Clair against
hostile Indians in the Northwest Territory in 1790 and 1791, respectively.
In July 1793, Hall was commissioned lieutenant colonel of a regiment of
mounted volunteers in Maj. Gen. Charles Scott's division of Kentucky mili-

tia. Hall later would serve as adjutant general in this same division in 1794. Capt. James Lanier was appointed commander of a company of volunteers in Hall's regiment on 15 July 1793 and subsequently was commissioned as regimental paymaster on 20 Sept. 1793 (Clark, *American Militia,* 12–24, 68, 89–91).

5. The expedition did not succeed, in part because Fauchet, the new French minister to the United States, issued a repudiation on 6 March, in which he declared that "EVERY Frenchman is forbid to violate the Neutrality of the United States. All commissions or authorizations tending to infringe that neutrality are revoked and are to be returned to the agents of the French Republic" (*General Advertiser* [Philadelphia], 7 March). On the administration's efforts to thwart this expedition, see Cabinet Opinion on Expeditions Against Spanish Territory, 10 March; and GW's Proclamation of 24 March. See also "An Act in addition to the act for the punishment of certain crimes against the United States," 5 June, which states that "if any citizen of the United States shall, within the territory or jurisdiction of the same, accept and exercise a commission to serve a foreign prince or state in war by land or sea, the person so offending shall be deemed guilty of a high misdemeanor, and shall be fined not more than two thousand dollars, and shall be imprisoned not exceeding three years" (*Stat.* 1:381–84).

6. GW's attempt in February 1793 to fill the position of U.S. district attorney for Kentucky failed when the nominee declined the office specifically because of difficulties in enforcing the collection of the federal excise tax on whiskey (Thomas Jefferson to GW, 19 June 1793 [first letter], n.3). An attempt in December 1793 to fill the vacancy also failed (GW to U.S. Senate, 27 Dec. 1793, and n.4 to that document). For the successful appointment of William McClung, see GW to U.S. Senate, 31 May.

Humphrey Marshall (1760–1841) was a native of Virginia and a veteran of the Revolutionary War. He moved to Kentucky in 1782, studied law, and began his practice in Fayette County. An ardent Federalist, he served in the Kentucky legislature, 1793–94 and 1807–9, and in the U.S. Senate, 1795–1801. *The History of Kentucky* (Frankfort, Ky., 1812) is among his published works.

7. Contrary to the opinion of the letter's author, Gov. Isaac Shelby was reluctant to interfere with Clark's expedition, as seen in his letter to Jefferson of 13 Jan. 1794 (*ASP, Foreign Relations,* 1:455–56).

From Andrew Ellicott

Sir   Philadelphia Feby 28th 1794

The enclosed letter was to have been delivered by me, to you, last June;[1] but from an expectation founded on my own feelings, I supposed that the commissioners for the public buildings in the City of Washington would certainly in the course of the summer go into an enquiry respecting the conduct of Mr Dermott; which was fully stated to them in several reports, particularly one bearing date June 17th, 1793, added to a wish that you might have no further trouble on my account with the embarrassing affairs of the City;[2] I have been induced to delay its delivery till this time; fully convinced that no transaction of Mr Dermott's, however injurious to the public, could induce the commissioners to institute an enquiry into his conduct.[3] I have the Honour to be Your very Hbe Servt

Andw. Ellicott

ALS, DLC:GW.

1. The enclosed letter was that from Andrew Ellicott, Benjamin Ellicott, and Isaac Briggs to GW of 29 June 1793, in which they presented their grievances against the continued employment, by the commissioners for the District of Columbia, of fellow surveyor James R. Dermott.

2. In his letter to the commissioners of 17 June 1793, Ellicott asserted that Dermott had made several erasures and alterations on "the plan from which we worked" in an effort to discredit Ellicott's work as chief surveyor (DNA: RG 42, Records of the Commissioners for the District of Columbia, Letters Received, 1791–1802).

3. While Andrew Ellicott was no longer employed by the D.C. commissioners, Dermott still was, and he retained his position in the surveyor's office until 3 Jan. 1798 (D.C. Commissioners to GW, 23 Dec. 1793, and n.8; 3 Jan. 1798 minutes, DNA: RG 42, Records of the Commissioners for the District of Columbia, Proceedings, 1791–1802).

From Andrew Ellicott

Sir   Philadelphia Feby 28th 1794

With this you will receive a copper-plate map of the territory of Columbia, which I find requires much larger paper than can be met with in this country, except amongst drafts-men who have imported it for their own use. It would therefore be necessary if the maps are intended for sale, to have some paper manufactured for that purpose of a proper size. I am in hopes the map will be found sufficiently correct, however if it should not, I have only to lament that it has been long out of my power to render it more accurate, in consequence of the original, together with my field notes, being more than a year ago privately carried away from the office.[1]

Although being one of those with whom the City of Washington may be said to have originated, I feel no desire of resuming my former station at that place, being convinced from severe experiance that no mans reputation can be safe, when in the power of men, who avail themselves of their right to censure, and remove from office, without allowing the object of their resentment the benefit of a scientific enquiry.[2] This has been my case; and nothing but a very extensive acquaintance with gentlemen of letters, and competent judges of my professional character, prevented its being sacrificed to the *private,* and I may confidently add, *misguided resentment* of the commissioners for the public buildings in the City of Washington, without, (so far as I can see,) the possibility of redress. "There are some subjects so circumstanced, that time alone can correct where man errs." I am willing to suppose my dispute with the commissioners are of that class, and feel entire confidence, that the injustice which I have experienced, will not only at some future period be manifest; but perhaps sap the foundation, and injure the whole business of the City in its infancy.

I think it my duty for your own satisfaction, to assure you, that the accuracy of the work is infinitely superior to any thing of the kind heretofore executed, and the methodical arrangement of the papers in the Office was not any where exceeded, when the commissioners for the second time, removed them for the City into Geo. Town! But notwithstanding this systematic arrangement of the papers, it will be found impossible for any person unacquainted with the detail of the business; however competent his abilities might have been to the execution of the plan of the City, to take up the work in its present state, and do justice to the public, and that part already completed. I have mentioned this circumstance for the purpose of preserving the character of the person who may be appointed to succeed me, and who will probably be charged with *ignorance, and neglect of duty,* on account of difficulties which will naturally arise out of the present state of the work.

I trust that my attachment to the City of Washington will be sufficiently manifest, when it is remembered that I declined entering into land concerns with some of the first characters in the U.S., (which would before this day, have secured to me ease, and independence,) for the express purpose of aiding an object, which I conceived of importance to the union: In return I have experienced the weight of *private resentment,* exercised officially by the commissioners, for the purpose of injuring my professional reputation!

I am informed that Mr Dalton is about resigning the office of Treasurer to the Mint. If this information should be true, I shall take the liberty of offering myself as a candidate for that appointment, and from the following consideration, (Viz.,) having undertaken to publish a Map of the U.S. I should thereby be enabled, tho' the salary is small, to discontinue my vocation for the present, which obliges me not only to be generally from home; but likewise to prolong the completion of that important work:[3] And I do not apprehend, that the business in the mint can possibly require so much time, as to preclude an attention of two, or three hours every day, to the compilation of the Map. With sentiments of gratitude for the klnd attention which I have received from you, I am Sir, Your Hble Servt

Andw. Ellicott.

ALS, DLC:GW.

1. The enclosed copper plate was for a typographic plan of the "Territory of Columbia." In a letter to the D.C. commissioners of 9 Dec. 1793, Ellicott wrote that this map "has been some months in the hands of an engraver, and will be finished early in the spring; but in order to make it useful, it will be necessary to have it accompanied with an explanation, and discription of the country, with the several advantages for atlantic commerce, and inland navigation" (DNA: RG 42, Records of the Commissioners for the District of Columbia, Letters Received, 1791–1802). The engraver has not been identified. The copper plate was copied in the early nineteenth century in order to produce the map featured in David B. Warden, *A Chorographical and Statistical Description of the District of Columbia* [Paris, 1816]). On the removal of papers from Ellicott's office, see D.C. Commissioners to GW, 13 March 1793, n.3, and 23 March 1794 (second letter).

2. On the dismissal in December 1793 of Ellicott as the chief surveyor for the District of Columbia, see D.C. Commissioners to GW, 23 Dec. 1793, and n.8.

3. For Tristram Dalton's resignation and the appointment of Nicholas Way as his successor, see Dalton to GW, 24 April, and GW to the U.S. Senate, 19 May 1794. Although Ellicott did not acquire the position at the U.S. Mint, he did publish *The American Atlas Containing the Following Maps.—Viz.--1. North-America 2. South-America 3. United States 4. New-Hampshire 5. Province of Maine 6. Massachusetts 7. Vermont 8. Rhode-Island 9. Connecticut 10. New-York 11. New-Jersey 12. Pennsylvania 13. Delaware and Maryland 14. Virginia 15. Kentucky, with the Adjoining Territories 16. North-Carolina 17. South-Carolina 18. Georgia 19. Tennessee 20. West-Indies* (New York, 1796).

From Alexander Hamilton

[Philadelphia] February 28. 1794.

The Secretary of the Treasury presents his respects to the President, & has the honor to send him a Communication from the Commissioner of the revenue, of this date, with its enclosures respecting the Survey comprehending Kentucke.[1] Also a letter from the Collector of Charlestown of the 6th instant, with its enclosures, respecting the case of the Spanish Vessel the St Joseph.[2] These dispatches appear to him important enough to be submitted to the particular attention of the President.

LB, DLC:GW.

1. The letter from Tench Coxe to Hamilton of 28 Feb. and its enclosures have not been identified. At this time, there was difficulty in collecting the federal excise tax on whiskey from the citizens of Kentucky, and this problem may have been the subject of this communication.

2. The letter from Isaac Holmes to Hamilton of 6 Feb. and its enclosures have not been identified, but they concerned the Spanish brigantine *San Josef,* under Capt. Castello, which had been captured by the French privateer *Aimée Marguerite* in September 1793 and brought first into the harbor of Wilmington, N.C. (see Spaight to GW, 21 Oct. 1793, 8 Feb. 1794 [second letter], and 16 Feb. 1794). Ensuing events are best described by Thomas Bee, the U.S. judge for the District of South Carolina, in the case of *Castello v. Bouteille et al.,* 18 March 1794: "The libel states that *Castello* was owner and commander of the brigantine *St. Joseph,* which was loaded in the port of *Carthagena* by himself and other subjects of *Spain,* which is in amity with the *United States.* That on the 22d of *September* last, in his way to *Cadiz,* he was captured on the high seas by the sloop *Fair Margaret,* commanded by *F. H. Hervieux,* and carried into *Cape Fear* river in *North Carolina.* That two days after their arrival within the bar of *Wilmington,* the said sloop and brigantine suddenly weighed anchor and proceeded to sea. This is said to have been in consequence of directions from the president of the *United States* to the governor of *North Carolina* to take possession of the brigantine and deliver her up to the libellant.

"The libel further states that *Hervieux* then proceeded to *Charleston,* where, upon some agreement between him and the defendant [Jean] Bouteille, the latter went to sea in the *Sans-pareille,* and, at some distance from the bar of *Charleston,* took possession of the brigantine, landed the Spanish crew in *Georgia,* and brought the vessel into *Charleston. Hervieux* and his people had previously quitted her.

"The libel also states some proceedings respecting the brigantine and cargo in consequence of directions from the president of the *United States* to the governors of *North* and *South Carolina,* the latter of whom declined all interference. And the collector of *Charleston,* not thinking himself authorized to detain the vessel, she was finally left in the hands of *Bouteille.* Whereupon, by a decree of the consul of *France* [Michel-Ange-Bernard de Mangourit], the said vessel and cargo were advertised and sold, except fifty bales of cotton, which were taken into the custody of the marshal [Daniel L. Huger] of this court by a warrant issued therefrom. The libel concludes by praying restitution of vessel and cargo, and compensation for the detention of the same" (Bee, *Reports of Cases*, 29–34).

From Henry Knox

Sir   War department February 28. 1794

I have the honor to submit to your consideration a request from the Governor of this State for the loan of four brass Nine pounders.[1] I have the honor to be with perfect respect Your obedient Servant

H. Knox

LS, DLC:GW; LB, DLC:GW.

1. Thomas Mifflin's brief letter to Knox of 28 Feb. asked for "the loan of 4 Brass nine pounders, to be employed in the defence of our Frontiers," which "shall be returned when required." In his reply of 1 March, Knox wrote that GW "regrets Sir, that the principles which have been invariably adopted, both under the old as well as under the present government relatively to keeping together the Ordnance and Stores in possession of the United States, notwithstanding the desire of many of the individual States, preclude his compliance in this instance" (both letters, PHarH: Executive Correspondence, 1790–99).

From James McGowan

Sir   Doun [Scotland][1] 28 February 1794

I beg your pardon for using the freedom of writing you about the following business. My Brother The Revd Mr Walter McGowan late Rector in the Parish of St James's in the County of Ann Aroundal in the Province of Maryland N. America died on the 4th May 1786—He was married to a sister in Law of Colonel John Winyess at or near the place where my Brother lived. I understand his wife is also dead, and I suppose her friends will be entitled to the one half of the subjects left by my Brother, But as to this you know better than I do.[2]

In the month of October 1786 I sent over a Power of Attorney to William Stewart Esquire Merchant in the City of Annapolis in the Provence of Maryland empowering him to be my true and lawfull Attorney for me and in my name to ask demand sue for levy, recover and receive all such sums & sums of money, Chattles, Goods, retale & Effects real and personal, and all other demands whatever which are or shall become due owing pay[ab]le or belonging to my Brother within the Province of Maryland or else where in North America.[3]

This Power I granted him on the faith of doing Justice to me, and I never had the least doubt but he would prove a faithfull Attorney to me seeing he was so very Kind as [to] write to this Country to his Brother the deceased George Hoome late Esqr. of Argaty saying that my Brother had left considerable sums of money, and that it would be my Interest to send over a Power of Attorney to some Person or come over myself. This Letter had no sooner arrived when the late Revd Mr James Smith Minister of the Parish of Killmadock (in which Parish I reside) got a Letter inclosing another for me from my Sister in Law Mrs McGowan offering me £500 Sterl. for my share if I choosed to take it, altho' she had every reason to believe my proportion might be more, She having understood that Mr Smith & my Brother having had a Correspondence which subsisted betwixt them for several years thought he would get me advised to take the offer, But having got a Letter from Mr Stewart saying that he recd my Power of Attorney I wrote my Sister in Law I would not accept of her offer—Which Letter of Mr Stewarts was dated 7 May 1787 saying that he had drawn for me Negroes & furniture wearing Apparel Watches &ca (the wearing apparel Watches and a small sum of money I have received) £580 Currency, which he had ardvirtized for sale, except the wearing Apparel—He having not got the Inventary compleated could not precisely inform what would be my proportion but from the idea that he had been able to form of it he thought I would have to receive between £1000 & £1200 Str.—From Letter of 25th April 1788 (which was the last Letter I recd from him) he mentions amount of Inventary returned to Commissarys Offie—

Curry £1955. 8.10
Amount of Debts upon Bond 1170.11. 6½
In all £3126.—. 4½

besides the apparel & Cash—From what I could learn from his Brother Mr David Stewart who came to Britain for some time and sometime after returned back to America I had reason to believe my proportion would amt nearly to £2000 Currency; however in this I may be misinformed, but as I have had no Letters from him for several years past, and altho I have wrote him repeatedly will not answer me a Letter, I have therefore every reason to believe he is using my property himself, and does not intend to let me know any thing about it unless he is brought to Account, which his Letters if produced will clearly show he is accountable to me for my Negroes & Cash—The Interest of the money will very near amount to the Stock, for he at any rate has either disposed of the Negroes, or has them himself—His connections and acquaintances in this Country is surprised at his conduct, and every person who knows of the business is of the opinion that he is using my property for his own purposes—As I am but a very poor man he thinks he may use me as he pleases—I therefore was advised by the Gentlemen in this place to Address you at present, as you have it in your power to do something for me, and as my Brother was Teacher in your ffamily for several years you will on his account give me some assistance as I am but a poor man weak in circumstance, & having become old I am not able to support myself & ffamily—If this you do it will be a great service done me, If you speak to any other Gentleman in case it be not convenient for yourself I will grant a new Power to him, or if Mr Stewart will account for his Intremissions, or let me know what he had done I will allow him a suitable gratifcation for his trouble out of the first end of the subject, But this I leave for you to Judge—I will be very much obliged to you to acknowledge the Receipt of this Letter, and if you'l do for me, and when you write direct to me James McGowan Residenter in Doun by Stirling N. Britain.[4] I am with the greatest respect Honourable sir Your most obedt & very humle Servt

James McGowan

LS, DLC:GW.

1. The town of Doune is in the central region of Scotland on the Teith River.

2. Walter Magowan served as a tutor to GW's stepchildren, Martha Parke Custis and John Parke Custis, from 1761 until early 1768, when he went to England for ordination in the Anglican church. In June 1769 he received an appointment to St. James Parish, Herring Creek, in Anne Arundel County, Md., where he served until his death in 1786. On 28 Oct. 1780, he married Elizabeth Dorsey Harrison, who was the sister of Mary Dorsey, the wife of

Col. John Weems (1727–1794) of St. James Parish. Weems is an anglicized spelling of the Scottish name Wemyss.

3. McGowan's choice of William Steuart (1754–1838) of Annapolis to act on his behalf may have reflected the close connection that the Steuart family had with Scotland. His father, George Steuart (1700–c.1784) emigrated to America from Perthshire, Scotland, circa 1721, and resided in Annapolis until returning to Scotland in 1775. William accompanied his father to Scotland in 1775, but by 1780 he had returned to Annapolis. His brother George Hume Steuart returned permanently to Scotland, settling at the family home in Argaty, Perthshire, and changing his name to George Steuart Hume. Another brother, David (1750–1814), fought for the British during the Revolutionary War, but later returned to Maryland. He is buried, along with William, at the family estate, "Dodon," located in present-day Davidsonville, Maryland. The various correspondence mentioned by James McGowan in this letter has not been identified.

4. The town of Stirling, located in central Scotland on the Forth River, is the site of Stirling Castle, a residence of Scottish kings and queens of the house of Stuart (Stewart). No reply from GW has been identified.

From Edmund Randolph

[Philadelphia] Feb. 28. 94. ½ past 11.

The Secretary of State has the honor of inclosing to the President two letters from Colo. Humphries, this moment received. His mission to Algiers is prohibited by the Dey, who refuses a passport. Colo. H: incloses two letters one in French, the other in a very cross hand; the former is translating; and the latter copying for the President; as they are connected with the Algerine affairs.[1]

As it is probable, that these papers will be sent to congress, Copies are directed for both houses.[2]

AL, DNA: RG 59, Miscellaneous Letters; LB, DNA: RG 59, GW's Correspondence with His Secretaries of State.

1. The enclosed letters from David Humphreys, the U.S. minister to Portugal and commissioner plenipotentiary to Algiers, were those to the secretary of state of 19 and 23 Nov. 1793, both written at Alicante, a Spanish port on the Mediterranean Sea. Humphreys' enclosures were in his letter of 23 November. The letter in French actually was a copy of two letters. One was from Mathias Skjöldebrand, the Swedish consul at Algiers, and the other was from his brother Pierre Eric Skjöldebrand, both written at Algiers on 12 Nov. 1793. The second letter also was a copy of more than one document, and it was written using a technique called cross writing, which is produced by turning a finished page and writing across the lines at right angles. This copy contained

a letter from Algerine captive Richard O'Bryen (O'Brien) to Humphreys of
12 Nov. 1793, and O'Bryen's detailed description of the "Algerine Maritime
Force" of the same date. A copy of Capt. John McShane's letter to Humphreys
of 13 Nov., describing the recent capture of his ship *Minerva* and containing a
list of other American ships and crews detained in Algiers, also was enclosed
by Humphreys. The letters received by Randolph on 28 Feb. are in DNA: RG
59, Despatches from U.S. Ministers to Portugal.

2. Copies of Humphreys' letters and the above enclosures were submitted
with GW's letter to the U.S. Senate and House of Representatives of 3 March
1794. For the copies and translations sent to Congress, see DNA: RG 233,
Third Congress, 1793–95, House Records of Legislative Proceedings, Journals; see also *ASP, Foreign Relations,* 1:413–18.

From John Jay

Dear Sir   New York 1 March 1794

When Mr Drayton of Charleston was here last Summer he
told me that the true nankeen Cotton was in So. Carolina. It
appeared to me to be a valuable acquisition, and I suggested to
him the Expediency of planting it always at so great a Distance
from *other* Cotton, as to avoid the Influence which many plants
of the same kind, tho' of different Species have on each other,
when very contiguous. whether that is the case with cotton, I am
uninformed; having very little knowledge of it as a Plant, or of
its Cultivation.[1]

I have just recd from Mr Drayton some of the seed mixed with
the cotton—I herewith send you half of it—Perhaps you have it
already—perhaps not. I think it worth having to those whose
Estates are in a Climate suited to its Growth. I suppose that to be
the Case with Mount Vernon's where you doubtless have a Gardener who will punctually observe your Instructions respecting
it.[2] with perfect Respect Esteem & Attachmt I am Dear Sir your
obliged & obt Servt

                                                    John Jay

ALS, DLC:GW; ADf, NNC: Jay Papers.

1. John Drayton (1766–1822), a planter, lawyer, and botanist, was at this time
a member of the South Carolina legislature. Drayton served as lieutenant governor, 1798–1800, and governor, 1800–1802 and 1808–10. He became a U.S.
district judge in July 1812 and served until his death. Drayton sent the cotton
to Jay in January (see Drayton to Jay, 29 Jan., and Jay to Drayton, 1 March, both
NNC). The original Nankeen cotton came from the Nanjing region of China,
and it produced a fiber that had a brown tint. On the various types of cotton

grown in South Carolina by 1802, see John Drayton, *A View of South-Carolina, as Respects Her Natural and Civil Concerns* (Charleston, 1802), 128–30.

2. For GW's thoughts on growing cotton at Mount Vernon, see his reply to Jay of 5 March. For his instructions on planting it, see his letter to William Pearce of 16–17 March.

From Edmund Randolph

Sir   Philadelphia March 1. 1794.

I made the informal communication to Mr Jaudenes. He expressed himself to be satisfied with the exertions of the general government; tho' he questioned, whether the governor of Kentucky has done, what he was commanded by the President to do.[1]

Mr Fauchet also was extremely frank in disavowing his predecessor's conduct. He says, that he will conform to any thing, which shall be prescribed to him by the United States; and at 6 o'clock this evening he is to meet me again at my house.[2]

The papers, which Colo. Smith delivered to you, fall within the arrangement of the *vexations and spoliations,* in which I am now employed. As soon as I can see him, I will explain the affair to him.[3] I have the honor, sir, to be with the highest respect yr mo. ob. serv.

Edm: Randolph

ALS, DNA: RG 59, Miscellaneous Letters; LB, DNA 59: GW's Correspondence with His Secretaries of State.

1. Randolph's informal communication with Spanish commissioner José de Jaudenes concerned a planned expedition led by American George Rogers Clark, and composed mainly of residents from the state of Kentucky, against Spain's Louisiana territory. Contrary to instructions written on 29 Aug. and 6 Nov. 1793 by former secretary of state Thomas Jefferson to Isaac Shelby, the governor was reluctant to interfere with Clark's preparations, as seen in his letter to Jefferson of 13 Jan. 1794 (*ASP, Foreign Relations,* 1:455–56).

2. Fauchet, the recently arrived French ambassador, disavowed the actions of his predecessor, Edmond Genet, who had encouraged Clark and others to prepare expeditions against Spanish territory. To this end, he issued a public declaration on 6 March declaring that "EVERY Frenchman is forbid to violate the Neutrality of the United States. All commissions or authorizations tending to infringe that neutrality are revoked and are to be returned to the agents of the French Republic" (*General Advertiser* [Philadelphia], 7 March).

3. According to GW's executive journal, the papers from Maryland congressman Samuel Smith were "sundry letters written by Capt. Joshua Barney and other papers relating to his being captured by a British frigate & carried into Kingston, Jamaica & treated in the most shameful manner" (*JPP,* 287).

These documents have not been identified. While returning from the French colony of Saint Domingue, Barney and his ship *Sampson* were captured on 6 Dec. 1793 by the British frigate *Penelope* and taken to Jamaica to stand trial. Although he was acquitted of the charges against him, his ship and cargo were condemned. The story of his capture and return to Baltimore on 16 May 1794 can be found in the various newspapers reports published about him in 1794 (*American Minerva* [Norfolk, Va.], 3 Feb.; *General Advertiser* [Philadelphia], 1 May; *Dunlap's American Daily Advertiser* [Philadelphia], 15 April; and *Baltimore Daily Intelligencer*, 19 May). On Barney's return, see also Randolph to Alexander Hamilton, 16 June (*Hamilton Papers*, 16:490–91). Randolph submitted an "abstract of vexations and spoliations of our commerce," which has not been identified, with his letter to the U.S. Senate of 20 May (*ASP, Foreign Relations*, 1:461).

From James D. Smith

Germantown Farqr County Virginia[1] 1st March 1794

Will your Excelly pardon the freedom I have taken, of Addressing you, & of inclosing a letter of introduction, from an Uncle of mine in Scotland—who says he has been acquainted with you, forty years ago[2]—I should have delivered it Personally, but time will not permitt me to go so fare as Philidelpha—& as your return to Mount Vernon being uncertain has made me take this liberty—I came into this Country shortly after the close of the late war with Thomas Montgomerie Esqr. as an assistant in the Store he keep't at Dumfries where I liv'd for five years— Afterwards went to Richmond & liv'd with my Cousin Alexander Donald for two years, & return'd again to Dumfries with a Small assortment of goods, but finding Trade dill, I retired to this place, which I find much the same, & not likely to be better.[3]

Being a Young man (& is now almost going idle) I wish to be in an actize life—As Congrass has proposed to raise a Body of Troops, I think that by joining them—or any other Line your Excelly may think proper under your Auspicious eye I can push my way thro: the worald with all propriaty—should your Excelly these requests—I will immediatly sell of all my property, Settle my Accts & with the greatest chearfullness Act as you may be pleased to desire—A letter Addressed to the Postmaster of Dumfries will be thankfully received by him[4] who has the honour to be with the greatest respect & Esteem Your Excellys Faithfull Servant

J.D. Smith

ALS, DLC:GW.

1. Germantown, an historic unincorporated community in Fauquier County, was about twenty-five miles northwest of Fredericksburg, Va., and near the present-day village of Midland.

2. For the enclosed letter of introduction, see Robert Donald to GW, 6 June 1793.

3. Smith may have left Dumfries because of the death of Thomas Montgomerie in 1792 (see James Keith to GW, 7 March 1793). The business misfortunes of his cousin, Alexander Donald, in the spring of 1793 may have prompted Smith to return to Dumfries. On these misfortunes and for Donald's description of his nephew "as too young to take the charge of my business" and as "a very fine young man," see Donald to Thomas Jefferson, 10 March 1793 (*Jefferson Papers,* 25:351–52).

4. A reply from GW has not been found, and Smith did not receive any federal appointment from GW.

From William Tilghman

Sir   Chester Town [Md.] March 1. 1794.

I have the honor of forwarding the inclosed copies of Sidney George's bond to J. West,[1] & of two letters from Mr George Chalmers to me, which I received a few days ago, by the December packet.[2] Mr Chalmers has been very obliging, & assiduous in searching for the bond, & appears to be very honorable in his proposals of settlement—I wait your instructions, whether to desire him to send the bond to me, or to retain it in his hands till the return of Peace shall make the conveyance less dangerous. I should suppose, that the certified copy of the bond which is now in my possession, would be a sufficient voucher to induce Mr George to make payment, without any writing of indemnification. You will observe that Chalmers authorizes me to draw for £100, tho' he seems confident that he has paid the money. Perhaps it might be worth while to apply to the representatives of Colonel Carlyle, to know whether his books or papers throw any light on this transaction.[3] I should rather think that it would be most prudent not to draw on Chalmers immediately. If however, you should be of a contrary opinion, you will be good enough to transmit me a writing of indemnity, to be forwarded to him agreeably to his request. I shall return him no answer till I receive your instructions on the subject.[4] Meanwhile I have the honor of remaining with the most perfect respect, yr obt Servt

Wm. Tilghman.

ALS, DLC:GW.

1. The copy of the bond from Sidney George, Jr., to John West, Jr., reads: "Maryland to wit. Know all men by these Presents that I Sidney George of Cecil County Executor of the last Will & testament of Sidney George Esqr. late of Cecil County & province aforesaid deceased; am held & firmly bound unto J[   ] West of Prince Williams County & Colony of Virginia in the full & just Sum of one hundred & eighty pounds pennsylvania currency, to be paid to the said J[   ] West his certain Attorney, Executors, Administrators or Assigns. To which payment well & truly to be made & done, I bind myself, my heirs Executors & Administrators firmly by these presents, sealed with my seal, & dated this thirtieth day of August in the year seventeen hundred & seventy four.

"The Condition of the above obligation is such, that if the above bound Sidney George, do & shall well & truly pay, or cause to be paid unto the aforesaid J[   ] West, his certain Attorney, Executors, Administrators or Assigns, the just & full sum of ninety pounds pennsylvania Currency at or upon the tenth day of June next ensuing the date hereof, with legal Interest for the same, then the above obligation to be void, else to remain in full force & virtue in Law." This bond was "Signed sealed & delivered in presence of G. Milligan [and] Robert Milligan," and attested as a "true Copy" by George Chalmers at Whitehall, London, on 3 Dec. 1793 (DLC:GW). For background on this bond, see Tilghman to GW, 16 Aug. 1793.

2. In his letter written at the "Office for Trade Whitehall" on 5 Nov. 1793, Chalmers acknowledged receipt of Tilghman's letter of 6 Sept. 1793. He then wrote that when he left Maryland for England in 1775, he turned over his papers to a "Doctor Stenhouse, who then resided in Baltimore Town. Upon my retirement, the Doctor gave public notice, that I had entrusted him with my Affairs, and any Person having any Claim on me might apply to him. In consequence, Clients called for Papers, and Creditors asked for their money. Some Years afterwards, the Doctor thought himself obliged to retire. And, since his arrival in this Country, about fifteen Years ago, I have seldom or never brought my mind upon affairs, which yielded to me no very pleasant Reflections; having had in the mean time neither any enquiry after Papers, nor any Demand for money.

"From those Circumstances you will easily suppose, that my Recollection, with regard to such distant objects, cannot be very minute, tho' from the Particulars which you mention, I immediately recollected the Transaction in general. I owe it however, to the nature of the Business, and to the respectability of the Parties to give every Information in my Power. With this view, I shall write to Doctor Stenhouse, who now lives on a farm in Fifeshire [in Scotland], and I shall ransack the Papers, which are in my Possession, and which, whatever may have been destroyed or lost, daily increase upon me" (DLC:GW).

The second letter, dated 4 Dec. 1793 and also written at the "Office for Trade Whitehall," reads: "I now sit down to fulfil, as well as I can, the promise that I made you in my Letter, dated the 5th of November, which was sent by the last mail, under cover to Mr Consul [Phineas] Bond, and a copy of which I enclose, in case of accident to the Original.

"Doctor Stenhouse wrote me, in answer to my letter, on this subject, That he could only remember, he had paid several sums of money for me, had delivered various papers to those who seemed to have a right to them, and had brought away with him such papers as still remained in his hands. . . . I now perceive, that the original Bond from Sidney George to Colo. [Thomas] Colville had been lost or mislaid, so that neither Mr George nor Mr West, knew any thing of it, before I had any concern in the business. And, Mr George refusing, or delaying, to satisfy the debt to Mr West, I was employed to file a bill of discovery in the Court of Chancery in Maryland, which still continued in Court, during the year 1774. But whether it was discontinued by the decease of Mr George, the original obligor, or was ended by Compromise, I am unable to tell. Nor, can I find, what expences, I incurred on account of this Chancery Suit, (the Attornies of Maryland being answerable for the Officers fees due from foreign Suitors) or what fees I may have received, or not, on account of this business. But, these are matters, which at this distance of time and place, are worthy of very little recollection.

"It is plain from the receipt, which you took the trouble to copy into your letter, though I had forgot the particulars of the transaction, that in September 1774, I must have received from Mr George, the Executor of the original Obligor, £100 Pensyla. Currency, and also a bond for £100. upon searching my papers, this bond I have happily found. And I have now enclosed you an exact copy of it: reserving the Original, as I did not think it prudential, at this season, to transmit the Bond without authority. I shall send it by the first packet, after I shall have received proper directions for that purpose.

"I can find nothing which satisfies me, to whom or in what manner, this money was discharged by me, after receiving it, though I am Sufficiently satisfied that I must have paid it. My recollection is, that I had more frequent intercourse with Colo. Carlyle of Alexandria, than with Mr West about this business. But at this distance of time, and without documents, I will not say, that I paid this money, to Colo. Carlyle. My notion is, that the remittance may have been made by letter, and that the acknowledgement may have been destroyed, while I was in the habit of destroying epistolary Correspondence, owing to the circumstances of the times.

"In this state of the business, and of the parties, I do not hesitate in saying explicitly, that I consider myself as answerable for the money, which was once in my possession, but which, after the expiration of nineteen years, and the loss of documents I am at present unable to trace out of it, so as to satisfy the Concerned and myself.

"I can only conceive, that the surviving Executor of Colo. Colville is anxious to close the Administration. I beg you will do me the justice to believe, that I too am anxious to have this transaction properly closed as far as depends on me. To these ends, I desire, that you will draw a Bill of Exchange on me for £100 Pensyla. Currency at the usual Exchange of 66⅔, at 30 days sight. And, I am also to request, that you will at the same time send me a letter of advice, with an acquittance, stating the facts, with a special Clause of indemnity, in case I should either by inquiry, or by Chance, discover documents to prove, that I had properly discharged the money, that had been paid to me.

This Condition I flatter myself, is so reasonable on both sides, that the mutual Anxiety to close the transaction may be gratified, without much difficulty.

"Having now answered satisfactorily, I hope, both the points of your letter, I will only beg leave to add my sincere wishes, that no misfortune has happened during the Sad Scenes at Philadelphia in September and October last, to the Personage, whose Life is so important to his Country and dear to the World" (DLC:GW).

3. John Carlyle (1720–1780), originally of Dumfrieshire, Scotland, was one of the founders of Alexandria, Va., and a prominent merchant of that town.

4. For GW's instructions, see his letter to Tilghman of 10 March.

To William Pearce

Mr Pearce,					Philadelphia March 2d 1794

Your letter of the 25th Ulto, & Reports of the preceeding week, came to hand this day.[1]

Enclosed, agreeably to the promise contained in my last, I send you the copy of an advertisement which the Printers of Baltimore & George Town have been directed to publish four times; in each of their Gazettes; alternate weeks; that is—to insert it one Week & leave it out the next, until it has been four times published. The same you may cause to be done in Alexandria, and where else shall be thought proper: among these Port Tobacco may be a good place. To Leesburgh (to the care of Colo. Ball) I will have one sent.[2]

I recommend particular care of the youngest Jack, that he may be made to grow large: I do the same of the Mules (which Peter knows) allotted for my own driving. Do not stint them in their feed to accomplish these purposes.[3]

Let there be an exact account kept of all the Mares & Jenneys that go to the Jacks; and to which, as well those belonging to myself, as others: the same with respect to the horse; but suffer no Mares to be taken away before the money is paid, unless by those who live near you, and from whom you can receive it at any time. A Mr Prescot of Loudoun (or Fauquier) owes yet for last year, so does some others; and as no regular accts were kept of these things, the money will be lost; for which reason, except as above, let no Mares or Jennies be taken away without payment. After knowing these to be the terms on which the Jacks and horses cover, those who do not comply with them, mean not to pay at all, unless compelled: and to bring suits will not be agreeable.[4]

You would do well to shew the horse at Public places. April Court at Alexandria would be a proper time and place, as it happens on Easter Monday, when, probably, many people will be there.[5]

I find by Mr Lewis's account, that the new Visto is opened much farther than I had the least intention to do. I had no idea of extending it farther than the other was; at no rate beyond Muddy hole Branch. Cease opening it any further until I can see it, & let me know how far it is got, and what has been done with the Wood that was cut down in its course?[6]

Buy as much good Oznabrigs in Alexandria as will enable the Gardeners wife to proceed in making linnen clothes for the Negros; and let me know on what terms you can get a full supply, that I may Judge whether it would be best to get the whole quantity there; or send it from hence. To know the width of the linnen, & if possible to obtain a sample of it, would enable me to decide with more accuracy.[7]

The price of Midlings & Ship stuff in Alexandria is greatly below the selling price in this market; especially the first, which is 5½ dollars the barrel of 196 lbs.—& the latter, from a dollar & half to two dollars pr hundred—but as these articles never are as high there as here, you must enquire the most favorable season to dispose of them, and do it to the best advantage. Keep me informed from time to time of the prices of Superfine & fine flour, that I may know when to strike, for mine; and ask the Miller why he does not, as usual, note in his weekly returns the number of barrels he has packed of *all* the different kinds.[8]

I forgot to observe to you in time, that if *all* the fields, intended for Crops this year could not be flushed up in due season, to let those intended for Corn be left to the *last* & *listed only,* rather than the whole work of the spring should be retarded, and the Crops put in late; in order to flush up the *whole.* You must act in this respect now from circumstances, & your own view of things. Had the ground been broke up in the fall, the amelioration it would have received from the frosts of the winter would have been of infinite service. Now, except the work is forwarded by it; I do not believe the Corn will receive any benefit from a flush plowing.[9] I wish you well and am Your friend

Go: Washington

P.S. How does the drilled wheat look?

ALS, ViMtvL; ALS (letterpress copy), DLC:GW.

1. Pearce's letter of 25 Feb. and its enclosed farm reports have not been found.

2. In his letter to Pearce of 24 Feb., GW promised to send copies of an advertisement offering the stud services of his horse Traveller and his jacks Knight of Malta and Compound. For this advertisement, see n.1 of Bartholomew Dandridge, Jr., to printers Angell & Sullivan and Samuel Hanson, 26 February. GW expected an ad to be placed in the *Columbian Mirror and Alexandria [Va.] Gazette*. Any newspapers being published in Leesburg, Va., where Burgess Ball resided, or in Port Tobacco, Md., have not been identified. On the jacks at Mount Vernon, see George Augustine Washington to GW, 16 July 1790, n.4, and Powell, *General Washington and the Jack Ass,* 176–90.

3. The slave Peter Hardiman was in charge of the stables on the Mansion House farm.

4. For Pearce's record of cash received for this season's covering services, beginning with a 15 May entry, see Mount Vernon Accounts, 1794–97. On the covering services provided in 1793, see GW to Anthony Whitting, 26 March 1793, and n.2 to that document.

5. Easter fell on Sunday, 20 April, in 1794.

6. GW's nephew Howell Lewis served as temporary manager of Mount Vernon until Pearce assumed this responsibility in January 1794 (Lewis to GW, 1 Jan. 1794; Mount Vernon Accounts,1794–97).

7. On GW's employment of Catherine Ehlers to oversee the production of clothing at Mount Vernon, see GW to Whitting, 14 Oct. 1792, and n.16.

8. A report from the miller, Joseph Davenport, was expected along with the other weekly reports from Mount Vernon. On 17 June, Pearce recorded receiving £34.14.0 Virginia currency from the Alexandria bakery firm of Joseph Korn and Jacob Weismuller (Wisemiller) "for midlings & Shipstuff," and that same month, he paid a total of £5.2.0 for shipping this flour via Dogue Run to Alexandria (Mount Vernon Accounts, 1794–97).

9. Flushing a field creates a smooth surface, while listing makes ridges and furrows.

From Edmund Randolph

Sir   Philadelphia March 2. 1794.

In your message to both Houses of Congress on the 5 of December 1793, you inform them that "the vexations and spoliations, understood to have been committed on our vessels and commerce, by the Cruisers and Officers of some of the belligerent powers appeared to require attention": that "the proofs of these, however, not having been brought forward, the description of Citizens, supposed to have suffered, were notified, that on furnishing them to the Executive, due measures would be taken to obtain redress of the past, and more effectual provisions against the future;"[1] and that "should such documents be furnished, proper representations will be made thereon, with a just reliance on a redress, proportioned to the exigency of the case."

On my succession to the department of State[2] I found a large volume of complaints, which the notification had collected, against severities on our trade, various in their kind and degree. Having reason to presume, as the fact has proved, that every day would increase the catalogue, I have waited to digest the mass, until time should have been allowed for exhibiting the diversified forms, in which our commerce has hourly suffered. Every information is at length obtained, which may be expected.

The sensations excited by the embarrassments, danger, and even ruin, which threaten our trade, cannot be better expressed, than in the words of the Committee of Philadelphia.[3] After enumerating particular instances of injury, their representation to Government proceeds thus—[4]

"On these cases which are accompanied by the legal proofs the Committee think it unnecessary to enlarge; as the inferences will of course occur to the Secretary; but they beg leave to be permitted to state other circumstances which tho' not in legal proof, are either of such public notoriety as to render legal proof unnecessary, or so vouched to the Committee as to leave them in no doubt of the truth of them.

"It has become a practice for many of the privateers of the Belligerent Powers, to send into Port all American Vessels they meet with, bound from any of the French Ports in the West Indies, to the United States, and it is positively asserted that the owners of some of them have given general instructions to their Captains to that effect—And tho' many of those Vessels have been afterwards liberated, yet the loss by plunder, detention and expence is so great as to render it ruinous to the American Owner—In many cases where the Cargoes have been valuable, the owners of the Privateers after acquittal have lodged appeals which they never intended to prosecute, but merely with a view of getting the property into their hands upon a valuation made so unfairly, as to insure them a considerable profit, even if they should be finally made liable.

"Fourteen days only are allowed to an American owner to make his claim which renders it impossible for him except he is on the spot, and every difficulty which a combination of interested persons can devise is thrown in the way to prevent his getting security; and in few instances can it be done but by making over his Vessel & Cargo to the Securities, and thereby subjecting himself to the heavy additional charge of Commission, Insurance &c.—it may be added that the most barefaced bribery is sometimes practised to prevail on unwary boys or those who know little of the obligation of an Oath to induce them to give testimony in favor of the Captors.

"Beside the cases here enumerated the committee have information of a number of vessels belonging to this Port, being captured, and carried into different Ports, but as the legal proofs are not come forward they forbear to mention them.

"It is proper however for them to add that besides the loss of property occasioned by those unjust captures & detentions the masters and crews of the Vessels are frequently subjected to insults & outrages that must be shocking to Americans. Of this the case of Captn Wallace is an instance, there are others within the knowledge of the committee of which they only wait the legal proof to lay them before the Secretary.[5]

"To this list of grievances the Committee are sorry to find it their duty to add that by reason of the vexation loss and outrages suffered by the Merchants of the United States it's commerce already begins to languish, and it's products are likely to be left upon the hands of those who raise them. Prudent men doubt the propriety of hazarding their property when they find that the strictest conformity with the laws of nations, or of their own Country will not protect them from the rapacity of men who are neither restrained by the principles of honor, nor by Laws sufficiently coercive to give security to those who are not subjects of the same Government.

"The Committee conclude this representation with an assurance that they have in no degree exaggerated in the statement they have made, and that they will continue to communicate all such information as they may further receive, of which nature before the closing of this report they are sorry to add is that of the irruptions of the Algerines from the Mediterranean in consequence of a truce concluded with that regency it is said by the British Minister on behalf of Portugal & Holland[6]—This alarming event to which some American Ships we hear have already become Victims is of so distressing a nature as must soon deprive us of some of the most lucrative branches of our Commerce, if not speedily checked or prevented. The immediate rise it has produced in Insurance and the fears it may instil into our Seamen and Commanders are of a nature highly deserving the serious consideration of Government, on whose protection and zeal for the interests commercial and agricultural of the Country the committee implicitly rely." [7]

In a supplementary letter the Committee of Philadelphia, make this conclusion; ["]that the cases, which they recite, and others less formally announced serve to shew, that there are frequent instances of suppression of papers, registers &c: very prejudicial to our shipping⟨,⟩ on their trials, and of injuries—by the destruction of Letters, to the general correspondence of the Country with foreign nations." [8]

When we examine the documents, which have been transmitted from different parts of the Union, we find the British, the French, the Spaniards and the Dutch, charged with attacks upon our Commerce.

It is urged against the British—

1. That their privateers plunder the American Vessels; throw them out of their cour⟨s⟩e, by forcing them upon groundless suspicions into ports other than those to which they were destined; detain them even after the hope of a regular confiscation is abandoned; by their negligence, while they hold the possession, expose the cargoes to damage, and the vessels to destruction—and maltreat their crews.

2. That British Ships of war, have forcibly seized mariners belonging to American vessels, and in one instance under the protection of a Portuguese fort.

3. That by British regulations and practice our Corn and provisions are driven from the ports of France; and restricted to ports of the British & those of their friends. [9]

4. That our vessels are not permitted to go from the British ports in the Islands, without giving security, (which is not attainable but with difficulty and expense), for the discharge of the Cargo in some other British or a neutral port.

5. That without the imputation of a contraband trade as defined by the law of nations, [10] our vessels are captured for carrying on a commercial intercourse with the French West Indies,

altho' it is tolerated by the laws of the French Republic: and that for this extraordinary conduct no other Excuse is alledged than that by some edict of a King of France, this intercourse was prohibited—and

6.   That the conduct of the British Admiralty in the Islands, is impeachable for an excess of rigor, and a departure from strict judicial purity; and the expences of our appeal to England too heavy to be encountered, under all the circumstances of discouragement.

Against the French it is urged.

1.   That their privateers harrass our trade no less than those of the British.

2.   That two of their Ships of war have committed enormities on our vessels.

3.   That their Courts of Admiralty are guilty of equal oppression.

4.   That besides these points of accusation, which are common to the French and British—the former have infringed the Treaty between the United States and them, by subjecting to seizure and condemnation our vessels, trading with their enemies in merchandize which that treaty declares not to be contraband; and under circumstances not forbidden by the law of Nations.[11]

5.   That a very detrimental embargo has been laid upon large numbers of American vessels in the French ports; (There is reason to believe that the embargo was removed in December last, and the detention compensated by an order of the Committee of public safety in France)[12]—and

6.   That a Contract with the French Government for Coin had been discharged with depreciated assignats.[13]

Against the Spaniards the outrages of privateers are urged; and against the Dutch one condemnation in the Admiralty is insisted to be unwarrantable.

Under this complication of mischief, which persecutes our commerce, I beg leave Sir, to submit to your consideration, whether as far as facts may justify, representations ought not to be immediately pressed upon the foreign Governments in those of the preceding cases for which they are responsible. Among these I class, first the violences perpetrated by public Ships of war; secondly prohibitions or regulations, inconsistent with the law of nations; thirdly the improper conduct of Courts; fourthly, infractions of treaty; fifthly—the imposition of embargoes; and sixthly—the breach of public Contracts. How far a government is liable to redress the rapine of privateers, depends upon the peculiarities of the case. It is incumbent upon it, however, to keep its Courts freely open; and to secure an impartial hearing, to the injured applicant. If the rules, prescribed to privateers, be too loose, and opportunities of plunder or ill treatment be provoked from that cause, or from the prospect of impunity, it is impossible to be too strenuous in remonstrating against this formidable evil.

Thus, Sir, have I reduced to general heads the particular complaints; without making any inquiry into the facts beyond the Allegations of the parties interested.

I will only add, that your message seems to promise to Congress some statement upon these subjects.[14] I have the honor, sir, to be with the highest respect yr mo. ob. serv.

Edm: Randolph

True copy
Geo: Taylor Jr. C.C.D.S.[15]

DS, DNA: RG 46, Third Congress, 1793–95, Senate Records of Legislative Proceedings, President's Messages; LB, DNA: RG 59, Domestic Letters; LB, DNA: RG 233, First Congress, 1789–91, House Records of the Office of the Clerk, Reports from Executive Departments.

1. Thomas Jefferson included the notification announcement in a circular letter of 27 Aug. 1793 that was addressed to specific American merchants in thirteen states and also widely printed in the newspapers (*Jefferson Papers*, 26:767–69).

2. Randolph succeeded Thomas Jefferson as secretary of state on 2 Jan. 1794 (Randolph to GW, 2 Jan. 1794).

3. The original letter from the Philadelphia committee has not been identified.

4. The following seven paragraphs are in a different clerk's handwriting.

5. This case may be that of William Wallace, master of the schooner *Dispatch* of Virginia, which was captured in October 1793, according to an article in the 22 Oct. 1793 issue of the *Gazette of the United States* (Philadelphia).

6. On the British role in obtaining a truce between Portugal and Algiers, which left American shipping in the Atlantic Ocean vulnerable to seizure, see n.9 of Tobias Lear to GW, 4 February. Great Britain did not negotiate a truce between the Netherlands and Algiers at this time.

7. The handwriting reverts at this point to that of the original clerk.

8. The supplementary letter has not been identified. The punctuation in angle brackets is from the letterbook at DNA: RG 233.

9. For the British order-in-council of 8 June 1793, which prohibited the shipment of U.S. corn, flour, or meal to France or French colonies, see *ASP, Foreign Relations,* 1:240.

10. This is a reference to Emmerich de Vattel's three-volume work, which was published in English as *The Law of Nations; or Principles of the Law of Nature: Applied to the Conduct and to the Affairs of Nations and Sovereigns* (London, 1760).

11. For the 1778 Treaty of Amity and Commerce between France and the United States, see Miller, *Treaties,* 2:3–34.

12. For French decrees currently affecting U.S. merchants, see the enclosed "translation of the French act of navigation," enclosed in Randolph's letter to the U.S. Senate of 28 Jan. (*ASP, Foreign Relations,* 1:316–23).

13. The contract for payment in specie, and not in paper assignats, has not been identified.

14. GW enclosed this letter in his letter to the U.S. Senate and House of Representatives of 5 March.

15. Taylor was the chief clerk at the Department of State, and the attestation and signature are his.

From Reuben Harvey

Respected Friend,   Cork [Ireland] 3d March 1794

Unwilling to break in upon thy Time which is so precious at this critical period, I have check'd a very ardent desire of addressing thee those some Months past, but as I conceive it my duty (considering the love & affection I have for America) to lay before thee some few observations that have occurr'd & impress'd my Mind, I trust there needs no farther apology for the liberty now taken.[1] I may therefore say that there is, in my poor opinion, a necessity for a residing American Consul in Ireland, And that such Consul should be a Native of America, For want of one, since my friend Knox's departure, many Ships & Vessels belonging to the United states have suffer'd injurys & insults from British Officers, by having their Seamen impress'd, & cajoled to enter in Men of War, whereby considerable losses befel the Owners, which would in a good degree have been prevented, had a Consul been in the Kingdom to interfere;[2] I believe there were many instances of most intolerable insolence & abuse offer'd American Masters of Vessels by Lieuts. & other Officers employ'd on the Impress Service; An unreasonable Quarantine was enforced here for many Months on all Vessels from New york, tho' no malignant Sickness prevail'd there, And it was only taken off about 2 Weeks ago, in consequence I am apt to think of a letter which I wrote to Thos Pinckney Esqr. the 28. of January, requesting his application to the British Minister (who governs every material Matter in both Kingdoms) to have the Quarentine removed, as the answer which I received dated Feby 7th mention'd that he expected Administration would shortly order it to cease.[3] It however gives me concern to inform thee that on another Affair of some Moment which I had occasion to trouble the Envoy about he has not been even so condescending as to answer any of the letters written him the 4: to the 13: Ultimo—The Affair is this; About 6 Weeks ago an American Brig, the Hannah of Kennebeck Wm Springer Mastr, laden with 280 pipes of Brandy from Bordx for Philadelphia, put into Kinsale a little leaky & rather short of Provisions, In 2 days after her arrival there she was seized by the Govr. Col. Browne, on an information, as he alleges, that the Cargoe was ship'd by Deputys of the National Convention, & that the Consignee at Phila. Thos Lee has been dead some time; The Brandy is mark'd T.L.[4] An Englishman named Thos Cox escaped by the aid of Capt. Springer, in the attire of a Sailor, And he is suspected of giving this information, as he pretends that the Convention deprived him of considerable property, & he hopes to recover some or all of it out of the present contested Cargoe, which is worth above £10.000 Stg: From what I can gather it seems likely that the Natl Convention ship'd this Brandy, & three more very large Cargoes at same time (all consign'd to Thos Lee) for remittance to Congress or for some reciprocal Concern of the two Governments, as the quantity of Brandy was very great in these 4 Vessels; I presume not far short of 2000 pipes.[5] I suggested to Thos Pinckney Esqr. that if he could prevail on the British Minister to direct a suspension of procedure respecting the Hannah's Cargoe until he could hear from Congress, it might answer a good purpose, as thereby the fact would be ascertain'd, but he has disregarded the Master's & my letters, And I have just now received a letter from the poor Man, acquainting me of the Business being put into the Proctor's hands in order to proceed, so that there needs no foresight to see that Condemnation will ensue, for Oaths in these Cases are easily had, & the temptation of Gain predominates in most trials of the kind, throughout the British Dominions, which I am grieved to observe has been fatally felt by too many suffering Americans. Indeed I cannot help (through long affection) saying that I was astonish'd at seeing American Ships seized & their Cargoes landed in England, when found carrying Wheat & flour, the produce of America, to France where they had been accustom'd to carry such Goods for many Years—I say I was astonish'd to find no publick remonstrance or retaliation or cessation of intercourse adopted by America, & I am convinc'd that if on the first capture, instant satisfaction had been insisted on, England would have relaxed & your Colours have been respected, equally with Russia & other Neutral Powers in the Years 1780 &c. Possibly your Patience will ultimately prove a wise Measure, & that the horrid plan (whoever effected it) of the Algerine business[6] may cause you to look for & to obtain ample Satisfaction which is the ardent wish of A true friend to America And Thy sincere Well Wisher

Reuben Harvey

P.S. The 3 other Vessels with Brandy, were
Ship Aurora
Ship Merchant
Brig Columbia[7]

ALS, DNA: RG 59, Miscellaneous Letters. GW's docket reads, "Receiv'd 21st of May 1794. refered to the Secy of State May 22d." No reply from Randolph to Harvey has been identified.

1. Merchant Reuben Harvey had been corresponding with GW for several years, beginning with his letter to GW of 12 Feb. 1783 (DLC:GW). The previous extant letter from Harvey is that of 1 March 1792.

2. On the departure of William Knox, see Thomas Jefferson to GW, 19 Aug. 1792, and n.2. Joseph Wilson was nominated on 28 May to be U.S. consul at Dublin (*U.S. Senate Executive Journal*, 1:158).

3. The quarantine on vessels sailing from New York may have been a response to the yellow fever epidemic that took place in Philadelphia during the late summer and fall of 1793. Harvey's correspondence with U.S. minister Thomas Pinckney, which is mentioned throughout this letter, has not been identified. William Pitt the Younger served as prime minister of Great Britain from 1783 until 1801.

4. The brig *Hannah* was under the command of Capt. William Springer of Pittson, Maine, which is located on the Kennebec River (*Daily Advertiser* [Philadelphia], 16 June 1792). This ship was one of many American vessels whose presence at the French port of Bordeaux was noted in the 17 Feb. 1794 issue of the *Philadelphia Gazette and Universal Daily Advertiser*. The port of Kinsale, Cork County, is on the south coast of Ireland. Browne probably was the British officer in command of Fort Charles, at the head of Kinsale harbor. The intended recipient of the brandy, Thomas Lee, has not been identified.

5. A pipe is a large cask used especially for wine and oil and often of a capacity equal to 2 hogsheads, or approximately 126 gallons.

6. On the British role in obtaining a truce between Portugal and Algiers, which left American shipping in the Atlantic Ocean vulnerable to seizure, see n.9 of Tobias Lear to GW, 4 February.

7. The ship *Aurora* sailed under Capt. John Seaward of Kennebunk, Me., the ship *Merchant* under Capt. John Jones of Portland, Me., and the brig *Columbia* under Capt. William Sole of Freeport, Me. (*Philadelphia Gazette and Universal Daily Advertiser,* 17 Feb. 1794; *General Advertiser* [Philadelphia], 18 Feb. 1794).

To John Jay and Rufus King

Philadelphia 3d March 1794

I certify, that the transcript below, which was permitted to be extracted from a report of the Secretary of State to the President of the United States, (dated the 10th of July 1793) by the Secretaries of Treasury and War, and inserted by them in a statement of certain facts published in Dunlap & Claypoole's American Daily Advertiser No. 4581. is a correct quotation from the original.

"On repeating to him" (the Governor, Mr Jefferson says) "and Mr Dallas what Mr Genet had said, we found that it agreed in many particulars with what he had said to Mr Dallas: but Mr Dallas mentioned somethings which he had not said to me, and particularly his declaration that he would appeal from the President to the People."[1]

B. D.
Secy to the P.U.S.

The above certificate was given to Mr Jay, Chief Justice of the United States, and Mr King, Senator from the State of New York, upon the Express condition that it should not be published, nor shewn, during my Continuance in the Administration of the Government of the United States; unless very imperious circumstances should arise to call it forth: nor then, or at any time thereafter, without first obtaining my consent. The object for requiring, & the motive to granting it, being, that it might remain with them as an evidence that they were not the *Authors* of the report "That Mr Genet had declared he would appeal from the President to the People."[2]

Go: Washington

ADS, NjP: de Coppet Collection. GW's docket reads, "Certificate &ca. To— Mr John Jay—& Mr Rufus King 3d March 1794."

1. For the report from which the following extract was made by Alexander Hamilton and Henry Knox, see Thomas Jefferson's Memorandum of a Conversation with Edmond Charles Genet, 10 July 1793 (*Jefferson Papers*, 26:463–67). The extract was included in an article printed on page 3 of the 17 Dec. 1793 issue, number 4581, of *Dunlap and Claypoole's American Daily Advertiser* (Philadelphia). The conversations alluded to in this extract are Jefferson's discussion with Pennsylvania governor Thomas Mifflin and Alexander J. Dallas and an earlier one between Edmond Genet and Dallas in which, allegedly, Genet made his controversial declaration.

2. GW personally handed the certificate to Rufus King on this same date (see GW to Knox, 15 Feb., and notes).

From James Muir

Sir: Alexandria [Va.] 3d March 1794

I have been favoured with yours of the 24th February; and this morning have seen your Manager Mr Pearce who discharged your annual donation for the education of Orphan Children or of the Children of indigent Parents who are unable to be at the expence themselves.[1]

The object of this charity is very worthy, as it rescues from ignorance a considerable number, and lays the foundation for their becoming useful Citizens.

I am sorry I cannot give you a particular account of this institution from its Commencement.[2] Mr McWhir who formerly had the direction of it, has removed to Georgia and no record remains from whence I can draw any information. I have reason to believe it was then conducted well. Mr McMath who taught the School was an eminent Teacher and produced accurate scholars.[3]

Since Mr McWhir went away the Academy has been on the wane, nor have the greatest exertions of the Trustees been able to produce a Teacher for the Washington School of any ability. Parents in good circumstances are unwilling that their Children should associate with those of a lower Class. This operates against the Washington School, and prevents its increase[.] Fifty Pounds alone will not procure the labours of an Accurate Scholar. Mr McWhir had address to keep out of view that they were poor Scholars, beside the whole direction of the Academy was in his hands. Since his departure the Trustees have thought proper that each School depend on itself without any Superintendent.[4] The Consequence to the Washington School has been unfavourable. A Twelve months advertisement in the Paper has not brought us an able Teacher.[5]

The Charity has certainly been useful:

J. Wiley went from this school, whose improvement has been such that Dr D. Stewart I am told has employed him as a Tutor to his Children.[6]

Thomas Sanford, son of a widow in Town has finished his education here with much applause.

At present the school consists of

1　John Smith, of indigent Parents, who is attentive, and makes progress.

2　Thomas Lowe, an Orphan who improves.

3.　Samuel Benton, his mother a widow, and indigent, his diligence is commendable.

4.　John Carey an orphan.

5　Henry Mars an Orphan.

These two have attended Ill during the winter being badly Clothed.

6　James Grimes, of indigent Parents, he is regular in his attendance and studious.

7　Thomas Pindal, his father dead, had fallen from easy to needy circumstances.

8　John ⎫

9.　Mary ⎬ Farmer a Widow's Children.

Both have made great progress in reading, writing and Cyphering, and are very deserving.

10.　Mary Stewart daughter of an Indigent widow, her progress is considerable.

11　William ⎫

12　John ⎬ Moore children of a widow beginning Spelling only, and their Letters.

13　William ⎫

14　Benjamin ⎬ Morley, their mother a widow a few miles from Town, the Children attend well, and begin to learn.

Such the present State of the School. The above are all who have lately been there, Of that number four only are advanced beyond their Spelling-book. Application is now making to the Trustees for the admission of two or three more.

I am sorry to say that the reputation of the School is not now, and has not for some time been such as I could wish. The cause I have already discovered.

Great benefit have numbers derived from the School, and now derive, but by no means such as ought to be. Painful is it to discover truths of this kind; nothing but your express desire could now have induced to that discovery.

Could a way be devised for Clothing as well as educating these Children, and could a person be prevailed upon, who is capable of Educating them, to attend to this, it would bring the School into repute.

The Trustees will neglect nothing which may be in their power to promote it's advantage.

I shall urge at the first meeting of the Trustees to Try the benevolent in Town to Complete this institution, raising a fund to Clothe such as it may embrace: and rather than allow the institution to continue in disrepute, I shall offer the Trustees to take the School under my own immediate inspection, although Parochial duties have made it convenient for some time past to decline Teaching I shall not think of inconvenience where so excellent an object is in view.

courage in the field; wisdom in the Council, are advantageous to Society, but Charities especially of this kind, have advantages which are of a very eminent and peculiar nature.

Our Academy it is to be dreaded will come to nothing. The house is built on land Subject to ground-rent. Considerable back-rents are due. The Trustees have no fund to discharge these, or to prevented them from accumulating. The Price of Education of itself is thought burdensome, and the Parents have expressed an unwillingness to add to their expence, already too great, by contributing any thing for rent. The Proprietor threatens to enter on the house to secure himself. Should he do so, the Trustees cannot prevent him. This circumstance has discouraged the Trustees and weakened their exertions.

What ever becomes of the Academy our attention to the Washington-School, shal⟨l⟩ be unremitting—Nothing in my power Shall be wanting, and I shall take care for the future, whilst

I continue a Trustee, that an exact statement of the school be regularly sent you. With great respect your humble Servt

James Muir.

ALS, DLC:GW.

1. GW instructed William Pearce in a letter of 24 Feb. to pay £50 Virginia currency to Muir for the support of the Alexandria Academy. Pearce recorded this payment on 1 March (Mount Vernon Accounts).

2. The academy had its beginning in 1785 when the cornerstone for the proposed school was laid on the east side of Washington Street, between Duke and Wolfe streets, in Alexandria, Va. (Brockett, *Lodge of Washington,* 44–45). In October 1786, the Virginia legislature passed "An act for incorporating the Academy in the town of Alexandria" (*Va. Statutes,* 12:392–93).

3. On the move of prior headmaster William McWhir to Georgia, see GW to McWhir, 17 Feb. 1793, and n.3. Mr. McMath has not been identified.

4. The Alexandria Academy and the charity school, or the Washington Free School, were united under the direction of a superintendent until McWhir's departure; shared the same building; and were administered jointly by the same board of trustees. Students of the charity school, however, were taught separately from the paying students (William Buckner McGroarty, "Reverend James Muir, D. D., and Washington's Orphan Wards," *WMQ,* 2d. ser., 20:511–23, and McGroarty, "Alexandria Academy," *WMQ,* 2d. ser., 20:253–60).

5. According to this advertisement, first placed in the *Virginia Gazette and Alexandria Advertiser* on 14 March 1793, a "Teacher is wanted to take charge of the Mathamatical School. He will be required to teach English, grammatically, Writing, Arithmetic, and the several Branches of Mathematics. Ample vouchers, respecting the moral character of the Candidate, will be obviously necessary."

6. Mr. J. Wiley, who may have served as a tutor for Dr. David Stuart's children, has not been identified.

Letter not found: from William Pearce, 3 March 1794. GW wrote Pearce on 9 March that "Your letter of the 3d instt is this moment received."

From Edmund Randolph

[Philadelphia] Monday Evening. 3d Mar. 94.

E. Randolph has the honor of informing the President, that he has shewn the draught of the letter, to Colo. Hamilton who approved it, except in a word, or two. The commercial resolutions being postponed to Monday, E.R. will take, with the President's permission, to morrow, in order to revise the letter, and examine some fresh complaints, which have come in to-day.[1]

AL, DNA: RG 59, Miscellaneous Letters; LB, DNA: RG 59, GW's Correspondence with His Secretaries of State.

1. The draft may have been Randolph's letter to GW of 2 March, which summarized merchant complaints about foreign interference with American trade and which GW enclosed in his letter to the U.S. Senate and House of Representatives of 5 March. The resolutions postponed until Monday, 10 March, were those introduced by James Madison on 3 January. These seven resolutions were designed to create a policy of commercial retaliation against the British and were prompted, in part, by British interference with American shipping (*Annals of Congress,* 3d. Cong., 155–56, 484–98).

From the United States House
of Representatives

Monday the 3d of March 1794.
Congress of the United States: In the House of Representatives,
Resolved, that the President of the United States be requested to cause to be laid before this House, a statement of the gross sum of money, which has been advanced by the United States, in making presents to the Creek and Cherokee Indians, since the treaty made at New York;[1] also, all expences incurred, and sums of money expended in making the said treaty.[2]

Extract from the Journal
John Berkley—Clerk.

LB, DLC:GW.

1. The Treaty of New York, with the Creek Indians, was signed on 7 Aug. 1790 (Kappler, *Indian Treaties,* 2:25–29). Following GW's instructions, Bartholomew Dandridge, Jr., enclosed this resolution with a brief cover letter of 4 March to Henry Knox requesting that the secretary of war provide the desired statements (DLC:GW).

2. Knox enclosed "A statement of the gross sum of money . . . and also of the amount of presents. . . ." with a brief cover letter to the U.S. House of Representatives of 10 March. According to the statement of 10 March, the expenses of the Creek treaty were $20,583.90. Since the treaty, "Indian goods and presents" for the Creeks and Cherokees had cost $22,279.99 and $18,217.56, respectively. The grand total came to $61,081.45. Knox noted that supplies forwarded to William Blount, governor of the Southwest Territory, "for the Cherokees, in the latter end of the year 1793, amounting to $5,230.75, and which were, by the last information, still remaining on hand, are included in the above, subject to the disposal of the Governor" (*ASP, Indian Affairs,* 1:476).

To the United States Senate
and House of Representatives

United States 3d March 1794.
Gentlemen of the Senate, and of the House of Representatives.

I transmit to you, an extract from a letter of mister Short, relative to our affairs with Spain; and copies of two letters from our Minister at Lisbon, with their enclosures, containing intelligence from Algiers. The whole of these communications are made in confidence, except the passage in Mr Short's letter, which respects the Spanish Convoy.[1]

Go: Washington

LS, DNA: RG 46, Third Congress, 1793–95, Senate Records of Legislative Proceedings, President's Messages; LB, DNA: RG 233, Third Congress, 1793–95, House Records of Legislative Proceedings, Journals; LB, DLC:GW.

1. For the extract of the letter from William Short to the secretary of state of 6 Nov. 1793, and for the letters and enclosures from David Humphreys to the secretary of state of 19 and 23 Nov. 1793, see *ASP, Foreign Relations*, 1:413–18; see also Randolph to GW, 27 Feb. (3d letter) and 28 Feb. 1794.

From Edmund Randolph

Sir   Philadelphia March 4. 1794.

I have to request you to issue a warrant on the treasury of the United States for the payment of so much of the sum, voted for the relief of the inhabitants of St Domingo, as you mean *now* to distribute. You will be pleased, sir, to recollect, that you determined the other day to apportion ten thousand dollars only. Since that time, a report has been made from Delaware, and an additional one from Connecticut, which will probably render it expedient to take for the former five hundred dollars, and for the latter One hundred dollars in addition, from the remaining five thousand dollars.[1] I beg leave to suggest the following form of a warrant.

United States March 4. 1794.

To the Secretary of the treasury.

Pay to the Secretary of State, in pursuance of the act providing for the relief of such of the inhabitants of St Domingo, residing within the United States, as may be found in want of support, ten thousand six hundred dollars; to be by him remitted according to his report to me on the 27th day of february last, and his letter to me of this date.

Given under my hand this fourth day of March 1794.[2]

I have the honor sir, to be with the highest respect yr mo. ob. serv.

Edm: Randolph.

ALS, DNA: RG 59, Miscellaneous Letters; LB, DNA: RG 59, Reports of the Secretary of State to the President and Congress; LB, DNA: RG 59, GW's Correspondence with His Secretaries of State.

1. "An Act providing for the relief of such of the inhabitants of Saint Domingo, resident within the United States, as may be found in want of support," 12 Feb. 1794, appropriated an amount not exceeding $15,000 for this purpose (*Stat.* 6:13). In his first letter to GW of 27 Feb. Randolph suggested that only $10,000 be distributed at first, thus reserving $5,000 "to redress any inequalities, which may be found on a more precise knowledge of the numbers." For the report from Delaware and the funds distributed as of 11 April, see Randolph's second letter to GW of 27 Feb., and n.1 of Cabinet Opinion, 22 April. The report from Connecticut has not been identified.

2. This suggested form was used for GW's letter to Alexander Hamilton of this date (LB, DLC:GW). The form does not appear in the letter book for GW's Correspondence with His Secretaries of State.

From Edmund Randolph

Philadelphia March 4th 1794.

The Secretary of State, having reviewed the Consular Appointments under the United States, has the honor of reporting to the President, as follows.

1. The Consul at Falmouth in Great Britain, has been commissioned in the name of *Edward* Fox; but he writes that his true name, is *Robert Weare* Fox. He was promised by the Secretary of State on the 12th of Septr 1793, that the error should be corrected.[1]

2. A letter has been received thro' Mr Pinckney, from a very respectable man in England; recommending a Mr Carpzaw,[2] as a proper person to be appointed a Consul at Bremen, one of the Hanseatic towns. It is certain, that some trade is carried on from the United States with Bremen. But Hamburgh where Mr John Parish is already fixed, as Consul seems to occupy the principal part of our trade in that quarter; and until

more accurate information can be obtained, whether the connection requires a Consul, the multiplication of useless Offices is of itself an objection. This Idea is confirmed by the opinion of an intelligent Mercantile Man in the City of Philadelphia, who doubts the extension, if not the continuance of our trade with Bremen.[3]

3. In the Consular establishments the following vacancies have occurred.

1. In Nantz by the resignation of Burral Carnes.[4]

2. In Rouen by the settlement of Nathaniel Barrett at New York.[5]

3. In Dublin, by the resignation of William Knox.[6]

4. In St Domingo by the resignation of Sylvanus Bourne.[7]

5. In Santa Cruz, by the resignation of James Yard;[8] and

6. In Surinam by the abandonment of Ebenezer Brush.[9]

It is submitted to the President, whether he will fill up the whole, or which of these vacancies.[10] An inquiry has been made into the necessity of increasing our Consulates in France. But under the present circumstances, and when it is probable, that new arrangements will be expedient, if the treaty of Commerce with that nation should be remodelled;[11] it is perhaps sufficient to do no more, than to supply the existing deficiencies.

Edm: Randolph.

LS, DNA: RG 59, Miscellaneous Letters; LB, DNA: RG 59, Reports of the Secretary of State to the President and Congress; LB, DNA: RG 59, GW's Correspondence with His Secretaries of State.

1. For the error in Fox's appointment, see GW to U.S. Senate, 19 Feb. 1793. GW corrected this error in his letter to the U.S. Senate of 29 May 1794. In a letter to Fox of 12 Sept. 1793, former secretary of state Thomas Jefferson promised that the error in Fox's "Christian name shall be duly attended to for correction at the next session of Congress" (source note, Circular to Certain Councils and Vice-Consuls, 12 Sept. 1793, *Jefferson Papers,* 27:95–96).

2. This name appears as Carpzow in the Reports of the Secretary of State to the President and Congress.

3. The letter recommending Mr. Carpzaw that Thomas Pinckney, the U.S. minister to Great Britain, forwarded to Randolph has not been identified. Bremen, a port city located on the Weser River in northwestern Germany, was at one time an independent city and a member of the Hanseatic League, a union of merchant associations from northern Germany and other nations along the North and Baltic Seas that flourished for over three centuries, beginning in the thirteenth. Contrary to Randolph's advice, GW appointed merchant Christoph Diedrich Arnold Delius (1742–1819), a native of Bremen, as the first U.S. consul at that port. After an unsuccessful business ven-

ture in the United States from 1783 to 1785, as an agent for the Bremen firm of Heymann & Talla, Delius returned to Bremen for a brief period and then went back to the United States, where he became a naturalized citizen in 1794 before returning to Bremen to fulfill his duties as consul (Delius to Benjamin Franklin, 7 Feb. 1783, *Franklin Papers*, 39:145–48; Sam A. Mustafa, "Arnold Delius and the Hanseatic 'Discovery of America,'" *German History* (2000), 18:40–59; GW to U.S. Senate, 28 May 1794).

4. On the resignation of Burrell Carnes, a native of Massachusetts, see Joseph Fenwick to Jefferson, 16 July 1792, (*Jefferson Papers*, 24:233). In 1793, Carnes was a merchant and paper manufacturer at 71 South Second Street in Philadelphia (*Philadelphia Directory, 1793*, 21).

5. In Memorandum on Consuls and Consular Appointments of 15 Feb. 1793, Jefferson noted that Barrett had "abandoned" his consulate at Rouen, France, and had "settled at New York" (*Jefferson Papers*, 25:202–3).

6. On William Knox's resignation as consul at the port of Dublin, Ireland, see n.2 of Jefferson to GW, 19 Aug. 1792.

7. For the resignation of Sylvanus Bourne as consul at Saint Domingue, see Bourne to GW, 28 Dec. 1791. GW appointed Bourne vice-consul at Amsterdam, Netherlands, later this year (GW to U.S. Senate, 28 May 1794).

8. According to Thomas Jefferson's Draft Memorandum on Consular Vacancies of 21 Nov. 1791, Philadelphia resident James Yard was a native of New Jersey, "wealthy, and connected by marriage" to the governor of St. Croix (Santa Cruz) in the Dutch West Indies, now the Virgin Islands. After receiving his consular appointment in February 1791, Yard offered his resignation in a letter to Thomas Jefferson of 30 Oct. 1792 (*Jefferson Papers*, 19:313–14, 24:545). Shortly afterwards, he advertised "PIMENTO and St. Croix SUGAR" for sale at 79 Arch Street, Philadelphia (*General Advertiser* [Philadelphia], 5 Nov. 1792). After Yard's resignation, GW appointed Henry Cooper of Pennsylvania as the consul at St. Croix, and as of November 1793, Cooper was on that island fulfilling his consular obligations (GW to U.S. Senate, 19 Feb. 1793; Cooper to Jefferson, 12 Nov. 1793, *Jefferson Papers*, 27:351).

9. On Ebenezer Brush's apparent abandonment of his consulate, see Jefferson's Circular to Consuls and Vice-Consuls of 31 May 1792 (source note, *Jefferson Papers*, 23:619).

10. The vacant positions at Rouen, Saint Domingue, and Surinam remained unfilled. For the appointment of Pierre Frédéric Dobrée and Joseph Wilson, respectively, to the vacant positions at Nantes and Dublin, see GW to U.S. Senate, 28 May 1794.

11. For the 1778 Treaty of Amity and Commerce with France, see Miller, *Treaties*, 2:3–34.

To John Jay

Dear Sir,   Philadelphia 5th March 1794.
    I thank you for the Nankeen Cotton-seed with which you had the goodness to furnish me. It shall be sent to Mount Vernon

with orders to my Gardener to be particularly attentive thereto, but with little hope, I confess, of success; that climate & country being too high & cold for this plant.[1]

The common cotten has frequently been tried on my estate, but hardly ever escaped the frost, of either Spring or Autumn. In the lower parts of Virginia where the climate is milder, and the soil has a larger proportion of sand in it, I have no doubt of its answering; and, accordingly, will furnish a gentleman of my acquaintance (living in that part of the state) with a few of the Nankeen Seed.[2] With very sincere esteem & regard I am—Dear Sir Your Obedt & Affecte Servt

Go: Washington

ALS (photocopy), ViMtvL.

1. For the letter accompanying the cotton seed, see Jay to GW, 1 March. GW forwarded part of the seed and provided instructions for its planting, in a letter of 16–17 March to his estate manager, William Pearce.

2. GW sent the remainder of the seed with his letter to Edmund Pendleton of 17 March.

Bartholomew Dandridge, Jr., to Henry Knox

United States 5. March 1794.

By the President's order Bw Dandridge has the honor to return to the Secy of War the letter of mr Seagrove of the 25 Decr 93 with its enclosures. Some parts thereof appearing to require particular attention, the President requests the Secretary to consider what is proper to be done in relation thereto.[1]

Bw Dandridge S.P.U.S.

ALS, DLC:GW; LB, DLC:GW.

1. The enclosed letter from Indian agent James Seagrove to Knox, written from the Creek village of Tuckabatchie on 25 Dec. 1793, has not been found (*JPP*, 288). For Knox's response, see his letter to GW of 6 March.

From Edmund Pendleton

Dear Sir   Virga March 5th 1794.

Unwilling as I am to trouble you with Applications respecting the Appointments to Public Offices, I feel it a duty I am inclined to fulfill, to mention my Nephew Mr Nathaniel Pendleton, the present Fedral District Judge of Georgia; who, having heard that you intended to supply the next Vacancy in the Supreme Court, by appointment of a resident of that state, wishes to be considered as a Candidate for that Office, and as such to be recommended to your notice.[1] He supposes that his only Competitor will be a Mr Houston, the State Chief Justice, before whom he thinks he stands in Grade, and modestly wishes to be refer'd to the Professional Gentlemen acquainted with both, for information as to Their comparative legal Abilities, & mentions amongst others Mr Baldwin, a Member of Congress from the State, as a good Judge & has an intimate knowledge of both.[2] Having thus mentioned him, I have only to Add that I am far from wishing him Success, unless the public good will be at least as well answered by him as another, but in that case shall esteem the prefference to him as a Singular favor to Dr Sir, Yr mo. Affe. Obt Servt

Edmd. Pendleton

ALS, NjMoHP.

1. The next vacancy on the Supreme Court did not occur until 1795, when Chief Justice John Jay of New York resigned (Jay to GW, 29 June 1795, DLC: GW). Nathaniel Pendleton never received an appointment to the Supreme Court, and the first justice from Georgia was James Moore Wayne, whom Andrew Jackson appointed in 1835.

2. For previous mention of John Houstoun as a potential candidate for appointment to the Supreme Court, see James Gunn's letters to GW of 7 March 1791 and 11 Feb. 1793. Abraham Baldwin currently was serving his third term in the U.S. House of Representatives.

To Charles Thomson

Dear Sir   Philadelphia 5th March 1794

Weeks have passed since I finished reading the first part of your translation of the Septuagent;[1] but having neglected (when I had the pleasure to see you last) to ascertain the medium through which I was to return it, and being unwilling to hazard the production to an uncertain conveyance, I give this letter to the Post Office in hopes of its reaching you, & of my receiving the information above.[2] 'Tis unnecessary to add that with much truth I am—Dear Sir Your Obedt Hble Servt

Go: Washington

ALS, Phi: Dreer Collection. The postal stamps on the cover read "5 MR" and "FREE." GW addressed the cover to "Charles Thompson, Esqr. Chester County."

1. The Septuagint is the oldest extant Greek translation of the Hebrew Bible, circa 250 B.C. Thomson later published a four-volume work entitled *The Holy Bible, Containing the Old and New Covenant, Commonly Called the Old and New Testament: Translated from the Greek* (Philadelphia, 1808).

2. Thomson currently resided near Philadelphia, at Harriton, his estate in Montgomery County, Pennsylvania.

To the United States Senate

Gentlemen of the Senate,　　　　United States 5. March 1794.

I nominate Josiah Tatnall, of Georgia, to be Marshal of and for the Georgia District; vice Robert Forsyth, deceased.[1] and

Laurence Muse, of Virginia, to be Collector for the District of Tappahannock; and Inspector of the revenue for the port of Tappahannock; vice Hudson Muse, superceded.[2]

Go: Washington

LS, DNA: RG 46, Third Congress, 1793–95, Senate Records of Executive Proceedings, President's Messages—Executive Nominations; LB, DLC:GW.

1. Josiah Tattnall (1764–1803) was born on the family estate of Bonaventure, near Savannah, Georgia. He enlisted in the Continental army in 1782, and after the war, as an officer in the state militia, he participated in expeditions against Creek Indians in 1788 and 1793. He later served in the Georgia House of Representatives, 1795–96, in the U.S. Senate, 1796–99, and as governor of Georgia, 1801–2.

2. On the removal of Hudson Muse from office for mismanagement of funds, and on the selection of Laurence Muse to replace him, see Hudson Muse to GW, 27 Jan., and Laurence Muse to GW, 1 February.

To the United States Senate
and House of Representatives

United States 5th March 1794
Gentlemen of the Senate, and of the House of Representatives.

The Secretary of State having reported to me upon the several complaints, which have been lodged in his office, against the vexations and spoliations on our commerce, since the commencement of the European war; I transmit to you a copy of his statement, together with the documents upon which it is founded.[1]

Go: Washington

LS, DNA: RG 46, Third Congress, 1793–95, Senate Records of Legislative Proceedings, President's Messages; LB, DNA: RG 233, Third Congress, 1793–95, House Records of Legislative Proceedings, Journals.

1. For the enclosed statement, see Edmund Randolph to GW, 2 March. The supporting documents have not been identified.

From Martin Van Butchell

Sir,   Mount-Street, London, 5 March, 1794.

I have a good Wife, and seven fine Children, (—healthy, well made—) four boys, and three Girls; the first born, a boy, full thirteen years old; the last born, a girl, just fourteen Months. I hope ere long we shall be all safe in the United States, for this Country is not the best place for brave fellows.

I have the pleasure to send this Letter and a parcel of News Papers, Pamphlets and Advertisements (—neatly sealed up—) by a well disposed young Man named Richard Rodgers, whom I cured of a Fistula about a year since. He was formerly employed in the farming line—latterly in a Sope Manufactory: Will bring with him Letters of Recommendation from his last Master, [   ] who was visiting America only ten Months ago.

Tho' my eldest son is not two Months more than thirteen years old, but Mind is so set upon going to America, that he would rather be there, bare foot, and penny less, than stay here. I took him on board the George Berkely, Captain Collet (—an American Vessel—) last Sunday, that he might learn how hard he must fare in the Steerage, but he has since cried very much, because his Mother wont let him go with Richard Rodgers.[1] I am, sir, Your respectful Servant,

Martin Van Butchell.

ALS, DLC:GW.

Martin Van Butchell (1735–1814) was a London dentist and maker of trusses as noted for his eccentricities as for his practice.

1. The *George Barclay,* under Capt. John Collet, arrived at Philadelphia in early May, having been at sea for forty-two days since leaving London. Richard Rodgers is not listed as one of the cabin passengers, but he may have been among the "32 in the steerage—all remarkably healthy" (*General Advertiser* [Philadelphia], 5 May 1794).

From Harriot Washington

Honord Uncle   Fredericksburg [Va.] March 5th 1794
It gives me pain to be obliged to apply to my dear Uncle, so soon after his kind present,[1] but embolden'd by your affectionate letter, I venture to ask you, if it is convenient, and you can spare the money, to let me have a peice of linnen, some dimmity to make me petticoat's and a great coat, I have not had a great coat since, the winter I spent at Shooters hill, mine is not entirely worn out, but it is so small, that I cant get it on.[2] I am not in immediate want of the linnen, but Aunt Lewis think's as it will take me a good while to make it up that if I could get it now, it would be better than some time hence.
Aunt Lewis join's me in love to you Aunt Washington and Nelly.[3] I am my dear Uncle Your affectionate Neice.
                                        Harriot Washington.

ALS, ViMtvL.

1. Harriot, who was now living with GW's sister Betty Washington Lewis in Fredericksburg, Va., had received a present from GW along with his letter to her of 3 Feb., which has not been found (Betty Washington Lewis to GW, 9 Feb. 1794).

2. It is not clear exactly when Harriot's coat was purchased, but she probably spent considerable time with distant cousins at the estate of Shuter's Hill, near Alexandria, Va., before living at Mount Vernon. On the shuttling of Harriot among various relatives after the death of her father, Samuel Washington, in 1781, and her residence at Mount Vernon, see source note, Harriot Washington to GW, 2 April 1790. In October 1792, Harriot left Mount Vernon to live with GW's sister (GW to Betty Washington Lewis, 7 Oct. 1792). According to two entries dated 11 March 1794 in GW's Household Accounts, GW paid $19.19 for "sundry articles" sent to Harriot and 25 cents for the freight to Fredericksburg of the box containing these articles.

3. Eleanor Parke "Nelly" Custis was the granddaughter of Martha Washington.

Bartholomew Dandridge, Jr., to Henry Knox

                                        United States 6. Mar: 1794.
By the President's order Bw Dandridge has the honor to transmit herewith enclosed, to the Secy of War a letter from the Governor of North Carolina, to the president; and sundry papers respecting the Spanish brig St Joseph.[1] The President

requests the Secretary to do with them what may be thought proper.²

Bw Dandridge S.P.U.S.

ADfS, DLC:GW; LB, DLC:GW.

1. The letter from Richard Dobbs Spaight to GW of 16 Feb., and its enclosures, concerned a Spanish request for restoration of the *San Josef* and its cargo.

2. In his letter to Spaight of 14 March, Knox acknowledged GW's receipt of the letter of 16 Feb. and its enclosures. "It is the instruction Sir of the President," Knox continued, "that the Marshal deliver up the money and other property belonging to the Spanish brig St Joseph without any deduction whatever. any claim he or any other person acting under your authority may have relatively to the said brig St Joseph must be properly authenticated & transmitted to this office where after examination it will be discharged.

"But any expenses incurred by Mr Jones agent of his Catholic majestys commissioners are not intended to be comprehended in this letter If such be founded they must be settled between the said commissioners & this government" (Nc-Ar: Governors' Letterbooks).

From Henry Knox

Sir,   War department March 6th 1794

I have the honor to submit the inclosed letter to Gove[r]nor Matthews relatively to the Indians in his possession requested by James Seagrove—Such other parts of Mr Seagroves letter, as require any further measures, will be considered & the result submitted to your consideration.¹ I have the honor to be with perfect respect Your obedient Servant

H. Knox

LS, DLC:GW; LB, DLC:GW.

1. Knox's letter of this date to Georgia governor George Mathews reads: "It appears by a letter from James Seagrove dated Tuccabackees, Upper Creeks, 7th of December that he is exceedingly desirous that the eight prisoners taken from the little Oakfuskie in September last by a party from the frontiers of Georgia should be instantly returned.

"It would appear from representations that the prisoners belonged to a Town under the direction of the White Lieutenant, who is esteemed one of our best friends in the Creek Nation.

"In addition to this circumstance, not only the release of all the white prisoners in the Creek Nation, but even the expected return of cordiality between the United States and the Creeks may be prevented by the continuing the Indian prisoners in their captivity.

"I am therefore instructed by the President of the United States to request that your Excellency would immediately cause the prisoners in question to be conveniently and safely transported to Fort Fidius upon the Oconnee, and there delivered to the commanding Officer for the purpose of being restored to their friends" (G-Ar: Georgia Executive Department, 1794–95). An unidentified letter from Indian agent James Seagrove to Knox of 25 Dec. 1793 was the reason for Knox's letter to Mathews (Bartholomew Dandridge, Jr., to Knox, 5 March 1794; *JPP*, 288).

From William Gordon

My Dear Sir   St Neots Hunts [England] March 7th 1794
    Your benevolence is so well established, that no apology is needful for my introducing to your notice, my friend the Revd Mr Hickman, who prefers living in a land of real liberty to remaining in his native country, where there is little of it, though great boastings about it.
    Being at Cambridge the beginning of the week, a gentleman of my acquaintance, Mr Flower, who has published upon the French Constitution of 1791, expressed his desire of notifying his regard to You, by sending You his work, did he know of a conveyance. I immediately told him that Mr Hickman would gladly take charge of it. He took the direction where to order it, & I conclude that before t⟨h⟩is reaches Mr Hickman, he will have received it.[1]
    I pray for your States as truly & steadily as an American, that you may be succeeded in warring with the Indians, till you have a safe lasting & honorable peace; & that You may be preserved from a war with G. Britain; but am afraid You will be driven into it by our ministry. Should the French give the allies a good hearty drubbing upon the ⟨opening⟩ of the campaign, so as to leave no reasonable hope of its being a successful one to the ⟨*mutilated*⟩rates, the ministry may accede to your just demands: for notwithstanding the contemptuous ⟨*mutilated*⟩gard they cast upon the voice of the public, a war with America will be so extremely unpopular, as to endanger their seats, which many think are more dear to them than their country. Wishing & praying that your Excellency may live to see the United States confirmed in the enjoyment of a safe peace with all the nations of the earth, & in the possession of a plan that shall secure the liberties of

America to the latest posterity, without exposing them to the wils of hereditary power in a single State, or a single President; & then finish your race with full glory, & remove to a better world through the merits of the Lord Jesus Christ. I remain My Dear Sir Your Excellency's affectionate friend & humble servant

William Gordon

Mrs Gordon joins me in the preceding paragraph, & in most cordial regards to your Lady, to whom Mrs Hickman will pay proper respect upon her arrival.

N.B. I shall enter my sixty-sixth year should I be spared till tomorrow. Am so favored, as to be able to write without spectacles, & to read without any kind of glasses.

ALS, DLC:GW. A notation on the cover reads, "Favored by the Revd Mr Hickman."

1. The Rev. Hickman and his wife have not been identified. On Benjamin Flower and his book on the French constitution, see his letter to GW of 17 March.

Henry Knox to Bartholomew Dandridge, Jr.

Dear Sir   Friday Evg 7 March 1794
Please to submit the enclosed letter from Genl Wilkinson of the 26th Jany together with the papers accompanying it to the President of the U.S.[1] Yours sincerely

H. Knox

ALS, DLC:GW; LB, DLC:GW.

1. James Wilkinson's letter to Knox of 26 Jan. and its enclosures have not been identified. According to an entry of 7 March in GW's executive journal, these documents were about the expedition being planned by Revolutionary War general George Rogers Clark and other Kentucky residents against the Spanish colony of Louisiana (*JPP,* 289). On this expedition, see Edmund Randolph to GW, 27 Feb. (fourth letter), and its enclosed extract of an anonymous letter dated 25 January.

From Alexander Hamilton

[Philadelphia] March 8th 1794.
The present situation of the United States is undoubtedly critical and demands measures vigorous though prudent. We ought

to be in a respectable military posture, because war may come upon us, whether we choose it or not and because to be in a condition to defend ourselves and annoy any who may attack us will be the best method of securing our peace. If it is known that our principal maritime points are out of the reach of any but formal serious operations—and that the Government has an efficient active force in its disposal for defence or Offence on an emergency—there will be much less temptation to attack us and much more hesitation to provoke us.

It seems then adviseable

1. to fortify the principal ports in the several States (say one in each State) so as to be able to resist a merely maritime attack or anything but a regular seige.[1]

2. to raise 20,000 Auxiliary Troops upon a plan something like the following (vizt)—To be divided into 10 Regiments—Each Regiment to consist of two Batallions and of the following Officers & men—1 Colonel 2 Majors 10 Captains 20 Lieutenants 2 Lieutenants & Adjutants 2 Serjeant Majors 40 Sergeants 4 Musicians & 1000 rank & file. These Troops to be engaged upon the following terms—to be inlisted for two years, but upon condition, that if a war should break out with any European Power, they shall be obliged to serve 4 years from the commencement of such war upon the same terms as the Troops of the establishment—To receive as a bounty Cloaths with 12 Dollars ℔ Man—To be under an obligation to meet 40 days in the year and 30 of these days to encamp—when Assembled to be paid Officers & men as the Troops of the establishment and to have the same subsistence & rations. To be furnished with arms & accoutrements by the United States, to be surrendered at the expiration of their term of service.

The Officers in time of war to rank & rise with the Officers of the Military establishment—The arrangement to cease ipso facto—at the expiration of a certain term (about two years.)

The expence of these operations would be—

For the Fortifications	Drs 150,000
For the Auxiliary troops ℔ annum	350,000
	Drs 500,000

In addition to this, the Legislature ought to vest the President of the United States with a power to lay an embargo partial or general and to arrest the exportation of commodities partially or generally.

It may also deserve consideration whether the Executive ought not to take measures to form some concert of the Neutral Powers for common Defence.[2]

Mr Hamilton presents his respects to the President, submits to him some reveries which have occupied his imagination. It may be interesting for the President to consider whether some such plan is not demanded by the conjuncture of affairs & if so, whether there ought not to be some executive impulse. Many persons look to the President for the suggestion of measures corresponding with the exigency of Affairs. As far as this idea may be founded, many important & delicate ideas are involved in the consideration.

The pains taken to preserve peace, include a proportional responsibility that equal pains be taken to be prepared for war.

Copy, DLC: Hamilton Papers. Hamilton's docket reads, "Thoughts submitted to The President March 8. 1794."

1. On federal legislation to fortify the U.S. coastline, which was passed later this month, see "An Act to provide for the Defence of certain Ports and Harbors in the United States," 20 March 1794 (*Stat.* 1:345–46).

2. Many of Hamilton's suggestions were incorporated in the eight resolutions made by Massachusetts congressman Theodore Sedgwick on 12 March (*Annals of Congress,* 3d. Cong., 500–501). For information that Secretary of War Henry Knox submitted to the House of Representatives concerning U.S. defensive measures and military preparedness, see his reports on: Fortifications, 28 Feb.; Arsenals and Armories, 5 March; Militia, 24 March; and Increasing the Army, and Calling into Service 80,000 Militia, 27 March (*ASP, Military Affairs,* 1:61–67). See also the joint resolution of Congress, which GW approved on 26 March, imposing a thirty-day embargo "on all ships and vessels in the ports of the United States" (*Stat.* 1:400).

From Richard Henry Lee

Dear Sir,   Chantilly [Va.] March the 8th 1794

Not having enjoyed one days health since I had the honor of seeing you at Shuters hill, and closely confined at home,[1] I knew not until yesterday that Mr H: Muse the Collector of Rappahanock had put his place in jeopardy by a conduct certainly very full of danger to the public affairs.[2] A young man of the same name and family has requested me to lay before you the reputation for fitness rightly to discharge the duties of this Office that he has acquired by doing the business of it for a considerable time past. That if you have not one more worthy in view he may have a chance to find favor with you.[3] Doctr Brokenbrough who lives in the Town where Mr Laurence Muse has kept the Office and whose judgement and opinion, I think, deserve attention,[4] writes thus to me. "If I had not been well satisfied of his merit, I should not have taken this liberty; but I know him to be a young Man of strict integrity, and that his abilities in this Line are at least equal to any persons on Rappahanock"—My brother Frank of Menoken who is not much disposed to give characters[5] writes me "This young man is generally very well spoken of, particularly for his diligence and punctuality[.]" It is true that I have not had much business with him: but at such times he has appeared expert and clever. Were I called upon to give my opinion concerning the late malversation in that Office, I think I could venture to say that I judged this person to have had no concern in the affair. I have spoken with him concerning his ability to give adequate security. Upon this point he appears to have no difficulty.[6]

I am very happy to hear of Genets recall. And hope it may prove a lesson to others, however justified by instructions, or seeming to be so, that they may not with impunity trample upon all the forms of decency and respect, that have hitherto been practised in the World.[7]

Is it possible that there can be any rational proof of the Court of London intriguing with Algier⟨s⟩ and Portugal to hound out the former against our Trade.[8] In any way that I can view the subject I cannot see the great interest that stimulate a conduct so unjustifiable, so contrary to Neutrality, and at a peculial crisis too, when our friendship not our enmity is to be desired. It is chiefly flour and grain that are sent to the South of Europe, in which articles, I believe, we have not the smallest competition with G. Britain. At the same time that the profits of this Trade enable our Merchants to pay for the immensity of British Manufactures that Messrs Jefferson & Madison say we import from thence. I confess that I do not by any means approve the Trade resolves introduced to Congress by the latter.[9] They appear to me to be partial, very ill timed, and totally unnecessary. Because, the fact, (admitting it to be one on which this whole

Theory, is built, and when by the bye Theories & the practise of Commerce have seldom agreed well) of our Commerce being so very highly beneficial to G. Britain as is stated, this fact, from the nature of things, must be continually increasing; so as to put the Gainers greatly too much in our power to permit them the idea of refusing our reasonable desires.

And this without proceeding, at a time and in a manner, evidently to shew a prejudiced, hostile temper of mind. But what astonishes me is, to see so many of our Virginia representatives voting for this most pernicious policy! For certainly Virginia will feel the ruinous consequences of this Crambo Trade fatally and quickly.[10] I hope your goodness will excuse my writing so much on this subject—The plan has often engaged the public attention, and been generally reprobated.

The Newspapers tell us that the present Minister of France condemns in toto the conduct of his predecessor, and in the same unlimited manner approves the proceeding of our government, especially in what relates to our avoiding War.[11] That he is right in both these points is incontestable. But attending to all we have seen, what consistent judgement can be formed to reconcile such contrarieties. There lay aside the Crafty, deep and intricate politics that have distinguished the genius of France thro all the Annals of history; by which she has duped so many Nations for her own advantage, and to their great injury. I have never heared it denied or doubted but that the instructions published by Genet were the genuine orders of his Masters, and altho in his conduct you discover the furious Zeal of a mad Precursor, yet it is impossible not to see thro the whole of the instructions the most decided determination to push us into the War by every possible means. The words of the instructions are, "We ought to excite by all possible means the Zeal of the Americans &c. &c.["][12] Fortunately, very fortunately for these States the Wisdom and Patriotism, firmness & vigilance of our Government hath frustrated the destructive design. But, is it possible that this Minister can speak the sentiments of his Masters when he approves the condemnation of what they so warmly & evidently deserved. It is here again lucky for us that we are fairly put upon our guard against all the Arts and Detours of the subtlest policy. The success & happiness of the United States is our care, and if the nations of Europe approve War, we surely may be permitted to cultive the arts of peace. And it is realy a happiness to reflect that if War should befall us, our Government will not promote it; but give cause to all who venerate humanity to revere the rulers here.

I beg leave to present my best respects, and those of this family to your Lady. I have the honor to be dear Sir with the most respectful sentiments of affection & esteem your friend & servant

Richard Henry Lee.

ALS, DLC:GW.

1. In 1792, ill health had forced Lee to retire from the U.S. Senate to his home, Chantilly, in Westmoreland County, Virginia. He died later this year on 19 June. The estate at Shuter's Hill, near Alexandria, Va., was currently the home of Lee's eldest son, Ludwell.

2. For the problems besetting Hudson Muse, the former customs collector for the District of Tappahannock, Va., see his letter to GW of 27 Jan., and n.3 to that document.

3. For the application of Laurence Muse, the deputy collector at Tappahannock, and other letters of recommendation for him, see his letter to GW of 1 Feb. and n.2 to that document. See also James Madison to GW, 12 Feb., and n.2 to that document.

4. Tappahannock physician John Brockenbrough (d. 1801) served as a justice of the peace in Essex County and as a surgeon in the Virginia navy during the Revolutionary War.

5. Francis Lightfoot Lee (1734–1797) represented Loudoun County in the Virginia House of Burgesses, 1758–68. He settled in Richmond County in 1769 on an estate called Menokin, and he represented that county in the House of Burgesses, 1769–76, where he became a leader of the opposition to British rule. He served in the Continental Congress, 1775–79, signing the Declaration of Independence in 1776, and in the Virginia Senate, 1781–82.

6. GW submitted Laurence Muse's nomination to the U.S. Senate on 5 March.

7. For the recall of Edmond Genet as the French minister plenipotentiary to the United States, see Provisional Executive Council of France to GW, 15 Nov. 1793. For the administration's decision to ask the French government to recall Genet, see the Cabinet Opinion of 23 Aug. 1793.

8. On the British role in obtaining a truce between Portugal and Algiers, which left American shipping in the Atlantic Ocean vulnerable to seizure, see n.9 of Tobias Lear to GW, 4 February.

9. The seven resolutions introduced in the U.S. House of Representatives by James Madison on 3 Jan. 1794 were designed to create a policy of commercial retaliation against the British and were a response, in part, to British interference with American shipping (*Annals of Congress*, 3d. Cong., 155–56, 484–98).

10. Crambo is a game in which one player gives a word or line of verse to be matched in rhyme by other players.

11. Fauchet publicly disavowed Genet's encouragement of military expeditions against Spanish territory that were to be organized and led by Americans. For one such expedition, see Edmund Randolph to GW, 27 Feb. (fourth letter), and its enclosed extract of an anonymous letter dated 25 January. In a public declaration of 6 March, Fauchet ordered Frenchmen not "to violate the Neutrality of the United States" and revoked all "commissions or authorizations tending to infringe that neutrality" (*General Advertiser* [Philadelphia], 7 March 1794).

12. Printed translations of "Instructions to Citizen Genet, Minister Plenipotentiary from the French Republic to the United States, from the Executive Council, and Minister of Marine" were included in Genet's *Correspondence between Citizen Genet, Minister of the French Republic, to the United States of North America, and the Officers of the Federal Government; to Which Are Prefixed the Instructions from the Constituted Authorities of France to the Said Minister. All from Authentic Documents* (Philadelphia, 1793).

From Edward Newenham

Dear Sir   Dublin [Ireland] 8th March 1794

The enclosed was left behind by the Captain of Ship, who promised to take it along with the papers & Magazines, which I had the Honor to send you last February.[1]

This goes by my Worthy Friend Mr Noble, who says he will have the Honor to deliver it personaly to you; he is a Neighbour of mine, & of a most respectable Character.

God forbid that there should be a War between your Country & this; it would be a Severe injury to both; I hope all concerned, on both sides, will act with that Magnanimity which marked your Conduct on a Late occasion; I read all the Letters & addresses, that passed on that Affair—they are universaly admired.

The War on the Continent, in my humble opinion, will be decisive this year on one side or the other; for Each are making their Utmost Efforts; France is Vastly Superior in Numbers & Artillery & there are so many Strong Towns to take before an Enemy can pene[t]rate into the Kingdom, that she may Still defy the Allies, if there are inward Dissentions; we thought all the Royalists in Le Vendee were Exterminated, but by the last papers it appears that 7000 of that Class of Men have rizen in Arms & were defeated[2]—it Shews that there is a latent convulsion ready to Break out, if Ever the Allies should prove Succesfull on the Frontiers.

It is thought, that, by this Time, the English are in Possession of Some of the French West Indies Islands,[3] & Stocks have rose a Little on that Account; but in my opinion, it would be of more consequence to Great Brittain to have Kept her fleet at home & sent her Soldiers to the Continent—for should France Succeed in Europe, all her Losses in the East and West Indies must be restored, as they could not be withheld from her; I am astonished that the Empress of Russia has not Sent a few Thousands of her Troopes by Sea to ostend.[4]

By a letter I lately received from Germany I hear that our most Worthy Friend the Marquiss Le Fayette is in health at Spandau & that the Marchiness is alive & well at her house in Auverne.[5]

our Parliament is near having done all Business in a Shorter Time than ever occurred before—all was Unanimous & firm in Support of the war—there has been only 2 Debates of any Consequence & the Minority very Small—our Minister cannot get the Supplies in this Kingdom under 6 ℔ Ct so he borrows in England at 5 & an annuity of 1 ℔ Ct for 15 years—the whole Militia of this Kingdom are training & on Constant Duty[6]—for Government is preparing for Defence in case the French should disturb us—though almost all our Regulars are gone Either to the West Indies or Flanders, which I think was bad policy.

A few Nights ago, this City was much alarmed; a fire Broke out Close to the Treasury & record office, & which brought to our remembrance the burning of the Parliament House, made us fearfull of a general Conflagration.[7] Wishing you every health & happiness of this Life, with Lady Newenhams best respects to you & Mrs Washington I have the Honor to be with Every sentiment of Respect & esteem Dear Sir your most faithfull & Affe. Hble Sert

Edward Newenham

ALS, DLC:GW.

1. The enclosure probably was Newenham's letter to GW of 11 Feb. 1794.

2. The Vendée region in western France was a center of opposition to the French republic. In March 1793, the peasant population of the area combined with Royalist forces to form an opposition army of nearly fifty thousand, the so-called Royal Catholic Army. This army had a series of victories throughout the summer and fall of 1793, but was decisively defeated at the Battle of Savenay on 23 Dec. 1793.

3. In the "Great Push" of 1793–94, British forces under Vice Admiral Sir John Jervis (1735–1823) and General Sir Charles Grey (1729–1807) over-

whelmed French positions throughout the Caribbean, seizing Barbados in January 1794, Martinique in March, St. Lucia and Guadeloupe in April, and parts of Saint Domingue by June 1794. However, setbacks soon occurred, less for French military resistance but more for slave uprisings and tropical disease (Jennifer Mori, *William Pitt and the French Revolution 1785–1795* [Edinburgh, 1997], 152, 212–13, 220–21; see also Michael Duffy, *Soldiers, Sugar, and Seapower: The British Expeditions to the West Indies and the War against Revolutionary France* [Oxford, 1987]).

4. At this time, the empress of Russia, Catherine II, failed to offer significant support to the First Coalition against France, being preoccupied with events in Poland following the Second Partition of Poland in January 1793. The North Sea port of Ostend, located in western Belgium, was under the control of France at this time, but Russian interests did not lie there. While Catherine II was opposed to revolutionary France ideologically, she hoped to gain territory for her empire in the east while France's neighbors were distracted in the west (Simon Dixon, *Catherine the Great* [Harlow, England, 2001], 169–73; Mori, *William Pitt,* 215–16).

5. Between January and May 1794, the Marquis de Lafayette was held prisoner by the Prussians in the fortress at Neisse in Silesia. The Marquise de Lafayette was not at the family estate of Chavanaic in Auvergne, but since mid-November 1793, she was incarcerated in the prison at the nearby village of Brioude.

6. On Ireland's pledge to help supply the British war effort against France, see n.2 of Newenham to GW, 11 February.

7. The Irish House of Parliament burnt on 27 Feb. 1792, destroying the dome and portions of the Commons' chamber (*Times of London,* 5 March 1792).

To John Cowper

Sir,   Philadelphia March 9th 1794.

After waiting several months from the time your bond, dated the 18th of May 1791, for £146.13.4 became due, to see if (without reminding you thereof) you would make payment, I hardly expected, when application was made, to learn that I was yet to wait many months more for the money.[1] As this, however, is the case, and you ask, "whether I chuse the payment to be made in Philadelphia, should you be as late as the last of June next in making it," my answer, and wish is, that this may be the case, unless you have other advice from me in the meanwhile.[2]

I never heard, before the receipt of your letter, of the claim of Jethro Ballard Esq: to any part of the land which was bought of Mr Marmaduke Norfleet; nor can I easily conceive that such a claim is founded in equity. For I recollect *well,* that all the *disput-*

able part of it, which was known to him, was given up. My opinion therefore is, that before any more of it is relinquished, he, or his heirs ought to be consulted; as they are certainly liable for any loss that may be sustained.

It appears a little extraordinary, that a claim of this sort should not have been known by Mr Norfleet; nor by Colo. Lewis & myself, whilst we had possession of the plantation—was shewn, & always viewed the contested spot as part of the premises, if Mr Ballard was the proprietor thereof in virtue of an elder patent—especially as I am very confident the lines & corners comprehending it, were ascertained to us by Mr Norfleet at the moment he announced a dispute in another part, which, as I have beforementioned, was given up with his consent, rather than embark in a contest.[3]

It is, however, the business of mister Jno. Lewis (from whom you purchased the land, or rather with whom you made the agreement) to examine into this matter; for I have not time, nor will my situation allow me to do it. and further because the land was disposed of contrary to my judgment, & given into, merely to accommodate the demand on his father's Estate. I am, Sir, &c.

Go. Washington

LB, DLC:GW.

1. For GW's earlier requests for payment of this bond, see his letter to Cowper of 26 Oct. 1793, and n.1. For the bond, see Indenture with John Cowper, 17 May 1791.

2. Cowper's letter to GW, from which this quote is taken, has not been found. GW received a partial payment in early September (GW to John Lewis, 8 Sept. 1794, ALS [letterpress copy], DLC:GW; LB, DLC:GW).

3. On the purchase of this tract of land in Gates County, N.C., from Marmaduke Norfleet of North Carolina, by GW and his brother-in-law Col. Fielding Lewis and, after the death of Fielding Lewis, its subsequent sale to Cowper by GW and John Lewis, see n.7 of George Augustine Washington to GW, 7 Dec. 1790. See also the Deed from Marmaduke Norfleet of 26 April 1766. Mr. Jethro Ballard's claim has not been identified.

To William Pearce

Mr Pearce   Philadelphia 9th Mar. 1794

Your letter of the 3d instt is this moment received. The badness of the roads has occasioned irregularity in the Post.[1]

I approve your repairing my house in Alexandria with my own People (preparing every thing that can be, at home) and of your doing it in the manner proposed; that is, to board between the houses in a neat & workman like manner & to do the three sides of the lot with White Oak Posts & Rails, well executed. Do not let the Posts be too far distant from each other—when this is the case the rails are apt to warp, & the fence is weakened by it.[2]

I am glad to hear that Green has, at length put a finish to the Barn at Dogue run farm.[3] I always supposed that shutters would be necessary to keep the weather from the floors, in driving Rain or Snow, & for comfort when working there when it is very cold; but these are soon done; and should be made to hang on substantial iron hooks, that when light, or air is wanting, they may be raised up; & hung to the foot of the rafters. If the windows below want shutters, the same may be done, & hung to the joice. But shoveling the grain as it falls from the treading floor, into the middle or octagon part of the building, will always preserve it from the weather. I want much to know how this mode of treading wheat answers.

If you conceive the Lucern in the Spring lot will come to any thing, I am well content that it should remain as it is, with the dressing you propose to give it. I directed Seed to be saved last year from that which grew in the Inclosure opposite to it, but whether it was done or not I am unable to say; if it was not I will send you two or three pounds to sprinkle over the ground. Running a harrow over the lot backwards & forwards, & every way in short, will do no injury to the Lucern as it has a long tap root, but may tare weeds & grass up, and prepare it better for fresh Seed. The St foin & India hemp may be sown in the lot which you have mentioned, as more secure perhaps than the other, against Hares; but how they will be annoyed by fowls you can judge better of than I. I wish to have the most that can be made of them.

It is very unlucky that the state of the Navigation has been such as to prevent my sending you the Clover & other Seeds; a vessel is now up, & talks of sailing this week for Alexandria, by which the things shall be sent.[4] I hope what clover seed you had (as you have pronounced it good) has already been sown on the grain, as far as it would go, as was directed. I am Your friend &ca

                                            Go: Washington

ALS, ViMtvL; ALS (letterpress copy), DLC:GW.

1. Pearce's letter to GW of Monday, 3 March, has not been found. According to the post office's schedule, GW should have received this letter on Thursday, 6 March (GW to Anthony Whitting, 2 Dec. 1792).

2. For GW's instructions to have his house and stable at the corner of Pitt and Cameron streets in Alexandria, Va., prepared for occupancy by Frances Bassett Washington, see his letters to Pearce of 12 Jan. and 16 February.

3. Thomas Green, overseer of the slave carpenters at Mount Vernon, was responsible for the construction of this barn. For the unique design of this barn, see GW to Anthony Whitting, 28 Oct. 1792, and enclosure.

4. In his letter to Pearce of 16–17 March, GW wrote that the clover seed had just been placed aboard a ship bound for Alexandria.

From Famine Savoy

Monsieur   Philadelphie ce 9 Mars 1794

La Citoyenne Savoye jeune habitante & propriétaire du Cap-francais, mère de deux enfans l'un âgé de six ans et démi et l'autre de quatre ans & demi mariée à un homme dont la vue ne lui permet pas de faire le plus petit travail pour soulager sa malheureuse famille se trouve dans la plus deplorable situation, il ne lui reste pas le moindre moyen pour subsister avec ses infortunés Enfans, la seule resource qui lui reste est d'avoir recours à vous pour la tirer de la détresse où elle se trouve elle n'a de droit aupres de vous pour l'autoriser a cette demarche que celle qu'ont tous les malheureux aupres des âmes généreuses, la bonte de votre coeur dont vous ne cessez de donner des preuves, lui fait esperer que vous voudrez bien avoir égard a se prière, en lui accordant quelques faibles secours pour lui éviter de mourir de faim et de misère avec sa famille, elle n'a à vous offrir que le tribut d'une reconnaissance proportionnée à un pareil Bien fait et elle adressera au ciel les voeux les plus sincères pour la conservation de vos Jours.[1]

famine Savoy

ALS (in French), DNA: RG 59, Miscellaneous Letters.

1. Famine Savoy describes herself as a young resident and landowner from Saint Domingue, with two young children, ages 6½ and 4½, and a husband whose poor eyesight prevents him from holding even the smallest job. No evidence has been identified to indicate that her request for financial assistance from GW was successful.

Letter not found: from Alexander Spotswood, 9 March 1794. GW wrote Spotswood on 15 March that "Your letter of the 9th instt is at hand."

Cabinet Opinion on Expeditions
Against Spanish Territory

[Philadelphia, 10 March 1794]

At a meeting of the heads of departments, and the attorney general at the President's on the 10th day of March 1794.

The intelligence from Kentucky, and the territory no. west of the Ohio, was laid before them;[1] whereupon it was advised

1.   that a proclamation issue against the expeditions, understood to be prepared in Kentucky, for the invasion of the Spanish dominions.[2]

2.   that a representation be made to the governor of Kentucky, upon the subject of his conduct, and giving information under proper guards of the steps, which have been taken by government as to the Mississippi:[3]

3.   that a representation be also made to congress:[4] and

4.   that General Wayne be instructed to post if compatible with his other operations a body of troops at Massac, in order to intercept by force, if necessary, any body of men, which may descend the river for the purpose of the invasion aforesaid.[5] From this fourth opinion the secretary of state dissents.[6]

Edm: Randolph
Henry Knox.
Alexandr Hamilton
Wm Bradford

DS (in Edmund Randolph's handwriting), DLC:GW. GW's docket reads, "Opinions 10th March 1794 respecting the threatned Invasion of the Spanish Dominions on the Mississippi by the People of Kentucky."

1. The intelligence presented about a proposed expedition by Kentucky residents against the Spanish colony of Louisiana probably included Edmund Randolph's fourth letter to GW of 27 Feb. and its enclosed extract.

2. See GW's Proclamation of 24 March.

3. For Randolph's letter of 29 March to Kentucky governor Isaac Shelby, see n.5 of Randolph to GW, 19 March (first letter).

4. Although the Kentucky expedition was mentioned in an enclosure that accompanied GW's letter to the U.S. Senate and House of Representatives of 12 March, the Kentucky expedition was addressed more fully in some of the enclosures that accompanied GW's letter to the U.S. Senate and House of Representatives of 20 May (*ASP, Foreign Relations,* 1:454–60).

5. Henry Knox wrote Anthony Wayne on 31 March: "The idea of a post to be established at Fort Massac was held forth in the seventeenth of May last, and left optional with you—But certain circumstances at that time prevented

your adopting the idea. The late intention of some restless people of the frontier settlements to make hostile inroads into the dominions of Spain, renders it indispensible that you should immediately order as respectable a detachment as you can take post of Fort Massac and to erect a strong redoubt and block house with some suitable cannon from Fort Washington. The officer who should command ought to be a man of approved integrity, firmness and prudence.

"Besides the directions for errecting the works, the supplies, discipline and police of his Garrison, he ought to be instructed somewhat in the following manner '*Secret and Confidential*' It has not be unknown to you that a number of lawless people residing on the waters of the Ohio in defiance of the national authority have entertained the daring design of invading the territories of Spain. The atrocity of this measure and its probable effects are pointed out in the Proclamation of the President of the United States herewith delivered to you.

"If this design should be persisted in or hereafter revived and any such parties should make their appearance in the neighbourhood of your garrison and you should be well informed that they are armed and equiped for war and entertain the criminal intention described in the Presidents proclamation you are to send to them some person in whose veracity you could confide, and if such person should be a peace officer he should be the most proper Messenger and warn them of their evil proceedings and forbid their attempting to pass the Fort at their peril. But if notwithstanding every peacable effort to persuade them to abandon their criminal design they should still persist in their attempts to pass down the Ohio, you are to use every military means in your power for preventing them—and for which this shall be your sufficient justification provided you have taken all the pacific steps before directed" (MiU-C: Wayne Letterbooks).

6. For Randolph's dissent, see his letter to GW of 11 March.

From James Duane

Sir   New York 10th March 1794.

I reflect with the utmost sensibility on the frequent instances I have experienced of your attention and benevolence, and particularly in the manner in which you was pleased to confer on me the office of Judge of this district. It manifested a mark of your esteem which I shall always prize as a distinguished honor.[1]

The disorder which I contracted by a sedentary habit, the effect of close application to business, is obstinately fixed in my stomach, and I have reason to believe that, if at all, it can only be mitigated by a relaxation from sollicitude and by regular exercise. I therefore propose to retire to my paternal estate where two of my children are already established, and which is too remote, if my health should be reinstated, to admit of the execution of any employment connected with even a periodical residence in this city.[2]

Upon these considerations, Sir, I most respectfully entreat your permission to resign my office, and shall deem myself happy if it meets your approbation which to me is of inestimable value.[3]

The appointment of a successor not later than the middle of April when the season will probably Favor my embarkation would be most convenient, and as soon as your pleasure is intimated I shall forward my commission or a more formal surrender if necessary.[4]

Permit me to add that however I may be disposed of, it will always be my fervent prayer that you may long continue to preside over our country, in health tranquillity and glory, supported by what you now so justly and eminently enjoy, the confidence attachment and affections of a grateful people. I have the honor to be with the most perfect attachment esteem & respect Sir your most obliged most faithful and most obedient servant

Jas Duane

LS, DNA: RG 59, Miscellaneous Letters; DfS, NHi: Duane Papers. The docket on the draft reads, "Sent ℔ Post 12th."

1. For Duane's nomination as a federal judge for the District of New York, see GW to U.S. Senate, 25 Sept. 1789.

2. Duane was preparing to retire to the family estate located just west of Schenectady, New York. During the 1760s, James Duane added over 30,000 acres to the 6,000-acre tract purchased in 1741 by his father, Anthony Duane (1682–1747). In 1765, New York State approved the creation of the township of Duanesburg from these lands. Duane's daughter Maria (Mary; 1761–1813) and her husband, William North (1755–1836), and James Chatham Duane (1770–1842) and his wife, the former Marianne Bowers (Mary Ann; 1773–1842), were already living in the township. See Edward P. Alexander, *A Revolutionary Conservative: James Duane of New York* (New York, 1938), 9, 41, 54–57, 216, map of Duanesburg facing 220, 235.

3. In his reply to Duane of 23 March, marked "Private," GW wrote: "I am sorry to find by it, that it no longer comports with your convenience to remain judge of that district; and am concerned that ill-health should be the cause of your resigning an Office, the duties of wch I am sensible require a residence in, or a very constant attendance at, the City of New York.

"For the flattering expressions of your letter, and the kind sentiments contained in it, I pray you to accept my best thanks. I wish, sincerely, that relaxation from business, in ease & retirement, may have the effect you hope" (ALS, NHi: Duane Papers; ALS [letterpress copy], DNA: RG 59, Miscellaneous Letters; LB, DLC:GW).

4. For the appointment of Duane's successor, see GW to U.S. Senate, 16 April (second letter). For Duane's official resignation, see his letter to GW of 8 April.

To John Gwinn

Sir,   Philadelphia March 10th 1794

In due course of Post I was favoured with your letter of the 25th of Jany, with the deed which it enclosed from Colo. Mercer & others, to me. This deed refers to a Survey of the Manor of Woodstock (in the year 1782) and to a division thereof made by Hezekiah Veatch, assistant Surveyor of Montgomery County, on the ⟨2⟩d day of January 1793.[1]

The latter (in the body of the deed) is said to be recorded. It is essentially necessary indeed that it should be so. But neither the original, nor a copy thereof was forwarded to me. This induces me to give you the trouble of informing me—whether the above Survey of Mr Veatch is admitted to record; and, in that case, that you would be so good as to furnish me with, either the original, or an attested copy thereof from your Office.[2] I am—Sir Your Obedt Servant

Go: Washington

ALS (letterpress copy), NN: Washington Papers; LB, DLC:GW. The text in angles brackets is from the letter-book copy.

1. John Gwinn (c.1756–1809) at this time resided in Frederick County, Maryland. A merchant by trade, he also served in the Maryland legislature (1788 and 1798), as a justice of Frederick County, and as the clerk of the Maryland General Court. His letter to GW of 25 Jan. has not been found. On GW's acquisition of 519 acres in Montgomery County, Md., and the deed of 1 April 1793, see n.1 of GW to John Francis Mercer, 7 Aug. 1793. On the survey of 2 Jan. 1793, see Francis Deakins and Benjamin W. Jones to GW, 20 Dec. 1792, and n.1.

2. For GW's receipt of the survey, see Mercer to GW, 13 April.

To William Herbert

Dear Sir,   Philadelphia 10th Mar. 1794

The only unsettled matter in my administration of the estate of Colo. Thos Colvill, is a bond of one Sidney George, of Maryland.[1] A Mr Chalme⟨rs⟩[2] (now of London) who was directed to institute a suit in chancery in this case, & who has been written to on the subject, thinks, as he was in the habit of corrisponding with Colo. Carlyle about that time (1774) there may be found some letter of his, or account relative to the payment of £100 to Mr Jno. West in part of this Bond.[3]

You would oblige me very much by examining, & giving me information on this head as soon it is convenient to you, as I am now about to decide something with Mr George respecting this bond. With great esteem & reg[ar]d I am, Dr Sir Yr Obedt Hble Servt

Go: Washington

ALS (letterpress copy), DLC:GW; LB, DLC:GW.

1. For the bond of Sidney George, Jr., to John West, Jr., see n.1 of William Tilghman to GW, 1 March. On the entangled estates of brothers John and Thomas Colvill, see John Montgomerie to GW, 24 Oct. 1788, source note. Alexandria, Va., merchant William Herbert had been hired in 1793 to review the financial accounts for the Colvill estate (James Keith to Tobias Lear, 15 July 1793, and notes 2 and 5).

2. A blank space appears in the letter-book copy in place of this name.

3. The information received from George Chalmers was contained in his letters to William Tilghman of 5 Nov. and 4 Dec. 1793 (see n.2 of Tilghman to GW, 1 March 1794). Herbert was married to Sarah Carlyle, the daughter of Alexandria merchant John Carlyle, who died in 1780.

To Robert Townsend Hooe

Dear Sir   Philadelphia Mar: 10th 1794

To the best of my recollection, when you paid me for my flour of last year, you asked the refusal of it this year.[1]

By the report from my Mill, I perceive about 3,000 bushels of Wheat has been manufactured; but how much flour it has made, and of what sort, I am yet to learn.[2] If you incline to purchase what there is, let me know the best price you will give; or to make the matter short, and to save time, you may have the Superfine (if any is made) and fine flour at what they sell for in this market with a deduction of the usual freight pr barrl from Alexandria to this place. The cash prices in this City ⟨are⟩

Superfine	50/
Common	47/6.

Two or three months credit I should not ob⟨jec⟩t to.

Your answer, as soon as it is convenient to you, will oblige[3] Dear Sir Your Obedient Servt

Go: Washington

P.S. I have more than what is mentd above to grind.

ALS (letterpress copy), NN: Washington Papers; LB, DLC:GW.

1. On the previous purchase of flour from Mount Vernon by Hooe, a merchant in Alexandria, Va., see Hooe to GW, 23 May 1793, and Tobias Lear to GW, 24 June 1793.

2. The report from miller Joseph Davenport has not been found.

3. In his reply to GW of 15 March, Hooe wrote: "I do myself the Honor to acknowledge the Reciept of Your Excellencys Letter of the 10th Inst.—and return you many thanks for the offer of Your Flour. At present I have a heavy quantity of both Wheat & Tobacco on my lands, which Articles not being able to get Vessells to carry off, & the great rumour of War with Britain—alarms me to such a degree, that I have Suspended my Purchases.

"This is very much the case with all the Merchts of this Town—I have made enquiry & cannot find any of them willing to Purchase" (DLC:GW).

To John Francis Mercer

Sir, Philadelphia Mar: 10th 1794

I have lately received from Mr Gwinn clerk of the Genl Court at Annapolis a Deed which has been enrolled in that Office from yourself & lady, Doctr Stuart and lady & Miss Sprigg, to me.[1]

As this is not the deed which you and Mrs Mercer executed in Philadelphia, and nearly a year posterior in date, I am at a loss to acct for these changes; & should be glad to be informed of the reasons which have induced them. Whether the present differs materially, or in any thing from the former, I am unable to decide; not having the means of comparing them. In date they do essentially.

No record of the Survey is annexed to the deed, which (a reference being made to it) induces me to believe it is imperfect, without; especially as the *division* of the Manor may be more of a private, than public act.[2] On this subject, however, I shall write to Mr Gwinn.

Your draught in favor of Dr Stuart was paid at sight. I am—Sir Your most Obedt Servt

Go: Washington

ALS (letterpress copy), DLC:GW; LB, DLC:GW.

1. John Gwinn's letter to GW of 25 Jan. has not been found. On GW's receipt of a deed from Mercer, Sophia Sprigg Mercer, James Steuart, and Rebecca Sprigg Steuart to a 519-acre tract in Montgomery County, Md., see GW to Gwinn, 10 March.

2. For GW's eventual receipt of the original deed and the survey, see Mercer to GW, 13 April.

From the Officers of the Grand Bailiwick of Nassau

Translation   Idstein near Maynz[1] March. 10th 1794.

Mr Frederick Christian Wernecke, a Native of this place, late a Colonel in the service of the United States departed this Life at Richmond in Virginia in the year 1783 and left a very considerable Estate in that country, the Administration whereof was that time granted by the competent public officer of that place.[2]

The sisters & brothers of the deceased being his legitimate heirs gave a power of attorney to Mr Leopold Nottnagel a Citizen and Merchant of Philadelphia authorizing him to settle matters in their behalf and generally to manage their Interests as to that Estate, but could not till now obtain the End desired, which could not but create Suspicion in Their Breasts.[3]

Now when in all cases, (which frequently occur) where Successions happen to escheat in this Principality to Citizens of the United States, such Estates have been delivered to them without the least difficulty; (as was lately done in the case of Mr Philip Henry Knapp: the heirs of Mr Wernecke first above mentioned did in their Petition, a copy whereof is annexed hereto,[4] implore the Interference of This Court praying to arrest and put under Sequestration all Property of that Kind belonging to citizens of America to serve as Security for their indemnification, until their just Claims to the Estate of the late Colo. Wernecke be discharged by legal Procedure.

This Court however forbore to the present granting their Request for the present being fully persuaded, that the matter has never reached Your Excellency's Knowledge; but, as we are bound in Duty of Office to befriend lawful Purposes of Supplicants by all means in our power, we most humbly pray Your Excellency please to cause the necessary Directions to be given conducive to promoting the final Settling of said Estate & the

Delivery of the same to the legitimate heirs of the deceased residing at this place; as in the contrary case we shall see ourselves under the painful Necessity, not only to put under Sequestration all Property of that Kind escheating in this Country to American citizens but also to publish for the general Concern of the German Empire The Rule observed by the Courts of Your Continent in that Respect.

Relying, however, on Your Excellency's well known and general Love of Justice We confidently expect The most effectual measures will be the Result of Our present most humble Application, offering Our best Services in the like occurrences, which to embrace we shall be the more ready, as we shall Thereby be enabled to show by our Exertions The unbounded Respect with which we beg Leave to remain Your Excy's most humble & devoted Sevts

"The officers composing the Grand Bailiwick
of the Principality of Nassow Saarbruck"

L (translation), DNA: RG 59, Miscellaneous Letters; copy, DLC:GW; copy (letterpress copy), DNA: RG 59, Miscellaneous Letters. The letterpress copy is from the manuscript at DLC:GW. The letter is addressed to "His Excellency George Washington President of the Congress of the United States of America."

The Grand Bailiwick of Nassau at this time was part of the German principality of Nassau-Usingen-Sasarbrücken.

1. The town of Idstein is located north of the German city of Mainz.

2. Frederick Christian Wernecke (d. 1783) served during the Revolutionary War as an "Engineer for" Virginia, with the rank of colonel (*Calendar of Virginia State Papers*, 3:96).

3. Leopold Notnagel was a partner in the Philadelphia mercantile firm of Notnagel, Montmillon & Co., located at 64 North Front Street (*Philadelphia Directory, 1794*, 114).

4. The translation of the petition, which was written at Idstein, 22 Feb. 1794, reads: "On the 20th of March of the year One Thousand seven hundred and Eighty four I made, according to Law the preliminary Distribution of the Estate left by Philipp Knapp, decd late Inhabitant of Beuerbach, to his children, when I found, that one of the Sons of the decd Philipp Henry Knapp a Taylor by Trade, had emigrated to America and is actually settled at Germantown near Philadelphia. To insure the preservation of that portion belonging to him I put it under Administration of Mr Philipp Lappach of Beuerbach he finding sufficient Security. Now said Philipp Henry Knapp by his Attorney Mr John Martin Gaul of Philadelphia demands the portion due him out of his late father's Estate authorizing his sd Attorney to receive the Amount thereof in his place & stead.

"Considering however, that Mr John Martin Gaul, of Philadelphia has on the 13th of Dec. of the Year 1789 furnished me with an authenticated

Copy of the Inventory made on the Estate of my Brother, the late Colo Fredk Wernecke, by which it appears, that he died on the 4th Day of July 1783, at Richmond in Virginia and left considerable Property in real Estates as well as money put out on Interest, said Mr Gaul adding the verbal Assurance that said Estate had been lawfully put under Administration to be delivered without difficulty to the next heirs of the deceased or their Lawful Attorney's.

"Considering further, that notwithstanding all my efforts to obtain any answer to my numerous Letters and recommendatory Addresses directed to the Administracy at Richmond, since that period I never could succeed.

"Therefore I most humbly pray this Honble Supreme Court of the Principality may please to cause all claims and property arising from Estates escheated to American Citizens to be stopped and to have the same detained within the Limits of this Jurisdiction, until the Magistracy of Richmond make known, whether they will see said Estate of my deceased brother duly administered and delivered to the next and legitimate heirs thereof, calling the Administrators formerly appointed to account for the Revenues of the Real Estates and the Proceeds of the monies put out on Rent, all which the better to prove I do not fail here to subjoin an authenticated Copy & respective translation of the Inventory made at Richmond, That a full official communication and Application may be affected to His Excellency, the President of the Congress of the United States and Lord Pearce—at Philadelphia the Directors of the Supreme national Court of the States of Maryland and Virginia. Expecting a kind Deference to the above I remain with due Respect &c. (signed) Wernecke" (DNA: RG 59, Miscellaneous Letters; copy, DLC:GW; letterpress copy, DNA: RG 59, Miscellaneous Letters).

The attached translation of the inventory reads: "taken by Matth: Patte and valued by the underwritten in conformity of an order of the Court for the County of Henrico.

    I. A real estate containing 5000 acres as p. deed dated June 14. 1783.
    II. Two certificates of military services of May 22d 1782. each for 300 pounds, interests paid to May 20th 1783.
    III. Amount of furniture valued at £7.14 s."

The inventory was signed by Richmond merchants Jesse Roper, Robert Boyd, and David Lambert. The inventory was presented at a court "held for Henrico County" on 2 Aug. 1784 and "ordered to be recorded." At another court hearing on 8 July 1783: "On representation of Ulrich Mark who took his oath according to law and found bail by Stephen Barkard [Tankard] and Wilm Tohlman [Coleman] who gave security on bond to the amount of £2000, as the law directs, the present has been granted, to qualify him for taking out in due form a letter of administration respecting the estate of Fredk Wernecke deceased." The translation was certified "to be a true & faithful translation conformable with its original" by "Th: Kobbê. Secry of the Grand Bailiwick of the principality of Nassow, Usingen," on 21 Feb. 1794 (copy, DLC:GW; letterpress copy, DNA: RG 59, Miscellaneous Letters).

From Edmund Randolph

Private.

Dear sir [Philadelphia, c.10 March 1794]

Whether the present deed from Mercer to you, differs in substance from the former, I do not recollect. But the date being a twelvemonth later, may be of serious consequence. It may let in creditors and subsequent purchasers.[1]

I beg leave therefore to suggest, that after acknowledging to Mercer the receipt of the deed, you remark, that upon observing the deed now sent not to be the same with that, which was here last year, you feel yourself under the necessity of asking, why the change was made: that you cannot carry in your head all the particulars of the former deed; but as it was the one, which you had upon examination approved, you were rather at a loss, how to act, until you should hear from him: that altho' no doubt was entertained of the propriety of any thing, contained in the new deed, yet the postponement of the date a year later might look as if your contract with him was made now for the first time: and that in the mean time you would keep the deed to be decided on by you.[2] I have the honor, to be, dear sir with sincere and affectionate attachment and respect yr mo. ob. serv.

Edm: Randolph

ALS, NN: Emmet Collection.

1. The two deeds from John Francis Mercer granted GW a 519-acre tract from Woodstock Manor in Montgomery County, Maryland. On the deed dated 1 April 1793, see n.1 of GW to Mercer, 7 Aug. 1793. The more recent version was enclosed in a letter from John Gwinn to GW of 25 Jan. 1794, which has not been found (see GW to Gwinn, this date).

2. Compare Randolph's suggestion with GW's letters to Gwinn and Mercer of this date.

From George Smith

Sir Galston Manse [Scotland] March 10th 1794

The subject of this Letter is a Gentleman, now no more Mr William Hunter a native of this place, & who some time ago died at the Town of Alexandria.[1] His Parents, though none of the richest, were as respectable, & as highly esteemed as any in this Parish. Mr Hunter, whom I personally knew, & whose good heart, & dutiful attention to his Parents, endeared him much to them, & all his ffriends, had for several years remitted Money for their Subsistence, & had promised to relieve his Brother Mr John Hunter of some incumbrances, which misfortunes in Trade, & his early Death prevented. In this Country much has been said of his extensive Trade & opulence; but by any accounts yet received, I am sorry to say that there appears little or no prospect of his Relations deriving any pecuniary advantage, from all the property which He possessed, in Land, Ships, Wharfs, Stock in Trade &c. &c. &c.—It is asserted here on the authority of his own Letters, that He had in property many thousands acres of Land & some of which was well cultivated, & a House & Stores in Alexandria.

By some extracts from his Will[2]—It appears, that there was a miniature picture of Himself, in Gold, a Lockett & two Gold Rings bequeathed to his near Relations, none of which, nor his Watch, nor indeed the Smallest remembrance of him, have reached this Country—Even the Silver plate, he possessed, would be a desireable acquisition to his ffriends—your Justice, & the known Benevolence of Character, have emboldened me to trouble You on the Subject, And as I am informed, that Your Excellency had admitted Mr Hunter to habits of Intimacy with You, I hope that you will take the trouble to cause any of Your secretaries enquire into his affairs at others, as well as his Trustees, & report to You.

Afterwards I shall flatter myself, that you will send me any intelligence, that may be for the information or advantage of his relations here.[3]

It is said that Mr Hunter sold 5,000 acres of his Land, but a great deal must yet remain. I have the Honour to be with much esteem of your elevated Character Sir Your Excellencie's most obt & obliged humble Servt

George Smith.

Please address to Me Mi⟨n⟩ister at Galston By Kilmarnock.

P.S. Mr Hunter's address was William Hunter Junr—This Letter is written at the desire of his Brother Mr John Hunter my Parishioner—and if your Excellency shall find that there is any considerable Subject, remaining of his Brothers property (though for some time lock'd up) He would instantly embark for America, if your Excellency approved of the Scheme. G.S.

ALS, DLC:GW. Postal notations on the cover read, "Alex. 1 June 94" and "Free."

The Rev. George Smith (1748–1823) was a Presbyterian minister at Galston, East Ayrshire, from 1778 until his death.

1. William Hunter, Jr. (1731–1792) was a Scottish-born merchant in Alexandria, Va., of which he served as mayor, 1788–90. He was a frequent visitor at Mount Vernon prior to GW's election to the presidency and a fellow member of Masonic Lodge No. 22 in Alexandria.

2. Hunter's will is on file in the Fairfax County Courthouse, Book F–1.

3. Upon receipt of this letter, GW enclosed it in a letter to Alexandria resident John Fitzgerald of 13 June asking for his assistance. Bartholomew Dandridge, Jr., then replied to Smith on 30 Aug.: "In answer to the enquiries made in your Letter of the 10 March last to the President of the U.S. The President directs me to transmit to you the Letters herewith enclosed; which contain the best information he is able to obtain relatively to the situation of the affairs of Wm Hunter jr decd" (ViMtvL). The enclosures, which probably came from Fitzgerald, have not been identified. Smith apparently did not receive Dandridge's letter, because he wrote to GW on 12 Feb. 1795 that he had never received a reply to his earlier letter. He therefore repeated much of the information in the letter of 10 March, asking again for GW's assistance (DLC:GW).

To William Tilghman

Dear Sir   Philadelphia 10th March 1794
Your favor of the 1st instt with its enclosures, I have duly received.

I shall, by this days Post, write to the representative of Colo. Carlyle (agreeably to the suggestion in Mr Chalmers' letter) to know if he (Mr Herbert) can throw any light upon the payment of £100 which Mr Chalmers conceives he must have made, on acct of Mr Sidney George's Bond.[1] When I receive the answer it shall be forwarded to you. 'Till then, the draught on Mr Chalmers may be suspended.[2]

I have no other object in this business than to bring every thing, which relates to it, to a speedy & equitable close so far as it respects the parties interested; and to a justifiable one, as it concerns myself. On these principals I should hope Mr George would not require (having an attested copy of it) the original bond in the possession of Mr Chalmers—especially as the receipt for the money might recite a statement of the fact, for his indemnification.

It is of moment, however, to me, to have it ascertained whether the sum of £100 recd by Mr Chalmers—& the bond due from Mr George for the payment of £90 ought not to be discharged with interest. The Administration accts which have been settled, will shew that interest has been paid by the estate of Colo. Colvill (Miss Andersons is an instance of it) and judgments in behalf of the estate have been obtained, in Virginia, with interest.[3] To act safely is all I aim at, for I neither gain or lose by the transaction. I am—Dear Sir Your Most Obedt & Very Hble Servant

Go: Washington

ALS, RPJCB; ALS (letterpress copy), NN: Washington Papers; LB, DLC:GW.

1. GW wrote William Herbert, the representative for the estate of John Carlyle, on this same date.

2. GW's letter to Tilghman of 16 March 1794 has not been found, but for Tilghman's response to it, see his letter to GW of 23 March.

3. For the financial accounts for the estate of Col. Thomas Colvill, of which GW was an executor and which was not finally settled until 1796, see Ledger C, 13–15, 25. For the payment of the legacy due Harriet Rebecca Anderson, see Tobias Lear to James Keith, 14 July 1793, and n.1 to that document.

Cabinet Opinion on the Payment of the U.S. Debt to France

[Philadelphia, 11 March 1794]

At a meeting of the heads of departments and the attorney general, on the 11th of march 1794.

It is advised unanimously, that Mr Fauchet be informed, that He shall be supplied with the instalments, due in September and November next, according to the manner, expressed in the report of the Secretary of the treasury to the President on this subject.[1]

It is proposed by the Secretary of the treasury and of war, and by the attorney general, that it be verbally stated to Mr Fauchet by the secretary of state, that notwithstanding the desire of the President to accommodate his request, the situation of the United States will not permit him to go farther, than as abovementioned.[2]

The Secretary of state proposes, that an attempt be made to satisfy Mr Fauchet verbally with the foregoing engagement; but if he does not relinquish his application, that it be forwarded to congress.[3]

Edm: Randolph

Approved   reserving the lastmentioned proposition of the Secretary of State for further consideration.[4]

A. Hamilton

H. Knox

Wm Bradford

DS (in Edmund Randolph's handwriting), DLC:GW.

1. For Hamilton's report on these installments, see his letter to GW of 18 March. Fauchet, the French minister to the United States, wrote Edmund Randolph on 1 March requesting "an advancement of the sum requisite to defray the expenses and preparations" for the return to France of those refugees from the French colony of Saint Domingue who were currently in the United States. On 2 March, in response to a request from Randolph, Fauchet wrote him that "I shall want at least a million of dollars, payable in six months, to satisfy the wants of Frenchmen at present in the United States" and to pay off other debts (both translations, DNA: RG 26, Third Congress, 1793–1795, Records of Senate Proceedings, Reports and Communications from the Secretary of State).

2. On 12 March, Randolph wrote Fauchet. "Your letters of the 1st and 2d instant, requiring the advance of a million of dollars, have been laid before the President of the United States.

"He instructs me to inform you, that the sum of one million, five hundred thousand livres, shall be paid to your order, as minister plenipotentiary of the French Republic, on the 3d of september next; and an additional sum of one million of livres, on the 5th of November next (1794): that for the present, all claim for the anticipations, which are understood to have been made by the United States, will be suspended; and that in the mean time any of your draughts within the above limits and epochs shall be registered at the treasury, in the order of their presentation.

"The President, in the determination now announced, has consulted a disposition to comply with your desire, as far as the situation and prospects of the United States have appeared to him at this juncture to permit.

"I shall be happy to have a personal interview with you upon this occasion. As two o'clock this afternoon and my office seemed, from what passed between us yesterday, to be an agreeable hour and place, I beg leave to expect you" (FrPMAE: Correspondance Politique, Etats-Unis, Supplement Volume 20; DNA: RG 46, Third Congress, 1793–95, Senate Records of Legislative Proceedings, Report and Communications from the Secretary of State).

Fauchet replied that same date: "I have received your letter dated to day, and I observe with chagrin the dispositions it contains.

"When I asked for the advance of a million of dollars I hoped that a part of that sum would be paid down to me, and the rest at different periods, the last of which should not exceed six months; but contrary to my hope, the first term of payment is indicated at that epoch only, and the advance to be made to me confined to half the sum which I had requested.

"I pray you, Sir, to observe to the President of the United States, that this determination will obviate none of the embarrassments in which I find myself: that I must pay cash to the captains of the vessels which may take the colonists to France, and for the subsistence, which those unfortunate people require; that I must advance to the latter for such stores, at least as are of the first necessity. I request you, Sir, to add also, that numerous drafts are drawn on me at sight, or within short periods of each other, by the different agents of the french Republic; either for articles of provision for the crews of vessels ready to sail; or for expenses incurred antecedent to my administration, and which it is impossible for me to postpone satisfying immediately.

"These various observations will without doubt operate a change in the resolution of the President which you have communicated to me; and the sincere picture, which I have traced to you, of my situation, will engage him to make an effort in favor of the allies of America" (translation, DNA: RG 46, Third Congress, 1793–95, Senate Records of Legislative Proceedings, Reports and Communications from the Secretary of State).

3. GW forwarded Hamilton's report, and the translations and copies of the correspondence between Fauchet and Randolph, to the U.S. Senate and House of Representatives on 18 March. For printed versions of the English translations and the copies of the French originals that were submitted to Congress, see, respectively, *ASP, Foreign Relations,* 1:427–28, and *Hamilton Papers,* 16:143, n.1. For the U.S. Senate's refusal to alter the payment schedules, see *Annals of Congress,* 3d. Cong., 129.

4. This modification is in Hamilton's handwriting.

Letter not found: from William Pearce, 11 March 1794. GW wrote Pearce in a letter of 16–17 March that "Your letter of the 11th with its enclosures came to hand at the usual time."

To Maria I of Portugal

Great and good Friend   [Philadelphia, March 11, 1794]

It was with the most sincere pleasure, that I was informed by your Majesty's highly-esteemed letter, of the addition made to your domestic happiness, and to the joy of your Kingdom, by the birth of the Princess of Beira. This event, so interesting in itself, is heightened by the favorable escape of the Princess of Brazil, from the danger attached to it.[1]

Your Majesty has a full claim upon the congratulations of the United States, in every instance of your prosperity, from the noble and friendly part, which you have lately adopted, by granting convoys to our Trade, against the Corsairs of Algiers.[2]

With the warmest hope, that the Amity, now subsisting between your Majesty and the United States, will be perpetual, I pray God to keep you, Great and good Friend, under his holy protection.

Written at Philadelphia the Eleventh day of March 1794. Your good Friend

Go: Washington[3]
By the President of the
United States of America
Edm: Randolph ⟨Secretary of State⟩

LS, Torre do Tombe: National Archives Institute, Lisbon, Portugal; LB, DNA, RG 59, Credences.

1. The birth of the Princess of Beira, Maria Teresa (d. 1874), on 29 April 1793 was announced in a letter to GW of that same date (LS [Portuguese], DNA: RG 59, Communications from Heads of Foreign States). The Princess of Brazil (Carlota Joaquina; 1775–1830) was married to the future John VI (1767–1826), who was a son of Maria I of Portugal (1734–1816).

2. On the protection offered to American shipping by Portugal, see David Humphreys to GW, 31 Jan., and n.1 to that document.

3. The following text and signature is in the writing of Edmund Randolph. The text in angle brackets is from the letter-book copy.

From Edmund Randolph

Sir   Philadelphia March 11. 1794.

The minutes, which were made yesterday at the conference in your room, did not permit an insertion of the reasons, upon which my dissent from the fourth proposition was founded.[1] As I shall always contend, for what I conceive to be the constitutional and legal powers of the government; so I beg leave to request, upon this truly important subject, that you will suffer this letter to be filed away, with the paper, containing the opinions.

My reasons against the instruction, advised to be given to general Wayne, to post a body of regular troops at Massac, and by force, if necessary, to prevent the party of Kentucky citizens, who are supposed to meditate an invasion of the Spanish dominions, from proceeding, are the following.

1.   Those troops were raised, and destined by law, exclusively for other purposes.

2.   The law of the land, and not an army, is to be resorted to, for the punishment of citizens of the U.S., who may be charged with crimes. Regular proof too ought to precede punishment.

3.   The sense of a committee at least of the senate appears to be the same; because a bill is actually depending before them for giving the power to the President to use military force on such an occasion. This would not have been necessary, if the power existed already.[2]

4.   The present case is not an invasion from a foreign nation, in the grammatical, legal or constitutional impo⟨rt.⟩

5.   If it were an insurrection, the President is restricted by a law of May 2. 1792 from interposing even with militia, except upon the application of the legislature or executive of Kentucky.[3]

6.   The marshals and their deputies have the same power, as sheriffs, to call out the posse comitatus.[4]

7.   If a combination to obstruct the laws be too powerful, the President cannot draw forth even the militia, but upon a notification from a judge of the supreme or district courts.[5]

8.   If the blood of the citizens of Kentucky should be shed under the order, now advised, it will I fear terminate in a revolt of that country, and a separation from the Union; and

9.   The probability is, that the attempt, which was begun, is at an end, for the present; and it is at any rate better to wait and see, what power congress may give, rather than to hazard so doubtful an one on so critical an occasion. I have the honor, sir, to be with the highest respect yr mo. ob. serv.

Edm: Randolph

ALS, DLC:GW; LB, DNA: RG 59, Domestic Letters. GW's docket reads, "Opinion of the Secretary of State 11th March 1794 against applying Military force to oppose the meditated Expedition from the State of Kentuck against the Spaniards on the Mississippi." The text in angle brackets is from the letter-book copy.

1. For these minutes, see the Cabinet Opinion of 10 March.

2. Section 7 of "An Act in addition to the act for the punishment of certain crimes against the United States," 5 June 1794, granted specific powers to "the President of the United States, or such other person as he shall have empowered for that purpose, to employ such part of the land or naval forces of the United States or for the militia thereof as shall be judged necessary . . . for the purpose of preventing the carrying on of any such expedition or en-

terprise from the territories of the United States against the territories or dominions of a foreign prince or state, with whom the United States are at peace" (*Stat.* 1:381–84).

3. See Section 1 of "An Act to provide for calling forth the Militia to execute the laws of the Union, suppress insurrections and repel invasions," 2 May 1792 (*Stat.* 1:264).

4. See Section 9 of "An Act to provide for calling forth the Militia to execute the laws of the Union, suppress insurrections and repel invasions," 2 May 1792 (*Stat.* 1:265).

5. For this provision, see Section 2 of "An Act to provide for calling forth the Militia to execute the laws of the Union, suppress insurrections and repel invasions," 2 May 1792 (*Stat.* 1:264).

From Edmund Randolph

[Philadelphia] Tuesday. 11. March. 1794.
E. Randolph has the honor of informing the President of the U.S., that he saw Mr Brown, of the senate, from Kentucky, yesterday afternoon: that Mr Brown informed him, that O'Fallon's letter in his possession, was the original; & that it was intercepted by one of his correspondents in going from O'Fallon to Capt. Herron.[1] Mr Brown did not mention the name of Belli or Wilkinson, in connection with this letter; nor did E.R. mention either of them to him.[2]

AL, DNA: RG 59, Miscellaneous Letters; LB, DLC:GW; LB, DNA: RG 59, GW's Correspondence with His Secretaries of State.

1. On the letter from James O'Fallon to Capt. Herron that was currently in the possession of Kentucky senator John Brown, see Randolph's fourth letter to GW of 27 Feb., and n.2 to that document.

2. GW apparently had questioned Randolph about deputy quartermaster general John Belli and Gen. James Wilkinson, both currently serving in the U.S. Army.

From Civis

Sir,   March 12th 1794.
As a Citizen of the United States, anxiously observing their critical Situation, and the hostile Measures pursued by one, at least, of the belligerent Powers—being perhaps more inclined to propose, than capacitated to suggest, the necessary Means of Relief, I yet take the Liberty of addressing your Excellency.

Without further Apology, permit me to submit to your Consideration, the following Propositions. viz.

1st. That an Embargo be laid upon all Shipping, & Exportations from the United States, for the term of six months.[1] 2d. That the Debts due [(] Vattel Book 3d Chap. 5th §. 77.[)] from the Citizens of the U.S., to the Subjects & Citizens of any of the belligerent Powers, be sequestered, or retained by Government, as a Pledge for the Restoration of the Property spoliated, and for the Injuries & Damages sustained by the Citizens of the United States, through any of the belligerent Powers, contrary to the Laws of Nations, or to the Faith of Treaties.[2] 3d. That the Citizens of the U.S. be required within a given, *short time,* to send forward to Commissioners to be appointed therefor, their Estimates of Losses, and Damages, to be accompanied with the best Evidences, which their Cases will admit of, in order that they may be arranged & transmitted to Europe, as expeditiously as possible. 4th. That special Commissioners be sent to the several belligerent Powers,[3] for the purposes of demanding in some Instances, and of stating in others, the losses & Damages sustained by the Citizens of the U.S. through Infractions of the Laws of Nations, & of assuring the said Powers respectively, of the pacifick Disposition of the United States, and of their determination to continue their impartial Neutrality, so long as it shall comport with the Honour of the Government, and the just Rights of the Citizens of the united States. 5th. That a Demand of an imediate Recall of all Orders, which are, or may be given to the Commanders of Ships of War, or Privateers, under the Authority of any of the belligerent Powers, contravening the Rights of Neutrality, according to the Laws of Nations, & that upon Refusal thereof, or upon the denial of Justice, in regard to the Injuries already sustained, to notify to the respective Governments, that the Government of the U.S. holds itself bound to its Interests, to retain the Debts due from the Citizens of the U.S. to their Citizens or Subjects, for the Purposes aforementioned, & to take such other Steps in the Premises, as their Honour & Interest may further dictate. 6th. That one or more Commissioners be sent to the Nations not engaged in the present War, for the Purpose of ascertaining, & vindicating the Rights of neutral Nations.

By a Policy of the kind before suggested, It is apprehended, the United States will gain Time, not only to recover their great

Property, but numerous Seamen now abroad, but will be enabled by the Events of the approaching Campaign to judge with more Certainty, of the Measures proper to be pursued.

Time does not permit me at present, to enter particularly into the Reasons, upon which the foregoing Propositions are grounded: It is, however my Opinion, that the Measures suggested are purely defensive, & can in no Construction of them, be considered as Acts of Aggression; but on the contrary result from the necessity of the case, & are both just & prudent, & will probably unite the Sentiments of the commercial Interest of the U.S. With Sentiments of the highest Respect & Esteem: I am, your Excellency's most obedet hble Servt

Civis.

ALS, DLC:GW.

1. On 26 March, GW approved a joint resolution of Congress that imposed a thirty-day embargo "on all ships and vessels in the ports of the United States" (*Stat.* 1:400).

2. This is a reference to Emmerich de Vattel's three-volume work, which was published in English as *The Law of Nations; or Principles of the Law of Nature: Applied to the Conduct and to the Affairs of Nations and Sovereigns* (London, 1760). Chapter five is entitled, "Of the Enemy, and of Things Belonging to the Enemy," and Section 77 is "Things due to the enemy by the third party."

3. On GW's appointment of John Jay as "envoy extraordinary of the United States" to Great Britain, see GW to U.S. Senate, 16 April (first letter).

From Gouverneur Morris

My dear Sir   Sainport [France] 12 March 1794

I send you herewith a Duplicate of my last Letter in the close of which I mention my Adherence to the Opinions exprest in my last but on recurring to my private Letter Book which was not then before me I find that the Letter I there alluded to was written on the eighteenth of October. It went by Captain Culver and has I hope arrived in due Season.[1] Every Day confirms what is contain'd in that Letter: but Parties are so ballanced, and the impending force from abroad is in such threatening Attitude, that the present State of Things drags on it's Existence rather from surrounding Circumstances than from internal Vigor— And Strange as it may seem the impending Change may arise from Victory or from a Defeat or from a famine.

The Gazettes tell us that Mr Jefferson is coming to Europe. Some of them say as my Successor others say it is a secret Mission. I have heard it said that he is to negotiate a Peace among the belligerent Powers.[2] For my own Part I hold in Politics the Opinions which prevail in Phisics among sound Philosophers viz. that it is proper to determine Facts before we attempt to discover Causes. I wait therefore patiently the Event. Major Jackson who has been here for some Time gave me two Successors first Mr Bingham and then Mr Pinkney giving in the latter Case Mr Pinkney's Place to Mr Bingham. So it is easy you see to fill up Vacancies.[3]

The probable Events of the Campaign about to open are not favorable to the french Republic.[4] It will be extremely difficult for them to subsist the Armies needful for their Defence and the extreme Severity exercised by the present Government will in Case of adverse Events excite an universal Insurrection. At present the People are restraind by Fear from shewing any Sentiment unfavorable to the existent Authorities but, as is usual in like Circumstances, should that Fear be remov'd it will be succeeded by sharp Resentment. If however the Armies of the Republic should prove successful they would in my Opinion be the first to overturn the Convention for such is the usual Course of Things. A terrible Perspective this my dear Sir for those who are at present in the Saddle⟨:⟩ no Wonder therefore if they ride hard. It is not the least of their Misfortunes to be fully sensible of their Situation and it results therefrom that as much Time is consum'd in providing for their Defence against Adverse factions and contingent Events as in preparing for the general Defence of the Country. More perhaps. How different was our Situation in America. Every one perform'd chearfully his Part nor had we any Thing to apprehend but from the common Enemy. Such is the immense Difference between a Country which has Morals and one which is corrupted. The former has every Thing to hope and the latter every Thing to fear. Adieu my Dear Sir. May god in Heaven bless and preserve and prosper you[5]

Gouv. Morris

ALS, DLC:GW; ALS (duplicate copy), DLC:GW; LB, DLC: Gouverneur Morris Papers. The text in angle brackets is from the duplicate ALS.

1. The enclosed duplicate was of Morris to GW, 5 February. The sloop *Hannah,* under William Culver, arrived at Philadelphia in mid-January (*Gazette of the United States and Evening Advertiser* [Philadelphia], 14 Jan. 1794).

2. The rumors that Morris would be replaced as minister to France were correct, but it was James Monroe, and not Thomas Jefferson, who replaced him (see GW to U.S. Senate, 27 May).

3. On William Jackson's visit with Morris, see Certificate for William Jackson, 12 June 1793, and Tobias Lear to Thomas Jefferson, 13 June 1793 (second letter). Philadelphia businessman and banker William Bingham's name appears on Alexander Hamilton's List of Candidates for Minister to France of 19 May 1794. For the suggestion that Thomas Pinckney, the current minister plenipotentiary to Great Britain, be reassigned to France, see GW to John Jay, 29 April.

4. France currently was at war with several nations, including Great Britain, Austria, and Prussia.

5. "I am very truly yours" appears at this point on the duplicate ALS.

From Marie Madeleine Rossignol Bancio Piémont

Monsieur le Général   Philadelphia le 12 Mars 1794

Je me Serais fait un devoir et un plaisir de vous porter moi-même le paquet dont Mr de Gimat m'avait chargé pour vous, Si ma Sante ne m'en eut privé dans ce moment. ⟨m⟩ais ne voulant pas différes plus long-temps ma Commission, j'ai l'honneur de vous l'envoier. j'ai bien du regret de ne pouvoir pas jouir de celui de voir moi même un homme tel que vous, dont la mérite reconnu de tout le monde lui à fait une réputation invariable.[1]

j'ai l'honneur d'étre, Monsieur le Général Votre très humble obéissant Servante

Rossignol Piémont

ALS (in French), DNA: RG 59, Miscellaneous Letters.

1. The writer of this letter has enclosed the letter from Gimat to GW of 5 Dec. 1793, along with its accompanying packet of letters. In this cover letter, she expresses her regret that ill health prevents her from delivering these papers personally.

From Edmund Randolph

[Philadelphia] Wednesday 12. Mar. 94

E. Randolph has the honor of sending to the President a message to accompany the papers from the Spanish commissioners[1]— Also the statement of general officers in the government.[2]

AL, DNA: RG 59, Miscellaneous Letters; LB, DNA: RG 59, GW's Correspondence with His Secretaries of State.

1. For this message and its accompanying papers, see GW to the U.S. Senate and House of Representatives, this date, and n.1.

2. The statement of general officers employed by the federal government has not been identified.

To the United States Senate
and House of Representatives

United States 12 March 1794.
Gentlemen of the Senate and of the House of Representatives.

I transmit to you the translations of two letters from the Commissioners of his Catholic Majesty to the Secretary of State, and of their enclosures.[1]

Go: Washington

LS, DNA: RG 46, Third Congress, 1793–95, Senate Records of Legislative Proceedings, Presidential Messages; LB, DNA: RG 233, Third Congress, 1793–95, House Records of Legislative Proceedings, Journals; LB, DLC:GW.

1. All the enclosures were translations of the original Spanish versions sent to Edmund Randolph by Spanish commissioners José de Jaudenes and José Ignacio de Viar. In their first letter, which is undated, the commissioners wrote that although a "circuitous course of the dispatches having retarded our receiving the Edict of His Majesty containing the declaration of War against the French in consequence of their having declared war against Spain and committed hostilities authorized by that Government even when War was not yet declared," they were now able to present "a printed Edict of that Monarch [Charles IV], which you will please to lay before the President of the United States in order to be communicated to Congress" (DNA: RG 46, Third Congress, 1793–95, Senate Records of Legislative Proceedings, President's Messages).

The second letter from Jaudenes and Viar, dated 5 March 1794, expressed concern about "those expeditions, which are in motion in the res[pectiv]e States of South Carolina, Kentuckey and Georgia" against nearby Spanish colonies. In their opinion, "the insufficiency of this government to enforce the execution of their laws and regulations as well as the notorious partiality of their Citizens and individual inhabitants in Favor of France tending to the open prejudice of the interests of Spain are likely to interrupt the good understanding and sincere amity, that happily subsisted between the two Nations to the present period, and which the United States cannot but look upon as a connexion of consequence." To support their claims about the hostile activities of individual Americans, they mentioned the involvement of James O'Fallon of Kentucky in a proposed expedition against Louisiana. They also enclosed a copy of a letter of 22 Jan. 1794 from the governor of

East Florida, Juan Nepomuceno de Quesada y Barnuevo, to the governor of Georgia, George Mathews, complaining about a "plot" by certain Georgia residents to invade East Florida, both by land and sea. Quesada requested Mathews "to exert your utmost efforts till the said plot shall be entirely destroyed. Meanwhile I make all possible dispositions to due defence to repel force by force, of all which I shall render an exact account to the King my master, enclosing for his superior consideration all proofs, I am possessed of and which ascertain the imminent danger of an approaching invasion of the royal flag and H. M[ajest]ys dominions, that his Majesty may cause such steps to be taken, as may secure due redress to Hs M[ajest]y" (DNA: RG 46, Third Congress, 1793–95, Senate Records of Legislative Proceedings, President's Messages). For the full text of the above four documents, see *ASP, Foreign Relations,* 1:425–27.

From Alexander Hamilton

The President of the United States   March 13. [17]94.

The Secretary of the Treasury presents his respects to the President. He sent yesterday for the papers necessary to furnish the particular instances of misconduct in certain officers of Pennsylvania, but on examination they prove not to be the right ones. There is probably not time to correct the error to-day; but the President may mention the circumstance to the Governor & inform him that he will direct me to communicate particulars.[1]

LB, DLC:GW.

1. The enclosed documents have not been identified. Hamilton's reference to misconduct may reflect the reluctance of some Pennsylvania officials to help enforce the collection of the federal excise tax on whiskey (see Thomas Mifflin to GW, 18 April 1794).

From Edmund Randolph

[Philadelphia] March 13. 1794.

E. Randolph has the honor of inclosing to the President two letters from our Consul at St Eustatius[1] with a draft of a letter, proposed to be written to Mr Van Berckell.[2]

AL, DNA: RG 59, Miscellaneous Letters; LB, DNA: RG 59, GW's Correspondence with His Secretaries of State.

1. David M. Clarkson's letter to Randolph of 15 Jan. reported that British vessels in the Caribbean Sea were "capturing all those of the United States of America, going either to or coming from any of the Islands belonging to

the Republic of France; several have been already libelled and condemned at Montserrat Vessels and Cargoes, altho it was made appear the property of American Citizens, at present there are at Montserrat & St Kitts between 20 & 30, which are libelled & which there is no doubt, from the general opinion will be condemned." Clarkson then cited a letter from a gentleman of St. Kitts describing the situation there: "There are now here 12 or 14 American Vessels, all which with their Cargoes will be condemned . . . The Brign. from Baltimore to Bourdeaux has been condemned and her Cargo landing—A Sloop from Virginia that carried Bread ⟨to⟩ Barbadoes for the British Navy, had taken in there 19 barrels ⟨of⟩ Sugar, fell in with a French Privateer that carried her to Guadaloupe, which they landed, he then took in some freight for an American at Guadaloupe & has been brought in here, where he wi⟨ll⟩ be condemned both Vessel and Cargo, the other Vessels are New England Vessels, except the Brign. Three friends, Captain Morris of Wilmington, with one hundred and odd hds Sugar, 30 hds Coffee & &ca which will be condemned without exception." Clarkson continued: "I take the liberty of enclosing you a News Paper of Antigu⟨a⟩ containing the statement of the case of Cargo of the American Ship Charlotte, Capt. Coffin, condemned there in a Vice Court of Admiralty—A British Fleet consisting of several Ships of the line & 10,000 troops have arrived at Barbadoes & at present the Island of Martinico [Martinique] is blockaded." In his letter to Randolph of 7 Feb., Clarkson mentioned again the seizure and condemnation of American vessels before writing: "Yesterday I received a possitive Order from the Governor & Council of this Island not to Act in any case whatever as Consul of the United States, as they had received directions to this effect from their High Mightinesses the States General. This is truly unfortunate for any Fellow Citizens ⟨as⟩ a Certificate from me of their having left this Port ⟨w⟩ould prevent their being molested by either French ⟨or⟩ British Privateers" (both letters, DNA: RG 59, Consular Despatches, St. Eustatius).

2. The letter-book copy has Van Bartkell. Randolph's letter of 13 March to Franco Petrus Van Berckel, the Dutch minister to the United States, referenced Clarkson's letter of 7 Feb. and its news that he had been ordered "not to act in any case whatever, as Consul of the United States." Randolph then wrote: "The disposition, which has been invariably manifested by the United States, to facilitate and improve the commercial intercourse between the two countries, gives them a title to hope for a correspondent disposition in the States General. But our expectation, that a Consul would be indulged in St Eustatius, is also supported by the 21st article of the treaty of commerce. It is there stipulated, that 'the two contracting parties grant to each other mutually, the liberty of having each in the ports of the other Consuls, Vice-Consuls' &c. After our conversation yesterday I cannot doubt, that directions, like those, which exclude Mr Clarkson, have not yet been made known to you by any authority of government, and if they exist, I cannot but hope, that being so extremely difficult to reconcile with the treaty they must have originated from misapprehension, and will be speedily rescinded" (DNA: RG 59, Domestic Letters). For the U.S. Treaty of Amity and Commerce of 8 Oct. 1782 with the Netherlands, see Miller, *Treaties,* 59–90.

From Edmund Randolph

[Philadelphia] March 13th 1794.

The President of the United States.

E. Randolph has the honor of transmitting to the President, a Letter on the subject of Mr Fauchet's demand, with three opinions[1]—The President will be pleased to say, whether the papers shall or shall not be prepared for Congress.[2]

LB, DNA: RG 59, Domestic Letters.

1. On the request of Fauchet, the French minister to the United States, for an advance payment of the U.S. debt to France, see Cabinet Opinion, 11 March, and notes 1–3. In an attempt to resolve this issue, Randolph met with Fauchet on 12 March. The enclosed letter may have been Randolph's letter to William Bradford, Alexander Hamilton, and Henry Knox of 13 March, in which Randolph reported on the failure of this meeting to resolve the matter to Fauchet's satisfaction. Randolph then wrote: "Permit me therefore to submit to your consideration my opinion, to be laid, with yours, before the President. I am of the opinion, that Mr Fauchet's application for money, ought to be transmitted to Congress. 1. Because the executive, as it is represented by the Secretary of the Treasury, cannot expect to modify the French debt by an further loans at present, altho' Congress have given the President special power to do so, and have expressed a desire, that it should be done. 2. Because Congress are the true Judges, whether the situation of the United States permits Mr Faucet's request to be complied with from other resources, besides loans. 3. Because the French debt is intitled to every exertion in our power, to relieve the embarrassments of the French government. 4. And because I do not discern any objection to submit to Congress a subject, so peculiarly within their province, as the raising of money" (DNA: RG 59, Domestic Letters). Opinions from any other individual cabinet member have not been identified.

2. GW enclosed the documents relevant to this issue in his letter to the U.S. Senate and House of Representatives of 18 March.

To the Commissioners for the District of Columbia

(Private)

Gentlemen,   Philadelphia, Mar. 14th 1794

My object in giving you a sight of the enclosed letters from Mr Ellicott, is merely to let you see the temper; and tendency of his views; and what may be expected from his representations to others. After reading the letters, be so good as to return them to me.[1]

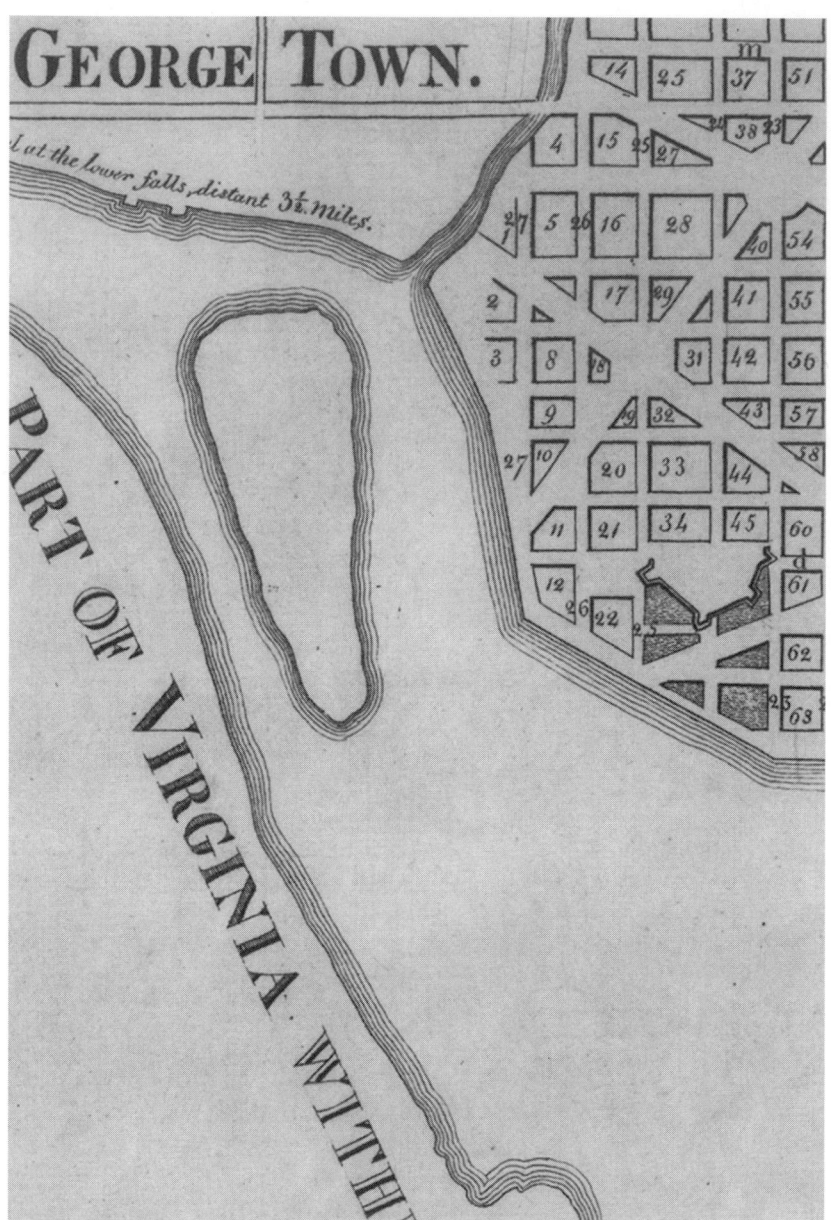

Fig. 1: Numbered lots on the west end of the District of Columbia, a detail of "Plan of the City of Washington in the Territory of Columbia," as drawn by Andrew Ellicott and engraved by Samuel Hill of Boston in 1792. (See back endpapers; Library of Congress, Geography and Map Division.) GW ultimately purchased square 21.

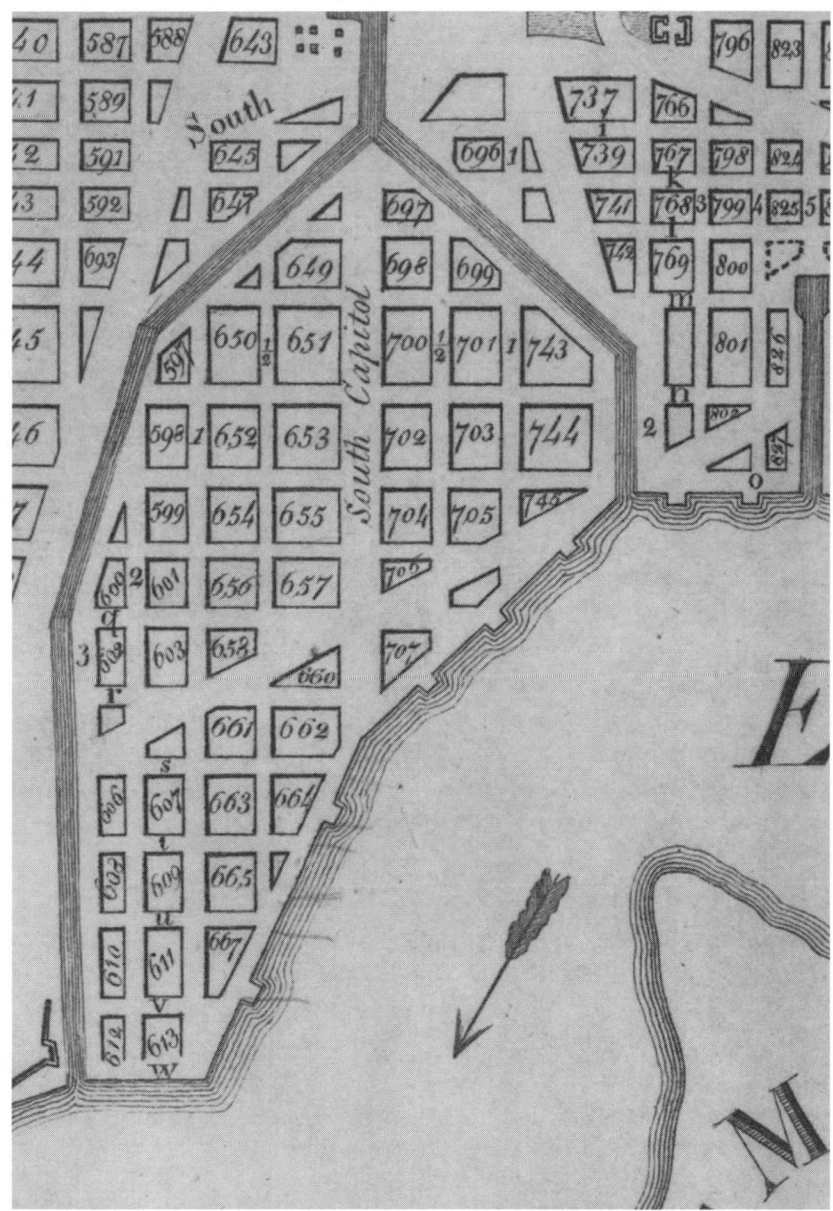

Fig. 2: Numbered lots on the south end of the District of Columbia, a detail of "Plan of the City of Washington in the Territory of Columbia," as drawn by Andrew Ellicott and engraved by Samuel Hill of Boston in 1792. (See back endpapers; Library of Congress, Geography and Map Division.) GW purchased square 667.

In September last, after having purchased four lots in Carrollsburgh (the doing of which was more the result of incident than premeditation); and being unwilling from that circumstance, it should be believed that I had a greater prediliction to the southern, than I had to the Northern part of the city, I proposed next day (the sale being continued) to buy a like number of lots in Hamburgh, and accordingly designated the spot;[2] but as little notice was taken of it then, and none since, that I have heard; and as the sale to Greenleaf & others may have thrown impediments in the way, I should be glad to know what my prospect is; adding, that I am as ready to relinquish, as I was to imbibe the idea, of this purchase.[3]

I had no desire at that time, nor have I any now, to stand on a different footing from every other purchaser. It was, and certainly would be convenient for me to know if there is a probability of my being accomodated agreeably to the enclosed from Mr Blodget; first, because the means of payment are to be provided, and secondly, because my object in fixing on the spot there-mentioned is to build thereon when I can make it convenient; provided the area described by him can be obtained: for less would not subserve my purpose.[4]

Whenever deeds to others issue, be so good as to direct those for the lots which I have bought on the Eastern branch, to be forwarded to me.[5] With great esteem & regard I am—Gentn Yr Obt Serv⟨t⟩

Go: Washington

ALS, Records of the U.S. Commissioners of the City of Washington, 1791–1869; LB, DLC:GW.

1. For these letters, which concern the long-running dispute between Andrew Ellicott and the commissioners, see Andrew Ellicott, Benjamin Ellicott, and Isaac Briggs to GW, 29 June 1793, and Andrew Ellicott's two letters to GW of 28 Feb. 1794.

2. On GW's purchase of four lots in square 667, south of the Capitol and along the Eastern Branch, see Certificate for Lots Purchased in the District of Columbia, 18 Sept. 1793, and notes. On rivalry between the proprietors of the towns of Carrollsburg and Hamburg, see n.2 of David Stuart to GW, 6 Feb. 1794.

3. GW was interested in purchasing lots in square 21, which was west of the President's House (D.C. Commissioners to GW, 23 March [first letter]). On land speculation in the Federal City by James Greenleaf, see n.1 of Edmund Randolph to GW, 3 January.

4. The enclosure from Samuel Blodget, Jr., has not been identified.

5. In lieu of a deed, the commissioners enclosed the certificate of 18 Sept. 1793 in their letter to GW of 23 March.

From John Gwinn

Sir,   Annapolis [Md.], March 14th 1794

The division made by Hezh Veach, as referred to in the Deed to you from Colo. Mercer & others, was not transmitted to me for enrolment, owing, I imagine, to its having been omitted by Doct. Steuart, with whom the Deed was left.[1]

I shall take the liberty to inform the Doctor of its being referred to in the Deed, and of your wish to have it enrolled; and shou'd he furnish me with it, it shall be forwarded to you immediately after it is enrolled.[2] I am, Sir, With great respect, your very Humble Servant

                                     Jno. Gwinn

ALS, NN: Washington Collection. A postal stamp on the cover reads, "ANNAPOLIS, March 15."

1. On GW's receipt of a deed to 519 acres in Montgomery County, Md., from John Francis Mercer, Sophia Sprigg Mercer, James Steuart, and Rebecca Sprigg Mercer, and his desire for a copy of the survey made of this land by Hezekiah Veatch, see GW to Gwinn, 10 March.

2. On GW's receipt of the survey, see John Francis Mercer to GW, 13 April.

From Thomas Mendenhall

Dear sir.   Philadelphia March 14th 1794

Being a considerable sufferer in the calamities which my fellow Citizens are at Present strugling with, has perhaps tempered my Disposition, and Excited sentiments of humanity towards the Injured Seamen of my Country, in proportion to the Indignation at the Cruel, and unpresedented Conduct of the British Cruizers which has brot these Misfortunes upon Us.

the deep Impression of this sentiments, and a real regard for the Interes and Dignity of my Country, I hope Sir will be an apolegy for this Freedom.

On Monday last[1] arived in Wilmington D. the Schooner Kitty Capt. Brinton from S. Eustatius who brought Six American Seamen in Passengers and informs that he left about Sixty or Seventy more there, (the Crews of Condemned Vessels,) in great Distress beging for Passages to America, and that others ware daily ariving from the Windward Ilands in hopes of meeting with homeward bound Vessels that would afford them a conveyance to this Continent, which could not be obtained but in a few Instances.[2]

The Loss of so many Brave Seamen as are now Driving about those Ilands and must eventually fall into the British Servis, or that of Other foreign Nations if some effacatious measures be not adopted is of a nature at this Moment which need only be hinted at.

If a Suitable Vessel could be provided and despatched Immediately for their releif, I should be Induced to offer my Servis in order to carry the Measure into Effect, nor would I Stipulate any thing for a compensation but the gratitude of those whom I might be Instrumental in releiving from their Distress. I have the Honour to be sir with the greatest respect your real friend, and that of my Country.[3]

Thomas Mendenhall
a Citizen of Wilmington Delaware

P.S. I have Just been Creditably Informd that the Brittish Agents in this Citty are takeing the Oath to the United States, and thereby Securing their Debts. yours Respectfully as above

T.M.

ALS, DNA: RG 59, Letters Received Regarding Impressed Seamen.

Thomas Mendenhall (1752–1843), of Wilmington, Del., served in 1775–76 aboard the brig *Nancy,* a privateer operating in the West Indies. After the war he began his mercantile career as the master of other merchants' trading vessels. By 1794 he was a prosperous merchant engaged in the West Indies trade. He also had extensive land holdings in Wilmington, including his townhouse at the corner of Front and Walnut streets (Bernard L. Herman, "Multiple Materials, Multiple Meanings: The Fortunes of Thomas Mendenhall," *Winterthur Portfolio,* 19:67–86). Stage boats between Philadelphia and Mendenhall's wharf in Wilmington ran back and forth on Monday, Wednesday, and Friday (*Philadelphia Gazette and Universal Daily Advertiser,* 29 March).

1. Monday last was 10 March.

2. For a recent list of American vessels detained by the British in the West Indies, see *Philadelphia Gazette and Universal Daily Advertiser,* 11 March. On the magnitude of this problem, see n.1 of GW to U.S. Senate and House of Representatives, 25 March.

3. No reply from GW has been found.

From Edmund Randolph

Sir   Philadelphia March 14. 1794.

I did myself the honor of informing you the other day, that the House of Representatives would probably remit to my office the documents, which related to the vexations and spoliations on our trade; conceiving, that they were of a nature, purely executive.[1] Yesterday the Senate, as if they meant to take up the subject in some shape or other, passed a vote, as I have heard, calling for an abstract, estimates of the value of the property injured &c. It is not understood, however, that this ought to arrest the proceedings of the President, if he should think a demand of compensation in behalf of each individual adviseable.[2]

You have already expressed your sense on that subject; and I shall begin immediately to prepare separate statements.

But, Sir, when I run over the long list of damage and confiscation, under which the citizens of the United States are now groaning; when I conjecture the amount of the mercantile capital, which must be lost to our country, already too deficient in that respect for it's own independence; when I know, that many individuals will actually become bankrupts by this unexpected invasion of their fortunes; I consider the tardy modes of ordinary negotiation, as a refinement in torturing them with a hope, which, if ever fulfilled, will be accomplished only after a series of years. Nay more. If the government shall suspend it's interposition, until all the expensive forms of the superior foreign courts shall be exhausted, it will, in many instances, produce no other effect, than to invite the possessors of a little remnant, to throw away even that also.

I must acknowledge, that the merchants, who have been impoverished by this highhanded rigor, seem to me to have a peculiar claim upon the most vigorous exertions of the executive. If the resolutions, proposed for adding 15000 men to the military establishment, should be carried; or a military countenance, for the purpose of defence, should be assumed by a proper modification of the militia, and a complete military apparatus; redress for past injuries will not be treated as hitherto: we shall not fear insults in our own borders, nor meet with it abroad, from an opinion of our impotence.[3] Under such circumstances, I submit, Sir, to your consideration, whether it may not be expedient, to send to England some temperate, and sensible man, without a particle of the diplomatic character, who, under the particular instruction of Mr Pinckney, may manage the discussion of the respective claims. The compensation for his services cannot be an affair of consequence: he will be a solicitor only, to execute the drudgery which Mr Pinckney cannot perform; and there will be no danger of his contravening any view of our Minister, as he will be always under his command. Such a person will go charged with all the necessary information; so as to render delay, unnecessary, for the collection of proof.[4]

There is another serious mischief which is a branch of the preceding. A large number of American Sailors are now wandering on foreign shores, anxious, but unable to return home. They will, undoubtedly be swallowed up, in foreign service, from distress; and that service may possibly be hostile to us. Whether a feasible scheme can be adopted, for facilitating their escape, or any pecuniary aids can be prudently and legally contributed to this end, I shall not undertake to determine. But I beg leave to offer the enquiry, as at least proper for reflection.[5] I have the honor, Sir, to be with great respect, & esteem, your most obedient Servant

Edm: Randolph

LS, DNA: RG 59, Miscellaneous Letters; LB, DNA: RG 59, GW's Correspondence with His Secretaries of State; LB, DNA: RG 59, Domestic Letters.

1. For the submission of these documents to Congress, see GW to U.S. Senate and House of Representatives, 5 March.

2. According to a 13 May resolution of the U.S. Senate, Randolph was ordered to provide "an abstract of the vexations and spoliations lately committed upon our commerce, and by whom, particularly noting the condemnations, as far as the documents in his office will enable him" (*Annals of Congress,* 3d Cong., 69). Randolph enclosed the required abstract, which has not been identified, in his letter to the Senate of 20 May. In this letter, he wrote that as of his letter to GW of 2 March, "the cases of complaint against the British were thirty-two; against the French twenty-six; against the Spanish ten; and against the Dutch one. The propriety therefore of what that letter contains, will not be determined by the great list, which has been exhibited since. . . . The abstract would have been drawn in the first instance; had it not been intended to endeavour to settle the business by representations to the foreign Courts. Unless the Senate desire, that the papers be retained here, it is probable that many of them will be sent abroad" (DNA: RG 59, Domestic Letters; *ASP, Foreign Relations,* 1:461).

3. In the first session of the Third Congress, there were several acts passed that were designed to bolster the defenses of the United States, including: "An Act to provide for the Defence of certain Ports and Harbors in the United

States," 20 March; "An Act to provide a Naval Armament," 27 March; "An Act to provide for the erecting and repairing of Arsenals and Magazines, and for other purposes," 2 April; and "An Act providing for raising and organizing a Corps of Artillerists and Engineers," 9 May. The pending legislation referenced by Randolph probably became "An Act directing a Detachment from the Militia of the United States," which authorized the president "to require of the executives of the several states, to take effectual measures, as soon as may be, to organize, arm and equip, according to law, and hold in readiness to march at a moment's warning . . . eighty thousand effective militia, officers included" (*Stat.* 1:345–46, 350, 352, 366–68).

4. John Jay was appointed, not as an assistant to U.S. minister Thomas Pinckney, but as an "envoy extraordinary" to Great Britain (GW to U.S. Senate, 16 April [first letter]).

5. On the problem of American sailors unable to return home, see Thomas Mendenhall to GW, this date, and GW to U.S. Senate and House of Representatives, 25 March, n.1.

From Edmund Randolph

Sir   Philadelphia March 14. 1794.

The director of the mint informs me, in the inclosed letter of the 12th instant, that the treasurer is in advance to a considerable amount: that sixteen hundred dollars will be sufficient, up to the first of April next, and three thousand more, up to the first of July. I called upon Mr Rittenhouse, and represented to him, that it would be better to go no farther at present, than the 1600 dollars; and to furnish the supply for the succeeding quarter at the beginning and middle of it. He acceded to the idea. I believe, sir, that you have the form of a warrant on such an occasion.[1]

Supposing, that no objection remains to the granting of Mr Cox's commission, I shall direct it to be prepared for your approbation.[2] I have the honor, sir, to be with the highest respect yr. mo. ob. serv.

Edm: Randolph

ALS, DNA: RG 59, Miscellaneous Letters; LB, DNA: RG 59, GW's Correspondence with His Secretaries of State; LB, DNA: RG 59, Domestic Letters.

1. David Rittenhouse's letter to Randolph of 12 March has not been identified. For GW's directive to pay Rittenhouse $2,600, see GW to Alexander Hamilton, 18 March.

2. For GW's nomination of Albion Cox as the assayer of the Mint, see his letter to the U.S. Senate, 3 April. GW signed Cox's commission, which has not been identified, on 5 April (*JPP*, 297).

From Charles Simms

Sir   Alexandria [Va.] March 14th 1794

Your Letter of the 29th of January inclosing a letter to Mr Keith, I received in due time, and immediately deliverd the Letter to him, who paid me the amount of my account against you as Executor of Colvils will and took my receipt for that Sum— and informd me that he should write to you by the then next succeeding Post. I therefore did not think it necessary to trouble you with a Letter on that subject[1]—I am Just informed by a Son of Mr Robert McCreas, who formerly resided in this Town, but for some years past has lived in the State of Georgia, that his Father has made or intends to make application for the Marshals Office in the State of Georgia, and requests that I would make mention of him to you—And altho I cannot suppose that my recommendation will promote Mr MrCreas success in his application, yet I cou'd not refuse to bear testimony of his great worth and merit⟨.⟩ His upright and exemplary conduct as a magistrate and a Citizen while he lived in this town, gained him the esteem and friendship of all his acquaintances, his losses during the War compel'd him to seek for a support for a very deserving and numerous family in a new country—And his appointment to the Office he solicits will I am persuaded give real satisfaction to all who know him.[2] I am with due respect Your Obedt Hbe Servt

Ch: Simms

ALS, DLC:GW. The postal stamp on the cover reads, "ALEX. Mar. 14."

1. GW's letter to James Keith of 29 Jan. was enclosed in GW's letter to Simms of 28 January. Neither Keith nor Simms acknowledged GW's letters or the payment of Simms's legal fees for work on the Colvill estate. This fact prompted GW's letter to Simms of 24 Feb., which elicited this reply. On GW's involvement with the tangled estates of John and Col. Thomas Colvill, see the source note for Thomas Montgomerie to GW, 24 Oct. 1788.

2. On the recent vacancy in the Georgia marshal's office, see James Hendricks to GW, 15 January. Former Alexandria, Va., merchant Robert Mc-Crea (died c.1804) was a native of Scotland and, along with GW, a member of Masonic Lodge No. 22, in Alexandria. By 1792, McCrea had settled in Wilkes County, Georgia. The son may have been John McCrea, who had been a schoolmate of GW's nephew George Steptoe Washington (*Virginia Journal and Alexandria Advertiser,* 9 Nov. 1787). McCrea also was recommended in David Stuart's letter to GW of 4 April. The letters from Simms and Stuart arrived too late to have any effect because GW had nominated Josiah Tattnall for the position in his letter to the U.S. Senate of 5 March.

From Pierce Butler

Sir   Philada March the 15th 1794

I am sensible You are troubled with the perusing of more letters than can be agreeable to You. I have therefore, to Crave your indulgence for intruding the inclos'd on You—It is an Act of Justice that I owe to the Citizens of So. Carolina to Convey to You their requests.¹

⟨mutilated⟩ ⟨h⟩ad the honor once before, to Name Mr James Simons to ⟨mutilated⟩ He served during the whole of the War in the Cavalry ⟨mutilated⟩ ⟨g⟩reat reputation.²

He is certainly well qualifie⟨d for disc⟩harging the duties of the Office He solicits.³ ⟨mutilated⟩ have the honor to be with great respect Sir, Yr Most Obedt humble Servt

P. Butler

ALS, DLC:GW.

1. Pierce Butler currently represented South Carolina in the U.S. Senate. For the enclosure, see note 3.

2. James Simons (1761–1815) was currently a merchant in Charleston, South Carolina. As part of his military service during the Revolutionary War, he served in the 3d Regiment of Light Dragoons in the Virginia Continental line under William A. Washington. He held a variety of local offices during his lifetime and served one term in the South Carolina legislature, 1785–86. Simons currently was seeking to replace Isaac Motte as the naval officer at Charleston. Any previous recommendation of Simons from Butler has not been identified.

3. Enclosed was a letter from Simons to Butler of 25 Feb., which was written at Charleston, S.C., and which begins: "The long and serious indisposition of Colo: Motte terminated a day or two ago in the palsy, and it is reported his recovery therefrom is not expected: I therefore take the earliest opportunity to give you this information, that you may be enabled at as early a period as possible to serve me.

"I have not nor shall I make application to any other person. Mr [Ralph] Izards knowledge of my character—his former strong recommendation in my behalf for the collectors place, Colo: Hambletons [Alexander Hamilton] promise to recommend me to the president for the next appointment—my being the oldest candidate—but Sir, what I value much more, your affectionate and friendly assistance, and a consciousness of the justice of my claim for an office encourages me to hope I may be successful.

"I am much hurt at the frequent trouble I have given you. An affectionate Wife and five small children the objects of my care and happiness, form at once my apology" (DLC:GW). Isaac Motte served as the naval officer at Charleston, S.C., until his death on 8 May 1795, and then Simons received the desired appointment. In 1797, President John Adams appointed Simons collector of the customs for the port of Charleston, a position he held until 1805 (*U.S. Senate Executive Journal*, 1:179, 181, 248).

Henry Knox to Bartholomew Dandridge, Jr.

Dear Sir   [Philadelphia] 15 March 1794

Be so good as to submit to the President of the United States the letter of Genl Chapin, with the accompanying speeches of the cheifs of the six nations at Buffaloe Creek on the 7th ultimo.[1] Yours

H. Knox

ALS, DLC:GW; LB, DLC:GW.

1. In his letter to Knox of 25 Feb., written at Canandaigua, N.Y., Israel Chapin wrote: "Inclosed are the proceedings of a Council holden at Buffaloe Creek, the 7th of this instant. There were present at the Council the principal Sachems Chiefs &c. of the Six Nations, together with one Shawane Indian, that attended the Council. There were a number of the British from Upper Canada also, who attended the Council, agreeable to the Indians request (Vizt) Major [Edward Baker] Littlehales, and others of the Indian department. I proceeded on business agreable to your direction. The Speach from the President was interpreted to them, and altho' a little different from what they expected (yet was gratified in the same). I also informed them respecting the supplies of Clothing &c. forwarded them by the Presidents directions, which they received with much gratitude, and as a new token of his Fatherly disposition towards them, but I believe had not the same effect with those who they at present call their Brothers, the other side of the water. They did not give me a direct answer to the President's speech, as they wanted some time for several reasons. Some of their Chiefs were absent, and some of them in the Shawanoe Country, in order to find out the disposition of them towards the States &c. Captain Brant was present at the Council, and from every information I can obtain, the Six Nations together with the Chippawas will undoubtedly agree to hold a Treaty next Summer agreable to the Presidents request." The enclosed proceedings recorded not only Chapin's speeches but also those of the Seneca chief Red Jacket and the Mohawk chief Joseph Brant (Phi: Wayne Papers, Large Miscellaneous Manuscripts, vol. 2; see also Jennings, *Iroquois Indians: A Documentary History*, reel 42, and a printed version in *ASP, Indian Affairs*, 1:479–80. On the speech from GW, see n.1 of Knox to GW, 23 Dec. 1793.

From Edmund Randolph

[Philadelphia] March 15. 1794.

E. Randolph begs leave to submit to the President the inclosed rough of a letter, just written to Mr Short,[1] in consequence of information of the immediate departure of a vessel for Spain, which was received last night from the Spanish commissioners.[2]

AL, DNA: RG 59, Miscellaneous Letters; LB, DNA: RG 59, GW's Correspondence with His Secretaries of State.

1. Earlier on this date, Randolph wrote GW that he "has the honor of sending to the President of the U.S. two letters, received last night from Mr Short," a U.S. commissioner currently conducting negotiations with Spanish officials at Madrid (DNA: RG 59, Miscellaneous Letters). The enclosed letters from William Short to the secretary of state were those of 20 and 27 Dec. 1793 (DNA: RG 59, Despatches from U.S. Ministers to Spain). The diplomatic news contained in these two letters concerned the receipt of a letter from the Duque de la Alcudia of 18 Dec. and the reply of Short and William Carmichael of 22 Dec. 1793, both of which revolved around Spanish insistence that difficulties over Indian relations could not be resolved until there was an acknowledged distinction between the Indians in Spanish territory and those within U.S. territory. This distinction, however, was impeded by "the want of fixing positively the limits" between the two nations (both letters, *ASP, Foreign Relations*, 1:439–40). Both of Short's letters to the secretary of state also contained news of recent military and political events in Europe.

The enclosed rough draft of Randolph's reply has not been identified, but the letter-book copy of his letter to Short of 16 March acknowledged the receipt of Short's letters of "Sept. 5. No. 128 (triple) Oct 22, No. 130.—Novr 6 No. 131—(dup). Decr 13th No. 133 (dup). Decr 20th No. 134 (dup). Decr. 27. No. 135. 1793. & Jany. 3 No. 136 (dup) 1794" (On the receipt of the letter of 3 Jan., see Randolph's first letter to GW of 16 March). Randolph then offered an explanation of recent events that could potentially affect U.S. relations with Spain:

"Mr. Genet, the late Minister here from the French Republic, had laboured to convulse our Country, by kindling parties, and forcing us from our neutrality. Among his other machinations was the raising of military corps within South-Carolina and Kentucky for the invasion of the dominions of his Catholic Majesty in Florida and Louisiana. The government of the former State has opposed itself firmly to these outrages, and altho' the Governor of the latter has been frequently pressed by the Executive of the United States to crush such attempts, even by military coercion, yet there is reason to fear, that a hostile descent down the Missisippi was lately meditated, and matured to an alarming height. Whether it escaped his notice, or from what other cause, we are not yet sufficiently apprized of the transaction, to transmit to you the particulars. We are tolerably certain, however, that the enterprize has been abandoned, and that the countenance, which some at least of the Confederates at first gave to it, was the effect of a supposition, wholly unfounded, that Mr. Genet could not have acted thus, without some connivance in the government. The truth is, that, as soon as a suspicion was entertained, on the 29th of August 1793, the Governor of Kentucky was admonished in terms of the greatest urgency; and at this moment, measures are in contemplation to repel with energy the repetition of such a combination. By this course of proceeding, we are intitled to full credit for the sincerity of our conduct; I mean the conduct of the federal government. The Spanish Commissioners in a conversation, which I held with them, on the first rumor of the movements in Kentucky expressed themselves satisfied of the candor and exertions of the President."

Randolph then offered his opinion on current problems in American shipping: "the authorized rapine of the British Cruisers and Courts have swept so much of our property on the water, as to impair our capitals, engross our Seaman, and chill, by the fear of seizure, the spirit of trade. What Congress, now in Session, may resolve, is a problem" (DNA: RG 59, Diplomatic and Consular Instructions, 1791–1801). For Randolph's reply to questions that GW raised about the draft, see Randolph's third letter to GW of this date.

2. The Spanish commissioners were José de Jaudenes and José Ignacio de Viar.

From Edmund Randolph

[Philadelphia] March 15. 1794.

E. Randolph has the honor of observing to the President in reply to his queries;[1] that the ruin of our merchants was expressed as strongly, as it is, in order to prepare Mr Short, in case some nervous measure should be adopted by government, with a general idea of the magnitude of the cause, before a particular explanation could be forwarded to him; and that, altho' the jealousy mentioned by the President occurred to him, as affording a fair opportunity of pushing our rights, yet it was not mentioned, as the dispatches will go thro' diplomatic hands here, and a public post-office in Spain. Confidence is due to the polite offer, made by the commissioners; but if by implicit confidence, the Spanish government were to seize a fact, which might fix a species of distrust in their integrity, a want of candor in us, and which, if it were even enveloped in cypher, might possibly be decyphered; I could not be sure of the consequence. Add to this, that the joint negotiation between the U.S. and Spain may possibly end, before the letter reaches Madrid; and it is very probable, that Mr Carmichael when alone, may not be equal to so delicate a game.[2]

E. R. will soften the strong paragraph; and if the President chooses, another will be added as to the jealousy, which may arise between G.B. & S. The messenger will bring the President's pleasure on this head.[3]

AL, DNA: RG 59, Miscellaneous Letters; LB, DNA: RG 59, GW's Correspondence with His Secretaries of State.

1. GW's queries concerned the draft of Randolph's letter to William Short of 16 March. For the contents of this letter, see n.1 of Randolph's second letter to GW of this date.

2. On the appointment of William Short and William Carmichael as commissioners to negotiate an agreement with the Spanish government, see GW to U.S. Senate, 11 Jan. 1792. On Short's concurrent appointment as the U.S. minister to The Hague, see GW to U.S. Senate, 22 Dec. 1791.

3. Any written reply from GW has not been found, but the paragraph on possible jealousy between Great Britain and Spain was not added.

From Richard Dobbs Spaight

Sir   No. Carolina 15th March 1794.

In the Secretary of wars letter to me of the 18th of January giving me instructions to cause the money detained in the hands of the Marshall of this district to be delivered to the agent of the Spanish Commissioners, He informed me that the expences which had or might be incurred in the prosecution of the business were to be defrayed by the general government, upon accounts which shall be authenticated by me and transmitted to the accountant of the war office.[1] Accordingly when I gave orders to the Marshal to deliver the money papers & other property taken from on board the Spanish brig St Joseph and then in his possession to the agent for the Spanish Commissioners; I likewise directed him to make out his account of the expences incurred by him in safekeeping the money, supported by proper vouchers and transmitt it, to me that I might send it forward to the war office.[2]

I now do myself the honor to enclose you a copy of his answer to my letter, declining to make out any account of his services but leaving it to the Government of the United States to make him such compensation for his trouble & expence as they may deem proper.[3] I am sir &c. &c.

R. D. Spaight

LB, Nc-Ar: Governors' Letterbooks.

1. Spaight is paraphrasing Knox's instructions regarding money and other property from the Spanish brig *San Josef* that were currently being held in protective custody by U.S. Deputy Marshal John Blakely. These instructions are in Henry Knox's letter to Spaight of 13 Jan. (see n.1 of Spaight's second

letter to GW of 8 Feb.). Edward Jones was hired by diplomats José Ignacio de Viar and José de Jaudenes to represent Spanish interests.

2. Spaight wrote Blakely on 11 Feb. to deliver the money and other property in his custody to Jones. He also instructed him "to make out your Account of the expenses incurred by you . . . and transmit the same to me with the necessary vouchers that it may be forwarded to the accountant of the War Office" (Nc-Ar: Governors' Letterbooks). Joseph Howell, Jr., was the accountant for the Department of War (GW to U.S. Senate, 8 May 1792 [first letter]).

3. In his reply to Spaight of 1 March, Blakely wrote that in compliance with the wishes of Mr. Jones, he had deposited the money in "the bank at Charleston. . . . With regard to the expences that accued on the safekeeping of the trunk which contained the Spanish gold, as I had no less than three times to open it, count it, and weigh it, I thought (& so did Mr Jones) I was entitled as marshal to 3 p. cent, but if this is not allowed I must leave it entirely to your Excellency & the Executive of the United States, what you choose to allow me for my personal services in taking care of it at my own risque from the 5th day of Oct: 93. to the 14 day of Feb: 1794 as the law has not pointed out any fixed payment for such services. the price for taking care of Vessels when seized is 150 cents ⅌ day. . . . I called out a guard as often as it appeared necessary I suppose about thirty nights six each night. I did not keep a regular account of them or the expences as we had no hope of being paid for it. . . . I believe I am far within bounds when I say it cost me out of my own pocket between thirty and forty dollars for fire room & refreshments for the guards at different times, besides many anxious nights and days, I being confined to my room every night during the time I had it in care. All this your Excellency will be so good as to take into consideration and report accordingly to the Secy of War what may appear to you right I have no doubt but the United States will allow me such a compensation as may appear to them just" (Nc-Ar: Governors' Letterbooks). Knox informed Spaight in a letter of 2 April that the "Statement made by the marshal and his claim founded thereon seemed to be so just that no objections are made thereto. accordingly I have directed the amount to be transmitted him by the present post" (Nc-Ar: Governors' Letterbooks).

To Alexander Spotswood

Dear Sir,   Philadelphia March 15th 1794

Your letter of the 9th instt is at hand.[1] Notwithstanding I have the best disposition to oblige you, & to promote the interest of your son John, yet it is impossible he can be contemplated by me as commander of one of the frigates (should the Bill now pending in Congress pass into a Law) because a number of the old Officers who served with great reputation through the whole of last war, thereby acquiring much experience, are tendering their services; & grounding their pretensions upon merit & the losses they have sustained.[2]

The most that can be done for your Son, would be to make him a second or third Lieutt—and even here I would not, at this time, be under any engagement until the matter is more unfolded than it is at present.

Mr Brooke, your Son in law, being one, among a great many others, who recommended in very strong terms Mr Lawrence Muse as Successor to Hudson Muse, it was thought best to appoint him to the Collectorship of Rappahannock.[3]

My love in which Mrs Washington unites is offered to Mrs Spotswood & the family. I am—Dear Sir Your Affecte & Obedt Servt

Go: Washington

ALS, PHi: Dreer Collection; ALS (letterpress copy), ViMtvL; LB, DLC:GW.

1. Spotswood's letter to GW of 9 March has not been found.

2. Spotswood was married to Elizabeth Washington, the eldest daughter of GW's half-brother Augustine Washington, and he was seeking a federal appointment for his son John Augustine Spotswood in the soon-to-be-established U.S. Navy. For the bill pending in Congress, see "An Act to provide a Naval Armament," 27 March 1794 (*Stat.* 1:350). For previous letters to GW seeking assistance in finding employment for his son, see Alexander Spotswood to GW, 27 Aug. 1793, and n.1 to that document. John A. Spotswood did not receive a federal appointment until President John Adams nominated him on 4 Feb. 1800 "to be Master Commandant in the Navy," which the Senate approved 10 Feb. (*U.S. Senate Executive Journal,* 1:337–38).

3. Any letter of recommendation from Francis T. Brooke to GW has not been found, but for Alexander Spotswood's recommendation of Brooke for a federal appointment, see his letter to GW of 15 Sept. 1793. For GW's recent appointment of Laurence Muse to the position of customs collector for the District of Tappahannock, Va., see GW to U.S. Senate, 5 March.

To Burgess Ball

Dear Sir,   Philadelphia 16th March 1794

At length your clover-seed, and chocolate Nut shells, are on Ship board for Alexandria; consigned to the care of Colo. Gilpin. The Vessel was to have sailed this day, but whether she is gone, or not, I am unable to say—she has been *going* every day for ten days, but I would not put your things nor my own Seeds on board until the last moment, lest they should get heated in the hold. yesterday they were embarked. It is to be regretted no opportunity offered sooner, but this is the first since I came to the City.[1]

The three bushels of clover seed, and freight of it to Alexandria (which is paid here) stands in Twenty three dollars—The Nut shells Fanny will accept as a present.[2]

I would thank you for causing the enclosed to be set up in Leesburgh; and if you chuse to send a Mare to either of the Jacks you are welcome or to the Horse.[3] The family here join in love to you & Mrs Ball and I am—Dear Sir, Your Affectionate Servt

Go: Washington

ALS, owned (1987) by William Hale Books, Washington, D.C. The cover is addressed to Ball at "Leesburgh," Va., and the postal stamps read, "17 MR." and "FREE."

1. For GW's previous promise to send these items to Ball and the reason for the delay in shipment, see GW to Ball, 24 February. At GW's request, Bartholomew Dandridge, Jr., wrote to Alexandria, Va., merchant George Gilpin on 17 March: "The President has directed me to transmit to you the enclosed bill of lading, & to beg the favor of you to receive from Captain [David] Denik⟨e⟩, when he arrives at Alexandria, the articles mentioned in the bill. Two of the barrels, Nos. 1 and 5. belong to Colo. B. Ball, who is informed that they will be consigned to your care. These you will be so good as to retain, 'till a safe conveyance for them can be had to Colo. Ball. All the others are to go to Mount Vernon, & Mr Pearce, the manager there, is directed where to call for them. The Captain has indeed promised, if possible to put them on shore at Mt Vernon; but it is very uncertain whether he will or not" (DLC: GW). On the shipment of these and other items on the *Sally,* see also GW to William Pearce, 16–17 March. On the arrival of these items, see Ball to GW, 5 April.

2. On 24 Feb., GW paid $2.20 for "2½ busls chocolate shels," and a barrel to contain them for shipment to Ball's wife and GW's niece, Frances Washington Ball (Household Accounts).

3. The enclosure was an advertisement offering the stud services of GW's horse Traveller and his jacks Knight of Malta and Compound. For a published text of this advertisement, see n.1 of Bartholomew Dandridge, Jr., to Angell & Sullivan and Samuel Hanson of 26 February.

To Robert Lewis

Dear Sir   Philadelphia 16th March 1794.

You have not informed me yet, in what condition, or under what circumstances you found my lots in the Towns of Winchester and Bath—and my land above the latter: or whether you have visited all, or any of them since I see you last.[1]

I wish also to be informed how your collection stands, that I may direct the application of the money: and request you will furnish me with a correct list of all my tenants entrusted to you—the amount of their Rents—and arrearages of them, if any, that I may have a more precise knowledge of this business than I am possessed of at present.[2]

I request you to have copies taken of the enclosed advertisement & set up at a few of the most public places in the part of the Country where you live; among these let Leesburgh & Fauquier Court Ho. be two of them.[3]

Mr Prescoat (unless he has paid lately, which I believe is not the case) owes for last year, & for a considerable length of Pasturage. Whether he had more than one Mare to the Jack, or not, I am unable to say; I presume he can tell; receive the money, & place it among your other collections—drawing a Commission thereon.[4] Your Aunt and the family (who are all well) join me in best wishes, for you & Mrs Lewis, and I am—Dear Sir Your sincere friend and Affectionate Uncle

Go: Washington

ALS (letterpress copy), ViMtvL; LB, DLC:GW.

1. On GW's two lots in Winchester, Va., the two lots in Bath, Va., (Berkeley Springs, W.Va.), and the lands owned in Berkeley County, Va. (now W.Va.), see the Schedule of Property enclosed in GW's Last Will and Testament, 9 July 1799, and notes (*Papers, Retirement Series,* 4:512–27). Lewis probably met with his uncle when GW was in residence at Mount Vernon from 14 Sept. until 28 Oct. 1793 (*JPP,* 239, 241). In his letter to GW of 5 Feb. 1794, Lewis promised to write "more fully & respecting to your business."

2. For Lewis's response to GW's request for information, see his letter to GW of 7 May (ViMtvL).

3. The enclosure advertised the stud services of GW's horse Traveller and his jacks Knight of Malta and Compound. For a published text of this advertisement, see n.1 of Bartholomew Dandridge, Jr., to Angell & Sullivan and Samuel Hanson of 26 February. Lewis lived with his wife, Judith Walker Browne Lewis, at The Exchange, his estate in Fauquier County, Virginia.

4. In his letter to GW of 7 May, Lewis wrote that "Mr Prescoat has not paid me for the season of his Mare to your Jack, nor for the pasturage; but promises it shall be done in a short time." Mr. Prescoat (Prescott) has not been identified.

From John C. Ogden

Sir   Hartland Vermont March 16th 1794

Foreign as the ecclesiastical affairs of our country may be from your immediate deliberation, yet as a member of the Church, it may not be unpleasant, to receive a line, on a new subject, which has excited some conversation.

The Revd Doctr Peters of London, formerly of Connecticut, is elected Bishop of Vermont.[1] The Revd Doctr Bass, knowing the embarrassments, as to The Church Land, and being unwilling constantly to reside in this State: declined our appointment. Doctor Peters, thus became a Candidate. His wealth, enables him to attend the duties of the function, without an instant dependence upon the income of our Glebes. The Church from want of possession of her Land has been led to abstain from pressing Doctr Bass's acceptance, and to take a Gentleman from the English Church, when the laws of that nation actually forbid Clergymen ordained in the State, from holding benefices in that kingdom or its provinces.[2]

Time may remove many remaining causes of sorrow in consequence of the revolution, both in Church & State—When America remonstrated against the machinations, and resisted the plans of men in Great Britain, to obtain an undue domination; When my own and Mrs Ogdens family connections embarked and lost their lives, in the war, on their countrys side, When we who survive them, in all cases, obediently followed the laws and regulations, which resulted from depreciated credit; and implicitly confided in the public honor and faith, untill we have thereby lost just and large reputations, I little thought that I should experience the sorrows, which are now my portion, and the notion of a family wanting bread and education, because of party usurpation and church plunderers in The States.

Many too partial friends, from pity, love and confidence, would have placed me in the station of Superintendant in the Church of Vermont, but that argument, which led us to resign our designs of enjoying the good offices of Doctr Bass, (from inability now to support him) influenced me in my abstaining from encouraging this design, which would otherwise have been most pleasing to me, and full of consolation to my family and friends.

This also in a State, by whose independence, ⟨dis⟩quieting acts, and other titles given by distressing times to trespassers, my wife has lost an handsome patrimony.

To recollect, and to feel, a necessary impulse, to state to Rulers, that the sacrilege upon Church property in Vermont & New Hampshire, is solely caused by the usurpation of a party, by Deists, Adulterers, & lax-principeled men, to purchase popularity, and secure wealth & power, wound more sensibly.[3]

This appointment of Doctr Peters, I trust will give the Church a Bishop, with out any charges to her, and consequently enable him more disinterestedly to seek the welfare of The Clergy.

We have evinced a magnanimous temper to the English Clergy, and placed a man of learning, abilities, zeal, and benevolence in the Episcopal Chair. If we have offended, it is unwished on our part. We first elected a man whose moderation is great.

In me, A citizen, intitled to just protection, and perhaps some attention for my familys sake, and my own obedience to the interests of The Church and Country, might have obtained the place. but in both these cases, for causes I have for several years stated, with an hope of redress by means of civil and ecclesiastical leaders, we are disappointed.

The alternative taken, must be supposed prudent, and I trust will be acquiesced in by all parties.

Hitherto, I see the lives of my relatives and the property of my family sacrificed by war & its events—by the consequences of revolution whic aggrandizes others. Their deaths are doubly poignant, because they have been made the causes of undesigned distress, in them, to those whom they loved, for whose protection they undertook the profession of arms, Was this the only case, in the State, it ought never to have been mentioned, but it is what I frequently meet among my extensive acquaintance, Soldiers & Citizens will unite with their sorrowing families, and complain, upon those events, which probe their wounds anew.

All this is repeated, merely, to excuse the Church in Vermont, from every suspicion of a want of attention to the principles, prejudices and interests of our Citizens in general. Her conduct is regular—Her principles good, and her sorrows great—To lessen her wants, she has chosen a Bishop—My duty and wish is to make him useful and happy as far as in my power.

That every satisfaction, in the power of mortals to enjoy, may be Your Excellencys portion is the devout prayer of a devoted servant

John Cosens Ogden

ALS, DNA: RG 59, Miscellaneous Letters. The postal stamps on the cover read, "RUTLAND" and "FREE." The date of "March 17" is handwritten on the cover.

1. Samuel Andrew Peters (1735–1826), a native of Connecticut, received a bachelor's and a master's degree from Yale in 1757 and 1760, respectively. In 1758 he went to England, and in 1759 he was ordained into the priesthood of the Anglican Church. He returned to Connecticut in 1760 and served as the rector of the Anglican church at Hebron. Persecution for his Loyalist sympathies caused him to flee to London, England, in 1774. On 27 Feb. 1794, Peters was elected as the bishop of the Protestant Episcopal Church of Vermont by a convention of clergy meeting at Manchester. The decision was negated when the Archbishop of Canterbury refused the convention's request to consecrate Peters.

2. Edward Bass (1726–1803), a native of Massachusetts, earned bachelor's and master's degrees in 1744 and 1747, respectively, from Harvard. Bass eventually left the Congregational Church, and in 1752 he was ordained in London, England, as priest in the Anglican Church. He then returned to the United States to became the rector of St. Paul's Church in Newburyport, Mass., a position he held until his death. Ogden was among those clergy who selected Bass to be the bishop of the Vermont diocese during their meeting at Pawlet, 18–19 Sept. 1793. His acceptance of this position was conditioned upon the availability of sufficient lands to allow him to live within the diocese. Given that the lands in Vermont of the former Anglican church, which was deemed loyal to the British cause during the Revolutionary War, had been seized by a combination of state and local governments, Bass's demand was impossible to meet. In 1797, however, he was ordained as the first bishop of the Protestant Episcopal Church in Massachusetts. On the selection of a bishop for the diocese of Vermont, see the *Documentary History of the Protestant Episcopal Church in the Diocese of Vermont* (New York, 1870), 14–60.

3. For earlier complaints by Ogden about the seizure of church lands, see his letters to GW of 9 Jan. 1791, 24 Nov. 1792, and 7 Feb. 1794.

From One of the People

Sir, [c.16 March 1794]

I need not, I trust, make any apology for the freedom I now take in sending you these few lines—They are well intended, and cannot, I think, in reason, give any offence.

The following truths are undeniable—There is a God—He is the supreme governor of the universe, both in a natural and moral sense—This God is holy, just, good, and merciful. Being holy, he cannot but hate sin; and being just, he cannot but punish obstinate sinners: But, being also good and merciful, he has provided a Saviour, through whom there is pardon for penitent offenders.

This God is to be worshipped and adored by all intelligent creatures; not merely in their individual, but also in their social, or national capacity. We have national mercies to acknowledge, national sins to confess, and national judgements to depricate.

This country has been repeatedly delivered from impending judgements: but we have been, and continue to be, unmindful of our Deliverer—While He has been adding mercy to mercy, we have been adding sin to sin.

God is again threatening us with the calamity of war. What is our duty in this situation? To use, no doubt, all the natural means in our power to ward off, or repel the blow. But is this all? No, it is not. Let a heathen prince, the king of Nineveh, instruct us on this head.[1] His city was threatened with destruction—He did not despise the threatening, nor trust to humans alone for its preservation. He proclamed a solemn fast, and exhorted the people "to turn, every one, from his evil way, and from the violence that is in his hands; adding, Who can tell if God will turn, and repent, and turn away from his fierce anger, that we perish not?" And the history informs us that "God saw their works, that they turned from their evil way, and God repented of the evil that he had said that he would do unto them; and he did it not."[2]

Imitate the pious example of this prince.

One of the people

AL, DLC:GW. GW's docket reads, "March--1794." The postal stamp on the cover reads, "16 MR."

1. On the king of Nineveh, see the third chapter of the Old Testament book of Jonah.

2. The quotations are from Jonah 3:8–10.

To William Pearce

Mr Pearce   Philadelphia 16th[–17] March 1794

Your letter of the 11th with its enclosures came to hand at the usual time;[1] but not so as that, enquiry co[ul]d be made into the prices of linnen, & you to be informed, by the Post of tomorrow (this day being Sunday)—Go on therefore, until you hear further from me, to get linnen as fast as it can be worked up. The 11½ d. linnen is as good as any for the boys, girls & small people, who do little or no work.

I was affraid to make the interstices between the pieces of the treading floor of the new barn at Dogue run too open, lest the straw should work into them, & choke the passage of the grain to the lower floor; or to emit so much straw between them, to that floor, as to make the difficulty of cleaning the grain much greater. Avoiding these two evils, the floor can not be too open, provided the horses feet or legs are not endangered; & this is not likely to happen unless the pieces were so far apart as for the hoof to pass through, or turn. If the section, or part of a section which you have left an inch a part, is not apt to choke or pass too much straw through try another section at an inch and half & so on, section after section, until you hit the mark exactly; & then regulate all the sections accordingly. This had better be done whilst you have Wheat with wch to make the experiment: & without loss of time, as not only an immediate advantage is to be derived from the *best* distance the pieces can be placed asunder, but that I may know better how to order another.[2]

Let the drilled wheat have all the cultivation you can give it, with convenience, that the most that can, may be made of it.

The Clover Seed, Furze & other articles, are on board the Sally Captn [   ] for Alexandria, the first Vessel that has offered since the breaking up of the frost. It is much to be regretted that the delay has been so great, but it was impossible to avoid it.[3]

I would not, by any means, have you sow the Eastern shore Oats—if these are what you depend upon Colo. Gilpin to get; because these, besides being almost as light as bran, are rarely, if ever, free from the Onion or wild garlick; with which my fields abound too much already, from this very cause. I had rather the ground intended for this Crop should receive Buck wheat, or any thing else; or indeed nothing, rather than be sown with such Oats as are generally brought to Alexandria from the Eastern shore of Virginia. It is possible you may get some Oats from Notley Young Esqr. near George Town. These will be good.[4]

I send you a few seeds of the Nankeen Cotton. let them be planted the first day of May in light & rich ground, well prepared—Put four Seeds in a hill.[5] I am Your friend &ca

Go: Washington

P.S. I have wrote Colo. Ball, & my Nephew Mr Robert Lewis, that they are welcome to send a Mare or two each, to either of the Jacks or the Horse.[6]

March 17th

P.S. The Vessel is not yet gone which has my Seeds &ca on board; and as she has been going every day for ten days past, there is no saying when she will go. The Captn *now* says to morrow. He has promised to land them, if he can, as he passes Mount Vernon; if not they are to be landed at Colo. Gilpins Warehouse. the Captn has one Bill of Lading, and another goes by this days Post to Colo. Gilpin. The two small Kegs contain the French furse seeds—Nuts & Garden Seeds; the two last may be given to the Gardener; the other you & Butler will manage as you shall judge best.[7]

One of the Casks contains five bushls of Plaster of Paris, which try on some of the clover, to see the effect—at the rate of about 5 bushls to the acre—spread a breadth, & leave a breadth, alternately; to shew more clearly, if any, what effect it will have.[8]

G.W.

ALS, ViMtvL, ALS (letterpress copy), DLC:GW.

1. The letter from Pearce of Tuesday, 11 March, has not been found. According to the post office schedule, if Pearce mailed this letter on Tuesday, GW should have received it on Thursday, but if Pearce did not post it until Thursday, GW would have received it on Saturday, 15 March (GW to Anthony Whitting, 2 Dec. 1792).

2. On the design of the treading barn under construction at Dogue Run farm, see GW to Anthony Whitting, 28 Oct. 1792, and enclosure.

3. On the shipment of these and other items aboard the *Sally*, Capt. David Denike, see GW to Burgess Ball, this date. For additional items included in this shipment, see GW's postscript to this letter.

4. In accordance with GW's instructions, Pearce did not purchase oats from Alexandria merchant George Gilpin, but instead bought 30 bushels of oats at 3/ per bushel from Notley Young (3 April entry, Mount Vernon Accounts, 1794–97).

5. On GW's recent receipt of these seeds, see John Jay to GW, 1 March.

6. GW wrote "Turn over" at this point. GW had enclosed an advertisement for the stud services of his horse Traveller and his jacks Knight of Malta and Compound in his letters of this date to Burgess Ball and Robert Lewis, but he had neglected to include the offer of free service in his letter to Lewis.

7. The nuts and garden seeds were intended for head gardener John Christian Ehlers, while Pearce and James Butler, the overseer of the Mansion House farm, were to oversee the planting of the furze seed. On the shipment

of these seeds and other items to the care of George Gilpin, see n.1 of GW to Burgess Ball, this date.

8. Plaster of paris, or calcined gypsum, can used as a fertilizer.

From Edmund Randolph

[Philadelphia] March 16. 1794.

E. Randolph has the honor of sending to the President a letter from Mr Short, received yesterday;[1] and two books, containing his shares in the companies. Those in the James river company are a hundred, and in Potowmac fifty—See page 26. in the blue book, and 12. in the red book.[2]

[P.S.] A letter from the Superintendants of the people of St Domingo at Baltimore is also ⟨e⟩nclosed.[3]

AL, DNA: RG 59, Miscellaneous Letters; LB, DNA: RG 59, GW's Correspondence with His Secretaries of State.

1. In his letter to Randolph of 3 Jan., William Short reported on the fall of the French port of Toulon, which is located on the Mediterranean Sea, on 19 Dec. 1793 and speculated on its military and diplomatic implications. Previous to its return to French control, Toulon had been occupied by French Royalists, with assistance from British and Spanish naval forces (DNA: RG 59, Despatches from U.S. Ministers to Spain).

2. The two books containing GW's shares in the James River Company and the Potomac Company have not been found.

3. This letter to Randolph concerning the refugees from the French colony of Saint Domingue who were residing in Baltimore has not been identified. On the state committee appointed by the Maryland legislature to oversee relief efforts and the effort by local citizens to assist the refugees, see William Patterson et al. to GW, 30 Jan., and notes 1 and 2 to that document.

From Edmund Randolph

[Philadelphia] March 16. 1794.

E. Randolph has the honor of informing the President, that the expression as to the merchants is changed, so as to give no possible offense, even if published.[1] But the fact is, that amongst others Colo. Sam: Smith, of congress, yesterday declared himself to be ruined.[2]

Cyphers, by way of figures, uniformly indicative of the same word, are not beyond the reach of *possible* discovery—But they have been always considered as safe enough, when combined with the usual precautions of conveyance. However, it cannot be foreseen, by how many ways the cypher may be obtained; and therefore it appeared adviseable to E.R., not to subject our candor to the danger of being blasted, by the opening of a letter, put into the hands of government.[3]

AL, DNA: RG 59, Miscellaneous Letters; LB, DNA: RG 59, GW's Correspondence with His Secretaries of State.

1. The questionable expression was in the draft of a letter to William Short of this date that Randolph enclosed in his second letter to GW of 15 March. The draft has not been identified, but the objectionable sentence probably was changed to this one that appears in the letter-book copy: "An embargo does not appear to be relished, and in this uncertainty, I can contribute to your information nothing more than this leading idea; that an indemnification to our merchants from British debts and property here is spoken of, out of doors, by timid men, who possess even Britannic affections" (DNA: RG 59, Diplomatic and Consular Instructions, 1791–1801).

2. Maryland merchant Samuel Smith currently represented his state in the U.S. House of Representatives.

3. Correspondence to and from U.S. diplomats was frequently enciphered, either in its entirety or in selected portions.

From George Lee Turberville

Sir   Richmond Co. Virginia March 16th 1794

Full of diffidence—And conscious of the multiplicity of essential concerns that occupy every moment of your important Life, believe me I do a violence to my feelings when I am tempted thus to tresspass on yr Leizure but the interests of a deserving and amiable Wife, and of a promising family of Children impell me to begin.

I sat out in Life with the fairest prospects, and for five years represented the County of Richmond, in Assembly. during that period (at least the latter three years of it), I cou'd have obtained almost any appointment I wanted, & I trust my Line of Conduct was such as will prove that disinterested & patriotic Conduct marked me whilst I was a public servant, for this I refer you to Doctor David stuart, and others who served with me. In 1790, I became a Martyr to the Gout, & was from that & the distressing situation of my Wife obliged to quit public Life. The loss of my house & one third of my property by Fire, in Books household Stuff, &c. &c. followed on in 1791. (Novr), & (as misfortunes seldom come single), I lost my own dear Mother in Janry following.

My Father (but a young man at least not much turned of 50) marrying again in a few months blasted all my hopes,[1] and altho I have a marriage settlement, which will enure to the benefit of me, or mine After my Father's demise, and ensures to my Children, (a son & two Daughters) an ample fortune hereafter. Yet still I am left in great measure distressed and destitute, & totally incapable of affording to my Children that Education of which they are at this time of an age to receive, & which can never be récalled.

Pardon me good sir for thus troubling you with private concerns, common to the rest of our Species, let it serve to inform you of the grounds of my present application & after informing you that Mr Madison, Mr New, Mr Nicholas of the lower house, indeed most of the Virga Delegation, & Messrs Munro, & Taylor of the senate will know me & my Character if you wish an enquiry thereinto, I will proceed to my requisition.[2]

I have heard that Mr Hudson Muse is about to be removed & indeed has actually been removed from his Office as Collector of Rappa. River[3] Shou'd this be the Case permit me to be an Applicant for that Office—but not in Opposition—to Anyone who from servitude in that Line has *Merited* such an Appointment, but shou'd none of that order present themselves or be thought adequate, I hope that the services of one thrown into obscurity at present only by infirmities that forbid Active Life may be remembered—I served my Country from 16 yrs of age to 22. in the Army, (& by my early exposure have brought on premature old age)—from 24 yrs of Age to 30 I was in the Assembly, & in ⟨*illegible*⟩ all the time in both Capacities I acted at least (I trust) without reproach if not with approbation.

Unfitted for Active Life I am still as able as ever to engage in sedentary business, & as I have others depending on me for support, & I am incapable from infirmity, & misfortune to do my duty, my Gout forbidding active exertion, I am induced to apply thus to you as my sole resource—Once more I sollicit yr pardon for this tresspass on yr Repose if the Appt I sollicit is conferred on me I shall know to whom Gratitude is due for to you alone I have applied, if not I shall be convinced greater merit than mine has obtained it,[4] in either Case nothing can alter the Sentiments of my heart in regard to you, Sir, for the Respect & admiration, of every true American, of every Patriot, & of every admirer of human Virtue Must coincide with that of sir Yr Obedt & respectful servant

George Lee Turberville

If this or any other appointment suiting an inactive man, either on this side or the other of the Atlantic, I live in Richmond Co. Virginia.

ALS, DLC:GW.

Attorney George Lee Turberville (1760–1798), resident of Epping, in Richmond County, was the eldest son of Col. John (1737–1799) and Martha Corbin Turberville (1738–1792). He married Betty Tayloe Corbin (1764–c.1797) in 1782, and they had three children: John, Martha Felitia (1786–1822), and Elizabeth Tayloe. A veteran of the Revolutionary War, rising to the rank of major, he represented Richmond County in the Virginia House of Delegates, 1785–89, and served as that county's sheriff in 1798.

1. Col. John Turberville married Anne Ballantine in December 1792.

2. Congressmen James Madison, Anthony New (1747–1833), and John Nicholas (c.1764–1819), plus Senators James Monroe and John Taylor (of Caroline), were some of the members of Virginia's congressional delegation.

3. On the removal of Hudson Muse as the collector of customs for the District of Tappahannock, Va., which was situated along the Rappahannock River, see Muse to GW, 27 January.

4. No reply from GW to Turberville has been found, and GW did not appoint him to any federal position. On the appointment of Laurence Muse to the collector's position, see GW to U.S. Senate, 5 March.

From Benjamin Flower

Sir   Cambridge [England], Mar. 17. 1794

I beg leave to present you with a performance which my Countrymen have favourably received, and which I request your acceptance of, as a small, though sincere token of respect, for a gentleman whose talents and virtues have excited the admiration of the great and the good, in every quarter of the Globe. I should not have presumed in the liberty I have now taken, had I not been assured by my Friend Dr William Gordon, that it would not only be excused, but that the mark would be favourably received.[1]

You will perceive at once Sir, that this tribute of respect does not come from a Statesman, or a Courtier, but from one who has nothing to recommend his performance, but an ardent zeal for the we[l]fare of his country, and of the whole human race. Was I to indulge my inclination at this moment, It would be impossible for me not to particularize the pleasure I receive when I hear of your exertions for the welfare of your country—Happily for you sir, and for that country! May the latter never shew the least degree of that insensibility and Ingratitude which has marked the conduct of the French Nation towards your excellent, persecuted Friend, Monsr De La Fayette[2]—May you—But my Book is such an intrusion that I will no longer intrude on you by letter than while subscribe myself with the most Respectful esteem Sir Your most obedient & most humble servant

Benjamin Flower

ALS, DLC:GW.

Benjamin Flower (1755–1829) was a British political writer known for his anti-government views. He was the editor of the liberal newspaper *Cambridge Intelligencer,* 1793–1803, in which he denounced the current war with France and promoted religious liberty. His *National Sins Considered* (London, 1796) continued to express his anti-war sentiments. In 1799 he was sentenced to jail for six months for remarks he printed about a bishop of the Anglican Church. He later settled at Harlow in Essex, where he published the monthly magazine *The Political Register,* 1807–11, and continued to champion religious toleration.

1. This letter was accompanied by a copy of Flower's book *The French Constitution; with Remarks on Some of Its Principal Articles,* 2d ed., London, 1792 (Griffin, *Catalogue of the Washington Collection,* 519). Both the letter and book were transmitted to GW though the agency of William Gordon (Gordon to GW, 7 and 25 March 1794).

2. On the series of Prussian and Austrian prisons in which the Marquis de Lafayette was held between August 1792 and May 1797, see n.7 of Marquise de Lafayette to GW, 12 March 1793.

Letter not found: to Betty Washington Lewis, 17 March 1794. Betty Washington Lewis wrote GW on 23 March that "Your letter of the 17th Came safe to hand."

From Pastor Americanus

GENTLEMEN,   Philadelphia, March 17, 1794.
    The reason of my presuming to address you on the subject of the culture of Wool, is, because it is a matter on which the

gradual abolition of our National Debt depend, i.e. upon industry and population of America, as the same is held forth in
the following observations. That it is the real fact, I shall now
undertake to prove: so always, and provided, That you will patronize the following scheme—What say you, Gentlemen, to this
matter?—Now this great principle of patriotism, I prove thus:

Permit me, gentlemen, in passing, just to observe, that here,
and no where else, lies all the *life* of our true policy—To cloath
and feed ourselves, and our neighbouring nations. I take this as
a *postulatum* that will without difficulty be granted.

Therefore,

Secondly, I shall, gentlemen, open myself fully on that important subject; not for the sake of telling you a long story (which I
know the genuine patriots, are not particularly fond of) but for
the sake of weighty instruction that I flatter myself, will necessarily result from our Shepherd's scheme. It shall not be longer
if I can help it, than so serious a matter requires. The American
Shepherd addresses us in this manner: He says, the reasons for
my preferring this Shepherd's scheme, are: *First,* I is because I
want to see a plan for improving the present condition of the
poor white people. *Next,* It is because I wish to be beneficial to
my country. *Thirdly,* It is because I wish to throw my mite into the
best public treasury, and therein improve it.

Come—help me raise the ever memorable Shepherd's Hall,
and the profit thereof will be commensurable to your public
spirit: yes, and will be your exceeding great reward. I labour not
for myself only, but for all them that patronize the said scheme.

He says, too, the position by me maintained is, that this scheme
is more excellent, than the Yankie's Tontine bank;[1] which is as
follows:

First, It is a scheme to increase the declining number of sheep
in America, and make wool our staple commodity.

Secondly, The short of the matter is this: Let it be supposed,
that a number of well disposed persons appropriate a *small sum*
of money each to the culture of wool.

Thirdly, Again, let it be supposed, that 6000 sheep may be pas-
tured three miles round the Shepherd's Hall. Now here arises a
necessary query to those well disposed persons, viz. What will
three years produce of the said pasture be?

That the culture of wool will produce an incredible treasury may be seen from the English manufactures. This scheme properly executed will make the American exports exceed her imports, which is the highest degree of our American patriotism. Q.E.D.

Again, let it be supposed, that government will be propitious to the said Shepherd's company, and given them a tract of land, &c. And that government will lend them a sum of money at 4 per cent. The reason whereof is, because the increase of the people will by industry reimburse the costs, and populate or furnish a barren part of our land with the best sort of people. Three things are here very remarkable: *First,* That the state will thereby obtain 4 per cent. *Secondly,* That government will thereby thus obtain a number of useful people. *Thirdly,* That government will thereby obtain the mechanic arts, and that this plan *properly executed* will employ a number of emigrants, viz. Shepherds, Ploughmen, and many other artificers, &c. in all an industrious and independent city.

To conclude: The jealous Britons[2] justly fearful lest they themselves should have lost their wool marts, made a law, *viz.*—That no English *ram* should be conveigled to North America; a plain proof of this, that we may make wool a staple commodity, and out-vie England: just in proportion to the differential quantity of the land in England, and the quantity of land in the United States of America. All that I would be understood to imply, is, that when the number of our sheep increase proportionable to the number of our acres of land; then we shall actually and *de facto* out-vie England, and thereby make ourselves independent, or not depend upon England, &c. or not depend upon manufactories. It is plain, therefore, that our imports of woollen drapery will thereby decrease, and our exportation of woollen drapery will thereby increase.

What has been said, respective to the nature of the preceding scheme implies its importance. But the way to facilitate it will more fully appear in considering the formation of the articles of the company of the American Shepherds.

N.B. Observe—that the subscription money *is not* to be paid until the said company shall be established with articles, and a power sufficient to take this matter in hand. When once a company can be established, with a fund sufficient to begin, there is no doubt but that it will have 6000 sheep in every county in each state: yes, 6000 sheep in every American township.

To constitute the capital of the said company, subscriptions for shares therein, at one Spanish dollar each, payable after the articles of the said company are made, and when a sufficient number of persons have subscribed, they will have the right to form the articles of constitution of their company of American Shepherds.

Any person, partnership, society, church, or body politic, may subscribe for as many shares as he, she, or they may think proper.

Books, for the purpose of subscribers entering their names, &c. will be handed about by divers well disposed persons. I am, with fidelity and consideration, Gentlemen, your well disposed, and most neglected servant,

PASTOR AMERICANUS.

Printed, in *The Shepherd's Contemplation: Or, An Essay on Ways and Means to Pay the Public Debt, and to Seat Congress-Men on Wool-Packs. In a Letter to George Washington, President of the United States of North-America, and to All The Other Genuine American Patriots* (Philadelphia, 1794). The letter is addressed "To George Washington, And To All The Other Genuine American Patriots." The broadside is dedicated "To the MEMBERS of the PHILADEL-PHIA COUNTY SOCIETY for Promoting AGRICULTURE and Domestic MANUFACTURES." The author, who describes himself as "A Patriot and the Poor Man's Friend," writes that "The following Letter, drawn up with a view of making American Wool our staple Commodity; and extend the Design of those concerned in the said Society, and in *our National Manufactory*—is earnestly Dedicated, by their Sincere Friend, Pastor Americanus. Patriots! By this short ensuing Scheme, you will perceive the subject of it, viz. a Plan calculated to thrive, without the assistance of the peculator's Bank, and the most effectual method of preserving the Commonalty or middling sort of People, and raising the Poor, which is congruous to the doctrine of Equality."

1. This may be a reference to the plan for a tontine that was contained in Alexander Hamilton's "Report Relative to a Provision for the Support of Public Credit," 9 January 1790 (*Hamilton Papers*, 6:51–168; see especially "Schedule H" on page 128).

2. A footnote indicated at this point reads: "*From the Maryland Journal.* NOTICE TO FARMERS.—HARRY D. GOUGH, has a number of fine Ram Lambs, of his broad-tailed Persian Breed. Those who wish to be supplied, must give information, in writing, before the 20th of April next, appointing some person, in Baltimore-Town⟨,⟩ to receive them, to whom they will be

delivered about the 15th of September. The price, as h⟨e⟩retofore, Twenty Dollars. Several gentlemen were disappointed last year, by not applying in time; for, after the 20th of April, no application can be attended to. Perry-Hall, Feb. 26, 1793."

To Edmund Pendleton

Dear Sir,   Philadelphia March 17th 1794

Your letter of the 5th instt came duly to hand. I know not from what source a report that, the next associate Judge was to be taken from the state of Georgia, could have been derived. Nothing from me, I can venture to say, gave rise to it; first, because there is no vacancy on *that* bench at present.[1] 2d because, whenever one does happen, it is highly probable that a geographical arrangement will have some attention paid to it; and (although I do—at all times—make the best enquiries my opportunities afford, to come at the fittest characters for offices, where *my own* knowledge does not give a *decided* preference) because, 3dly, no one knows my ultimate determination until the moment arrives when the nomination is to be laid before the Senate.[2] My resolution, not to create an expectation, which thereafter might embarrass my own conduct (by such a commitment to any one as might subject me to the charge of deception) is co-eval with my inauguration; and in no instance have I departed from it. The truth is, I never reply to any applications for offices by letter; nor verbally, unless to express the foregoing sentiments; lest something might be drawn from a civil answer, that was not intended.

A gentleman of my acquaintance has presented me with a little of the Nankeen cotton with the Seed in it; half, or more, I enclose to you; and it might have been better, perhaps, if I had sent you the other half also; as the climate & soil at Mt Vernon is too cold, I conceive, for this plant; but it is due to the donor, that I should make an experiment.[3] With very great esteem & regard I am—Dear Sir Your Most Obedt & Affe H. Ser.

Go: Washington

ALS, MHi: Washburn Papers; ALS (letterpress copy), DNA: RG 59, Miscellaneous Letters; LB, DLC:GW; copy, CSmH.

1. Pendleton had written GW on 5 March to recommend a Georgia resident for appointment to the U.S. Supreme Court.

2. The current justices of the Supreme Court were James Wilson of Pennsylvania, John Jay of New York, William Cushing of Massachusetts, John Blair of Virginia, James Iredell of North Carolina, and William Paterson of New Jersey. When Jay resigned in 1795, GW nominated John Rutledge of South Carolina to replace him (*U.S. Senate Executive Journal*, 1:194).

3. For GW's receipt of this cotton seed, see John Jay to GW, 1 March. GW sent the other half of this seed to his estate manager at Mount Vernon (GW to William Pearce, 16–17 March 1794).

To Alexander Hamilton

United States 18 Mar. 1794
Pay to the Director of the Mint the within[1] sum of sixteen hundred dollars—and also the further sum of one thousand dollars for the purposes of that establishment.[2]

Geo: Washington.

LB, DLC:GW.

1. An asterisk at this point refers to the following copy of an account from David Rittenhouse of 17 March, which appears at the bottom of this letter.

Expenses of the Mint for the present quarter, ending Mar. 31. 1794.

	Dols.Cts
Including all the arrears due to Albion Cox, Assayer, since he was first engaged by Mr [Thomas] Pinckney	3315.02
balance in the Treasurer's hands Jan. 1. 1794	1715.02
Remains to be covered by Warrt	1600.

Edmund Randolph forwarded Rittenhouse's "statement" to GW with a brief cover letter of 18 March (DNA: RG 59, Miscellaneous Letters).

2. On the request for this money, see Edmund Randolph to GW, 14 March (second letter).

From Alexander Hamilton

Treasury Department March 18th 1794
I certify that the installments which according to the contracts respecting the Debt to France accrue in the present year are 1,500,000 livres on the 3rd of September, and 1,000,000 of livres on the 5th of November: which, was there no anticipation, would be payable on those days respectively. The amount antici-

pated, there being some unsettled items, cannot be pronounced until a definitive settlement shall have been had.[1]

Alexandr Hamilton
Secy of the Treasy

LS, DNA: RG 46, Third Congress, 1793–95, Senate Records of Legislative Proceedings, President's Messages.

1. On the reason for this report, see Cabinet Opinion on the Payment of the U.S. Debt to France, 11 March. This report was enclosed in GW's letter to the U.S. Senate and House of Representatives of 18 March.

To the Newport, R.I., Artillery Company

Gentlemen   [Philadelphia, c.18 March 1794]

For your kind congratulations on the anniversary of my birth day, and the other obliging expressions of your address, I pray you to accept my grateful thanks.[1]

To cherish those principles which effected the Revolution, and laid the foundation of our free and happy Government, does honor to your patriotizm; as do the sentiments of comiseration for the sufferings of the unfortunate, and the good wishes for the happiness of the great family of mankind, to your philanthropy.

Your prayer for me, is reciprocated by the best vows I can offer for your welfare.

Go: Washington

ALS, RiNA; LB, DLC:GW.

1. This letter is a reply to the address of the Newport, R.I., artillery company to GW of 22 February.

Letter not found: from William Pearce, 18 March 1794. In a letter to Burgess Ball of 23 March, GW mentioned "a letter I have just received from my Manager, Mr Pearce, dated the 18th instt."

From Edmund Randolph

[Philadelphia] March 18th 1794.

E. Randolph, thinking that the inclosed letters from Simpson & Church contain some interesting matter, has the honor of sending them to the President.[1]

A letter from Mr Brown is also inclosed with O'Fallan's letter.[2]

LB, DNA: RG 59, Domestic Letters.

1. The letter from James Simpson, the U.S. consul at Gibraltar, to Randolph was that of 3 Jan., which is docketed as received on "March 18. 94." Simpson wrote that he had received a letter from Capt. Richard O'Bryen, one of the Algerine captives, reporting on recent captures of American ships and the conditions for a truce between Algiers and the Netherlands (DNA: RG 59, Consular Despatches, Gibraltar). The letter from Edward Church, the U.S. consul at Lisbon, Portugal, to the secretary of state probably was that of 2 Dec. 1793, since its cover bears a postal stamp of "N.YORK MR 13." Church reported his concerns about the form and effectiveness of U.S. passports and on the danger to American shipping posed by Algeria and the Barbary pirates (DNA: RG 59, Consular Despatches, Lisbon).

2. The letter from Kentucky senator John Brown to Randolph has not been identified, but it probably was a cover letter for James O'Fallon's letter to Capt. Herron of 18 Oct. 1793 concerning a planned expedition by Kentucky residents against the Spanish colony of Louisiana (see Randolph's letters to GW of 27 Feb. [fourth letter] and 11 March 1794).

To the United States Senate and House of Representatives

United States 18 March 1794.
Gentlemen of the Senate, and of the House of Representatives.

The Minister Plenipotentiary of the French republic having requested an advance of money, I transmit to Congress certain documents, relative to that subject.[1]

Go: Washington

LS, DNA: RG 46, Third Congress, 1793–95, Senate Records of Legislative Proceedings, President's Messages; LB, DLC:GW.

1. For the enclosed documents, see Cabinet Opinion on the Payment of the U.S. Debt to France, 11 March, and notes 1–3, and Alexander Hamilton to GW, 18 March.

From John Barry

Sir— March 19: 1794
Finding that Government have partly determined to fit out Some Ships of War for the protection of our Trade against the Algerines,[1] I beg leave to offer my self for the Comd of the

Squadron conceiving my self competent thereto assuring your Excellency that should I be honored with your approbation, my utmost abilities and the most unremitting attention shall be exerted for the good of my Country, and also to approve my self Worthy of the high honor shown by your Excellency.[2] Im your Obedient Humbl. Sert

					J.B.

Copy

Copy (in John Barry's handwriting), Nhi: Barnes Collection.

Ireland native John Barry (1745–1803) was settled in Philadelphia by 1760, where he became a prosperous captain and merchant ship owner. During the Revolutionary War he had a successful career as a captain in the Continental navy (see n.1 of Lt. Col. Anthony Walton White to GW, 20 Sept. 1777). During the Quasi-War with France, 1798–99, he commanded U.S. naval forces in the West Indies and remained in the Navy until his death.

1. For the creation of an American navy, starting with four ships of forty-four guns and two ships of thirty-six guns, see "An Act to provide a Naval Armament," 27 March 1794 (*Stat.* 1:350).

2. GW nominated Barry to be a captain in the new navy in his letter to the U.S. Senate of 3 June.

From Henry Knox

Private.

Sir,					War Department March 19. 1794

As it is understood that the bill for fortifying the ports and harbours has passed into a law, I beg leave respectfully to lay before you the following thoughts upon the manner of executing this business.[1]

The operation of the federal Government upon the State Governors and State Officers it is well known has been in general rather irksome than otherwise as it has tended to lessen their patronage and influence, and perhaps in their opinion of course somewhat to impair their dignity, when compared with their situation under the confederation.

The Governors are commanders in chief of the Militia of their respective states and as such were the last year called upon in the name of the President of the United States to perform certain unpleasant duties relatively to the preservation of our neutrality.[2]

These observations are made with this view that it would most probably be a conciliatory and grateful measure to them as Commanders of the Militia to be the Agents of the United States in a certain degree of the proposed fortifications. For instance the Engineers might be directed to consult and take the opinions of the Governors upon the points most proper to be fortified and to report to them the reasons on which their opinions should be founded, which opinions the Governors might confirm or reject and transmit the result to the Secretary of War in order to be submitted to the President of the United States. The Governors might also be requested to appoint some suitable person to superintend the erection of the works, the keeping of the accounts &c. and also of the mounting of such of the Cannon as are to be mounted in or furnished by the respective States—By an arrangement of this sort it is conceived that the Governors would be kindly brought to act by system to support the general government and that unless something of this nature should be devised that they might be displeased and disgusted—Some Agents must be appointed The Governors are on the spot and well acquainted with characters and really possess higher responsibility than any other individuals— It may therefore perhaps be expedient in an oeconomical as well as a political view to request their assistance on this occasion.[3]

Whether these ideas be well founded or not is respectfully submitted. I have the honor to be with perfect respect Your obedient Servant

H. Knox

LS, DLC:GW; LB, DLC:GW.

1. The act just passed by both houses of Congress was "An Act to provide for the Defence of certain Ports and Harbors in the United States," 20 March 1794 (*Stat.* 1:345–46).

2. For examples of the neutrality measures that the governors of the maritime states were expected to enforce, see Cabinet Opinion on the Rules of Neutrality, 3 Aug. 1793, and n.3 to that document; and Knox to Tobias Lear, 17 Aug. 1793, n.1.

3. No written reply to Knox has been found, but GW apparently approved Knox's suggestion, as seen in Knox's letter to New Hampshire governor

Josiah Bartlett of 24 March: "I am instructed to transmit to your Excellency the enclosed copy of a law relatively to the fortifications of the ports and harbours therein mentioned.

"And as a judicious choice of the places to be fortified and vigorous prosecution of the works may be of great importance to the State of New Hampshire the President of the United States requests that your Excellency as the Commander in chief of its Militia would please to take upon you the general direction of the business.

"An Engineer will as soon as possible be appointed. He will be directed to prepare and submit plans of the works to your consideration and upon your approving thereof to have them put into a train of immediate execution some suitable provision will also be soon made to obtain the necessary materials and workmen.

"The number of Men and Cannon designed for Portsmouth and also the amount of the expence to be incurred at that place will hereafter be transmitted.

"If the State of New Hampshire is in possession of any good Cannon of and above the Caliber of eighteen pounds and which could be appropriated to the fortifications within the said State a return of them is requested together with the condition of their carriages and apparatus in order that the necessary repairs be provided without delay" (NIC). See also the letters from Knox to Richard Dobbs Spaight, 24 March, in n.1 of Spaight to GW, 27 April, and from Knox to Thomas Mifflin, 27 March, in n.1 of Mifflin to GW, 28 March.

From Henry Knox

Sir,   War department March 19th 1794

I have the honor to submit to you a return of the commissioned Officers who served in the Navy during the late War, including the Officers of the Marines, together with a list of applicants for Offices in the Navy made out by Mr Lear & the documents accompanying the same.[1] I have the honor to be with perfect respect Your obedt Servant

H. Knox

LS, DLC:GW; LB, DLC:GW.

1. The enclosures have not been identified. Knox probably prepared these lists in anticipation of the passage of "An Act to provide a Naval Armament," 27 March 1794 (*Stat.* 1:350). For GW's decision to nominate only the requisite captains at this time, see his letter to the U.S. Senate of 3 June.

From William Maunsell

Limerick [Ireland] March 19th 1794

Your Excellency will be pleased to pardon the liberty I have taken in Sending you the inclosed two Letters, on the Culture of Potatoes from the Shoots, a discovery heretofore unknown, & which I have reduced to as perfect & Simple System of Agriculture, as any other Branch in that Science.[1]

Your Excellencys great Abilities as a Statesman, a Soldier, & the Founder of a great Empire, deserve every tribute of respect; you will please to Accept this Small one from me.

As the providing the lower orders of the people with food at a cheap rate, is an object of great magnitude, so it shd be an object of great attention in every Legislator; as it will be the means of keeping them quiet, & contented in their present Situations; I am Satisfied your Excellencys Patronage of the Culture, will stamp a value on the discovery, & give it Currency in America.

If we can cre[d]it tradition, Sr Walter Rawleigh first Introduced Potatoes, & their culture into great Britain & Ireland, from America, it is more than probable, that my mode of culture was practised at that early period;[2] if not, I shall claim the merit of introducing a new Species of Agriculture, and of giving Existence, (if I may use the Expression) & value to what heretofore had been thrown away as useless.

I do Suppose your Excellency is Patron of all the Agricultural Socictys in America;[3] your communicating my mode of Culture to them, with my best wishes for its Success, will be a high obligation conferred on me, by your Excellency; my exertions in reducing the Culture to a perfect System, was really disinterested, actuated only by the Love I bear to Society, as an Individual.

May your Excellency live long, & enjoy good health, and be a wittness of the encrease of my mode of Culture in America for many years.[4] I am with the highest & most profound respect your Excellencys most obedt Servt

William Maunsell

ALS, DLC:GW.

GW's docket reads: "From The Revd Mr Wm Maunsell." This individual may be the same as the "Rev William MAUNSELL, LLD," who died in 1804 "in the 79th year of his age" (*Limerick General Advertiser or Gazette,* 31 Dec. 1804).

1. Maunsell enclosed a pamphlet he wrote titled *Letters to the Right Honour-*

able and Honourable the Dublin Society, on the Culture of the Potatoes from the Shoots* (Dublin, 1794). He also wrote a second pamphlet, *An Essay on Raising Potatoes from Shoots, . . . and a Letter from Alderman Alexander, on Potatoes, Addressed to the Dublin Society* (Dublin, 1802).

2. A long tradition associates Sir Walter Raleigh (Ralegh; 1554–1618), an English explorer, courtier, and soldier, with the introduction of the potato to the British isles, but the evidence is scanty and the conclusion speculative.

3. GW was a member of the Philadelphia County Society for the Promotion of Agriculture and Domestic Manufactures and the Philadelphia Society for Promoting Agriculture.

4. GW replied to Maunsell on 20 Feb. 1795: "At the moment I acknowledge the receipt of your obliging favor of the 19th of last March, I find it incumbent on me, to apologize, for delaying so long to offer you my thanks for the interesting pamphlet you had the goodness to send me, on the cultivation of Potatoes, from the shoots.

"Your discovery of this mode is novel; and it must be of great utility if it can be carried into extensive practice. I shall make trial of it myself the ensuing season, and will recommend it to others to do the same, by laying your experiments before them.

"It is to be regretted, that we have not more agricultural societies established in this country; and it is to be lamented that those wch are formed, are not sufficiently attended to. but in this, as in other things we must have a beginning. I pray you to accept my particular thanks for your kind wishes for me—& to accept mine in return" (ADfS, DLC:GW; LB, DLC:GW).

From Edmund Randolph

[Philadelphia] March 19. 1794.

E. Randolph has the honor of inclosing to the President a letter and list, from Mr Fenwick, consul at Bourdeaux, stating the affair of the embargo there.[1]

The vessel from France, which arrived here yesterday brought no letters from Mr Morris, except triplicates and duplicates. But among these is his No. 34. which was missing, when the rest of his correspondence was sent in to the Senate.[2]

The committee at Baltimore for superintending the unfortunate people of St Domingo, were informed yesterday, that the further sum of two thousand dollars would be furnished to them. The President will therefore be pleased to have a warrant on the treasury sent to E.R.[3]

Mr Bradford brought the proclamation yesterday. Some amendments were suggested; and it is probable, that it will be completed to-day.[4]

The letter to the governor of Kentucky is completed; except a paragraph or two, which waits, until I finish the Spanish papers, to see, how much of the negotiation may be communicated. It will probably be completed to-day. The mail for Kentucky goes on tuesday.[5]

Mr Fauchet is to call upon me at 9 O'clock this morning, to speak about the embargo in France.[6]

AL, DNA: RG 59, Miscellaneous Letters; LB, DNA: RG 59, GW's Correspondence with His Secretaries of State.

1. The letter from Joseph Fenwick to Randolph of 4 Jan. is docketed as "recd March 19. 94." Fenwick devoted much of this letter to the efforts he and others had made to persuade the French government to repeal a measure designed to punish the citizens of Bordeaux for their political opposition to the National Convention. This June 1793 law forbid all vessels from carrying cargo out of this port city (see Gouverneur Morris to Thomas Jefferson, 26 Nov. 1793, *ASP, Foreign Relations* 1:400). To illustrate these efforts, Fenwick enclosed copies of his correspondence with Morris, the U.S. minister to France, from 30 Oct. to 30 Dec. 1793; "a remonstrance from me to the Representa⟨tives⟩ of the Convention at Bordeaux" of 21 Nov. 1793 and 12 Dec. 1794; an address of 12 Oct. 1793 "To the Representatives of the French People now in Commission at Le Recole from the Captains of Vessels of the United States of America detained at Bordeaux in Consequence of the Embargo"; and a letter of 31 Dec. 1793 from several of the American captains giving instructions to "their Deputies sent to Paris the 1 Inst.," in which they list their rationale for requesting monetary compensation from the French government. Fenwick also enclosed a list of "American Ships clear'd out from 1st January to 30th June 1793," which gives specific information about each vessel, including its name, classification, captain, size of crew, and cargo, and a list of the thirty-nine American vessels "now in port" (DNA: RG 59, Consular Despatches, Bordeaux).

2. The letter marked No. 34 was a "Duplicate" of Morris's letter to Jefferson of 7 Aug. 1793, which is docketed as "recd March 19. 94." Morris discussed the depreciation in the value of the assignat, France's paper money, and enclosed a table showing the specie value of the assignat from June 1792 to June 1793. The original No. 34 had been received by Jefferson on 11 Nov. 1793 and submitted to GW on that same day (DNA: RG 59, Despatches from U.S. Ministers to France; *Jefferson Papers,* 26:635–38; *JPP,* 251). The other Morris correspondence was enclosed in GW's letter to the U.S. Senate of 26 Feb. 1794.

3. On the allocation of federal money for the relief of refugees from the French colony of Saint Domingue, see Edmund Randolph to GW, 27 Feb. (first and second letters). For GW's instructions to have a warrant issued, see GW to Alexander Hamilton, 21 March.

4. William Bradford brought a draft of the proclamation that GW issued on 24 March.

5. The unfinished letter was that of Randolph to Gov. Isaac Shelby of 29 March, which missed the post of Tuesday, 25 March. The topic addressed by this letter was an expedition being planned against the Spanish colony of Louisiana by George Rogers Clark and other residents of Kentucky. After reviewing previous correspondence on this matter, Randolph urged Shelby to take measures to prevent the plans of Clark and others from being fulfilled. After reviewing the legal basis for using force to do so, Randolph wrote: "Thus far have I addressed your Excellency upon the constitutional and legal rights of the government. . . . But, as it may not be known, that the navigation of the Missisippi has occupied the earliest labours of the Executive, and has been pursued with an unremitted sincerity, I will lay before you a sketch of the pending negotiations," which included the efforts by commissioners William Carmichael and William Short to negotiate with officials at Madrid for free navigation of the Mississippi River by Americans. Randolph continued: "Let this communication then be received, Sir, as a warning against the dangers, to which these unauthorized schemes of war may expose the United States, and particularly the State of Kentucky. Let not unfounded suspicions of a tardiness in government prompt individuals to rash efforts, in which they cannot be countenanced, which may thwart any favorable advances of their cause; and which by seizing the direction of the military force, must be repressed by law, or they will terminate in anarchy" (DNA: RG 59, Domestic Letters; *ASP, Foreign Relations*, 1:456–57). On Carmichael and Short's commission to negotiate an agreement with the Spanish government, see GW to U.S. Senate, 11 Jan. 1792.

6. Fauchet, in a letter of 4 April to François-Louis-Michel Chemin Deforgues, France's minister of foreign affairs, requested that the French government consider lifting the embargo on the port of Bordeaux, particularly because of its negative effects on relations with the United States and its detrimental effect on the acquisition of supplies for France (Turner, *Correspondence of the French Ministers*, 320–21). In his letter to Randolph of the 7th Germinal, or 27 March 1794, Fauchet wrote: "it is the intention of the Committee of Public Safety, the actual centre of the French Government, to indemnify all the owners or captains, who by the operation of the embargo, have been obliged to remain a length of time in France" (*ASP, Foreign Relations*, 1:431).

From Edmund Randolph

[Philadelphia] March 19. 1794.

E. Randolph has the honor of informing the President, that in a conversation last evening with Mr Madison, he was of opinion, that, altho' the President had a legal right to dispose of the shares in the two companies, as he pleased; still it might be an unpleasant thing to Virginia to have them given to a *continental,* instead of a *state* object. Considering, that Virginia would have a participation in the fruit of an university, placed in the fœderal city, E.R. should not have concluded, as Mr Madison has, from the mere words of the law, that Virginia would Object: but he, (Mr M.) being present at the passage of the law, may probably be a better judge of the prevailing sense of the time.[1]

AL, DLC:GW.

1. In 1784 the Virginia legislature gave GW one hundred shares in the James River Company and fifty shares in the Potomac Company (*Va. Statutes*, 11:525–26). He was reluctant to accept these shares and induced the legislature to agree in 1785 that the shares and any future profit from them "shall stand appropriated to such objects of a public nature, in such manner, and under such distributions, as the said George Washington, esq., by deed during his life, or by his last will and testament, shall direct and appoint" (*Va. Statutes*, 12:42–44). For his bequest of the fifty shares in the Potomac Company "towards the endowment of a UNIVERSITY to be established within the limits of the District of Columbia," see his Last Will and Testament of 9 July 1799 (*Papers, Retirement Series*, 4:482–83). On his gift of the one hundred shares in the James River Company to Liberty-Hall Academy, present-day Washington and Lee University in Lexington, Va., see GW to Robert Brooke, 15 Sept. 1796 (ALS, Vi; LB, DLC:GW).

From George Clinton

Sir   Albany [N.Y.] 20th March 1794.
    I conceive it to be my duty to communicate for your Information the Copy of a Speech made to me this Morning by Colo. Louis Cook, who with four other Indians of the Villages of St Regis is now at this Place;[1] and also a Copy of a Speech, of Lord Dorchester to the Chiefs of the Seven Villages or Nations of lower Canada—The latter I this Moment received inclosed in a Confidential Letter from a Gentleman, in Vermont, and I believe the Authenticity of it may be relied on.[2] I am with the highest Esteem and Respect Your Most Obedient Servant
                                    Geo: Clinton

ALS, DNA: RG 59, Miscellaneous Letters.

1. Clinton's enclosed memorandum of 20 March, which contains the speech of Caughnawaga Indian Louis Cook (Atoyataghroughta), reads: "Coll. Louis waited upon Govr Clinton on Thursday the 20th march 1794. with Mr Gray his Interpretator. He mentioned that he had called upon him yesterday but he was out on business—That he had again called this morning His object was to communicate the Contents of a Letter which he had received

from their chiefs (of the Seven Nations) They are as follows to wit. It acknowl-
edges the Receipt of a Letter from Coll. Louis dated at this place—mentions
that they had lately been with Lord Dorchester about certain Business with
which he was acquainted. That they had delivered a speech to him and received his answer with which they were well satisfyed—That they were also
well satisfyed with his conduct here and hoped he would receive a satisfactory
answer from their Brothers here—That they were well when their council
broke up and presented their Compliments to their Brothers at this place.

"Coll. Louis then addressed the Governor as follows.

"Brother. I will now mention to you what I have not done to any Body
before—Our people are your friends. we have been faithful to the united
States—we wished to bring about peace between them and the Indians. And
we should have been able to have effected it for all of them (5 nations excepted) were disposed to listen to our advice but [Joseph] Brant by the assistance of the British Government puts the Tommyhawk in their hands and
urges them to war. Brother rely on it this is true, let them pretend to what
they will.

"Brother. The Business which the Chiefs of our seven nations went upon
was at the request of the nations to the westward who are disposed for peace
to know of Lord Dorchester whe⟨n⟩ they were urged to war and the Tommyhawk put into their hands against the Americans, and why their Lands
were taken from them and no Boundary fixed between them and the Americans—I do not know what his answer was because I have not heard it—My
Letter says it was satisfactory that is all I know about it" (DNA: RG 59, Miscellaneous Letters).

2. The enclosed copy of the speech given at Quebec on 10 February 1794
reads: "Reply of his Excellency Lord Dorchester [Guy Carleton] to the Indians of the seven Villages of Lower Canada as Deputies from all the Nations
who were at the General Council held at the Miami in the year 1790 except
the Chawanois [Shawnees], Miamis, and Loups.

"Children I have well considered your words and am now prepared to
reply.

"Children, You have informed me that you are deputed by the seven Villages of Lower Canada and by all the Upper Country which sent Deputies to
the General Council held at the Miamis Except the Chawanois Miamis and
Loups.

"Children, You remind me of what passed at the Council Fire held at Quebec just before my last departure for England, when I promised to represent
their situation and wishes to the King their Father and expressed my hope
that all the grievances there complained of on the part of the United States
would soon be done away by a just and lasting peace.

"Children I remember all very well—I remember that they pointed out
to me the line of seperation which they wished for between them and the
United States and with which they would be satisfied and make peace.

"Children I was in expectation of hearing from the people of the United
States what was required by them—I hoped that I should have been able to
bring you together and make you freinds.

"Children I have waited long and listened wi⟨th⟩ great attention but I have not heard a word from them.

"Children I flattered mysef with the hope that the line proposed in the year 1783 to sepera⟨te⟩ us from the United States, which was immediately broken by themselves as soon as the peace was signed, would have been mended or a new one drawn in an amicable manner—Here also I have been disappointed.

"Children Since my return I find no appearance of a Line remains and from the manner which the people of the States pass on and act and talk on this side and from what I learn of their conduct towards the Sea, I shall not be surprised if we are at war with them in the course of the present year and if we are, a line ought then be drawn by the Warriors.

"Children You ask for a Passport to go to New York—A passport is useless in peace—It appears therefore that you expect that we shall be at War with the States before you return. You shall have a passport, that whether peace or war you shall be well received by the Kings Warriors.

"Children You talk of selling your lands to the State of New York. I have told you there is no line between them and us. I shall acknowledge no land to be theirs which have been encroached on by them since the Year 1783—they have broken the peace and as they kept it not on their part, it doth not bind on ours.

"Children They have destroyed their right of pre-emption—therefore all their approaches towards us since that time and all the purchases made by them I consider as an infringment on the King's rights and when a line is drawn between us, be it peace or war, they must lose all their improvements and houses on our side of it—The people must all be gone who do not obtain leave to become the King's subjects—what belongs to the Indians will of course be confirmed and secured to them.

"Children, What further can I say to you—You are are witnesses that on our part we have acted in the most peacable manner and borne the language of the People of the United States with patience but I believe our patience is almost exhausted" (DNA: RG 59, Miscellaneous Letters).

Letter not found: to William Tilghman, 20 March 1794. Tilghman wrote GW on 23 March "acknowledging the receipt of your favors of the 10th & 20th instant." This one-page ALS of "about 35 words" was sold at auction in 1938 (*American Book Prices Current*, 45 [1939]: xx, 361).

To Alexander Hamilton

United States, 21 Mar. 1794.
Pay to the Secretary of State, in pursuance of the Act providing for the relief of such of the Inhabitants of St Domingo, resident within the U.S. as may be found in want of support, two

thousand dollars;[1] to be by him remitted to the Committee at Baltimore, appointed to superintend the unfortunate people of the above description at that place.[2]

Geo: Washington

LB, DLC:GW.

1. For this law, see "An Act providing for the relief of such of the inhabitants of Saint Domingo, resident within the United States, as may be found in want of support," 12 Feb. (*Stat.* 6:13). On the allocation of money to Baltimore, see Edmund Randolph to GW, 27 Feb. (first and second letters) and 19 March.

2. On the state committee appointed by the Maryland legislature to oversee relief efforts, and the attempts by local citizens to provide relief for the French refugees residing in Baltimore, see William Patterson et al. to GW, 30 Jan., and notes 1 and 2.

From Alexander Hamilton

Sir,   Treasury Depart. Mar: 21st 1794.

A law having passed to inable the President to cause a loan to be made in aid of the current receipts from the Public revenues, it is urgent that measures should be taken without delay for carrying it into effect.[1]

The enclosed statement shews the probable situation of the Treasury to the end of the ensuing quarter as far as materials are now possessed and manifests the necessity of an immediate aid by Loan.[2]

I therefore submit to the President the draft of a Power in the usual form to authorise the making of the Loan.[3] With perfect respect &c.

Alexander Hamilton. Secy of the Treasy

LB, DLC:GW.

1. The legislation recently passed was "An Act authorizing a Loan of one million of Dollars," 20 March 1794 (*Stat.* 1:345).

2. The enclosed statement (DLC:GW) reads:

"Probable State of Cash up to the 1. July 1794.

Treasury Department March 21. 1794.

Probable demands on the Treasury to the first of
    July 1794—Vizt.

For the Departmt of War by estimation   400,000
For the payment of foreign officers   127,474.75.

For sums informally advanced by the bank of the U.S. for the public service for want of Appropriation.		99,543.05.
For bills purchased & to be purchased to remit to Amsterdam for payments of interest & instalment falling due on the foreign debt to the 1. July 94.		784,560.
For the last instalment of a loan of 800,000 dollars of the bank of the U.S. obtained pursuant to an Act of the last Session		200,000
For two quarters Interest on the public debt payable within the U. States		1,094,000.
Amount of Civil List for two quarters		256,360.
	Dollars	2,961,937.80
Amount of Cash in the several banks per Treasurers return of 7 Mar. 1794		674,621.68.
Amount of Cash in the hands of the several Collectors of the Customs & Supervisors per abstract of returns rendered, dated 7 Mar. '94		130,726.29.
Amount of sums receivable for duties on Imports & tonnage in the months of march, april May & June per abstract of returns of bonds made up the 7. of March 1794		806,307.31.
Amount of additional return since received from the Custom house of New York		60,877.57.
Sums receivable from the duties on Imports & Tonnage of distilled Spirits not ascertainable by reason of deficient returns ⟨&⟩ by estimation		300,000.
Deficiency of Cash towards answering the probable demands on the Treasury		989,404.95
	Dolls	2,961,937.80

Alexander Hamilton"

3. The enclosed draft has not been identified, but the authorization that GW returned to Hamilton on 22 March reads: "For carrying into execution the provisions of the Act of the twentieth day of this present month, whereby the President of the United States is authorised & empowered to borrow a certain sum of money on the credit of the United States.

"I do hereby authorise you the said Secretary of the Treasury in the name and on the credit of the United States to borrow of the bank of the United States, or of any other body or bodies politic, person or persons whomsoever a Sum not exceeding one million of dollars, at any interest not exceeding five per centum per annum; and to enter into such agreements for the reimbursement thereof as shall be needful & proper; hereby promising to ratify whatever you shall lawfully do in the premises.

"In testimony whereof I have here unto subscribed my hand at the City of Philada the 22d day of March 1794" (LB, DLC:GW).

From Henry Knox

Sir,   War department March 22d 1794
    I have the honor to submit to your consideration the proposed draft of an introductory letter to the Governors of the respective States relative to the intended fortifications.[1]
    If you should approve thereof, Copies shall be prepared for the distant States by the Mondays posts. I have the honor to be with perfect respect Your obedt Servant
                                        H. Knox secy of war

LS, DLC:GW; LB, DLC:GW.
    1. Knox wrote the enclosed draft, which has not been identified, in response to the passage of "An Act to provide for the Defence of certain Ports and Harbors in the United States," 20 March 1794 (*Stat.* 1:345–46). The draft probably was similar to the letter that Knox wrote to New Hampshire governor Josiah Bartlett on Monday, 24 March (see n.3 of Knox to GW, 19 March [first letter]).

To Burgess Ball

Dear Sir,   Phila. March 23d 1794.
    By a letter I have just received from my Manager, Mr Pearce, dated the 18th instt I find he had received no more at that time, than 131 bushls of the Buck Wheat you were to procure for me. I hope there will be no disappointment of the remainder. It would fall hard upon me, as I have not the quantity of Seed Oats necessary to carry my plan into affect this year; a failure of both would leave my grounds unoccupied.[1]
    My love, in which Mrs Washington & the family unite is tendered to Mrs Ball & yours.[2] I am—Dear Sir Your Affecte
                                        Go: Washington

ALS (letterpress copy), NN: Washington Papers; LB, DLC:GW.
    1. William Pearce's letter of 18 March has not been found. For Ball's promise to send buckwheat seed to Mount Vernon, see his letter to GW of 21 January. Contrary to GW's expectation, Ball sent the buckwheat seed in several shipments that extended from late January until early April (Pearce to GW, 4 Feb.; Ball to GW, 13 Feb. and 5 April). In a letter to Pearce of 12 Jan., GW indicated that he would need 340 bushels of oat seed and 363 bushels of buckwheat.
    2. The letter-book copy has "yourself."

From the Commissioners
for the District of Columbia

Sir,   City of Washington 23d March 1794
We inclose you a Certificate of your Purchase of Lots, and payment of the price, which by a late Act transfers the Title without the formality of Deeds—This is a Duplicate, the Original is lodged in the Office of the recording Clerk, to be entered by him, and will be returned to our Office.[1]

We were not unmindful of your intention of becoming a Purchaser of a Situation in the other end of the City—we enquired for the Spot you had fixed on, but could get no certain information of it, else it would have been mentioned in the exceptions from Greenleaf's Choice; it was mentioned to him, and we have not only his promise, but his wish that we may dispose of the Ground you may chuse, let it be more or less—if you can rely on Mr Blodget's description, it Shall be finished on Mr Greenleaf's coming down, otherwise it may be kept open till we have the pleasure of seeing you here: at all Events, the Quarter of the Square No. 21 on the N.E. Corner, will not be disposed of, though we Suspect as it affords a north front and an East front only, Mr Blodget may be mistaken.[2]

The Season is already fine enough to resume the Survey of the City. we had an Idea to employ some Gentleman of Service and talents, and Mr Revardi had made so favorable an Impression on us, that we mentioned him to you for your Consideration—we do not wonder in your Situation, you should not always retain on your mind every minute Thing—one Mr Vermanet is here, he is said to have been an Engineer in the Time of the War—We have a letter from Mr Revardi which refers to some Conversation with Mr Blodget, and offers his Services;[3] but unwilling to enter into engagements with any body, without your approbation, or enter on the work with a common Surveyor only we shall decline coming to any decission; 'till our next meeting about the 12th of April; when we Should with pleasure receive a line from you on this Subject.[4] We are Sir very respectfully Your obed. hble Servts

Th. Johnson
Dd Stuart
Danl Carroll

LS, DLC:GW; LB, DNA: RG 42, Records of the Commissioners for the District of Columbia, Letters Sent, 1791–1802. Johnson wrote the closing line on the receiver's copy.

1. The enclosed certificate of 18 Sept. 1793 was for GW's purchase of four lots in square 667, which lay south of the Capitol and along the Eastern Branch.

2. On GW's intention to purchase lots in square 21, west of the President's House, see GW to D.C. Commissioners, 14 March and 11 April, and D.C. Commissioners to GW, 23 April, and n.2. On the offer of James Greenleaf and Robert Morris to purchase 6,000 lots in the District of Columbia, see D.C. Commissioners to GW, 23 Dec. 1793, and n.1 to that document. Samuel Blodget, Jr., was the former superintendent of the District of Columbia.

3. For an earlier mention of John Jacob Ulrich Rivardi by the commissioners, see their letter to GW of 28 January. Neither Rivardi nor John Vermonnet was employed by the commissioners. Rivardi was hired by the War Department as an engineer in charge of building fortifications at the ports at Baltimore, Md., and Norfolk, Va., and Vermonnet was similarly employed at Annapolis, Md., and Alexandria, Va. (*ASP, Military Affairs,* 1:87–95). For Rivardi's letter to the D.C. Commissioners of 10 March, see DNA: RG 42, Records of the Commissioners for the District of Columbia, Letters Received, 1791–1802.

4. For GW's reply, see his letter to the D.C. Commissioners of 11 April.

From the Commissioners
for the District of Columbia

Sir,   City of Washington March 23d 1794

Major Ellicott's, Briggs's and Benjamin Ellicott's Letters of the 29th of June, and 28th of February which you inclosed to Us assert so many untruths, artfully combined that an unusual lengthiness is required to draw the Circumstances into view which have happened for two or three years past.[1]

We certainly best know the real State of our own minds with regard to this Corps and Dermott, and of course know the falsity of the Suggestions which impute to us malicious or dishonourable Motives—nor did we enquire whether Mr Dermott was a Man of Courage as a necessary Qualification for the Division of Squares but we should have thought before the 28th of last month the Major's Ideas of Mr Dermott's prowess were corrected.[2] Nor is the Major better grounded in his charge against Dermott of habitual Drunkeness, we were unwilling to take his Malice or the Mouthing of some of the people of George town as evidence of it we were well informed that he had now and then drank to excess and when inebriated that he is unruly and quarrelsome but we did not perceive that it's frequency injured the business he was engaged in; we made inquiry and formed an opinion not that he was the most discreet nor faulty in this particular to a very uncommon degree; he has since tabled at Sims's for near a year with Gentlemen of as much Sobriety and propriety of Conduct in every respect as any in George Town who Speak well of him—The Major would be far from gaining, by placing his moral Character in one Scale and Dermotts in the other—The Major is always giving verbal Evidence of his attachment to the Interest of the City but neither he nor any body introduced by him has purchased a Lot—Dermott says nothing about his attachment that we have ever heard, but out of his Savings on moderate wages, tho' a Drunkard, has purchased Several Lots and is improving according to his Ability. The occasion and manner of Mr Dermott's coming into Employment and the manner of his being dismissed differ widely from the Representation in the Letter. You may recollect that several Things in the Course of the Quarrel with L'Enfant strongly pointed to a duplicity and ill intentioned conduct of Ellicott[3]—you may recollect too tho' Ellicott would save twenty shillings a day by discharging Dermott and putting a double and impossible duty on Fenwick—the Commissioners because of the extravagance of the Surveyors and their Slow Movements declared they would not pass the preceeding Accounts or have any thing to do with them in future unless those employed were on a different footing so far at least as that they should live at their own Expence.[4]

Mr Jefferson had intercourse with Ellicott on this Subject and the Major agreed; we presume, tho' we do not know it, that more expedition was promised for about the time of a letter from Mr Jefferson,[5] we received one from Major Ellicott dated 7th March 1792, to an extract of which we refer you.[6] Mr Johnson did not attend the meeting when this Letter was received—Doctr Stuart did not even know Dermott by sight, but having heard of his being employed in the Farquair and afterwards in the Alexandria Academies—that he was a man of Science and going to the Southward, mentioned him and the Circumstances to Mr Carroll in Consequence of that letter of Elliotts—they both thought it best that Doctr Stuart Should endeavour to engage him—and he was engaged accordingly.[7]

The Temper and view of the Commissioners appear by their Letter of the 14 March 1792 to Major Ellicott (see the Extract).[8]

Major Ellicott cannot but remember that more than once he spoke of Dermott as the readiest Calculator he had met with; and though in the Succeeding Summer he employed him wholly, or nearly so, as an Overseer to overlook the Negroes in cutting down the trees in the Streets and Avenues, previous to the Sale in the fall and preparatory to it, he employed him in calculating the Areas and dividing the Squares.[9]

The Commissioners saw the impropriety of employing Dermott to overlook the cutting down the Avenues and Streets at his wages, and especially as he was an European, he had probably never had any thing to do of the kind: they perceived too, Dermotts uneasiness at his situation, and were glad to see that Ellicott had changed it.

Major Ellicott asserts that he communicated his intention to discharge Dermott, to Doctr Stuart who pointedly opposed his dismission—Doctr Stuart neither remembers or believes it—nor does Mr Johnson or Mr Carroll recollect they ever heard any thing of it. On some joyous Occasion, We believe on the laying a Stone of the Bridge,[10] Dermott was in Liquor and in that State intimated to Doct. Stuart that there were inaccuracies in the work, but so far from a disposition to pick up Matter against Ellicott, Doctr Stuart let Dermott know, that he should take no notice of what he said unless he would at a more Seasonable time address himself to the Commissioners—Dermott did not and nothing more was done at that time—Not long afterwards as Ellicott said, he had discharged Dermott: and as Dermott said Ellicott told him, that there was no present business for him but to be ready against the Axmen should go to Work in the Spring—Ellicott 29th January 1793 desires the Commissioners to order Dermott to deliver up Papers—5th February Doctr Stuart and Mr Carroll write to Dermott to deliver them (see the Extracts)[11]—the Commissioners then looked on Dermott as discharged without any inquiry into the Cause of it.

Afterwards on his way to attend as a Commissioner Doctr Stuart met with Dermott in Virginia, who then again entered on the Subject of Errors—Doctr Stuard unwilling to Act at all on verbal information to him Singly, and thinking it necessary there should be some Examination, desired Dermott to address what he had to say in writing to the Commissioners and to attend, himself, the meeting in George town; he did so.[12]

Major Ellicott was expected to be at George town by a particular day—the Commissioners met and received Dermotts letter—they all thought it best to say nothing of it 'till Major Ellicott came; had resolved to mention it to him in a private way, and if mistakes were really committed to have them rectified, if it could be done, without saying a word about them—their motives need not be mentioned, and Dermott had a caution accordingly—The Commissioners waited from Monday 'till *Friday*[13] in Expectation of Ellicotts coming, but the sickness of his wife kept him back—On friday the Commissioners gave orders to Mr Fenwick to remeasure in a Cursory way, the Squares pointed out and except in an Instance, where the number of one was mistaken, they were erroneous and some very considerably so.[14]

Major Ellicott however returned from Philadelphia on Monday Night before we Separated—he was undoubtedly soon notified of the inaccuracies and it is equally true that his answer was desired in writing—we do not recollect that he was limited in time and if we remember right Thomas Curtis who was Measurer under Ellicott did the Same Service under Mr Fenwick[15]—We desired the answer in writing to prevent shuffling and do not yet see that the Manner required would have given extraordinary trouble—The letters which passed between Us will shew the Temper and views of each—Indeed Major Ellicott in his verbal explanations to the Commissioners has taken liberties under a presumption of their ignorance and he deals with the same freedom towards others who are easier satisfied, and he is of so compliant a Temper that he would talk whole Days of altered Stakes, and altered figures and trifling inaccuracies but he was too Cunning to commit himself in writing.[16]

On Major Ellicott's evading the delivery of the papers we went with Colo. Deakins to Prouts house, where he then kept his Office, and made a personal demand of them[17]—he then told us that Dermott had stolen a plan of the City, describing it, Mr Johnson remarked it was a Severe charge for which he ought to be well grounded before he made it—Major Ellicott said he had stolen it; that it was in his trunk and he could prove enough to obtain a search warrant, and if we would break open his trunk we should find it—Mr Johnson replied that the End might perhaps be answered by milder Measures without going to that violence—on turning off he proposed to Doctr Stuart and Mr Carroll to send for Dermott immediately on their return and question him about the plat and if he denied his having it, to desire him to submit his trunk to their Search—it was agreed to—Dermott was sent for and attended: Mr Johnson asked him if he had the plat,[18] describing it, he answered yes. where is it? in my trunk—the Commissioners wish to see it—I will bring it to you immediately Sir—Major Ellicott knows very well I have it, and that I would deliver it to him at any time that he'd ask for it—He expressed astonishment at Major Ellicott's making, (in his expression) a fuss about it, for he knew, he offered to deliver him any Papers he had and that Major Ellicott said it was no Matter then, it would do as well some other time—(see Dermotts letter to Ellicott 6 Feby 1793)[19]—He brought the Plat immediately, and believing it to be a public paper we ordered our Clerk to keep it[20]—this was known publicly—Sometime after Major Ellicott's last return from Philadelphia an Advertisement appeared in the George town paper in the name of Benjamin Ellicott, though said to be inserted by Joseph, offering a Reward for apprehending Dermott as a Thief in stealing the plat and in the same paper under the same Date a Letter was addressed by him to the Commissioners containing an infamous insinuation against them[21] In consequence of our letter to Benjamin Ellicott, inclosed, he and Joseph attended—the plat was produced; Hallet's Certificate, inclosed was put into Benjamin's hands, and he was told the Commissioners had no wish to surprize him:[22] The end of their inquiry was to discover to whom the Paper, important only from Circumstances, really belonged—Joseph said that the Letter was not to be justified that his Brother was sorry for it and would make any Concessions the Commissioners required—he was told the Commissioners did not want Concessions: they instantly withdrew and the paper was put up again—Dermott's letter to Major Ellicott, as it imports on his receipt of the Commissioners Order to deliver papers, must evince that he came to the possession of the papers in the Course of his Service under Ellicott in a way not reprehensible and was willing to deliver all up, and on the Contrary it Seems that Ellicott rather sought for cause of Complaint than for the papers else he would have taken the Short way of inquiring of Dermott if he had any particular paper which he wanted—The charge of Theft against Dermott is in a way of being examined into in a Suit he has brought against Hanson the printer—the removal of the Corps has prevented a writ being served on some of them also—they will now have an opportunity of adducing their evidence before an impartial tribunal.[23]

Another Charge against Dermott was his changing and maliciously misplacing Stakes: we heard nothing of that 'till we perceived the greater part of a Succeeding Summer was spent in going over the work of the preceeding and then the excuse was that Some body had altered the Situation of Stakes and it must be maliciously done because the alteration was so systematic that the greater part of a Season was spent before it could be discovered—Dermott was said to know nothing of the System but it was Dermott because he was malicious and he was malicious because he did it—it was first Suspicion afterwards certain, it was first several stakes afterwards one and now amongst all Dermott's Crimes this the most capital is omitted—Briggs at several times mentioned to Doctr Stuart *his Suspicion* that Dermott had altered the Stakes, the Doctor inquired if he had any proof of it Briggs acknowledged that he had not but suspected it the Doctr remarked it was a very delicate thing and that it would be unjust to act on Suspicion—when in Briggs's altercation with the Commissioners he recurred again to the Story of the Stakes—as an evidence of Dermotts infamous Conduct Doctr Stuart lost his Temper and spoke to him very roughly—The truth is the Commissioners had their Suspicions too whether ill or well founded they cannot say but they suspected that the whole story was invented to cover a mistake which had happened accidentally or for want of care.

If the charge of altering the work, of stealing or maliciously secreting a paper or misplacing a Stake was Substantiated the result would surely be against Dermott—We have seen Strong marks of Candour in this Man: we have no reason to suspect his telling us a lie. he shews an attention to the public interest in his divisions, has his business in good order and gives us and others such ready answers that he must have the clearest and most comprehensive view of his department—We had a good deal of trouble with Briggs before he was out of employ it was obviously necessary to return the length of line to the water and the width of the Streets to know whether the returns were accurate and what part was land and what was water but an affected misunderstanding of applications kept up a dodging for two or three meetings.

We had determined to separate the platting and dividing Squares from the execution of the field work and were confirmed in it by Major Ellicott's making a merit of his preparing the Divisions because it was, as he said, out of the line of his duty and he intimated too his not being therefore accountable for their accuracy the check has proved useful, several inaccuracies, not more than might be expected, have been discovered in time and been rectified.[24]

The more perfect the work done may be found the better we shall be pleased but the experience we have had in marking out the lots on the lines of Squares does not lead us into Major Ellicott's opinion that his is the most accurate work of the kind, and he is mistaken if he supposes we shall impute all future embarrasment to the ignorance or negligence of his Successor for we know that lines designed to be paralel so far as they differ from a paralel will grow narrower or wider by extending their length; and that there will be the like increase of error by extending diverging lines partly run on undue quantity of difference.

Is it possible that Major Ellicott believes his own insinuation that the Commissioners had any pleasure in the Baltimore publication against him? they had spoken their disapprobation of it severally and their joint letter to him of the 6th February last gave him, we believe, no new information on this head[25]—Major Ellicott has good reason to be satisfied that we dispise libellous publications. We are sir with the truest Respect Your most obedt Servants

Th Johnson
Dd Stuart
Danl. Carroll

LS, DLC:GW; LB, DNA: RG 42, Records of the Commissioners for the District of Columbia, Letters Sent, 1791–1802. Johnson wrote the closing on the receiver's copy. None of the enclosures identified as "A" to "K" has been identified, but other versions of these documents, if known, are identified in the notes below.

1. For these letters, see Andrew Ellicott, Benjamin Ellicott, and Isaac Briggs to GW, 29 June 1793, and Andrew Ellicott's two letters to GW of 28 Feb. 1794. GW enclosed these three letters in a letter to the D.C. commis-

sioners of 14 March. The long-running dispute between the commissioners and Andrew Ellicott, the former chief surveyor for the district, involved Ellicott's accusations of incompetence and malfeasance against James R. Dermott, who also worked in the surveying department, and the commissioners' countercharges of incompetence against Ellicott.

2. For some of the aspersions made against the commissioners, especially David Stuart, see Stuart to GW, 18 Feb. 1793, and n.1 to that document. At this point in the letter-book copy, the letter contains the following text: "Nor could we have transactions with Major Ellicott or Briggs for any length of time without discovering their disregard to truth. From dates and other circumstances it may fairly be inferred that from the time, 10th April [1793], of them entering anew on the Surveying Department Major Ellicott, Benjamin and Briggs were preparing to have the Work of the City wholly in their Hands. we had no meeting in May; our first, was the 17 June there was no new complaint but that contained in the extract of the report of that date, which stated the Evil as remedied at a considerable expence by a resurvey though in the Majors letter to you of the 28th [Feb. 1794], he would have you impute any inaccuracy to the loss of the field notes without intimating any thing of a Resurvey—The Major knows that he employed a person at first to do the greater part of the field work who he represented to us before he employed him as not to be trusted for either Skill or Care in any thing we had but a very indifferent opinion of him from our own observation, the Resurvey may have added to the expence and ought to be much more accurate than the first Survey—The Majors Military achievements did not recommend him to the Head of the Surveying Department." On Andrew Ellicott's initial resignation and his subsequent return to the surveying department, both in 1793, see GW to D.C. Commissioners, 3 April 1793, and n.6 to that document.

3. On the dismissal of Pierre L'Enfant, see editorial note, L'Enfant to GW, 21 Nov. 1791, and GW to L'Enfant, 28 Feb. 1792.

4. On the employment of George Fenwick in the surveying department, see D.C. Commissioners to GW, 23 April, and n.3 to that document.

5. For this letter, see Thomas Jefferson to D.C. Commissioners, 6 March 1792 (*Jefferson Papers*, 23:224–25). The commissioners had this letter by the time they met on 13 March 1792 (DNA: RG 42, Records of the Commissioners for the District of Columbia, Proceedings, 1791–1802).

6. An "A" appears in the left margin to indicate which enclosure is the extract of Ellicott's letter to the D.C. commissioners of 7 March 1792. In this letter, Ellicott requested an assistant who was "acquainted with practical Astronomy and expert in the use of Instruments" (DNA, RG 42, Records of the Commissioners for the District of Columbia, Letters Received, 1791–1802).

7. During their meeting on 26 March 1792, the commissioners voted to hire Dermott as an assistant surveyor (DNA: RG 42, Records of the Commissioners for the District of Columbia, Proceedings, 1791–1802).

8. A "B" appears in the left margin to indicate the appropriate extract. The letter from the D.C. commissioners to Ellicott of 14 March 1792 is in DNA: RG 42, Records of the Commissioners for the District of Columbia, Letters Sent, 1791–1802.

9. On the sale of lots in the Federal City, which commenced on 8 Oct. 1792, see GW to D.C. Commissioners, 29 Sept. 1792, and n.1 to that document; and Broadside: Sale of Lots in the Federal City, 8 Oct. 1792.

10. On the building of Rock Creek Bridge and the laying of the cornerstone of the eastern abutment on 4 July 1792, see n.1 of GW to Jefferson, 21 March 1792, and *Maryland Journal and Baltimore Advertiser,* 10 July 1792.

11. Letters "C" and "D" appear in the left margin to indicate the extracts, respectively, for Ellicott to D.C. Commissioners, 29 Jan. 1793, and D.C. Commissioners to Dermott, 5 Feb. 1793. The complete texts of these letters can be seen, respectively, at DNA: RG 42, Records of the Commissioners for the District of Columbia, Letters Received, 1791–1802, and DNA: RG 42, Records of the Commissioners for the District of Columbia, Letters Sent, 1791–1802.

12. A written report on the various surveying errors from Dermott to the commissioners has not been identified, but the minutes for the meeting of the commissioners on 13 March 1793 recorded the receipt of "a List of public papers from James Dermott" (DNA: RG 42, Records of the Commissioners for the District of Columbia, Proceedings, 1791–1802).

13. The original *"Tuesday"* was altered at this point. According to their minutes, the commissioners began their March 1793 meeting on Monday, 4 March, and ended it on Thursday, 14 March (DNA: RG 42, Records of the Commissioners for the District of Columbia, Proceedings, 1791–1802).

14. On the reaction of Ellicott and the commissioners to Dermott's suggestion of inaccurate surveys and subsequent correspondence on this issue, see D.C. Commissioners to GW, 11–12 March 1793, and notes 8 and 11 to that document. On Friday, 8 March, the commissioners instructed George Fenwick to measure "several squares alledged to be erroneous," and received his report the next day. On 14 March, he was directed to "remeasure the squares with a chain and to report to the Comrs from time to time their agreement or disagreement with the plats of those squares" (DNA: RG 42, Records of the Commissioners for the District of Columbia, Proceedings, 1791–1802).

15. On 14 March 1793, the commissioners directed "Mr Curtis and Mr Bennett Fenwick to proceed in measuring" (DNA: RG 42, Records of the Commissioners for the District of Columbia, Proceedings, 1791–1802).

16. On Ellicott's return from Philadelphia on 12 March and his subsequent conversation with the commissioners, see the postscript to D.C. Commissioners to GW, 11–12 March 1793. In his letter to the commissioners of 12 March 1793, Ellicott wrote: "If I am to understand your letter of yesterday, that no work will be done in the surveying department, until you receive a particular explanation with respect to some errors which you were pleased to enclose; it will in my opinion be most proper, and expedient, to have the explanation immediately at the office in the City, where all the necessary papers may be immediatly recurred to." In a postscript he added: "It is my meaning, that the explanation should be personal much information may be given by few words which would take much writing" (DNA: RG 42, Records of the Commissioners for the District of Columbia, Letters Received, 1791–1802).

17. On Ellicott's rental of a house from William Prout, see n.9 of D.C. Com-

missioners to GW, 11–12 March 1793. William Deakins, Jr., was the treasurer for the federal district.

18. On the missing plat, see note 22.

19. An "E" appears in the right margin to indicate Dermott's letter to Ellicott of 6 Feb. 1793.

20. John Mackall Gantt was the clerk for the D.C. commissioners.

21. For Andrew Ellicott's "last return," see D.C. Commissioners to GW, 28 Jan. 1794. On the final dismissal of Andrew Ellicott in December 1793, see D.C. Commissioners to GW, 23 Dec. 1793, and n.8 to that document; see also D.C. Commissioners to Ellicott, 17 Dec. 1793 (DNA: RG 42, Records of the Commissioners for the District of Columbia, Letters Sent, 1791–1802). An "F" appears in the left margin to indicate the enclosed advertisement, which probably appeared in the *Columbian Chronicle* (Georgetown) along with Benjamin Ellicott's unidentified letter to the D.C. commissioners, which is indicated by a "G" in the left margin.

22. An "H" appears in the left margin to indicate the letter from the D.C. commissioners to Benjamin Ellicott of 25 Jan., in which they wrote that they had seen his letter in the newspaper demanding "a plan of the City." After objecting to the publication of his request, they invited him to their office, "where the plan which has occasioned so much heat, has been deposited ever since the Spring, and shall order it to be delivered to you on your Substantiating your claim to it" (DNA: RG 42, Records of the Commissioners for the District of Columbia, Letters Sent, 1791–1802). In his reply of 25 Jan., written at the "Surveyor's Office," Ellicott acknowledged being the author of the advertisement and letter appearing in the Georgetown newspaper. He also wrote: "my aim so far as related to you was only to obtain a Map which had hitherto give me much pain and anxiety—being accountable to Majr L. Enfant for it." He then agreed to meet with the commissioners (DNA: RG 42, Records of the Commissioners for the District of Columbia, Letters Received, 1791–1802).

An "I" appears in the margin to indicate a letter from Stephen Hallet to Dermott of 25 Jan. 1794, the so-called certificate given to Ellicott, in which Hallet wrote: "Being called upon by the Commissioners to examine a fragment of a Plan in their Office. I acknowledged that which has been laid before me to be the same Reduction of Major L Enfant's Plan of the City, which I once undertook at his requisition from a GREAT Map he intrusted to me. . . . It was done on Silk paper in order to save time, but Major L'Enfant being at a Hurry took back his Original before the Reduction could be finished. And I delivered it in the same state to Mr Lear, upon his application in the name of the President" (DNA: RG 42, Records of the Commissioners for the District of Columbia, Letters Received, 1791–1802).

23. Samuel Hanson was the publisher of the *Columbian Chronicle*, a Georgetown newspaper, which was printed from 3 Dec. 1793 to 10 May 1796. On the dismissal of Andrew, Benjamin, and Joseph Ellicott, see D.C. Commissioners to GW, 28 Jan. 1794, and notes 1 and 2 to that document.

24. On the allocation of work assignments according to this plan, see the minutes of the commissioners' meeting on 25 March (DNA: RG 42, Records of the Commissioners for the District of Columbia, Proceedings, 1791–1802).

25. The letter "K" appears in the left margin to indicate the letter from the D.C. commissioners to Ellicott of 6 Feb., which has not been identified.

From Betty Washington Lewis

My Dear Brother   March 23th 1794

Your letter of the 17th Came safe to hand the inclos'd letter will meet with a Convayance in a few dayes by my Son George as he will Call on Robert in his way to Kaintucky he sets of in a few daye on Busness, at the same time takes Negroes to settle a Place there, and I believe in a few years intends liveing there as Chief of the Property he Possessis is in that Part of the World,[1] I am inform'd that the Vessel that brings Harriots Box is in the River,[2] we are Extreamly alarm'd here for fear of a War the Merchants here say that it is Inevitable I Expect it is to raise the Price of Goods which has allredy taken Place in regard to Westindia goods, I wish to here from you as I then shall be satisfied of the truth of it, I was in hopes I should never live to see any more of those troublesome times.[3]

My Dear Brother I am going to ask a great favour of you that is to give me a Mule, if you have one that you Can spear without disfirnishing your self if you Can let me have one & I will send for it.[4] I am Joind in love by the Girls to you and my Sister Washington with the family your Affectionate Sister

Betty Lewis

ALS, MH: Sparks Collection.

1. GW's letter to Betty Washington Lewis of 17 March has not been found. For the letter to be conveyed by George Lewis, see GW to Robert Lewis, 16 March. George Lewis (1757–1821) was the fourth son of Betty Washington Lewis and her husband, Fielding Lewis. During the Revolutionary War he served as the captain of GW's Life Guard in 1776 and in the 3d Continental Dragoons, 1777–79. He did not settle permanently in Kentucky because in 1797 he purchased Marmion Plantation in King George County, Va., where he resided until his death.

2. For the contents of the box sent to Harriot Washington, which was now aboard a vessel in the Rappahannock River, and for its receipt, see Harriot's letters to GW of 5 and 24 March.

3. GW's reply of 30 March has not been found (see Betty Washington Lewis to GW, 13 April).

4. For GW's gift of a mule, see Betty Washington Lewis to GW, 13 April.

To William Pearce

Mr Pearce   Philadelphia 23d March 1794

The weekly reports, and your letter of the 18th instant, came regularly to hand.[1]

The insufferable neglects of my Overseers in not plowing as they ought to have done in the Fall, begins now to be manifest; for I perceive by the account given of the plowing, that I am driven to the alternative of putting my Oats into ground not half plowed, & prepared, & thereby little to expect from it; or, in order to do this, be so late in sowing, as to hazard an entire loss of the Crop, if the Spring is not very moist and dripping; for I have seldom succeeded with Oats unless they were *sown* before the middle of March.

It did not occur to me in time, to advise running the rollers over your grass grounds, & even the Wheat, after the frosts had come fairly out of the earth; nothing would have recovered both more. The roots (even of that which had been thrown entirely out) would have been pressed in such a manner to the earth as to have shot forth fibres to restore the plant. now, I presume it is too late.

I do not, in the first place believe Spring Barley is to be had in that part of the Country, as little of it is grown there; and in the next place, it is not likely it would succeed, as I tried it two or three years unsuccessfully. If it is to be had at all, it is most likely to come from Wayles the Brewer in Alexandria;[2] and you might, as Oats are scarce, make another experiment, if Seed is to be had. How does the Winter Barley look?

I am sorry to find Colo. Ball is so tardy in forwarding the B. Wheat—I shall remind him of it by tomorrow's Post.[3] What quantity of Wheat is supposed to be in the Straw at the several farms? Before it is all out at Dogue run, take up one section after another and new lay it; 'till you are able to ascertain the true distance the pieces ought to be asunder; for the reasons mentioned to you in a former letter; attending particularly to the circumstance I mentioned, and am apprehensive of, viz.—that of the straw working between & choaking.[4]

Mr Smith has, I believe, been furnished with fish from my landing, and if he will give as much as another, ought to have the preference; but before you positively engage, enquire what the other fisheries were disposed to sell at. 4/ pr thousand for the Herrings, and 10/ pr hundred for shad, is very low. I am, at this moment, paying 6/ a piece for every shad I buy.[5] I am entirely against any Waggons coming to my landing; but there is one thing which Mr Smith, or any other with whom you engage, must perfectly understand, if they agree to take *all* (over what I want for my own use) that is, when the glut of the fish runs, he must be provided to take every one I do not want, or have them thrown on his hands: the truth of the case is, that in the height of the fishery, they are not prepared to cure, or otherwise dispose of them, as fast as they *could* be *caught;* of course the Seins slacken in their work, or the fish lye & spoil, when that is the only time I can make any thing by the Sein—for small hauls will hardly pay the ware & tare of the Sein & the hire of the hands—your account of the dificiency of Sein rope would have surprized me if it had not been of piece with the rest of the conduct which has waisted every thing I had, almost: whatever is necessary must be got, & I shall Depend upon your care and attention, now, to guard me against destruction of my property, while it is entrusted to your management.[6]

Secure a sufficiency of fish for the use of my own people from the first that comes, otherwise they may be left in the lurch, as has been the case heretofore, by depending on what is called the glut.

What quantity of Wheat have you yet in the straw, according to the conjectures of the Overseers, at whose farms it is? If you can get Six dollars a barrel for the superfine, & thirty four shils. for the common flour, in good hands, let it go, at Sixty days credit.

I have 25 Hds of Tobacco in the Warehouses in Alexandria; examine what condition they lye in, & see that they are safe. not having been able to obtain the price I set upon them they have lain there five or six years, at least. I have held these at a guinea a hundred, and would take it.[7]

Is your family arrived at Mount Vernon?[8] you have said nothing about them in your last letters.

The Vessel with the Clover Seed &ca left this City on Tuesday last, and is, I hope, with you before this—Another goes tomorrow, on board which I send you (directed to the care of Colo. Gilpin) nine bolts of Oznabrigs, finding it cheaper to buy here than in Alexandria.[9]

Enclosed you have a bond of Colo. Lyles, who lives on Broad Creek (between you & Alexandria)—receive the amount with interest to the day of payment, & place it to my credit. If the money is wanting for paying the Overseers, or for other purposes, it may be applied accordingly; otherwise, when more can be added to it, I will direct the application another way. Remember it is Virginia money you are to receive, that is dollars at Six shillings. The readiest way of getting to Colo. Lyles is in your own Boat; & by so doing you can touch at the fishing landings between, & learn their expectations with respect to the prices of Fish.[10]

I send you 3 lbs. of Lucern Seed to sprinkle over the spring lot, where the former grew. The ground ought to be well torn with a sharp toothed harrow, in order to prepare it for the Seed, otherwise much of it will miss.[11]

With Colo. Lyles bond I send you a letter to him, which seal before delivery; you have also a statement of the account, as far as I have any knowledge of it. Receive nothing short of the whole sum which is due; unless you have no other means of discharging any demands upon me, for receiving a bond in driblets, is, in a manner, sinking it; and the amount of this bond, if it can be spared from other uses, I want to apply in discharge of another bond, which is also carrying interest.[12] I am Your friend &ca

Go: Washington

ALS, ViMtvL; ALS (letterpress copy), DLC:GW.

1. Pearce's letter of 18 March and the enclosed reports have not been found.

2. Andrew Wales owned a brewery and distillery on South Water Street and a tavern on Union Street in Alexandria, Virginia.

3. GW wrote Burgess Ball on this date to ask about the promised buckwheat seed.

4. For GW's instructions regarding the spacing between the threshing boards at the new barn at Dogue Run farm, see his letter to Pearce of 16–17 March.

5. For Alexandria merchant Alexander Smith's proposed fishing contract with GW, see his letter to GW of 3 July 1793. On 15 May, Smith paid Pearce

£29.10.08 "for 147676 Herrings @ 4 ℔ thousand," and £17.10.06 "for 3295 Shad @ 10/ ℔ hundred" (Mount Vernon Accounts, 1794–97).

6. In preparation for the fishing season, Pearce paid £22.15.00 on 3 Feb. to Robert Hamilton for 182 lbs of "Seine Twine @ 2/6 ℔ lb.," £60 on 1 April to Smith for 200 bushels of "Salt for fish" at 6/ per bushel, £13.09.04 to Lawrence McGinnis on 1 April for "kniting A new Seine & putting a piece in the Old Shad Seine," and £14.05.4 to James Irvin on 6 May for "Seine Rope &c." On 13 May, he paid £15 to Thomas Dyer "for hauling the Seine During the fishing Season" and £5.12.00 to "the People for hauling the Seine on Holyday Sundys & Sundy Nights" (Mount Vernon Accounts, 1794–97).

7. On the 25 hogsheads of tobacco currently stored in warehouses in Alexandria, see GW to Alexandria, Va., Inspectors of Tobacco, 21 Oct. 1792, and notes 1 and 3 to that document; and GW to John Fitzgerald, 28 April 1793, and n.3 to that document.

8. On Pearce's family, see n.2 of Benjamin Chew, Jr., to GW, 16 Aug. 1793.

9. On the shipment of clover seed and other items aboard the *Sally,* which set sail on Tuesday, 18 March, see GW to Burgess Ball, 16 March, and GW to Pearce, 16–17 March. On 19 March, GW paid $80.91 to merchant Robert Smith for 3 bolts of oznabrig and $163.25 to the Philadelphia firm of Todd & Mott for 6 bolts of oznabrig; on 24 March, he paid $2.75 for its freight to the care of George Gilpin in Alexandria (Household Accounts).

10. Alexandria merchant William Lyles lived in Prince Georges County, Md., on his estate of Want Water, which was located along Broad Creek, a tributary of the Potomac River. In 1789, he assumed responsibility for the payment of £795.15.4 that Robert Alexander owed to GW (Lyles to GW, 3 April 1789). According to his agreement with GW, Lyles paid £300 to GW in three payments of £100 each, on 7 May, 2 June, and 31 July 1789. Lyles then posted a bond for £495.15.04 on 19 Sept. 1789. This bond was to be paid in "four annual payments of £123.18.10 each on the 19th day of Septr in the years 1790, 1791, 1792, & 1793." As of this date, payments had been made on 19 Oct. 1790 in the amount of £123.18.10 plus interest of £6.3.11; on 24 Nov. 1791 in the amount of £93.11.08; and on 1 Oct. 1792 in the amount of £105. An undated notation in GW's ledger reads, "This acct settled by the payment of the above Bond with interest" (Ledger B, 361).

The enclosed statement of 24 March (ADS [letterpress copy], DLC:GW) reads:

Willm Lyles Esqr. in acct with G: Washington

Dr.		Virga Curry	
1789 Sepr 19th	To yr Bond of this date for	£495.15.4	
1790 Octr ⟨19⟩	Int[eres]t thereon	26.17.	
			522.12.4
1790 Oct. 19	To Bal[anc]e pr Contra	392. 9.7	
1791 Nov. 24	Interest thereon	23. 3.5	
			415.13.0
1791 Novr 24	To Bale pr Con:	322. 1.4	
1792 Oct. 1	Intt thereon	12. 6.1	

			334. 7.5
1792 Oct. 1st	To Bale pr Con.	229. 7.5	
1794 Aprl 1st	Intt to this date	17. 4.0	
			£246.11.5—due
	Cr.		
1790 Octr 19	By Cash	£130. 2.9	
	Bale	392. 9.7	
			522.12.4
1791 Nov. 24	By Cash	93.11.8	
	Bale	322. 1.4	
			415.13.0
1792 Oct. 1st	By Cash	105.	
	Bale	229. 7.5	
			334. 7.5

E[rrors] Excepted—March 24th 1794.

Go: Washington

The enclosed letter to Lyles was also dated 24 March. In a letter to Pearce of 23 Nov. 1794, GW indicated that a payment from Lyles had been received earlier that month, but the amount was not specified (ALS, ViMtvL).

11. On 24 March, GW paid $1 for "3 lbs. Lucerne seed to send to Mo. Vn" (Household Accounts).

12. The other bond may have been for money owed Lund Washington. Upon receiving notification that money received from Lyles had been deposited in a bank in Alexandria, GW enclosed "money to discharge my bond to Mr Lund Washington" in a letter to Pearce of 23 Nov. 1794 (ALS, ViMtvL).

From William Tilghman

Dear Sir   Chester Town [Md.] March 23. 1794.

I have the honor of acknowledging the receipt of your favors of the 10th & 20th instant. Mr Herbert's letter, which was inclosed in your last, shall be safely kept amongst the other papers relating to the debt due from Sidney George to the estate of Col. Colvill.[1] There is no doubt but interest must be paid on Mr Georges bond, subject to a small deduction during the late war, according to the law of Maryland. The case is different with respect to the £100 received by Mr Chalmers. He is to be considered as a British subject; & as our Courts have determined that British creditors are not entitled to interest during the war, on their debts due from American citizens, I suppose it would be inferred from the same principle, that Americans cannot recover interest on debts due before the revolution, from British subjects. Mr Chalmers seems to view it in this light, as his order authorizing me to draw on him, extends no farther than £100[2]—I must confess however, that tho' the law may be so, I see no good reason in point of Justice, why he should not pay interest. As it is not probable that any further information can be obtained as to the payment which Mr Chalmers supposes he must have made, all that now remains, is to decide, whether I shall draw on him for the value of £100 currency, agreeably to his order. It will occasion a small embarrassment in your final settlement of Col. Colvills estate—because if Chalmers should hereafter be able to prove that he paid the money before the War, you will have to make him restitution—You must guard yourself against this contingency, by taking a refunding bond from the persons interested in the estate of Col. Colvill. I shall wait your orders on this subject, & if you conclude that I had better draw, you will be so obliging as to send me a short writing, binding yourself to refund the money, if it should hereafter be proved that Chalmers paid it before.

I have seen Mr George, since I last wrote to you. He promises to pay £100 this Spring, & I submit it to your consideration, whether it will not be adviseable to take a new bond for the balance, payable next fall, to yourself, as surviving Executor of Col. Colvill. I think this will place the debt on a better footing than it stands at present, & I dare say Mr George will have no objection. He is apt to be a little tardy in his payments, but the security of his bond is equal to that of any man. I shall delay my answer to Mr Chalmers's letters till I receive your instructions.[3] I have the honor to be with every sentiment of the most respectful regard Yr most ob. Servt

Wm Tilghman.

ALS, DLC:GW.

1. The enclosure in GW's letter to Tilghman of 20 March, which has not been found, was GW's letter to William Herbert of 10 March.

2. For this authorization, see George Chalmers to Tilghman, 4 Dec. 1793, in n.2 of Tilghman to GW, 1 March 1794.

3. For GW's instructions, see his letter to Tilghman of 31 March.

From the Democratic Society of Washington County, Pa.

Washington [Pa.] March 24th 1794.
To the President and Congress of the United States of America.

The Remonstrance of the Democratic Society of the County of Washington, in Pennsylvania, Respectfully sheweth

That your Remonstrants are entitled by nature and by stipulation, to the undisturbed Navigation of the river Mississippi, and consider it a right inseperable from their prosperity.[1] That in colonizing this distant and dangerous desart, they always contemplated the free enjoyment of this right, and considered it as an inseperable appendage to the Country they had sought out, had fought for, and acquired. That for a series of years during their early settlement, their petetions to government to secure this right, were answered by its alledged weakness, and your Remonstrants taught to expect, that the time was approaching fast, when both power and inclination would unite to establish it on the firmest grounds. In this anxious expectation they waited, and to the insolence of those who arrogated its exclusive exercise, they patiently submitted, till the government of America had so strengthened itself as to hold out an assurance of future protection to all its citizens, and of redress for all their wrongs.[2]

That protection has not been extended to us, we need only refer to our present situation, and that that situation has not been concealed from, or unknown to, Congress, we appeal to its Archives. We have, without ceasing, deplored to you our degraded situation, and burdened you with our humble petitions and requests. But alas! we still experience, that the strong nerved government of America, extends its arm of protection to all the branches of the Union, but to your Remonstrants. That it is competent to every end, but that single one, by which alone it can benefit us: the protection of our Territorial rights. It is competent to exact obedience, but not to make that return which can be the only just and natural exchange for it.

Long have your Remonstrants been anxiously in quest of the obstacles that have stood in your way to the establishment of this our right; And as long has their pursuit been fruitless. Formal and tardy negociations have no doubt been often projected, and have as often miscarried. It is true, some negociations were once attempted, that were neither *formal* nor *tardy*, and gave an early shock to our encreasing population and to our peace of mind; but your Remonstrants are constrained to be of opinion, that the neglect or local policy of American councils, has never produced one single effort to procure this right. Could the Government of America be for Ten years seriously in pursuit of the establishment of a grand Territorial right, which was arrogantly suspended, and return to that quarter of the Union to whom it was all-important, but an equivocal answer?[3] We think it high time that we should be thoroughly informed of the situation on which your negociations, if any, have left this right: for apathy itself has grown hopeless from long dissappointed expectation.

Your Remonstrants yield not in patriotism to any of their fellow-citizens: but patriotism, like every other thing, has its bounds. We love those states from which we were all congregated, and no event (not even an attempt to barter away our best rights) shall alien our affections from the individual members who compose them: But attatchment to governments cease to be natural, when they cease to be mutual. To be subjected to all the burthens, and enjoy none of the benefits arising from government is what we will never submit to.[4] Our situation compels us to speak plainly. If wrechedness and poverty await us, it is of no concern to us how they are produced. We are gratified in the prosperity of the Atlantic states, but would not speak the language of truth and sincerity, were we not to declare our unwillingness to make any sacrifices to it, when their importance and those sacrifices result from our distresses. If the interest of Eastern America requi⟨res⟩ that we should be kept in poverty, it is unreasonable from such poverty to exact contributions. The first, if we cannot emerge from, we must learn to bear; but the latter, we never can be taught to submit to.

From the General Government of America, therefore, your Remonstrants now ask protection, in the free enjoyment of the navigation of the river Mississippi, which is withheld from them by the Spaniards. We demand it as a right which you have the power to invest us with, and which not to exert, is as great a breach of our rights, as to withhold. We declare, that nothing can retribute us for the suspension or loss of this inestimable right. We declare it to be a right which must be obtained; and do also declare, that if the General Government will not procure it for us, we shall hold ourselves not Answerable for any of the consequences that may result from our own procurement of it. The God of nature has given us both the right and means of acquiring and enjoying it: and to permit a sacrifice of it to any earthly consideration, would be a crime against ourselves and against our posterity.[5]

Teste.   By order of the Society
W. McCluney   James Marshel[6]
Secretary.   President.

DS, DNA: RG 59, Miscellaneous Letters.

1. William Carmichael and William Short, commissioners plenipotentiary to Spain, were currently negotiating with officials in Madrid for the American right to free navigation on the Mississippi River. On their appointment, see GW to U.S. Senate, 11 Jan. 1792.

2. This paragraph may refer to the change that occurred in 1788 with the ratification of the U.S. Constitution and the abandonment of the Articles of Confederation as the foundation of the national government.

3. Article 8 of the 1783 peace treaty between the United States and Great Britain reads: "The Navigation of the River Mississippi, from its source to the Ocean shall for ever remain free and open to the Subjects of Great Britain and the Citizens of the United States" (Miller, *Treaties*, 2:155). It was not until the U.S. treaty with Spain of 27 Oct. 1795, that Spain, which controlled the mouth of the Mississippi River, agreed that navigation of the Mississippi would be free to the citizens of the United States (Article 4, Miller *Treaties*, 2:321–22).

4. This may be a reference to the federal excise tax on whiskey that was opposed, sometimes violently, by many residents of Washington and other western counties in Pennsylvania (see GW's Proclamation of 24 Feb.).

5. GW submitted this letter to Edmund Randolph, along with a brief cover letter of 11 April.

6. James Marshel (1753–1829) was born in Lancaster County, Pa., but by the Revolutionary War he had settled in what is now Cross Creek township in Washington County. He served in the county militia and as justice of the peace during the war. He held the office of registrar of wills and recorder of deeds, 1781–84 and 1791–95. He served as sheriff, 1784–87, and as a delegate to the state ratifying convention in 1787, where he opposed the adoption of the U.S. Constitution. He was a delegate to the Pennsylvania Assembly, 1789–90. In 1795, he moved to what is now Brooke County, West Virginia. William McCluney (1770–1856) later became Marshel's son-in-law.

From Alexander Hamilton

Sir,   Treasury Dept. Mar. 24 1794

A Committee of the House of Representatives appointed to enquire into the state of the Treasury Department, is charged among other things to enquire into the authorities from the President to the Secretary of the Treasury respecting the making and disbursement of the Loans made under the act of the 4th and 12 of August 1790. You will perceive by the enclosed copy of a paper of this date delivered to the Committee, the opinion I entertain of the proper limits of a Legislative enquiry on that subject.[1]

But in the event of a determination that the enquiry should be general it becomes proper to fix with the President the true view of facts.

The real cause of the transaction has been this. Before I made the disposition of any Loan I regularly communicated to the President my ideas of the proper disposition, designating how much it would be expedient to pay to France—how much to draw to the United States—and always received his sanction for what was adopted & afterwards carried into execution. The communication & the sanction were verbal whenever the President was at the seat of Government. In a case of absence they were in writting. This will appear from my Letters of the 10th & 14. April 1791 and from the President's answer of the 7 of may following. My Letters of the 29 July & 22d of September 1791, and of the [   ] of August[2] & 22d of September 1792 contain a further illustration of the general spirit of proceeding in the case, in regard to the consultation of the President.

The sanctions of the President were sometimes expressly and always, as I conceived in their spirit, founded in a material degree on the confidence, that the measures proposed were guided by a just estimate on my part of circumstances, which from situation must have been best known to me—and that they would be always in conformity to the Law. With the most perfect respect &c.

Alexander Hamilton
Secy of the Treasy

LB, DLC:GW.

1. For the resolves passed by the House of Representatives on 24 Feb. and the appointment of a committee "to examine into the state of the treasury department," see *U.S. House Journal*, 6:147–49. For "An Act making provision for the (payment of the) Debt of the United States," 4 Aug. 1790, and "An Act making Provision for the Reduction of the Public Debt," 12 Aug. 1790, see *Stat.* 1:138–44, 186–87. For disbursements made on the domestic and foreign debt of the United States, see Hamilton's "Report on the Receipts and Expenditures of the United States from the Commencement of the Present Government to the End of the Year 1793," of 18 March 1794, which he sent to the Select Committee Appointed to Examine the Treasury Department. For the enclosure, see Hamilton's letter to the Select Committee of 24 March (*Hamilton Papers*, 16:165–81, 193–95).

2. This probably is Hamilton's letter to GW of 27 Aug. 1792.

From Henry Knox

Sir   War department March 24. 1794
I think it necessary that you should be acquainted with the following information received this day from Doctor Hutchins who set out from Fort Washington on the 17 of February and arrived at George Town in Kentuckey 12 Miles from Lexington on the 19th and remained in several parts of Kentucky among which two days were passed in Lexington which he left on the 24th of Feby. From the best of his information in conversing with all classes of people and particularly with some Gentlemen from Louisania the Doctor was convinced that Clarks expedition was at an end, the causes he was not particularly acquainted with, but it was supposed owing to a want of confidence in the French Agents. he heard nothing of Colonel Montgomery who was said to have taken post at the Mouth of Cumberland.[1] I have the honor to be with perfect respect Your obedt Servant
H. Knox

LS, DLC:GW; LB, DLC:GW.
Thomas Hutchins of Pennsylvania served as a surgeon's mate for the troops currently under the command of Gen. Anthony Wayne in the Northwest Territory from 11 April 1792 until his resignation on 14 Dec. 1793.
1. On the expedition being planned against the Spanish colony of Louisiana by Kentucky residents George Rogers Clark and John Montgomery, see Edmund Randolph to GW, 27 Feb. (fourth letter) and its enclosure. On the French agents sent to Kentucky to encourage this expedition, see n.2 of Edmund Randolph to GW, 15 February.

To William Lyles

Sir,   Philada 24th March 1794.
Mr Pearce, my Manager will present this letter to you; with your Bond—for payment. I should be obliged to you for making it. He is furnished also with a statement of the receipts, as far as I have any knowledge of them.[1] I am, Sir Your Obedt Hble Servt
Go: Washington

ALS (letterpress copy), DLC:GW. This letter was enclosed in GW's letter to William Pearce of 23 March.
1. On the money owed to GW, the statement given to William Pearce, and the eventual payment of this bond, see n.10 of GW's letter to William Pearce of 23 March.

Proclamation on Expeditions
Against Spanish Territory

[Philadelphia, 24 March 1794]
BY THE PRESIDENT OF THE
UNITED STATES OF AMERICA
A PROCLAMATION.[1]

WHEREAS I have received information that certain persons in violation of the laws, presumed under colour of a foreign authority to enlist citizens of the United States and others within the state of Kentucky, and have there assembled an armed force for the purpose of invading and plundering the territories of a nation at peace with the said United States:[2] And whereas such unwarrantable measures, being contrary to the laws of nations and to the duties incumbent on every citizen of the United States, tend to disturb the tranquility of the same, and to involve them in the calamities of war: And whereas it is the duty of the Executive to take care that such criminal proceedings should be suppressed, the offenders brought to justice, and all good citizens cautioned against measures likely to prove so pernicious to their country and themselves, should they be seduced into similar infractions of the laws;

I have therefore thought proper to issue this proclamation hereby[3] solemnly warning every person not authorised by the laws, against enlisting any citizen or citizens of the United States, or levying troops, or assembling any persons within the United States for the purposes aforesaid, or proceeding in any manner to the execution thereof, as they will answer the same at their peril: And I do also admonish and require all citizens to refrain from enlisting, enrolling or assembling themselves for such unlawful purposes and from being in any wise concerned, aiding or abetting therein, as they tender their own welfare, in as much as all lawful means will be strictly put in execution for securing obedience to the laws, and for punishing such dangerous and daring violations[4] thereof.

I do moreover charge and require all courts magistrates and other officers, whom it may concern, according to their respective duties, to exert the powers in them severally vested to prevent and suppress all such unlawful assemblages and proceedings and to bring to condign punishment those who may have been guilty thereof, as they regard the due authority of Government, and the peace and welfare of the United States.

In testimony whereof, I have caused the seal of the United States of America to be affixed to these presents, and signed the same with my hand. Done at the City of Philadelphia, the twenty fourth day of March, one thousand seven hundred and ninety four, and of the Independence of the United States of America, the eighteenth.

Go: WASHINGTON,

By the President,

EDM: RANDOLPH,

Printed, *Gazette of the United States and Evening Advertiser* (Philadelphia), 27 March 1794; Df, CSmH; Df, PHi: Wallace Collection. The draft at CSmH is in the writing of William Bradford, has interlineations by Alexander Hamilton and Edmund Randolph, and is signed by Hamilton, Randolph, and Henry Knox (see *Hamilton Papers,* 16:162–64). For Bradford's submission of the draft at CSmH for approval by the other cabinet members, see Randolph to GW, 19 March (first letter). The draft at PHi, which is also in Bradford's handwriting, precedes the draft at CSmH.

1. On the decision to issue this proclamation, see Cabinet Opinion, 10 March. Randolph enclosed this proclamation in his letter to GW of 24 March.

2. On the proposed expedition against Spanish territory, see Randolph's fourth letter to GW of 27 Feb. and its enclosed extract.

3. Randolph, Hamilton, and Knox indicated on the draft at CSmH that GW might not want to use the original wording at this point. Therefore, GW substituted the following four words for "strictly prohibit and forbid any person or persons."

4. In response to a suggestion offered by Randolph, GW changed the original word "infractions" to this one.

From Edmund Randolph

[Philadelphia] March 24. 1794.

E. Randolph has the honor of inclosing to the President the fair copy, as well as the rough draft of the Proclamation. It was transcribed upon the supposition, that the President would direct it to issue in the form, which the three other gentlemen had approved; and the rough is sent; in order that the President may decide, whether there be any propriety in the two amendments, which have been suggested.[1]

AL, DNA: RG 59, Miscellaneous Letters; LB, DNA: RG 59, GW's Correspondence with His Secretaries of War.

1. The enclosed "fair copy" has not been found. On the enclosed draft, which was composed by William Bradford and revised by other cabinet members, and for the two suggested amendments, see GW's Proclamation of 24 March, and notes 3 and 4.

From Harriot Washington

Fredericksburg [Va.] March 24, 1794

I received the box which contained the thing's My dear Uncle was so kind as to send me, how shall I express my gratitude to my beloved Uncle for so much kindness.[1] I hope my dear Uncle will not be displeased if I beg him for as much money, as will make my great coat, & will purchase thread and tape to make my linnen, I am affraid you will attribute my not making my great coat to laziness, but I can assure you I would make it with a great deal of pleasure, as it wuld save you the trouble of sending money, if I could get it cut out. but there is not a Taylor in town that will cut it out unless we will consent to let them make it. I was very much in want of a few thing's some time ago, & was obleiged to borrow 24 shilling's from Aunt Lewis. she is in want of money just now and wishes me to pay her; I shall be much obleiged to you for as much as will do that.[2] Aunt Lewis join's me in love to you and Aunt Washington. I am my dear Uncle Your affectionate Neice

Harriot Washington.

ALS, ViMtvL.

1. For Harriot's request for the linen and other material contained in the box, see her letter to GW of 5 March.

2. Betty Washington Lewis reported in her letter to GW of 13 April that the requested money had been safely received.

From William Gordon

My Dear Sir   St Neots [England] March 25. 1794

The goodness of my intention will apologize for the present letter. The purport of which, I conceive, may not be known to any

American. You may possibly be under the disagreeable necessity of appointing military officers for active service in dangerous warlike undertakings. I have a great regard for Genl Otho Williams, & am under peculiar obligations to him; but if what our deceased friend Genl Greene told me, has not been mentioned to You, it is proper, I apprehend, to acquaint You with it. When conversing about him the words of Genl Greene were nearly to this purpose—"Williams does not want for courage, he will fight any thing; but he has no fortitude, & cannot bear up under disasters; he was so dispirited by the rapid pursuit of Cornwallis before he joined me, that I would have beaten him with forty old squaws."[1]

You had the blessing of being endued from above, with both courage & fortitude. Greene's distinction between the two qualities pleased me so much, that I have never forgotten it. Wishing your Excellency all that special wisdom which is wanted, for guiding the state helm in this critical period; & that You may have the guidance of the supreme Governor of the universe, I remain Your affectionate friend & humble Servt

William Gordon

Mrs Gordon joins in most cordial regards to Self & your Lady.

P.S. My friend the Revd Mr Hickman who is intrusted with this has one of an earlier date, together with Flower upon the French Constitution of 1791, a present from the author, if sent in time.[2]

ALS, DLC:GW.

1. In preparation for writing *The History of the Rise, Progress, and Establishment, of the Independence of the United States of America: Including An Account of the Late War; and of the Thirteen Colonies, From their Origin to that Period* (N.Y., 1789), Gordon had interviewed Gen. Nathanael Greene (1742–1786) at his home in Newport, R.I. (Greene to Henry Knox, 25 March 1784, *Greene Papers*, 13:275–76). After receiving an appointment from Washington, in October 1780, to replace Gen. Horatio Gates as commander of the southern army, Greene was successful in gradually forcing the British troops under the command of Gen. Charles Cornwallis to retreat from previously held territory in the southern states of Georgia, South Carolina, and North Carolina. Prior to Greene's appointment, Otho Holland Williams, then a colonel, evidently had been discouraged by his participation in the ill-fated campaign led by Gates, but he performed well, both on and off the field, under Greene's leadership. Williams was in poor health by 1794, in part because of his experience as a prisoner of war, 1776–78, and he died on 15 July at about 45 years of age.

2. The other letter entrusted to the Rev. Hickman was Gordon's letter to

GW of 7 March. The second edition of *The French Constitution; With Remarks on Some of Its Principal Articles* was accompanied by Benjamin Flower's letter to GW of 17 March.

From Henry Knox

Sir.   War Department, March 25 1794.

I have the honor to submit, the copy of a letter intended to be sent to the Secretary of the Treasury, relatively to arrangments to be made, for procuring the Iron Cannon and shot; contemplated in the Act, entitled, "An Act to provide for the defence of certain Ports and Harbors in the United States."[1] I have the honor to be Sir, with the greatest respect, Your most obedt Servt

H. Knox

LS, DLC:GW; LB, DLC:GW.

1. The draft was of Knox's letter to Alexander Hamilton of 29 March and concerned the execution of the provisions in "An Act to provide for the Defence of certain Ports and Harbors in the United States," 20 March 1794 (*Hamilton Papers*, 16:209–11; *Stat.* 1:345–6). Knox added two enclosures to his letter to Hamilton. The first, dated 28 Feb., was an estimate of expenses for each location, with a total of $172,698.52 for erecting fortifications and providing the necessary cannon and military stores and $90,349.25 for the troops needed to garrison the fortifications (*ASP, Military Affairs*, 1:62–65). The second was a draft of a letter dated 29 March and intended for use by the Treasury Department when appointing someone at each location to obtain the labor and materials needed (*ASP, Military Affairs*, 1:104–5).

Bartholomew Dandridge, Jr., wrote Knox later this same date, enclosing Knox's draft and informing him that "the President approves thereof, provided the treasury be the proper Department from whence the articles mentioned in the letter are to be furnished" (DLC:GW).

Letter not found: from William Pearce, 25 March 1794. GW wrote Pearce on 30 March that "The Reports, and your letter of the 25th instt have been duly recd."

To the United States Senate
and House of Representatives

United States 25. March 1794.

Gentlemen of the Senate, and of the House of Representatives,

The two letters, which I now forward to Congress, were written by a Consul of the United States;[1] and contain information, which will probably be thought to require some pecuniary provision.[2]

Go: Washington

LS, DNA: RG 46, Third Congress, 1793–95, Senate Records of Legislative Proceedings, President's Messages; LB, DNA: RG 233, Third Congress, 1793–95, House Records of Legislative Proceedings, Messages; LB, DLC:GW.

1. Fulwar Skipwith, U.S. consul to the French isle of Martinique, wrote Edmund Randolph from the Dutch colony of St. Eustatius on 1 March that: "The Ship Delaware in which I had taken passage for Philadelphia was on the *7th Inst.* captured by the Experiment privateer of Bermudas and carried into Mon[t]ser[r]at, on her arrival stript of her sails, and by order of the Judge, the Captain's [James Art] papers and mine were peremptorily demanded. I waved a compliance, and at the instant waited on the Judge, and in the mildest terms, observed the impropriety of my exposing by compulsion public papers, which, if the U. States were not at War with England, ought to be deemed sacred, or my private papers, which did not in the most indirect manner relate to the Ship or Cargo in question. Such assurances did not satisfy the curiosity of the Judge, and the next day my Desk was seized and forced. The Ship Delaware with thirty three other American Vessels have been condemned in the Vice-Court of Admiralty of Monserat—about the same number have been also in St Kitts, and upwards of one hundred and fifty more have been arrested and carried into the different Ports of the English Windward Islands, and no doubt will share the same fate. . . . The Ship Sidney of Baltimore cleared for this place, had arrived two weeks since under the cannon of one of it's Fortresses, and was there captured by a small English Privateer, carried into St Kitts, is libelled, and in the general opinion of that Island, will be condemned. Other Vessels from America, cleared and actually on a direct passage to Neutral and British Ports, have been likewise taken and libelled in British Courts of Admiralty; and Judges, Sir, have been heard to say, that altho' no Documents could be found to prove that such Vessels intended to trade with the French; yet it was reasonable to suppose that such might have been their designs." He reported that he had assisted some of the American seamen in finding safe passage home, and that, if necessary, he would charter a vessel to bring the remainder to the United States (DNA: RG 46, Third Congress, 1793–95, Senate Records of Legislative Proceedings, President's Messages; *ASP, Foreign Relations,* 1:428–29). For "an accurate List of the American Vessels taken by British Cruisers, and carried into different Ports of the West-Indies," as well as the names of their captains and owners, see the 1 Sept. 1794 issue of the *Philadelphia Gazette and Universal Daily Advertiser.*

On 7 March, Skipwith wrote Randolph that "about two hundred and twenty sail of American vessels" had been seized by the British and carried into different ports. "The whole of those vessels with thirty others, which have been captured since my last respects, were immediately on their arrival in those different Ports, libelled; but only those in Dominique, Antigua, Monserat, and St Kitts have been condemned—making in the whole about one hundred and fifty sail—The greater part of the people belonging to those vessels have rendezvoused here in order to obtain passages for America, and having been stript, many of them, of the little resources they had possessed I have ventured to procure on acct of the U. States a sufficiency of bread, beef, and water to support them to their respective homes—Vouchers and receipts of which, I will have the honor to lay before the Executive of the U. States on my arrival in Philadelphia, and I flatter myself that the step will meet their approbation, when they become satisfied that my sole motive for undertaking the measure, has been to guard our seamen, many of whom would have entered into foreign service" (DNA: RG 46, Third Congress, 1793–95, Senate Records of Legislative Proceedings, President's Messages; *ASP, Foreign Relations,* 1:429).

2. "An Act providing for the payment of certain expenses incurred by Fulwar Skipwith, on public account," 19 May, authorized GW to direct that payment be made to Skipwith (*Stat.* 6:15). The amount reimbursed came to $900 (Randolph to Alexander Hamilton, 16 May [first letter] and 2 July [second letter], *Hamilton Papers,* 16:417–18, 558–59).

Cabinet Opinion on Enforcing the Embargo

[Philadelphia, 26 March 1794]

At a meeting of the heads of departments, and the Attorney general of the U.S. at the President's, on the twenty sixth day of march 1794.[1]

The resolution of congress, of this date, being submitted to them by the President, for their opinion as to the best Mode of executing the same;[2]

It is advised unanimously, that the governors of the several States ought to be called upon, to enforce the said embargo by the militia, whensoever it may be necessary to appeal to force.[3]

Edm: Randolph
A. Hamilton
H. Knox
Wm Bradford.

LS (in Edmund Randolph's handwriting), DLC:GW. GW's docket reads, "Opinion 26th–March–1794 On the proper mode for carrying the Embargo into effect."

1. Randolph wrote GW earlier this day that he had "the honor of informing the President, when the gentlemen are assembled. E. Randolph took the liberty of mentioning his office, on the supposition, that it might be more agreeable to the President, that the meeting should be there. But, as the

President wishes to be present, it is submitted, whether it may not be more convenient to him, that they should wait upon him at his house" (DNA: RG 59, Miscellaneous Letters).

2. The joint resolution of Congress, approved on this date, imposed a thirty-day embargo "on all ships and vessels in the ports of the United States" (*Stat.* 1:400).

3. On GW's acceptance of the cabinet's advice, see his letter to the U.S. Senate and House of Representatives, 28 March.

From Frederick Frelinghuysen

Sir,   [Philadelphia] Wednesday Morning 26. Mar. 1794

After repeated disappointments, a Barrel with the *heavy* Oats has at length arrived, containing 3½ bushels.[1] It is at Mr Pearson Hunt's Store, in Water-Street, near Market Street, where it will be delivered to your order.[2] I am, Sir, Your most obedient Servant

Fred: Frelinghuysen.

ALS, DLC:GW.

Frederick Frelinghuysen (1753–1804), a native of Somerset County, N.J., graduated from the College of New Jersey (now Princeton) in 1770 and was admitted to the New Jersey bar in 1774. He served in the state militia and the Continental Congress during the Revolutionary War and in the New Jersey assembly, 1784 and 1800–1804. He represented New Jersey in the U.S. Senate, 1793–96.

1. In a letter to William Pearce of 12 Jan., GW indicated that he would need 340 bushels of oat seed for his fields at Mount Vernon. On 19 May, GW paid Frelinghuysen $2 for a barrel of "Seed Oats bo't for the President by him" (Household Accounts).

2. Pearson Hunt (d. 1829) was located at 9 South Wharves and 7 South Front Street according to the *Philadelphia Directory, 1794*, 74. He later moved to Trenton, N.J., where he became the first cashier of the Trenton Banking Company in 1805.

From Edmund Randolph

[Philadelphia] March 26. 1794.

The Secretary of State has the honor of sending to the President the translation of a declaration from Spain;[1] And the President will be pleased to say, whether it be important enough to be sent to Congress.[2]

AL, DNA: RG 59, Miscellaneous Letters; LB, DNA: RG 59, GW's Correspondence with His Secretaries of State.

1. The undated document begins with an expression of sorrow and indignation by Charles IV (1748–1819) of Spain at the execution of Louis XVI of France and an acknowledgment that he has been "necessitated to defend himself against the same Frenchmen, who, usurping the royal Authority and tyrannizing their fellow Subjects declared War to him, has resolved to make war in Opposition to his own natural and decided Reluctance to every Infringement of peace." He also has decided to support those members of the royal family in prison and those Frenchmen who have rebelled against, or who will in the future rise up against, the current French government, and "to reinstate them in the unmolested Enjoyment of their Habitations and Property. . . . His Majesty is persuaded, that the Views of His Majesty, the King of Great Britain [George III] His Alley coincide therein, and does also not doubt but the other Powers that took up Arms in Combination against France, will on their part coöperate in supporting and protecting those Frenchmen, that will come forth ready to support So beneficial a Plan" (translation, DNA: RG 59, Miscellaneous Letters).

2. No written reply from GW has been found. The declaration was not sent to Congress.

From Edmund Randolph

[Philadelphia] March 26. 1794.

The Secretary of State has the honor of returning to the President Govr. Clinton's letter &c. It was the opinion, that the Speech of Ld Dorchester, tho' important, is sufficiently promulgated in the Newspaper.[1]

The gentlemen have agreed to the letter to the governor of Kentucky, without any amendment.[2]

They have suggested an amendment to the third paragraph of the proposed message; which will be corrected, to be laid before you tomorrow.[3]

AL, DNA: RG 59, Miscellaneous Letters; LB, DNA: RG 59, GW's Correspondence with His Secretaries of State.

1. For the speech given by Lord Dorchester (Guy Carleton) on 10 Feb., see n.2 of George Clinton's letter to GW of 20 March. Randolph and other members of the cabinet apparently did not see the need to submit a copy of this

speech to Congress because of its widespread publication in the newspapers. For a publication of this speech, see the 26 March issue of the *Gazette of the United States* (Philadelphia).

2. For the letter from Randolph to Isaac Shelby of 29 March, see n.5 of Randolph to GW, 19 March (first letter).

3. For the proposed message, see Randolph to GW, 27 March (second letter).

Cabinet Opinion on the
Conyngham and the *Pilgrim*

[Philadelphia, 27 March 1794]

At a meeting of the heads of departments and Attorney general. March 27. 1794.

The Secretary of War, the attorney general and the Secretary of State advise, that the Conyngham be not delivered up to the British owners; the secretary of the treasury dissenting.

The Secretary of the Treasury, the Secretary of war, and the attorney general advise, that the Pilgrim be delivered up to the British owners; the Secretary of State dissenting.[1]

Alexandr Hamilton
H. Knox
Wm. Bradford.
Edm: Randolph.

DS (in Edmund Randolph's writing), DLC:GW.

The British brigs *Conyngham* and *Pilgrim* were captured in October 1793 by the French privateer *Sans Culottes de Marseilles* and brought into the port of Baltimore (*Counter Case*, 612–13). The British claimed that both vessels had been captured within three miles of the U.S. coastline and thus were not subject to condemnation and sale according to the policy set by the United States. For the establishment of this policy, see Record of Cabinet Opinions, 22 Nov. 1793; for its application to these two cases, see Thomas Sim Lee to GW, 18 Oct. 1793, and notes 1 and 3 to that document; Thomas Jefferson to GW, 16 Nov. 1793, and notes 1, 2, and 9 to that document; and Alexander Campbell to Edmund Randolph, 6 Feb. 1794 (DNA: RG 59, Miscellaneous Letters; see also *Hamilton Papers*, 16:202–3).

1. Randolph wrote to British minister George Hammond on 5 April: "The President of the United States having taken into consideration the cases of the Brigs Pilgrim and Conyngham; has instructed the Secretary of war to cause the former to be restored to her former British owners. The latter, not

being proved to have been taken within the protection of our coasts, will no longer be detained from the Captors" (DNA: RG 59, Domestic Letters).

From Thomas Mifflin

Sir.   Phil: 27 Mar. 1794

As soon as I recd the communication of your arrangements, for laying an Embargo on the trade of this Port, I issued instructions to the Commanding Officer at Fort Mifflin upon the subject; and of those instructions I have now the honor to inclose you a copy.[1] I am, with perfect respect, Sir Yr most obed. H. Servt.

Df, PHarH: Executive Correspondence, 1794; LB, PHarH: Executive Letter-Books.

1. A joint resolution of Congress of 26 March imposed a thirty-day embargo "on all ships and vessels in the ports of the United States" (*Stat.* 1:400). On the implementation of this resolve by the administration, see Cabinet Opinion, 26 March. Mifflin's copy of the circular letter that Henry Knox sent to the governors of the maritime states has not been identified. This letter, which was printed and dated "8 o'clock P.M. 26 March 1794," reads: "I am instructed by the President of the United States to transmit to your Excellency the inclosed resolve of Congress passed this day, laying an embargo for Thirty days, upon all vessels bound to any foreign port or place. The President requests that you will please to enforce the prompt execution of the said resolve by the aid of the militia in all cases where the same may be necessary." A hand-written postscript on the letter sent to North Carolina governor Richard Dobbs Spaight reads, "All armed vessels possessing pubic Commissions from any foreign power (letter of marque excepted) are considered as not liable to the embargo" (DSoC).

The enclosed copy of Mifflin's letter of 26 March to Capt. John Rice, commander at Fort Mifflin, reads: "The enclosed Letter from the Secretary of War I have this moment received. You will comply lierally with the Instructions therein contain'd and not permit any vessel bound to any foreign Port to pass the Port, unless furnished with a Special passport from the President of the United States" (PHarH: Executive Correspondence).

From Edmund Randolph

[Philadelphia] March 27. 1794.

The Secretary of State has the honor of informing the President, that the gentlemen are of opinion, that the rates of the ships be the same, as those marked out by law; and that they ought to be *built* instead of being *purchased*. But whether they had better be built by contract, general or particular, they prefer reserving, until information can be obtained from those, skilled in the art.[1]

AL, DNA: RG 59, Miscellaneous Letters; LB, DNA: RG 59, GW's Correspondence with His Secretaries of State.

1. This cabinet opinion refers to provisions contained in "An Act to provide a Naval Armament" and may have been issued in advance of GW's signing of it on this date (*Stat.* 1:350).

From Edmund Randolph

[Philadelphia] March 27th 1794.
Message proposed by E. Randolph, some days ago
to the President; but now rendered unnecessary by
Congress having proceeded to vigorous measures.[1]

Although I cannot doubt, that from the sources of information possessed by Congress themselves, and the communications, which I have occasionally made to them, they feel the crisis in our public affairs; yet at no time have I seen the necessity of exercising the right of recommendation, more strongly than present.

It is now almost five years, since our government was organized. Its sufficiency for the happiness of the Union has been tried; and stands approved by the friends of liberty and order. No people can ever have a deeper or more solemn interest in defending with firmness and with zeal their country already flourishing under the influence of such a Constitution; no people can, with better reason expect, from the progress of its operation, the completion of their welfare, and none ought to be more cautious, in trusting themselves to uncertain changes.

Notwithstanding, after an honorable and scrupulous conduct towards all nations, we have arrived at the hour of suffering and of danger. Many of our fellow Citizens are now languishing in slavery and chains, our commerce has been ravaged, our Seamen dispersed by captures in foreign lands, or compelled into foreign service; and our peace threatened.

The fate of our brethren groaning under a cruel bondage, will, I am persuaded, receive a sincere attention.

To prevent a repetition of insult and violence; to meet the increasing hostility against us; and to be indemnified for the past; are cares, great indeed, in themselves, but involving the highest responsibility to our Constituents.

We can never hope to obtain the respect which is due to us; to secure our peace or an exemption from plunder but by demonstrating our means to resist. The stability of public credit, and an adequate and regular revenue, constitute an essential article in the work of defence. You, Gentlemen, who so well understand the capacity of our fellow Citizens for taxation, and the calls of justice, honor and good faith, will adapt the fiscal arrangements accordingly. I trust too, that, when a question shall arise on the form, which the public force shall assume for our defence, it will not be forgotten, that principles of real efficiency ought to be consulted, and that it is our policy, and ought to be our character, to bid defiance to invasion from any of the powers of the earth.

Without preparations, like these, the demand of retribution for past injuries would be an absurd waste of time. It will be treated with contempt if we remain in that painful situation of public weakness, which first invited attack.

I must, therefore, lay before Congress my sense of this awful period, record to my fellow Citizens, that I have not neglected it; and declare again, that my co-operation with your labors shall be prompt, and persevering. There are certain moments in human affairs, when harmony among the persons, administering them, create an irresistable energy; and to cultivate it is patriotism. That this is the moment in the affairs of the United States, must be pronounced by all.

When we shall be armed against the events of war, peace, that blessing to our rising Nation, will be at our command; and it shall be my constant effort to cherish it, with all the world.

LB, DNA: RG 59, Domestic Letters.

1. On Randolph's intention to submit this proposed message, for GW to send to Congress, see Randolph to GW, 26 March (second letter). Randolph is referring to the earlier passage of "An Act to provide for the Defence of certain Ports and Harbors in the United States," 20 March, and "An Act to provide a Naval Armament," which GW signed on this date (*Stat.* 1:345–46, 350).

From Alexander Hamilton

Treasy Dept. Mar. 28 1794.

The Secretary of the Treasury presents his respects to the President of the U. States and encloses herewith the draft of a passport for Capt. Montgomery, to which (if found right) the President's signature is requested, in order that the vessel may be dispatched.[1]

LB, DLC:GW.

1. The enclosed passport for Capt. James Montgomery of the *General Greene,* the revenue cutter for Pennsylvania, has not been identified. The passport, which GW signed on this same date, allowed the *General Greene* to travel to Charleston, S.C., in order to carry a notice of the congressional resolution of 26 March, which established a thirty-day embargo on American vessels bound for foreign ports (*JPP*, 293; *Stat.* 1:400).

Bartholomew Dandridge, Jr., to Henry Knox

[Philadelphia] 28 March 1794

By the President's order Bw Dandridge has the honor to inform the Secretary of War that the President thinks the fortification of New York much more difficult to be accomplished than that of any other place intended to be fortified—he therefore thinks it proper that the most skilful of the engineers should be selected for that purpose.[1]

ADf, DLC:GW; LB, DLC:GW.

1. On the proposed fortification of U.S. ports, see "An Act to provide for the Defence of certain Ports and Harbors in the United States," 20 March (*Stat.* 1:345–46). On those intended for New York City and for Knox's instructions to engineer Charles Vincent, see Knox's report on fortifications submitted to the House of Representatives on 19 Dec. 1794 (*ASP, Military Affairs,* 1:71–72, 77–81).

From Henry Knox

Sir.   [Philadelphia] March 28 1794

The enclosed, being the opinion of the Secretary of State, and the Secretary of the Treasury, I pray your directions whether the three French Gentlemen shall be employed as temporary Engineers—They are to be with me at 12 o'clock.[1] The same direction is requested with respect to three Artillerists now at Baltimore.[2] I have the honor to be Sir, With the greatest respect, Your most obt Servt

H. Knox

LS, DLC:GW; LB, DLC:GW.

1. The enclosed opinion of this date, which was written by Edmund Randolph and signed "Agreed" by Alexander Hamilton, reads: "I could not see Mr Fauchet yesterday; and indeed I would prefer saying nothing more about. My opinion is, that the government ought to avoid employing French Engineers notoriously obnoxious to their Republic; but not to go in quest of disqualifications. If the Minister complains, he may be told of our distress for such characters, and the protection which French vessels will receive from our fortifications. At any rate, it will be true enough to recede, if this should be necessary, when the complaint comes—As to Vincent, he is clear, to my mind, in consequence of Sonthonax's certificate" (DLC:GW).

Four French refugees received appointments. Charles Vincent became the temporary engineer responsible for fortifying the harbor and city of New York (Knox to Vincent, 1 April). Nicholas-Francis Martinon served as the temporary engineer for the fortifications at Wilmington and Ocracoke, N.C. (Knox to Martinon, 11 April). Paul Hyacinte Perrault (d. 1834) later served as an engineer in the U.S. Army during the War of 1812, continuing in service until at least 1817. He was appointed the temporary engineer for the fortifications at Charleston and Georgetown, S.C., and at Savannah and St. Mary's, Ga. (Knox to Perrault, 11 April). John (Jean-Baptiste-Arthur) Vermonnet (b. 1750) served with U.S. forces during the Revolutionary War, and he came to the United States in 1793 after being stationed in Saint Domingue. He received an appointment as the temporary engineer for the fortifications at Annapolis, Md., and Alexandria, Va. (Knox to Vermonnet, 12 May). For Knox's letters of appointment and his later correspondence with these engineers, see *ASP, Military Affairs*, 1:72–81, 93–104.

2. The artillerists at Baltimore have not been identified.

From Thomas Mifflin

Sir.   Phil: 28 Mar. 1794

The Secretary at war, has transmitted to me, by your instructions, a copy of a law relatively to the fortification of the Ports and harbours therein mentioned; and he has, at the same time, communicated your request, that, as Commander in Chief of the Militia of Pena., I would take upon me the general direction of the business, as far as respects the works to be established within this State.[1]

I undertake the proposed trust with great chearfulness; and

you may be assured, Sir, that on this, and on every other occasion, I shall be happy to facilitate the execution of the duties of your arduous station.

Permit me to take the present opportunity of transmitting for your information, a copy of an Act of the Ge[nera]l Ass[embly] of Pena., entitled "An Act["] &c (define law)[2] of an Act for laying out a town at Presqu' Isle,[3] and of the proceedings which have been instituted, for the purpose of carrying those laws into effect.[4]

I have, likewise, inclosed a statement of the number & condition of the Cannon, belonging to the State of Pena., that are above the calibre of Eighteen pounds, and fit to be appropriated to the Fortification of the Port of Philadelphia.[5] I am, with perfect respect, Sir—

Df, PHarH: Executive Correspondence; LB, PHarH: Executive Letter-Books; Copy (extract), DNA: RG 46, Third Congress, 1793–95, Senate Records of Legislative Proceedings, President's Messages.

1. Knox wrote Mifflin on 27 March: "I am instructed to transmit to your Excellency the enclosed Copy of a law relatively to the fortifications of the ports and harbours therein mentioned.

"And as a judicious choice of the places to be fortified and vigorous prosecution of the works may be of great importance to the State of Pennsylvania the President of the United States requests that your Excellency as the Commander in chief of its Militia would please to take upon you the general direction of the business.

"An Engineer will as soon as possible be appointed. He will be directed to prepare and submit plans of the works to your consideration and upon your approving thereof to have them put into a train of immediate execution—some suitable provision will also be soon made to obtain the necessary materials and workmen.

"The number of Men and Cannon designed for the Port of Philadelphia, and also the amount of the expence to be incurred at that place will hereafter be transmitted.

"If the State of Pennsylvania is in possession of any good Cannon of and above the Caliber of eighteen pounds and which could be appropriated for the fortifications within the said State, a return of them is requested, together with the condition of their carriages and apparatus in order that the necessary repairs be provided without delay" (PHarH: Executive Correspondence). For "An Act to provide for the Defence of certain Ports and Harbors in the United States," 20 March, see *Stat.* 1:345–46.

2. The letter-book copy at PHarH contains the full title of this legislation. For the provisions of "An ACT for more effectually securing the trade, peace and safety of the port of Philadelphia, and defending the Western Frontiers of the commonwealth," 28 Feb., see *Acts of the General Assembly of the Common-*

wealth of Pennsylvania, passed at a session, which was begun and held at the city of Philadelphia on Tuesday, the third day of December, in the year one thousand seven hundred and ninety-three (Philadelphia, 1794), 463–65.

3. For the provision of "An ACT for laying out a town at Presqu'-Isle," 8 April 1793, see *Acts of the General Assembly of the Commonwealth of Pennsylvania, passed at a session, which was begun and held at the city of Philadelphia on Tuesday, the fourth day of December, in the year one thousand seven hundred and ninety-two* (Philadelphia, 1793), 346–48.

4. According to an entry in GW's executive journal of 31 March, Mifflin also enclosed "Appointmts. in the four defence Companies & the Detachment fo Presqu' isle," a letter from Mifflin to the captains of the four companies, and a letter from Mifflin to Ebenezer Denny "Capt. of the Alleghany Co. &c." (*JPP*, 294). For these and other documents, dated from 1 to 28 March, concerning the establishment of a town at Presque Isle and the defense of western Pennsylvania, see *Pa. Archives*, 2d. ser., 6:673–84.

5. According to a report of this date by Alexander J. Dallas, on "the number and condition of the Cannon belonging to Pennsylvania, at Fort Mifflin," there were nine eighteen-pounders and four twenty-four-pounders, all "well mounted on Garrison Carriages," and one thirty-two-pounder, "Without Trunnions and not mounted" (PHarH: Executive Letter-Books). For GW's response to the information contained in this letter, see Bartholomew Dandridge, Jr., to Knox, 30 March.

From Edmund Randolph

Sir   Philadelphia March 28. 1794. ½ past nine.

I do myself the honor of inclosing to you two letters from the Minister of the French Republic.[1]

Upon the first, the opinion of the gentlemen was against mine, that a passport ought not to be granted. I thought it so urgent, a case, that ⟨I⟩ sent the letter immediately to them.

This moment I have received another letter from Mr Fauchet. He represents his embarressment so strongly, that I cannot forbear to lay both letters before you without delay.[2]

I understand, that the vessel had actually cleared out and got as far as Newcastle, when she was stopped.[3] I have the honor, sir, to be with the highest respect yr mo. ob. serv.

                                        Edm: Randolph

The translations of the letters are sent.[4]

ALS, DNA: RG 59, Miscellaneous Letters; LB, DNA: RG 59, GW's Correspondence with His Secretaries of State. The text in angle brackets is from the letter-book copy.

1. Neither Fauchet's original letters nor the enclosed translations have been identified. However, copies of Fauchet's two letters to Randolph of this date are to be found in FrPMAE, Correspondance Politique, Etats-Unis, 40. The first letter reported that the snow *Camilla,* while waiting at New Castle, Del., for dispatches from Fauchet, had been detained by officers enforcing the recent embargo. Fauchet requested an immediate presidential order to allow the captain to continue his voyage so that the dispatches could be delivered. The second letter reinforced the first by declaring "positivement" that delay of the ship would harm the French Republic because of the importance of Fauchet's dispatches, which, he added, the consul had sent to the captain before learning of the embargo resolution (for that resolution of 26 March, see *Stat.* 1:400).

2. For GW's opinion on this situation, see his letter to Randolph of 29 March. For Randolph's reply to Fauchet, written after consulting with other members of the Cabinet and GW, see n.1 of his second letter to GW of that date.

3. On the departure of the *Camilla* from Philadelphia, see the 25 March issue of the *Philadelphia Gazette and Universal Daily Advertiser.* On the detention at New Castle of the *Camilla,* "bound to France with a cargo of flower," see the 1 April issue of the *Philadelphia Gazette and Universal Daily Advertiser.*

4. This sentence does not appear in the letter-book copy.

To the United States Senate
and House of Representatives

United States 28. March 1794.

Gentlemen of the Senate, and of the House of Representatives.

In the execution of the resolution of Congress, bearing date the 26. of March 1794, and imposing an embargo, I have requested the Governors of the several States to call forth the force of their militia, if it should be necessary for the detention of vessels. This power is conceived to be incidental to an embargo.[1]

It also deserves the attention of Congress, how far the clearances from one district to another, under the law as it now stands, may give rise to evasions of the embargo. As one security, the Collectors have been instructed to refuse to receive the surrender of coasting licences for the purpose of taking out registers, and to require bond from registered vessels, bound from one district to another, for the delivery of the cargo within the United States.[2]

It is not understood, that the resolution applies to fishing vessels; although their occupations lie generally in parts beyond the United States. But without further restrictions there is an opportunity of their priviledges being used as means of eluding the embargo.

All armed vessels, possessing public commissions from any foreign power (letters of marque excepted) are considered as not liable to the embargo.

These circumstances are transmitted to Congress for their consideration.[3]

Go: Washington

LS, DNA: RG 46, Third Congress, 1793–95, Senate Records of Legislative Proceedings, President's Messages; LB, DNA: RG 233, Third Congress, 1793–95, House Records of Legislative Proceedings, Journals; LB, DLC:GW.

1. For the resolve of Congress, see *Stat.* 1:400. For the administration's decision to call upon state governors to assist in enforcing the embargo, see Cabinet Opinion, 26 March. For the circular letter of 26 March that Knox sent to the governors of the maritime states, see n.1 of Thomas Mifflin to GW, 27 March.

2. For these instructions, see Alexander Hamilton's circular letter to the collectors of customs of 26 March (*Hamilton Papers,* 16:199–200).

3. For clarification of the restrictions imposed by the embargo, see the congressional resolution that was approved on 2 April (*Stat.* 1:400–401).

From Henry Knox

Sir.   [Philadelphia] March 29th 1794

I have the honor to submit to your consideration, a letter just received from Major Gaither dated at St Mary's the 8th instant.[1] I am, most respectfully, Sir, Your obedient Servt

H. Knox secy of war

LS, DLC:GW; LB, DLC:GW.

1. The letter from Henry Gaither to Knox of 8 March, written from Saint Marys, Ga., has not been identified. GW returned this letter to Knox on this same day (*JPP,* 294).

To Edmund Randolph

Sir   Philadelphia 29 March 1794

It is to be regretted that the Snow Camilla had not got off before she was arrested by the Revenue Officer. To permit it now as she is a loaded Vessel might be a delicate, if not an unjustifiable measure, under the Act of Congress laying an Embargo.[1]

Whether the representation of the French Minister in his *second* application is of weight sufficient to induce a departure from the obvious meaning of the Embargo, is worthy of consideration, under the peculiar circumstances which are related.[2]

I am *well disposed,* and think we *ought* to comply with Mr Fauchets request, if it can be done without envolving unpleasant consequences. I am &ca.

ADf, DNA: RG 59, Miscellaneous Letters; LB, DNA: RG 59, GW's Correspondence with His Secretaries of State.

1. On the sailing of the French snow *Camilla,* contrary to the embargo imposed by Congress, see Randolph to GW, 28 March, and notes 1 and 3. For Randolph's denial of French minister Fauchet's request that this vessel be issued a passport, see n.1 of Randolph's second letter to GW of 29 March.

2. For Fauchet's second letter to Randolph of 28 March, see n.1 of Randolph's letter to GW of that date.

From Edmund Randolph

[Philadelphia] March 29. 1794

E. Randolph has the honor of informing the President, that Mr Hammond has given him a duplicate of the letter to the governor of Jamaica, concerning Barney; but that Colo. Hamilton says, that the cutter going to Charleston is too infirm to proceed to Jamaica.[1] The President will therefore be pleased to determine whether it be worth while to send a cutter from Baltimore for this special purpose, *at this late day; when Barney's fate must be decided one way or the other, before she can arrive.*[2]

AL, DNA: RG 59, Miscellaneous Letters; LB, DNA: RG 59, GW's Correspondence with His Secretaries of State.

1. The letter from British minister George Hammond to Adam Williamson (1734–1798), who served as governor of Jamaica from 1791 to 1795, has not been identified. On the detention of Capt. Joshua Barney on the British island of Jamaica after the seizure of his ship *Sampson* in December 1793, see n.3 of Randolph to GW, 1 March. On the imminent departure of the *General Greene,* the revenue cutter for Pennsylvania, to Charleston, S.C., see Alexander Hamilton to GW, 28 March, and n.1.

2. Barney returned to Baltimore on 16 May aboard a pilot boat that had been hired specifically for this purpose (*Baltimore Daily Advertiser,* 19 May; see also Randolph to Hamilton, 16 June, *Hamilton Papers,* 16:490–91). On the passport issued by GW to the pilot boat, see *JPP,* 293.

From Edmund Randolph

[Philadelphia] March 29. 1794.

The Secretary of State has the honor of submitting to the consideration of the President two drafts of letters to the French minister The substance of the one concerning the passport to a vessel *in ballast* was agreed this morning between Colo. Hamilton and E.R. It is also submitted to the President, whether Mr Fauchet's two letters for the Passport ought not to be sent to congress, that, if they should think proper to pass a general or particular modification of their resolution, they may have an opportunity of doing so.[1]

Since writing the above, a passport has been requested for a vessel, belonging to John Brown, a merchant of this place, *in ballast,* and destined for St Domingo with some of its former inhabitants, who are anxious to return. The President will be pleased to express his pleasure as to this vessel.[2]

AL, DNA: RG 59, Miscellaneous Letters; LB, DNA: RG 59, GW's Correspondence with His Secretaries of State.

1. In a letter to Fauchet of this date, Randolph wrote: "With every disposition in the executive to serve the French Republic, the resolution, which imposes the embargo, is so imperious in its terms, as to leave no discretion as for granting a Passport or license to depart to the Snow Camilla, *with a Cargo on board.* If however it should be thought adviseable by you, that she or any other vessel be sent in ballast with your dispatches, a Passport will be readily granted" (DNA: RG 59, Domestic Letters). On the embargo imposed by a resolution of Congress, see *Stat.* 1:400.

Randolph's second letter responded to a letter from Fauchet of this date that reads: "Je vous avais demandé par ma lettre du 16 Ventose (6 Mars) de vouloir bien me désigner les agens de la République française dont le Gouvernement des Etats-unis avait à se plaindre; je n'ai point reçu de réponse à cette lettre; votre silence, Mr, me laisse dans une incertitude que je vous prie de faire cesser; vous m'obligerez beaucoup" (FrPMAE, Correspondance Politique, Etats-Unis, 40). Randolph wrote: "I have delayed an answer to your Letter of the 16th instant, requiring me to name those Agents of the French Republic, who were obnoxious to the government of the United States, from a persuasion, that you would of your self remove those, against whom we have cause to complain. And in this I have not been mistaken. You have superseded, if I am rightly informed Mr Mangourit of Charleston, Mr Hauterive of New York, and Mr Dannery of Boston. I do not class among these Mr Moissonnier of Baltimore, because it is hoped, that he has been sensible of the impropriety of his conduct, and more particularly because I entertain a confidence, that you will restrain all future Consuls within the limits of due respect of the United States" (DNA: RG 59, Domestic Letters).

For a previous suggestion from GW that the congressional embargo needed further clarification, see GW's letter to the U.S. Senate and House of Representatives, 28 March. For GW's approval of the drafts and his reply to Randolph's question, see his letter to Randolph of 30 March.

2. Merchant John Brown conducted his import/export business from the Walnut Street wharf in Philadelphia (*Philadelphia Directory, 1794,* 18; *Federal Gazette, and Philadelphia Evening Post,* 16 Jan. 1793). For his advertisement offering passage to Saint Domingue aboard the brig *Sally,* see the 2 May issue of the *Philadelphia Gazette and Universal Advertiser.* For GW's reply, see his letter to Randolph of 30 March. For GW's granting of a passport for this ship on 22 April, see *JPP,* 300.

To Joseph Barrell

Sir   Philadelphia March 30th: 1794

Your favor of the 25th of Novr last, and the Sea Otter skin with which you were pleased to present me by the hands of Colo. Sergant, were not (as he probably has informed you) received at this place until a few days ago; or I should, most assuredly, have thanked you 'ere this for your kind and polite attention to me.[1]

I now pray you to accept my acknowledgment of the favor—and the assurance of the esteem with which I am—Sir Your Most Obedt Servt

Go: Washington

ALS (letterpress copy), ViU; LB, DLC:GW.

1. On Massachusetts merchant Joseph Barrell's acquisition of a sea otter skin and for Winthrop Sargent's presence in Philadelphia, see Barrell's letter to GW of 25 Nov. 1793, and notes.

Bartholomew Dandridge, Jr., to Henry Knox

[Philadelphia] 30th March 1794

By the President's order Bw Dandridge has the honor to transmit to the Secretary of War the Letter herewith enclosed from the Govr. of Pennsylvania—dated the 28 instant—together with its enclosures, numbered from 1 to 7.[1] The President requests the Secretary to take into consideration the Act No. 1—for raising four defence companies—and if he should entertain any doubt with respect to the constitutionality thereof, to take the opinion of the Atty Genl upon it—and report the result to the President.[2]

AL, DLC:GW; LB, DLC:GW.

1. For the numbered items, see the notes for Thomas Mifflin to GW, 28 March, and *JPP*, 294.

2. Item 1 was a copy of "An ACT for more effectually securing the trade, peace and safety of the port of Philadelphia, and defending the Western Frontiers of the commonwealth," 28 Feb. 1794. This act provided: "That the Governor shall raise, by voluntary enlistments from the militia of this commonwealth, three infantry companies of active and experienced rifle-men, and one company of artillery, to serve, under his orders and instructions, for a term of eight months . . . but if the state of war in Europe, and on the frontiers of this commonwealth, shall be such as, in the judgment of the Governor, to require the continuance of the said companies in the service of the said commonwealth, after the expiration of the said term of eight months, it shall be lawful for him to continue the same accordingly" (*Acts of the General Assembly of the Commonwealth of Pennsylvania, passed at a session, which was begun and held at the city of Philadelphia on Tuesday, the third day of December, in the year one thousand seven hundred and ninety-three* [Philadelphia, 1794], 463–65).

Knox wrote Attorney General William Bradford on 31 March, enclosing a copy of the act and expressing concern "whether this measure of Pennsylvania is not incompatible with the constitution of the United States" (*Pa. Archives*, 2d. ser., 6:684). For Bradford's reply, see n.1 of Knox to GW, 7 April (second letter).

Letter not found: From Le Brun, 30 March 1794. An entry of 15 May in GW's journal of proceedings of the presidency reads: "Recd. a letter from Mr. Le Brun dated 30. March 94 & sent it to the Secy. of State for consideration" (*JPP*, 302).

Letter not found: to Betty Washington Lewis, 30 March 1794. Betty Washington Lewis wrote GW on 13 April that "Your letter of the 30th of march came safe to hand."

From John Page

Sir   Philadelphia March 30th 1794

The Multiplicity & importance of Business in which I have been engaged, prevented my making the Extracts from Mr Anderson's Letter which I promised you on Tuesday last, till unfortunately it was mislaid so that I have not yet found it—but I recollect that he gave me his Opinion freely that Mr Gayle was an honest punctual Man, & he supposed capable of making such Payments as you might require—& that *he* made an Offer of his Services to negotiate the Business for you, if you had no particular Person in View on whom you might rather rely.[1] I have received another Letter from Mr Anderson, in which he desires me to inform you, that he finds others besides Gayle are disposed to purchase your Land—He thinks that fifty Shillings per Acre, on long Credit, the Interest paid annually, & Payment well secured, are the best Terms that can now be had.[2] I am Sir your most obedient humble Servant

John Page

ALS, DLC:GW.

1. Page, who was currently representing Virginia in the U.S. House of Representatives, may have given a verbal promise, rather than a written one, on Tuesday, 25 March, since no written letter from him of that date has been found. His correspondence with Mr. Anderson has not been identified. On the offer from Joshua Gayle to purchase a 400-acre tract owned by GW in Gloucester County, Va., see Gayle to GW, 8 Dec. 1793, and n.1.

2. GW did not sell this property until 1797, when George Ball agreed to purchase it for £800 (GW to Ball, 6 March 1797). At the time of his death on 14 Dec. 1799, GW still had not received full payment from Ball (see the Schedule of Property enclosed in GW's Last Will and Testament, 9 July 1799, and n.6 [*Papers, Retirement Series*, 4:513, 521]).

To William Pearce

Mr Pearce,   Philadelphia Mar. 30th 1794

The Reports, and your letter of the 25th instt have been duly recd.[1]

If you are satisfied from repeated trials, that the pieces of the treading floor at Dogue run Farm, are well placed at an inch and half a part, it would be well to lay them all at that distance, that you may derive as much benefit as you can from it in the present Crop, and that it may be ready against the next year.[2]

The Oats might also be tread out on the same floor; and the sooner the better, as you will then know precisely the quantity which you will have to depend upon; and when known, inform me thereof. I have three and half bushls of a peculiar kind of Oats which I will send by the first Vessel bound to Alexandria: unfortunately they came to my hands too late for the Vessels which have lately departed from hence for that Port; but I would have you reserve and keep about two acres of ground in a good state of preparation for sowing the moment the seed shall reach you.[3]

I am sorry to hear your drilled and other Wheat, makes but an indifferent appearance. I was in hopes such extreame fine weather as we have had during the whole month of March would have occasioned a pleasing change in both. As grain puts on different looks at this season, according as the weather, while growing happens to be, let me know from time to time how mine comes on. If it stands thick enough on the ground, such uncommon mildness & warmth as we have had since February, must have recovered that Crop greatly, as well as the Winter Barley.

I doubted the Gardeners information at first, when you reported a pottle of St foin seed; because the few plants could not bare so much; and next, because he did not take care *in time* to save what they did bare. Be the qty little or much, make the most of them & of the Hemp—and also the other seed he took for St foin that you are able.[4]

Let Abram get his deserts when taken by way of example; but do not trust to Crow to give it him; for I have reason to believe he is swayed more by passion than judgment in all his corrections.[5]

All the labour that can be spared from more pressing & important work should be employed on the Mill Race; otherwise when the springs get low you will have no water for grinding; it being but a poor stream at best, and many leaks in the old part which will be avoided by the new, whilst those in other parts of the race should be carefully sought after, & effectually stopped.[6]

If my Sister Lewis of Fredericksburgh should send for it, let her have one of the unbroke Mules of midling quality and size.[7] I am your friend &ca

Go: Washington

ALS, ViMtvL; ALS (letterpress copy), DLC:GW.

1. Pearce's letter of 25 March and its enclosed reports have not been found.

2. On the design of the new threshing barn at Dogue Run farm, see GW to Anthony Whitting, 28 Oct. 1792, and enclosed plan.

3. On GW's recent acquisition of "*heavy* Oats," see Frederick Frelinghuysen to GW, 26 March.

4. The report on the sainfoin seed from head gardener John Christian Ehlers has not been found. A pottle is equal to two quarts.

5. Abram was among the slaves whom GW leased from Penelope Manley French. He is listed on GW's Slave List of June 1799 as the husband of Nancy, a slave owned by GW who was twenty-eight years old and assigned to the Muddy Hole farm. Hiland Crow was the overseer of the Union farm, which was created by joining the farms previously known as French's and Ferry (see GW to Whitting, 16 Dec. 1792).

6. For GW's previous instructions regarding the race for the gristmill, see his letter to Pearce of 19 January.

7. For the request of Betty Washington Lewis for the gift of a mule, see her letter to GW of 23 March.

To Edmund Randolph

Sir,   Phila. March 30th 1794

The Letters *to* the Minister of the French republic, appears proper. The propriety of laying those *from* him, before Congress, I will converse with you upon tomorrow morning at Eight o clock.[1]

By whom is the request made for a Passport for a Vessel belonging to Mr Jno. Brown to go to St Domingo? I have no objection to the measure if such cases are within the contemplation of the Resolution laying the Embargo—but great care shd be used or a Vessel may I conceive clear in Ballast & meet a load or part of one below the Custom Houses.[2]

As one Pa⟨ss⟩port has already been granted to carry Mr Hammonds letter to Jamaica I do not think the Revenue Cutter from Baltimore ought to be sent.[3] If the one belonging to this Port was in condition to proceed from Charleston thither, it would have met my appro⟨bation⟩, because a double purpose wd have been answered—and I confess I see no cause why a Vessel capable of the Voyage to the latter place might not ⟨be⟩ adequate to the other also.[4] Yr[5]

ADf[S], DNA: RG 59, Miscellaneous Letters; LB, DNA: RG 59, GW's Correspondence with His Secretaries of State. The text in angle brackets is from the letter-book copy.

1. For Randolph's two letters to Fauchet of 29 March, see n.1 of Randolph to GW, 29 March (second letter). For Fauchet's two letters to Randolph of 28 March, see n.1 of Randolph's letter to GW of that date. Fauchet's letters were not submitted to Congress (see Randolph's first letter to GW of 31 March).

2. On the request by Philadelphia merchant John Brown for a passport for the brig *Sally*, see Randolph to GW, 29 March (second letter), and n.2. On GW's granting of this passport on 22 April, see *JPP*, 300. The request for a passport was necessitated by the recent congressional embargo "laid on all ships and vessels" in U.S. ports (*Stat.* 1:400).

3. For the ship bound for Jamaica and the letter from British minister George Hammond, see Randolph to GW, 29 March (first letter), and notes; see also *JPP*, 293. The revenue cutter stationed at Baltimore was the *Active*.

4. On the passport granted to the Pennsylvania revenue cutter *General Greene* to sail to Charleston, S.C., see Alexander Hamilton to GW, 28 March, and n.1 to that document.

5. The closing and signature have been clipped.

From Edmund Randolph

Sir   Philadelphia March 30. 1794.

The application for the passport to St Domingo is made by the Refugees themselves. It was in French, and could not be immediately translated; or it would have been sent.[1]

Inclosed is another application of the same kind from Mr Hammond.[2] I have the honor, sir, to be with the highest respect Yr Mo. ob. serv.

Edm: Randolph.

ALS, DNA: RG 59, Miscellaneous Letters; LB, DNA: RG 59, GW's Correspondence with His Secretaries of State.

1. On the application for a passport for the brig *Sally*, which would take French refugees back to Saint Domingue, see Randolph to GW, 29 March (second letter), and GW to Randolph, this date.

2. In his letter to Randolph of 29 March, British minister George Hammond wrote: "at the moment it is necessary for me to have an immediate communication with my Court." Therefore, he asked Randolph to procure from GW a passport "for a vessel which I intend to engage, for the *sole* purpose of conveying to Halifax [Nova Scotia] a messenger, who will be charged with my dispatches (DNA: RG 59, Notes from Foreign Legations: Great Britain). Randolph replied to Hammond on 31 March that GW had granted the passport "for an advice boat to Halifax" (DNA: RG 59, Domestic Letters).

From Edmund Randolph

(Private) Sunday. [Philadelphia, c.30 March 1794]

The intelligence, as derived from Mr G. thro' Mr N——s, stands thus:[1]

Colo. H. was asked by the committee, what authority he had for drawing the money borrowed in Europe, over here. His answer was, "I have verbal authority from the President, and fortunately written also"—It is supposed by Mr G., that the written authority, or rather the letter from Mount Vernon, which is referred to, does not support the assertion; but that a reliance will be wholly placed on the verbal.[2]

A question is now depending, (as is further said) before the committee, whether they have any right to inquire into a verbal authority, given by the President. It is also said, to be one, made by Colo. H.[3] The next week must bring this business to a point; when we shall be able to ascertain facts, without drawing them from any source, which is not well-affected to the gentleman in question. The object in mentioning the thing to the President was to give him time to examine into the fact, from his own memory, and papers.[4]

AD, DLC:GW. The cover is marked "Private."

1. The intelligence derived from Virginia congressman William B. Giles probably came through Vermont congressman Nathaniel Niles. Both men served on the Select Committee Appointed to Examine the Treasury Department. On this committee and its interest in the foreign loans arranged by Alexander Hamilton, see Hamilton to GW, 24 March, and n.1.

2. James Madison, in his letter to Thomas Jefferson of 26 March, wrote that when the subject of "the authority for drawing the money from Europe into the Bank" was raised by the Select Committee, Hamilton "endeavored to parry the difficulty by contesting the right of the Committee to call for the authority. This failing he talks of constructive written authority from the P. but relies on parol authority" (*Madison Papers*, 15:294–96). On the progress of the Select Committee's investigation and Hamilton's responses to its questions, see Introductory Note, Hamilton to Frederick A. C. Muhlenberg, 16 Dec. 1793 (*Hamilton Papers*, 15:460–65).

Among the written documents giving Hamilton authority to arrange the various foreign loans was GW's first letter to him of 7 May 1791, which was written at Charleston, S.C., not Mount Vernon. For other documents used to support Hamilton's claims, see his letter to GW of 24 March 1794.

3. On Hamilton's constitutional objection, see his letter to the Select Committee of 24 March (*Hamilton Papers*, 16:193–95).

4. On the committee's attempt to ascertain the extent of Hamilton's authority by appealing to GW for information, see Abraham Baldwin to GW, 5 April, in n.1 of Hamilton to GW, 7 April.

From Alexander Spotswood

Dear Sir   March 30th 1794.

your favour of the 15. Inst. came to hand yesterday. and altho I have the highest Opinion of my Sons Abilities, as a perfect Seaman and able Navigator; (not from any knowledge which I have in the Bussiness) But from my Knowledge, of his haveing had a very good Nautical Education—and the High Terms in which, many Nautical men of Abilities Speak of him. Yet it never was my wish, to ask of you impropper promotion for him—But still hope, that circumstances, may yet Turn out, so as to put it in your power, without doing Injustice to others, to make him a first Lieutenant; However, what pleases you, he must receive; and in future, Endeavour by assiduity & merrit to push himself forward.[1] I am dr Sr yr affect. & obt St

                                                           A. Spotswood

ALS, DLC:GW.
1. GW's letter of 15 March explained why he was unable to give John Augustine Spotswood a commission in the new navy at this time. It was John Adams, and not GW, who finally gave the younger Spotswood the desired appointment in the U.S. Navy (see *U.S. Senate Executive Journal*, 1:337–38).

To George Clinton

(Private)
Dear Sir,   Philadelphia Mar. 31st 1794.

Your favor of the 20th instt, with its enclosures, came duly to hand; and for which you have my particular thanks.

As there are those who affect to believe that Great Britain has no hostile intention towards this Country, it is not surprizing that there should be found among them characters who pronounce the Speech of Lord Dorchester to the Indians to be spurious. No doubt however remains in my mind of its authenticity: but as it is of importance to be satisfied (as far as the nature of the thing will admit) of the fact, I would thank you for such information as you are enabled to give, respecting this matter.[1]

How far the disappointments, experienced by the combined powers in Europe, may have wrought a change in the political conduct of G. Britain towards this Country, I shall not take upon me to decide. That it has worn a very hostile appearance latterly, if it has not been so uniformly, no one, I conceive, will be hardy enough to deny: and that Lord Dorchester has spoken the sentimts of the British cabinet at the period he was instructed I am as ready to believe. But, foiled as that Ministry has been, whether it may not have changed its tone, as it respects us, is problamatical. This, however, ought not to relax such enquiries on our part into the existing state of things, as might enable us, if matters should come to extremity, to act promptly, and with vigour.

Among these enquiries, it appears important to me to know the present state of things in upper and lower Canada—that is the composition of the Inhabitants (especially in upper Canada): how they stand affected to their Government; What part they would be disposed to act if a rupture between this Country & G. Britain should take place, &ca. The proximity of our settlements from the Northwestern to the North Eastern parts of the State of New York with the Lake Ontario & River St Lawrence; the strength thereof; and of their neighbours on the other side of the line—Regulars & Militia—especially about Niagara—and Oswego.

As you have, I am certain, a pretty accurate knowledge of many of these matters yourself; and have the means from your acquaintance with characters (on whose adroitness and integrity you can rely) bordering on the British settlements, to obtain information from others, you would oblige me very much by such communications as relate to the above, or any other points that you may conceive worthy of attention.[2] With great esteem & regard I am—Dear Sir Yr Obedt & Affecte Sert

Go: Washington

ALS, NHi: George and Martha Washington Papers; ALS (letterpress copy), DNA: RG 59, Miscellaneous Letters; LB, DLC:GW.

1. For Clinton's response on the authenticity of Lord Dorchester's speech to the Indians of 10 Feb., see Clinton to GW, 7 April.

2. Clinton promised to make the requested inquiries and provided some information on British military strength in his letter to GW of 7 April.

To Alexander Hamilton

United States 31. March 1794.
Pay to The Secretary of State, in pursuance of the Act providing for the relief of such of the Inhabitants of St Domingo, resident with the United States, as may be found in want of support,
Six hundred dollars; to be applied to the relief of persons of the
above description in the City of Philadelphia.[1]

Geo: Washington

LB, DLC:GW.
    1. For the relevant legislation, see "An Act providing for the relief of such
of the inhabitants of Saint Domingo, resident within the United States, as
may be found in want of support," 12 Feb. (*Stat.* 6:13). On the original apportionment of $1,000 in federal funds to relief efforts in Pennsylvania, see
Edmund Randolph's first letter to GW of 27 February. On the disbursement
of a total of $1,600 to a relief committee in Philadelphia, see Cabinet Opin-
ion of 22 April, n.1.

From James McHenry

(private)
Sir.   Fayetteville [Md.] 31 March 1794.
    I have very often troubled you respecting others; will you
excuse me for speaking a little concerning myself. My health
which has suffered a considerable shock by an autumnal fever in
1792 & 1793, I am pretty well persuaded might be benefited by a
change of climate for a short time. It has struck me that the new
situation in which the United States may find itself will require
additional diplomatic appointments to forward or attend to its
interests abroad, at least till peace and order shall take place in
Europe. Should this be the case, and any opening occur where
the little talents I may possess could be rendered useful it would
greatly oblige and gratify me to be considered by you as a proper
person to fill one of them. I hope I need not say that a vain ambition has had no share in this application, and my own interest
as little. Had either any influence over my conduct it is no ways
likely that I should have waited for ill health to have stimulated
them into action.[1] Wishing you most sincerely in this difficult
moment a continuance of your wonted health I have the honor
to be very respectfully & affectionately your ob. st
James McHenry

ALS, DLC:GW.

1. On 3 April, James McHenry wrote another letter to GW, in which he expanded on his request for a diplomatic appointment. For GW's reply to both these letters, see his letter to McHenry of 8 April.

From Edmund Randolph

Sir   Philadelphia March 31. 1794

The laying of Mr Fauchet's letters before congress came into my mind.[1] But I did not observe upon it; because he has given no answer, whether a passport for the dispatches on board may not be sufficient, or how he would wish the business to be modified. When that comes, it will probably be time enough to consider, how far the President ought to be sending every application for relaxing the embargo to congress; and whether there is not something too strong in excepting by a new resolution a vessel, *notoriously loaded with flour for France,* from the operation of the embargo.[2] I thought, that the liberal construction of the resolution would permit her to procccd. But as you have determined otherwise, I cannot see the propriety of making a special rule for her, or of the President being the vehicle to congress of such a proposition.[3] Possibly Mr Fauchet may place the subject upon other ground. I speak only upon the case, as it now exists. I have the honor, sir, to be with the highest respect yr mo. ob. serv.

Edm: Randolph

AL, DNA: RG 59, Miscellaneous Letters; LB, DNA: RG 59, GW's Correspondence with His Secretaries of State; LB, DNA: RG 59, Domestic Letters.

1. For the letters from French minister Fauchet to Randolph of 28 March, see n.1 of Randolph's letter to GW of that date. For Randolph's suggestion that these letters might be laid before Congress, see Randolph's second letter to GW of 29 March.

2. On the embargo recently imposed by Congress, see *Stat.* 1:400.

3. GW may have expressed this opinion at his 8 a.m. meeting with Randolph on this day (GW to Randolph, 30 March).

From Edmund Randolph

[Philadelphia] March 31. 1794.

E. Randolph has the honor of submitting the inclosed application for a passport to the President, and whether if all the ministers of foreign nations here should assent, most of the objections will not be overcome.[1]

AL, DNA: RG 59, Miscellaneous Letters; LB, DNA: RG 59, GW's Correspondence with His Secretaries of State.

1. The enclosure came from Louis Osmont, who emigrated from France in 1790. At this time, his mercantile business was located at 117 North Second Street in Philadelphia (*Philadelphia Directory, 1794,* 110). His letter to Randolph of this date requested a passport in order to circumvent the recent embargo enacted by Congress (see *Stat.* 1:400). Osmont's intention was to send a ship full of French refugees to their homes in Saint Domingue. "I was about fitting out a Vessell to carry them," he wrote. "They are about Fifty in Number, have nothing left in this part of the World; what they have paid me for the Consideration to be paid here, the remainder being payable at Hispaniola, would not by any means be sufficient to support them one Week; their resources are at home, & they can no longer support themselves without Assistance or liberty to go with their Wives and Children now in distress, & take possession again of their Properties; I myself should be a great sufferer, If I was to make void the Contract; They join themselves to me, Sir, to beg of the executive power of the United States to permit me to send out a Vessell for the only purpose of carrying them. I shall give full and sufficient Security to the United States, (tho' I have sworn fidelity & obedience to their Constitution and Laws) that I do represent you nothing but the truth. I shall take in no Cargo whatsoever, but the necessary Victuals for the Voyage, and the Vessell shall not go out, except We can obtain of all and every the Ministers of other Courts or Nations to the United States, a passport of such nature as can prevent any Insults from the Privateers or Men of War of the Belligerent Powers.

"I shall further engage, if required, to send those Passengers in a french Bottom, shall also transact the whole Business in any Shape you may think proper to prevent demands of the same sort from being asked upon the Grounds of this being granted" (DNA: RG 59, Miscellaneous Letters). On 2 May, GW granted a passport to Osmont's ship *America,* Capt. Edward Rice, "to proceed to the West Indies in ballast to carry french passengers" (*JPP,* 301).

The cabinet opinion on granting Osmont's request was written below Osmont's signature:

Randolph, Alexander Hamilton, and Henry Knox signed the following opinion, of which the beginning text is in Randolph's handwriting and the text after the colon is in Hamilton's: "I am of opinion that a passport ought to be granted, under the restrictions, proposed by the petitioner: (viz.) the vessel to be American, in ballast & to have passports from the several foreign Ministers."

William Bradford then wrote and signed his dissenting opinion: "I am inclined to think that the Embargo extends to all vessels which are not in some degree or other considere⟨d⟩ as under the direction of the President of the U.S."

To William Tilghman

Dear Sir,   Philada March 31st 1794
   Your favor of the 23d instt came duly to hand.
   The laws, in the cases of both Mr George and Mr Chalmers must regulate ⟨my con⟩duct. To do all that these will permit, is enough for my justification—more I shall not covet. If, however, as I conceive the fact assuredly is, the latter Gentleman has actually received, and did not pay a hundred pounds which was put into his hands as *part* of a *Bond* due to the estate of Colvill (and was then bearing interest) it would seem but justice that he should allow interest for that sum when applied to his own use—but if there is a principle arising from analogy or reciprocity opposed thereto I must be content with what Mr Chalmers will pay, and this I am disposed to in order that my administration of the estate of Colo. Colvill may be finally closed.[1]
   With respect to Mr George, I had rather his acct should be settled & a new bond taken for the *whole* balance payable at a given time (when he will be punctual, & by which the money can be drawn from Mr Chalmers) than to receive part this spring and the residue in the Fall; because the demands upon Colvills estate (except the residuary legacy) have all been discharged; and because the money which is due had better remain at interest than lye dead in my hands or subject me perhap to the payment of it.
   If the law of Maryland has stopped interest during a certain period of the War, the estate of course must (as I have observed before) lose it. The case however, was otherwise in Virginia for there I have lately recovered a pretty heavy debt with interest from the date of the bond which was taken before the war. With very great esteem & regard I am, Dear Sir Your Obedt Hble Sert
                                             Go: Washington

ALS (letterpress copy), DLC:GW; LB, DLC:GW. The text in angle brackets is from the letter-book copy.
   1. An entry of 17 June 1795 in the account of Thomas Colvill reads: "By Cash received of George Chalmers of London formerly an Attorney employed by the Executors of Thomas Colvill to recover of Syndey George of Maryland a debt due from him to the Estate of which he received in Maryland money £100.—which sum he alledges to have paid soon after the receipt, to one of the Executors, but from the great length of time since the transaction the receipt has been mislaid, but the sum received by him he has agreed to pay upon Condition of having the same refunded when ever he can produce

the Receipt, and directed a Bill to be drawn for the said £100—at par being £60 Stg which at an Exchange of 1% produced £105.12.0 Maryland money equal to £84.7.7¼" Virginia currency. The estate was not settled until 18 July 1796, when £932.17.3¾ was paid "into the Bank of Alexandria agreeably to a Decree of the High Court of Chancery of Virginia, being the balance due from me as Surviving Executor to this Estate as ﷼ Settlement with the Court of Fairfax" (Ledger C, 15).

From Gustavus F. Goetz

[Philadelphia, March 1794]

P.S. The person, that has the honor to submit the above Translations, the theme whereof he has published in the German gazette annexed hereto along with the french Translation made by him, begs Leave to observe: that he is brought up regularly to the Bar in Germany, that he is ready to produce a formal Certificate on his Examen, he underwent there, in the Civil Law and the Laws of Nations, that he is well acquainted with the antient as well as modern diplomatic stile of nations (being intimately acquainted with the latin language), that he has taken, before this the Oath to support the Constitution, being employed by the Post Master General of the U.S. to whom he has been favoured to exhibit Vouchers for his Integrity, Secrecy and accuracy in business.[1]

Gustavus F. Goetz

He understands to translate from Dutch and now is employed to attain a more sufficient Knowledge of the Spanish.

ALS, DLC:GW. The docket reads: "March [   ] 1794. Candidate for office of Translator to Dep. of State."

1. Gustavus F. Goetz may have been referring to something he published in the German newspaper *Philadelphische Correspondenz,* but the enclosed translations have not been identified. Goetz was mentioned in an advertisement for *Vorlesungen über Philosophische Sittenlehre von Johann Macpherson, übersetzt durch G.F. Goetz* (Philadelphia, 1792), a German translation of John Macpherson's *Lectures on Moral Philosophy* (Philadelphia, 1791). In this ad in the 4 May 1792 issue of the *Federal Gazette, and Philadelphia Evening Post,* Macpherson states that the translator, Goetz, "shews himself to be a complete master of our copious and expressive language, and appears to possess besides the talents of an able and accurate translator." Goetz was also the translator of Aesop's fables in *Auserlesene Fabeln des Esop und andrer vorzüglichen Fabeldicter, Zur Bildung des Verstandes und Herzens* (Philadelphia, 1794).

The current postmaster general was Timothy Pickering. No reply has been found.

From Anne Sauvage

[March–April 1794]

Anne Sauvage habitante du Cap français, ayant echappé au fer, & a l'Incendie de cette infortunée ville,[2] amena avec elle, trois jeunes Demoiselles, orphelines, dont l'Éducation, lui avait eté confiée, (des leur Berceau) par leurs Péres, & Meres. a leur arrivée dans Ce Continant, elle obteint des secours, pour elle, et ses trois orphelines, on les leur continua, jusqu'a Ce que les fonds destinés a une si belle action, fussent épuisés. aprés, on leur donna d'autres secours, provenant d'une quétte, que des personnes charitables,[3] avaient faite, en dernier lieu, sous le Ministère de Mr Genet, elles sollicitérent, et obteinrent de nouveaux secours; ils continuaient encore, a l'Epocque qu'il a êté remplacé par Mr Faucher. Nous nous sommes présentées a ce nouveau Ministre, pour lui exposer nos malheurs, et nos préssants besoins, il nous a repondu que la Republique française ne pouvait donner des secours que dans son sein. en consequense il nous a offert de nous envoyer en Europe.[4] nous l'avons remercié sans acccptcr son offre par rapoil a notie age, et par la raison que notre proprieté n'est pas en Europe et que nous ne Conaissons pas les parents que nous pourrions y avoir. il nous a paru plus naturel, de rester dans ce Continent. afin d'etre plus aportée de retourner a St Domingue, ou nous trouverons les débris de notre fortune. puisque le Ministre de la République française ne peut pas nous secourir, dans ce Pays, que deviendrons nous helas! Si les sanglots, et les soupirs douloureux de l'indigence, ne pénétraient pas la sensibilité des belles ames. Vos vertus honorées de toutes les nations, nous font espérer que vous voudrés bien nous faire participer aux Secours destinés pour les Malheureux,[5] jusqu'a ce que nous puissions retourner ou sont nos propriétés. Cet acte de Générosité, de justice, gravera dans nos Coeurs, et pour toujours, les traits inéfassables de la reconaissance; nos voeux seront Constents pour la durée de vos jours, si precieux au bonheur d'un Peuple dont vous etes chery.

anne Sauvage

ALS, DNA: RG 59, Miscellaneous Letters. Sauvage, a refugee from Saint Domingue with three orphaned young ladies in charge, explains that she has been surviving on charity and some assistance provided by the previous French minister, Edmond Genet. The new minister, Jean-Antoine-Joseph

Fauchet, has told her that France will offer aid only if they return to Europe, but they would prefer to remain in America, hoping to return to Saint Domingue. She asks that GW allow them to participate in the benefits offered the poor.

2. During the conflict between rival factions in Saint Domingue, the town of Cap Français was burned in June 1793.

3. For the ongoing charitable efforts to assist the Saint Domingue refugees in Baltimore, Md., see William Patterson et al. to GW, 30 Jan., and notes. For a similar effort at Philadelphia, to which GW contributed, see GW to Laurent De Saxÿ and Laurent De Verneüil, 26 Dec. 1793, and n.1 to that document.

4. Fauchet, who arrived at Philadelphia on 21 Feb., issued a notice on 28 Feb.: "The unfortunate inhabitants of the French colony of St. Domingo, who in the conflagration of the Cape, came to seek an asylum in the United States, are informed, that the Republic grants them a passage for France. They are invited, in consequence, to apply for this purpose, during eight days from this time, to the Consuls of the Republic in the different ports of the United States" (*The American Star, or, Historical, Political, Critical, and Moral Journal* [Philadelphia], 8 March).

5. Sauvage may have been asking to be included among the beneficiaries of "An Act providing for the relief of such of the inhabitants of Saint Domingo, resident within the United States, as may be found in want of support," 12 Feb. (*Stat.* 6:13). The act appropriated $15,000 to be "placed under the direction of the President." On the arrangements for distribution of those funds, see Edmund Randolph to GW, 27 Feb. (first letter).

Alexander Hamilton's Proposed Presidential Message to Congress

Gentlemen   [Philadelphia, March–May 1794]

In my speech to the two houses of Congress at the opening of the session I urged the expediency of being prepared for war as one of the best securities to our peace[1]—Events which seem dayly to be unfolding themselves press still more seriously upon us the duty of being so prepared, indicating that the calamities of war may by a train of circumstances be forced upon us, notwithstanding the most sincere desires and endeavours to cultivate and preserve peace.

I cannot therefore withold from congress the expression of my conviction that the united States ought without delay to adopt such military arrangements as will enable them to vindicate with vigour their rights and to repel with energ⟨y⟩ any attacks, which may be made upon them: and that it may be advisable to add some dispositions calculated to exempt our commerce from being the prey of foreign depredation.

The blessings of peace are in my view so precious that they will continue to engage my most zealous exertions for their continuance—under this impression the suggestions I have made are influenced as much by a persuasion of their tendency[2] to preserve peace as by a sense of the necessity of being prepared for events which may not depend on our choice.[3]

Copy, DLC: Hamilton Papers. Hamilton wrote on the back of this document: "Copy of a message drafted at the desire of the President for his consideration. Deposited in my Pigeon Hole." At a later date, someone else wrote "[20 May, 1794?]" on the top of this document.

1. For this speech, see GW to the U.S. Senate and House of Representatives, 3 Dec. 1793. This draft may have been inspired by Hamilton's letter to GW of 8 March, in which Hamilton argued that the United States needed "to be in a respectable military posture" and offered his ideas on how to achieve this state.

2. This word is in Hamilton's handwriting.

3. By early May, this address probably was deemed not necessary due to the passage of several defense-oriented laws by Congress. For this legislation, see "An Act to provide for the Defence of certain Ports and Harbors in the United States," 20 March; "An Act to provide a Naval Armament," 27 March; "An Act to provide for the erecting and repairing of Arsenals and Magazines, and for other purposes," 2 April; "An Act providing for raising and organizing a Corps of Artillerists and Engineers," 9 May, and "An Act directing a Detachment from the Militia of the United States," also 9 May (*Stat.* 1:345–46, 350, 352, 366–68).

From Alexander Hamilton

Philadelphia April 1 1794.

The Secretary of the Treasury presents his respects to the President & transmits the copy of a paper, which he proposes to communicate to the Committee on the state of the Treasury Department[1] and which he hopes will be found by the President conformable with what passed in the interview of yesterday.[2]

LB, DLC:GW.

1. On the request by the U.S. House of Representatives for the enclosed "Report on Principles and Course of Proceeding with Regard to the Disposition of the Moneys Borrowed Abroad by Virtue of the Acts of the Fourth and Twelfth of August 1790, as to the Point of Authority," see Hamilton to GW, 24 March, and n.1. The report, dated 1 April, reads: "Principles and course of proceeding, with regard to the disposition of the monies borrowed

abroad, by virtue of the Acts of the 4 and 12 of August 1790, as to the point of authority.

"It was conceived by the Secretary of the Treasury, to be a clear principle resulting from the constitution of the Treasury Department, and from the several provisions of that Act, collectively taken, that all public monies, once obtained, and destined for disbursement within the United States, came, of course, under the direction of the officers of that Department, according to their respective functions; and that no special authority, extrinsic to the Department, was, in strictness, necessary to enable them to draw money, from whatever source originating, into the Treasury, or to issue it thence, for the purposes designated by Law.

"It was also conceived by him, to be, tho' a less clear principle, one most agreeable to the true spirit of the constitution of the Department, as well as essential to the preservation of order and due accountability in the money-transactions of the Country, that even monies procured abroad, and to be disbursed abroad, were, as to their application, to be under the direction of the same Department.

"Under the influence of these principles, thus entertained with different degrees of assurance (the President having determined to place the procuring of the loans under the direction of the Secretary of the Treasury) the following course of proceeding was pursued.

"The Secretary obtained from the President, in the first place, a general Commission to him to make the Loans authorised by the two Acts of the 4th & 12th of August. A copy of this Commission was communicated to the House of Representatives in the last session, No. 1 and is dated the 28. of August.

"He also obtained from the President, an instruction, dated the same day, to guide and justify him; 1st. with regard to the person to be employed in Europe in negotiating the Loans, and 2dly. with regard to the extent, to which, the loans under the first Act, and payments on account of the foreign debt, should be carried, at all events, exclusively of the consideration of the advantageousness of the terms of the loans.

"But under the influence of the first mentioned principle, he neither asked, nor obtained any general instruction from the President, as to the sums to be drawn to the United States, for the purpose of the second Act.

"Nevertheless, from the special connection of the President with the subject, owing to the authority to borrow being immediately vested in him; from the circumstance of the existence of a particular discretion to be exercised by the President, as to anticipated payments of the foreign debt; and from the official relation of each head of a department to the President; The Secretary of the Treasury considered it, as his duty, from time to time, to submit the disposition of each Loan to the consideration of the President, with his reasons for such disposition, & to obtain the sanction of the President, previous to carrying it into effect, which was always had.

"The communications to the President and his sanctions were, for the most part, verbal. Two exceptions appear from letters (herewith shewn) of the Secretary to the President, of the 10 and 14 of April, and 22d of September 1791; and from the President to him of the 7 of May '91, relating to a case of absence from the seat of Government. These Letters are evidence of the course and spirit of proceeding.

"It is to be understood, that the sanctions of the President were always bottomed upon the representations of the Secretary, and were always expressly or tacitly qualified with this *condition*-that whatever was to be done, was to be agreeable to the Laws" (DLC:GW).

2. GW submitted Hamilton's report to Edmund Randolph for his opinion before replying to Hamilton in two letters of 8 April (see Randolph's second letter to GW of 1 April).

Letter not found: from John Hunter, 1 April 1794. Tench Coxe wrote John Hunter of South Carolina on 3 May: "I have the honor to inform you that a letter of the 1st Ulo from you to the President has been this day transmitted to this office." Coxe continued by asking a series of questions about the manufacture of cordage at the Columbia Mill (DNA: RG 75, Letters of Tench Coxe, Commissioner of the Revenue, Relating to the Procurement of Military, Naval, and Indian Supplies).

Letter not found: from William Pearce, 1 April 1794. GW wrote Pearce on 6 April acknowledging receipt of "Your letter & Reports of the 1st instant."

To Edmund Randolph

Sir,   [Philadelphia] Tuesday April 1st 1794

I think the United States will be benifited by granting the request of Louis Osmont[1]—but, as applications have been, and probably will be frequent—I conceive it will be advisable to ascertain as nearly as may be the *precise* objects of the Embargo[2]— and havg so done to establish rules or principles that will meet cases as they shall occur which will save trouble at the same time that it will be a mean of facilitating business.[3] Yrs

G. W——n

ADfS, DNA: RG 59, Miscellaneous Letters; LB, DNA: RG 59, GW's Correspondence with His Secretaries of State.

1. On the request of Louis Osmont for a passport, see n.1 of Randolph's second letter to GW of 31 March.

2. For the thirty-day embargo of 26 March that Congress imposed on "all ships and vessels" in U.S. ports, see *Stat.* 1:400.

3. Any written reply from Randolph on this subject has not been found. For clarification of the restrictions imposed by the embargo and its eventual extension until 25 May, see the congressional resolutions of 2 and 18 April and 7 May (*Stat.* 1:400–401).

From Edmund Randolph

[Philadelphia] April 1. 1794.

E. Randolph would ⟨have⟩ done himself the honor of waiting on the President with the inclosed, to know his pleasure as to sending the two letters to the Senate and house of representatives, if he was not under a very severe pain of the head.[1] Besides the letters, now sent, he has received by the mail of to-day from Colo. Humphreys, seven others, but containing no recent or important intelligence; and therefore they will not be sent, unless the President should think proper to call for them.[2]

AL, DNA: RG 59, Miscellaneous Letters; LB, DNA: RG 59, GW's Correspondence with His Secretaries of State. The text in angle brackets is from the letter-book copy.

1. According to GW's executive journal, the enclosed letters from David Humphreys to Randolph were those written at Madrid, Spain, on 25 Dec. 1793, and at Lisbon, Portugal, on 30 Jan. 1794. Both letters pertain to Humphreys' efforts to relieve the immediate suffering of Americans held captive by Algiers and to obtain their eventual release (*JPP*, 296). These letters and their enclosures are in DNA: RG 59, Despatches from U.S. Ministers to Lisbon; see also *ASP, Foreign Relations*, 1:418–23.

2. David Humphreys' letter to Randolph of 7 Dec. 1793 reported on his inability to leave Alicante, Spain, because of the "uncommonly heavy rains which have fallen." The enclosures were copies of his letters of 29 Nov. 1793 to: Mathias Skjöldebrand, consul general of Sweden; Pierre Eric Skjöldebrand; Capt. Richard O'Bryen, marked "Secret & Confidential"; "Captn Obrien, Captn Stevens [Isaac Stephens], & the other Captains & Officers, Citizens of the U.S. of America, now Prisoners at Algiers"; and a letter of 30 Nov. 1793 to "the Mariners, Citizens of the U.S. of America, Prisoners at Algiers." These letters were numbered, respectively, from one to five. The letter of 7 Dec. and its enclosures are in DNA: RG 59, Despatches from U.S. Ministers to Portugal; see also Humphreys, *Life and Times of David Humphreys*, 2:191–95. Apparently GW did call for this letter and its enclosures, because he returned these six items to Randolph on 2 April (*JPP*, 296).

From Edmund Randolph

Sir   [Philadelphia] Tuesday afternoon April 1. 1794.

The distraction of my head from pain scarcely enables me to hope for tolerable exactness in my remarks. If therefore it were possible to let the paper rest with me, until the morning, I could better fulfil your wishes.[1]

According, however, to the view, which I now take of the subject, the seven first paragraphs appear unexceptionable, so far as respects the President.

I am extremely dissatisfied with the manner of the three last clauses. The first of those three, which is the eighth in order, states that he always had the President's Sanction for disposing of the money, as he did. So far he had the sanction, "*I approve if it be agreeable to law.*" At first sight, it would seem "that the last line in the paper was tantamount to this idea. But the positive assertion, that your sanction was always given to the disposition; including the drawing of the money over here, implies, that you considered this act as lawful.

Permit me to suggest this mode of answer, to be given verbally. "I have read the paper, but not distinctly recollecting all the circumstances, I can only say, that I do not discover any thing Which I am to object to as to myself, unless the manner, in which you speak of my sanction in disposing of the loans, implies that I meant to give an opinion how far it might or might not be lawful. I presume however, that you do not mean this, as you say at the close, that my san⟨c⟩tion was always expressly or tacitly qualified with the condition that whatever was to be done was to be agreeable to the law. I imagine that you sent me the paper, only to determine, what related to myself, and therefore I did not undertake to judge of other parts."[2] I have the honor sir, to be with sincere attachment & respect yr mo. ob. serv.

Edm: Randolph.

ALS, DNA: RG 59, Miscellaneous Letters; LB, DNA: RG 59, GW's Correspondence with His Secretaries of State.

1. The paper under consideration, which carries this date, was Alexander Hamilton's "Report on Principles and Course of Proceeding with Regard to the Disposition of the Moneys Borrowed Abroad by Virtue of the Acts of the Fourth and Twelfth of August, 1790, as to the Point of Authority." For this report, see n.1 of Hamilton's letter to GW of this date.

2. For GW's eventual response to Hamilton's report, see his two letters to Hamilton of 8 April.

From Joseph Brown

No. 3. Lower Terrace Islington (near London)
Honoured Sir   April 2 1794
A few years ago I had the honour to address to your Excellency a pair of Prints, one of Yourself, another of the late General

Green, the receipt of which you did me the favour to acknowledge, another pair of them very elegantly framed were sent to
Congress, whose acceptance of them, I requested on condition
of their being hung up in some public part of the Building
wherein they held their deliberations; I afterward reced. a Letter in which these prints were mentioned by the Secretary, but
whether Captn Cooper of the Edward New York Trader (a lying
Scot!) did not as I believe he was very capable of doing, play me
a trick, by assuming to himself whatever merit could be due to
the present, I never had any opportunity of knowing.[1]

It is with unspeakable pleasure that I have since observed
Sir, that the homage which is so justly due to your Character &
Talents, has been so generally displayed by every Class of your
Fellow Citizens, who with so much honour to themselves & ad-
vantage to the Common-Wealth, have repeatedly testified their
grateful sense of your eminent services to your Country & to
Mankind by re-electing You the Chief of Freemen.[2]

May America long enjoy the benefit of your wise & salutary
Council, & as she is the depository of rational Freedom and the
Asylum of persecuted Merit every Country, I trust your eforts to
preserve Peace will be attended with success. Genet, the super-
cillious Frenchman was kept at a prudent distance, & at the time
he was endeavoring to be troublesome by his teezing impertinence, I observed that nationalists described a species of Cats,
by his name.[3]

Long 'ere this you must have been informed that "in the hour
of our insolence" when we were in possession of Toulon;[4] when
the combined powers upon the European Continent were likely
to penetrate France, our Court were not only endeavoring to
bully Sweden, Denmark, the Swiss Cantons and the Republic of
Genoa to become parties in a War, begun under a pretence of
the love of Order & humanity, but in reality design'd to tear up
every vestige of European Liberty & to perpetuate the reign of
Popery & Superstition; our Cabinet (the 6 of Novr last) issued
a most arbitrary Edict, to seize your Vessels in defiance of the
law of Nations:[5] Toulon however being about to be disgracefully
abandoned, and the Forces of the Crowned Conspirators being
constrained by the French Republicans to retreat beyond the
Rhine, Pitt and his detestable Junto were under the necescesity
of lowering their haughty & unjust pretentions, but no doubt

many vessels belonging to the subjects of the United States have been seized in consequence of the arrogant Orders sent from hence & tyrannically detained in the West Indies;[6] 'tis therefore with pleasure that I have read of your pacify plan of Reprisals viz. That of levying a duty on British Ships & British Merchandize to reemburse those who may be sufferers by British depredation.[7]

When *Bowles,* was in this Country I expected that he & his wretched associates would only return to America to stimulate the Savages (less savage than they who prompted the Massacres which have happened on your Frontiers) to give every annoyance & check to the rising Greatness of your Country,[8] which excites in the bosoms of your antient Enemies in this, the most malignant sensations, in as much as those who are best acquainted with the insidious Arts of the vile Hypocrite—the successful Apostate who now directs the public Measures of this Kingdom, are at no loss to conjecture, by whom the Algerines have been stimulated to harrass & to plunder your Commerce.[9]

The Empress of Russia who held during our wicked war with North America, very different opinions respecting the Rights of Neutral Nations in one of her late Manifestos declared that "no Faith was to be held with Rebels," hence it is easy to perceive that if the confedracy of "crowned Robbers," could succeed in their impious endeavors to legislate for the Republic of France, nothing but the weakness & poverty of "the high contracting Parties", would prevent their undertaking a Cruisade to give or rather in the hope of giving a Monarchical form of Government to your United States:[10] May divine Providence grant, that their Republican Government may be incorruptible & immortal. Liberty is in this Country in a most drooping and retrograde State: free & liberal discussions are no longer safe & under the pretext of accusations of Sedition, several worthy Persons are suffering fine & imprisonment, and four worthy persons are sentenced to 14 years transporation, for no other offence than insisting on the necessity of a more equal representation of the people, which about 11 years ago lifted the Duke of Richmond and Mr Pitt, into the most lucrative & distinguishd offices in the Kingdom,[11] verifying the words of Dr Garth,

    Here little Villains must submit to fate

    That Great Ones may enjoy the World in state.[12]

The worthy & justly celebrated Dr Priestley justly alarmed at these sentences & having for some time been harrassed, vilified & persecuted by the venial tools of Government has determined to expatriate himself & to seek a peaceful asylum in the united States; the circumstances that occasion his departure are a disgrace to the Age & Nation[13]—"whose Sons will blush their Fathers were his Foes".[14] Nothing should have prevented my following his example, but the insuperable aversion to a Sea Voyage entertained by my Wife, the amiable constant & affection partner of my sufferings when in consequence of events connected with the late war I lost a respectable Fortune.

If by the mysterious dispensations of Providence I should have the misfortune to be bereaved of my dear Consort, the best the most precious gift which Heaven ever bestowed on me although I am near 50 years of Age I shall wish & endeavour that my last sleep shall be in America.

A Friend is this moment come in, who tells me that an Article is entered on Lloyds' Book,[15] that is intended to inform the Underwriters the Algerines have fitted out Sixteen sail of Ships to cruise against the Ships belonging to the United States; if that is true & I fear 'tis too probable however humiliating the measure may appear, the most prudent step that appears to us possible for the preservation of your Trade, is to give the Pirates a *larger* Bribe than they have obtained to stimulate them to this plan of Robbery. There is every reason to believe that the Prussian Monarch sick of the disasters of the War & probably gained over by an enormously doucer is about to withdraw the greater part of his Troops from the frontier of France, but the inveteracy of our Court to the principles of Freedom will nevertheless determine them to try the fortune of another (fruitless) Campaign.[16]

Fearing that I have treaspassed too long on your valuable moments I beg leave to subscribe myself with the most profound veneration & gratitude Honoured Sir Your most obedt & very humb. Servt

Joseph Brown

N.B. You will probably Sir before the receipt of this Letter have heard that an ineffectual attempt has been made in our Ho. of Commons to stir the Governmt to interfer in behalf of your ill-fated Friend (my respectable & ⟨va⟩lued Correspondent) M. de la Fayette: Burke opposed it on the ground of his having been in Arms against this Country: whereas he saw no improperiety *formerly* in himself moving for the enlargemt of Mr Laurens, who had been a President of Congress from the Tower, & afterwards meeting him at my House, though the motion was not immediately successful.[17]

ALS, DLC:GW.

1. The letter from British publisher Joseph Brown to GW of 12 Sept. 1785 has not been found. On the creation of the "mezzotinto" prints of GW and Nathanael Greene that were sent to GW, on the portraits sent for display in the chambers of Congress, and for Brown's correspondence in 1785 and 1786 with Charles Thomson, the secretary of Congress, see the notes for GW to Brown, 30 May 1786 (*Papers, Confederation Series,* 4:84–86).

2. On GW's election to a second term as president, see n.1 of a Conversation with a Joint Committee of Congress, 9 Feb. 1793.

3. Edmond Genet was the former French minister to the United States. On the Washington administration's decision to ask the French government for Genet's recall, see Cabinet Opinion, 23 Aug. 1793. The genet is a small, catlike creature of the family *Viverridae,* which also includes civets and mongooses. The common species, *Genetta vulgaris,* is found in the south of France. It can emit a foul-smelling substance to deter its enemies.

4. The French port of Toulon was briefly controlled by the Royalist party with the aid of the British navy, but after a prolonged siege by the forces of the French republicans, the port fell on 19 Dec. 1793.

5. The edict of 6 Nov. 1793 instructed the commanders of British ships of war and privateers "That they shall stop and detain all ships laden with goods the product of any colony belonging to France, or carrying provisions or other supplies for the use of any such colony, and shall bring the same with their cargoes, to legal adjudication in our courts of admiralty." On 8 Jan. 1794 the government issued new instructions, in which the edict of 6 Nov. was revoked. These new instructions, however, contained more detailed regulations that required the capture of vessels engaged in trade with the French West Indies, thereby still leaving American shipping subject to British seizure (*ASP, Foreign Relations,* 1:430–31). Emmerich de Vattel's three-volume work on international law was published in English as *The Law of Nations; or Principles of the Law of Nature: Applied to the Conduct and to the Affairs of Nations and Sovereigns* (London, 1760).

6. William Pitt the Younger served as prime minister of Great Britain from 1783 until 1801. At this point in time, the First Coalition, composed of the kingdoms of Austria, Prussia, Sardinia, Great Britain, the Netherlands, and Spain, was actively engaged in the war with France. French victories over Austrian and Prussian forces at Wattignies on 16 Oct., Fröschwiller on 22 Dec., and Geisberg on 26 Dec. 1793 bolstered republican spirits. For a recent list of American ships detained in the West Indies, see *Philadelphia Gazette and Universal Daily Advertiser,* 11 March 1794.

7. On 3 Jan., James Madison introduced in the U.S. House of Representatives seven resolutions that were designed to create a policy of commercial retaliation against the British. For these resolutions, see *Annals of Congress*, 3d. Cong., 155–56.

8. On the intrigues of William Augustus Bowles among the Creek Indians, see the source note for the Secret Article of the Treaty with the Creeks, 4 Aug. 1790, which was enclosed in GW to the U.S. Senate, 4 Aug. 1790, and n.1 of Henry Knox to GW, 14 Nov. 1791. Bowles was arrested by the Spanish in late February 1792 and spent the next five years in a series of Spanish prisons.

9. On the British role in obtaining a truce between Portugal and Algiers, which left American shipping in the Atlantic Ocean vulnerable to seizure by the Algerines, see n.9 of Tobias Lear to GW, 4 February.

10. In a proclamation of 29 Feb. 1780, Catherine the Great of Russia helped define the concept of armed neutrality, which was then incorporated in a defensive treaty between Russia, Denmark, and Sweden that was designed to protect neutral shipping during a time of war. Other European nations later joined the League of Armed Neutrals. See Samuel Flagg Bemis, *A Diplomatic History of the United States* (rev. ed., New York, 1947), 38–41. On 25 March 1793, however, Russia and Great Britain signed a convention in which both parties agreed to stop all shipment of provisions or military supplies to French ports (Parry, *Consolidated Treaty Series*, 51:491–97; *ASP, Foreign Relations*, 1:243).

11. Charles Lennox, the third duke of Richmond, was currently a member of Pitt's cabinet and the master-general of ordnance for Great Britain.

12. The quotation is from *The Dispensary*, a mock heroic poem written by English physician and poet Sir Samuel Garth (1661–1719) and published in London in 1699.

13. Theologian, scientist, and radical thinker Joseph Priestley and his wife, Mary, left England in April 1794 for the United States, where they settled in Northumberland, Pa., for the remainder of their lives.

14. This quotation is a slight variant of a verse from the fourth epistle of *An Essay on Man*, which the English poet Alexander Pope (1688–1744) published in 1734.

15. By 1794, Lloyd's Coffee House, located in the Royal Exchange, London, no longer served coffee, but instead consisted of a society of insurance underwriters for ships and cargoes. Lloyd's eventually was incorporated by an act of Parliament in 1871.

16. Frederick William II was the current ruler of Prussia, which, as an ally of Austria, had been at war with France since 1792. Prussia, however, agreed to a separate peace with France in the Treaty of Basle, 5 April 1795.

17. The Marquis de Lafayette currently was being held prisoner by the Prussians in the fortress at Neisse in Silesia. On the recent debate in the House of Commons on whether the British government should undertake a diplomatic effort to obtain Lafayette's release from prison, see *Parliamentary History of England*, 31:28–54. Henry Laurens had been captured at sea by the British on 3 Sept. 1780 and subsequently held prisoner in the Tower of London, from 6 Oct. 1780 until 31 Dec. 1781. On Edmund Burke's presentation

of Lauren's petition for release, dated 1 Dec. 1781, to the House of Commons on 20 Dec. 1781, see *Parliamentary History of England*, 22:877–78.

Cabinet Opinion on Granting a Passport

[Philadelphia] 2 April 1794

We are of the opinion, that a passport ought to be granted for a vessel under the above restrictions.[1]

Edm: Randolph
Alex. Hamilton

I am inclined to think the vessel ought sail not only by the *permission*, but in consequence of the *directions* of the President.[2]

Wm. Bradford

The same opinion.[3]

H. Knox

DS, DNA: RG 59, Miscellaneous Letters.

This opinion appears at the bottom of a letter from Philadelphia merchant Thomas FitzSimons to Edmund Randolph of 2 April, in which he wrote: "I am among the unfortunate Merchts of the U.S. who has suffered by the depredations of the British Cruizers, a Vessell of mine with a Very Valuable Cargo having been Carryd into Bermuda on the 7th Last Month. as a No. of Vessells as well as mine were Carryd in under the instructions of the 6th November and it is more than probable those of the 8 January may not be sent there officially to prevent this Condemnation, I submit it to your Consideration Sir Whether it may not be proper to send an Express-boat to that Island for the purpose of Carrying that information . . . for if the Cargoes & Vessells are Condemned and Restitution should hereafter be decreed, the Captors will have possession of the property and will only account for it at a Valuation Less than half the Real Cost. . . . There is a further Reason which I hope may have its Weight, the Necessity the American Seamen are under of entering onboard the British privateers for want of Subsistence." To support this contention, FitzSimons enclosed a letter from a Mr. P. Hayes that was written at Bermuda the previous month. He then continued: "If permission will be given, for sending a Small Pilot boat the most satisfactory Security will be given, that no goods Wares or Merchze of any Kind or nature, Will be sent, and the boat so permitted shall bring back any American Seamen that are there. I beg the favor of you Sir to Lay this Subject before the President." For the British orders in council of 6 Nov. 1793 and 6 Jan. 1794, see *ASP, Foreign Relations*, 1:430–31.

1. This sentence is in Randolph's handwriting.

2. This sentence is in Bradford's handwriting.

3. This sentence is in Knox's handwriting. Randolph enclosed this opinion and the letter from FitzSimons in his first letter to GW of 2 April.

From Alexander Hamilton

Sir,   [Philadelphia] 2d April 1794.

Two persons have been mentioned to me as qualified & probably willing to go—one Mr Ralston, merchant;[1] the other Mr Higginson, Lawyer. The latter is supposed to be the most competent, & would probably be in all respects acceptable. I mentioned them half an hour ago to the Secy of State. Upon an enquiry of his—he prefers the latter.[2] Respectfully &c.

                                                        A. Hamilton.

LB, DLC:GW.

1. Robert Ralston (1761–1836) was a Philadelphia merchant who amassed a fortune in the East Indian trade and was known for his philanthropic activities, including large contributions to the Widows' and Children's Asylum, the Mariners' Church, and the Philadelphia Bible Society.

2. Massachusetts native Nathaniel Cabot Higginson (1768–1794) practiced law in Philadelphia, where he had married Sarah Rhea in 1792. He died at Roseau, a port city in the British colony of Dominica, in July 1794 (*Gazette of the United States* [Philadelphia], 9 Aug. 1794). Acceding to the cabinet opinion contained in Edmund Randolph's first letter to GW of this date, GW appointed Higginson a special agent assigned to the State Department. Higginson then was sent to the British West Indies to file appeals in British admiralty courts on behalf of American ships being held in those islands (GW to Hamilton, 16 April 1794; see also Hamilton to Higginson, 16 April 1794, *Hamilton Papers*, 16:288–91).

From Henry Knox

Sir.   War Department, April 2d 1794.

I submit to, you the draft of instructions prepared for Mr L'Enfant—Similar instructions were yesterday transmitted, by the post, to Mr Vincent at Brunswick, and I presume he will be to day, or to morrow morning, in New York—I also submit, the copy of a letter to Governor Clinton, by Mr Vincent.[1]

Under therefore the circumstances of the case, I respectfully submit to your consideration, whether it may not be proper for Mr L'Enfant to go forward, and make his plan, and let the person whose plan should be adopted, execute the works—If Mr L'Enfants plan should be adopted, I presume he might, without injury, be suffered to repair here, for a day or two, once or twice in the course of a month.[2] I have the honor to be Sir, most respectfully, Your obedient Servt

H. Knox.

LS, DLC:GW; LB, DLC:GW.

1. In order to implement "An Act to provide for the Defence of certain Ports and Harbors in the United States," 20 March 1794 (*Stat.* 1:345–46), the United States employed Pierre L'Enfant as a temporary engineer for the fortifications at Philadelphia and at Wilmington, Delaware. Charles Vincent, residing in New Brunswick, N.J., became the temporary engineer responsible for fortifying the harbor and city of New York. For the instructions sent by Knox, see his letters to Vincent of 1 April and to L'Enfant of 3 April, *ASP, Military Affairs,* 1:72–73, 82. Knox's letter to George Clinton has not been identified.

2. Knox's instructions to L'Enfant stated that he was "to proceed in the execution of this business, under the general directions of the Governors respectively of the States of Pennsylvania [Thomas Mifflin] and Delaware [Joshua Clayton]. . . . The choice of the ground on which the batteries and works are to be erected, together with all the combinations and effects dependent thereon, will rest upon your judgment under the directions of the Governors." For the assignment of the general oversight of this construction to the state governors, see Knox to GW, 19 March (first letter), and n.3.

From Henry Knox

Sir,   War department April 2d 1794

I have the honor to submit to your consideration the draft of a proposed letter to General Wayne.[1]

It appears that Colonel Pickering would not dislike the proposal of joining him provided the arrangements consequent upon the Post Office Bill now under consideration would permit the measure which however he doubts.[2]

If the purport of the letter should meet your approbation it may either be forwarded immediately or wait a few days under the expectation of further information from General Wayne.[3] I have the honor to be with perfect respect Your obedient servant.

H. Knox secy of war

I also submit a letter to General Wilkinson.[4]

LS, DLC:GW; LB,DLC:GW.

1. Knox enclosed his letter to Anthony Wayne of 31 March for GW's approval. Because this letter is a reply to letters written by Wayne to Knox of

15 Nov. and 4 Dec. 1793, and 10 and 18 Jan. 1794, it covers a wide variety of topics, including provisions and supplies; the apparent "little service" provided by the Kentucky volunteers, desertion among their ranks, and questions about payment for their services; and the promotion of officers. It also touched upon relations with the Indians: "If . . . it should be that the Shawanese, Miamies, Delawares and Wyandots are desirous of permanent peace it would be a most acceptable event to the President of the United States and to every class of Citizens. And as it is possible that from some motives or other such a desire on their part may exist, the instructions marked A. have been matured in order to govern your conduct, if you should hold a treaty with them. At present it is a questionable point whether Colonel [Timothy] Pickering or some other person as a Commissioner may not be sent to assist you provided the proposals should have a serious aspect." Knox informed Wayne that if the Indians prove intransigent, then the decision to move the troops forward was being left to Wayne's judgment. He then wrote that the expeditions being planned against Spanish territory by "some restless people of the frontier settlements" mandated that Wayne "immediately order as respectable a detachment as you can to take post at Fort Massac and to erect a strong redoubt and block house with some suitable cannon from Fort Washington," and he enclosed a copy of GW's proclamation of 24 March to illustrate this potential problem. He also instructed Wayne that, given the current state of U.S. relations with Great Britain, "you may see the perfect propriety of abstaining from every step or measure which could by possibility be construed into any aggression on your part against either Spain or England. If a War should ensue, timely notice will be given to you. . . ." He also assured Wayne that it was "with great pleasure, Sir, that I transmit you the approbation of the President of the United States of your conduct generally since you have had the command and more particularly for the judicious and military formation and discipline of the Troops, the precautions you appear to have taken in your advance, in your fortified camps, and in your arrangements to have full and abundant supplies of provision on hand" (Knopf, *Wayne,* 313–20).

2. The bill currently under discussion in Congress was "An Act to establish the Post-office and Post-roads within the United States," which GW approved on 8 May (*Stat.* 1:354–66). Pickering currently was serving as postmaster general under "An Act for the temporary establishment of the Post-Office," 22 Sept. 1789 (*Stat.* 1:70). GW nominated Timothy Pickering as postmaster general, under the terms of the 1794 act, in a letter to the U.S. Senate of 10 Dec. 1794 (copy, DNA: RG 46, Third Congress, 1793–95, Senate Records of Executive Proceedings, President's Messages—Executive Nominations; LB, DLC:GW).

3. GW approved Knox's draft and returned it to him this same day (*JPP,* 296). Knox probably waited to post this letter until he finished his "Private and Confidential" letter to Wayne of 3 April (Knopf, *Wayne,* 321).

4. This sentence is in Knox's handwriting. For this letter, drafted by Knox, see GW to James Wilkinson, this date.

From Edmund Randolph

[Philadelphia] April 2. 1794

The secretary of State has the honor of inclosing to the President the opinions of the gentlemen upon two cases of passports. If the President should decide in their favor, it will be a relief to the parties that they should be issued without delay.[1]

The gentlemen also agree in the propriety of Mr Higginson, a young lawyer here, being sent to the West Indies to enter the appeals. If this be agreeable to the President, E.R. will speak to him to understand his terms &c.[2]

AL, DNA: RG 59, Miscellaneous Letters; LB, DNA: RG 59, GW's Correspondence with His Secretaries of State.

1. For the cabinet's reaction to a request by Thomas FitzSimons for a passport, see the Cabinet Opinion of this date. In agreement with this opinion, GW issued a passport for the sloop *Independence* on 5 April (*JPP*, 297). The second request has not been identified.

2. On the appointment of Nathaniel C. Higginson, see Alexander Hamilton to GW, this date, and n.2. Randolph met with Higginson later this day, and the following evening Higginson wrote Randolph to accept the appointment "with a compensation in a sum not less than $2500 Dollars, admitting the term of absence to be four months only, that either all actual expences be paid or some daily & competent allowance be made for those expences together with such other incidential charges as the objects of the mission might make it necessary to incur" (DNA: RG 59, Communications from Special Agents).

From Edmund Randolph

Sir   [Philadelphia] Wednesday afternoon [2 April 1794].

The message and papers appear to me to be right. The Minister of France has certified a copy of the letter, the original of which is sealed. To say therefore that the sealed letter shall not be sent, seems to argue such a distrust of his veracity, that it would be very unkindly received. It was not the opinion of Colo. Hamilton or myself, that it should be suppressed, after this assurance was given.[1]

The sealed letter is in fact the highest original; having been written by the commission of Guadeloupe—The letter from them to Mr Genet is also original, so far as relates to me; it being that paper, from which I made the translation. I have the honor sir to be with the highest respect yr mo. ob. serv.

Edm: Randolph.

P.S. I have seen Mr Jay and General Knox. But nothing very marked or particular occurred.

ALS, DNA: RG 59, Miscellaneous Letters; LB, DNA: RG 59, GW's Correspondence with His Secretaries of State.

1. The documents under discussion in this letter have not been identified, but they may be related to Fauchet's request for a passport so that diplomatic dispatches could be sent during the recently enacted American embargo (see Randolph's first letter to Fauchet of 29 March, in n.1 of Randolph to GW, 29 March [second letter]). For the embargo, see *Stat.* 1:400.

To James Wilkinson

Sir,   United States April 2. 1794.

I have received the letter which you addressed to me, accompanied by a new map of the present theatre of War North West of the Ohio, which I consider as the best description extant of the Country to which it relates.[1]

The value of the object is greatly enhanced in my estimation by its being the production of the Officer second in the command of the American legion.

This desire of being useful in the highest degree to the service, in which you are employed, affords me great satisfaction: Nothing should have prevented my having it published, but an apprehension that an improper use may be made[2] of the information it contains in this apparently eventful moment. This apprehension however may be obviated at a future period. I am Sir[3] Your most obedt Sevant

Go: W——n

Df, DLC:GW; LB, DLC:GW. The draft, in the handwriting of a War Department clerk, was prepared by Knox and enclosed in his second letter to GW of this date.

1. Wilkinson's letter to GW and the enclosed map of the Northwest Territory have not been found.

2. A second hand struck out "had" and inserted this word on the draft.

3. At this point on the draft, a second hand struck out "I have the honor to be with great respect" before inserting the preceding three words before

the rest of the closing, and he then added the abbreviated signature to the document.

From Henry Knox

Sir   War Department April 3rd 1794
I have the honor to submit a letter from Governor Blount dated 10th March 1794. with the enclosures.[1] I have the honor to be with perfect respect Your obedient servant
H. Knox secy of war

LS, DLC:GW; LB, DLC:GW.
1. The 10 March letter to Knox from William Blount, the governor of the Southwest Territory, and its enclosures have not been identified. GW returned these documents to Knox on 4 April (*JPP*, 297).

From James McHenry

Sir.   Fayetteville [Md.] 3d April 1794
I ought to have mentioned in the letter which I took the liberty to write to you a few days since what I had then chiefly in my mind abstracted from the personal consideration of health.[1]

I thought that perhaps it might come within your view at this juncture to send a commissioned person to Vienna to solicit the release of Mr la Fayette with powers to proceed to France on a like errand in favor of his wife and children, in order that the whole might be removed to this country.[2]

I perceive by the act of Congress for discharging his pay during the war the new obligation you have laid up on your unfortunate friend.[3] If it is possible to go beyond pecuniary aid, or so far as to restore him to liberty and his family how would he rejoice to owe that blessing to the man he affectionates most upon earth; and what sublime pleasure to me to be an humble instrument in its accomplishment. The friendship he has always expressed for me; the friendship I feel for him; a conviction of the patriotism of his principles and purity of his motives; the esteem in which he is still held by America; a remembrance of the moment and his youth when he embarked in our cause, and the services he rendered it in the course of our revolution, all conspire to make such a project peculiarly interesting to the feeling heart: at the same time, Sir, you must be sensible, you who on former occasions have not deemed me unworthy some portion of your confidence, that such a mission would reflect upon you its author, and from whom alone it ought to proceed, as long as exalted friendship shall be ranked among the virtues, a lustre which philosophy must delight to contemplate and history to diffuse among mankind for their benefit or instruction. The friendship of Achilles for his dear Patroclus, as celebrated by Homer, has survived the fate of empires and the charges of time, as if destined to serve as a perpetual monument sacred to friendship.[4] May not another Homer arise to consign yours for Fayette to equal immortality, and tears of pleasure flow at its recital like an exhaustless stream through the long period of future ages.

But if all this should prove no more than a dream of friendship, I hope for the sake of the object, that you will excuse the dreamer for troubling you with his vision,[5] who be assured when awake, is and has always been affectionately and truly your most obt & hble st

James McHenry

ALS, DLC:GW; ADfS, DLC: James McHenry Papers.
  1. See McHenry's letter to GW of 31 March.
  2. The Marquis de Lafayette currently was being held by the Prussians in the fortress at Neisse in the province of Silesia, and the Marquise de Lafayette was incarcerated in a prison at Brioude, France.
  3. "An Act allowing to Major General La Fayette his pay and emoluments while in the service of the United States," 27 March 1794, granted Lafayette $24,424 for his service during the Revolutionary War (*Stat.* 6:14).
  4. On the friendship between the mythical Greek heroes Achilles and Patroclus, see the *Iliad,* an ancient Greek epic poem attributed to Homer.
  5. McHenry did not receive a special commission to negotiate Lafayette's freedom. For a personal attempt by GW to obtain Lafayette's release from prison, see his letter to Frederick William II of Prussia of 15 January. Lafayette, however, remained incarcerated until 1797.

From Edmund Randolph

Thursday [3 April 1794].
  E. Randolph has the honor of sending to the President in another parcel three letters from Mr Pinckney.[1] A large bundle has

arrived from Mr Short; many of which are triplicates; the others are probably interesting; but the whole have been in salt water are barely legible yet, and in some instances will require to be decyphered.[2]

Copy, DNA: RG 59, Miscellaneous Letters; LB, DNA: RG 59, GW's Correspondence with His Secretaries of State.

1. The brief cover letter from Thomas Pinckney to the secretary of state of 26 Dec. 1793 enclosed the British order of 6 Nov. 1793, which instructed the commanders of British ships of war and privateers "That they shall stop and detain all ships laden with goods the product of any colony belonging to France, or carrying provisions or other supplies for the use of any such colony, and shall bring the same with their cargoes, to legal adjudication in our courts of admiralty." His letter of 2 Jan. 1794 reported on his inability to meet with Lord Grenville, the British foreign secretary, in order to obtain an "explanation" of these instructions.

Pinckney's letter to Randolph of 9 Jan. contained a report on his recent conversation with Grenville and enclosed another set of orders, dated 8 Jan., which announced the revocation of the orders of 6 Nov. and substituted new restrictions on trade with the French West Indies. Pinckney expressed the U.S. position "that we did not admit the right of the belligerent powers to interfere farther in the commerce between neutral nations & their adversaries, than to prevent their carrying to them articles which by common usage were ⟨de⟩emed contraband & any articles to a place fairly blockaded." Grenville assured Pinckney that it "was the sincere desire of the Administration ⟨to⟩ maintain the best understanding & harmony with the United States." All three letters and the enclosed copies of the British instructions are in DNA: RG 59, Despatches from U.S. Ministers to Great Britain; see also DNA: RG 46, Third Congress, 1793–95, Senate Records of Legislative Proceedings, President's Messages and *ASP, Foreign Relations*, 1:430–31. GW submitted these letters and their enclosures with his letter to Congress of 4 April.

2. A letter from William Carmichael and William Short, U.S. commissioners to Spain, to Randolph of 7 Jan. and two letters from Short to Randolph of 9 and 17 Jan. were given to GW at some time before 7 April, when GW returned them to Randolph (*JPP*, 297–98). The letter of 7 Jan. discussed their problems in pursuing negotiations with Spain, particularly on the subject of the American right to free navigation of the Mississippi River (*ASP, Foreign Relations*, 1:440–42). The letter of 9 Jan. reviewed the effects of the current European war on diplomacy, while the letter of 17 Jan. contained a chart showing ships that entered the Bay of Cadiz in 1793 and the value of the gold and silver brought in them, and another chart showing the prices of wheat in Spain during January 1793 and January 1794. For the two letters from Short, and the enclosed charts, see DNA: RG 59, Despatches from U.S. Ministers to Spain; see also *ASP, Foreign Relations*, 1:442–45. GW submitted these letters and their enclosures with his letter to U.S. Senate and House of Representatives, 15 April.

To the United States Senate

United States 3d april 1794

Gentlemen of the Senate,

I nominate Albion Cox, to be Assayer for the Mint of the United States.[1]

Go. Washington

LB, DLC:GW.

1. Albion Cox had been working as the assayer for the U.S. Mint on a temporary basis since the spring of 1793 (*JPP,* 141). The Senate approved Cox's appointment on 4 April, and GW signed his commission on 5 April (*U.S. Senate Executive Journal,* 1:149; *JPP,* 297).

From Benevolence

Sir   Connecticut Apr. 4th 1794

I have lately travelld through the N. England States Vermont—&c. The Generale topick was the times but principally the Sufferings of our Citizens among the Algerines—At Several places the Generale wish was that the President Would Issue his proclamation for a generale Contribution for their Relief—I heard one farmer Say he would give 5 Guinies another 2. no person said under a Dollar.[1]

Upon the principles of Compassion I have thus made Bold to write you I am myself an Obscure Charactor, & I would not Even wish to Dictate the President, But if I am in the Wrong, it must be imputed to my Feelings.

however I am Confident that if the President Should only Issue his proclamation Ordering it to be Read preparatory one week in all Religious Assemblys in the Union that a Prodigious Sum would be Raised Voluntarily—if any thing will touch the feelings of mankind that will—I will give 10 Guinies now sir if this Aynominus letter will be Recd & the proclamation Comes forth I will do all in my power to promote it[2]—I have no Relation Neither acquantance among the Prisoners. I am Sir—a True Friend & Republican

Benevolence

ALS, DNA: RG 59, Consular Despatches, Algiers. There is no inside address or cover for this letter.

1. On the efforts of U.S. commissioner David Humphreys to relieve the suffering of the American captives in Algiers and to obtain their eventual release, see his letters to the secretary of state of 19 and 23 Nov. and 25 Dec. 1793, and 30 Jan. 1794, and the enclosures to these letters, in *ASP, Foreign Relations*, 1:413–23.

2. Although GW did not issue the desired proclamation, civic and religious groups collected money for the "relief and redemption of all American captives in *Algiers*" (see "Theatrical" and Samuel Haven to "Mr. Printer," *Columbian Centinel* [Boston], 17 May and 11 June).

From William Jackson

Paris, April 4th 1794.

France, at this moment, exhibits such scenes as the pencil of Salvator Rosa would have been well employed to delineate—abounding in light and shade, which is at once splendid and awful.[1]

To use the language of a living Artist, and One fonder of gilding than Salvator, France is, in truth, "an armed Nation." Her exertions and firmness seem well proportioned to the resistance, which her situation requires, and far exceed the expectations, which our limited acquaintance with the power and resources of such a Nation, resolved to be free, could have excited.

No longer resembling Venus attended by the Graces, She now represents Minerva followed by the Fates.[2] You must pardon this imagery—it is really necessary to convey an idea of facts, or to describe the change, which has here taken place—indeed, it is only by what, in common parlance, would be accounted extravagant hyperbole, that One can express the situation of this most extraordinary people.

Wherever you move, or to whatever quarter your attention is turned, nothing meets the view but warlike preparation. Every consideration is sacrificed to public exigence, every contribution of property or service, which the public necessity requires appears to be cheerfully made—and in the few instances, where reluctance may exist, terror supplies the absence of patriotism, and operates its full effect.

Age and infancy are employed in extracting from the earth, and, by a late refinement in chemistry, from vegetables, the thunders, which youth and manhood are to direct, while the cares of domestic life are altogether devolved on the female part of the Society.

Fifteen armies, forming a force, which I do not think exaggerated, of twelve hundred thousand men, are now in the actual service of the Republic—and it has been surmised that a part of the second requisition would be made before the opening of the campaign—Should this additional effort be deemed necessary, the coalesced nations of Europe must unquestionably yield to the momentum of an individual power, exceeding in numbers and array all that the world has hitherto exhibited.

Perplexed by the variety of interesting objects, which attract my attention, I am really at a loss where to begin in giving you the details of these formidable and stupendous preparations.

The first requisition has been carried into complete effect— that is to say, all the unmarried men of this extensive nation, from the age of eighteen to twenty five years, whatever their situation or fortune (for neither money nor substitutes would exempt them from service) have joined the several armies of the Republic, which they have augmented with Six hundred thousand. These levies have been incorporated with the ancient Corps, and have been under a strict discipline for several months.

The Cavalry has been so considerably encreased as to require that the swords, exceeding thirty inches in blade, should be taken from the Infantry for their use. The augmentation is upwards of fifty thousand—and the remounted exceeds thirty thousand⟨.⟩ The whole force in Cavalry being at least One hundred thousand. So that in this arm, which, during the last campaign, was the weakest part of their composition, I am persuaded the french will be superior to the combined forces.

The artillery, so formidable in the last campaign, has received an addition of Two thousand pieces, for field service, and, judging from its former effect, must, I think, be absolutely irresistible.

The fuel, which is to nourish this immense volcano, is, as I have already intimated to you, prepared by those hands, which are otherwise unable to serve their country; and, under the direction of persons well skilled in the process, saltpetre is produced in astonishing quantity[3]—I have daily opportunity of observing its product in the several sections of Paris, and the operation is the same throughout the Republic.

The public founderies and manufactories of small arms, aided by the mechanics, who work in metals, and who, for this purpose, are all in requisition, are constantly employed, and furnish immensely.

And yet, amidst all this din and preparation of arms, the Country more carefully and extensively cultivated than in any former period. You will ask by whom? By old men, by women, and the youth of both sexes, under the age of eighteen years.

This I can assure you, from personal observation, wherever I have travelled not a single spot is neglected—The very avenues and approaches to the Chateaux are ploughed—even walks in the gardens of the Tuilleries are sown and planted[4]—and no Country presents a more promising appearance, in agriculture, than France does at this moment.

It has become a public care, with the several municipalities, to plant those grounds, which were formerly appropriate to pleasurable purposes, with useful vegetables, and, to this end, regular institutions are established.

The value of the potatoe is known, and sufficiently appreciated to remove every apprehension of want. Indeed so promising is the grain now in the ground, that I am persuaded, from my information of the present state of their granaries, the quantity on hand and the ensuing crop, will furnish an advance of provision for at least two years.

You may be assured the idea of starving France is as unfounded as it is unworthy—The variety of soil and climate, in this extensive country, reduces the chance of a general failure in their crops, to a very remote possibility—And the invigorating energies of property and freedom have more than balanced the deductions from their agriculture, occasioned by the call of their Peasantry to the frontiers. Indeed a very considerable proportion of their farming was always done by the women of France, who still continue to cultivate the ground.

Take a single illustration of my supposition that their Granaries are well stocked—The price of bread in Paris, at this time, is not half as much as in London. True it is brown, but it is equally nutritious.

Extensive manufactures of useful fabrics continue to flourish—and even the most refined articles of luxury are not neglected.

Of the former, I have attentively observed the cloth-manufacture at Abbeville, which is in vigour—and of the latter I have visited the Eobelius, where the most exquisite productions of the needle and the shuttle, still continue to charm and astonish. This last is continued as a public establishment.[5]

Even the palaces and pleasure grounds of the ci-devant royalty are respected as national property, and, as such, are carefully preserved.

The greater part of the furniture has been removed from Versailles—some of the paintings remain. Those by the best Masters have been sent to the Gallery of the Louvre, which is now the National Museum, where the collection greatly exceeds any other exhibition of the fine arts in the world. It is under the care of a Committee, appointed to protect the arts, and is maintained in the most superb style. Such is the war, which these Goths and Vandals wage against the arts!

The late Queens favorite residence of St Cloud remains as when She occupied it.[6] The paintings will be sent to the Museum, and the furniture will be sold.

In remarking on the agriculture and manufactur⟨e⟩s I have digressed from the subject of the public force⟨,⟩ to which I return.

The operations of the northern army appear to engage the greatest degree of attention, and from its composition, as well as its situation, this part of their force seems destined to the most arduous service.

Including the detachments on the side of Dunquerque, and the garrisons, which, without hazard to their posts, may be called into field service with the main body, I do not suppose this army amounts to less than Two hundred and fifty four thousand men, composed nearly as follows

Brigaded Infantry	170,000.
Light Corps	20,000
Cavalry	44,000
Brigaded artillery	15,000
Artillery attached to Corps	5,000
	254,000

In addition to this immense force, no less formidable by the decided superiority of their artillery, the improved state of their arms, discipline, and œconomical arrangements of supplies, than by their numbers—The armies of the Moselle and Ardennes may, by rapid movements to their left, be brought into full co-operation, and at very short notice, with the army of the north—for experience has demonstrated that they are capable of forming these sudden junctions, by transporting their troops in carriages.

That they are disposed to effect, whatever a profuse application of money can accomplish, must be admitted—and that the means are in their power cannot be denied.

Their treasury is, at this time, by far the richest in Europe—perhaps more abundant than all the rest of Europe. And, immoderate as their expenditure appears, the sources of their supplies seem but to increase with the streams that flow from them—The taxes, that are collected, with the donations, crown and church property, and money received for Emigrants estates form altogether an inordinate mass.

On this subject, also, it is fair to remark that the Persons, who direct their fiscal arrangements, have been long enough in office to give to them all the advantages, which result from method and established order. Of this a very strong proof was lately given by Cambon, in his report on the State of their finances: He therein asserts (which he dared not to do without foundation) that a diminution, of One hundred and seventy millions of livres per month, had been made in their disbursements, leaving the actual expenditure about fifty four millions sterling ⅌ annum.[7]

Enormous as this sum may appear, it is not immoderate compared with their resources—for, however extraordinary, it is true that, including the estates of the Crown, the Clergy, and the Emigrants⟨,⟩ at least one third part of the whole property of France is in confiscation. Such had been the tendency of the ancient regime to absorb, and concentrate the national wealth in the hands of the few!

This fact is well understood by the men of property, who are now in France, and the reflections which arise from it, have fully decided them to go with the revolution, and to support it at all hazards. They are now aware of the worst that can happen to them under the Republic, and they know full well that the confiscated property is more than competent to the expences that have been, or may be, incurred to maintain the war—Whereas a counter-revolution would not only place the expences of the war to their charge as holders of the public Securities but prostrate the residue of their property to the indemnity of those, who have emigrated.

These influential considerations of property, by which the more wealthy part of the people, now in France, are actuated, aided by the enthusiasm of some, the fears of others, and the resentments of all, against their external enemies, have not only subdued all spirit of revolt, and condensed the public opinion in favor of the revolution, but appear to me to have decided the nation, literally to adhere to their declaration "to live free or die."

This reasoning may seem on first view to be too positive—but, compared with facts, and analysed by the test of experience, I am persuaded, and I venture to predict, it will be found true in every result.

I would now state the respective strength and composition of the other armies of the Republic—but, as their operations are not likely to be equally interesting or decisive with that of the north, I have been at less pains to obtain particular information respecting them. That which is intended to act against Spain will, I think, be the next efficient in force, and impressive in its operations.

The direction of the military measures of the Republic are said to be confided to a Committee of Officers, of high professional talents and distinguished service. Two of them, it is thought, will go to the army of the North—The others will remain at Paris.

Besides this Board of Officers, there are Commissioners from the Convention, with each of the Armies, who superintend the œconomy of the staff-arrangements and watch over their supplies.

A controuling authority, that may be termed almost unlimited, is vested in the Committee of Public safety, which is composed of the following Members, classed according to the influence, which, I think, they respectively possess.

Robespierre, Billaud de Varennes, St Just, Couthon, Collot d'Herbois, Jean Bon St André, Barerre, Carnot, Lindet, and Prieur.[8]

Robespierre is certainly the apex of this pyramid—Barerre, in point of talents, may, I think, be considered as one of its ablest supports—Lindet, whose application is even distinguished

where all are unremitting, is the Member, to whom the department of subsistence is devolved—St Just is very eloquent and
popular with the Convention—Jean Bon St André has been selected for his energy of character to regenerate the marine; and
is now at Brest, Billaud de Varennes and Carnot, it is said, are
to go to the army of the North—Couthon and Collot d'Herbois
are very influential with the popular assemblies—Prieur is less
distinguished than either of his Colleagues.

The removal of Danton, La Croix, and the other Deputies,
who were executed with them—and the extinction of Heberts
party, will give a stability to the power of this all-influential Body,
which nothing will be able to shake—and will enable them to
call forth the resources of this inexhaustible people—and to direct the application of them, if possible, more efficiently than
they have even yet done.[9]

Since the recovery of Toulon the marine has obtained
great attention, and will, it is said, within a short time, be very
respectable.[10]

Regulations for the government of the navy, calculated to in-
vigorate the discipline, have been lately enacted by the Convention, and are now in force. Every sea-faring person, including
the fishermen, are in requisition for public service.

Viewed in the light I have here placed it, the picture of France
is pleasing and splendid. But there are shades, which abstract
from its beauty, and which a regard to truth makes necessary to
confess and to expose.

Proceeding less from native defect than from accident, they
may be greatly softened, perhaps be entirely removed.

In a course of conquest, it is to be apprehended that the lust
of dominion may lead this People, already the happiest nation
on the globe, in geographical position, to grasp at possessions,
which, far from encreasing, would eventually abridge their
power and their happiness.

The retention of Savoy I regard as a decided affair, and ir-
revocable—and unless negociations for peace are soon entered
upon, I should consider the annexation of Austrian Flanders,
and the Dutchy of Luxembourg, to the french Republic, as neither improbable nor remote.[11]

This conquest, should it be made, (and that a nation of twenty
eight millions of People, situated as the french are, becoming a

nation of Soldiers, should, within a very short period, atchieve whatever conquest they attempt, is but too probable)—This conquest, I say, may be more susceptible of restitution in exchange for her Islands[12]—but even that, I think, would be problematic, as, with the extension of her territory, her other means of obtaining their restoration must be dangerously encreased.

This is a case for the consideration of those, whom I have neither the power nor the wish to influence; but I am satisfied, from what I see and know, that more political reflection ought immediately to attach to it, than they to whom it is most interesting seem disposed to bestow upon it.

As inauspicious to the happiness of France, and the peace of Europe, I can only regret and deprecate the near possibility of such an event.

The difficulty of organising the government of France, after peace, would form a darker shade than it does, but for the reflection that the constitution is already prepared—that the nomination to office, and the knowledge, which qualifies to select characters, would be almost exclusively in the possession of the Comité de Salut Public—and that a long continuance in office has already designated the individuals for the offices, which they ought respectively to fill. This is nevertheless a source of serious apprehension, as it regards the internal tranquillity of France, and will be deserving of all the attention, which philosophy and philanthropy can bestow upon it.

To the assuasive touch of time we must refer the obliteration of those remembrances, which may nourish individual resentments, for some years to come. They will not extend beyond the present generation—perhaps they will be extinguished with the war, which occasioned them.

It is however to be confessed and lamented that they cloud the prospect.

W. Jackson

ALS (retained copy), PHi: Society Collection. The docket reads: Original Copy letter Major William Jackson to General Washington Which Major Jackson Cut out of his Copybook and handed to ⟨illegible⟩ on March 17th 1810."

1. On William Jackson's presence in France, see Certificate for William Jackson, 12 June 1793, and n.3. Italian painter Salvator Rosa (1615–1673) was known for his romantic landscapes, marine paintings, and pictures of battle scenes.

2. This probably is a reference to the 1486 painting by Sandro Botticelli (c.1445–1510) entitled "Venus and the Graces Offering Gifts to a Young Girl." Minerva was the Roman goddess of war.

3. Saltpeter is the common name used for the chemical compound potassium nitrate, which is used as an oxidizing component in gunpowder.

4. The Tuileries Palace was located on the right bank of the Seine River in Paris. Although it was destroyed in 1871, its extensive gardens are still maintained today. It served as the headquarters for the assemblies, conventions, and councils that governed France from 1789 until 1798, and later as the official residence of Napoleon Bonaparte.

5. The town of Abbeville, located on the Somme River in northeastern France, was home to the Van Robias textile mills.

6. The royal Château de Saint-Cloud, overlooking the Seine River at Saint-Cloud in the Hauts-de-Seine *département,* was a favorite residence of Queen Marie-Antoinette.

7. On the report of Pierre-Joseph Cambon (1756–1820), the chair of the Finance Committee, see *Le Moniteur Universal* (Paris), 24 March.

8. The *Comité de Salut Public,* or committee of public safety, included Maximilien-François-Marie-Isidore de Robespierre (1758–1794), Jacques-Nicolas Billaud-Varenne (1756–1819), Louis-Antoine-Lèon Florelle de Saint-Just (1767–1794), Georges-Auguste Couthon (1755–1794), Jean-Marie Collot d'Herbois (1749–c.1796), Jean-Bon Saint-André (1749–1813), Bertrand de Barère de Vieuzac (1755–1841), Lazare-Nicolas-Marguerite Carnot (1753–1823), Jean-Baptiste-Robert Lindet (1746–1825), and Prieur de la Marne (Pierre-Louis Prieur; 1756–1827).

9. Newspaper publisher Jacques-René Hébert (1755–1794) and eighteen of his supporters were guillotined on 24 March, but Georges-Jacques Danton (1759–1794) and Jean-François Delacroix (Lacroix; 1753–1794) were not executed until 5 April.

10. The French port of Toulon was under the control of the Royalists from late August 1793 until a prolonged siege by the forces of the French republicans forced its surrender on 19 Dec. 1793.

11. Savoy, located on the southeastern border of France, was annexed in 1792. The Austrian Netherlands, or Belgium, was annexed in 1795 by a vote of the National Convention on 1 October. The Grand Duchy of Luxembourg came under French rule in 1795. French control of all three territories ended with the fall of Napoleon in 1814.

12. On the British seizure of French colonies in the West Indies, 1793–94, see n.3 of Edward Newenham to GW, 8 March.

From Henry Knox

Sir   [Philadelphia] 4h April 1794

Capt. Williamson who is settled in the Genesee Country has given me the enclosed intelligence,[1] and in a subsequent conversation which I have had with him he seems impressed with the

Authenticity of the speech of Lord Dorchester, and also of his general ill dispositions towards this Country.[2] I am sir respectfully Your humble Servant

H. Knox

ALS, DLC:GW; LB, DLC:GW.

1. Charles Williamson (1757–1808), a native of Scotland, came to the United States in 1791 as the land agent for a London investment group known as Pulteney Associates. Most of this company's land lay in the present-day New York counties of Allegany, Livingston, and Monroe, all of which incorporated a portion of the Genesee River, and the counties of Schuyler, Steuben, Wayne, and Yates. Williamson became a U.S. citizen in 1792, and by 1793 he was a resident of Ontario County, where he was active in local politics. He later represented Steuben County in the state assembly, 1796–1800. The enclosed intelligence has not been identified.

2. For the speech given by Lord Dorchester on 10 Feb., see n.2 of George Clinton's letter to GW of 20 March.

To Henry Knox

Sir,   Philadelphia 4th Apl 1794

Your letter of this date, enclosing one from Captn Williamson, is received. I have never entertained any doubt myself of the genuineness of the Speech which is published as Lord Dorchester's; nor of the intentions of the B—— Government to keep this Country in a state of disquietude With the Indian nations; and also to alter the boundary between them and us, if, by any means, they can effect it.

For this reason, I repeat in this manner, what I have two or three times done before, verbally, that Genl Chapin should be instructed to leave no means unessayed to keep the Six Nations well disposed towards the U.S.—and to buy Captn B——t off at almost any price.[1] Captn Williamson affords, I presume, a Safe conveyance to him Yrs &ca

Go. Washington

ALS, sold (1973) by Kenneth W. Rendell, Inc., catalog 86, item 155, p. 67; ADfS, DLC:GW; LB, DLC:GW.

1. Israel Chapin, Sr., served as the U.S. Indian agent to the Iroquois Indians. Mohawk leader Joseph Brant, who had fought on the side of the British during the Revolutionary War, was involved in the U.S. attempt to negotiate a peace treaty with the Indians in the Northwest Territory (Knox to Tobias Lear, 19 July 1793, n.1, and Knox to GW, 10 Aug. 1793, n.1).

From David Stuart

Dear Sir,   Alexa. [Va.] April 4th 1794

Coll Little & Mr Minor have just informed me, that the trespasses committed on your land near Alexa., have much exceeded this winter what has been usual in that way—that the hoop timber of which there was a good deal is entirely gone—that, as if it was not enough to get fire wood without molestation from it, it has now become a practice to cut down & carry off the best timber trees—On asking Coll: Little's opinion on the best mode of preventing such practices in future—he observed, that Mr Minor who lived convenient to the land, would be the most proper person to give an eye to it; and that he was sure he would do it at your desire.[1]

I then applied to Mr Minor to know whether he would or not; his reply was, that he would do it with pleasure if it was your desire—From my knowledge of Mr Minor, I really think him the most proper person you can employ for the purpose, as he lives very near if not adjoining to the land; and is very active and stirring.[2]

I expect it is no news to you to be informed, that our small grain at present, has but a bad appearance.

I have just recieved a letter from Mr Macrae of Georgia formerly an inhabitant of this place, requesting me to mention him to you as a Candidate for the office lately filled by Mr Forsyth in that State—From the impression, that you will be aided in making your appointment, from the variety of characters presented to you; I take the liberty of recommending him to your consideration—He was much respected in this place, as an intelligent honest man.[3] I am Dr: Sr, with the greatest respect Your Affecte: Serv:

Dd: Stuart

ALS, DLC:GW.

1. For earlier problems with timber being removed from GW's land on the north side of Four Mile Run and for Charles Little's attempt to assist GW in preventing such trespasses, see GW to Bushrod Washington, 8 Jan. 1792, and notes. Fairfax County resident George Minor also owned a large tract near Four Mile Run. The flexible stems of the hoop-ash, *Fraxinus sambucifolia*, were used to make barrel hoops.

2. For GW's request for assistance from Minor, see his letter to Minor of 13 April; see also GW's reply to Stuart of 13 April.

3. The letter from former Alexandria merchant Robert McCrea to Stuart has not been identified, but for a letter recommending McCrea's appointment as the new U.S. marshal for Georgia, see James McHenry to GW, 18 February. On the death of Robert Forsyth, the former marshal, see n.1 of James Hendricks to GW, 15 January. Stuart's recommendation of McCrea arrived too late for GW's consideration (see GW to U.S. Senate, 5 March 1794).

To the United States Senate and House of Representatives

United States 4 April 1794.
Gentlemen of the Senate, and of the House of Representatives.

I lay before you three letters from our Minister in London;[1] advices concerning the Algierine Mission, from our Minister at Lisbon and others;[2] and a letter from the Minister Plenipotentiary of the French Republic to the Secretary of State, with his answer.[3]

Go: Washington

LS, DNA: RG 46, Third Congress, 1793–95, Senate Records of Legislative Proceedings, President's Messages; LB, DNA: RG 233, Third Congress, 1793–95, House Records of Legislative Proceedings, Journals; Df, DNA: RG 59, Reports of the Secretary of State to the President and Congress; LB, DLC:GW.

1. For the letters from Thomas Pinckney, see Randolph to GW, 3 April, and n.1.

2. For the letters from David Humphreys, see Randolph to GW, 1 April, and n.1 to that document.

3. Fauchet's letter to Randolph of 27 March was a response to complaints about the French embargo imposed on the port of Bordeaux (see Randolph to GW, 19 March [first letter], and n.6). For this letter and Randolph's response of 3 April, see DNA: RG 46, Third Congress, 1793–95, Senate Records of Legislative Proceedings, President's Messages; *ASP, Foreign Relations*, 1:431–32.

From Burgess Ball

Dear sir,   Leesburg [Va.]--5th Apl 94.

The Clover Seed & Chocolate Shells came safe to Hand yesterday[1]—I recd yours of the 23d ult. on the same day, wherein you seem to despond abt the Buckwheat; but I'm happy now to inform you that, with 98. Bush: which went off today, I have deliver'd 454½ Bush:, which I hope is in full time for sowing— The Ball: of 44½ Bush. shall be sent down in the Course of the running of the Fish; and, as I expect you intend to keep some to sow in the proper Season to make Seed for another year, I hope this Ball: will not be so immediately wanting[2]—I have wrote to Mr Pearce, informing him of this Arrangement, and that I shall want for my own use a considerable quantity of Fish for which I will settle with him, or, be accountable for in the Settlement of the Buckwheat with you.[3] I am sorry I have it not in my power to embrace the kind offer of sendg a mare to one of the Jacks, as I have not one in the World, but hope by another Season I shall.[4] War, in this part of the Country is the general Topic, and, I think never were People more united than at present, in shewing their Contempt for the Brittish. Miss Milly & Sammy have just arrived among us, and unite with Fanny & myself in best respects & good Wishes for you & Family,[5] & I am Dr sir yr Affect. Hbe. st

B: Ball

ALS, DLC:GW.
  1. On GW's shipment of the clover seed and chocolate, see his letter to Ball of 16 March.
  2. On Ball's promise to provide buckwheat sccd for GW, see his letter to GW of 21 January.
  3. Ball's letter to William Pearce, GW's estate manager, has not been identified.
  4. On GW's offer of the stud services of one of his jackasses, see GW to Ball, 16 March.
  5. Mildred Gregory Washington, a frequent guest of her sister Frances Washington Ball, was accompanied on this visit by her brother Samuel Washington.

From Alexander Hamilton

Philada April 5. 1794.

The Secretary of the Treasury presents his respects to the President & encloses the draft of a Passport for the vessel of Mr Fitzsimons which he understands the President had agreed to give. Mr Fitzsimons states that there will be on board, 8 barrels bread, 3 bbls Beef, 1 bbl Pork & 1 barrel hams. all the articles but the last are understood to be intended for the subsistence of such of our seamen as may incline to come in the vessel—the barrel of hams destined for a present.[1]

The vessel only waits it is said for the Passport.[2]

LB, DLC:GW.

1. On the request by Thomas FitzSimons for a passport for the sloop *Independence* to sail to Bermuda and the purpose of this trip, see the source note for the Cabinet Opinion of 2 April.

2. GW issued the desired passport on 5 April (*JPP*, 297).

From Henry Knox

Sir   Philadelphia 5th April 1794

I beg leave respectfully to submit as my opinion that General Chapin should be authorised to offer Captain Brant, an Annuity for life, a sum not less than One thousand nor more than one thousand five hundred Dollars, agreable to the tenor of the letter herewith submitted to General Chapin. If this letter sir should receive your approbation Captain Williamson will undertake to deliver it safely.[1] I have the honor to be sir Your obedient Servant

H. Knox.

ALS, DLC:GW; LB, DLC:GW.

1. Knox's letter to Israel Chapin, Sr., of this date, which has not been identified, was written in response to the instructions contained in GW's letter to Knox of 4 April. GW wrote Knox later this day that "The Letter appears to me to be very proper, but Genl Chapins negotiations with the Six Nations ought to be apart from British Agents or Spies—I mean with the chiefs— otherwise they can come to nothing" (ALS, NNGL: Knox Papers; Df, DLC: GW; LB, DLC:GW). On the unsuccessful efforts by the War Department and its agents to bribe the Mohawk chief Joseph Brant, see Kelsay, *Brant,* 472, and Cruikshank, *Simcoe Papers,* 2:116. On Charles Williamson's presence in Philadelphia, see Knox to GW, 4 April.

From John Francis Mercer

Sir   Philadelphia, April. 5th 94.

I have been delayd unexpectedly in the receit of Money which I had a right to expect here, & am now called home by an express giving me very disagreable news from my family[1] I therefore enclose you the order on Mr Jones for one half the Rents of 92 & 93 & consider myself engaged that they shall produce you 56£ V⟨iga⟩ Cur., & Interest or be liable therefor.[2] I am respectfully Yr Ob. hle Ser.

John F. Mercer

ALS, DLC:GW.

1. Mercer, who resided in Anne Arundel County, Md., was in Philadelphia to attend the current session of Congress. The family crisis has not been identified, but it evidently prompted his resignation from Congress on 13 April 1794.

2. The enclosed copy of a letter from Mercer to Benjamin W. Jones was written at Philadelphia on this date. It reads: "The President of the United States having agreed with me for the purchase of a moiety of the tract of Land in Montgomery County called Woodstock Manor, in the year 1792, became thereby entitled to receive the rents accruing that year. You'll therefore account with him for one half of the rents of 1792 & 1793, and I suppose he will give such orders respecting the future disposition of his Land as will render any farther attention, to the part purchased by him, unnecessary on the part of Mr Sprigg or those claiming under him" (DLC:GW). The docket reads, "Please to pay the contents of the within order to Colo. Willm Deakins. signed. G. Washington." GW enclosed this letter in one to William Deakins, Jr., of 11 April.

From John Nicholas

Sir   Sunday [6 April 1794]

In a crisis like the present nothing can require apology which may proceed from patriotism. The object of my letter may perhaps induce a suspicion that I am governed by party views, but when I disclaim the influence of numbers I may expect so far to escape imputation as to leave my opinions in their just force—I claim your attention from the motive which determined me to make this address rather than promote the united expression of a sentiment, common to many, which might have wounded your feelings and in the end committed your reputation—whatever may be my reception I hold it a duty to proceed under an impression that your information of the public opinion must be partial & that to forbear would be to expose you to censure for a conduct which may be proper in the supposed state of things.

It is rumoured in the city that you are about to send an Envoy to the court of Great Britain and that your choice will probably fall on the Secretary of the treasury[1]—You will pardon me for saying that the measure in itself is improper because unnecessary and that when connected with the instrument it bodes infinite mischief to yourself and your country.

I consider the measure as improper in the present state of things because they are liable to change at the will of the legislature & your own and the public dignity would be involved in the revocation of his authority—I cannot conceive it to be practicable to make a special mission which will not be liable to this fate, for I cannot conceive it be possible that Congress will adjourn without doing something which will no longer leave it optional with Great Britain to do us justice—If a measure of this sort should be adopted the mission will be improper because America will be the most convenient place for settling our losses & it is most honorable for us to extort in appearance as well as reality, the compensation we claim—If the operation of the measure is limited by law to the time when the British Court shall engage to make satisfaction, it is presumed that no executive declaration will be necessary on that subject & that, aided by the law the national honor will rest safely on our present minister[2]—When ostensible reasons fail for any measure secret ones will be sought after & these will be found in those subjects on which the public are most jealous and for which the appointed instrument will be most solicitous—at all events, with so little appearance of necessity, you must expect to incur the blame of every exceptionable act of his whether authorized or not.

I confess myself astonished to hear the nomination which is made for this office—at a time when perhaps more than half America have determined it to be unsafe to trust power in the hands of this person however remotely it is connected with many of the odious traits in his character—at a time when at least one half the legislature are afraid to exert themselves in the most trying situation of their country, lest his present powers should enable him to wrest them to purposes which he is supposed by them to entertain & which they dread more than the open attack of Great Britain—at a time when this person is the avowed friend of Great Britain in the most infamous contest, when all his measures have tended to throw this country into her arms & many entertain suspicion with some grounds that the present hostility of that country to this is partly intended to aid his well known attachment to it—to appoint him to an office in which he could immediately & successfully advance his purposes would be to stake the American happiness on the justice of one of two opinions where both are advocated by equal numbers—every man in a republic is a centinel on public safety and the warnings of danger should [be] listened to rather than the assurances of

safety from the importance of the consequences which may follow—I confess my expectation was of a very different kind, that
he who was elected to office by the love of the people would not
exercise his power to the destruction of their happiness & is it
less when he who is suffered to shares most of the authority of
the government is suspected of undermining the public happiness—I may be told that these suspicions are groundless and that
an equal number of men in America are strongly attached to
him—both may be true & yet the injury remain unimpaired—if
there are deep rooted prejudices which visibly gain strength is it
not inhuman to continually resist them—if children are afraid
of hobgoblins is it not unwise and cruel to cherish and alarm
their fears—it is immaterial what is the truth unless it can be
conveyed to our minds—let the rate of understanding be what
it will men must be governed on an estimate of what it is & not
what it might be—but he is supported by equal numbers—this
if an argument at all will be found a strong one for his dismission—one side hopes an accession of good the other side the
loss of all that is dear to them—is there an equality in these pretensions—there certainly would not be if the makers were unequal—the government no body will say depends on him—one
half America determine that it will be ruined by him—In all
governments it has been found necessary to consult the public
opinion on the persons employed & it has ever been concluded
that a continued favor to an unpopular servant ought to involve
the master in the blame. In America this has not yet happened
altho' I greatly fear it is rapidly in progress—the unexampled
affection of the people to you requires more to shake their confidence than is usually necessary but natural causes must operate
& it is a well known principle that small injuries obliterate important services—this is not contradicted by present experience,
for there is rather a suspension of opinion than a disregard of
wrong—the present moment may determine the mind & to be
sure the love of our country will fully justify the decision—to
put a drawn sword into the hands of a suspected madman is
to expose every body in his way to ruin & when the mischief
shall happen it will be a poor satisfaction to say you did not believe it—the affection of the people has hitherto prevented their
blame of your measures from lessening their confidence in you,
but it will be a poor return for what should excite your gratitude

to persevere in what is disagreable to them—the strongest affection cannot withstand injury whetted by insult—did it never occur to you that the divisions of America might be ended by the sacrafice of this one man—I do sincerely believe from my own knowledge of the causes of divisions & the obvious interest that his partizans have to unite in any mode of executing the government which will preserve it's credit, that they would & to a heart solicitous for it's countrys happiness the event must be most desireable.

I have extended this subject to great length without saying half that occurs & indeed it was only my intention to have given a testimony to public opinion which you may perhaps not have heard—I aver it to be as I have stated it—the consequences must be obvious to you—if the mission should be unfortunate you will bear the undivided odium—if it should be successful it will do you no service, for the event will be too late to stop the opinion that you are determined to govern America according to your own inclination & that of one half it's inhabitants and in contempt of the most rooted opinions of the other half— Among them at present you possess almost universal confidence & it should be rendered dear to you by the reflection that it has stood the conflict of opinions unaided by the smallest dependence on your influence—I myself am one of those who have hitherto shut my eyes on those events which could even shake my confidence in your discernment & I declare I shall meet the event with grief which will persuade me that you are no longer your countrys bulwark.

Are you apprized of the clamour which is raised against the government by Mr Morris being employed in a service for which his principles render him so unfit[3]—Mr H. is understood to have the same wishes with respect to France & a position at London will be infinitely more favorable for their gratification than at Paris—faction has doubted whether you could be a friend to the revolutionary principle & throw such a stumbling block in it's way—a second appointment of that sort will give distrust to every jealous defender of the right of self government.

Can you justify to America increasing the power of a man who is now under question for that which he already has?[4] with so many objections to him will it not shew an excess of favoritism to appoint him to an office inconsistent with the duties of that which he already fills? May it not deserve consideration whether you can dispense with the exercise of official duty as you will do by sending the officer from America.

When the above was written it was my intention as you will perceive by the contents to have sent it without a signature & on one account I wished for concealment, but reflection tells me that I do justice neither to my principles nor present intentions in supposing that one or the other can be doubted—If the spirit in which it is written should be conveyed by it I shall have no reason to regret the want of those expressions of respect which I could honestly have mixed with my political opinions—If there is any information which I may be supposed to possess which is desireable to you I shall take pleasure in attending you[5]—I am with the greatest respect yr mo. ob. servt

John Nicholas

ALS, DLC:GW. GW's docket reads, "6th Apl 1794."

Attorney John Nicholas (c.1764–1819), a graduate of the College of William and Mary, was a brother of Edmund Randolph's wife, Elizabeth "Betsy" Nicholas Randolph (1753–1810). He represented Virginia in the U.S. House of Representatives, 1793–1801, before moving to Geneva, New York. He served in the New York State senate, 1806–9, and as a judge of the court of common pleas, 1806–19.

1. For GW's nomination of John Jay, and not Alexander Hamilton, as a special envoy to Great Britain, see his first letter to the U.S. Senate of 16 April.

2. Thomas Pinckney was the U.S. minister plenipotentiary to Great Britain.

3. Gouverneur Morris was the U.S. minister plenipotentiary to France. For GW's nomination of James Monroe to replace Morris, see his letter to the U.S. Senate of 27 May (LS, DNA: RG 46, Third Congress, 1793–95, Senate Records of Legislative Proceedings, President's Messages—Executive Nominations).

4. On a recent inquiry by Congress into Hamilton's conduct as secretary of the treasury, see Hamilton to GW, 24 March, and n.1 to that document.

5. Nicholas wrote another letter to GW the following evening, 7 April, which reads: "As the anxiety occasioned by the subject on which I took the liberty of addressing you yesterday subsides, my apprehensions increase that in doing it I have violated the respect for you which no body feels more than myself—my pretensions to interfere in so important a deliberation were estimated by myself as small as they could be by any other person, but it was not possible for me to resist the incitement of zeal for my country & for the continuance of that public happiness to yourself which I consider as the most honorable testimony of the virtue of its citizens—hurried by feelings which have the utmost power over me it is not impossible that my sentiments may have been trusted with too little caution in expressing them & that an enthusiasm in the cause may have made me regardless of the conduct of it; but of this be assured that I never should have run the risque of contempt if I had

not thought as an American I owed every thing to you from whom I received every thing—In any proper occasion I doubt not that I may convince you that altho' the opinions are deeply rooted in me a want of respect never accompanied them" (DLC:GW). GW showed both letters to Randolph and asked him if he had encouraged Nicholas to write. For Randolph's reaction, see his first letter to GW of 9 April.

To William Pearce

Mr Pearce,						Philadelphia April 6th 1794

Your letter & Reports of the 1st instant I have received, and am glad to find by the first that you have got your family safe to Mount Vernon; as, unquestionably, it will be a satisfaction to you to have them along with you. Change of Air may, and I hope will, restore your eldest daughter to health again.[1]

I had no doubt but that the late capture of our Vessels by the British Cruisers, followed by the Embargo, which has been laid on the Shipping in our Ports, wd naturally occasion a temporary fall in the article of provisions;[2] yet, as there are the same mouths to feed as before; as the demand, consequently, will be as great; and as the Crops in other parts of the world will not be increased by these means, I have no doubt at all, but that, as soon as the present impediments are removed the prices of flour will rise to what it has been (at least) for which reason hold mine up to the prices mentioned in my last; & if they are offered, make a provisory agreement, to be ratified, or not, by me; an answer to which can be obtained in a week.[3] With respect to the Wheat on hand, you must (if you hear nothing to the contrary from me) be governed by circumstances & your own judgment, in getting it out of the straw; but, at any rate, remove it into the Barns for the purpose of threshing in weather when the people cannot work out.

When salt, or any other article of which you are in want, gets to a high price, provide for the present occasion *only* unless there is a moral certainty of their rising still higher; in that case prudence would direct otherwise.

It was not my expectation that either grass or grain could be rolled at the expence of stopping the Ploughs; consequently, if the Oxen were not in a condition for the accomplishment of this work the execution of it was not to be expected: but is not this an instance among a variety of others, of the impolicy of not breaking a great number of Steers at each of the Farms? which would prevent the few that are broke from being reduced too low for the services thereof. Twenty Oxen are not more expensive than ten broke, & ten unbroke Steers, because you feed them as Oxen only when they are worked; and unbroke steers must be fed, as well as Oxen (though not in the same manner) at other times. By this means there never would be a want of draught Cattle for Cart, Harrow or Roller.

How does the young grass which was sown in the new meadows, last fall, and the clover come on? Was the latter injured much by the Winter?

Besides the number of Stacks which are yet in Wheat, I wanted to know what those stacks are supposed to contain; and this the Overseers, by comparing the size of them with those which have been tread out, may certainly give a pretty near guess at.

The three bushels & half of Oats, mentioned to you in my last, are not of such superior quality as I had been led to expect from the account given of them; yet, notwithstanding, ground may be kept sometime longer for them, or until you hear further from me, on this head.[1]

The imposition with respect to the Garden seeds, is very unjustifiable; 'tis infinately worse than simple robbery, for there you loose your money *only*, but when it is given for bad seed you lose your money, your labour in preparing for the reception of them, and a whole season.

Cloaths must be provided for the Young Gardener at Alexandria. Those for work to be strong, & substantial. Sunday, or holliday Cloaths to be decent, and such as may please without going to more expence than is necessary: but of the latter class I should conceive he can be in no want *now*, unless he has made an improper use of a whole suit (of very good Cloaths) which were given to him the latte end of October last.[5]

I am sorry to find that my chance for Lambs this year, is so bad. It does not appear to me by the Reports that I shall have more than a third of what I had last year: what this can be ascribed to is beyond my comprehension, unless it be for want of Rams, or bad Rams. Let therefore, at Shearing time, a selection of the best formed, & otherwise promising ram lambs be set apart (in sufficient numbers) to breed from; & when they are fit for it, cut the old ones and turn them aside, to be disposed of.

At Shearing time also, let there be a thorough culling out, of all the old, and indifferent sheep from the flocks, that they may be disposed of, & thereby save me the mortification of hearing every week of their death! which is the more vexatious as I was taught to believe that every indifferent sheep was drawn for this purpose last Spring, notwisthstanding the loss of them which has been sustained the past winter; and indeed unto the present moment.

When you go next to Alexandria take the exact dimensions of the rooms in my house at that place, that I may send paper for them. Give the length & breadth of each. and height from the wash board to the Chair board (as they are commonly called) and thence to the Cornish, if any, with the doors and windows, & size of them, in each room or passage. If there is occasion to make good the plastering in any of the rooms, no white wash is to be put thereon; because it is improper for paper. Thomas Davis must paint the outsides of both houses there; the lower part of a stone colour, and the roofs red. the Inside of the dwelling house is also to be painted. The whole in short is to be put in very good, & decent condition. If the planking between the two houses is plained, this also should be painted.[6] I am Your friend &ca

Go: Washington

ALS, ViMtvL; ALS (letterpress copy), DLC:GW.

1. Pearce's letter to GW of 1 April and the enclosed farm reports have not been found.

2. For a list of American ships detained by the British in the West Indies, see *Philadelphia Gazette and Universal Daily Advertiser,* 11 March. On the embargo imposed by Congress, see *Stat.* 1:400.

3. The suggested prices of flour are contained in GW's letter to Pearce of 23 March and not in his letter of 30 March. For the postal schedule between Philadelphia and Alexandria, Va., see GW to Anthony Whitting, 2 Dec. 1792.

4. On GW's recent shipment of oat seed to Alexandria, see his letter to Pearce of 30 March.

5. On GW's acquisition of gardener John Gottleib Richler in July 1793, see n.8 of GW to Frances Bassett Washington, 28–29 July 1793. On 14 July 1794, Pearce paid £2.00.6 to "Neil & Tomsons" and £4.10.5 to "Riddle & co." for clothing for the "young Gardener" (Mount Vernon Accounts, 1794–97).

6. For earlier instructions from GW to have his house and stable in Alexandria, Va., prepared for occupancy by Frances Bassett Washington, see his letters to Pearce of 12 Jan. and 16 February. According to GW's Household Accounts for 28 May, GW paid $22 for "paper hangings" sent to Virginia. Thomas Davis was a dower slave assigned to the Mansion House farm.

From Edmund Randolph

Sir   Philadelphia April 6. 1794.

I conclude from what you observed yesterday, that in the nomination of an envoy extraordinary to London, you prefer some statement more special, than is customary in nominations. I beg leave therefore to present to you a short review of the subject; that you may determine, whether the occurrences in the legislature are ripe for such a statement.[1]

I believe, that I was among the first, if not the first, who suggested this mission to your consideration; and I am still its advocate. I was induced to think favorably of the measure; 1. because the representations, made by our minister in ordinary,[2] seemed to rest on the British files among the business, which, if ever entered upon, would be entered upon, at extreme leisure; 2. because the recent accumulations of injuries called for pointed notice; 3. because the merchants and insurers would suspect an inattention in government, if their interests were left to the routine and delays of common affairs, and would on the other hand be highly gratified by the movement; 4. because the British nation, without whose affections the British Minister[3] can do nothing of importance in war, ought to be retained by the strongest demonstrations in the persuasion, that we mean peaceable negotiation, rather than war; and 5. because a distinguished character, sent fresh from the feelings of the U.S., would with more confidence assert, and with more certainty impress.

I confess, that two remarks, which came from yourself, had for some time employed my thoughts. These related to the sensations, which might be excited in Mr Pinckney, and to those, which may be excited in the people of our country.

To wound unnecessarily a valuable and meritorious officer, as Mr Pinckney is, may be affirmed to be a public mischief. But this will not be the case, I hope. He will admit, that on great occasions, such missions are often instituted; that they are never interpreted by the diplomatic world, as a disparagement of the minister resident; and that a step of so much eclat will rouse the British court from their profound slumber over our various applications. He may moreover to receive s⟨uch⟩ declarations of continuing confidence, as to calm little possible inquietudes.

The same kind of considerations will satisfy the animadversions of our citizens. For, if a man, the most conspicuous for talents and character were now the stationary representative of the U.S. at London, the efficacy of a solemn and special mission may still upon the foregoing principles, be easily conceived.

And yet, the difference between one grade and another is not so powerful as of itself to secure a difference of reception to our demands. The Envoy will be impotent, if he is to carry with him only the language of rhetoric, or of menaces without the power of revenge. To fulfil the purpose of his creation, he must shew, that the U.S. can and will vindicate their rights. But measures of this kind depend on congress alone; and from them we have the embargo alone.[4] They are employed in discussions, leading to these Objects.[5] To nominate an envoy immediately, or until you see the nature and extent of the preparations, may perhaps be to nominate an useless officer; and, if by such a nomination it is proposed to give a direction to the views and deliberations of congress, may it not be better to send a message to them, urging them to adopt the preparatory steps, than to run the risque of appointing a gentleman, who, if our state of imbecility is to remain, cannot, except from personal qualities, have more influence, than Mr Pinckney. It would be unusual too, to expect by an act done to the Senate in its executive capacity, that its influence should extend to the other house in its legislative.

I believe indeed, that to postpone the nomination will be attended with two advantages; the one is, that after congress shall have given nerve to our affairs, the propriety of the mission will no longer be questionable; nor will it require those arguments, which in the present state of things will not be sufficiently apparent; the other is, that the person nominated will then be able to decide, whether he would choose to be the missionary, after certain acts of congress. For example, it might not accord with the opinions of some gentlemen, to go, with an act of Sequestration in their hands.[6]

Notwithstanding the suspension of the nomination, you may perhaps approve of mentioning in the mean time your intention eventually to the person, whom you contemplate.[7] I must request your instruction, whether I am to prepare the message to the senate immediately. I have the honor, sir, to be with the highest respect yr mo. ob. serv.

Edm: Randolph

ALS, DNA: RG 59, Miscellaneous Letters; LB, DNA: RG 59, GW's Correspondence with His Secretaries of State; LB, DNA: RG 59, Domestic Letters. The text in angle brackets is from the letter-books.

1. For the nomination of John Jay as an envoy extraordinary to Great Britain, see GW to U.S. Senate, 16 April (first letter). Among the unresolved issues that led to this appointment were British orders-in-council that adversely affected U.S. shipping, and the continued British occupation of military posts located within the United States, contrary to the Treaty of Paris that ended the Revolutionary War in 1783 (Miller, *Treaties*, 2:151–57). On British interference with U.S. shipping, see Randolph to GW, 2 March; see also the British order-in-council of 8 Jan. (*ASP, Foreign Relations,* 1:431).

2. Thomas Pinckney was the U.S. minister plenipotentiary to Great Britain.

3. William Pitt the Younger was the British prime minister.

4. For the congressional resolve of 26 March that imposed an embargo on all ships in U.S. ports that were bound for foreign ports, see *Stat.* 1:400.

5. On 12 March, Massachusetts congressman Theodore Sedgwick introduced eight resolutions designed to create a program of national defense (*Annals of Congress,* 3d Cong., 500–501).

6. Jonathan Dayton of New Jersey offered a resolve on 27 March that would have provided for "the sequestration of all the debts due from the citizens of the United States to the subjects of the King of Great Britain" (*Annals of Congress,* 3d Cong., 535).

7. GW wrote to John Jay on 15 April, and he sent Jay's nomination as envoy extraordinary in his first letter to the U.S. Senate of 16 April.

From George Clinton

Dear Sir   New York 7th April 1794

I had the honor of receiving your Letter of the 31st Ultimo a few Days ago—Could I have had reason to suppose that the Authenticity of Lord Dorchester's Speech to the Indians would have been doubted by any I presume I might have procured at the Time the most unquestionable Testimony respecting it.[1]

A Deputation from the St Regis Indians arrived at Albany some Time in the Month of February—Their Object was to sollicit the State to appoint Commissioners to negotiate with their Tribes about certain Lands they claim within Our Limits[2]—They informed me that the Chiefs of the seven Villages of lower Canada were deputed by the Western Nations (mentioned in his Lordships Speech) to confer with him on the very Subject referred to in it, and that some short Time before they left Home those Chiefs had set out for Quebec with this Object in View. They also told me a few Hours before my getting the Copy of the Speech that they had received a Letter from their Chiefs stating that they had conferred with Lord Dorchester and obtained a satisfactory Answer; which was afterwards explained to me by them as only meaning an explicit, not a satisfactory Answer; but my Informants pretended Ignorance of it's Contents—Colo. Louis mentioned to me in Confidence his Apprehensions of a War between the British & Americans and seemed desierous of sending to St Regis for his Wife and Children instead of returning there; which he would have done had I not advised him to the contrary and gave him Assurances that should a War take Place I would take Measures for removing his Familly to Oneida[3]—From these Circumstances—From the Confidence I reposed in the Discernment & Integrity of Colonel Udney Hay who transmitted me the Speech and from its coincidence with Sentiments of Lord Dorchester and Governor Simcoe respecting their being no acknowledged Boundary Line as avowed to Colo. Samuel Ogden in a Report made by him to me a Duplicate whereof I believe was delivered to the Secretary at War[4]—There was no Room for Doubt left on my Mind, and a Letter from Colo. Joseph Fay which I now inclose will serve to coroberate the Fact.[5]

I shall not fail to pay the earliest Attention to the interesting Inquieries which you wish me to make and I shall endeavour to conduct them in such a Manner as to prevent any Alarm and ensure a Reliance upon the Result—In the Mean Time it may not be amiss to communicate the following Circumstances.

Quebec Isle à Noux & St Johns are the only fortified Places in Lower Canada. Chamble & Montreal are not in a state of defence[6]—All the armed Vessels employed on Lake Champlain last War are condemned. A new one has been lately built & now traverses that Lake—I have not been able to learn the Number of regular Troops in that Province—The Militia is by no Means formidable but their Numbers I cannot with any accuracy ascertain.

The antient Inhabitants are disatisfied with the Government— and in Case of a Rupture I have good Reason to believe would be disposed to act in our Favour—A proclamation of Lord Dorchester which I understand has been forwarded to the late Secy of State evinces in some degree his Apprehensions on this Subject.[7]

The Vermont Militia in the Neighbourhood of the British Lines is formidable—The Settlements of Clinton County on our Side are recent and dispersed, and do not exceed 500 enrolled Militia—The greater Part of these however are contiguous to the British Lines and are well disposed.

As to Upper Canada—The Fortresses are much decayed and thinly garrisoned, altho they have lately made some Repairs to the Fort at Niagara—The Fort at Oswego is utterly defenceless and only garrisoned by a single incompleat Company and I presume at this Moment might be taken without the effusion of a single drop of blood—Governor Simcoe is erecting a Fortress at Torronto (now called the City of York) on the West End of Lake Ontario—I understand that he has established in his Government a Regiment of about 1000 Men on a Plan similar to the Feudal System and consisting chiefly of the Officers & Soldiers of the irregular Corps that served under the British last War—They occupy the Settlement of Catteraqui & consist of about 5000 Souls.[8] The Regular Troops in that Province consist of three Regiments, one stationed at the City of York another at Niagara & the third at D. Troit but neither of them are compleat that at York is greatly reduced by a Fever that prevailed among them last Summer.

Our nearest Settlements to the Line of thei⟨r⟩ Provinces are in the Vicinity of the Oswego Falls[9] Fort Stanwix and the Genesse River The enrolled Militia of the Counties of Herkimer Onondago and Ontario in which these Places are situated consist of between 4 & 5000 Men as nearly as I can compute but they are very deficient in Point of Arms, and live considerably dispersed. I am with the highest Respect & Esteem, your Most Obedient Servant

Geo. Clinton

ALS, DLC:GW.

1. For the speech given at Quebec by Lord Dorchester to the Seven Nations of Lower Canada on 10 Feb., see n.2 of Clinton to GW, 20 March.

2. According to the 8 March 1794 issue of *Greenleaf's New York Journal & Patriotic Register* (New York City), Caughnawaga Indian Col. Lewis Cook of St. Regis, Canada, and "three other warriors" arrived at New York in February "as a deputation from the chiefs of the seven villages or nations of Lower Canada." Clinton submitted their speech to the New York State legislature on 22 Feb., and on 5 March, the legislature reported that "they have enquired into the several circumstances relative to the claim of the said Indians, to

certain lands within the jurisdiction of this state, and are of opinion that it will be necessary to appoint commissioners to treat with the said Indians, and to authorize, by law, to extinguish the said claim; or take such measures . . . as shall be most beneficial to this and to the United States" (*American Minerva* [New York], 19 March 1794). On Clinton's meeting with Cook and the other Indians from St. Regis, see also Clinton to GW, 20 March. For extinguishment of the claim by the Seven Nations to lands in New York State, see the U.S. Treaty with the Seven Nations of Canada of 31 May 1796, Kappler, *Indian Treaties,* 2:45–46.

3. After the Revolutionary War, Cook lived with the Oneida Indians for a time and then briefly with the Onondagas at their village near Syracuse, N.Y., where he married his second wife, Marguerite (Monique) Thewanihattha (Tewennihata), before returning to St. Regis around 1789.

4. Clinton enclosed Udny Hay's letter to him of 13 March, which accompanied Lord Dorchester's speech (DLC:GW). John Graves Simcoe was the lieutenant-governor of Upper Canada. During the Revolutionary War, Samuel Odgen (1746–1810) owned an iron foundry on the Rockaway River, near Morristown, N.J., from which he supplied ammunition and iron to the Continental army. He also served in the New Jersey militia, rising to the rank of lieutenant colonel in 1777. In 1791, he served as Robert Morris's agent in the purchase of land in western New York. In 1792–93, he speculated in land located in present-day St. Lawrence County, New York. Ogden's report, which has not been identified, may have been submitted after his return from Quebec in October 1793 (*Diary or Loudon's Register* [New York], 14 Oct. 1793).

5. The letter from Vermont resident Joseph Fay to Clinton of 5 April is at DLC:GW.

6. Fort Lennox was located on Île-aux-Noix, an island in the St. Lawrence River. The French fort of St. Jean, known to the English as St. Johns, was situated on the west bank of the Richelieu river, southeast of Montreal. The site is now contained within the city of Saint-Jean-sur-Richelieu. The city of Chambly, on the Richelieu River, is east of Montreal. An earlier fort on this site was destroyed by the Americans in 1776.

7. This proclamation has not been identified.

8. Many Loyalists moved to Canada during and after the Revolutionary War, including those from New York who served in a corps of rangers named for its commander, John Butler. After the war, Butler and many of his rangers settled at present-day Niagara-on-the-Lake, which is in Ontario Province and opposite Fort Niagara. Other Loyalists served in the King's Royal Regiment of New York, which was under the command of Sir John Johnson. Kingston, also known as Cataraqui in 1794, is located at the eastern end of Lake Ontario, at the head of the St. Lawrence River. It was settled primarily by Loyalist refugees from the United States, including Mohawk Indians from New York State.

9. The Oswego Falls, in the Oswego River, were at the site of the present city of Fulton in central Oswego County.

From Alexander Hamilton

[Philadelphia] Monday April 7. 1794.
The Secretary of the Treasury presents his respects to the President and has the honor to transmit a resolution of the Comittee of Inquiry into the state of the Treasury Department, of the 5. instant which came to his hand this morning, together with the paper to which it relates.[1] The Committee meet again tomorrow Evening.

LB, DLC:GW.
1. The enclosed resolve of 5 April, signed by Abraham Baldwin, chair of the select committee appointed to examine the Treasury Department, reads: "Resolved, that it would be satisfactory to the Committee, that the paper submitted to them, April 1st 1794, by the Secy of the Treasury, respecting the point of authority, under which, monies borrowed abroad, have been drawn to the United States, should be presented to the President of the United States; and that the Secretary should obtain from him, such declaration concerning the same, as the President may think proper to make" (DLC:GW). For the enclosed paper, which already had been submitted to the committee, see "Report on Principles and Course of Proceeding with Regard to the Disposition of the Moneys Borrowed Abroad by Virtue of the Acts of the Fourth and Twelfth of August, 1790, as to the Point of Authority," of 1 April 1794, in n.1 of Hamilton to GW, 1 April. For the political background on the creation of this committee, see the source note for Hamilton to Frederick A. C. Muhlenberg, 16 Dec. 1793, *Hamilton Papers*, 15:460–65. For GW's response to this resolution, see his letters to Hamilton of 8 April.

From Carl Andreas Kierrulf

Sir   [c.7 April 1794][1]
Some time ago I took the Liberty To present to Your Excellency in Your quality as a Citizen and Chief magistrate of the United States a Petition and Some memoirs annexed thereto, respecting the deserved and undeserved Distress heaped on me by the fury of Despotism, flattering myself, to obtain thereby a Resolution agreeable to my Wishes.[2]
Your Excellency caused my Papers to be returned to me by Mr Jefferson, the late Secretary of State, without resolving any Thing on my Petition or paying any Regard to my distressed Situation, as a friend to humanity a Freeman and President of a free Empire.

A mistake must have taken place, I suppose, or Your Excellency have, misled by an incomplete or even a false Report made on my Papers by the late Secretary of State, determined, to abandon myself to my unhappy situation.

For, imagining any other reason would compromitting the glory of a Washington So celebrated in Europe, of a personage of his manner of thinking, who has announced himself as a learned man as a Doctor in Philosophy and Theology and as a Statesman whose Faculties were improved by travelling, so, that even to suppose an other motive, would be insulting Humanity the Rights of Man and Liberty in Your Excy's Person.

Please Your Excellency, to grant Pardon to the frank Language of an upright Man; I am induced to think the Chief of a free Empire blest with so high a Degree of generosity as not to disdain placing himself for a moment in my Situation, and he will be convinced of the property of my Conduct, that prompts me to proceed without forms, as it becometh to a free Man.

I could wish to request of Your Excellency the granting of an Audience, that would enable me with Assistance of an American, serving as an Interpreter, to explain my Situation, my Pretensions and what little merit I claim, Certainly, no European has before me, visited this Continent, who Suffered so much by Persecution on account of the good Cause and who might yet do So much in behalf of the same. Therefore I again recommend myself as a Patriot, as a man of merit and an Unfortunate to the benevolent attention of the Chief of the first Republic as being principally concerned in patronizing the affairs of Humanity. remaining Your Excellency's most devoted and humble Servant

(signed) Carl Andreas Kienalf[3]

Living in Front-street No. 77. at the french Coffee-house.

P.S. In order to rectify the Translation of Mr Kienalf's Letter I beg Leave to observe:

1) I qualified the Translation, as the Civilists use to say: "Sern perande verba in factum."

2) In case the Writer thereof pretends to be a Native of Germany, h⟨e⟩ by no means can, by his stile be looked ⟨u⟩pon as a Man of sufficient Knowledge, to manage a beneficial Resolution, so, that, while his own Indiscretion spares him from being called a mere Enthousiast, he does not in the least display those

grand Abilities, a Man ought to possess, that has done or will be in future able to do much good in the important but delicate Cause of Liberty.

The Translator.

L, translation, DNA: RG 59, Miscellaneous Letters. The internal address reads, "George Washington President of the United States of America and Commander in Chief of Their Forces." The cover is addressed to "The Honorable the Secretary of State."

1. The date of "Apr. 7. 1794." was added by someone other than the translator. On the date of this letter, see also note 3.

2. On Kierrulf's petition asking for government support as a professor of moral philosophy, and Jefferson's reply of 20 Dec. 1793, see Kierrulf to GW, 10 Dec. 1793, and notes. The U.S. House of Representatives read and tabled Kierrulf's petition on this date (*U.S. House Journal*, 6:242).

3. The translator incorrectly transcribed Kierrulf's name.

From Henry Knox

Sir. War Department, April 7th 1794.

I have the honor to submit to your consideration, the propriety of embarking a detachment of recruits, of about fifty, now in this place, either for Charleston, or Georgia; in order to guard the batteries, for the present, which are to be erected upon the Sea coast of those States.[1] I am Sir, Most respectfully, Your obedient Servant.

H. Knox

LS, DLC:GW; LB, DLC:GW.

1. On the erection of coastal fortifications in South Carolina and Georgia, see "An Act to provide for the Defence of certain Ports and Harbors in the United States," 20 March (*Stat.* 1:345–46). For specific details about the fortifications being planned in these two states, see *ASP, Military Affairs*, 1:101–2. For GW's reply, see his letter to Knox of this date.

To Henry Knox

Sir, Philada April 7. 1794.

If the number of recruits in the Atlantic States, can afford a detachment of fifty men to the southward without too great an exposure of more important objects, it will accord with my opinion that that number should be sent thither. And they may be designated for Charleston or Savannah, as shall appear most

eligible to you from the information that is to be obtained.[1]
Yours &c.

G. W——n

Df, DLC:GW; LB, DLC:GW.

1. For Knox's request to post fifty men in either Charleston, S.C., or in
Georgia, see his first letter to GW of this date.

From Henry Knox

Sir.   War Department, April 7 1794.

I have the honor to submit to your consideration the opinion
of the Attorney General upon the act of the legislature of Pennsylvania for securing the trade, peace and safety of the port of
Philadelphia, and defending the Western frontiers of the Commonwealth.[1] I am Sir, Most respectfully, Your obedient Servant

H. Knox

LS, DLC:GW; LB, DLC:GW.

1. Knox wrote Attorney General William Bradford on 31 March to ask for
his opinion on a Pennsylvania law of 28 Feb. entitled "An ACT for more effectually securing the trade, peace and safety of the port of Philadelphia, and
defending the Western Frontiers of the commonwealth" (*ASP, Indian Affairs,*
523). On this legislation and GW's concerns about its constitutionality, see
Bartholomew Dandridge, Jr., to Knox, 30 March, and n.2.

Bradford's signed reply to Knox of 2 April begins with a restatement of
the act in question and then continues: "By the Constitution of the U.S. it is
provided 'That no State shall without the consent of Congress lay any duty of
Tonnage, keep troops or ships of war in time of peace' &c. This restriction
on the power of keeping Troops, I am of opinion, is not *absolute;* but that the
natural & grammatical construction of the words connect the qualification
intended by the terms—'in time of peace'—with this restriction, as well as
with that on keeping ships of War. There is therefore nothing in the constitution which prohibits the states from keeping Troops *in time of War.*

"So far, therefore, as the act in question contemplates the defence of the
Western Frontiers against the hostilities of the Indians now at War with the
United States, I consider it as within the strictest limit of the Constitution.
Such measures have heretofore been pursued by the state of Pennsylvania
without objection; & a practical construction of this clause in the Constitu-
tion has thus been given.

"The rest of the act however, is questionable and it is not without some
great hesitation that I decide upon it. The spirit of a prohibition to keep
troops in time of peace seems to imply that the Troops raised and kept in
time of War, ought to be raised, kept, & employed, with reference to the
objects of that war. It is easy to perceive that the dangers which it is notable
the people of the United States, intended to guard against this prohibition,

will exist, if on every breaking out of indian or other hostilities, the separate states may raise troops, & build ships of war for any object but that of
repelling such hostilities. But altho' these consequences are evident, I cannot find in the constitution itself, any thing which prohibits the states from
stationing & employing the troops which they have a right to keep in time of
war, in what manner they please, within the bounds of their respective states.
I consider those clauses in the constitution, which restrict the powers of the
several states, as subject to a *strict* construction; and that the prohibitions are
not to be extended by implication, nor is the natural & obvious meaning of
the words to be enlarged by a consideration of inconveniences which may
possibly result from adhering to it.

"But as the state of Pennsylvania has no power to keep troops when the
United States are not at war, so much of the act as goes to authorize the Governor 'to keep up those companies if the circumstances of the war in Europe
should in his Opinion require it' is not, I apprehend compatible with the
Constitution of the United States. If Peace shall be made with the Indians, &
no other war, these troops cannot be constitutionally kept up by Pennsylvania, altho' the war should continue, & the terms of the inlistment should be
unexpired" (NNGL: Knox Papers; see also *ASP, Indian Affairs,* 1:523–24, for
a version that contains some modifications in phrasing and word choice and
is dated 3 April).

Joseph Robinson's Affidavit

[Salisbury, N.C., 7 April 1794]

This day settled with John Steele Esqr. and reced. from him
Thirty pounds in full satisfaction and payments of all accompts,
dcbts, dues, notes, bonds, bills, or dealings whatsoever, but particularly in full for, and in discharge of a certain paper now in
the hands of John Haywood Esqr. purporting to be an obligation upon George Washington late of Virginia, and John Steele,
which said obligation as well as all others I do herby release, and
therefore acknowledge myself perfectly satisfied.[1]

In witness whereof I have hereunto affixed my hand this 7th
day of April, at Salisbury in the year 1794 in presence of Henry
Giles.[2]

his
J. ⟨Rob⟩inson Robin⟨son⟩
mark

D (in Henry Giles's writing), NcU. An unidentified person wrote the docket
that reads, "Joseph Robinson's Release from an obligation against John Steele
& George Washington for £10,000 currency."

1. Neither Joseph Robinson nor the reason for the financial obligation that

North Carolina congressman John Steele and GW apparently owed Robinson have been identified. Either of two men named John Haywood may be the individual mentioned in this affidavit. The first is attorney John Haywood (1762–1826), who was a native of Halifax County, North Carolina. He was elected the state's solicitor-general in 1790, became the attorney general in 1791, and served on the bench of the superior court, 1793–1800. He later moved to Tennessee, where he continued the practice of law and served on the Tennessee supreme court, 1816–26. The second John Haywood (d. 1827), of Edgecombe County, N.C., served as the state treasurer from 1784 until his death.

2. Henry Giles appears on the 1790 census as a resident of the Salisbury District in Rowan County, N.C. (*Heads of Families* [North Carolina], 175).

From Robert Rutherford

Dear Sir   Philadelphia April 7th 1794

I address you with reluctance, with unease that you are too often beset, while the momentous Concerns of your Very important trust are pressing.

Soon after Coming to this place,[1] I saw a letter to Colo. Parker from Mr D. Bedenger at Norfolk in which he says "I have been informed that Mr Fitzsimmons in presence of Majr Frazier of Pittsburgh and in public Company declared that a Certain Mr Bedenger of Norfolk was the author of the publication under the signature of Veritas, and as I have reason to believe this story was invented to injure me I feel myself obliged to make inquiry respecting the Authority upon which that Gentleman made the declaration. In short I wish to know of whom Mr Fitzsimmons had his information and must rely on your friendship in procuring a sattisfactory answer from that gentleman."[2]

I went immediately to Mr Fitzsimmons with the above extract under which he wrote. "I never said to any person or in any Company that either Mr Bedenger or any particular person was the author of the pieces under the Signature of Veritas nor was the name of the writer of these papers inquired after by me directly or indirectly.["] This he Signed and dated Philada January 3d 1794,[3] and I inclosed a Copy to Mr Bedenger, who tho a perfect Stranger to the author of this publication, has Several times mentioned the nature of a Certain party in that place, who regularly Correspond with those of their sentiments here and elsewhere, that I am induced to trouble you with a State of real facts. Mr Bedinger my son in law,[4] as myself, is a warm friend to his Country & it's goverment, he therefore of Course is looked upon with an evil Eye by these Silken Commercial birds of passage, who are for the most part factors, and as far as they have influence, emessarys of Brittain, and too much infect our States while they are Malignant in their hate. But I am happy to know beyond a possibility of doubt, that the most disinterested paternal regards for the rights of the people & well being of this our Common Country fill your mind with the ardor of a patriot, and an honest man, the noblest of all charactors, and this Conscious evidence of mind is all powerful with my brother & all our Connections, Mr Peyton Clerk of the Winchester Scottish Court and who acted as clerk when the Resolutions of that place were entered into, and Mr Conrad Mare of the town are of my family as is Colo. Morrow of Shepperds Town, and Mr Hite, who with Mr Bedinger were officers in the Continental army, where Mr Hite sufferd much by a wound.[5]

Capn Christie of this place has often expressd his desire to obtain some appointment. Certificates in his favour are full. he is Cousin to Mr Christie from the State of Maryland. His Connections here are honest people. He is poor & his family rather suffering, a wish to be with them & the attair of the Algerene war having deranged his usual mode of life. He served through the last war as Capn of one of the Galley's, was wounded at red bank & mud Island. an appointment at the arsenals or where his family Can be with him appears to be most his wish. I beg pardon for detaining you tho it is perhaps less troublesome than waiting on you as at several times when I attended you were engaged.[6]

Pray accept my sincere good wishes while I have the honor to be with every Sentiment of real respect Dear Sir Your Most Hble Sert

R. Rutherford

ALS, DLC:GW.

1. Virginia congressman Robert Rutherford arrived at Philadelphia in time to attend the opening on 2 Dec. 1793 of the first session of the Third Congress (*Annals of Congress,* 3d Cong., 133).

2. The letter from Daniel Bedinger, the current surveyor of customs for the port of Norfolk, Va., to Virginia congressman Josiah Parker has not been identified. Thomas FitzSimons of Philadelphia also was a member of the current House of Representatives. For the anonymous letters, which were critical of GW, see Veritas to GW, 30 May, 3 June, and 6 June 1793.

3. The extract with the signed affidavit from FitzSimons of 3 Jan. 1794 has not been identified.

4. Bedinger married Sarah Rutherford (born c.1770) in April 1791.

5. Thomas Rutherford (1729–1804) represented Hampshire County, now

in West Virginia, in the Virginia House of Burgesses, 1761–68. Rutherford's connections probably included: John Peyton, who served as the clerk of the town of Winchester, Va., after the Revolutionary War (Norris, *Lower Shenandoah Valley,* 160, 180); Col. John Morrow of Shepherdstown, Va., who served as a colonel in the Virginia militia, 1778–81, and later represented Virginia in the U.S. House of Representatives, 1805–9; and one or more members of the Hite family of Virginia, of whom several served as officers in the Continental army (Heitman, *Historical Register,* 292).

6. Capt. Christie may be the John Christie (born c.1746) who was commissioned in 1776 to command the fire brig *Vesuvius* of the Pennsylvania navy, and in 1781 to command the armed sloop *Sally* (Claghorn, *Naval Officers of the American Revolution,* 59). Christie remained active in the maritime trade despite his desire for a federal appointment (*Philadelphia Gazette and Universal Daily Advertiser,* 20 Sept. 1794; *Finley's American Naval and Commercial Register* [Philadelphia], 29 Jan. 1796). On the October 1777 attack on Fort Mercer, overlooking the Delaware River at Red Bank, N.J., see Charles Stewart's two letters to GW of 22 Oct. 1777, and Samuel Ward, Jr., to GW, 23 Oct., and n.2 to that document. On the subsequent attack on Fort Mifflin, located on Mud Island in the Delaware River, see GW to George Clinton, 26 Oct. 1777. Gabriel Christie (1755–1808) represented Maryland in the U.S. House of Representatives, 1793–97 and 1799–1801.

From John Wanton

Sir   Newport Rhode Island April 7th 1794

Much has been said concerning the detention of the Schooner, Bayonne, Thomas Greene Master, from St Johns, Nova Scotia. I wish to give your Excellency as just account of the transaction as I can nearly recollect,[1] at 10 oClock A.M. the 1st day of April, arrived here the Schooner Bayonne as abovemention'd. and the Custom house boat went onboard her & brought her Register on Shore, & deliver'd to the Collector; at 4 OClock P.M. I was informd by the Pilot the said Schooner Intended to sail Immediately back to St Johns, I thought it my duty to acquaint the Collector (Wm Ellery Esqr.) with the Circumstance, accordingly I waited on him, & inform'd him what I had heard respecting her, & wished to know if he wanted my assistance to stop her, he answered that he wanted none of my assistance, she might go when & where she pleased, for he shou'd not stop her, I then inform'd him I must, as I thought it my duty, accordingly I got a Boat & Manned her with some Gentlemen of the Town who offerd their Service to assist me. & went onboard & weighed her Anchor & brought her into the wharf, & the next Morning onbent her

Sails, which I now have in Custody. I acquainted the Governer & Company of this State & they approvd of my Conduct;[2] I shou'd be glad of your Excellencys advice in the matter.[3] I must inform you there has Sail'd from this Port, Since the Embargo tooke place, One Brig bound to Turtola, & a Schooner to Hispaniola, I informed the Collector of their Intention, that I had it from good Authority, they informed me they where going to Providence, not to Sea, altho' they had their papers onboard, & Shipt a new hand, & paid him his Months advance, which might have informd them they intended for Sea as they have since Saild.[4]

I offerd my Service in the same way last Summer, when the Ship from Jamaica run away that had Robbed one of our Vessels, but I was informed it was none of my business, they wanted none of my assistance, but about 8 oClock in the Evening the Marshall waited on me to know if I commanded the Fort. I inform'd him I did, he acquainted me he had a Warrant against the Capt. of the Ship for Piracy, & wished my assistance to take him, or stop her which I Afforded with chearfulness but the Wind soon sprung up to the Northward. & she cut her Cable & got out after my firing two Shot at her.[5] as I have ever Served my Country with Fidelity I still wish to serve it but it hurts my feelings to see things go on in this manner. I am Your Excellencys Most Obdt humble Servt

John Wanton.
Capt. of Fort Washington

ALS, DNA: RG 59, Miscellaneous Letters. Post office notes on the cover read "Newport 7th April" and "*Free.*"

1. Capt. John Wanton commanded at Fort Washington, which was located on Goat Island in Narragansett Bay and guarded the entrance to Newport's harbor. For other accounts of this incident, see the letters from collector of customs William Ellery to Alexander Hamilton of 8 and 14 April (*Hamilton Papers*, 16:246–48, 256–57).

2. Wanton detained the schooner *Boyne* in conformity with the embargo of 26 March, which was "laid on all ships and vessels in the ports of the United States . . . bound to any foreign port or place" (*Stat.* 1:400). Henry Knox had informed Gov. Arthur Fenner of the embargo in a circular letter of 26 March (R-Ar: Letters to Governors).

3. On GW's decision allowing the *Boyne* to depart Newport, see Hamilton to GW, 19 April (first letter), and notes 2 and 3.

4. The islands of Tortola and Hispaniola are located in the Caribbean Sea, while Providence is another port in Rhode Island. Knox informed Fenner in a letter of 18 April that the embargo was to be continued until 25 May, in accordance with the enclosed congressional resolution of 18 April. He also enclosed a copy of the resolution of 2 April, which contained detailed

instructions for the collectors of customs to use in enforcing the embargo (R-Ar: Letters to Governors; *Stat.* 1:400–401).

5. For this earlier incident, including the actions of Wanton and deputy marshal Jabez Champlin, see Henry Marchant to GW, 3 Aug. 1793 (first letter).

From James Duane

Sir   New York 8th April 1794

Be pleased to accept my most thankful acknowledgments for the honor done me by your favor of the twenty third of March, the concern you are pleased to express for my ill State of health, and your benevolent wishes for my recovery—They are fresh proofs of the Attention with which you have always had the goodness to distinguish me, and which I shall not cease to remember with the utmost gratitude and sensibility.[1]

I now sir after a conference with Judge Willson (with respect to the manner most proper) beg leave to present to you an Act of Surrender of my office as Judge of this district.[2] It would have been transmitted at an earlier day, had not the state of the business of the Court prevented it.[3]

I flatter myself that if I regain my health, I shall soon be placed in a situation to extend my usefulness as a Citizen, and steadfast friend, to the general Government, on which the dignity, safety and prosperity of our Country evidently depends.[4]

Permit me to assure you that amongst a People so eminently benefited by your military atcheivements, and civil administration, there is no man who prays with more sincerity, and ardor, that you may uninteruptedly, enjoy every honor and every blessing which an indulgent heaven can bestow, than him who is—with the utmost attachment respect and esteem Sir your most obliged most faithful and most obedient Servant

Jas Duane

LS, DNA: RG 59, Miscellaneous Letters; ADfS, NHi: Duane Papers.

1. Duane had mentioned his ill health in a letter to GW of 10 March.

2. The enclosed signed resignation of this date, which was written at New York, reads: "To all People who shall see these presents I James Duane Judge of the United States of America for the New York district send greeting: Whereas the President of the said United States, by Letters patent bearing date the twenty Sixth day of September in the year of our Lord One thousand Seven hundred and eighty nine sealed with the seal of the United States, did by and with the advice and consent of the Senate, appoint me Judge of the

district court, in and for the New York district, authorizing me to execute and fulfil the duties of that office, and to hold the same with the powers, previledges, And emoluments thereunto appertaining during my good behaviour, as fully appears by the said Letters patent: Now know ye that I do by these presents freely, voluntarily, and absolutely, resign, relinquish, and surrender the said office of Judge of the New York district with all the powers, previledges, and emoluments, to the same appertaining." The resignation was "Sealed and delivered in the presence" of his son, James Chatham Duane, and John M. Bowers, and was attested by James Wilson, an associate justice of the Supreme Court (DNA: RG 59, Miscellaneous Letters).

3. Duane struck out the remainder of this paragraph on the draft: "We thought it necessary that the original Commission should be retained as evidence of the Authority by which I have hitherto officicated: Nor did I wish if it could be dispensed with unnecesserily to part with so flattering a testimonial of your Attention to me. Least however a different opinion might prevail To prevent all difficulty I have delivered to the Judge the Commission itself to be ⟨*illegible*⟩ed or."

4. At this point the draft has "will be enlarged."

To Alexander Hamilton

Dr Sir, [Philadelphia] Tuesday 8th April 1794
Annexed to your Statemen⟨t⟩ of "Principles and course of Proce⟨ed⟩ings" I have given the certificat⟨e⟩ required.[1] I am yours always

Go: Washing⟨ton⟩

ALS, DLC: Hamilton Papers.
1. For Hamilton's "Report on Principles and Course of Proceeding with Regard to the Disposition of the Moneys Borrowed Abroad by Virtue of the Acts of the Fourth and Twelfth of August, 1790, as to the Point of Authority," of 1 April 1794, see *Hamilton Papers*, 16:231–33. For the attached certificate, which is in the form of a letter, see GW's second letter to Hamilton of this date.

To Alexander Hamilton

Sir, United States April 8. 1794
I cannot charge my memory with all the particulars which have passed between us, relative to the disposition of the money borrowed. Your letters, however, and my answer; which you refer to in the foregoing statement, and have lately reminded me of, speak for themselves, and stand in need of no explanation.[1]

As to verbal communications, I am satisfied, that many were made by you to me on this subject; and from my general recollection of the course of proceedings, I do not doubt, that it was substantially as you have stated it in the annexed paper, that I have approved of the measures, which you, from time to time, proposed to me for disposing of the Loans, upon the condition, that what was to be done by you, should be agreeable to the Laws.[2]

Go. Washington

LB, DLC:GW; copy, DNA: RG 233, Third Congress, 1793–95, House Records of Legislative Proceedings, Committee Reports and Papers; Broadside, DLC: Jefferson Papers.

1. For background on this letter, see Hamilton to GW, 24 March. The statement is Hamilton's "Report on Principles and Course of Proceeding with Regard to the Disposition of the Moneys Borrowed Abroad by Virtue of the Acts of the Fourth and Twelfth of August, 1790, as to the Point of Authority," of 1 April 1794 (*Hamilton Papers,* 16:231–33). GW consulted with Edmund Randolph before writing this letter. For Randolph's suggested reply, see his second letter to GW of 1 April.

2. The laws authorizing federal loans were "An Act making provision for the [payment of the] Debt of the United States," 4 Aug. 1790, and "An Act making Provision for the Reduction of the Public Debt," 12 Aug. 1790 (*Stat.* 1:138–44, 186–87).

From Alexander Hamilton

Sir   Philadelphia April 8 1794

I have analised the declaration which you have been pleased to make upon the copy of the paper of the first instant delivered by me to the Committee of Inquiry into the state of the Treasury Department—and find, with regret, that the terms used are such as will enable those, who are disposed to construe every thing to my disadvantage, to affirm "That the Declaration of The President has intirely waved the main point and does not even manifest an *opinion* that the representation of the Secretary of the Treasury is well founded."[1]

To this it would be added, that the reserve of the President is a proof that he does not think that representation true—else his justice would have led him to rescue the officer concerned even from suspicion on the point.

That this will be the Interpretation put upon your declaration, I have no doubt, and in justice to myself I cannot forbear to make this impression known to you, and to bring the declaration under your revision.

I am the more certain that this construction will be put upon the fact from what has heretofore taken place. In the course of the discussion of the last session, an argument of this kind was, in private, urged against me. "If Mr Hamilton had really acted by the authority of The President, or in due communication with him would not the President take some method either directly to Mr Madison or through Mr Jefferson or Mr Randolph to make known to him, that this ground of accusation did not exist? His not doing it, which may be inferred from Mr Madison's urging the point, is a proof that there was no cooperation on his part."[2]

In addition to this, I have learnt from an authentic source that a particular Gentleman,[3] supposed to possess good opportunities of information has intimated in a manner to induce a belief of its having come from you—That it never was your intention that any of the loans which were made should have had reference to the Act making provision for the Reduction of the public Debt[4] and that you never knew any thing of the operation while it was going on.

Under all that happened Sir, I cannot help entertaining and frankly expressing to you my apprehension, that false and insidious men, whom you may one day understand, taking advantage of the want of recollection, which is natural, where the mind is habitually occupied with a variety of important objects, have found means by artful suggestions to infuse doubts and distrusts very injurious to me.

My consciousness of what has been the real tenor of my conduct and my conviction of the fairness and rectitude of your mind compel me to this conclusion.[5]

Upon this as upon every other occasion my desire is to encounter directly and without detour whatever embarrassment may stand in my way—If contrary to what I understood from Mr Lear during the discussion of the matter in Congress,[6] and what I inferred from the late conversations with you—the affair does not stand *well* in your mind—I request the opportunity of a full and free conference on the subject, to recapitulate and go over all the circumstances which have occurred, in the hope of recalling to your Memory what may have escaped it—and with a wish to abide the result in an explicit form; that is, by a declaration which shall render the main fact unambiguous or shall record the doubt.

As on the one hand I expect what is due to the situation—so on the other I seek no palliation of delinquency, no cover for any defect of conduct.

The situation is indeed an unpleasant one—Having conducted an important piece of public business in a spirit of confidence dictated by an unqualified reliance, on the ⟨one⟩ hand, upon the rectitude, candour and delicacy of the person under whom I was acting, on the other, by a persuasion that the experience of years had secured to me a reciprocal sentiment (whatever imperfections it may have otherwise discovered) and by the belief likewise that however particular instances might be forgotten, the general course of proceeding in so important an affair could not but be remembered—I did not look for a difficulty like that which now seems to press me. Knowing too that there existed in my written communications with The President (not only those which have been specified but others) so many direct and indirect indications of what was truly the course pursued—I still less apprehended a difficulty of that nature when the occasion for explanation should occur.

Not seeking to escape responsibility for any improper execution of the laws, if any has happened, I did not imagine that want of immediate authority from the President to do what they would justify would be suffered to remain (the appeal being made to him) a topic of objection to my conduct.

In the freedom of these remarks, I flatter myself, Sir, that you will perceive nothing but that just sensibility which a man of honor, who thinks his veracity exposed to question, ought to feel, and that you will be persuaded I continue yet to retain undiminished all that respect which a long established conviction of the existence of an upright and virtuous character ought to inspire. With this sentiment I have the honor to remain Sir Your most Obedient & most humble servant

Alexand⟨e⟩r Hamilton

ALS, DLC:GW; ALS, DLC: Hamilton Papers; ADf, DLC: Hamilton Papers. Hamilton wrote "Copy" on the ALS at DLC: Hamilton Papers. The text in angle brackets is from the draft.

1. For the declaration that was attached to Hamilton's "Report on Principles and Course of Proceeding with Regard to the Disposition of the Moneys Borrowed Abroad by Virtue of the Acts of the Fourth and Twelfth of August, 1790, as to the Point of Authority," of 1 April 1794, see GW's second letter to Hamilton of this date.

2. On the investigation of Hamilton undertaken in 1793 during the second session of the Second Congress, see the U.S. House of Representatives to GW, 23 Jan. 1793, n.1.

3. In the draft, this paragraph appears in the left margin to replace the following text, which Hamilton initially wrote and then excised: "In addition to this, Mr [William Branch] Giles lately in a conversation with the Committee intimated in a manner which was well understood—That he had good information that I had never had your sanction verbally or otherwise for what was done. Your own reflections will make the proper comment on an insinuation of this kind!"

4. See "An Act making Provision for the Reduction of the Public Debt," 12 Aug. 1790, *Stat.* 1:186–87. At this point in the draft, Hamilton wrote: "or should have been brought to the U.S."

5. The draft continues with another paragraph at this point: "Whether these men may have misrepresented any expressions of yours, or betrayed any declarations which you may have made through want of recollection, you will best judge from what has been the conduct of particular individuals and from the information which I have stated."

6. This is a reference to the investigation conducted during the second session of the Second Congress, 5 Nov. 1792–2 March 1793, when Tobias Lear was still serving as GW's secretary.

From Henry Knox

Sir.   War Department, April 8th 1794.

I have the honor to enclose, the copy of a letter, just received from the Governor of Maryland, dated the 3rd instant,[1] and submit to your consideration, whether any measures ought to be taken respecting the defence of the harbor at Annapolis.[2] I am Sir, Most Respectfully Your obedt: Servt:

H. Knox secy of war

LS, DLC:GW; LB,DLC:GW.

1. The letter to Knox from Thomas Sim Lee, written "In Council, Annapolis" on 3 April, acknowledged receipt of Knox's recent letter "enclosing the Act of Congress, to provide for the defence of certain Ports, and Harbours in the United States." Lee's copy of the circular letter of 26 March that Knox sent to the governors of the maritime states has not been identified, but for its content, see n.1 of Thomas Mifflin to GW, 27 March. Lee also acknowledged the receipt of a second letter from Knox of 26 March, which has not been identified,

"requesting an authority from this Board to Captain Stricker to mount eleven eighteen-pounders, belonging to the State of Maryland at Whetstone-point; and in conformity with the request contained in the last mentioned letter, we have written to Captn Stricker, giving him the permission required." The letter from Lee to Capt. John Stricker (1759–1825) of 27 March is at MdAA: Executive Records, Letterbooks of Governor and Council, 1787–1820.

Lee continued: "We are not at present in a situation to transmit a complete return of the Ordnance belonging to this State, as some of them are at a distance from Annapolis; but we inclose you a list of such as are here; only three of which are of the Calibre wanted.

"As the object of requesting this return, appears to be the appropriation of these Cannon to the fortifications contemplated by the Act of Congress, and as the Port of Annapolis is entirely omitted in that Act, it becomes proper as connected with the subject, to suggest that the Board will not hold itself authorized to permit the whole of the heavy Ordnance of the State to be applied to the defence of one place, to the exclusion of another, rendered important by circumstances, and much exposed by situation.

"The City of Annapolis is the seat of the State Government, and of course the repository of the public records; the residence of many of the public Officers concerned in the immediate discharge of the important departments of Government: the place where the Legislature, and Superior Judicatures assemble, and where the Executive is stationary.

"It contains also the public Treasury, and property of the State, and of Individuals, to a large amount. By reason of its situation, immediately on the Chesapeak, it is peculiarly liable to annoyance from an enemy, if left unfortified; but it is at the same time easily capable of being placed in a very respectable state of defence: In every view its protection is of consequence: detached from the propriety of sheltering the Capital of the State (where so much is deposited to excite attack) from injury and depredation, the security of this City is in a great degree connected with the convenience of Baltimore, and the general welfare. If fortified, the harbour, and the river which contributes to form it, would in case of pursuit be an asylum for our Vessels, superior in strength and convenience to any in the State: On the other hand, if permitted to remain defenceless, and left to the mercy of an Enemy, the property of Government and of Individuals, must be withdrawn from it, at a very heavy expence, and great inconvenience; the Records of every description must be removed, at the hazard of irreparable injury, and our Vessels in the Chesapeak deprived of the refuge, which a harbour in all respects commodious, and made peculiarly defensible by nature would present to them in the moment of danger.

"From these and a variety of other considerations, it will readily occur to you that some part of the State's Cannon ought to be reserved for the defence of Annapolis, even if the General Government should not on reconsideration deem its security an object of national concern, and should refuse to take it under its protection: We have no doubt however that Congress will provide for it's safety, if it should be certain that defensive operations are indispensable" (DLC:GW). The enclosed return of ordnance has not been identified.

2. For GW's reply, see his letter to Knox of 9 April.

To James McHenry

(Private)

Dear Sir, Philadelphia 8th April 1794

Your private letters of the 31st of March & 3d instt have been duly received.

Although it is a rare, if not an entire new thing with me, to answer letters applying for appointments, yet from motives of esteem & regard, & our former connexion in public life,[1] I shall acknowledge the receipt of yours on this head; although I can say nothing more on the subject than to explain the motives which have imposed silence upon me on these occasions.

They are.

1st because letters of this sort are so numerous, that to give them a civil answer woud employ too much of my time. 2d. because civil answers might be construed to mean more than was intended; and 3d because, coeval with my inauguration, I resolved—firmly—that no man should ever charge me *justly* with deception. Abundant reason I have had to rejoice at this determination, for I have experienced the necessity in a variety of instances of hardening my heart against indulgences of my warmest inclinations & friendships; and from a combination of causes, as well as mere fitness of character, to depart from first impressions, & first intentions with regard to nominations: which has proved, most unequivocally, the propriety of the maxim I had adopted, of never committing myself until the moment the appointment is to be made, when, from the best information I can obtain, & a full view of circumstances my judgment is formed.

With respect to your second letter of the 3d of April, I have only to add—and this in confidence—that every thing which friendship requires, and which I could do without committing my public character or involving this Country in embarrassment is, and has been for sometime in train, though the result is, as yet, unknown.

I am very sorry to hear of your bad state of health, but hope the approaching pleasant season & warm weather will restore you.[2] With very great Esteem I am—Dr Sir—Yr Affect⟨e⟩

Go: Washington

ALS (letterpress copy), ViMtvL; LB, DLC:GW.

1. This probably is a reference to McHenry's service during the Revolutionary War as one of GW's secretaries, from May 1778 to August 1780.

2. Although McHenry did not receive the desired diplomatic appointment, GW nominated him to be secretary of war on 26 Jan. 1796 (*U.S. Senate Executive Journal*, 1:198).

From James Monroe

sir,   Philada April 8. 1794

Having casually heard that it was requested by many of Col. Hamilton's political associates, that you would nominate him as Envoy to the Court of Great Britain, and as I should deem such a measure not only injurious to the public interest, but also especially so to your own, I have taken the liberty to express that sentiment to you & likewise to observe farther, that in case it is your wish I should explain to you more at large my concern for this opinion, I will wait on you at any hour you may appoint for that purpose.[1] With great respect & esteem, I am sir, Yr most humble servt

Jas Monroe.

L, Sprague transcript, DLC:GW.

1. Before replying to Monroe on 9 April, GW showed this letter to Edmund Randolph and asked if he had encouraged Monroe to write it (Randolph to GW, 9 April [first letter]).

Report from the Commissioners of the Sinking Fund

[Philadelphia, 9 April 1794]

At a Meeting of the Commissioners of the Sinking fund, mentioned in the Act making provision for the reduction of the public debt,[1] at the Senate Chamber, April 9. 1794.

Present,

The Vice-President of the United States,
The Secretary of the Treasury,
The Secretary of State,
The Attorney General.

A report from Joseph Nourse, register of the Treasury, was read, stating that the dividend of interest arising on the first quarter of the present year on the stock standing to the credit of the said Commissioners, and also to the credit of Samuel Meredith, Treasurer, in trust for the United States, amounted to sixteen thousand five hundred & fifty eight dollars & seventy seven Cents.[2]

Whereupon, Resolved, that the same be forthwith applied towards sinking the public debt by purchasing stock upon rules & principles conformable to the last resolution of the board.[3]

Resolved, that the sum of fifty thousand dollars be also appropriated & applied in like manner.

Resolved, that Samuel Meredith, be the Agent for making the said purchases of Stock.

Signed by order of the board,   John Adams.[4]

Approved, April 12. 1794   Geo. Washington

LB, DLC:GW.

1. See "An Act making Provision for the Reduction of the Public Debt," 12 Aug. 1790, *Stat.* 1:186–87.

2. See Joseph Nourse to Alexander Hamilton, 27 March, *Hamilton Papers,* 16:203–4.

3. For this resolution of 13 July 1792, see n.1 of Hamilton to GW, 16 July 1792.

4. This report was enclosed with a brief cover letter from Alexander Hamilton to GW of 12 April (DLC:GW).

To Henry Knox

Sir,   [Philadelphia] April 9th 1794.

In reply to your letter of yesterday, I observe, that to fortify Annapolis is, in my judgment, a very proper measure. But I do not see that the Executive of the U. States can take any steps towards it until the result of the motion, now pending in the House of Representatives, be known.[1]

It is my desire that you would examine carefully the Speeches which have been made in this City, & elsewhere, to the Tribes of Indians now in amity with us that unfulfilled promises (if any) may be complied with.[2]

I desire also, that the requisites of such laws as have passed this Session (not already in execution) within the purview of the Department of War, may be reported to me, that directions may issue accordingly.[3]

Go: Washington

ALS (letterpress copy), DLC:GW; LB, DLC:GW.

1. On 8 April, the House of Representatives ordered that "a committee be appointed to bring in a bill to fortify the city of Annapolis," and on 9 May,

GW approved "An Act supplementary to 'An Act to provide for the Defence of certain Ports and Harbors in the United States,'" which provided for the fortification of the "port and harbor of the city of Annapolis" (*Annals of Congress,* 3d. Cong., 563; *Stat.* 1:367).

2. Any written reply from Knox on this subject has not been identified.

3. For the relevant laws, see "An Act to provide for the Defence of certain Ports and Harbors in the United States," 20 March; "An Act to provide a Naval Armament, 27 March; and "An Act to provide for the erecting and repairing of Arsenals and Magazines, and for other purposes," 2 April (*Stat.* 1:345–46, 350, 352). For Knox's response to this request, see his letters to GW of 10 April and 5 June (DLC:GW).

From Henry Knox

Sir,   War department April 9. 1794

I have the honor to submit to your consideration a letter from Doctor White who has come forward from the Southwestern Territory to solicit protection for Mero district.[1]

Governor Blount has a power to order the Militia of the said district into service at the expence of the United States in proportion to the danger. But the inhabitants request something further, the protection of permanent troops. This will be difficult to accomplish with the present number of Troops notwithstanding the perfect propriety of the measure, until the operations in which General Wayne is engaged should have a favorable termination.[2] I also beg leave to submit a letter from General Arthur Campbell.[3] I have the honor to be, Sir with perfect respect Your obedient Servant

H. Knox

LS, DLC:GW; LB, DLC:GW.

1. James White (1749–1809), a native of Pennsylvania, studied at the Medical School of the College of Philadelphia. A veteran of the Revolutionary War, he later settled in Davidson County, N.C., which he represented in the state legislature in 1785. After Davidson County became part of the newly created Southwest Territory in 1790, he was elected in 1794 to the first territorial assembly. He served as a territorial delegate to Congress from 3 Sept. 1794 until 1 June 1796, when the territory was admitted to the union as the state of Tennessee. He moved to Louisiana in 1799.

The enclosure from White, which has not been identified, was a copy of a memorial asking for federal assistance in defending the Mero District from hostile Indians. On White's delivery of this memorial to the U.S. House of

Representatives and for its response, see Carter, *Territorial Papers*, 4:331–33, 335–36. For recent accounts of Indian depredations in this area, see the 23 April issue of the *Independent Gazetteer* (Philadelphia), which reprinted an earlier article from the *Knoxville Gazette*.

2. Gen. Anthony Wayne did not achieve a decisive victory over the hostile Indians of the Northwest Territory until the Battle of Fallen Timbers on 20 Aug. 1794. A peace treaty would not be signed until the Treaty of Greenville of 3 Aug. 1795 (Kappler, *Treaties*, 2:39–45). For GW's response to the memorial, see his letter to Knox of 10 April 1794.

3. The letter from Arthur Campbell to Knox has not been identified.

To James Monroe

Sir,   Philadelphia April 9th 1794

In reply to your letter of yesterday, I can assure you with the utmost truth, that I have no other object in nominating men to offices than to fill them with such characters as, in my judgment, or (when they are unknown to me) from such information as I can obtain from others, are best qualified to answer the purposes of their appointment.

Having given you this assurance, I request, if you are possessed of any facts or information, which would disqualify Colo. Hamilton for the mission to which you refer, that you would be so obliging as to communicate them to me in writing. I pledge myself, they shall meet the most deliberate, impartial & candid consideration I am able to give them.[1]

Colo. Hamilton & others have been mentioned, & have occurred to me as an Envoy for endeavouring by negotiation, to avert the horrors of War.

No one (if the measure should be adopted) is yet absolutely decided on in my mind; but as much will depend, among other things, upon the abilities of the person sent—and his knowledge of the affairs of this Country. And as I *alone* am responsible for a proper nomination, it certainly behoves me to name such an one as in my judgment combines the requisites for a mission so peculiarly interesting to the *peace* & happiness of this country.[2]

With great esteem & regard I am—Sir Your Obedt Hble Servt

Go: Washington

ALS, DLC: Monroe Papers; ADfS, DNA: RG 59, Miscellaneous Letters; LB, DLC:GW.

1. For Monroe's objections to Hamilton's appointment, see his letter to GW of 11 April.

2. For GW's nomination of John Jay, and not Alexander Hamilton, as a special envoy to Great Britain, see his first letter to the U.S. Senate of 16 April.

Letter not found: from William Pearce, 9 April 1794. GW wrote Pearce on 13 April that "your letter of the 9th instt (which with the weekly reports) have been duly received."

From Edmund Randolph

Sir   Philadelphia April 9. 1794.

Among my first reflections upon the two letters, which you did me the honor of shewing to me yesterday and the day before, I could not forget, that they produced a degree of delicacy to myself.[1] The authors of them are of the number of my friends; and one is closely connected with me by other considerations. However, I did not rest long upon any idea of this kind; being persuaded, that after my declaration of the most absolute and unequivocal ignorance of what was meditated, and of what was done, you would not for a moment believe, that I had resorted to those expedients for conveying to you sentiments, which I was unwilling to deliver to you in person. This never has been, and never can be, a recourse of mine; altho' I have no doubt, that both parties have more or less Endeavoured to forward their views, by occasionally, and as it would seem without concert, by making communications of the supposed opinion of the public.

I cannot learn, that any body has undertaken to say, that you had determined to nominate any particular gentlemen. At any rate nothing has fallen from me except the conversation, which you permitted me to hold, upon the Affair; and in which *the individual* was spoken of, only as a character, which stood forward.

The first of the two letters appears to be settled; that is, it has been so considered and explained, as to prove, that the writer is not, (and I affirm it) inferior to any man in the U.S. in attachment to yourself.[2]

The letter of the second gentleman creates the difficulty: and these seem to be the leading ideas.

Is no person to write to the executive upon public subjects, but an acquaintance? The answer will immediately be, that the President will receive information from every quarter.

Is the President to answer these letters? Undoubtedly not, for reasons too obvious to need an enumeration.

Is there any line to be drawn between matter proper and improper for such communications? They may speak of facts, or of public opinion; but they ought to be disregarded, if they go beyond these.

But what kind of attention is to be paid to these facts, and this public opinion? An inquiry into both.

Suppose charges are brought against public officers, and the writers offer themselves, as witnesses? I presume they will be heard, and called upon to produce proofs, if the character of the informer be not such, as to render it disgraceful to listen to him.

Suppose a particular appointment be apprehended; and a *stranger* shall arraign it, without making charges against the person? The letter ought to be treated with silent contempt; unless an occasion should arise for expressing a particular disapprobation.

This is a course of thinking for cases in general. But that of a senator has other aspects.

If I were to examine the question upon abstract principles, I would say, that no senator ought to recommend, or oppose a candidate by any representations, except of fact, made beforehand to the President. For he will have his vote upon the nomination; and to recommend is to promise to support, and to oppose, is a declaration to thwart the nomination; neither of which is exempt from indecorum.

The letter of Colo. M. does not relate to fact; as far as I can discover from its language. But he shews, that he wishes an interview; and an interview for the purpose of communicating facts would, I suppose, be admissible.

How is it to be brought about? The mode ought to be well considered. To refuse to receive information would be food for clamor; to admit the offers to give it, without restrictions and in full latitude, hazards the independance of the executive.

The following therefore is the best style of proceeding, which occurs to me.

"That the secretary of state inform Colo. M. verbally, that his station entitles his communications to atte⟨ntion⟩ that it is presumed, that he has considered and made up his mind as to the kind of interference, which a senator ought to make in a nomination beforehand: that upon this idea, the President would be ready to afford an interview at a given time.[3]

It may be added in the course of conversation as the opinion of the Secretary, that facts are the principal things to be consulted.

Should he place his advances upon the ground of private friendship or regard, then I think, that he may be told, that any letter, going upon this ground, ought to be worded in such a manner as demonstrably to shew, that he intended it in that and no other light. I have the honor, sir, to be with the most respectful and sincere attachment yr mo. ob. serv.

Edm: Randolph

ALS, DLC:GW.

1. GW showed Randolph the letters received from Congressman John Nicholas, who was Randolph's brother-in-law, of 6 April and from Senator James Monroe of 8 April. In these letters, both men responded negatively to rumors that GW was planning to nominate Alexander Hamilton as a special envoy to Great Britain.

2. For an expression of this attachment, see Nicholas to GW, 7 April, in n.5 of Nicholas to GW, 6 April.

3. GW did not offer Monroe an interview, as Randolph suggested, but instead decided to compose a written reply on this date.

From Edmund Randolph

Sir   Philadelphia April 9. 1794.

I do myself the honor of inclosing for your consideration the request of Mr Philip Mark to be appointed consul of the United States in the Germanic Empire.[1] His recommendations are also forwarded, and will be found to be satisfactory. As before an office is instituted, it ought to be seen to promise public utility, I have inquired into the effect of the establishment solicited. The benefits proposed are the aid, which a consul, fixed at Nuremberg in Franconia may give to Emigration; the facility, which he may afford to the remittances of property from thence; and a certain portion of intercourse carried on, as Mr King represents to me, between New-York and Nuremberg.[2] The only question therefore of serious consideration in this business seems to be; whether any political objections exist against the sending of a consul for the first time *now* into Germany? or whether an offence even to the caprice of any other government, when so small a public good is to be produced, ought to be hazarded? These are subjects of expediency only; and do not operate very strongly upon my own mind; altho' I thought it proper to lay them before you.[3] I have the honor, sir, to be with the highest respect Yr mo. ob. serv.

Edm: Randolph.

ALS, DNA: RG 59, Miscellaneous Letters; LB, DNA: RG 59, GW's Correspondence with His Secretaries of State; LB, DNA: RG 59, Domestic Letters.

1. Philip Mark, a native of Germany, was a partner in the New York City mercantile firm of Jacob and Philip Mark, at 241 Queen Street, until early in 1793, when the partnership was dissolved because Philip Mark was returning to his native Germany to live (*Daily Advertiser* [New York City], 23 April 1793). Before leaving, he wrote then Secretary of State Thomas Jefferson on 2 May 1793 to solicit a consular appointment in either Nüremberg, in Franconia; Frankfurt am Main; or the Palatine Electorate, including the bishopric of Franconia (DLC:GW; extract, *Jefferson Papers*, 25:640).

2. Randolph apparently enclosed Mark's letter of application to Jefferson and a letter of recommendation from New York merchant John Murray to Alexander Hamilton of 3 May 1793 (DLC:GW; *Hamilton Papers*, 14:410–11). A letter of recommendation of circa 2 May 1793 from Murray and other prominent New York City businessmen, which was enclosed in the letter to Jefferson, has not been identified. Another letter from Mark, of 12 May, and a letter from Rufus King of 17 July 1793, which were received by Jefferson on 25 July 1793, also have not been identified (Chronological Index of Letters, DLC: Jefferson Papers).

3. On GW's appointment of Mark as U.S. consul "in Franconia, in Germany," see GW to U.S. Senate, 28 May (DNA: RG 46, Third Congress, 1793–95, Senate Records of Executive Proceedings, President's Messages—-Executive Nominations).

To Henry Knox

Sir,   Philada April 10. 1794

After giving the application contained in the Memorial of Doctr White (herewith returned) all the consideration it deserves, you will report what you think can & ought to be done for the protection of the District of Mero under present circumstances.[1] I am &c.

G. W.

Df, DLC:GW; LB, DLC:GW.

1. On the memorial presented by James White, which requested federal assistance in the defense of the Mero District in the Southwest Territory, see Knox to GW, 9 April. For Knox's report, see his letter to GW of 11 April.

From Henry Knox

War Department April 10. 1794
The Secretary of War respectfully reports to the President of the
United States[1]

That it appears from an examination of the Acts which have
passed during the present session of Congress, that the duties
hereinafter enumerated to be performed by the said Secretary
under the directions of the President of the United States
   to wit

1st.   The act for the defence of certain ports & harbors.[2]

The purchase of the lands on which the fortifications are to
be erected, provided such lands shall be private property, and
shall not be ceded by the respective states, conformably to the
third section of the said Act.

It is presumed however that those purchases are not[3] to be
made until a sufficient time shall elapse to ascertain whether the
respective states will make, or not, the cessions in question. The
other parts of the said Act are in a train of execution.[4]

2d.   The act relatively to the naval armament.[5]

Preparatory arrangements are making by the master builders
of this city to ascertain the sizes of the ships and to have drafts
and models made of the same. The sizes of the cannon and the
places where it may be expedient under all circumstances to build
the frigates contemplated are also under consideration. As soon
as these particulars shall be satisfactorily ascertained (which will
be very shortly) a particular report thereon will be submitted to
the President of the United States.[6] But it is doubted whether any
considerable progress can be made in this business until there
shall be an appropriation to defray the expenses thereof.[7]

3d.   The act for erecting and repairing of Arsenals and Magazines, and for other purposes.[8]

The first section of this act requires two places to be designated as Arsenals and Magazines in addition to Carlisle and
Springfield either or both of which may be continued as part of
the number of three or four setts of Arsenals and Magazines at
the discretion of the President.

Springfield seems to combine all the requisite qualities of a
permanent Arsenal and Magazine, but there are certain repairs
which will be necessary.[9]

But a question arises as to Carlisle. The subscriber submits the opinion that the buildings there be put into repair which probably may be done in a respectable degree for one thousand or one thousand five hundred Dollars. This measure seems necessary whether the buildings be retained or sold. No doubt exists as to the defective qualities of the place as a national repository on account of the locality of the situation and the expences which would accrue in transporting the stores by land to and from the said place. At present however it does not seem that any authority is vested for the purpose of selling the buildings. The repairs therefore seem indispensible upon œconomical principles.[10]

If the idea of a permanent establishment at Carlisle be upon mature consideration deemed inadmissible then it would seem most proper to form a Magazine upon the Potowmac above the falls. The place most suitable to be sought, combining the greatest facilities of water transportation, populousness of the neighbouring country, and water for the necessary works. A person of accurate judgment ought to be appointed for this purpose, and to report the place for the decision of the President.[11]

The southern Magazine and Arsenal may probably be fixed upon the Santee so as to combine all the water communications, water for the works, and other advantages which properly belong to the establishment, and in like manner to report for decision. It would seem proper for the person or persons who should perform this business ought to be an able surveyor who should return an accurate plan of the proposed scites and of the elevation of the grounds and all other circumstances in the vicinity.[12]

A question may arise whether the Armouries specified in the second section of the said Act should be immediately commenced in the places which shall be decided upon and the proportions of stores destined to each place transported thereto with all convenient expedition. These measures seen to be the natural and immediate consequences of the places being fixed. And also that prompt measures should be adopted to have the permanent buildings erected of the nature and form which shall be adopted to the quantity of stores intended to be deposited. If these ideas should be approved proper characters for Superintendants and Master Armourers will be sought after and their names submitted.

The third section specifies a person to superintend the

receiving safe keeping and distribution of Stores, and also for the due accounting of the same. It would seem by the law that this appointment is vested solely in the President of the United States, and it is so explained by the members of both houses. Samuel Hodgdon is submitted as the person most proper for this office. He has been in the practice of some of the most essential of its duties for sixteen years, and his integrity and competency appear to have been amply tested by experience.[13]

It is submitted that the arms ammunition and military stores contemplated the fourth section of the said Act should be purchased according to the following list.

Estimate of the expence of purchasing the following articles—

| 7000 Muskets and Bayonets | at 9 Dolls. | 63000 |

It is presumed the above number added to the good muskets in possession of the United states together with those which are deemed worthy of repair will amount to 50,000 the number directed.

2000	spare bayonets	at 1 Doll.	2000
1000	large horseman's pistols	at 4 Dolls.	4000
10000	Knapsacks	at 50 Cents	5000
10000	Cartridge boxes	at 1 Dollr	10000
2000	Soldiers Tents	at 10 Dolls.	20000
100	Horseman's do for company Officers	at 20 Dolls.	2000
20	Marquees for General & Field Officers	at 150 Dolls.	3000
20	eight inch brass howitzers each weighg 1500 lb	at 50 Cents	15000
20	field carriages for ditto	at 180 Ds.	3600
100	tons of Saltpetre or 100 tons powder at 400 Ds. ℔ ton or 20 D. ℔ Cwt		40000
200	tons of Lead at 173. D. 20 C. ℔ ton or 8 66/100 ℔ Cwt		34640
		Dolls.	202,240

It is to be understood that all these articles are additional to any contained in preceding estimates.

The above is a copy of an estimate laid before Congress on the 4th march last,[14] and therefore ought to be provided, and as they have appropriated the sum of three hundred and forty thousand Dollars it is submitted that the excess be expended in the purchase of one hundred and fifty tons of Powder, or Saltpetre and Sulphur equal thereto.

150 tons of Powder	at 400 Dolls.	60000
400 tons of Lead		69280
		129,280

But it is to be apprehended that the rise of the above articles will greatly diminish the quantities specified in the estimate.

As the article of ammunition is now under consideration. This will not be an improper place to bring to the view of the President of the United States the following general ideas upon this subject.

The United States have now in store about four thousand four hundred barrells of powder, but the four hundred may be considered as in a train of expenditure, a considerable proportion thereof being with the army. If to this quantity be added the two hundred and fifty tons for which the appropriations are made, there then would be about nine thousand barrells. This quantity would have been pretty respectable were it not for two circumstances which have been created by late laws to wit—

The first is the fortification of certain ports and harbours.

The second, the creation of six frigates.

These objects will require and bring into use seven hundred pieces of cannon, which may be averaged as of the caliber of twenty four pounders. Each of these pieces ought to be provided with two hundred pounds of powder each round of eight pounds. This additional demand alone requires a provision of five hundred and sixty tons which with the consumption for experiments signals &c. ought to be encreased to six hundred tons or twelve thousand barrells.

If we are to make provision for a war we ought to have in possession for all purposes the amount of twenty four thousand barrells of powder; from this quantity is to be deducted the quantity on hand and the quantity for which appropriations are made amounting to nine thousand barrells.

The quantity then of fifteen thousand barrells would remain to be provided. The cost of this quantity at five hundred Dollars per ton would amount to the sum of four hundred thousand Dollars for which an appropriation by law will be necessary.

It may however be doubted whether the powder could be obtained for the five hundred Dollars per ton unless arrangements shall be made for procuring it from abroad.

The following is a Summary View of this subject.

	Required		
		tons	barrels
A provision of two hundred rounds for the frigates & sea coast		560	11200
contingencies		40	800
For the troops which may be raised, estimated at three years supply at 10 pounds ℔ man.		300	6000
One half being estimated for exercise for the artillery		300	6000
		1200	24000
On hand	200		
Appropriation for	250	450	9000
Deficient and to be provided		750 or	15000
			barrels

A question arises on this statement whether any further measures should be taken for to obtain an appropriation for this essential article to carry on a war.[15] All which is humbly submitted to the President of the United States.

H. Knox

LS, DLC:GW; LB, DLC, GW. The docket reads, "Report of the Secy of War 10 April 1794. of things required by law to be done by the President."

1. GW requested this report in his letter to Knox of 9 April.

2. See "An Act to provide for the Defence of certain Ports and Harbors in the United States," 20 March (*Stat.* 1:345–46).

3. The word "not" is missing from the letter-book copy.

4. For the cessions of land made by Maryland and North Carolina and for Knox's efforts to implemented this act, both now and throughout the remainder of 1794, see *ASP, Military Affairs,* 1:71–107.

5. See "An Act to provide a Naval Armament," 27 March (*Stat.* 1:350).

6. Knox's report, if written, has not been identified.

7. Section 3 of "An Act to authorize the President of the United States during the recess of the present Congress, to cause to be purchased or built a number of Vessels to be equipped as Galleys, or otherwise, in the service of the United States," 5 June, provided an appropriation of $80,000 (*Stat.* 1:376).

8. See "An Act to provide for the erecting and repairing of Arsenals and Magazines, and for other purposes," 2 April (*Stat.* 1:352).

9. The repair of the Revolutionary War-era magazine and armory at Springfield, Mass., probably was approved at some point later this year, because David Ames received an appointment as its superintendent in July (Knox to GW, 17 July, DLC:GW). On the operation of this armory from 1795 until 1 Oct. 1799, see James McHenry's report of 6 Jan. 1800 (*ASP, Military Affairs,* 1:130–32).

10. Carlisle, Pa., was the site of a British post during the French and Indian War, and the British built an armory there in 1769. Under American control during the Revolutionary War, it continued to serve as armory and was the Quartermaster Supply Headquarters for the Western Department. It was not until 1801 that the federal government acquired this site, but a federal armory or arsenal was not built on it (Roberts, *Historic Forts,* 675–77). Instead, a location on the Schuylkill River near Philadelphia was designated for a new federal arsenal (see Knox to GW, 17 July, DLC:GW).

11. John Hills subsequently was appointed to report on proper spots for erecting arsenals (Knox to Bartholomew Dandridge, Jr., 13 June, DLC:GW). About his report, see GW to Burgess Ball, 27 June (NNGL); Knox to GW, 14 June (second letter, DLC:GW); and GW to Knox, 30 Sept. (DLC:GW). On the selection of a specific site, see Timothy Pickering to U.S. Senate, 12 Dec. 1795 (*ASP, Military Affairs,* 1:109–10; see also GW to James McHenry, 13 Dec. 1798 [source note to first letter, *Papers, Retirement Series,* 3:250–65]). In 1796, the federal government purchased a 125-acre tract bounded by the Potomac and Shenandoah Rivers, and construction of the armory began at Harper's Ferry in 1799.

12. On the selection of a location in South Carolina, see Pickering to U.S. Senate, 12 Dec. 1795, *ASP, Military Affairs,* 1:109–10. The proposed site was situated near Columbia, S.C., which lies at the head of navigation on the Congaree River (Knox to GW, 14 July 1794 [third letter, DLC:GW]; see also GW to McHenry, 13 Dec. 1798 [source note to first letter]). The confluence of this river with the Wateree River forms the Santee River. The eventual site chosen for a federal arsenal was at Rocky Mount on the Wateree River, but construction did not begin until 1803 (Statement of Sums Expended . . . on Fortifications, Arsenals, Armories, and Magazines, 6 Feb. 1805, *ASP, Military Affairs,* 1:178–84).

13. Samuel Hodgdon's experience included his service as field commissary, deputy commissary general, and commissary general of military stores during the Revolutionary War. During the Washington administration he served as commissary of military stores, 1788–91, and then as quartermaster general, 1791–92, before becoming commissary of military stores again. He received the title of superintendent of military stores later in 1794 and retained this position until 1800.

14. See Knox's report to the U.S. House of Representatives of 5 March (*ASP, Military Affairs,* 1:65–66).

15. "An Act making appropriations for certain purposes therein expressed," 9 June, provided additional funding for War Department expenses connected with the defensive measures passed in the first session of the Third Congress (*Stat.* 1:394–95).

From James McHenry

Sir.   Fayetteville [Md.] 10 April 1794.
I am extremely obliged to you for your letter of the 8th and received the exposition of your motives as a fresh mark of that confidence with which you have so often favored me. I should indeed, if I know myself, be the last person in the United States, who on a *public account* would wish you to feel any other; and as it respects your *personal fame,* I beleive the first to regret their being intrenched on to gratify mere inclination or friendship. In all appointments it is undoubtedly proper that superiour merit, and fitness of character, and aptitude of talents to the office to be filled should govern. This is a rule that cannot be too rigidly obeyed, and which I am sure no good man will ever blame you for observing.[1]
What you have been pleased to communicate to me respecting an unfortunate person has releived me from a great deal of anxiety. I shall now not only sleep a sounder but be happier when awake.[2] With real wishes for your health, I am very truely and affectionably Sir your most ob. st
                                                  James McHenry

ALS, DLC:GW; ADfS, MdAA: McHenry Collection.
    1. In response to McHenry's letters of 31 March and 3 April requesting a diplomatic appointment, GW expounded in a letter of 8 April on the method he usually employed in dealing with letters of application.
    2. McHenry's relief came from the knowledge that GW had made an effort to obtain the release of the Marquis de Lafayette from a Prussian prison (see GW to Frederick William II of Prussia, 15 Jan. 1794).

From Richard Dobbs Spaight

Sir   No. Carolina New Bern 10th April 1794
In the course of the last month I received the Secretary of wars letter of the 22nd Feb: respecting the sloop L'amee Margueritte;[1] but as I had on the 8th Feb: forwarded on to you copies of all the papers then in my possession relating to her;[2] and as Mr Hill the Atto. of the United States had informed me in his letter of the 12th of the same month, that he had sent by post to the Secretary of State, the examination which he had taken relative to her capture, I did not think it prudent either to take

off the arrest or to restore her to her former owners till I had received your ultimate decision thereon she therefore still continues in the custody of the militia.[3]

Some days ago I received from Mr Severin Erickson a letter dated the 27th March, enclosing Capt: Hervieux's statement of facts relative to the Capture of the sloop Providence attested by Mr Mangourit the french Consul at Charleston, I do myself the honor to enclose you copies of both: I shall direct the marshall to restore to Captain Hervieux his trunk, papers and cloths, which I hope will meet with your approbation.[4]

Agreable to the Secretary of wars letter of the 26th of March, which I received by express the 3rd inst: I immediately issued orders to the commanding officers of the counties in which the different ports lay, that they should in all cases where application was made to them, by the revenue officers, assist with the militia under their command in carrying the embargo into full force and effect.[5] I have the honor &c.

R.D. Spaight

LB, Nc-Ar: Governors' Letterbooks.

1. For Henry Knox's letter to Spaight of 22 Feb. concerning the privateer *Aimée Marguerite,* the former British sloop *Providence* before its capture by the French, see n.1 of Knox to Bartholomew Dandridge, Jr., the same date.

2. For the various papers forwarded to GW, see Spaight's first letter to GW of 8 February.

3. The letter from U.S. District Attorney William H. Hill to Spaight of 12 Feb. and the "examination" sent to Edmund Randolph have not been identified.

4. In his letter to Spaight of 22 March, Severin Erickson wrote: "At the Request of Mr Mangourit Consul of the French Republic at Charleston, I do myself the honour to forward you the legalized copy of the Procés-verbal of Captn Hervieux and his Officers relative to the Capture of the Sloop Providence last June, which will serve to convince your Excellency of the distance the said Sloop was taken from the Shores and Territory of the United-States. As Captain Hervieux's Agent here, I was likewise directed to demand the Redelivery of his Trunk, Clothes, Commission and the Consul's dispatches, which have been so long detained by the Marshall here. Mr Blakely professed his Willingness to return the said Effects, but said that he could not do it without your Excellency's Approbation" (Nc-Ar: Governor's Papers, Richard Dobbs Spaight). The enclosed statement from Hervieux and his officers has not been identified. U.S. deputy marshal John Blakely had been charged with responsibility for the confiscated items (Spaight to GW, 8 Feb. [second letter]).

5. Knox's letter to Spaight of 26 March was the circular letter sent to the governors of the maritime states informing them of the embargo established by the congressional resolution of 26 March (Nc-Ar: Governors' Letterbooks; *Stat.* 1:400; see also n.1 of Thomas Mifflin to GW, 27 March).

To the Commissioners
for the District of Columbia

Gentlemen,   Philadelphia April 11th 1794.

Your letter of the 23d Ulto came duly to hand, but as you did not expect to meet again until the 12th instt I have, accordingly, postponed my reply to the contents of it 'till now.

I am sensible that the No. East quartr of square Number 21. is subject to the disadvantage of a North and East front (not desirable I confess) but these are more than counterpoised in my estimation by the formation of the ground, which, though expensive to improve, on account of a steep declevity on the other two sides, can never (if a quarter of the square is taken, and improved) have the view from it obscured by buildings on the adjoining lots. I was on the ground, and examined it in company with Mr Blodget during the Sale in September last; and after comparing the advantages and disadvantages, resolved to fix on that spot if a quarter of the square could be obtained, and the price not run upon me, beyond the usual Sales; for doing which there could be no just cause; for, as I have observed before, it is not less than the area mentioned that would secure my object; and to improve it would be expensive, from the shape of the ground. If, after this explanation, I can be accomodated without involving inconveniences, I would rather the matter should be fixed *now* than delayed to a *future* period—first, because I had rather be upon a certainty (one way or other) than remain in doubt; and 2dly because it would be convenient to me to know, whether there would be a call (for some money which I expect to receive in a few days) for that purpose, or that I might apply it to some other.[1]

I was not unmindful of your communication respecting Major Rivardy; but, unluckily, the Secretary of State mistook (as I have lately discovered) the purport of my direction to him on this head.[2] It was, that your employing the Major for the purposes designated, wd be perfectly agreeable to me if you were satisfied with his character, and that he had abilities adequate to the undertaking; that he was an entire stranger to me; and that I had rather you should pursue your own judgment in, than be prompted to, a choice by me. He understood these sentiments as applying to the measure (of the utility and ind⟨ee⟩d necessity of which I had no doubt) and not to the man. Hence the mistake has happened, nor should I have discovered it, had not our late enquiry for Engineers brought to view that nothing had been concluded between you and Majr Rivardy. The employment as Engineer may occupy him three or four months—The fortifications at Baltimore, Alexandria and Norfolk were assigned to him that you might be enabled to judge whether under these circumstances it would be best to adhere to the Major, or employ Mr Vermanet, or any other[3]—Your more perfect knowledge of the business—and of the situation of things than I possess will direct you better than any advice I could give; for in truth I have little knowledge of characters proper for such Surveying, levelling &ca as the City requires; and besides, I have been unfortunate hitherto in those whom I have been instrumental in bringing forward for the subordinate Offices in the City.[4]

Mr Greenleaf is here, and told me on tuesday last that he should set out for George town as yesterday or today, but if he does not call upon me before eleven oclock (Post hour) this letter will go by the Mail.[5] With very great esteem & regd I am— Gentlemen Your Obedt Servt

Go: Washington

ALS, Records of the U.S. Commissioners of the City of Washington, 1791–1869; ALS (letterpress), DLC:GW; LB, DLC:GW. The text in angle brackets is from the letter-book copy.

1. GW met with Samuel Blodget, Jr., the former superintendent for the District of Columbia, during the public sale of lots, which began on 17 Sept. 1793 (D.C. Commissioners to GW, 16 Sept. 1793). On GW's purchase of this lot in square 21, see the letter to GW from the D.C. commissioners of 23 April, and n.2 to that document. Perhaps GW expected to receive prompt payment on a debt owed by William Lyles (GW to Lyles, 24 March 1794).

2. On the intention of the D.C. commissioners to employ the Swiss engineer John Jacob Ulrich Rivardi, see their letter to GW of 28 January.

3. On the appointment of Rivardi in March as the engineer in charge of fortifying the ports at Baltimore, Md., Alexandria, Va., and Norfolk, Va., and the hiring of John Vermonnet in May to supervise the fortifications at Annapolis, Md., and Alexandria, which had been reassigned to Vermonnet, see *ASP, Military Affairs*, 1:87–95.

4. This may be a reference to the problems encountered earlier with Pierre L'Enfant and Andrew Ellicott. Both had been hired as chief surveyors for the District of Columbia, and both had been dismissed from their positions after prolonged disagreements with the D.C. commissioners. On the firing of L'Enfant, see GW to L'Enfant, 28 Feb. 1792. On the dismissal of Ellicott in December 1793, see D.C. Commissioners to GW, 23 Dec. 1793, and n.8.

5. On James Greenleaf's financial investment in the Federal City, see GW to the Commissioners for the District of Columbia, 20 Aug. 1793, and n.3 to that document. Tuesday last was 8 April.

To William Deakins, Jr.

Dear Sir,   Philadelphia 11th Aprl 1794
   You would oblige me by receiving the contents of the enclosed order;[1] and then, by informing me of the price the Tobacco would fetch.[2] With esteem, I am Sir Your very Hble Servt
                                                       Go: Washington

ALS (letterpress copy), ViMtvL; LB, DLC:GW.
   1. For the enclosed order from John Francis Mercer to Benjamin W. Jones of 5 April, authorizing the payment of past rent due on GW's land in Montgomery County, Md., see n.2 of Mercer to GW, 5 April.
   2. Deakins made no mention of tobacco in his reply of 30 April, in which he wrote: "Your much Esteemd favor of the 11th Current, with an Order on Mr Benjamin Jones for Rents, came to hand in due time, but my Indisposition has prevented my Answe⟨r⟩ring it till now. I have not yet seen Mr Jones, but will call on him soon, and do the Needfull" (DLC:GW). It was not until 31 May that he notified GW that the rent due him amounted to 4,500 lbs. of tobacco per year.

From José de Jaudenes

                                    [Philadelphia] Friday the 11th April 1794
   Don Josef de Jaudenes presents his most respectfull Compliments to the President of the U.S. and his Lady.
   Longing for the honor of introducing Doña Matilde Stoughton de Jaudenes (his Lady) to their valuable acquaintance begs them the favor of appointing the hour that would be more Convenient tomorrow morning if possible, when both will have the honor of waiting on them in due form.[1]

L, DLC:GW.
   1. GW's reply reads: "The Compliments of the President of the U. States & Mrs W., are presented to Don Josef de Jaudenes—Informing him that they will with pleasure, receive the introduction of Doña Matilda Stoughton de Jaudenes his Lady at 12 Oclock tomorrow" (ADf, PWacD: Sol Feinstone Collection. This draft is written on the back of a cover for another letter sent to GW). Matilda Stoughton (b. 1778) of New York City married Jaudenes on 25 March.

From Henry Knox

                                          War department April 11. 1794
The Secretary of War respectfully reports to the President of the United States.[1]

That he has had further conversations with Doctor White, and also perused a report of a Committee of Congress herein enclosed relatively to the defence of Mero district.[2]

That the Inhabitants of the said district amounting to about fifteen thousand, thrust out into the Wilderness and one hundred & sixty Miles from any succour and greatly exposed to Banditti Indians seem intitled to receive a due proportion of protection from the United States.

That under the present circumstances of imminent danger and until regular troops can be had for the purpose, resort must be had to the militia of the said district.

The following temporary arrangement is therefore submitted.

That Governor Blount be authorized if he judges the measure indispensible for the safety of the Inhabitants of the said Mero District to call into service until the first day of next December unless sooner discharged the following portions of Militia upon the pay and rations allowed by law.

A post and Garrison to be established at the ford at the crossing of Cumberland River of 1. Subaltern 2 Scrjeants 2. Corporals and 26 privates

For the protection of Tennessee County and the Inhabitants of Red River running into Cumberland--1 Subaltern 2 Serjeants 2 Corporals and 21 privates.

Davidson County--1 Subaltern 2 Sergts 2 Corpl and 26 privates the chief post to be in the front of Nashville

Sumner County--1. Subaltern. 1. Serj. 2 Corporals and 17. Privates

That besides these 2 Subalterns and thirty mounted Militia be allowed the district.

That six small iron howitzers with one hundred rounds of ammunition each be transported immediately from Philadelphia to Fort Pitt and thence to Nashville by water.

That also two hundred of the old muskets wanting repair at Fort Washington be ordered to the same place.[3] These may be repaired at Nashville by the Inhabitants—That these stores be put under the orders of General Robertson who is already in the pay of the United States as a Sub Agent of Indian affairs.[4] All which is respectfully submitted to the President of the United States.[5]

H. Knox

LS, DLC:GW; LB, DLC:GW.

1. On GW's request for this report, see his letter to Knox of 10 April.

2. On the memorial submitted by James White requesting federal assistance in defending the Mero District in the Southwest Territory from Indian attacks, see Knox to GW, 9 April, and n.1 to that document. For the text of the congressional report of 8 April, see Carter, *Territorial Papers*, 4:335–36.

3. Fort Washington was located at present-day Cincinnati, Ohio.

4. On the appointment of James Robertson as a "temporary agent" to the Chickasaw Indians at a salary of $400 per year, see Knox to William Blount, 22 April 1792 (Carter, *Territorial Papers*, 4:139–42).

5. For GW's reply, see his letter to Knox of 12 April.

From James Monroe

Sir   Philadelphia April 11. 1794

My letter of the 8th, and to which I was on the succeeding day honored with a reply, was written in the belief that great exertions were made to convince you that it was the general wish of the community Colo. Hamilton should be appointed Envoy extra[ordinar]y to G. Britain upon the present occasion. As I knew that this was not the case, but on the contrary was persuaded that a great majority of the people of America would not only disapprove the nomination, but deem it likely to produce much mischief, I thought it consistent with the duty I owed the publick, and that respect I have always personally entertained for you, to apprize you of it. A knowledge of truths and even of opinions upon this subject, might be serviceable & could not be injurious; and in point of propriety I could perceive no difference in communicating them, as well against, as for a nomination: otherwise indeed than as the latter is the more pleasant service to the person rendering it. I am therefore happy to find that the part I have taken in this respect, was received in that confidential & friendly manner it was intended, and shall accordingly proceed to state to you in writing the objections which have occurred against the nomination.

I am led to conclude from the liberal stile of your letter that you are willing I should state to you generally the objections which have been urged against it. Upon that principle this reply will be founded. In case however I have misapprehended your intention, I beg you to ascribe it to that consideration alone, and not to a desire to obtrude any opinions of mine upon you.

That there exists among us a party, not to be slighted for its talents or numbers strongly attached to the British monarchy & nation, is a fact which I presume no address has been able to hide from your view. The demonstration of such a party is to be trac'd from an early period of the government, and is to be found in its uniform partiality for both upon every occasion which occurred; in declarations innumerable both in publick & private; but above all in its constant & systematic enmity to the French nation & revolution, of which latter disposition, not to go further back, sufficient proof has been furnished during the present session alone.

This single consideration is sufficient to excite a suspicion of the views of this party. To patronize and support G. Britain when appear[an]ces would allow it, & when her dangerous projects are unmasked, & the publick mind wounded with accumulated injuries is inraged against her, and to discountenance France the friend and ally of America, in every instance, must have something in view unfriendly to the liberty & safety of these States.

That Colo. Hamilton is a member of this party, active in its councils and devoted to its interests is generally and well known. The particular proofs of it are numerous, positive, & satisfactory. The free disclosure of his sentiments upon these subjects, in conversations, anonymous publications (known however to be his) and in his intrigues, have pretty generally explained his true character to the publick.[1] Tis manifest that at present his prospects are founded upon the British & monarchic interests here alone, and in proportion as the confidence of the country has been withdrawn from him, he has more entirely thrown himself upon the support of the former.

Should a person therefore of such character & principles be sent to England, and upon an occasion so attractive of the publick notice, it would not only furnish an opportunity for political intrigue against republicanism here, and against our connection with France, but as I have reason to believe, be regarded in America in a light, unfavorable to the authority appointing him. Nor could it fail to be viewed by France, in respect to the byas of our publick councils, otherwise than with the strongest jealousy and dissatisfaction. and if the mission should not succeed in its object, and a state of things ensue so as to require the friendship and co-operation of that country with this, our situation would be as mortifying as it would be alarming. nor could neither ask with propriety for aid, nor could she with pleasure grant it afterwards.

That an understanding subsists at the present time between this party and the British administration is not improbable and generally inferred, from the late communications of Mr Pinckney. The footing of intimacy upon which it is known to stand with their minister here, is a circumstance which naturally cherishes the suspicion.[2]

That the views of this party have been latterly better understood by the community at large and its influence greatly diminished, is to be plainly seen, by the present state of the legislation. Indeed it is obvious that whenever any of those whose principles are best known, revolve back on their constituents, especially in the Senate, they are superseded. The publick mind is rapidly forcing its way in opposition to the views of this party and so far as a respect is due to that consideration a strong objection arises against the nomination.

Perhaps it would be improper for me to suggest any doubt of the propriety of the mission itself. I wish however that it be not inferred that my judgment balances in its favor. on the contrary I consider it as liable to strong & serious objections, & which have not been removed by the most recent events.[3]

Since I have been plac'd here by my country you will do me the justice to remember that I have, at no time heretofour trespassed on yr attention.[4] I have done so at present from a conviction of the importance of the present crisis, & the delicacy of the measure contemplated. and I trust you will be satisfied I have been induc'd to it from my regard for the publick interest & the most friendly & respectful considerations for yourself. I have the honor to be with the greatest respect & esteem yr Most obt & very humble Servant

Jas. Monroe

ALS, PHi: Gratz Collection; ALS (photocopy), DLC:GW.

1. For the most recent anonymous essays published in the newspapers by Alexander Hamilton, see "Americanus No. I," 31 Jan., and "Americanus No. II," 7 Feb. (*Hamilton Papers*, 15:669–78; 16:12–19).

2. Thomas Pinckney was the U.S. minister plenipotentiary to Great Britain, and George Hammond was the British minister to the United States. GW had submitted three letters from Pinckney to Edmund Randolph in his letter to the U.S. House of Representatives and Senate on 4 April. For these letters, see Randolph to GW, 3 April, and n.1 to that document. Monroe,

however, may have been referring to another Pinckney letter, which had not been made public (see Randolph to GW, 19 April [second letter]).

3. For GW's nomination of John Jay as an envoy extraordinary to Great Britain, see his first letter to the U.S. Senate of 16 April.

4. Monroe represented Virginia in the U.S. Senate, 1790–94.

To Edmund Randolph

Sir   [Philadelphia] Friday 11th April 1794

The fruit of the Democratic Society begins, more and more, to unfold itself. You will report what is necessary to be done with the specimen of it which I herewith send; as it is not only addressed to the Executive, but to the Legislat⟨ure also⟩.[1] Yours ⟨*mutilated*⟩

AL[S], DNA: RG 59, Miscellaneous Letters; LB, DNA: RG 59, GW's Correspondence with His Secretaries of State. The text in the first set of angle brackets is from the letter-book copy.

1. The enclosure was a letter from the Democratic Society of Washington County, Pa., to GW of 24 March. For Randolph's response, see his third letter to GW of 19 April.

From John Hurt

Sir   Philadelphia 12th April 1794

The enclosed are copies of letters, one of which I desired General Knox to present to you at the time of my resignation:[1] from some circumstances, I have been led to suppose it had been omitted; and for fear this should have been the case, I have, for the satisfaction of my own mind, & that I might not stand in a worse light with you than I deserve, enclosed a certificate with them, signed by Doctor Wistar, of the same purport with one in the former letter, signed by Doctor Rush.[2]

I beg pardon for what may perhaps, appear to you to be an unnecessary trouble. I am Sir, with great respect your most Obedient servant

John Hurt

ALS, DNA: RG 59, Miscellaneous Letters. The cover has a notation that reads, "Favor'd by Mr [John] Page," who currently represented Virginia in the U.S. House of Representatives.

1. Virginia clergyman John Hurt received a chaplain's commission in the U.S. Army in 1791 (see GW's second letter to the U.S. Senate, 4 March 1791). According to his letter to Knox of 31 Dec. 1793, which he wrote while at Philadelphia, Hurt had been "afflicted with pain or sickness since the month of July 1791" and was unable to perform his military duties (DNA: RG 59, Miscellaneous Letters). In his letter to Knox of 6 Jan. 1794, also from Philadelphia, Hurt enclosed his commission, "with a declaration—that if for some time past, I have failed in the attendance required of me, it has been owing, not to want of inclination & good wishes, but to bad health & bodily infirmities" (DNA: RG 59, Miscellaneous Letters).

2. The enclosed certificate from Philadelphia physician and professor Caspar Wistar, Jr., of 11 April certified that Hurt "is affected with the disease known by the name of Hernia, which renders it necessary for him to avoid violent exertions of every kind, & also the effects of Cold, which, by producing Coughing might be very injurious to him" (DNA: RG 59, Miscellaneous Letters). The certificate from Dr. Benjamin Rush has not been identified.

To Henry Knox

Sir,   [Philadelphia, 12 April 1794]

Your report, dated the 11th instt, respecting the defence of Miro district is approved, and the Governor of the South Western Territory may be authorized to carry it into effect.[1] Given at Philadelphia this 12th day of April 1794.

Go: Washington

ALS, DLC:GW; LB, DLC:GW.

1. Knox included the defensive measures suggested in his letter to GW of 11 April in a letter to William Blount of 14 April (Carter, *Territorial Papers*, 4:339).

To Richard Peters

Dear Sir,   Saturday. 12th Aprl [1794]

If you are done with the Pamphlets & Papers which I put into your hands, be so good as to return them, as the Gentleman from whom they were taken, when sent to you, has had no opportunity yet of forming an opinion on them.[1]

Such observations as you have made I would thank you for.[2] Yours &ca

G: Washington

ALS, PHi: Peters Manuscripts.

1. The requested agricultural pamphlets and papers originally had been loaned to James Madison (GW to Madison, 8 Feb., and notes 2 and 3).

2. For Peters' delay in making any observations on the returned publications, see his letter to GW of 14 April.

From Betty Washington Lewis

My Dear Brother   April 13th 1794
  Your letter of the 30th of march came safe to hand,[1] I should of acknowledg'd the receipt of it before this had it not been Owing to my haveing a very severe Ague and fever which Confin'd me to the House for a fortnight, a Complaint tho subject to in the fall, I never had in the spring of the Year before this, it has reduc'd me very much but thank God I am now able to see after my Busness again.
  I have now My Dear Brother to thank you for your kind Preasent of a Mule, as you think it best to send in the Fall I shall defer it till that time,[2] I am very happy to here that you all keep your Helths, as it is reported here that some Dye in that Sitty at this time of that fever which Rag'd there last Fall[3] I hope it is not true, Harriot got her money safe for which she is mutch Ooblig'd to you,[4] she Joines me in Love and Best wish's for you and all our Friends. I am Dear Brother Your Affcte Sister
                                                            Betty Lewis

ALS, ViMtvL.
  1. GW's letter to his sister of 30 March has not been identified.
  2. For the request of a mule, see Betty Washington Lewis to GW, 23 March. On the selection of a specific mule to be sent, see GW's second letter to William Pearce of 28 Sept. (ViMtvL).
  3. On the yellow fever epidemic in Philadelphia during the late summer and fall of 1793, which did not return in spring 1794, see n.19 of GW to Howell Lewis, 25 Aug. 1793.
  4. For Harriot Washington's request for money, see her letter to GW of 24 March.

From John Francis Mercer

Sir   Marlbro. [Md.] April. 13th [17]94.
  I have this day enclosed Mr Gwinn Clerk of th[e] G.C. of Maryland, the Original Survey of partition of the Lands you purchased of me—& directed him to record the same & then transmit it to you—I now herewith transmit you the first deed executed to you, the record was delay'd untill the Deed ran out

of date[1]—I then consulted Mr J.T. Chace, Judge of the G.C. of M. who it is to be observ'd took all the acknowledgements, if it wou'd not be possible to alter the dates or render it efficient in some other manner, but after mature reflection he judged it necessary to execute another Deed entirely anew, & this was the sole cause why it was so done.[2] I am with sincere respect & esteem Yr Ob. hbl. Sert

John F. Mercer

ALS, NN: Washington Collection.

1. GW had requested a copy of the original survey of the partition of Woodstock Manor in Montgomery County, Md., in a letter of 10 March 1794 to John Gwinn, clerk of the Maryland General Court. The 2 Jan. 1793 survey was recorded on 18 April 1794 (ViMtvL). On the original deed of 1 April 1793 for the 519 acres belonging to GW, see n.1 of GW to John Francis Mercer, 7 Aug. 1793.

2. Mercer had consulted with Jeremiah Townley Chase.

To George Minor

Sir,   Philadelphia 13th Aprl 1794

From a letter which I have lately received from Doctr Stuart, I learn that depredations continue to be made upon my land on four mile run, in the County of Fairfax; & that you were so obliging as to inform him, that you would use your endeavours to rescue it from further injury if I should request it.[1]

This offer is kind, and I thank you for having had the goodness to make it; and do hereby vest you with power to watch over, & punish in any manner the Laws will authorise, any, and every person whatsoever who shall be found trespassing thereon.

The growth on the land, I always considered as the most valuable part of the property; stripped of this, as there appears to be a strong disposition to do by lawless people, and the value of it is reduced in the ratio of the Trespasses.

Sometime since, perhaps two or three years, I desired my Nephew Mr Bushrod Washington to bring suits against those who had been detected in taking off Wood, Hoop poles, &ca but what, or whether any thing resulted from it, is unknown to me at this moment.[2]

Nothing short of vigorous measures, I am now persuaded, will stop the injustice I am sustaining, and these I am resolved to pursue. any reasonable expence therefore which may be in-curred in carrying this resolution into effect, & for your trouble, will be cheerfully paid by Sir Your Obedient Hble Servt

Go: Washington

P.S. I have directed Mr Wm Pearce my Manager to converse with you on this business when he shall see you in Alexandria.[3]

ALS (letterpress copy), DLC:GW; LB, DLC:GW. GW enclosed this letter in his letter to David Stuart of this date.

1. Stuart informed GW in a letter of 4 April that timber, especially the hoop-ash trees, was being removed from GW's land at Four Mile Run.

2. For GW's charge to his nephew and for Bushrod Washington's response, see GW to Bushrod Washington, 8 Jan. 1792, and notes 3 and 4.

3. GW gave these directions in a letter to Pearce of this date.

To William Pearce

Mr Pearce,   Philadelphia April 13th 1794

By your letter of the 9th instt (which with the weekly reports) have been duly received,[1] I find you wish to open a communica-tion between the lower rooms, in what is called the Servants Hall, and to make a closet therein: against the latter I have no objection at all—nor against the first provided the doing it does not cut away a brace, and thereby weaken the house. If the chim-neys project into the rooms (as I think they do) a closet may be conveniently made in one of the recesses, between the jamb and the side of the house; and if two closets are not made, the one that is put up, would look better, and be more out of the way, in the back side, than front of the room. However, unless I was to examine it with a particular eye to this measure, I may be mis-taken in my judgment of it; & therefore leave it to you to fix it where it shall be found most convenient.

As I have mentioned in one of my former letters to you, so now I repeat, that it is not my wish that more important work, that is, work which cannot be delayed without producing injuri-ous consequences, should be put aside or neglected on account of the Mill Race. The completion of the latter, though very de-sirable had better be postponed than many other things which might involve the loss, or diminution of the ensuing Crop.[2] I expected, & believe I mentioned in one of my letters to you, that the digging of this Race would prove laborious after the wet of the winter should have passed away—much of my land has that hard bottom to it, wch is the cause of its being so wet in winter & hard in Summer.[3]

Does it appear to you that the grain can be tread out much faster upon the open floor in the New Barn at Dogue run, than it can be in the usual way on the ground? What are the advantages and disadvantages, if any, of treading the grain out in this manner? It wd be well to examine them closely, that I may not only be able to decide on the utility of the plan, but to improve on the good parts and avoid the bad ones, if there be such, in future.[4]

Unless the weather grows warmer, your fishing, this season, will, I fear, prove unproductive; for it has always been observed, that in cold & windy weather the fish keep in deep water, and are never caught in numbers, especially at shallow landings.

In a letter which I have lately received from Colo. Ball, he informs me that he had, at that time, sent off (in the whole) 454½ bushls of Buckwheat for Mount Vernon; & that the remainder of the 500 bushls viz. 44½ should be sent to you during the fishing season; and, that he had written to you, he should want a quantity of fish for his own use. How far your engagement with Mr Smith, or any other, will enable you to comply with his request remains for yourself to decide. If the doing of it would interfere with no contract I could wish to oblige him; but contracts must always be fulfilled.[5]

Whenever a field—a lot—or any spot of ground is sown with either grain or grass—let the time when finished, and the quantity of seed sown therein, be entered in the Weekly report of the place where it happens—for, as these reports are in the nature of a record, of the occurances on each farm—to be resorted to at any time hereafter—it will be very satisfactory to know when the fields—the meadows—Lots, or other ground were sown; with what; & the quantity of seed bestowed thereon.

I have a tract of Woodland of 1200 acres about 4 miles from Alexandria, on the great Road to Leesburgh, whose principal value is on acct of the Timber, wood & Hoop poles—and of all these, I am informed it has been most shamefully pillaged. I have by this days Post, by the advice of, & under cover to, Doctr Stuart, wrote to a Gentleman of the name of Minor (who lives near to it) requesting the favor of him to have an eye to the land;

Whenever you may see Mr Minor (wch may be at the Courts in Alexa.) spk to, & concert measures with him, for putting a stop to the continual depredations which I am told a parcel of trespassers are making on the land, by absolute Sales of the articles beforementioned, to the very great injury of the property.[6] I remain Your friend

Go: Washington

ALS (letterpress copy), DLC:GW.

1. Pearce's letter of 9 April and the enclosed farm reports have not been found.

2. For this previous instruction, see GW to Pearce, 24 February.

3. For GW's previous observations on the difficulty of digging the race, see GW to Pearce, 19 Jan. and 24 February.

4. For the design of the new treading barn at Dogue Run farm, see the plan enclosed in GW to Anthony Whitting, 28 Oct. 1792.

5. The letter from Burgess Ball was that of 5 April. Ball's letter to Pearce has not been identified. On the fishing contract with Alexander Smith, see Smith to GW, 3 July 1793, and GW to Pearce, 23 March 1794, and n.5.

6. On the removal of timber from GW's land on Four Mile Run in Fairfax County, Va., see David Stuart to GW, 4 April; GW to George Minor, this date; and GW to Stuart, also this date.

To David Stuart

Dear Sir, Philadelphia 13th Aprl 1794

I have been favored with your letter of the 4th instt and thank you for the information respecting the depredations on my land, lying on four miles run. Mr Bushrod Washington a year or two ago, was desired to commence a suit or suits against some of the Trespassers; but whether he did, or not, or what the result was, I do not recollect ever to have heard.[1] The growth of the land, is more valuable than the land itself; to protect it therefore is important.

Not knowing the christian name of Mr Minor, or whether there may not be more than one of that name—I am at a loss how to direct to him; and indeed for a safe mode of conveying a letter to him; and therefore take the liberty of putting the enclosed under cover to you, with a request (after putting a wafer in it) that you would be so good as to have it safely conveyed to the right person.[2]

The accounts which I receive from Mount Vernon, respecting

my Wheat, are very unfavorable. They could not, indeed, be otherwise, after the effect, occasioned by drought in the fall had become apparent, which was the case before I left home in the latter part of October.[3]

The appointment of a Marshal, for the District of Georgia, had taken place before your letter came to my hands: but if the case had been otherwise, Mr McCrea, however well known in Virginia, was too new a settler, and too little known in Georgia to have become an acceptable man for that office when half the State (in a manner) was in hot pursuit of it. & many of the ancient inhabitants & repectable characters were pressing forward by themselves, & friends, on this occasion.[4]

My best wishes attend Mrs Stuart and the rest of the family, & with very great esteem & regard—I am—Dear Sir Your Affecte Servant

Go: Washington

ALS (letterpress copy), NN: Washington Papers; LB, DLC:GW.

1. For GW's instructions and the results, see GW to Bushrod Washington, 8 Jan. 1792, and notes 3 and 4.

2. The enclosure was GW's letter to George Minor of this date.

3. Recent farm reports from Mount Vernon have not been found. The previous extant reports are those for 2–8 Feb., and the next extant reports are those for 25–31 May (both DLC:GW).

4. Stuart's letter of 4 April, in which he recommended former Alexandria merchant Robert McCrea for appointment to the position of U.S. marshal for the District of Georgia, came too late for consideration (see GW to the U.S. Senate, 5 March).

Bartholomew Dandridge, Jr., to Henry Babcock

Sir,   Philada 14 April 1794.

The President of the United S. directs me to thank you for the tender of your services to your Country; and, agreeably to your request, to return the Certificate herewith enclosed.[1] I am, Sir, Your obt Servt

B. Dandridge
Secy to the Prest U.S.

ALS, DNA: RG 59, Miscellaneous Letters; LB, DLC:GW.

1. Henry Babcock (1736–1800), a native of Rhode Island and a 1752 graduate of Yale, fought in the French and Indian War, 1755–59. He served briefly

in 1776 as a colonel in the Continental army during the Revolutionary War, but he was dismissed from service for health reasons. At this time, he resided in Stonington, Connecticut. The enclosed certificate has not been identified.

From Jeremy Belknap

Sir   Boston April 14. 1794

The favourable reception which you gave to my History of New Hampshire encourages me to present you the first volume of an American Biography.[1]

In the 326th page I have given a particular description of the place *originally* called St Croix, in hope that it might throw some light on the Controversy with the British Government respecting the Eastern boundary of the United States.[2]

The prosecution of this work will probably employ a great part of the remaining years of my life—and any assistance which can be afforded me will be very acceptable.[3] Should you find leisure from your public duties to furnish me with any communications in this way, the favour will be gratefully acknowledged by sir Yr very humble servt

Jeremy Belknap

ALS, DLC:GW.

1. GW thanked Belknap for volume 1 of the *History of New Hampshire* in a letter of 5 Jan. 1785. The current gift was volume 1 of *American Biography: or, An historical account of those persons who have been distinguished in America, as adventurers, statesmen, philosophers, divines, warriors, authors, and other remarkable characters. Comprehending a recital of the events connected with their lives and actions* (Boston, 1794). Both volumes were in GW's library at the time of his death. GW also possessed a complete three-volume set of the *History of New Hampshire,* and an additional volume 1 and a volume 2 of *American Biography* (Griffin, *Catalogue of the Washington Collection,* 508–9).

2. The chapter on the early French explorers de Monts, Poutrincourt, and Samuel Champlain includes a lengthy footnote that gives a detailed description of the island of Saint Croix and its surrounding waters, that is, the Saint Croix River in Maine (*American Biography,* 1:326–30). This island was assigned to the United States in 1798, and the river serves as a boundary between Maine and the Canadian province of New Brunswick (Miller, *Treaties,* 2:427–32).

3. GW's reply of 9 May reads: "Your letter of the 14th Ulto, and the first Vol. of an American Biography, came safe to my hands. For both I pray you to accept my thanks; and to consider me as a subscriber for the latter."

"I wish it was in my power to afford you any aid in the prosecution of so desirable a work. But I do not see wherein I can; and if I did, my avocations are of such a nature as to allow me no time to profit by the means. My good wishes therefore seems to be all that is left me, on this occasion" (ALS [photocopy], Profiles in History, catalog 15 (1992), item 10; ALS [letterpress copy], NN: Washington Papers; LB, DLC:GW; copy, MHi: Belknap Papers).

From John Fitzgerald

Dear Sir   Alexandria [Va.] Aprill 14th 1794

When I last had the honor of dining with you in this town, I mention'd the information given by some people in Maryland to the executive of that state respecting the Estate of Thomas Digges, & wishing to bring it under the confiscation Law[.][1] This Business is now drawing to a Crisis, & it may possibly be brought to trial next Month in the General Court[.] I am possess'd of a great variety of Proofs in support of Mr Digges's Agency & Activity during the American War, which I believe were exerted at the utmost peril, as he was strongly suspect'd & narrowly watched in England at that time[.] Upon mentioning the observations you were pleased to make respecting Mr Digges's conduct my Lawyers think it highly essential that your testimony on this matter should be obtained, as that will immediately silence the Gentry who wish to enrich themselves in this summary way[.] Your love of Justice I well know, would induce you to set matters right on any common occasion, where circumstances happen'd within your knowledge but in this I feel a flattering confidence, that you will with pleasure step forward, & testify what you know of Mr Digges during & since the War, as you will thereby not only do justice to his patriotic Character, but perhaps save an Estate to the Descendants, of an old friend & Neighbour, & to a family which from a strong habit of intimacy with yours, I have every reason to believe you honor with your friendship[.] I take the liberty of giving you this previous information that you may at any leisure moment make a memorandum of what has come to your Knowledge on this subject, & have no farther trouble than delivering it to the Commissioners appointed.[2]

I think you will be so good as to believe me when I declare that it is with the most painful reluctance I give you this trouble, well knowing the weight of Business with which your mind must be oppressed at this particular time but the greatness of the Object & the iniquity of the claim will I hope plead my excuse[.] that you may long enjoy health & happiness is the most sincere & ardent Wish of Dear Sir your mo. Obedient Hble Servant

John Fitzgerald

ALS, DLC:GW. The cover has "private" written on it.

1. GW was at Mount Vernon between mid-September and 28 Oct. 1793, and he probably dined at Alexandria with Fitzgerald during this time period (*JPP*, 239–41). For the complicated and precarious economic history of Thomas Attwood Digges and the family disputes over ownership of Warburton Manor, the family estate located across the Potomac River and within sight of Mount Vernon, see the "Introduction" in Elias and Finch, *Digges Letters*. Digges had been in England when the Revolutionary War broke out, and during this time, he assisted American prisoners of war in England. He did not return to the United States until late 1798, when he settled at Warburton Manor. He visited Mount Vernon several times before GW's death in December 1799 (*Diaries*, 6:333, 346, 351, 361).

2. For GW's favorable comments about Digges, see his letter to Fitzgerald of 27 April.

From Alexander Hamilton

Sir   Philadelphia April [14] 1794

The present is beyond question a great, a difficult & a perilous crisis in the affairs of this country. In such a crisis it is the duty of every man, according to situation, to contribute all in his power towards preventing evil and producing good. This consideration will I trust be a sufficient apology for the liberty I am about to take of submitting without an official call the ideas which occupy my mind concerning the actual posture of our public affairs. It cannot but be of great importance that the chief Magistrate should be informed of the real state of things; and it is not easy for him to have this information but through those principal officers who have most frequent access to him—Hence an obligation on their part to communicate information on occasions like the present.

A course of accurate observation has impressed on my mind a full conviction, that there exist in our councils three considerable parties—one decided for preserving peace by every effort which shall any way consist with the ultimate maintainance of the national honor and rights and disposed to cultivate with all nations a friendly understanding—another decided for war and resolved to bring it about by every expedient which shall not too directly violate the public opinion—a third not absolutely desirous of war but solicitous at all events to excite and keep alive irritation and ill humour between the U. States and Great Britain, not unwilling in the pursuit of this object to expose the peace of the country to imminent hazards.

The views of the first party in respect to the questions between G. Britain and us favour the following course of conduct— To take effectual measures of military preparation, creating in earnest force and revenue—to vest the President with important powers respecting navigation and commerce for ulterior contingencies—to endeavour by another effort of negotiation confided to hands able to manage it and friendly to the object, to obtain reparation for the wrongs we suffer and a demarkation of a line of conduct to govern in future—to avoid 'till the issue of that experiment all measures of a nature to occasion a conflict between the motives which might dispose the British Government to do us the justice to which we are intitled and the sense of its own dignity—If that experiment fails then and not till then to resort to reprisals and war.[1]

The views of the second party, in respect to the same questions favour the following course of conduct—to say and to do every thing which can have a tendency to stir up the passions of the people and beget a disposition favourable to war—to make use of the inflamation which is excited in the community for the purposes of carrying through measures calculated to disgust Great Britain and to render an accomodation impracticable, without humiliation to her, which they do not believe will be submitted to—in fine, to provoke and bring on war by indirect means without declaring it or even avowing the intention; because they know the public mind is not yet prepared for such an extremity and they fear to encounter the direct responsibility of being the authors of a War.

The views of the third party lead them to favour the measures of the second—but without a perfect coincidence in the result. They weakly hope that they may hector and vapour with success—that the pride of Great Britain will yield to her interest—and that they may accomplish the object of perpetuating animosity between the two countries without involving War.[2]

There are some characters, not numerous, who do not belong to either of these classes—but who fluctuate between them as in the conflict between Reason & Passion, the one or the other prevails.

It may seem difficult to admit in the situation of this Country that there are parties of the description of the two last; men who can either systematically meditate war or can be willing to risk it otherwise than by the use of means which they deem necessary to insure reparation for the injuries we experience.

But a due attention to the course of the human passions as recorded in history and exemplified by daily occurrences is sufficient to obviate all difficulty on this head.

Wars oftener proceed from angry and perverse passions than from cool calculations of Interest—This position is admitted without difficulty when we are judging of the hostile appearances in the measures of Great Britain towards this country.[3] What reason can there be why it should not be as good a test of similar appearances on our part? As men, it is equally applicable to us—and the symptoms are strong of our being readily enough worked up into a degree of rage and phrenzy, which goes very far towards silencing the voice of reason and interest.

Those who compose the parties whose measures have a War-Aspect are under the influence of some of the strongest passions that can actuate human conduct. They unite from habitual feeling in an implacable hatred to Great Britain and in a warm attachment to France. Their animosity against the former is inflamed by the most violent resentment for recent and unprovoked injuries—in many instances by personal loss and suffering or the loss and suffering of intimate friends and conections. Their sympathy with the latter is increased by the idea of her being engaged in defending the cause of liberty against a combination of despots who meditate nothing less than the destruction of it throughout the world.[4] In hostility with Britain they seek the gratification of revenge upon a detested enemy with that of serving a favourite friend and in this the cause of liberty. They anticipate also, what is in their estimation a great political good, a more complete and permanent alienation from Great Britain and a more close approximation to France. Those even of them who do not wish the extremity of war consider it as a less evil than a thorough and sincere accomodation with Great Britain and are willing to risk the former rather than lose an opportunity so favourable as the present to extend and rivet the springs of ill will against that Nation.

However necessary it is to viel this policy in public—in private there are not much pains taken to disguise it. Some Gentlemen do not scruple to say that pacification is and ought to be out of the question.

What has been heretofore said relates only to persons in public character. If we extend our view from these to the community at large, we shall there also find a considerable diversity of opinion—partizans of patience negotiation and peace, if possible, and partisans of war. There is no doubt much of irritation now afloat—many advocates for measures tending to produce war. But it would be a great mistake to infer from these appearances that the prevailing sentiment of the Country is for war—or that there would be either a willing acquiescence or a zealous cooperation in it if the proceedings of the government should not be such as to render it manifestly beyond question, that war was inevitable but by an absolute sacrifice of the rights and interests of the Nation—that the race of prudence was completely run and that nothing was done to invite hostility or left undone to avoid it.

It is to my mind unequivocal, that the great mass of opinion in the Eastern States and in the State of New York is against War if it can be avoided without absolute dishonor or the ultimate sacrifice of essential rights and interests—and I verily believe that the same sentiment is the radical one throughout the U. States, *some* of the towns perhaps exepted, where even it is much to be doubted whether there would not be a minority for the affirmative of the naked question of war or of measures which should be acknowleged to have a tendency to promote or produce it.

The natural inference from such a state of the public mind is—that if measures are adopted with the disapprobation and dissent of a large and enlightened minority of Congress, which in the event should appear to have been obstacles to a peaceable adjustment of our differences with Great Britain—there would be under the pressure of the evils produced by them a deep and extensive dissatisfaction with the conduct of the Government—a loss of confidence in it—and an impatience under the measures which War would render unavoidable.

Prosperous as is truly the situation of this country, great as would be the evils of War to it, it would hardly seem to admit of a doubt, that no chance for preserving peace ought to be lost or diminished, in compliance either with resentment or the speculative ideas, which are the arguments for a hostile course of conduct.

At no moment were the indications of a plan on the part of Great Britain to go to War with us sufficiently decisive to preclude the hope of averting it by a negotiation conducted with prudent energy and seconded by such military preparations as should be demonstrative of a Resolution eventually to vindicate our rights. The revocation of the instructions of the 6th of November even with the relaxation of some pretensions which Great Britain has in former wars maintained against Neutral Powers is full evidence that if the system was before for War it was then changed.[5] The events which have taken place in Europe are of a nature to render it probable that such a system will not be revived and that by prudent management we may still escape a calamity which we have the strongest motives internal as well as external to shun.

I express myself thus—because it is certainly not an idle apprehension that the example of France (whose excesses are too many an object of apology if not of justification) may be found to have unhinged the orderly principles of the People of this country and that War by putting in motion all the turbulent passions and promoting a further assimilation of our principles with those of France may prove to be the threshold of disorganization and anarchy.

The late successes of France have produced in this country conclusions much too sanguine with regard to the event of the Contest—They no doubt afford a high probability of her being able eventually to defend herself especially under a form of administration of such unexampled vigour as that by which she has of late managed her affairs. But there will be nothing wonderful in a total reverse of fortune during the ensuing campaign. Human nature must be an absolutely different thing in France from what it has hitherto shewn itself to be throughout the globe and in all ages if there do not exist in a large proportion of the French Nation germs of the profoundest discontent ready to burst into vegetation the moment there should appear an efficacious prospect of protection and shade from the progress of the invading armies—And if having possessed themselves of some of the keys of France the principle of the commencing campaign should be different from that of the past—active field operations succeeding to the wasteful and dilatory process of seiges[6]—who can say that Victory may not so far crown the enterprises of the coalesced powers as to open the way to an internal explosion which may prove fatal to the Republic? Tis now evident that another vigorous campaign will be essayed by the Allies. The result is and must be incalculable.

To you, Sir, it is unnecessary to urge the extreme precariousness of the events of War. The inference to be drawn is too manifest to escape your penetration. This Country ought not to set itself afloat upon an ocean so fluctuating so dangerous and so uncertain but in a case of absolute necessity.

That necessity is certainly not yet apparent. The circumstances which have been noticed with regard to the recent change of conduct on the part of G. Britain authorise a strong hope that a negotiation conducted with ability and moderation and supported at home by demonstrations of vigour and seriousness would obviate those causes of collision which are the most urgent—might even terminate others which have so long fostered dissatisfaction and enmity. There is room to suppose that the moment is peculiarly favourable to such an attempt. On this point there are symptoms of a common sentiment between the advocates and the opposers of an unembarrassed attempt to negotiate—the former desiring it from the confidence they have in its probable success—-the latter from the same cause endeavouring either to prevent its going on under right auspices or to clog it with impediments which will frustrate its effect.

All ostensibly agree that one more experiment of negotiation ought to precede actual war; but there is this serious difference in the practice. The sincere friends of peace and accomodation are for leaving things in a state which will enable Great Britain without abandoning self-respect to do us the justice we seek— The others are for placing things upon a footing which would involve the disgrace or disrepute of having receded through intimidation.

This last scheme indubitably ends in War. The folly is too great to be seriously entertained by the discerning part of those who affect to believe the position—that Great Britain fortified by the alliances of the greatest part of Europe will submit to our demands urged with the face of coertion and preceded by acts of reprisal. She cannot do it without renouncing her pride and her dignity, without losing her consequence and weight in the scale of Nations—and consequently it is morally certain that she will not do it. A proper estimate of the operation of the human passions must satisfy us that she would be less disposed to receive the law from us than from any other nation—a people recently become a nation, not long since one of her dependencies, and as yet, if a Hercules—a Hercules in the cradle.

When one nation inflicts injuries upon another, which are causes of war, if this other means to negotiate before it goes to War, the usual and received course is to prepare for War and proceed to negotiation—avoiding reprisals till the issue of the Negotiation. This course is recommended by all enlightened Writers on the laws of Nations as the course of moderation propriety and wisdom and it is that commonly pursued except where there is a disposition to go to war or a commanding superiority of Power.

Preparation for War in such cases contains in it nothing offensive. It is a mere precaution for self defence under circumstances which endanger the breaking out of War. It gives rise to no point of honor which can be a bar to equitable and amicable negotiation. But acts of reprisal speak a contrary effect—they change negotiation into peremptory demand and they brandish a rod over the party on whom the demand is made. He must be humble indeed, if he comply with the demand to avoid the stripe.

Such are the propositions which have lately appeared in the House of Representatives for the sequestration or arrestation of British Debts—for the cutting off of all intercourse with Great Britain till she shall do certain specific things. If such propositions pass they can only be regarded as provocatives to a Declaration of War by Great Britain.[7]

The sequestration of Debts is treated by all writers as one of the highest species of Reprisal. It is moreover contrary to the most approved practice of the present century, to what may be safely pronounced to be the modern rule of the law of Nations— to what is so plainly dictated by original principles of Justice and good faith that nothing but the barbarism of times in which war was the principal business of man could ever have tolerated an opposite practice—to the manifest interest of a people situated like that of the U. State; which having a vast fund of materials for improvement in various ways ought to invite into the channels of their industry the Capital of Europe, by giving to it inviolable security—which, giving little facility to extensive revenue from taxation, ought for its own safety in war to cherish its credit by a religious observance of the maxims of credit in all their branches.

The proposition for cutting off all intercourse with G. Britain has not yet sufficiently devellopped itself to enable us to pronounce what it truly is. It may be so extensive in its provisions as even to include in fact though not in form sequestration by rendering remittances penal or impracticable. Indeed it can scarcely avoid so far interfering with the payment of debts already contracted as in a great degree to amount to a virtual sequestration. But however this may be—being adopted for the express purpose of retaliating or punishing injuries to continue until those injuries are redressed it is in the spirit of a reprisal—Its principle is avowedly coertion—a principle directly opposite to that of negotiation, which supposes an appeal to the reason and justice of the party. Caustic and stimulant in the highest degree, it cannot fail to have a correspondent effect upon the minds of those against whom it is directed—It cannot fail to be viewed as originating in motives of the most hostile and overbearing kind—to stir up all the feelings of pride and resentment in the nation as well as in the cabinet—and consequently to render negotiation abortive.

It will be wonderful if the immediate effect of either of these measures be not either War or the seizure of our vessels wherever they are found, on the ground of keeping them as hostages for the debts due to the British Merchants and on the additional ground of the measures themselves being either acts of hostility or evidence of a disposition to hostility.

The interpretation will naturally be that our views originally pacific have changed with the change in the affairs of France, and are now bent towards War.

The measures in question, besides the objection to them resulting from their tendency to produce war, are condemned by a comprehensive and enlightened view of their operation in other respects.

They cannot but have a malignant influence upon our public and mercantile credit—They will be regarded abroad as violent and precipitate. It will be said there is no reliance to be placed on the steadiness or solidity of concerns with this people— Every gust that arises in the political sky is the signal for measures tending to destroy their ability to pay or to obstruct the course of payment. Instead of a people pacific, forbearing moderate and of rigid probity we see in them a people turbulent hasty intemperate and loose—sporting with their individual obligations and disturbing the general course of their affairs with levity and inconsiderateness.

Such will indubitably be the comments upon our conduct— The favourable impressions now entertained of the character of our government and Nation will infallibly be reversed.

The cutting off of intercourse with Great Britain to distress her seriously must extend to the prohibition of all her commodities indirectly as well as directly. Else it will have no other operation than to transfer the Trade between the two countries to the hands of foreigners to our disadvantage more than that of Great Britain.

If it extends to the total prohibition of her commodities, however brought, it deprives us of a supply, for which no substitute can be found elsewhere, a supply necessary to us in peace and more necessary to us if we are to go to War. It gives a sudden and violent blow to our revenue—which cannot easily if at all be repaired from other resources. It will give so great an interruption to commerce as may very possibly interfere with the payment of the duties which have heretofore accrued and bring the Treasury to an absolute stoppage of payment—an event which would cut up credit by the roots.

The consequences of so great and so sudden a disturbance of our Trade which must affect our exports as well as our Imports are not to be calculated. An excessive rise in the price of foreign commodities—a proportional decrease in price and demand of our own commodities—the derangement of our revenue and credit—these circumstances united may occasion the most dangerous dissatisfaction & disorders in the community and may drive the governt to a disgraceful retreat—independent of foreign causes.

To adopt the measure in *terrorem* and postpone its operation will be scarcely a mitigation of the Evil. The expectation of it will as to our imports have the effect of the reality; since we must obtain what we want chiefly upon credit. Our supply and our revenue therefore will suffer nearly as much as if there was an immediate interruption.

The effect, with regard to our peace will be the same. The principle being menace and coertion will equally recommend resistance to the policy as well as the pride of the other party. Tis only to consult our own hearts to be convinced that nations like individuals revolt at the idea of being guided by external compulsion. They will at least only yield to that idea after resistance has been fruitlessly tried in all its forms.

Tis as great an error for a nation to overrate as to underrate itself. Presumption is as great a fault as timidity. Tis our error to overrate ourselves and to underrate Great Britain. We forget how little we can annoy how much we may be annoyed.

Tis enough for us, situated as we are, to be resolved to vindicate our honor and our rights in the last extremity. To preci⟨p⟩itate a great conflict of any sort is utterly unsuited to our condition to our strength or to our resources. This is a truth to be well weighed by every wise and dispassionate man as the rule of public action.

There are two ideas of immense consequence to us in the event of War. The disunion of our enemies—the perfect union of our own citizens—Justice and moderation united with firmness are the means to secure both these advantages. Injustice or Intemperance will lose both.

Unanimity among ourselves, which is the most important of the two ideas, can only be secured by its being manifest, if war ensues, that it was inevitable by another course of conduct. This cannot and will not be the case, if measures so intemperate as those which are meditated take place. The inference will be that the war was brought on by the design of some and the rashness of others. This inference will be universal in the Northern States, and to you Sir I need not urge the importance of those states in war.

want of unanimity will naturally tend to render the operations of War feeble and heavy—to destroy both effort and perseverance. War undertaken under such auspices can scarcely end in any thing better than an inglorious and disadvantageous peace. What worse it may produce is beyond the reach of human foresight.

The foregoing observations are designed to convey to the mind of the President information of the true state of things at the present juncture and to present to his consideration the general reasons which have occurred to me against the course of proceeding which appears to be favoured by a majority of the House of Representatives.

My solicitude for the public interest, according to the view I have of it, and my real respect and regard for him to whom I address myself lead me to subjoin some reflections of a more delicate nature.

The crisis is such a one as involves the highest responsibility on the part of every one who may have to act a part in it—It is one in which every man will be understood to be bound to act according to his judgment without concession to the ideas of others—The President, who has by the constitution a right to object to laws, which he deems contrary to the public interest, will be considered as under an indispensable obligation to exercise that right against any measure, relating to so vast a point as that of the peace of the Country, which shall not accord with his opinion[8]—The consideration of its having been adopted by both Houses of Congress and of respect for their opinion will have no weight in such a case as a reason for forbearing to exercise the right of objection—The consequence is that the not objecting will be deemed conclusive evidence of approbation and will implicate the President in all the consequences of the measure.

In such a position of things it is therefore of the utmost importance to him as well as to the community that he should trace out in his own mind such a plan as he thinks it would be eligible to pursue and should endeavour by proper and constitutional means to give the deliberations of Congress a direction towards that plan.

Else he runs the risk of being reduced to the dilemma either of assenting to measures, which he may not approve, with a full responsi[bi]lity for consequences—or of objecting to measures which have already received the sanction of the two houses of Congress with the responsibility of having resisted and probably prevented what they meditated. Neither of these alternatives is a desireable one.

It seems adviseable, then, that The President should come to a conclusion, whether the plan ought to be preparation for war and negotiation unincumbered by measures which forbid the expectation of success—or immediate measures of a coercive tendency to be accompanied with the ceremony of a demand of redress. For I believe there is no middle plan between these two courses.

If the former appears to him to be the true policy of the Country, I submit it as my conviction that it is *urgent* for him to demonstrate that opinion as a preventive of wrong measures and future embarrassment.

The mode of doing it which occurs is this—to nominate a person, who will have the confidence of those who think peace still within our reach, and who may be thought qualified for the mission as envoy extraordinary to Great Britain—to announce to the one as well as the other House of Congress with an observation that it is done with an intention to make a solemn appeal to the justice and good sense of the British Government to avoid if possible an ulterior rupture and adjust the causes of misunderstanding between the two Countries—and with an earnest recommendation that vigorous and effectual measures may be adopted to be prepared for war should it become inevitable—abstaining for the present from measures which may be contrary to the spirit of an attempt to adjust existing differences by Negotiation.

Knowing as I do Sir that I am among the persons who have been in your contemplation to be employed in the capacity I have mentioned, I should not have taken the present step, had I not been resolved at the same time to advise you with decision to drop me from the consideration and to fix upon another character. I am not unapprised of what has been the byass of your opinion on the subject—I am well aware of all the collateral obstacles which exist—and I assure you in the utmost sincerity that I shall be completely and intirely satisfied with the election of another.[9]

I beg leave to add that of the persons whom you would deem free from any constitutional objections—Mr Jay is the only man in whose qualifications for success there would be thorough confidence and him whom alone it would be adviseable to send. I think the business would have the best chance possible in his hands. And I flatter myself that his mission would issue in a manner that would produce the most important good to the Nation.[10]

Let me add Sir that those whom I call the soberminded men of the Country look up to You with solicitude upon the present occasion. If happily you should be the instrument of still rescuing the Country from the dangers and calamities of War, there is no part of your life, Sir, which will produce to you more real satisfaction or true Glory than that which shall be distinguished by this very important service.

In any event I cannot doubt Sir that you will do justice to the motives which impel me and that you will see in this proceeding another proof of my sincere wishes for your honor & happiness and anxiety for the public weal. With the truest respect and attachment I have the Honor to be Sir Your most obedient & humble servant

Alexand⟨e⟩r Hamilton

ALS, DLC: Hamilton Papers. GW's docket reads, "recd 14th April 1794."

1. Massachusetts congressman Theodore Sedgwick introduced eight resolutions in the House of Representatives on 12 March that were designed to create a program of national defense (*Annals of Congress,* 3d Cong., 500–501).

2. Virginia congressman James Madison proposed seven resolutions on 3 Jan. that would have created a policy of commercial retaliation against Great Britain (*Annals of Congress,* 3d Cong., 155–56).

3. On British interference with U.S. trade, see Edmund Randolph to GW, 2 March.

4. This is a reference to the coalition forces of Austria, Prussia, Great Britain, and other monarchial European nations that were currently at war with the Republic of France.

5. On the revocation of the 6 Nov. 1793 British order-in- council, and its replacement by instructions dated 8 Jan. 1794, see n.1 of Edmund Randolph to GW, 3 April.

6. For a contemporary account of the successful siege and recapture of the port of Toulon by the Republic of France on 19 Dec. 1793, see the 11 March 1794 issue of the *Gazette of the United States* (Philadelphia).

7. Jonathan Dayton of New Jersey offered a resolve in the House of Representatives on 27 March that would have provided for "the sequestration of all the debts due from the citizens of the United States to the subjects of the King of Great Britain." New Jersey congressman Abraham Clark's proposals of 7 April called for an end to all commercial intercourse with Great Britain until the British government caused "restitution to be made for all losses and damages sustained by the citizens of the United States" from British seizures of American ships and cargo and until "all the posts now held and detained by the King of Great Britain, within the territories of the United States, shall be surrendered" (*Annals of Congress,* 3d Cong., 535, 561). None of these proposals became law.

8. Section 7 of Article I of the U.S. Constitution gives the president the power to veto a law passed by both houses of Congress.

9. For objections to Hamilton's nomination, see John Nicholas to GW, 6 April, and James Monroe to GW, 8 April.

10. For GW's nomination of John Jay as envoy extraordinary to Great Britain, see his first letter to the U.S. Senate of 16 April.

To Henry Knox

Sir,   [Philadelphia, 14 April 1794]

Consider, and report such an answer to the letter herewith enclosed (from the Governor of the State of Pennsylvania of this date) as the contents in your judgment may require.[1]

Given at Phila. this 14th day of April 1794.

G. W——n

ADfS, DLC:GW; LB, DLC:GW.

1. For the enclosed letter and Knox's reply to Thomas Mifflin of 15 April, see Mifflin to GW, 14 April, and n.3.

From Thomas Mifflin

Sir.   Philadelphia: 14th April 1794.

A body of about 120 Seamen, who declared to me that they were British subjects, deprived of employment in consequence of the Embargo, having paraded with colours flying through the streets of the City, and intending (as several respectable Citizens informed me) to address Congress, and yourself, for relief, I deemed it incumbent upon me to take proper precautions for preventing any outrage upon the occasion; and, accordingly, ordered out a party of the Militia. The present cause of apprehension being removed, it is only necessary to communicate to you, that, for a short time, a small guard from the Militia will be stationed at the State-house; and to assure you I shall ever be prompt, on the first symptoms of riot or disorder, to interpose with all my constitutional power, for preserving the public peace, and the dignity of the Government inviolate.[1]

It may be proper, by this opportunity to submit to your consideration, the memorial whch I had recd, previously to the occurrence above mented, from a number of Sailors, founded on the same cause of complaint.[2] As I have promised that an answer shall be given on the day after tomorrow, I wish to be apprised of your sentiments on the subject.[3] With perft respt, I am yr Excys. most obt humble Servt

Thos. Mifflin.

Df, PharH: Executive Correspondence, 1790–99; LB, PHarH: Executive Letter-Books.

1. The embargo of 26 March was "laid on all ships and vessels in the ports of the United States . . . for a term of thirty days" (*Stat.* 1:400). According to an article in the 15 April issue of the *General Advertiser* (Philadelphia), "Yesterday a number of sailors made a procession throughout the streets of this city to remind the inhabitants that they are *out of employment.*"

Mifflin's second set of orders of 14 April to Josiah Harmar, the adjutant general of the Pennsylvania militia, reads: "In consequence of the riotous appearance of a considerable body of British seamen, I gave you a parol order, this day, for drafting a party from the Militia: but as the seamen have dispersed, you will dismiss all the party . . . except twelve men from the Artillery, and twenty five from the Infantry, who are to be stationed, with two field-pieces at the State House, until further orders (PHarH: Executive Letter-Books). The Pennsylvania State House, known today as Independence Hall, is located at 520 Chesnut Street.

2. The enclosed memorial has not been identified.

3. Henry Knox's letter to Mifflin of 15 April reads: "The President of the United States has instructed me to acknowledge the receipt of your letter of yesterday informing him of the measures you had been pleased to adopt for the preservation of the police of the City and also transmitting a memorial addressed to you by a number of Sailors who being out of employ pray for relief.

"If the distresses of the Petitioners are as great, and are owing to the cause stated, and even if it should appear upon full investigation that they are really proper objects for a general provision there are no public funds at the disposal of the President of the United States which could be appropriated to their subsistence" (PharH: Executive Correspondence, 1790–99).

From Richard Peters

Dear Sir   Monday 14. Apl 94

Your Note lay, without my Knowledge, on my Table, 'till last Evening, or I should have sent the Agricultural Papers before this Time.[1] I am much obliged & gratified by the Perusal of them. I had formed a Plan of abstracting Parts of these Papers for Observation, & Part for Publication. But there seems a Fatality attendant on my Plan, for I have met with Interruptions in every Attempt I have made to execute it. Some Parts would be very useful if published here. I must postpone my Design for the present, & live in Hopes that, one Day or other, these Papers, with those to complete Sr J.S.'s System, will be published & find their Way here.[2] Much useful Knowledge will be propogated, & the whole will contain the best Body of agricultural Information founded on Fact, every yet extant. I wish you could prevail on Sr J., if the Request would not produce unnecessary Obligation, to send a few Copies of the Statistical Reports as they are published.[3] They would be of infinite Importance to our agricultural Concerns, as well as in other Respects. They would assist the Efforts of those who wish to promote a Spirit of good Husbandry, by adding Knowledge to their Zeal. Much might be done in this Way under all our Disadvantages—But I fear the Dream will call off our Labourers from the Plough. I am with sincere Esteem & Respect Your obedt Servt

Richard Peters

ALS, DLC:GW.

1. For the note from GW, see his letter to Peters of 12 April. The papers returned probably consisted of those that British agriculturist John Sinclair enclosed in his letters to GW of 15 June, 15 Aug., and 11 Sept. 1793.

2. For Peters' eventual observations, see his letter to GW of 16 July 1794 (DLC:GW). On Sinclair's plan for an agricultural survey of Great Britain, see his letter to GW of 15 Aug. 1793.

3. When GW wrote Sinclair on 20 July 1794 (UkLBM: Add MS 5757), he did not ask for additional copies of any reports. For a list of the agricultural surveys and essays published by Sinclair and the British Board of Agriculture and sent to GW, including Sinclair's *Specimens of Statistical Reports* (London, 1793), see Griffin, *Catalogue of the Washington Collection,* 89–95, 183.

To John Jay

Dear Sir,   [Philadelphia] Tuesday Morng 15th Apl 94

At as early an hour this morning, as you can make convenient to yourself, I should be glad to see you. At eight o'clock we breakfast. Then, or after, as suits you best, I will expect to have the satisfaction of conversing with you on an interesting subject.[1] Yours always & sincerely

Go: Washington

ADfS, DLC:GW; LB, DLC:GW.

1. The subject for discussion was GW's desire to appoint Jay a special envoy to Great Britain (GW to U.S. Senate, 16 April [first letter]).

From Henry Knox

Sir,   War department April 15th 1794

I submit to your consideration a proposed answer to the Governors letter of yesterday.[1] The object really seems more of a local than of general nature, and therefore nothing is hinted of an application to Congress, who if the object is of a general nature are alone competent to grant relief—But although the Petitioners are probably British subjects yet it is highly probable that they are sailing in the ships of Americans as eight tenths of the Sailors out of this port are probably Europeans.

If Congress should interpose in this case it would form a precedent for similar applications from every other part of the Union. I have the honor to be with perfect respect Your obedient servant

H. Knox

LS, DLC:GW; LB, DLC:GW.

1. Pennsylvania governor Thomas Mifflin's letter to GW of 14 April enclosed a petition from unemployed sailors asking for financial support from the federal government during the embargo imposed on 26 March (*Stat.* 1:400). For Knox's letter to Mifflin of 15 April, see n.3 of Mifflin's letter.

From Henry Knox

War Department April 15. 1794

The Secretary of War respectfully submits to the President of the United States, the following ideas relatively to the frigates authorised by the law for providing a naval armament.[1]

That the said frigates be constructed upon the principles which shall after the most mature information and consideration appear to combine the greatest possible force, with adequate strength, and swiftness of sailing, so as to render them equal or superior to any ships of their description belonging to the powers of Europe.

That therefore the largest of the ships of forty four guns be constructed to carry thirty cannon of the calibre of twenty four pounders upon one deck, each cannon to weigh about two tons. Formerly cannon of this calibre weighed forty eight hundred, which indeed is the weight at present in France, but then they are ten feet in length whereas it is proposed to make our's of about eight feet.

That in order to complete the force of the ship the following ordnance be added to the twenty four pounders—eight twelve pounders—four eight inch howitzers—two five inch and an half howitzers, besides smaller cannon or carronades for the tops and forecastle.

That the forty four gun ships be one hundred and forty seven feet keel for tonnage—forty three feet beam—fourteen feet hold below the gun deck, and including the orlop deck, six feet in the clear between the gun and spar deck and seven feet waist.

That taking into consideration the great length proposed it will be necessary to devise certain braces and riders in order to give a just strength and prevent the accidents to which vessels are generally liable, of being hogged, or broken backed, which causes the vessel from weakness to droop at both ends.

That Mr Joshua Humphreys and Col. Marsh eminent master shipbuilders in Philadelphia, and Mr John Wharton formerly also an eminent shipbuilder, and a member of the navy board during the late war, have each given to the subscriber their opinions of the propriety of the proportions before specified,[2] but Mr Thomas Penrose, Mr John Bowers, and Mr Samuel Bowers, also all excellent shipbuilders, are of opinion that twenty eight twenty four pounders on one deck will be sufficient, and that it would be difficult to secure a ship of thirty twenty four pounders against the broken back before mentioned.[3] As it is important to be certain of the principles, Mr John Hacket an eminent shipbuilder in Massachusetts who constructed the Alliance frigate during the late war, has been invited to repair to this city in order to be consulted on this business. It is asserted by Captain Barry and seems conceded by the builders that the Alliance was one of the best constructed frigates in all respects of the late war. Besides Mr Hacket's, other opinions will be sought in order to furnish materials for a solid judgment upon the subject.[4]

It is proposed the frigates of thirty six guns shall carry the same weight of metal of the forty four gun ships, but only to have twenty eight guns upon one deck, of course eleven feet shorter. But Mr Penrose is of opinion that these frigates should have one hundred and twenty feet keel for tonnage, thirty five feet beam, twelve feet hold, six feet between decks, and six feet waist, and one hundred and sixty three feet on the gun deck, and the largest guns to be twelve pounders.

The manner in which these vessels ought to be built has been under consideration; that is, whether the hull and other parts susceptible of the measure should be built by contract, or by a capable agent or agents appointed for the purpose of procuring the labor and materials. Upon enquiry however it appears improbable that a contract could be formed with the shipbuilders in this place for any which may be directed to be built here. They alledge that if a contract was offered and accepted by two, three, or more, it would excite the ill will and envy of those who had no part in it, and as the frigates would require many hands the price of that sort of labor would rise, and that therefore it would be in the power of those not employed to raise the wages of Journeymen a shilling or two per day which would occasion great embarrassment if not ruin to the undertakers. Hence it would appear to follow as a consequence, that if the shipbuilders of Philadelphia some of whom have considerable capitals would decline a contract, that it would be almost, or quite impracticable to obtain the building by contract elsewhere. If this should be so, then Agents respectable for their intelligence, activity, and integrity must be sought in the places in which it shall be decided to build the said frigates.

If the principles of oeconomy alone were to predominate in determining the places where the said vessels were to be built and equipped, it is not improbable the arrangement might be different from the one hereinafter submitted.

But as the government is the government of the whole people, and not of a part only, it is just and wise to proportion its benefits as nearly as may be to those places or states which pay the greatest amount to its support. It is conceived the saving of a few thousand dollars in the expences will be no object compared with the satisfaction a just distribution would afford. Under these impressions the following are submitted as places at which it might be proper to build the said frigates, to wit

Charleston South Carolina	1	36 Gunship
Norfolk or Portsmouth, Virginia	1	36
Baltimore Maryland	1	44
Philadelphia Pennsylvania	1	44
New York New York	1	44
Boston Massachusetts	1	44

The information which the subscriber has hitherto received is by no means accurate as to the price at which the said vessels could be built at either of the two southern places, nor the time in which they could be finished, but it seems to be pretty well ascertained, that it would be practicable to build them as specified, although it may and probably will require that some additional artificers should be sent from the northward, particularly to Charleston. It is to be understood that the enhanced prices particularly at Charleston will relate principally to the hull, provided the communication is kept open, as the guns, anchors, and a variety of other articles may be sent to that port from other parts of the United States. Perhaps articles must be imported from Europe for all the places, particularly copper for the bottoms, hemp for the cordage, and sail cloth.

It will however be of the utmost consequence to the construction of the vessels, that the timber should be cut with all possible expedition, as it is estimated by a master builder here, that it will require the labor of three hundred men two months to cut the live oak and cedar necessary for the said ships.

The estimate which accompanies the report, is made in Philadelphia. But if the appearance of our being involved in the European war should continue it is very questionable whether the actual cost will not considerably exceed the estimate.[5] All which is humbly submitted

H. Knox secy of war

LS, DLC:GW; LB, DLC:GW. The closing on the LS is in Knox's writing.

1. "An Act to provide a Naval Armament," 27 March, provided for "four ships to carry forty-four guns each, and two ships to carry thirty-six guns each" (*Stat.* 1:350).

2. Shipwright Joshua Humphreys (1751–1838), at 218 Swanson Street, received an appointment as naval constructor for the 44-gun frigate *United States,* which was built at Philadelphia (*Philadelphia Directory, 1794,* 74; and Knox to Humphreys, 28 June, DNA: RG 45, Letters Sent by the War Department Relating to Naval Matters). Col. Joseph Marsh was located at 23 Christian Street, Southwark (*Philadelphia Directory, 1794,* 95). John Wharton (c.1732–1799), a Philadelphia shipbuilder, served on the Continental Navy Board, 1778–80.

3. Thomas Penrose (1734–1815) was at 27 Swanson Street, Southwark, and also at 85 Penn Street. Knox presumably meant Joseph (d. 1797) and Samuel Bowers, shipbuilders at Point Pleasant, near Kensington (*Philadelphia Directory, 1794,* 15, 119).

4. In the 1770s, John Hacket was associated with his relative William Hacket in shipbuilding at Salisbury, Massachusetts. For Knox's letter to John

Hacket of 1 April, see DNA: RG 45, Letters Sent by the War Department Relating to Naval Matters. The Revolutionary War frigate *Alliance* was a 36-gun frigate. Originally named the *Hancock,* it was launched in 1778. Capt. John Barry commanded the *Alliance* from September 1789 until its sale to private owners after the war.

5. The enclosed estimate of 15 April (DLC:GW) reads: "Estimate of the building and fitting a frigate of 1430 51/95 tons the proposed size of a forty four gun ship—and also one of 1145 25/95 tons, the proposed size of a thirty six gun ship—

	Pennsa. Curry
Carpenter's bill complete	£9.—.—
Smith's bill including Anchors	4. 5.—
Joyner's bill for stuff & work	—.17.6
Boat builder's bill	—. 3.6
Painter & Plumber's bills	—. 7.6
Carver's bill	—. 4.6
Cooper's do for 6 months water	—.12.6
Blockmaker's bill	—. 7.6
Mast maker's bill	—.11.3
Rigger's bill with Cordage	3.—.—
Sail Cloth & Sailmaker's bill, 2 suits	3. 5.—
Chandler's bill for locks, hinges, colors and other small charges	1. 2.6
The cannon & ordnance stores are not included in this estimate	
For one ton	£23.16.9

		Pennsa. Curry
44 Guns	1430 51/95 tons at £23.16.9	£34.100. 8. 5¼
36.	1145 25/95 tons at do	27.300.12. 6"

To Richard Henry Lee

Dear Sir,   Philadelphia 15th April 1794.

    I have been favored with your letter of the 8th of March from Chantily. It did not, however, (by the Office mark thereon) leave Westmoreland Court House until the 16th of that month. Previously to the receipt of it, the nomination of Mr Lawrence Muse to the Collectorship of Rappahannock had been made, consequent of strong testimonials in his favor.[1]

    The manners of Mr Fauchet, and Mr Genet, the present & former Ministers of France, appear to have been cast in very different moulds. The former has been temperate & placid in all his movements, hitherto; the latter was the reverse of it in all respects. The declarations made by the former, of the friendly dispositions of his Nation towards this Country, and of his own inclinations to carry them into effect, are strong & apparently sincere. The conduct of the latter is disapproved in toto, by the Government of both. yet, it is *time only,* that will enable us to form a decisive judgment of each; and of the objects of their pursuits.

The British Ministry (as you will have perceived by Mr Pinckneys letter to the Secretary of State, which has been published) disclaim any hostile intentions towards this Country, in the agency they had in bringing about the truce between Portugal & Algiers;[2] yet, the tenour of their conduct in this business has been such—added to their manœuvres with our Indian neighbours— but more especially with respect to the late orders of the King in council, as to leave very unfavorable impressions of their friendship, & little to expect from their justice; whatever may result from that of the interest of their Nation.[3]

The debates, on what are commonly called Mr Madison's resolutions, which no doubt you have seen (having been published in all the Gazettes) will give you the pro & con of that business more in detail than I could do if my leisure was greater than it is; but these resolutions, like many other matters, are slumbering in Congress; and what may be the final result of them no mortal, I believe can tell.[4]

I learn with regret that your health has continued bad ever since I had the pleasure of seeing you at Shuters hill.[5] Warm weather I hope will restore it: if my wishes could be of any avail you assuredly would have them. With best respects to Mrs Lee and the rest of your family, in which Mrs Washington unites, I am with very great esteem and regard, Dear Sir, Yr Obedt and Affecte Hble Servt

Go: Washington

ALS (photocopy), DLC:GW, series 9; ALS (letterpress copy), DNA: RG 59, Miscellaneous Letters; LB, DLC:GW.

1. Lee's estate of Chantilly was in Westmoreland County, Virginia. For GW's recent appointment of Laurence Muse as the customs collector for the District of Tappahannock, Va., see GW to U.S. Senate, 5 March.

2. This is a reference to Thomas Pinckney's letter of 25 Nov. 1793, which GW enclosed with his letter to the U.S. Senate and House of Representatives of 24 Feb. 1794. On the British encouragement of a truce between Portugal and Algiers, which left American shipping in the Atlantic Ocean vulnerable to seizure by the Algerines, see n.9 of Tobias Lear to GW, 4 February.

3. For the British order-in-council of 8 Jan., which adversely affected American shipping, see *ASP, Foreign Relations,* 1:431.

4. On 3 Jan., Virginia congressman James Madison proposed seven resolutions that would have created a policy of commercial retaliation against Great Britain (*Annals of Congress,* 3d Cong., 155–56; *Gazette of the United States* [Philadelphia], 4 Jan.). None of the resolutions was adopted by Congress.

5. Lee retired from the U.S. Senate in 1792 due to ill health, and he would die on 19 June 1794. GW may have stopped at Shuter's Hill, near Alexandria, Va., to visit with Lee and his wife, Anne Gaskins Pinkard Lee, in late October 1793 (see Lee to GW, 23 Oct. 1793, and GW to Lee, 24 Oct. 1793).

Letter not found: from William Pearce, 15 April 1794. GW wrote Pearce on 20 April acknowledging receipt of "Your letter of the 15th, with the weekly reports."

To Edmund Randolph

Dear Sir,   [Philadelphia] Tuesday morng 15th Aprl 1794

Let me know whether the message (which in the evening of yesterday) I requested you to draw, will be ready by 11 o'clock this forenoon?

If you answer in the affirmative, I shall require the Gentlemen with whom I usually advise on these occasions, to attend me at that hour; for I consider that message (both as to matter & form) of such importance as to make it necessary that every word of it should undergo due consid⟨eratio⟩n.

My objects are, to prevent a war—if justice can be obtained by fair & strong representation (to be made by a special Envoy) of the injuries which this Country has sustained from G.B. in various ways—To put it in a complete state of military defence. And to provide *eventually,* such measures as seem to be now pending in Congress for execution, if negotiation, in a reasonable time proves unsuccessful.[1]

Such is the train of my though⟨ts;⟩ but how far all, or any of them, except the first, ought to be introduced into the message, in the present stage of the business, in Congress, deserves, as I have said before—due consideration.[2] Yours always & sincerely

Go: Washington

ALS (letterpress copy), DNA: RG 59, Miscellaneous Letters; LB, DNA: RG 59, GW's Correspondence with His Secretaries of State. The text in angle brackets is from the letter-book copy.

1. The measures pending in Congress may refer to the program of national defense contained in eight resolutions introduced on 12 March in the House of Representatives by Massachusetts congressman Theodore Sedgwick. Other resolutions probably were also on GW's mind. Jonathan Dayton of New Jersey offered a resolve on 27 March that would have provided for "the sequestration of all the debts due from the citizens of the United States to the subjects of the King of Great Britain." Abraham Clark of New Jersey proposed on 7 April that the United States end all commercial intercourse with Great Britain until the British government caused "restitution to be made for all losses and damages sustained by the citizens of the United States" from British seizures of American ships and cargo and until "all the posts now held and detained by the King of Great Britain, within the territories of the United States, shall be surrendered" (*Annals of Congress*, 3d Cong., 500–501, 535, 561). Neither of these resolves was passed by both houses of Congress.

2. After meeting with the cabinet, GW decided upon only one topic for his first letter to the U.S. Senate of 16 April—the appointment of a special envoy to Great Britain.

To the United States Senate and House of Representatives

United States 15 April 1794.

Gentlemen of the Senate, and of the House of Representatives.

I lay before you a Letter from the Minister plenipotentiary of his britannic majesty to the Secretary of State;[1] a Letter from the Secretary of the territory South of the river Ohio, enclosing an ordinance and proclamation of the Governor thereof;[2] the translation of so much of a petition of the Inhabitants of Post Vincennes, addressed to the President, as relates to Congress;[3] and certain dispatches lately received from our Commissioners at Madrid. These dispatches from Madrid being a part of a business, which has been hitherto deemed confidential, they are forwarded under that view.[4]

Go: Washington

LS, DNA: RG 46, Third Congress, 1793–95, Senate Records of Legislative Proceedings, President's Messages; LB, DNA: RG 233, Third Congress, 1793–95, House Records of Legislative Proceedings, Journals; LB, DLC:GW.

1. For the letter from George Hammond to Edmund Randolph of 11 April, defending the British right "to detain, and even seize" provisions transported on American ships bound for France, see *ASP, Foreign Relations*, 1:432–33.

2. Gov. William Blount's ordinance of 19 Oct. 1793 provided for the elec-

tion of representatives to the first general assembly of the Southwest Territory. The proclamation of 1 Jan. 1794 announced that the newly elected assembly would convene at Knoxville on 24 February. For both documents and the cover letter from Daniel Smith to Randolph of 1 March, see Carter, *Territorial Papers,* 4:309, 319, 330.

3. For the enclosed petition, see Post Vincennes citizens to GW, 20 Nov. 1793.

4. The enclosed dispatches from Madrid, reporting on the state of U.S. negotiations with Spain, were from William Carmichael and William Short to the secretary of state, 7 Dec. 1793, and from Short to the secretary of state, 9, 17, and 21 Jan. 1794. For these letters and their enclosures, see *ASP, Foreign Relations,* 1:438–46. On Randolph's receipt of these letters, see his letter to GW of 3 April.

To Alexander Hamilton

[Philadelphia, 16 April 1794]

Having thought fit to appoint Nathaniel Cabot Higginson, of the City of Philadelphia, attorney at law, as an Agent on behalf of the United States, to proceed to the british West India Islands for certain purposes relating to the Ships or vessels of the United States, which have been, or may be seized & sent into the ports of any of those Islands by british cruisers, since the commencement of the present war between great britain & France:[1]

I do hereby direct you to cause to be advanced to the said Nathaniel Cabot Higginson, Five thousand dollars, out of the fund of ten thousand dollars, appropriated for defraying the contingent charges of Government, on account of his compensation & expenses as Agent, and the expenses of his said agency, for which he is to be held accountable.[2]

Given under my hand the 16 day of April 1794.

Geo: Washington.

LB, DLC:GW.

1. On the appointment of Higginson, see Hamilton to GW, 2 April, and n.2 to that document.

2. For the establishment of a contingency fund for use by the president, see section 3 of "An Act making appropriations for the support of government for the year one thousand seven hundred and ninety," 26 March 1790 (*Stat.* 1:105). Hamilton acknowledged GW's request in a letter written later this day: "The Secretary of the Treasury presents his respects to the President of the United States and encloses herewith the draft of a Warrant for five thousand dollars, relating to Mr Higginson's mission, for the Presidents sig-

nature" (LB, DLC:GW). For the instructions that accompanied this warrant, see Hamilton to Higginson, this date (*Hamilton Papers,* 16:288–91).

To Henry Knox

Sir,   [Philadelphia, 16 April 1794]
I have considered your report of the 15th instt relatively to the Frigates which are to be built; and as soon as the important points on which the master builders have differed, is settled by the expedient you have had recourse to; and you can obtain the means for carrying the law into effect, it is my desire that the work ⟨may be entered upon⟩ without delay; in the manner, and at the places which you have suggested; with this alteration however—that if Baltimore does not possess advantages which Norfolk has not, that the 44 gun ship shall be built at the latter, & the one of 36 guns at the former. The wealth, and populousness of the two states will not only warrant, but require this change if there is an equality in other respects.[1]
Given at Philadelphia this 16th day of April 1794.
Go: Washington

P.S. At nine o clock tomorrow, I shall want to converse with you on your other report of the 10th instt.

ALS (letterpress copy), DLC:GW; LB, DLC:GW.
1. In a report to the U.S. House of Representatives of 27 Dec. 1794, Knox identified Baltimore, Md., as a site for the construction of a 36-gun frigate and either Norfolk or Portsmouth, Va., for a 44-gun frigate (*ASP, Naval Affairs,* 1:6).

Isaac Mansfield, Jr., to Tobias Lear

Sir,   Marblehead [Massachusetts] Apr. 16. 1794
Early in the late War, James Mugford Commander of the Schooner Franklin was killed in an Engagement *in taking* the Powder Ship; the Powder Ship at that time you may recollect was a very important Acquisition.[1]
The Administrator on Mugford's Estate has applied for a Bounty provided for in such Case; the application was dated in December last, we received an answer from Treasury Depart-

ment auditors office dated Feb. 13, a Reply to which directed to Richard Hamilton Auditor of the Treasury bears date Mar. 10.[2]

Another Matter in which I am personally interested is this; having served in the capacity of a Chaplain, after repeated applications I have obtained my Wages; but, my Rations were not included from a mistaken apprehension that my first application was so late that I was barred by the Statute of Congress of March 27. 1792. To rectify this Apprehension I addressed Mr Howell the paymaster in a Letter dated March 7.[3]

Both these Letters we forwarded to Mr Goodhue to be communicated to the persons to whom they were directed[4]—We have been delayed, (I do not say, *unreasonably*) and are *now* amused with an Idea that we are barred by the Statute of Mar. 27. 1792 which Suspended Limitations of Claims till Mar. 27. 1794.

Our Letters were in the Office at Philadelphia some days before the 27th.

If it may comport with the Dignity of The President, with all dutiful Respect we request his Attention to the Subjects beforementioned. I subscribe myself Your Friend & H. Servant,

Isaac Mansfield

ALS, DNA: RG 59, Miscellaneous Letters.

1. While in command of the armed schooner *Franklin*, James Mugford, Jr. (1749–1776), of Marblehead, captured the British ordnance storeship *Hope*, Alexander Lumsdale, master, on 17 May 1776. This ship "had on board 1500 Barrils of powder & 1000 Stand of Arms" (Richard Devens to John Adams, 17 May 1776, *Naval Documents*, 5:133; Artemas Ward to GW, 17 May 1776). Mugsford was killed in another naval battle on 19 May 1776 (Ward to GW, 20 May 1776).

2. The administrator of Mugford's estate sought payment according to a bounty approved by the Continental Congress on 15 Nov. 1776, which authorized that "20 dollars be paid to the commanders, officers, and men of such continental ships or vessels of war, as shall make prize of any British ships or vessels of war, for every cannon mounted on board each prize, at the time of such capture, and 8 dollars per head for every man then on board and belonging to such prize." Congress repealed this bounty on 10 July 1782 (*PCC*, 6:954, 22:380). The auditor of the Treasury was Richard Harrison. The December 1793 application and the correspondence of 13 Feb. and 10 March 1794 have not been identified.

3. For a previous letter containing this same complaint, see Mansfield to GW of 19 Sept. 1792. Even if Mansfield's letters were received by the deadline of 27 March 1794 that was imposed by "An Act for providing for the settlement of the Claims of Persons under particular circumstances barred by

limitations heretofore established," 27 March 1792, Section One of that act expressly states that "nothing herein shall be construed to extend to claims for rations or subsistence money" (*Stat.* 1:245). Joseph Howell, Jr., served as the acting paymaster general in GW's administration until replaced by Caleb Swan on 8 May 1792, when he became accountant to the Department of War (GW to U.S. Senate, 8 May 1792 [first letter]). Mansfield's letter to Howell of 7 March 1794 has not been identified.

4. Congressman Benjamin Goodhue, of Salem, Mass., was currently in Philadelphia to attend the first session of the Third Congress.

To the United States Senate

Gentlemen of the Senate,   United States 16. April 1794.

The communications, which I have made to you during your present session, from the dispatches of our Minister in London, contain a serious aspect of our affairs with Great Britain.[1] But as peace ought to be pursued with unremitted zeal, before the last resource, which has so often been the scourge of Nations, and cannot fail to check the advanced prosperity of the United States, is contemplated; I have thought proper to nominate, and do hereby nominate,

    John Jay, as envoy extraordinary of the
    United States, to his britannic Majesty.

My confidence in our Minister plenipotentiary in London continues undiminished. But a mission, like this, while it corresponds with the solemnity of the occasion, will announce to the world a solicitude for a friendly adjustment of our complaints, and a reluctance to hostility. Going immediately from the United States, such an envoy will carry with him a full knowledge of the existing temper and sensibility of our Country; and will thus be taught to vindicate our rights with firmness, and to cultivate peace with sincerity.[2]

Go: Washington

LS, DNA: RG 46, Third Congress, 1793–95, Senate Records of Executive Proceedings, President's Messages—Executive Nominations; copy, DNA: RG 46, Fourth Congress, 1795–97, Senate Records of Executive Proceedings, President's Messages—Foreign Relations; LB, DLC:GW; copy, Nc-Ar: Governor's Papers, Richard Dobbs Spaight.

1. Thomas Pinckney was the U.S. minister plenipotentiary to Great Britain. Among the serious problems was Great Britain's interference with American shipping. On this and other unresolved issues with Great Britain, see n.1 of

Alexander Hamilton to GW, 23 April; and Instructions to Jay, 6 May (NHi: Jay Papers; *ASP, Foreign Relations,* 1:472–74).

2. Although the Senate received this letter on 16 April, it did not immediately approve Jay's nomination. On 18 April it approved a resolution "That the President of the United States be requested to cause to be laid before the Senate the reports of John Jay to Congress while Secretary of Foreign Affairs [1784–90], and in case the books in which the same are recorded are transmitted to the Senate, that the same be returned by the Secretary of the Senate [Samuel A. Otis, Sr.] to the office of the Secretary of State." Edmund Randolph submitted the desired reports to the Senate on 19 April along with a cover letter of that same date, which has not been identified, and the Senate approved Jay's nomination on 19 April by a vote of 18 to 8 (*U.S. Senate Executive Journal,* 1:150–52).

To the United States Senate

Gentlemen of the Senate.   United States 16. April 1794.

I nominate Richard Harrison, attorney for the District of New York, to be Judge of the District of New York, vice James Duane, who has resigned.[1]

Go: Washington

LS, DNA: RG 46, Third Congress, 1793–95, Senate Records of Executive Proceedings, President's Messages—Executive Nominations; LB, DLC:GW.

1. For James Duane's official resignation, see his letter to GW of 8 April. After the Senate ordered on 19 April that further consideration of GW's nomination of Richard Harison "be postponed," Harison wrote GW on 21 April asking that his nomination be withdrawn (*U.S. Senate Executive Journal,* 1:152).

From Alexander Hamilton

Treasy Dept. April 17. 1794.

The Secy of the Treasury presents his respects to the President of the U.S. & encloses herewith the draft of a Passport, requested by mister Hammond for a vessel intended by him to be dispatched to Halifax, and which the Secretary understood from the Secy of State was to be granted by the President.[1]

LB, DLC:GW.

1. For the request for a passport by British minister George Hammond "for the *sole* purpose of conveying to Halifax [Nova Scotia] a messenger, who will be charged with my dispatches," see his letter to Edmund Randolph of 29 March (RG 59, Notes from Foreign Legations: Great Britain). Randolph

submitted Hammond's letter to Hamilton with a cover letter of 16 April (*Hamilton Papers,* 16:291–92). The enclosed passport has not been identified, but it probably was for the schooner *Margery,* which sailed from New York "with the MAIL, for Halifax," on 20 April (*Daily Advertiser* [New York], 21 April).

From Reuben Harvey

Respected Friend   Cork [Ireland] 17th April 1794
   I took this liberty last Month by way of Baltimore, And I am sorry that a similar cause for troubling thee has so soon occurr'd at Kinsale, where a fine Philadelphia Ship, the Molly Capt. Farrel, having put in the 3d Curr[en]t to procure Bread & Beef, has been detain'd by Lieut. Govr Brown, on suspicion that her valuable Cargoe of 450 pipes Brandy, 150 Casks of Wine & Vinegar, & other Articles, is the property of the Convention;[1] Seven of her Crew were press'd & afterwards by threats & cajolings induced to enter, And the Master of the Molly is threaten'd with Jail unless he pays these Men what Money appears to be due them; The Brig Hannah & Cargoe have been orderd to proceed to Falmouth, & it is probable that the British Government will give the same orders respecting the Molly;[2] I exceedingly regret that no Consul had been sent to Ireland when War commenced 'twixt Great Britain & France, as that Event alone must necessarily produce many instances wherein the interposition of a *Native* Consul would be wanted; Indeed it is surprizing that this Measure has been so long omitted.[3] The Molly's Cargoe is mark'd DM & consign'd to Daniel Marian Mercht at Newyork, The Ship belongs to Philip Care Mercht at Philadelphia, She carry'd 4500 barrels of flour from Baltimore to Nants & Bordeaux last Summer:[4] I shall not trouble thee farther on this Subject, but just to say that your Envoy at London never answer'd the letters I wrote him concerning the Hannah, which was not kind, as I had no other Motive therein than regard for America.[5] With sincere regard I remain Thy affte. Friend

                                                        Reuben Harvey

ALS, DNA: RG 59, Miscellaneous Letters; LS (identified as "1st Coppy"), RG 59, Miscellaneous Letters; LS (identified as "2d Coppy"), RG 59, Miscellaneous Letters. Postal stamps on the ALS read "June 1⟨7⟩" and "FREE." A notation on the cover of the ALS reads, "Newyork 14 June 1794 recd under cover & forwarded by Sir your very Hble servant W. Wilson." William Wilson, a New York City merchant at 217 Pearl Street, may have forwarded this letter

(*New-York Directory, 1794,* 206). The docket, which probably was added at the Department of State, reads, "recd 28th June."

1. The National Convention was the governing body of the French Republic from September 1792 until October 1795.

2. In his letter to GW of 3 March, Harvey had written about the retention of the *Hannah* and three other ships, all carrying cargoes of brandy and all having set sail from the French port of Bordeaux (*Philadelphia Gazette and Universal Daily Advertiser,* 17 Feb.).

3. The post of consul at Dublin had been vacant since the departure of William Knox in 1792. GW nominated Joseph Wilson for the post on 28 May (*U.S. Senate Executive Journal,* 1:158).

4. Philadelphia merchant Philip Care was located at 15 South Water Street (*Philadelphia Directory, 1794,* 22).

5. On Harvey's letters to Thomas Pinckney, the U.S. minister plenipotentiary to Great Britain, see Harvey to GW, 3 March. Upon receipt of this letter, GW forwarded it to Secretary of State Edmund Randolph (GW to Randolph, 25 June, DLC:GW). GW also forwarded one of the copies to Randolph on 12 July (*JPP,* 312).

From Alexander Hamilton

Philada 18 April 1794.

The Secretary of the Treasury presents his respects to the President. the enclosed permit has been prepared on the intimation of the Secretary of State, for the Spanish Comissioners.[1] The Secretary is not informed whether the doubt on the subject of mister Hammond's application was removed. The return of the enclosed will be considered as the evidence that it was.[2]

LB, DLC:GW.

1. The enclosed passport was for the Spanish ship *Nuestra Senora del Carmen,* master Prospero Farrayolo (Ferrola), "to proceed in ballast from Philadelphia to Havanna," Cuba (*JPP,* 299; *Philadelphia Gazette and Universal Daily Advertiser,* 29 April). For Randolph's request on behalf of José Ignacio de Viar and José de Jaudenes, see his letter to Hamilton, 17 April (*Hamilton Papers,* 16:293–94).

2. For George Hammond's application for a passport, see Hamilton to GW, 17 April. The enclosure has not been identified.

From Henry Knox

Sir,   War department April 18. 1794

I have the honor to submit a draft of a letter to the Governors, and to the commanding Officers of Militia of certain Ports to the southward, which are out of the route of the residence of the Governors.[1] I have the honor to be Sir with perfect respect Your obedient Servant

H. Knox secy of war

LS, DLC:GW: LB, DLC:GW.

1. In a circular letter of this date to the maritime governors and militia officers, Knox wrote: "The president of the United States has directed me to inform Your Excellency of the Continuance of the Embargo upon Vessels bound to any foreign port or place, untill the 25th of next Month; And that the same be regulated conformably to the former Resolve of the 26th ultimo, and to the enclosed Resolves of the 2nd instant—and of this date.

"And he requests that the co-operation of Your Militia may be afforded, if necessary, as mentioned in my former Letter of the 26th ultimo (Knox to Arnoldus Vanderhorst, 18 April, ScCoAH: Governor's Messages; see also Knox to Arthur Fenner, 18 April, R-Ar: Letters to Governors). For the congressional resolves of 26 March, imposing an embargo on "all ships and vessels in the ports of the United States"; the resolve of 2 April, giving detailed instructions for the collectors of customs to use in enforcing the embargo; and of 18 April, extending the embargo until 25 May, see *Stat.* 1:400–401. For Knox's circular letter of 26 March, see n.1 of Thomas Mifflin to GW, 27 March.

From Thomas Mifflin

Sir   Philadelphia 18. April 1794

In answer to a circular letter, which I addressed to the Officers of this Commonwealth, enjoining, among other things, an implicit obedience to the laws of the Union, I have received a variety of communications of a very patriotic and satisfactory nature:[1] and the inclosed Extracts from the letters of Judge Addison and Mr Reddick (the Prothonotary of the County of Washington) relatively to the Excise, appear to me to contain information of sufficient moment, to excuse my submitting them to your consideration.[2] I am, with perfect respect, Sir, Your most obedt Servt

Tho. Mifflin

LS, DNA: RG 59, Miscellaneous Letters; Df, PHarH: Executive Correspondence; LB, PHarH: Governor's Letter-Books.

1. In his circular letter of 21 March, Mifflin wrote: "In the present state of our National affairs, relatively to the Belligerent powers of Europe, I think it my duty to call the attention of the Officers of the Commonwealth of Pennsylvania to the prospect of such events, as cannot fail to interest the patriotism

of every good Citizen; and which, if not happily averted, will, I anxiously hope, produce that unanimity of sentiment and conduct among the people, that is obviously essential to give energy and success to the exertions of a Republican Government, created by their will, and only to be supported by their confidence. . . . The disposition that has appeared in some of the Counties, to resist and counteract the execution of the Excise Law of Congress, will attract particular notice. Whatever diversity of opinion may arise as to the policy of imposing that tax; the propriety of acquiescing in it, while sanctioned by the Legislative authority, cannot be controverted, by any friend to the peace and happiness of his Country. The same Constitution that gave the power to lay a tax, has designated the mode in which original impolicy, or oppressive operation, may be represented to that tribunal which can, and, in the case of real grievance, is bound, to grant redress. As Freemen, let us always remonstrate against actual wrongs; but, as Citizens, let us always obey existing Laws" (PHarH: Executive Correspondence). The federal excise tax on whiskey was opposed, sometimes violently, by many residents of the western counties in Pennsylvania (see GW's Proclamation of 24 Feb.). For the excise tax, see "An Act repealing, after the last day of June next, the duties heretofore laid upon Distilled Spirits imported from abroad, and laying others in their stead; and also upon Spirits distilled within the United States, and for appropriating the same," 3 March 1791, and "An Act concerning the Duties on Spirits distilled within the United States," 8 May 1792 (*Stat.* 1:199–214, 267–71).

2. Alexander Addison (1759–1807) a native of Scotland, attended the University of Edinburgh and was a licensed Presbyterian preacher when he emigrated to the United States in the early 1780s. After preaching for a short time in Pennsylvania, he studied law and was then admitted to the bar in Washington County. He served as the chief justice on the state's fifth district court, 1791–1803. The extract of his letter to Mifflin of 31 March reports that nothing "of a criminal nature" has "come within my cognizance," except for "the conviction of Samuel Wilson, and the submission of the other rioters in Allegheny county. . . . In private conversation I have endeavoured to inculcate that constitutional resistance, which alone is justifiable in a free people. The Constitution, however, ordaining an equal Excise, renders it impossible to make this an equal tax, in the estimation of the people of this Country. Were I to express an opinion, I would say, that if the Collection of the Excise were in proper hands, it might now be made; but it seemd to be intrusted to men without spirit or discretion, and in whose principles the people have no confidence. They seem tamely content with the enjoyment of their appointments; or, if they have discovered any acts of decision and vigor, it is, I conceive, in unlawful and oppressive stretches of authority and in the commission of trespasses" (DNA: RG 59, Miscellaneous Letters).

Attorney David Redick (d. 1805), a native of Ireland, originally lived in Lancaster County, Pa., after emigrating to the United States, but circa 1780 he settled permanently in the town of Washington, Pa., in Washington County. He represented Washington County in the Supreme Executive Council of Pennsylvania, 1786–89, and served briefly as the state's vice president in 1788. The extract of his letter to Mifflin of 8 April reads: "I had conversations with many of the People on the subject matter of your letter—Generally I found a disposition to comply; but I found one very considerable obstacle in their way—they fear a vindictive spirit in the Collector [Robert Johnson], which may prompt a rigorous hand, in order to retaliate for past disappointments and affronts—however they may be mistaken in the Man, I have no doubt but a change would have very happy effects. Indeed, I have reason to believe, at least, to fear, that altho' a general compliance should take place, that as the minds of many being heated, ungovernable spirits would now and then boil over and scald the head of the present Officer—Whereas if another should be appointed to supercede him, one who would not only have spirit, but dignity of manners, all might be well" (DNA: RG 59, Miscellaneous Letters).

From Gouverneur Morris

My dear Sir   Sainport [France] 18 April 1794.

In a Letter which I had the Honor of writing to you on the 10th of January 1793, I gave you some Traits respecting Mr Westerman, and as my public Dispatches had already communicated the Plans of Mr Danton, you will not have been surpriz'd at what has lately happened to them.[1] I wrote to you on the 25th of June that those who rul'd the Roast had just Ideas of the Value of popular Opinion. Also that should they reach a Harbor it would be as much by good Luck as by good Management, and that at any Rate Part of the Crew would be thrown overboard. Those I had then particularly in View were Chabot & Company of which Company a Part still exists.[2] On the Eighteenth of October I gave you a short View of the nature of the then Government, and added what seem'd to be the probable Termination. I therein observd that whether France would pass to that Point thro the Medium of a Triumvirate, or other small Body of Men seem'd as yet undetermin'd but that I thought it most probable she would. At that Period Things were wound up very high, and ever since the utmost Uncertainty has prevaild as to the Stroke which would be given. I enclose herein a Copy of what I wrote on the twelfth of last Month⟨,⟩ since which both the Dantonists and Hebertists are crush'd.[3] The fall of Danton seems to terminate the Idea of a Triumvirate⟨.⟩ The Chief who would in such Case have been one of his Colleagues has wisely put out of the Way a dangerous Competitor. Hence it would seem that the High road must be laid thro the Comité de Salut public[4]: Unless indeed the Army should meddle. But as to the Army no Character seems as yet to have appeard with any prominent Feature; neither is there so much Discipline as would give an aspiring Character just Ground of Hope. It is a wonderful Thing Sir that four years of Convulsion among four and twenty Millions of People has brought forth no one either in civil or military Life whose Head could fit the Cap which fortune has woven. Roberspierre has been the most consistent, if not the only consistent. He is one of those of whom Shakespeare's Cæsar speaks to his frolicksome Companion. "He loves no Sports as thou dost Anthony."[5] There is no Imputation against him for Corruption. He is far from rich, and still farther from appearing so. It is said that his Idol is Ambition; but I think that the Establishment of the Republic would (all Things considered) be most suitable to him. Whether he thinks so is another Question which I will not pretend to answer, nor how far such Establishmt may appear to him practicable. If it be supposed that a Man in his situation should absolutely despair of the Republic, and have so much Diffidence either in his Abilities, or his Influence, as to despair also of obtaining, much less of preserving the supreme Power, then it might be supposd that Danton's Plan would be by such Person carried into Execution. Yet all this Supposition is but conjectural Foundation of new Conjecture. And what are the Allies about? Forming Schemes to be executed if they should continue to be Allies.[6] I am dear Sir very truly yours.

Gouv. Morris

ALS, DLC:GW; LB, DLC: Gouverneur Morris Papers.

1. François-Joseph Westermann and Georges-Jacques Danton were guillotined on 5 April.

2. François Chabot (1756–1794), who was a member of the *Comité de sûreté générale* (Committee of General Security) from 21 Jan. 1793 until its reorganization in September of that year, was executed on 5 April.

3. On the fall of Jacques-René Hébert and his followers, see William Jackson to GW, 4 April, and n.9.

4. For members of the *Comité de Salut Public* (Committee of Public Safety), see n.8 of Jackson to GW, 4 April.

5. Robespierre, another member of the *Comité de Salut Public*, was guillotined on 28 July. "He loves no plays, As thou dost, Anthony" appears in Act 1, scene 2, of William Shakespeare's *Julius Caesar*.

6. Great Britain, Austria, Prussia, Portugal, Russia, and Spain were mem-

bers of the First Coalition, a military alliance formed in opposition to the Republic of France.

Bartholomew Dandridge, Jr., to Alexander Hamilton

Sir,   United States 19. April 1794.

The President directs me to send the letters herewith enclosed, from Governor Mifflin and John Wanton, for your perusal; and desires, if any measures are necessary to be taken relative to them, that you will report the same to him.[1] I have the honor to be &c.

Bw. Dandridge

LB, DLC:GW.

1. For the enclosed letters, see Thomas Mifflin to GW, 18 April, and John Wanton to GW, 7 April. For Hamilton's response, see his first letter to GW of this date.

From Alexander Hamilton

Sir,   Treasury Departmt April 19. 1794.

I have received a letter of this date from Mr Dandridge transmitting me two letters to you, one from Governor Mifflin, the other from John Wanton; and desiring that if any measures should be necessary to be taken relative to them, they should be reported to you.

With regard to the communication from Govr Mifflin, the subject of it will be put in a train of examination and the result will be communicated.[1]

With regard to that from Mr Wanton I had received from Mr Thornton the british Vice Consul the enclosed state of the case of the schooner Bayonne or Boyne—which as you will perceive has been submitted to the Attorney General for his opinion; which is, that the schooner Boyne under the circumstances stated in that paper "is not within the meaning of the resolves of the Legislature laying an Embargo and that she ought to be permitted to proceed on her voyage to New York."[2]

It was my intention to have sent this morning to the Secretary of war in order that what was proper further to be done might be determined and correspondent instructions given to the military Officer and to the Collector.[3]

I believe the opinion of the Attorney General is right though it puts the effect of the Embargo in some jeopardy as to vessels arriving from abroad.

Perhaps the most adviseable course is to permit the present vessel concerning which there has been some irregularity to proceed to the port of her destination without any condition and to consider & establish some rule of proceeding with proper guards for future cases.[4]

I retain a copy of mister Wanton's letter to be sent to the Collector of New Port as it contains an impeachment of his conduct that calls for inquiry.[5] With the highest respect, I have the honor to be &c.

Alexandr Hamilton

LB, DLC:GW.

1. According to GW's third letter to Hamilton of 29 May (DLC:GW), Hamilton failed to provide any further information for GW regarding a response to the information contained in Thomas Mifflin's letter to GW of 18 April.

2. On the retention of the British schooner *Boyne* at Newport, R.I., see John Wanton to GW, 7 April; see also the letters from the collector of customs at Newport, William Ellery, to Hamilton of 8 and 14 April (*Hamilton Papers*, 16:246–48, 256–57). Edward Thornton, the British vice-consul at Baltimore, was transferred in early April to Philadelphia, where he currently was serving as secretary to British minister George Hammond (Hammond to Edmund Randolph, 2 April 1794, DNA: RG 59, Notes from Foreign Legations: Great Britain). Neither the enclosed statement from Thornton nor a written opinion from Attorney General William Bradford has been identified. For the resolves of 26 March and 2 April establishing an embargo on ships in U.S. ports, see *Stat.* 1:400–401.

3. In a letter to Rhode Island governor Arthur Fenner of late April, which has not been identified, Henry Knox wrote that it had been determined that the *Boyne* was not liable to detention and that GW had given instructions that the vessel be allowed to depart. For Knox's instructions, see Ellery to Hamilton, 5 May (*Hamilton Papers*, 16:376–77). Hamilton's letter to Ellery of 22 April has not been identified. The *Boyne* cleared Newport on 5 May (*Newport Mercury*, 6 May).

4. Bartholomew Dandridge, Jr., wrote Hamilton on 21 April: "By the President's order Bw Dandridge has the honor to inform the Secretary of the Treasury, that the President desires measures may be pursued in the case of the schooner Boyne as advised in the Secretary's letter to the President of the 19 instant, relative to that subject" (LB, DLC:GW). One more resolve respecting the embargo was subsequently passed. The resolve of 7 May authorized the president "to direct clearances" for vessels owned by U.S. citizens and bound for any port beyond the Cape of Good Hope (*Stat.* 1:401).

5. Hamilton enclosed a copy of Wanton's letter in a letter to Ellery of 1 May (*Hamilton Papers,* 16:363).

From Alexander Hamilton

[Philadelphia] April 19. 1794.
The Secretary of the Treasury presents his respects to the President of the United States, and encloses herewith the draft of a passport for the Sloop Dove for the President's signature.[1] It will be forwarded by Mr Goodhue, who will call for it at the Secretary's Office.[2]

LB, DLC:GW.
1. GW signed the enclosed passport, which has not been identified, later on this date. The sloop *Dove,* Capt. Friend Dole, was granted permission to sail from Newburyport, Mass., "in ballast," to any island in the West Indies (*JPP,* 299–300).
2. Massachusetts congressman Benjamin Goodhue was currently in Philadelphia to attend the first session of the Third Congress. Hamilton's office was at 100 Chesnut Street.

From Howell Lewis

Dear Sir,   Philadelphia April 19th 1794.
It is with extreme regret that I am under the necessity of informing you that I intend leaving your family on the 15th of next month, as at that time I shall have been with you two years.[1] The reason why I have taken this resolution is because I find that 300 dollars does not support me here by two hundred; my property also in Virginia through bad management is running me in debt, & I do not make enough to pay you my rent & other expences which are necessary; My Brother Robert wrote me the other day,[2] that my Overseer had not paid the rent nor was there produce of any kind on the farm sufficient to discharge the Same; my negroes Clothing unpaid for, so that I am now obliged to sell some of them (the negroes) to pay what I owe there and here; I have sunk 300 dollars since I have been here, & about £45 in Virginia. & have with the advice of my mother & Brothers taken this step; & also have determined to give up the place which I have of yours, & move with the small remains of my fortune which are but a few negroes, the next spring with my

Brother George to Kentuckey, & there try if I can make something, or at least have it in my power to look after my lands which I have in That Country.[3]

For your attentions to me whilst in your family I hope it is unnecessary for me to say I entertain the deepest sense of gratitude. To dwell on this subject & to make a long acknowledgment of the obligations under which I feel myself laid by your & family's kindnesses must to a mind like yours be tedious and painful. I will only add that, it has made an impression on my mind which, I trust time itself cannot obl⟨i⟩terate. I am Dear Sir your affe[ctiona]te Nephew

Howell Lewis

ALS, ICHi.

1. On GW's employment of his nephew Howell Lewis as a recording secretary for a salary of $300 per year, see GW to Betty Washington Lewis, 8 April 1792. He served briefly as the temporary manager of Mount Vernon during the latter half of 1793, returning to Philadelphia in early January 1794 (GW to William Stuart, Hiland Crow, and Henry McCoy, 14 July 1793; and to William Pearce, 12 Jan. 1794).

2. The letter from Robert Lewis has not been identified.

3. Howell had received seventeen slaves and 15,000 acres in Kentucky from the estate of his father, Fielding Lewis, Sr. Neither Howell nor his brother George settled permanently in Kentucky (Felder, *Fielding Lewis*, 300, 312–15).

From Edmund Randolph

Philadelphia Saturday afternoon [19 April 1794]

The secretary of state has the honor of informing the President of the U.S., that the commission for Mr Jay is preparing, and he is notified by letter, that it is preparing; no time being to be lost.[1]

Perhaps the President will find it necessary to have a ship, taken for the voyage and to fix the salary at once. E.R. will therefore talk with Mr Jay.[2]

An express is sent off to Mr Patterson, with a letter from Mr Wilson, to stop his journey hither, as being more convenient to the other plan.[3]

AL, DNA: RG 59, Miscellaneous Letters; LB, DNA: RG 59, GW's Correspondence with His Secretaries of State. The docket on the AL reads, "19 April 1794."

1. The commission for John Jay reads: "Reposing especial Trust and Con-

fidence in your Integrity Prudence and ability, I have nominated, and by and with the advice and Consent of the Senate do appoint you the said John Jay, Envoy extraordinary from the United States of America to the Court of his Britannic Majesty, authorizing you hereby, to do and perform all such matters and Things, as to the said Place or Office doth appertain, or as may de duly given you in Charge hereafter. And the said office to hold and exercise during the Pleasure of the President of the United States for the Time being.

"In Testimony whereof I have caused the Seal of the United States to be hereunto affixed.

"Given under my Hand at the City of Philadelphia, the nineteenth Day of april in the Year of our Lord one thousand seven hundred and ninety four, and of the Independence of the United States of America the Eighteenth" (copy, DLC:GW).

2. For Alexander Hamilton's role in arranging passage for John Jay, see Hamilton to William Seton, 22 April, 2 May, and 21 June, and Hamilton to Jay, 28 April (*Hamilton Papers*, 16:312, 350–51, 371, 510). On 12 May, Jay departed from New York City for Great Britain on the *Ohio,* Capt. John Kemp (*Daily Advertiser* [New York], 13 May; *New-York Directory, 1794,* 100).

3. In a letter of 16 April to William Paterson of New Jersey, Randolph notified the Supreme Court justice of Jay's nomination and its expected approval by the U.S. Senate. "In that event, Mr. Jay will be immediately occupied with preparations for a hasty departure" and cannot continue serving on the circuit court for the District of Pennsylvania, which was currently in session. "The President has therefore determined to submit this intelligence to you, that you may judge, how far it may be convenient and necessary for you to go thro' the remaining Courts, and what remains of the Pennsylvania term. He instructs me to add, without presuming, however, to exercise any right on this occasion, that your presence here immediately will be very agreeable to him, and that he hopes, that you will, when you arrive here, be able to make such arrangements for prosecuting Mr Jay's tour, as will be acceptable to yourself." The letter from Supreme Court justice James Wilson of Pennsylvania to Paterson of 19 April, which has not been identified, probably stated that Wilson would finish Jay's current assignment, because Wilson took Jay's seat on the circuit court on Monday, 21 April, and the court continued its session until adjourning on 26 April. For the plan adopted for covering the other circuit court sessions, see Wilson to William Cushing, 27 April (*Documentary History of the Supreme Court,* 2:445–47, 450).

From Edmund Randolph

(Private)
Dear sir   Philadelphia April 19. 1794.
I called upon Mr Monroe, and obtained his promise, to explain the manner of his procuring the extract, as it was in truth,

without my privity and against the rule of the office. But I find, that Mr King was employed in the examination of the same books, at the same time; so that in this instance, the want of equal measure cannot upon any ground be suspected.[1]

Your friendly remarks add to the many obligations, which I owe to you; and also present an opportunity, which I cannot forego, of unbosoming myself to you without reserve.

I have often said, I still say—that nothing shall sway me, as nothing has yet swayed me, to depart from a long-settled determination, never to attach myself to party. I believe, that I might appeal to you, Sir—nay I should not distrust an appeal to any man, with whom I have acted, that this determination has been conscientiously pursued. What has been the consequence? I know it—that my opinions, not containing any systematic adherence to party, but arising solely from my views of right, fall sometimes on one side, and sometimes on the other; and the momentary satisfaction, produced by an occasional coincidence of sentiment, does not prevent each class from occasionally charging me with instability. But I had much rather submit to this tax, than to the more painful sensations, which a contrary conduct would excite.

I am no less apprized, that my connections by friendship, by marriage, by country, and by a similitude of opinions, where republicanism and good order meet, with the leaders of the southern politicks, give birth to suspicions.[2] But if I were here to enumerate the great subjects, which, since the organization of the government, have agitated the public mind, it would appear that even those connections have not operated upon me, beyond the weight of their reason. They are inestimable to me; and while I retain a consciousness of my ability to resist an undue influence, I cannot deny the satisfaction, which I feel in maintaining them. And yet, sir, there is one fact, of which I beg you to be persuaded; that with them I have no communication on matters of government, which I would not have with others: I converse freely, but without imparting official intelligence, which is not of an absolutely public nature—I commit myself by no opinions—and above all, I shall never attempt to use those persons, as engines of any measure, which is a favorite with me. While I was writing this last sentence, a question springs up, "what views can I have"? The answer is, peace, liberty and good government.

When I contemplate the other party, I see among them men, whom I respect, and who, if their duplicity be not extreme, respect me. I see others, who respect no man, but in proportion to his subserviency to their wishes. Some of these are well informed, that I have opposed in several instances things, which they had at heart. I have no reason to suspect Colo. Hamilton of any unkind disposition towards me—he has none on my part with relation to himself—Even to your confidential ear have I never disclosed an idea concerning him, which he might not hear, and which in many instances and particularly a late one he has not heard from my own mouth. But I have reason to suspect others—if you pause upon a measure, which they are anxious for, I am supposed to embarrass you with considerations of a popular kind.

But I have said enough—perhaps too much. Suffer me, however, to add one word more, of the sincerity of which I ask no other judge than yourself. Your character is an object of real affection to me. there is no judgment, no disinterestedness, no prudence, in which I ever had equal confidence. I have often indeed expressed sentiments contrary to yours. This was my duty, because they were my sentiments. But, sir, they were never tinctured by any other motive, than to present to your reflection the misconstructions, which wicked men might make of your views, and to hold out to you a truth of infinite importance to the United States, that no danger can attend us, as long as the persuasion continues, that you are not, and cannot become the head of a party. The people venerate you, because they are convinced, that you choose to repose yourself on them. Let me intreat you, only to look round the continent, and decide, if there be any other man, but yourself, who is bottomed upon the people, independent of party? There is surely none; and the inference, which I submit to your candor, is, that the measures, adopted by you, should be tried solely by your own pure and unbiassed mind. I have the honor, to be dear sir with the most affectionate attachment and respect yr mo. ob. serv.

Edm: Randolph

ALS, DLC:GW.

1. The extract examined by Senators James Monroe and Rufus King has not been identified, but it may have been a letter to Randolph from Thomas Pinckney, the U.S. minister to Great Britain, that had not been made public (see Monroe to GW, 11 April).

2. On Randolph's connections to critics of the Washington administration, particularly those from his native Virginia, see John Nicholas to GW, 6 April, source note.

From Edmund Randolph

Saturday [Philadelphia, 19 April 1794]

The Secretary of state has the honor of sending to the President the opinions of the gentlemen on the address from the democratic society in Washington.[1]

AL, DNA: RG 59, Miscellaneous Letters; LB, DNA: RG 59, GW's Correspondence with His Secretaries of State.

1. GW enclosed the address from the Democratic Society of Washington County, Pa., of 24 March with his letter to Randolph of 11 April. Randolph then wrote a letter to William Bradford, Alexander Hamilton, and Henry Knox on 14 April asking for their opinions on a proper response to the address. As Randolph's letter circulated from one cabinet member to another, each man wrote his opinion directly below Randolph's signature. For this cabinet opinion, see the enclosure below.

Enclosure
Cabinet Opinion on an Address from the
Democratic Society of Washington County, Pa.

Gentlemen   Philadelphia April 14. 1794.

The President wishes your opinion, as to the step, proper to be taken, upon the inclosed address. To send to congress, what the President thinks unfit for himself, will be unkindly received; being uncivil in itself. To acknowledge the body, as such, is in every view inadmissible. So that the question seems to turn upon this; whether it be better to treat the paper with unqualiffied and silent contempt; or to return it to James Marshal, as an individual, to this effect; "that the President receives no applications from a body, as such, whose constitution is not known in the laws; and that the paper is therefore returned to him, as the individual, from whom it came"—Silent contempt I prefer. I have the honor, gentlemen, to be with great respect Yr. mo. ob. serv.

Edm. Randolph

I am of opinion that no answer should be given but that the Paper should be referred to the Atty General to examine carefully if it does not contain criminal matter & that if it does it ought to be put in a train of prosecution.

A. Hamilton

No prosecution—but no answer of any sort.

H. Knox

The Language of the petition is exceedingly reprehensible and improper: but I doubt whether it would be considered *per se,* as a proper subject for a criminal prosecution, without some *extrinsic* proof of a seditious intention. The "right of petitioning for redress of grievances" is so solemnly gaurantee'd by the Constitution and so jealously guarded, that Juries are apt to consider an attempt to correct it[s] abuses, unless very flagrant, as an attack upon the right itself; & they regard those improprieties merely as excrescences which it is dangerous to touch. More exceptionable matter appears frequently in the public prints: but these abuses are endured from a fear of injuring the freedom of the Press.[1] An unsuccessful prosecution from seditious writings generally does harm: and independant of any legal doubt, this does not seem to be a case that will *certainly* ensure a conviction. I therefore think it best to treat the paper with the contempt it deserves.

Wm Bradford

DS, DNA: RG 59, Miscellaneous Letters. GW's docket reads, "Opinions of the Heads of Depts. relative to a remonstrance of the Democ. Society of Washington Coty—Pennsylvania 14th April 1794."

1. The first amendment to the U.S. Constitution states that "Congress shall make no law . . . abridging the freedom of speech, or of the press; or the right of the people peaceably to assemble, and to petition the Government for a redress of grievances."

To William Pearce

Mr Pearce   Philadelphia 20th April 1794

Your letter of the 15th, with the weekly reports, came to hand as usual, yesterday. I was sorry to learn by the first that you had been unwell.[1]

It is almost impossible for me to say, with exactness, what I owe the Estate of Mr Anthony Whitting, because his accounts do not appear to have been regularly kept, but rather in detached Memms. More than his wages from the first of Jany until the day of his death (which I think was about the middle of June) at the rate of One hundd pounds Virga Curry pr annum, I cannot owe him;[2] because my Nephew when his health obliged him in November 1792 to spend the Winter with his father in law Colo. Bassett, paid Mr Whitting, and all the under Overseers (as he did not expect to be back again if ever, in less than Six months) their full wages for the year, ending the last of December. More therefore than from the close of that year, until the time of his death, in the succeeding one, can[not],[3] as I have observed before, be due to the Estate; and this, rather than do it a *possible* injury, you may pay his Exrs or Admrs; although (as he always had money of mine in his hands) it is probable he might, as it became due to him, have applied part to his own use.[4]

With respect to the Bond which you say his Exrs are enquiring after, I never saw, or heard of such an one; except whilst I was in Virginia last;[5] when I was told by some one, what you have mentioned in your letter. Mr Lear (who at that time was my Secretary) being called to the Federal City on business, & hearing that Mr Whitting was dead, or at the point of death (I am not sure which) and knowing that my affairs at Mount Vernon would, by this event, be thrown into great disorder, went down there (which he had not intended to do when he left Phila.) and remained there until I got home; at which time he gave me all the Papers he had found belonging to Mr Whitting. The private papers in one bundle—and those which concerned my business in another.[6] In neither of these was there any bond, nor did I ever hear the circumstance mentioned, until I went to Virginia last Fall. If such a bond did exist, it certainly can be no difficult matter to learn from whom it was obtained; & whether it has been discharged, or not; if discharged, the person paying it will know to whom; without which the bond will be of no use to any one. All Whittings private papers were, to the best of my recollection, turned over to Mr Ring; who, by a non-cupitive Will, was made his heir.[7]

I am glad to find you are upon the point of sowing Buck wheat at all the Farms. It is essential it should be in the ground without delay, if two Crops are to be plowed in, before the Wheat is sown thereon. Does the Oats which you have sown, and the grass-seeds, come up well? and how are your seasons, and the temper of the ground? By the last Reports you appear to have had rain twice during the week they were made.[8] In this neighbourhood the earth is dry, & rain wanting. Did you allow a plenty of seed to the ground that was resown with grass, as well as the other, for the first time.

As the Embargo is continued until the 25th of next month, I think you had better grind no more Wheat until you hear further from me; & let that which is in the straw, remain there; as the safest mode of keeping it; unless you should discover any appearance of the fly about the stacks; in that case, it might be proper to get it out, & grind it as speedily as possible.[9]

I do not know how much ground you have sown with flax; but as there is no foreseeing what our disputes may end in, it is my wish that you would add a good deal more (if not too late) to what you have already sown; that, let what will happen, I may make a shift to cloath my Negros. This makes it peculiarly necessary also to be extremely attentive to the Wool; for I am satisfied that a tenth part of what is sheared, in bringing it home, and after it is in the usual place, where it is kept, is stolen from me. To guard against both these modes of pilferring, will require much caution; & a strict watch.[10]

Has there been many Mares, or Jennies, sent yet to the Jacks or Horse? or have you reason to expect that many Will be sent this Season, besides my own?[11]

Enclosed you will find a letter of complaint—Butler against Crow[12]—I do not see that it is in my power, or yours, to interfere in the matter otherwise than in an amicable manner. If this fails, the Courts of Justice are equally open to both, and that must be the resort of the injured party. If however, Butler is acquainted with any mal-conduct in Crow, & is able to prove it, he ought, as an honest man, to come forward with it; but he should take care to advance nothing that he is unable to support, lest it should recoil upon himself. When I was last at Mount Vernon, I received numerous complaints from my Negros of their not having been supplied as usual with Fish, & strong insinuations were held out that breaking open the house, in which they were deposited, was no other than a pretence to cover a more nefarious mode of disposing of them. In short it was hinted that Crow had sold them. but as there did not appear any proof of the fact, I set on foot no enquiry, but resolved to lay in a sufficiency for my people this year; secure them well; and let only one person have access to them for delivery, & to be responsible. The Key to be locked up with others at the mansion Ho., and a periodical time for issuing a certain number to each farm, to be distributed by the Overseers in certain proportions to the old & young thereon.

I hope, as the weather seems to be turning warm, that the fish will run more abundantly. Keep a regular acct of this business, that, when it is closed and everything charged, & every thing credited that appertains to it the profit or loss may be ascertained.[13] I wish you well & am Your friend

Go: Washington

P.S. Since writing the foregoing letter I have received one from Mr Lear (now in London) containing the following paragraph.

"I have engaged 5000 of the white thorn plants which will be put on board the Ship Peggy bound to George Town, she will sail by or before the 10th of February and is addressed to Colo. Deakins."[14]

Make diligent enquiry for the Vessel if she is not already arrived, as the Season is advanced & the plants will be much injured, if not lost, if not soon got into the ground. I conceive they had better be placed at once where they are finally to remain— and as many may die, plant them thicker on that account. You may have the ground prepared against the plants arrive that not a moment may be lost that can be avoided—plant them where, in your own opinion, they will answer best; Or if Butler, who ought to understd this business thinks they had better go into a nursery in the first instance, let it be so.[15]

G. W——n

AL (fragment), ViMtvL; ALS (letterpress copy), DLC:GW.

1. Pearce's letter of 15 April and the enclosed farm reports have not been found.

2. Anthony Whitting, GW's previous estate manager, had died on 21 June 1793 (Tobias Lear to GW, 24 June 1793).

3. On the letterpress copy, GW corrected "can" to "cannot."

4. On the departure of George Augustine Washington and his family from Mount Vernon in October 1792 in order to spend the winter months at the home of Burwell Bassett, Sr., see GW to Betty Washington Lewis, 7 Oct. 1792. According to GW's financial records, Whitting received £42.13.5 on 5 Oct. 1792 as payment "in full" for his services from 3 Sept. through 25 Dec. 1792 (Ledger B, 310). On 2 Aug. 1794, £40 in cash was paid to Whitting's executors (Mount Vernon Accounts, 1794–97).

5. GW was last at Mount Vernon between mid-September and 28 Oct. 1793 (*JPP*, 239, 241).

6. On Lear's presence at Mount Vernon, see Lear to GW, 19 and 24 June 1793. GW visited Mount Vernon between 27 June and 7 July 1793 (*JPP*, 189–90).

7. On William Ring, see n.6 of GW to Howell Lewis, 4 Aug. 1793. A nuncupative will is one that is declared orally before witnesses.

8. The previous farm reports, which were enclosed in Pearce's letter to GW of 9 April, have not been found.

9. On the thirty-day embargo, which was placed on all ships and vessels in U.S. ports, and its extension to 25 May, see the congressional resolutions of 26 March and 18 April (*Stat.* 1:400–401).

10. The remaining text is taken from the letterpress copy.

11. For the fees charged by GW for the stud services of his horse Traveller and the jacks Knight of Malta and Compound, see n.1 of Bartholomew Dandridge, Jr., to Angell & Sullivan and Samuel Hanson of 26 February.

12. The letter from James Butler, the overseer of Mansion House farm, in which he complained about Hiland Crow, the overseer of Union farm, has not been found.

13. For Pearce's record of the expenses and income generated by GW's fishery, see Mount Vernon Accounts, 1794–97.

14. The quotation is based on a passage in the postscript to Lear's letter to GW of 26–30 January. For additional mention of this shipment, see Lear to GW, 12 February.

15. On the receipt of the white thorn plants and their planting at Mount Vernon, see the farm reports for 25–31 May (DLC:GW).

From Noah Webster

Sir.   New York April 20th 1794

At the perfect critical juncture of our political affairs, it appears to be the duty of every good citizen to use his influence in restraining the violence of parties & moderating the passions of our injured fellow-citizens. For this purpose a just estimate of the Revolution in France, & the danger of *faction* may not be without its effects in this country, in determining the people to resist any intrigues that may be hostile to our government. The enclosed is intended to aid the cause of government & peace.[1] Should it have the least influence for this purpose I shall be satisfied—Be pleased to accept it as a proof of my attachment to you & the Constitution of the United States, & believe me with sincere wishes for your personal happiness & a firm resolution to support your administration,[2] Your most obedient and most hume Servant

Noah Webster, Jun.

ALS, DNA: RG 59, Miscellaneous Letters.

1. The enclosed pamphlet was *The Revolution in France, Considered in Respect to Its Progress and Effects* (New York, 1794).

2. GW's reply to Webster of 9 May reads: "I have received, though realy it has not been in my power yet to read, the Pamphlet you were so obliging as to send me. Your motives to writing it are highly laudable, and I sincerely wish they may meet the reward which is due to them. I pray you to accept my thanks for the work" (ALS [letterpress copy], NN: Washington Papers; LB, DLC:GW).

From Alexander Hamilton

Sir,   Treasy Departmt April 21. 1794.

I lately communicated to you a letter from our Comissioners at Amsterdam announcing the undertaking of a Loan on account of the U. States for three millions of Florins.[1] I submit the following application of that loan as the one which appears to me most conducive to the good of the public service. One million of Florins to be appropriated to the payment of an instalment of an equal sum of the Dutch debt payable on the first of June next[2]—the residue of the loan to be transferred here for the purposes either of payments to France,[3] or purchases of the Debt as circumstances shall dictate.[4]

I had begun remittances & made a provisional arrangement for the purchase of bills of the Bank of the United States, toward payment of the June instalment.[5] But the loan supercedes the necessity of the former and the bills remitted will serve to pay interest & premium of the old loans due and becoming due.[6] With the highest respect &c.

                                              Alexr Hamilton

LB, DLC:GW.

1. This probably is the letter from the Dutch banking firm of Willink, Van Staphorst, and Hubbard to Hamilton of 27 Dec. 1793 (*Hamilton Papers,* 15:593–96).

2. The payment due on 1 June 1794 was for the 1782 Dutch loan of 10 million livres (5 million florins). On this loan, see Bayley, *National Loans,* 15–17.

3. For a description of the French loan of 6 million livres, see William Short to Hamilton, 30 Nov. 1789, n.3 (*Hamilton Papers,* 5:570–71). On the French loans of 18 million and 10 million livres, see Bayley, *National Loans,* 11, 13–14.

4. Section 4 of "An Act making Provision for the Reduction of the Public

Debt," 12 Aug. 1790, authorized the president to borrow $2 million for the payment of this debt (*Stat.* 1:187).

5. The Bank of the United States was to "furnish Bills of Exchange on Amsterdam for the use of the Government" (Hamilton to Thomas Willing, 3 March, *Hamilton Papers,* 16:105–6).

6. For an account of the various loans and debts of the United States and the payments made on them in 1794, see Statements A, B, C, D, and E enclosed in Hamilton's Report on a Plan for the Further Support of Public Credit, 16 Jan. 1795 (*Hamilton Papers,* 18:130–44).

From Richard Harison

Sir,   Philadelphia 21st April 1794

Having been informed that your Excellency has nominated me as Successor to Mr Duane in the Office of District Judge for the New York District, I think it my Duty to mention that from professional Engagements, and the Situation of my private Affairs, I am under the Necessity of declining the Appointment. I should have felt greater Reluctance to this Measure had I not been convinced that there were several Persons, differently situated, who may be disposed to accept the Office, and are qualified to fill it with Reputation to themselves and Advantage to the Public.[1]

Your Excellency may be assured that the Honor conferred upon me by your late Nomination, as well as the former Marks of your favorable Opinion have made an indelible Impression upon my Memory.[2] It will be my Study to merit, and my greatest Pride to maintain a Continuance of your Approbation, the Confidence of my Country, and the Esteem of it's most virtuous Citizens; and I shall ever remain, with the highest Respect, Sir, Your Excellency's most obliged and obedt Servt

Rich: Harison

ALS, DNA: RG 59, Miscellaneous Letters.

1. For the nomination of Harison, see GW to U.S. Senate, 16 April (second letter). Harison also may have been influenced by the Senate's decision on 19 April to postpone further consideration of his nomination (*U.S. Senate Executive Journal,* 1:152). For GW's subsequent nomination of John Laurance as judge of the District of New York, see his letter to the U.S. Senate of 5 May (DNA: RG 46, Third Congress, 1793–95, Senate Records of Executive Proceedings, President's Messages—Executive Nominations).

2. Harison currently was serving as the U.S. district attorney for New York (see GW to U.S. Senate, 25 Sept. 1789).

Cabinet Opinion on Funds for French Refugees

[Philadelphia] April 22. 1794.

We do ourselves the honor of advising the President of the U.S. to apply the remainder of the money, given by law to the indigent of St Domingo, resident here,[1] to the furnishing of them with the means of going thither, it being known, that several vessels are now bound thither from different parts of the U.S. with passports, for the purpose of conveying them.[2]

Edm: Randolph.

H. Knox

Alexandr Hamilton.

DS (in Edmund Randolph's handwriting), DNA: RG 59, Miscellaneous Letters; LB, DNA: RG 59, GW's Correspondence with His Secretaries of State.

1. "An Act providing for the relief of such of the inhabitants of Saint Domingo, resident within the United States, as may be found in want of support," 12 Feb., provided "a sum not exceeding fifteen thousand dollars" (*Stat.* 6:13). On 11 April, Randolph submitted to GW a list of the money distributed to that date (DNA: RG 59, Miscellaneous Letters):

"Sent to [William] Patterson, [Gustavus] Scott & [Samuel] Sterrett of Baltimore	2,000
to Jed. Huntington of Connect thro Col. [Jeremiah] Wads[wor]th	150
to Delaware by [William] Hemphill	500
to [Jabez] Bowen of R. Island	1000
[Thomas] Russell of Massa.	250
[Guilian] Verplan[c]k of N. York	1750
[Daniel] De Saus[s]ure of So. Caro.	1750
[Donald] Campbell & others of Virga	1450
[John] Vaughan & others of Phila.	1600
	Dollars $\overline{10,450}$
Patterson in addition	2000.
	$\overline{12,450.}$
Georgia	500
No. Carolina	250
	Dollars. $\underline{13,200}$"

See also Randolph's accounts of 10–20 March 1794, DNA: RG 59, Miscellaneous Letters.

2. For some of the vessels scheduled to transport refugees to Saint Domingue, see Hamilton to GW, 22 April. In response to this opinion, GW instructed Hamilton in a second letter to him of 24 April to "Pay to the Secretary of State in pursuance of the Act providing for the relief of such of the Inhabitants of St Domingo, resident within the U.S. as may be found in want of support, one thousand eight hundred dollars; being the remainder of the sum granted for that purpose by the above Act, and to be applied to the furnishing the said Inhabitants with the means of returning to Saint Domingo" (LB, DLC:GW).

To Alexander Hamilton

Sir,   Philada the 22 day of April 1794

Upon examining my letter to you of the 27 June '93, and my two powers of the 8th of August 1793, the one for making a loan of one million of florins,[1] and the other for making a loan of 1,515,[0]98 dols. & 11 Cents,[2] I wish to have some explanation upon the subject of your letter of yesterday's date.[3] The questions which arise are these: whether the million of Florins, to be borrowed for the instalment, payable to Holland in June next, be not already appropriated for that purpose; and whether the appropriation now proposed of the three millions of florins will not in some measure be contrary to the appropriation contained in my power of the 8th of August 1793. For it appears to me, that I have directed the money to be borrowed under that power, to be applied to the purchases of the public Debt.[4]

Geo: Washington

LB, DLC:GW.

1. GW's second letter to Hamilton of 8 Aug. 1793 authorized him to borrow 1 million florins "to be applied to the payment" due on 1 June for the Dutch loan of 1782.

2. In his first letter to Hamilton of 8 Aug. 1793, GW authorized a loan of $1,515,089.11 and stipulated that it "be applied to purchases of the public debt."

3. GW apparently questioned the contents of Hamilton's letter of 21 April, after receiving Edmund Randolph's letter of 22 April, which reads: "E. Randolph requests the President to let him see the instructions, which he gave to Colo. Hamilton in the course of the last summer for borrowing more money. If E.R. is not greatly mistaken, there was some special appropriation made of it there" (DNA: RG 59, Miscellaneous Letters).

4. For Hamilton's reply, see his second letter to GW of 23 April.

From Alexander Hamilton

[Philadelphia 22 April 1794]

The Secretary of the Treasury presents his respects to the President ⟨&⟩ has the honor to transmit sundry drafts of Passports in cases which have been handed to him for that purpose by the Secretary of State. In some instances though the names of the vessels appear in the documents, those of the masters do not. If the President thinks fit to sign them as they are care will be taken that they are properly filled.[1]

	Recovery	Baltimore	
Schooner	Providentia	Do	
Ship	Govr. Hamilton	Charleston, Richd West, Master	
Brigte	Sally	Philadelphia	
Brigt.	Betsey	Ditto	Thos Adams, Master
Brigt.	Franklin	Ditto[2]	

LB, DLC:GW.

1. According to his executive journal, GW signed passports on this date for all six vessels listed below, allowing them to proceed to Saint Domingue, "in ballast with liberty to take in such Inhabitants of sd. Island as may choose to go as passengers, with their baggage & seastores" (*JPP*, 301).

2. According to an advertisement in the 3 May issue of *The American Star, or, Historical, Political, Critical and Moral Journal* (Philadelphia), the brig *Sally*, Capt. Stephen Parsons, was scheduled to sail for Saint Domingue, with passengers, on Thursday, 8 May, and the brig *Franklin* on Wednesday, 7 May.

Letter not found: from William Pearce, 22 April 1794. GW wrote Pearce on 27 April that "Your letter of the 22d instant with its enclosures came duly to hand."

From Bushrod Washington

Dear Uncle   Richmond [Va.] April 22d 1794

I find that there is an injunction in the High Court of Chancery obtained against you, which I am employed by those interested in the Judgment at law, to dissolve—to do this, your answer is necessary. I send you a Copy of the Bill;[1] if upon the reciept of this letter, you will immediately communicate to me the substance of your answer, I will save you the expence of applying to Counsel, and will draw it in form, & forward to you to be sworn to. the Court sits on the 12th of May, & the answer if possible ought to be filed before that time; so that if I draw it, and return it to you to be sworn to, we shall have no time to spare in getting it prepared.[2] with great sincerity I am dear Uncle Yr Affect: Nephew

Bushd: Washington.

ALS, ViMtvL.

1. The enclosed bill has not been identified.

2. For GW's reply and his explanation of the circumstances surrounding the suit brought by John Henshaw, see GW to Bushrod Washington, 30 April.

From Baron Otto de Wurmser

Par francfort au Duché de Wirtemberg

Monsieur   à Louisbourg[1] ce 22 avril 1794

C'est avec une Confiance Sans Bornes, et avec une profonde veneration pour les vertus et les Sublimes qualités de vôtre Excellence, que je prend la liberté de m'adresser à elle, pour la prier de m'aider dans la pénible recherche de la malheureuse mere de ma femme. Cette respectable femme S'apelle Md. de Bayeux, agé de 84 ans, habitante du Cap françois Côtes et Isle de St. Domingue; Elle etoit Sur Son habitation du Port Margot paisible et tranquille lors de la premiere revolte des Negres; elle a été Sauvé comme par miracle du feû qui avoit été mis aux quatre coins de Sa maison, d'oû on là emportée en chemin, pour l'embarquer pour la ville du Cap; depuis le Sac de cette malheureuse ville, nous n'avons Sçu nous en procurer aucune nouvelle; et comme l'on dit que quelques habitans de ces malheureuses contrées ont eu le bonheur de Se Sauver à Philadelphie, et ne connoissant personne dans cette ville, J'ose implorer les bontés et l'humanitée de Vôtre Excellence, et la pries de faire faire la recherche de cette tendre mere parmi les refugiés françois de cette Colonie, la prendre Sous Sa protection; Si parmi le nombre de ces malheureux Colons refugiés, il y en avoit une du nom de chabert et petite fille de nôtre mere, J'ose egalement la recommander aux bontés de Votre Excellence. La faveur Seroit complette Si elle daignoit me faire instruire du Sort de ces malheureux mais bien chers Parens. Je ne cesserai de faire des voeux pour la prosperité et la Conservation des jours précieux de vôtre Excellence. Ma reconnoissance egalera le profond Respect avec le quel Je Suis. Monsieur de Vôtre Excellence le trés humble et trés obeissant Serviteur

Le Baron Otto de Wurmser
aide Mareschal General des Logis des Armées du Roy
de france et chambellan de L'Electeur de Saxe.

ALS (in French), DNA: RG 59, Miscellaneous Letters.

Wurmser, who served in the French army and as chamberlain for Friedrich August III (1750–1827), the elector of Saxony, requested GW's assistance in finding family members who might be among the French refugees from Saint Domingue that were currently in the United States. He was anxious to find his mother-in-law, Madame de Bayeux of Port Margot, who was 84 years old, and her granddaughter Chabert.

1. Wurmser wrote this letter while in the German city of Ludwigsburg in the duchy of Württemberg.

From Samuel Campbell

Hond Sir   New York 23d April 1794

Having lately printed an American Edition of the Trial of Thomas Muir, please allow a copy thereof a place in Your Library.[1]

Mr Muir since he received his rigorous sentence, intimated indirectly to me a desire that a Copy of his Trial might be presented to You, but was disappointed in sending out one of the British Editions.[2]

It is peculiarly gratifying to me, to have it in my power to accomplish his wish, in sending the present. I am most respectfully Hond Sir, yr hble Sevt

Samuel Campbell

ALS, DLC:GW.

1. Bookseller and printer Samuel Campbell (1765–1836) was a native of Scotland. Formerly a partner in Hodge, Allen, and Campbell, he was now operating independently at 37 Hanover-Square in New York City. He sent GW a copy of *An Account of the Trial of Thomas Muir, Esq. Younger, of Huntershill, before the High Court of Justiciary at Edinburgh, On the 30th and 31st days of August, 1793, for Sedition* (New York, 1794). This book was in GW's library at the time of his death (Griffin, *Catalogue of the Washington Collection*, 529).

2. Thomas Muir (1765–1799), a lawyer in Edinburgh, Scotland, was charged with sedition in 1793 for advocating radical political reform in Scotland and Ireland. Although he was found guilty on 31 Aug. 1793 and sentenced to fourteen years in the penal colony of Botany Bay, Australia, it was not until 2 May 1794 that he was put aboard a ship bound for this colony. He managed to escape in 1796 and eventually settled in France, where he died.

From the Commissioners
for the District of Columbia

Sir   City of Washington April 23d 1794

We take the Liberty to inclose you a Letter for Messrs Richard Harrison and George Taylor Jr, which we beg you to read and send to them: it will apprize you of our very difficult Situation with Mr Blodget, who has come hither without any Thing nearly, but evasions and excuses—we have past by the Secretary, because we imagine his time will not allow this to be a first object to him as it is unfortunately to us.[1]

You have inclosed, a Duplicate of the certificate for the N.E. Corner of Square 21—the other quarter on the same North line belongs to the public and may be joined to your part if you should desire it.[2]

We have had Conversations with Mr Fenwick, who has been a good while in the Surveying Department, and a Mr Freeman, who has been lately taken into it—the Conduct of the first, and a Specimen of the Abilities of the last, with their general View, and Idea disclosed of the manner of continuing the work, lead us to expect, they are competent to do it, and they are proceeding; if they should meet with unexpected difficulties, we have no doubt but they will apprize us of such with Candor, and Sincerity, and we leave the Surveying Department with them for the present under this Confidence.[3] we are sir most respectfully Your obedt Servants

Th. Johnson
Dd: Stuart.
Danl Carroll

LS, DLC:GW; LB, DNA: RG 42, Records of the Commissioners for the District of Columbia, Letters Sent, 1791–1802.

1. The enclosed letter of 23 April was addressed to Richard Harrison, auditor of the Treasury Department, and George Taylor, Jr., chief clerk of the Department of State. This letter was prompted by problems with a lottery conducted by Samuel Blodget, Jr., the former superintendent of the Federal City. On this lottery and Blodget's delay in selecting and paying the winners, see D.C. Commissioners to GW, 9 April 1793 (second letter); Thomas Johnson to GW, 23 Dec. 1793, and n.2 to that document; and GW to Johnson 23 Jan. 1794, and n.4.

After explaining the current financial state of the lottery, the commissioners requested Harrison and Taylor "to examine and compare Mr Blodget's redeemed tickets with the Book of prizes and to retain the Tickets carefully so that they may be recurred to on occasion if under a second ticket of the same number a prize should be demanded." The commissioners also requested that if Harrison and Taylor found the "state of things" such that legal proceedings were justified, they should file charges against Blodget "in the federal Court—his refusal to give the farther Security on Demand will be a breach of his covenant as well as not paying off the Prizes in Time." The commissioners further noted that Blodget "has planned a second Lottery, he has not had our Consent for that, or indeed any second Lottery but on Terms he has not complied with—we hear he is selling tickets, he may perhaps give it the Air of Connection with the Commissioners to prevent the public being misled we disavow it, and as soon as you obtain the Tickets and Security if the State of the account should make it proper on the principles stated we wish you to have the inclosed advertisement published in all the Philadelphia papers for we are determined to have nothing to do with this Lotteries—If any Embarrassment should occur we wish you to advise with the President who will be prepared for such event and will we are sure afford any aid he can to get us out of this difficulty" (DNA: RG 42, Records of the Commissioners for the District of Columbia, Letters Sent, 1791–1802).

For the enclosed disavowal, see the minutes for the commissioners' meeting of 15–24 April (DNA: RG 42, Records of the Commissioners for the District of Columbia, Proceedings, 1791–1802). For the acceptance of this request from the D.C. commissioners, see Harrison to D.C. Commissioners, 30 April, and Harrison and Taylor to D.C. Commissioners, 10 May (DNA: RG 42, Records of the Commissioners for the District of Columbia, Letters Received, 1791–1802).

2. On GW's desire to purchase the lot on the northeast corner of square 21, see GW to D.C. Commissioners, 11 April. The sale was recorded by the commissioners on 23 April: "George Washington Esquire now President of the United States, purchased of the Commissioners at private sale Lot Number four in square Twenty one for Two Hundred pounds current money, and a Duplicate certificate thereof transmitted to him" (DNA: RG 42, Records of the Commissioners for the District of Columbia, Proceedings, 1791–1802). He followed their suggestion and purchased as well the lot on the northwest quarter, Lot 1 (GW to D.C. Commissioners, 1 June).

3. Thomas Freeman (d. 1821) emigrated from his native Ireland to the United States in 1784. He resigned as a surveyor for the Federal City in 1796 to accept a commission as one of the U.S. surveyors charged with establishing the boundary line between the United States and Spain. Although he did not complete this survey, he was employed to survey other locations in the Southwest by the administrations of Thomas Jefferson and James Madison, and in 1811, he received a commission as the surveyor of public lands south of Tennessee.

According to the minutes for the commissioners' meeting of 19–25 March, "The Commissioners retain Mr Thomas Freeman as an Assistant Surveyor on the usual terms of Twenty Shillings per day, he defraying his own Expenses of living." In the minutes for 15–24 April, the commissioners noted that "Mr George Fenwick is appointed to lay off Lots for improvement East of the Capitol" (DNA: RG 42, Records of the Commissioners for the District of

Columbia, Proceedings, 1791–1802). On Fenwick's prior employment by the commissioners, see Andrew Ellicott, Benjamin Ellicott, and Isaac Briggs to D.C. Commissioners, 29 June 1793, and n.9.

From Alexander Hamilton

[Philadelphia] April 23d 1794

Mr Hamilton presents his respects to The President—In compliance with the desire expressed by him, Mr H—— has made a memorandum of certain points for consideration in preparing instructions for Mr Jay, which are herewith sent.[1]

LB, DLC:GW.

1. For the appointment of John Jay as a special envoy to Great Britain, see GW to U.S. Senate, 16 April (first letter). Hamilton's memorandum of this date reads:

"Points to be considered in the Instructions to Mr Jay.

Envoy Extraordinary to G.B.

"I. Indemnification for the depredations upon our Commerce according to a rule to be settled.

"The desireable rule is—that which theoretical Writers lay down as the rule of the law of Nations (to wit) that none but articles by general usage deemed contraband shall be liable to confiscation and that the carrying of such articles shall not infect other parts of a cargo, nor even a vessel carrying them where there are no appearances of a design to conceal.

"Our Treaties contain a good guide as to contraband articles Which fall under the general denomination of *instrumenta belli* instruments of War.

"But if it should be found impracticable to establish this rule, the following qualifications of it occur to consideration.

"1. Whether *Provisions* (defining what shall be deemed such) may not be excepted so far as to render them liable, when going to an enemy's port not blockaded, to be carried into the port of the other enemy and converted to his use *paying the full value*. A good rule for estimating this value would be the cost & charges at the place of exportation with the addition of [   ] per Cent?

"2dly. Whether Colony produce going directly from the colony to the mother Country may not be added to the list of contraband articles?

"Or in the last resort whether the rule in this ⟨particular,⟩ resulting from the instructions of the Eighth ⟨of⟩ January last may not be admitted? to wit—that colony produce goin⟨g⟩ from the colony to any port in Europe may be ⟨confiscated.⟩ This is a principle which it is understood has been long adher⟨ed to⟩ by Great Britain and finds a sanction in prece⟨dents under⟩ the antient Governm⟨ent of⟩ France and other maritime powers.

"The indemnification for prizes made by proscribed vessels of which an expectation has been given by the President may be confirmed by convention.

"II.   Arrangement with regard to the future.

"The basis to be the rule already quoted of the general law of Nations.

"But it is probable that the same exceptions which may be insisted upon as to indemnification for the past will also be insis⟨ted⟩ upon as to the future.

"The idea of a ⟨place⟩ blockaded or besieged by construction which ⟨is⟩ not actually so ought to be excluded ⟨in either⟩ case.

"A stipulation against th⟨e sale⟩ of prizes in our ports will probably be ins⟨isted⟩ upon and it is just that it should be ⟨made.⟩

"A stipulation that in case of war with any Indian Tribe, the ⟨other⟩ party shall furnish no supplies whatever to such Tribe except such and in such quanti⟨ty only,⟩ as it was accustommed to furnish previ⟨ous to the⟩ war and the party at war to have a right to keep an agent or agents at the posts or settlements of the other party nearest to such Indians to ascertain the faithful execution of this stipulation.

"Grounds of adjustment with regard to the late Treaty of Peace
on the part of the British
"I.   Indemnification for our negroes carr[i]ed away
"II.   Surrender of our Posts
On the part of the U. States
"I.   Indemnification for the obstructions to the recovery of debts not exceeding [   ] Sterling.

"It may be desired and would it not be our interest to agree that neither party shall in time of peace keep up any armed force upon the lakes nor any fortified places nearer than [   ] miles to the lakes except small posts for small guards (the number to be defined) stationed for the security of trading houses?

"Would it not also be our interest to agree to an arrangement by which each party shall permit to the other, under due precautions and regulations a free trade with the Indian tribes inhabiting within the limits of the other?

"Treaty of Commerce—
"The statu quo may be taken with the following exceptions—
"A privilege to carry to the West India Islands in our vessels of certain burthens (say not less than 60 Tons nor more than Eighty Tons) all such articles as may now be carried thither from the U. States in British Bottoms and to bring from thence directly to the U. States all such articles as may now be brought from thence to the U. States in British bottoms.

"The privilege of carrying to G. Britain & Ireland manufactures of the U. States similar to those which now are or hereafter may be allowed to be carried thither by other nations who stand on the footing of the most favoured nation and upon terms of admission equally good.
"As equivalents—
"The extra Tonnage and duties on British vessels and goods imported in British vessels to be done away & if desired a stipulation to be entered into that the commodities and manufactures of Great Britain & Ireland may be imported into the U. States upon terms equally good with the like commodi-

ties & manufactures of any other nation and that the duties upon such of them as now pay ten per Cent ad valorem & upwards shall not be increased and that the duties upon such of them as now pay under 10 ℔ Cent ad valorem shall not be increased beyond 10 ℔ Cent.

"A Treaty on these Terms to be made for any term not exceeding [   ] years.

"But if such a Treaty cannot be made it deserves consideration whether a Treaty on the basis of the *statu quo* for a short term (say five years) may not be adviseable as an expedient for preserving peace between the two Countries" (DLC: Hamilton Papers. The text in angle brackets is from John C. Hamilton, ed., *The Works of Alexander Hamilton; Comprising His Correspondence, and His Political and Official Writings, Exclusive of the Federalist, Civil and Military* [7 vols., New York, 1851], 4:536–39). For the final version of the instructions sent to Jay, see Edmund Randolph to Jay, 6 May, NHi: Jay Papers; see also *ASP, Foreign Relations*, 1:472–74.

From Alexander Hamilton

Sir,   Treasury Departmt April 23d 1794

When I wrote my letter of the 21st instant I had intirely forgotten the existence of your two instructions of the 8 of Augt, owing probably to the effect upon my memory of my sickness which soon after ensued.[1] I only recollected that the loan had been authorised by me pursuant to your special direction, and I conceived that the subject of it's disposition was wholly open. I regret this circumstance, though no inconvenience could have ensued.

For I am of opinion, that until the actual investment of the monies in purchases, they remain liable to any disposition which you may think proper, with reference to either of the two Acts of the 4th & 12th of August 1790.[2] The loan has been made without particular reference to either of them, agreeably to the intimation in your letter of the 27 of July, namely, that it was not your purpose by seperate instructions to prevent the loans from being carried on without distinction in Holland.[3] Accordingly no distinction has been made—And as the Contract for the loan will not be specially bottomed upon either of the Acts, I conceive the instructions which have been given may be varied so as to accommodate the application to the purposes of both or either.

It is not, however, essential that any alteration should now be made. If the whole sum is to be drawn for here, as I should have to remit from hence what remains to complete the million of Florins towards the payment of the next June instalment, I can fulfil this object, with convenience to the public service, by drawing upon the fund created by the last loan[4]—which will leave in the Treasury here an equivalent sum applicable to purchases. This will be the same thing in principle, (without the inconvenience of a double operation) as to draw bills upon that fund to be sold here, in order to place the proceeds in the Treasury, and to purchase other bills to remit to Holland, in order to place there a fund for the payment of the June instalment.

But if it is your intention at all events to *attach* the proceeds of this loan to purchases and to exclude absolutely the future application of any part of it towards payments to France or otherwise on account of the foreign debt, I will thank you to signify your pleasure accordingly. And then the Accounts of the Treasury will be so regulated as to fix that course of proceeding irrevocably.[5]

But I think embarassments may be found to attend this course, which prevent me from recommending it. With the highest respect, I have the honor to be &c.

Alexandr Hamilton

LB, DLC:GW.

1. Hamilton is responding to a letter that GW wrote to him on 22 April. For the two instructions regarding the application of the funds to be obtained by a loan from the Dutch banking firm of Willink, Van Staphorst, and Hubbard, see GW's first and second letters to Hamilton of 8 Aug. 1793. On Hamilton's contraction of yellow fever in early September 1793, see GW to Hamilton, 6 Sept. 1793.

2. See "An Act making provision for the [payment of the] Debt of the United States," 4 Aug. 1790, and "An Act making Provision for the Reduction of the Public Debt," 12 Aug. 1790 (*Stat.* 1:138–44, 186–87).

3. See GW to Hamilton, 27 July 1793, and its enclosed letter to Hamilton of the same date.

4. For a description of the Dutch loan of 1792, see Ratification Statement, 5 Nov. 1792, and n.3 to that document.

5. For GW's response to this suggestion, see GW to Hamilton, 24 April (first letter).

From Thomas Johnson and David Stuart

Sir,   Washington April 23th 1794

Mr Greenleaf has had a Conversation with us before Mr Carroll on the subject of new Commissioners[1]—You will I am sure do the Doctr & myself the Justice to believe that our Declarations to you are real and not calculated on Ideas of our own Importance to eat into the funds—Mr Greenleaf mentions

Mr Dalton and Mr Baldwin as proper with your Approbation to fill our places and speaks an intention of proposing them to you—it is under an expectation of their coming here in July or August to reside[2]—the sooner we are relieved the more pleasing to us but if it is necessary we will continue till August—Mr Greenleaf wishes to know our Ideas of Compensation; considering ourselves as unconnected with it, we are of opinion £600 a Year is far from extravagant this without Agency for which or rather for nothing we paid £600 to Mr Blodget[3]—and indeed we are Satisfied that Commissioners on the Spot may do better than any Agent. We are Sir with high Respect Your affectionate Servt

Th. Johnson
Dd: Stuart.

LS, DLC:GW.

1. Commissioners Daniel Carroll (of Rock Creek), Thomas Johnson, and David Stuart met with James Greenleaf in the course of conducting a regular business meeting in the Federal City, 15–24 April (DNA: RG 42, Records of the Commissioners for the District of Columbia, Proceedings, 1791–1802). On the resignations of Johnson and Stuart, see their respective letters to GW of 23 Dec. 1793 and 6 Jan. 1794.

2. For Tristram Dalton's resignation as treasurer of the U.S. Mint, see his letter to GW of 24 April. Dalton became a partner with Greenleaf and Tobias Lear in the mercantile firm of Lear and Company, located at the intersection of G and 27th streets in the northwest quadrant of the Federal City (Clark, *Greenleaf and Law,* 147). GW did not appoint either Dalton or Baldwin. Dalton, however, received an appointment to the commission from John Adams shortly before Adams left the presidency in March 1801 (D.C. Commissioners to Thomas Jefferson, 28 March 1801, *Jefferson Papers,* 33:480–82). For the individuals who replaced Johnson and Stuart as commissioners, see n.2 of GW to Johnson, 23 January.

3. Samuel Blodget, Jr., was the recently fired superintendent for the District of Columbia. On the dissatisfaction of both GW and the commissioners with Blodget's performance, see D.C. Commissioners to GW, 23 Dec. 1793, and n.7, and GW to Thomas Johnson, 23 Jan. 1794, and n.4.

From Alicia McKenna

Honoured Sir   New york April the 23d 1794

Nothing Could Make Me trouble your Excellency with this Request, but My very great uneasyness about tow Children, I left in Ireland ten years ago one a Girl, your Amiable Charecter and Goodness, has induced Me to Make So Bold, as to Request your leave to go in the Vessell that Mr Jay goes to England in,[1] I would not trouble him in the Cabbin, any Place I would be Private from the Sailors I would be happy to get, My Anxiety is so great to go for My Children before any Farther troubles take Place—I have been ten years liveing in Alexandria have the Pleasure of being very well acquainted with Doctor and Mrs Steward, Mrs Herbert, and Many Others My Husband and Six Children are there he has an Employment in the Bank of that town, three of My Sons are in the Militia in Baltimore[2]—I Came to New York to go in a Vessell going to Dublin a Week before the Embargo in March took place, Since that I have been at Lodgeings here waiting for it being off but was dreadfully disappointed at it being laid on again, as I hope to be back in the Fall[3]—I humbly beg your Excellency will forgive My Presumption Nothing but the Feelings of a Mother Could Make Me trouble you let that Plead My Excuse.

Mrs Harison—she that Was Miss Craig knows Me—if you Can grant My Request and allow one of your Domesticks to let Me know at No. 56 Water Street New York I Shall Ever Pray for your Happyness and long Life, let Me intreat your Pardon.[4] I am Sir your Obedient Humble Servant

Alicia McKenna

ALS, DLC:GW. Postal stamps read, "N York. Apr 23" and "FREE."

1. On John Jay's approaching departure for England, see n.2 of Edmund Randolph to GW, 19 April (first letter).

2. Eleanor Calvert Custis Stuart, the wife of physician David Stuart, was the former daughter-in-law of Martha Washington. Sarah "Sally" Carlyle Herbert was the wife of Alexandria merchant William Herbert. Both couples were frequent visitors to Mount Vernon. James L. McKenna (d. 1813) was a cashier in the Bank of Alexandria.

3. For the congressional resolve of 26 March, which established a thirty-day embargo on "all ships and vessels" in U.S. ports, and the resolve of 18 April, which extended the embargo until 25 May, see *Stat.* 1:400–401.

4. This probably is Ann "Nancy" Craik, who was the daughter of GW's friend and physician James Craik and married to Richard Harrison, a partner in the Alexandria mercantile firm of Hooe and Harrison and currently the auditor of the U.S. Treasury Department. No reply from GW has been found.

From Edmund Randolph

Sir   Philadelphia April 23. 1794

I do myself the honor of submitting to your consideration a few reflections on the manner of appropriating the three millions of florins, lately borrowed.[1]

In your power of the 8th of August 1793. you expressly say, that the present being likely to continue for some time a favorable season for the purchases of the public debt, you therefore direct the secy of the tr⟨e⟩asury to obtain a loan to be applied to the purchases of the public debt, pursuant to the act of the 12th of Aug: 1790.

Under this power, and this power only the loan of three millions of florins has been accomplished.

The Secretary of the treasury thinks that embarrassments may be found in excluding absolutely the future application of any part of this sum towards payments to France or otherwise on account of the foreign debt.

I cannot see the propriety of now altering the appropriation.

1.　because it is plain by consulting the power of the 8th of August 1793, under which the three millions of florins were borrowed, that it is the act of the 12th of August 1790, and no other, upon which the loan was bottomed. So that the Secretary appears to be mistaken, when he says, "that the loan has been made without particular reference to either of them."

2.　because, if the President in his letter of July 27th did even insert the clause, which says *that it was not his purpose to separate instructions to prevent the loans from being carried on without distinction;* still that same clause directs, that the monies, as they are received, shall be considered as first applicable to the sinking fund.

3.　because the Secretary of the Treasury, tho' requested by your private letter to make objections, to the plan, which you marked out, did not object to the appropriation of the loan to the sinking fund.

4.　because the appropriation to the sinking fund is a beneficial and favorite one to all classes of men.

There remains even yet a sufficient scope for borrowing, as far as law is concerned. But probably it is not easy to effect a loan. If therefore the Secretary of the Treasury will specify the embarrassments, to which he alludes, they may be judged of; and I am sure, that I shall not now undertake to say, that they may not be as strong as he thinks them.

If therefore the President wishes, as Mr Dandridge intimated, that I should speak to Colo. Hamilton, I will do so.[2] If he prefers to write, (as perhaps is the better way) the following may be an adviseable form for a letter.

"It appears to me, that my instructions on the 8th of Aug: 1793 have fixed the appropriation of the money to the sinking fund; and I have considerable difficulty in being convinced of my power to change it at this time. However as I wish to see the whole subject together, it may be well for you, to state to me what the embarrassments are, which you suppose will arise from confining the money borrowed to the purchase of the public debt *which* I own I am very desirous of seeing effected as fast as it can be done advantageously for the public."[3] I have the honor sir to be with the highest respect Yr mo. ob. serv.

Edm: Randolph

ALS, DNA: RG 59, Miscellaneous Letters; LB, DNA: RG 59, GW's Correspondence with His Secretaries of State. The text in angle brackets is from the letter-book copy.

1. GW evidently had asked Randolph for an opinion on a dispute between GW and Alexander Hamilton over the application of funds from a recent Dutch loan for 3 million florins. For the arguments raised by each side, see Hamilton to GW, 21 April and 23 April (second letter), and GW to Hamilton, 22 April. Randolph apparently had access to these three letters before writing his letter.

2. Bartholomew Dandridge, Jr., was GW's secretary.

3. For GW's written response, see his first letter to Hamilton of 24 April.

Cabinet Opinion on Submission of Letters to Congress

[Philadelphia] April 24. 1794.

The Secretary of state submits to the Secretaries of the treasury and war, whether the inclosed letters from Mr Pinckney or either of them shall be sent to congress.

E.R. is of opinion, that the letter of the 28th of Jany, and not the other ought to be sent.[1]

I am [of] opinion that it is not adviseable to send either—That of the 28th of January contains no new substantive matter material to the information of Congress & mere stimulants do not seem to be necessary.

A. Hamilton[2]

I do not conceive the propriety of transmitting these letters to Congress.

H. Knox[3]

DS, DLC:GW. GW's docket reads: "Opinion 24th April 1794. respecting the laying certain letters of the American Minister before Congress." The dateline and the first two paragraphs are in the handwriting of Edmund Randolph.

1. Randolph received two letters dated 28 Jan. from Thomas Pinckney, the U.S. minister to Great Britain. The first letter was written originally in cipher. A decoded version is entitled "Explication of a Letter from Mr Pinckney dated London 28th Jany 1794." Pinckney wrote that he had no role in obtaining the revocation of the order-in-council of 6 Nov. 1793 because he had been unable to obtain a meeting with Lord Grenville until the British "cabinet had determined on the measure." Pressure from British merchants, concern over a possible war with the United States, and recent French military victories had prompted this decision. "I have confined myself to requiring ⟨a⟩ verbal explanation of what is past because if the President thinks proper to demand an explanation I presume he will ⟨d⟩irect it to be made in different terms from what I might use without special instruction . . . I intreat that my instructions may be full and precise."

A postscript written without code on the ciphered letter reads: "I repeat for the greater certainty that I am to expect no answer here ⟨to⟩ my memorial on the additional Instructions of June last Ld Grenville having ⟨tol⟩d me that he would send his answer to Mr Hammond to be by him forwarded to you" (both, DNA: RG 59, Despatches from U.S. Ministers to Great Britain). The letter from George Hammond to Randolph of 11 April, defending British policy, was enclosed in GW to the U.S. Senate and House of Representatives, 15 April, and is printed in *ASP, Foreign Relations,* 1:432–33. On the British order-in-council of 6 Nov., see n.5 of Joseph Brown to GW, 2 April, and n.1 of Randolph to GW, 3 April.

The second letter of 28 Jan. was a brief cover letter enclosing a copy of Pinckney's June 1793 memorial to Lord Grenville in which Pinckney stated U.S. objections to the British order-in-council of 8 June 1793 authorizing the seizure of American ships carrying provisions to France (both, DNA: RG 59, Despatches from U.S. Ministers to Great Britain). For the British order-in-council, see *ASP, Foreign Relations,* 1:240. GW submitted the second letter of 28 Jan. and its enclosed memorial with his letter to the U.S. Senate and House of Representatives of 12 May (see also *ASP, Foreign Relations,* 1:448–49).

It is probable that the "other" letter under consideration was Pinckney's letter of 29 Jan., in which he reported on the political state of Europe and recent French military victories (DNA: RG 59, Despatches from U.S. Ministers to Great Britain).

2. This paragraph was written and signed by Alexander Hamilton.

3. This sentence was written and signed by Henry Knox.

From Tristram Dalton

Sir   Philadelphia April 24th 1794
    The arrangements of my private Affairs demand my attention, and will call me from this City[1]—I am, thereby, constrained to

request Your permission to resign my Office, as Treasurer of the Mint of the United States—from the performance of the duties of which place I ask the favor to be released, as soon as You may find it convenient to nominate a Sucessor.[2]

My very grateful Acknowledgments are presented to You, Sir, for the many marks of publick and private Favors, that You have been pleased to honor me with. I shall ever remain, with the greatest Respect, Sir Your most obliged, and most obedient humble, Servant.

Tristram Dalton

ALS, DNA: RG 59, Miscellaneous Letters.

1. On Dalton's plans to relocate to the Federal City, see Thomas Johnson and David Stuart, 23 April, and n.2.

2. For GW's appointment of Nicholas Way as Dalton's successor, see GW to U.S. Senate, 19 May (*U.S. Senate Executive Journal,* 1:156).

Letter not found: from Jean-Baptiste Ducoigne, 24 April 1794. On 16 July, GW sent Henry Knox "a letter from Baptiste Ducoigne, Kaskasias, 24 April '94" (*JPP,* 314).

To Alexander Hamilton

Sir,   Philadelphia 24. April 1794.

It appears to me that my instructions on the 8 of August 1793 have fixed the appropriation of the money to the sinking fund; and I have considerable difficulty in being convinced of my power to change it at this time. However, as I wish to see the whole subject together it may be well for you to state to me what the embarrassments are which you suppose will arise from confining the money borrowed to the purchase of the public debt, *which* I own I am very desirous of seeing effected as fast as it can be done advantageously for the public.[1]

Geo: Washington

LB, DLC:GW.

1. On the drafting of this letter by Edmund Randolph in response to a dispute between GW and Alexander Hamilton over the application of funds from a recent Dutch loan, see Randolph to GW, 23 April.

To Thomas Jefferson

Dear Sir,   Phila. 24th April 1794.

The letter herewith enclosed came under cover to me in a packet from Mr Lear, accompanied with the following extract of a letter, dated—London February 12th 1794.[1]

"A Mr Bartraud, a famous Agriculturalist belonging to Flanders, put into my hands a few days ago several papers for Mr Jefferson on the subject of manuring & vegitation, requesting that I would forward them to him by some vessel going to America; being uncertain whether Mr Jefferson is in Philada or Virginia, I have taken the liberty of putting them under cover to you."[2]

Nothing, is more wanting in this Country, than a thorough knowledge of the first; by which the usual, and inadequate modes practiced by us may be aided—Let me hope then, if any striking improvements are communicated by Mr Bartraud on the above important subjects that you will suffer your friends to participate in the knowledge which is to be derived from his instructions.

We are going on in the old way "Slow" I hope events will justify me in adding "and sure" that the proverb may be fulfilled. "Slow and Sure."[3] With very great esteem and regard I am—Dear Sir Yr Obedt & Affecte Hble Servt

Go: Washington

ALS, DLC: Jefferson Papers. Jefferson docketed this letter as received on 6 May.

1. See Tobias Lear to GW, 12 February.

2. On the papers sent by O. A. Bertrand, see his letter to Jefferson of 8 February. GW also enclosed Lear's letter to Jefferson of 12 February. For both letters, see *Jefferson Papers,* 28:16–20.

3. GW may be referring to the English proverb "slow and sure, like Pedley's mare."

From Alexander Hamilton

Sir,   Treasury Department April 25. '94

I beg leave by way of explanation to submit the grounds of my opinion, that the President may vary his instructions of the 8th of August last in reference to the application of the last loan obtained in Holland.[1]

A summary of the preceding transactions will serve to throw light upon the subject.

The President by his Commission of the 28 of August 1790, gave full power to the Secretary of the Treasury to make the whole of the two loans contemplated by the Acts of the 4th & 12th of August.[2]

When in the beginning of June last certain considerations rendered it in my judgment expedient to obtain a further loan; I concluded to address myself to the President, not for want of power to proceed in the business, but to obtain the sanction of his opinion and instruction as to the eligibility of the measure. This will appear from my letter of the 3d of that month.

After some explanatory communications, I received from the President his letter of the 27 of July, informing me of the shape the business had taken in his mind.

On the basis of that letter, I prepared the instructions of the 8 of August, which I considered merely as directions to me from the President in the execution of the general power of the 28th of August 1790, to be understood in connexion with the letter of the 27 of July.

The proposition in my report of the 15th of June was that the proposed Loan⟨s⟩ should be made upon the authority of both Acts, and the letter of the President just mentioned precisely declares he did not intend by separate instructions to prevent the loans from being carried on without distinction in Holland.[3]

Accordingly I sent no new *powers* for making a further loan, but merely an additional *instruction* to make a loan of three millions of Florins on the basis of the former powers. This additional instruction too made no special reference to either act, but left the matter to proceed as before, *without distinction.*[4]

The consequence will be that the loan as in all preceding cases will be founded upon both the acts. I send for your inspection all the contracts heretofore made as the evidence of what will be the form of the one not yet forwarded; all of which expressly and indiscriminately refer to both the Acts.[5]

The inference is that according to the contract itself (the formal obligatory Act) the loan will be placed upon the joint foundation of the two Acts, equally applicable therefore to the purpose of either.

This being the case it is in my mind a clear proposition, that the money remains in that state liable to be applied according to either or both the Acts, 'till one of two things happens; an actual investment, or the being carried in the books of the Treasury specifically to the account of the particular appropriation.

It appears to me that there are but two circumstances which can attach irrevocably a similar fund to a particular destination—either its being so attached in its original creation by the formal obligatory Act, (to wit—the Contract for the loan)—or its having receiv'd in the treasury its ultimate form by being carried to the account of the particular appropriation. This last, where the fund in its creation is liable to different destinations is, as I suppose, the only thing which consummates & fixes the precise destination—'Tis the record, so to speak, of the sentence or *direction* of the law, ascertaining its application.

If this position be as solid as I believe it to be, it will follow, that all collateral instructions of the President intervening between his original power to make the loan, and the final application of the loan, are mere directions to the Secretary of the Treasury, binding on him until they are revoked, but revocable at pleasure by the President until they are definitely acted upon at the Treasury.

This is my view of the subject; for troubling the President with which, I have no other motive than merely to explain the ground of an important opinion.

I proceed now to execute the order of the President contained in his letter of yesterday.

The embarrassments which I suppose may possibly arise from fixing at this time the destination of the fund, are connected with the following considerations.

The laws, except by the means of loans, make no provision for the payment of any part of the *principal* of the foreign debt. Instalments of the principal of the Dutch debt are falling due yearly—The same is the case of the Debt to France, deferring the computed anticipations as has been heretofore done.[6] Perhaps it may become the policy of the Country in a short time to accelerate in the latter case.

The state of European affairs forbids a *reliance* on further loans there. The actual situation of the United States (and a *fortiori*[7] its possible one) is likely to call for all the aid of domestic loans, which is obtainable, for domestic purposes. This resource therefore could not be depended upon as a substitute for foreign Loans for foreign objects. Still less, & for the same among other reasons, could additional taxation be counted upon.

Our credit therefore and in certain events our security in a degree, may depend on retaining a part of the resource in question in a situation to come in aid of both Our credit entirely, and our security, in a very small degree, are of far greater consequence, than the savings to be made by the investment of 1,200,000 Dollars in purchases.

Past experience admonishes to caution. The last loan of a million of Florins,[8] and the present one of three millions are in some sort accidents. Antecedent intelligence had in each case forbidden the expectation of either, as the President will see from the letters herewith transmitted.[9] Had these not happen'd, & had the monies originally drawn to this Country for purchases been hastily so invested, our credit would in all probability have been lost, and things, which we believe it of importance to have been done, would have been impracticable.

A considerable defalcation of Revenue, this year seems probable.

I feel in a manner not less interesting to my own reputation than to the public interest, the advantage of extensive purchases at the existing juncture—and though I think the opportunity will not escape, it enters into the plan which I should approve to proceed gradually & circumspectly in availing ourselves of the advantage. But I do not incline either wholly to tie up the fund at this time, or to precipitate its application to that single object. I think the matter had better be left open to be governed by circumstances as things shall unfold.

It appears to me better at the hazard of some criticism to wave or defer an advantage inferior in magnitude, rather than incur a probable risk of a disadvantage of much greater magnitude.

It appears by the letter from the Commissioners announcing the loan already communicated to the President, that the receipts on account of it may be considerably protracted.[10] This is a circumstance of some weight in the decision.

I submit these observations with all deference to the decision of the President,[11] and have the honor to, with the highest respect &c.

Alexandr Hamilton

LB, DLC:GW.

1. This is one of several letters exchanged between Hamilton and GW about the correct use of the 3 million florins acquired as a 1794 loan from the Dutch banking firm of Willink, Van Staphorst, and Hubbard (Hamilton to GW, 21 April and 23 April [second letter], and GW to Hamilton, 22 April and 24 April [first letter]). For another opinion on this issue, see Edmund Randolph to GW, 23 April. For a description of this loan, see Willink, Van Staphorst, and Hubbard to Hamilton, 27 Dec. 1793 (*Hamilton Papers,* 15:593–96).

2. For this commission, see GW's second letter to Hamilton of 28 Aug. 1790, which appears in n.1 of GW's first letter to Hamilton of that date. See "An Act making provision for the [payment of the] Debt of the United States," 4 Aug. 1790, and "An Act making Provision for the Reduction of the Public Debt," 12 Aug. 1790 (*Stat.* 1:138–44, 186–87).

3. For Hamilton's report of 15 June 1793 on obtaining new foreign loans, see the enclosure in Hamilton to GW of that date.

4. For this additional instruction, see Hamilton to Willink, Van Staphorst, and Hubbard, 12 Aug. 1793 (*Hamilton Papers,* 15:231–32).

5. The enclosed contracts probably included that of 9 Aug. 1792 with Willink, Van Staphorst, and Hubbard (see Ratification Statement, 5 Nov. 1792, and n.3 to that document).

6. For a summary of the foreign debt of the United States as of 31 Dec. 1794, see Statements B, C, and D, enclosed in Hamilton's Report on a Plan for the Further Support of Public Credit, 16 Jan. 1795 (*Hamilton Papers,* 18:132–41).

7. The Latin phrase *a fortiori* means "even more so."

8. On this loan, see Willink, Van Staphorst, and Hubbard to Hamilton, 1 May 1793 (*Hamilton Papers,* 14:364–67).

9. The specific letters enclosed have not been identified.

10. The letter from Willink, Van Staphorst, and Hubbard to Hamilton of 27 Dec. 1793 was enclosed in Hamilton's letter to GW of 21 April.

11. For GW's reply, see his letter to Hamilton of 27 April.

From Alexander Hamilton

[Philadelphia] April 25. 1794.

The Secretary of the Treasury presents his respects to the President of the United States & encloses the drafts of two passports for the President's signature. One for the Schooner Commerce, now in this Port; and the other for the Schooner Eagle at Baltimore.[1]

Colo. Smith of Baltimore has applied, thro' the Secry of State, for a Passport for a small vessel (name & Captain not known) to be sent to Bermuda in ballast, for certain purposes explained in the letter herewith transmitted;[2] the draft of which passport is also enclosed, & if granted by the President will be sent to the Collector of Baltimore, with instruction to fill the blanks with the names of the master and vessel.[3]

A. Hamilton

LB, DLC:GW.

1. According to GW's executive journal, he signed the passports for these two vessels on 26 April. They were cleared to sail to Saint Domingue, in ballast, and to carry as passengers any inhabitants of that island wishing to return, along "with their clothing, baggage & seastores" (*JPP*, 300).

2. In his letter to Edmund Randolph of 23 April, Maryland congressman Samuel Smith wrote: "I send you Inclosd Mr Patterson's Letter—& hope you will be so Obliging to apply to the President for Permission for a Vessell to depart for the purpose he describes so that the same may be sent by tomorrow's Post." Smith's enclosure has not been identified, but it probably concerned the ship *Betsey,* owned by George Patterson of Baltimore, which currently was detained in Bermuda by the British (Moore, *International Adjudications,* 179–290).

"It will give You pleasure," Smith continued, "to be Informed'd that Capt. Barney was cleared by the Petty Jury after Ten Minutes Consideration (DNA: RG 59, Miscellaneous Letters). On the detention of Capt. Joshua Barney on the British island of Jamaica after the seizure of his ship *Sampson* in December 1793, see n.3 of Randolph to GW, 1 March.

3. GW signed the enclosed passport on 26 April, and Hamilton sent it with a letter of that date to collector of customs Otho H. Williams (*JPP*, 300; *Hamilton Papers*, 16:345–46).

From Alexander Hamilton

[Philadelphia] April 25. '94.

The Secretary of the Treasury presents his respects to the President & sends a letter to him from Captn Cochran. The manner in which it appears explains the error of having opened it.[1]

LB, DLC:GW.

1. The enclosed letter from Capt. Cochran to GW has not been found. It may have been from Robert Cochran, the captain of the South Carolina revenue cutter.

From Alexander Hamilton

[Philadelphia] April 25. '94

The Secretary of the Treasury presents his respects to the President. has the honor to transmit a Memorial from Colo. Waissenfelt, which came enclosed to him.[1]

LB, DLC:GW.

1. The enclosed memorial from Frederick Weissenfels has not been found, but it may have been a letter requesting appointment to a federal position (see Weissenfels to GW, 2 May 1789, and notes).

From Presley Nevill

Sir   [Philadelphia] Friday Morng Apl 25th 1794

Your Excellency, when last I had the honor of waiting on you, hinted a wish to change your Agent in Washington County; I believe it would be prudent to do so; the present one is considerably involved, he wants method, & I fear punctuality, of which I had no Idea, till lately.[1]

There is in the neighbourhood a certain Charles Morgan, whose Integrity & attention may be depended on, if he will undertake the business, I think you will be satisfied. If your Excellency thinks proper to instruct me for the purpose, I will engage him or some other fit person.[2]

I shall leave Phila. on Monday Morning, and shall be glad to receive your Excellys Commands here or in Pittsburgh. With great respect & Attachment, I've the honor to be your very Obt Sert

                                                    Presley Nevill

ALS, DLC:GW.

1. John Canon was responsible for collecting the rents from GW's tenants in Fayette and Washington counties, Pennsylvania. On GW's desire to replace Canon, see his letter to Tobias Lear, 8 April 1793.

2. GW replied in a letter to Nevill of 16 June (ALS, [letterpress copy], DLC:GW; LS [duplicate], NN: Myers Collection; LB, DLC:GW). In this letter, GW enclosed a power of attorney of 16 June authorizing Charles Morgan, or whomever Nevill selected, to collect the rents. He also enclosed a letter to Canon of the same date dismissing him from service (both enclosures, ALS [letterpress copy], ViMtvL; LB, DLC:GW). Nevill selected Morgan, who accepted the position (Morgan to GW, 26 Nov., DLC:GW).

From Alexander Hamilton

                                        [Philadelphia] April 26. 1794.

The Secretary of the Treasury presents his respects to the President of the U. States, & encloses the draft of a Passport for the American sloop Eliza, now in this port, bound for St Domingo with Passengers, for the Presidents signature.[1]

A. Hamilton

LB, DLC:GW.

1. GW signed the enclosed passport for the sloop *Eliza,* Capt. William Davis, on this date (*JPP,* 300).

Bartholomew Dandridge, Jr., to Henry Knox

[Philadelphia] Saturday 26th Aprl 1794.

By the President's order B. Dandridge sends the enclosed letter &c. from the Govr. of No. Carolina to the President, to the Secretary of war.[1] The President wishes the Secretary to inform him what has prevented a final settlement of the business respecting the Sloop L'Amie Marguirette, & what is necessary to be done in order to an ultimate decision relatively thereto.[2]

ADf, DLC:GW; LB, DLC:GW.

1. For the enclosed letter, see Richard Dobbs Spaight to GW, 10 April.

2. No written reply from Knox to GW has been identified, but in a letter of 12 May to Spaight, Knox wrote: "I have the honor to inform your Excellency that in pursuance of your letter of the 10th ultimo the President has decided that the L'amee margueritte having been taken by the illicit privateer Vanqueur de Bastille is to be given up to her previous owners or to the persons appointed by the British minister or Consul for that purpose, & the President requests that your Excellency will please cause her to be restored accordingly.

"An account of the expenses which have been incurred in this business to be authenticated and transmitted to this office" (Nc-Ar: Governors' Letterbooks).

To Edmund Randolph

Sir,   Philadelphia April the twenty Sixth 1794

Herewith you will receive two resolves—one of the Senate, dated the 24th; the other of the House of Representatives, dated the 25th instant;[1] accompanying a letter from the Committee of public Safety of the French Republic to Congress requesting the President of the United States to cause the same to be answered, on their behalf.[2]

This answer you will prepare accordingly, in terms expressive of their desires.[3]

Go: Washington

ALS (letterpress copy), DNA: RG 59, Miscellaneous Letters; LB, DNA: RG 59, GW's Correspondence with His Secretaries of State.

1. The resolve from the U.S. Senate of 24 April, which was attested by Samuel A. Otis, reads: "Ordered, that the Letter of the Committee of public safety of the French Republic, addressed to Congress be transmitted to the President, and that he be requested to cause the same to be answered on behalf of the Senate of the United States, in such manner as shall manifest their sincere friendship and good will, for the French Republic" (DNA: RG 59, Miscellaneous Letters).

The resolve from the U.S. House of Representatives of 25 April reads: "Resolved unanimously, that the letter of the Committee of Public Safety of the French Republic, addressed to Congress, be transmitted to the President of the United States, and that he be requested to cause the same to be answered, on behalf of this House, in terms expressive of their sensibility for the friendly and affectionate manner, in which they have addressed the Congress of the United States, with an unequivocal assurance, that the Representatives of the People of the United States have much interest in the happiness and prosperity of the French Republic." Speaker of the House Frederick Augustus Muhlenberg signed the resolve, which was attested by John Beckley (DNA: RG 59, Miscellaneous Letters).

2. The enclosed translation of the letter of 10 Feb. from the French Committee of Public Safety to the U.S. Senate and House of Representatives reads: "The Representatives of the French People, Members of the Committee of public safety—To the Citizens, Members of the Congress of the United States of America.

"After having laid the foundation of our liberty, it became incumbent on us to secure it. A national government is born and with it victory. Emanating from the will of the people it has their energy. For the salvation of the State it has been resorted to, and the State is saved. At its voice 15 Armies are in motion and triumph: at its signal, interior order is restored—fruitful industry is expanded: The Conspirators fall.

"We impart the news of the success of our armies to a people who, having obtained Liberty in a similar manner with ourselves, cannot learn but with enthusiasm, of the victories of Republicans and the downfall of Tyrants.

"Policy already appreciates the advantage of the retaking of Toulon! Already have the neutral powers proclaimed themselves; and Genoa, indignant at the atrocity of our enemies, who have sullied her territory by the vilest and blackest of crimes; Genoa has resumed all her energy, and driven the English and Spaniard from her ports.

"In the North, our triumphs, not less brilliant, have given the combined powers some severe shocks.

"They had dared to menace Dunkirk, Maube[u]ge, and Landau. Every where they have been beaten, every where they have been put to flight; and even towards the Rhine, our army in pursuit of them had advanced to the very Gates of Mayence.

"Such is the long catalouge of success which unfolds itself at the same moment at every point to which the French Republic sends her invincible Phalanxes.

"So many Victories will convey nothing astonishing to you; You, magnanimous Republicans, who will easily conceive the prodigies which liberty is capable of performing, after having in this vast career, left to the defenders of the people memorable examples.

"You had already participated in our Triumphs, as well in thought as political Union. Our successes reverberate in you, and the fall of our eternal and implacable enemies, will be as satisfactory to America, as to outraged France. Our cause is reciprocal; it is that of every people who honor humanity.

"It is under these glorious auspices that the Representatives of the French People are pressed by the desire of drawing closer more than ever, the bonds of friendship which unite two great, generous and free Nations.

"Thus liberty will have two points of fixture in the world; and being an immoveable Colossus, she will rest one foot in each Hemisphere.

"At her voice let Agriculture and Commerce, these two services of national prosperity, pouring out under our hands their mutual exchanges—multiply, aggrandize and cement our friendly relations and public felicity.

"Let us discard every thing which may disturb that necessary harmony pointed out by the nature of things, still more than by a reciprocal interest, that harmony which has not a cautious, selfish, mercantile policy for its principle, but the esteem, the fraternity, all the social and benificent virtues, which flow from liberty.

"Honor, Prosperity, Safety and Fraternity.

"The Representatives of the French People, Members of the Committee of public safety." The men who signed this letter were: Jean-Bon Saint-André, Claude-Antoine Prieur-Duvernois (Prieur de la Côte-d'Or; 1763–1832), Bertrand de Barère de Vieuzac, Jacques-Nicolas Billaud-Varenne, Jean-Baptiste-Robert Lindet, Maximilien-François-Marie-Isidore de Robespierre, Georges-Auguste Couthon, Lazare-Nicolas-Marguerite Carnot, and Jean-Marie Collot d'Herbois (DNA: RG 59, Miscellaneous Letters).

3. Randolph wrote two letters to the Committee of Public Safety on 10 June. The first was an answer on behalf of the U.S. Senate and the second an answer on behalf of the U.S. House of Representatives. In both letters, he wrote that GW had transmitted to the secretary of state the "honor" of replying. He acknowledged the assistance provided by France to the United States during the Revolutionary War and noted the continued friendship between the two nations, before extending wishes for the future happiness and prosperity of the French nation (*ASP, Foreign Relations*, 1:674).

From Edmund Randolph

Saturday evening [Philadelphia, 26 April 1794]

E. Randolph has the honor of inclosing to the President of the U.S. a letter from General Wilkinson, which, tho' of a factious cast, is still proper to be submitted to the President. The parts of a public nature are included in the black line.[1]

E.R. will be obliged to the President for the bundle of papers, relative the *additional* loan.[2]

AL, DNA: RG 59, Miscellaneous Letters; LB, DNA: RG 59, GW's Correspondence with His Secretaries of State. The docket on the AL reads, "26. April 1794."

1. The letter from James Wilkinson to Randolph has not been identified.

2. The specific papers requested have not been identified, but they probably included the various documents mentioned in Alexander Hamilton's first letter to GW of 25 April, which concerned a recent Dutch loan of 3 million florins. For Randolph's opinion, see his first letter to GW of 27 April.

To the Commissioners for the District of Columbia

Gentlemen,   Philadelphia April 27th 1794

The Post of yesterday brought me your favor of the 23d instant.

I am obliged to you for the early attention which you have given to the request contained in my letter of the 11th preceeding, and I am perfectly well satisfied with the price which you have affixed on the lot, I have obtained.

If it be necessary for me to decide at this moment, whether I will avail myself of the offer you have made me of the No. West quarter of the same square, I shall answer in the affirmative; but it would be more agreeable to me (if no inconvenience would result from delay) to suspend my determination until I could examine, & form my plan on the spot; for as it is for the purpose of improvement I fix on that site, whensoever my finances will enable me, I should like to see in what manner this can be done most advantageously. Had the So. East, instead of the No. West quarte⟨r⟩ of this square fallen to the public, I should have embraced your offer with avidity; not that I think it of more intrinsic value than the other (if I recollect the ground rightly) but because the hill declining that way also, it would have laid me entirely open to the South, and have given a fine exposure for a Garden.[1]

As soon after the rising of Congress as the business of the public will allow, I intend a visit to Mount Vernon for a few days; and if I knew the time appointed for your next meeting at George Town, a few days delay on my part, in order to meet you there, would be attended with no inconvenience to me.[2]

Your letter to Messrs Harrison and Tayler was sent to them as soon as I had read it. I sincerely wish you were rid of that business to your intire satisfaction. I fear, however, you will have some trouble in it before this happens.

I shall not, at this time, enter upon the subject of the letter written to me by Mr Johnson & Doctr Stuart, further than to express my wish that they would remain in Office until August, if it can be made to comport with their convenience.[3] The reasons for this shall be assigned when we meet, or in another letter, if this is not likely to happen soon. With very great esteem & regd I remain Gentlemen Yr Obedient Servt

Go: Washington

ALS, Records of the U.S. Commissioners of the City of Washington, 1791–1869; ALS (letterpress copy), DLC:GW; LB, DLC:GW. The text in angle brackets is from the letterpress copy.

1. On GW's subsequent purchase of Lot No. 1 in square 21 of the Federal City, see his letter to the commissioners of 1 June.

2. The first session of the Third Congress ended on 9 June. GW departed Philadelphia for Mount Vernon on 17 June, and he arrived back in Philadelphia on 7 July (*JPP*, 310–11). GW was unable to meet with the commissioners during their meeting of 22–28 June because of a riding accident on 22 June (GW to Henry Knox, 25 June; DNA: RG 42, Records of the Commissioners for the District of Columbia, Proceedings, 1791–1802).

3. See Thomas Johnson and David Stuart to GW, 23 April. GW addressed the issues of appointing new commissioners and questions about financial compensation for the new commissioners in a letter to Johnson of 27 June. For the new commissioners appointed later this year, see n.2 of GW to Johnson, 23 January.

To John Fitzgerald

Dear Sir   Philadelphia 27th April 1794

Your letter of the 14th instant ⟨ca⟩me to hand in due course of Post, and ⟨w⟩ould have received an earlier acknowledgment had I not been pressed with other business.

I have no hesitation in declaring, ⟨t⟩hat the conduct of Mr Thomas Digges towards the United States during the War (in which they were engaged with Great Britain) and since, as far as the same has come to my knowledge, has not only been friendly, but I might add zealous.

When I conversed with you on this subject in Alexandria,[1] I thought I recollected a special, & pointed instance of beneficial service he had rendered this Country in sending me, between the leather & paste-board cover of a book, ⟨some⟩ important intelligence; but upon ⟨ref⟩lecting more maturely on the matter since, I am unable to decide *positively* whether it was from him, or another gentleman this expedient was adopted, to elude the consequences of a search. Be this however as it may, it is in my recollection that various *verbal* communications came to me, *as from him,* by our captives who had escaped from confinement in England;[2] and I think I have received written ones also: but the latter, (if at all) must have been rare on account of the extreme hazard of discovery, & the consequences which would follow, both to the writer and bearer of such corrispondences.

Since the war, abundant evidence might be adduced of his ac⟨ti⟩vity and zeal (with considerable risk) in sending artisans and machines of public utility to this Country—I mean by encouraging and facilitating their transporta⟨tion⟩ as also of useful information to the Secretary of State, to put him on his guard ⟨aga⟩inst nefarious attempts to make Paper &ca, for the purpose of counterfeiting our money.[3] Until you mentioned the doubts which were entertained of Mr Digges's attachment to this Country, I had no idea of its being questioned. With esteem and regard I am—Dear Sir Your Obedient Hble Servt

Go: Washington

P.S. Since writing the foregoing letter, I have seen & conversed with Mr John Trumbull respecting Mr T. Digges. The former, before he was committed to the Tower of London, was well acquainted with the latter, in England, and much in his company. To him, Mr Digges always appeared well attached to the rights & Interests of the United States. *Knows* that he was active in aiding our citizens to escape from their confinement in England; and *be⟨lieve⟩s* he was employed to do so by Doctr ⟨Fran⟩klin. Mr Trumbull has never seen Mr Digges since he left the Tower, but has heard that a difference arose between him and the Doctr not from any distrust entertained by the latter ⟨of⟩ disaffection in the former; but on the ⟨s⟩ettlement of their accounts.[4]

G. W——n

The preceeding statement is made from the best recollection I have of the Subject. The expression might (if I had had more leisure) been more correct, but not more consonant with truth. Such as it is you are welcome to make what use you please of it.

Go: Washington

ALS (letterpress copy), ViMtvL; LB, DLC:GW. The text in angle brackets is from the letter-book copy.

1. GW may have conversed with Fitzgerald at Alexandria, Va., while he was at Mount Vernon between mid-September and 28 Oct. 1793 (*JPP*, 239–41).

2. One prominent American captive was Henry Laurens, the former president of Congress, 1777–78, and later one of the commissioners who signed the preliminary peace treaty with Great Britain in 1782. He was held prisoner in the Tower of London from 6 Oct. 1780 until 31 Dec. 1781.

3. On Digges's encouraging skilled artisans to emigrate to the United States, see Digges to Thomas Jefferson, 28 April 1791, and editorial note. His letter to Thomas Pinckney of 13 Aug. 1793 and its enclosed memorandums on counterfeiting were enclosed in Pinckney's letter to Jefferson of 28 Aug. 1793 (*Jefferson Papers*, 20:313–22; 26:776–82).

4. The artist John Trumbull, the youngest son of former Connecticut governor Jonathan Trumbull, was studying in London in November 1780 when he was arrested and tried on suspicion of treason before being released. On the assistance that Digges provided Americans during the Revolutionary War and his relationships with John Trumbull and Benjamin Franklin, see "Introduction," Elias and Finch, *Digges Letters*, xxxviii–lv.

To Alexander Hamilton

Sir,   Philadelphia April the 27th 1794.

I cannot, under all the circumstances of the case, satisfy myself, that I am at liberty to go contrary to my last instructions; and that I have authority to direct the money, which I have expressly directed to be applied to the purchase of the public debt, to be applied to any other object.[1]

Still, however, I am willing, that the embarrassments, which you *Stat.*[2] shall be communicated to Congress; and I have no objection to recommend to them to order the money to be reserved for the exigencies which you point out.[3]

Go: Washington

ALS, CtHi: Oliver Wolcott, Jr., Papers; LB, DLC:GW.

The draft of this letter appears in the body of Edmund Randolph's first letter to GW of this date.

1. On the subject of this letter, see Hamilton to GW, 21 April, 23 April

(second letter), and 25 April (first letter), and GW to Hamilton 22 April and 24 April (first letter).

2. Hamilton mentioned the possibility of "embarrassments" in his first letter to GW of 25 April.

3. Hamilton replied to this suggestion in a letter of 28 April, which reads: "I should not advise a present reference to the Legislature on the subject of the application of the loan; as under the circumstances of that body at this moment much debate would probably ensue and perhaps no decision.

"I am the less induced to advise this step; as the expedient itself will be hereafter practicable, if it shall appear to be necessary. It will be some time before the proceeds of the loan will be realised in the Treasury. When there, though the appropriation will be fixed to the sinking Fund, the actual disbursement of the monies may be accelerated or retarded as may be judged adviseable according to the developpement of circumstances" (CtHi: Oliver Wolcott, Jr., Papers).

To William Pearce

Mr Pearce,   Philadelphia 27th April 1794.

Your letter of the 22d instant with its enclosures came duly to hand.[1]

Thomas Green's account of the dimensions of the Rooms in my house in Alexandria, is so confused & perplexed, that I can make neither head nor tail of it. The length, breadth & height of each, with the distance from the washboard to the Chairboard, & the number of doors & windows in each room, was all I wanted; instead of these he has attempted to draw a plan which no one can understand, and has given an explanation of it that is still more incomprehensible.[2]

I am very glad to find that you have caused so much flaxseed to be so⟨wn,⟩ as appears from the Memorandum se⟨nt⟩ me; but have you not departed from the plan which was to regulate the gra⟨ss-⟩lots at Dogue run Farm?[3] As well a⟨s I reco⟩llect, these were to succeed each ot⟨her in Po⟩tatoes—and one after another to ⟨be sown⟩ with Oats & Clover; and this rotine was to be persevered in. As the case now is, neither the lot East of the New Barn,[4] nor that in number 3, can be touched next year; and neither of them, I fear, will be in condition to yield much clover. My intention with respect to these lots was, by soiling the Plow horses with the Clover, cut green, to save the great expense of grain. By having one of them therefore in Potatoes; another in Oats, sown also with Clover; and the third in Clover, there would always have been one (which is sufficient for this purpose) handy to the Stable; more would be unnecessary, as there will be such a quantity of mowing ground on the Farm for the support of the Stock, the Mansion house, & for Sale.

Particular attention will be paid I hope to penning of the Stock, an⟨d⟩ shifting the Pens—nothing has been mo⟨re⟩ neglected—general as neglects have hit⟨her⟩to been on my estate—than the latter, m⟨ere⟩ly to avoid the trouble of removing the [Posts].

How does the White thorn⟨, and t⟩he cuttings of the Willow & other sets⟨, which hav⟩e been put out this Spring, loo⟨k? & ap⟩pear to have taken, & to be in a thriving condition?

I mentioned to you in my last that 5000 plants of the White thorn was to be sent to me, by Mr Lear in the Ship Peggy, from London to George Town. I have advice of the Sailing of the Ship, and hope it is arrived. No time should be lost in getting the Plants home (to Mt Vernon) as every day's delay will put th⟨em⟩ more & more in jeopardy. Mr Lear in his last letter informs me that he had by the same Vessel, sent some fruit trees for his own use, wch he requests my care of: let these also be taken to Mount Vernon & put into a nursery for his use; & the Gardener⟨'s⟩ particular care of them is required.[5] I am your friend &ca

Go: Washington

P.S. With this letter you will receive a paper of Lima beans, which the Gardener will p⟨lant⟩ the first of May; seperate from any oth⟨ers; and be⟩ particularly careful of them.

ALS, ViMtvL; ALS (letterpress copy), DLC:GW. The postscript does not appear on the letterpress copy. The text in angle brackets is from the letterpress copy.

1. Pearce's letter of 22 April and its enclosures, including the farm reports for the previous week, have not been found.

2. GW requested the dimensions of the rooms in his house in Alexandria, Va., in his letter to Pearce of 6 April. The report from Thomas Green, the overseer of carpenters at Mount Vernon, has not been found.

3. For a plan of crop rotation for Dogue Run farm, see Crop Rotations for Mount Vernon Farm, enclosed in GW to Pearce, 18 Dec. 1793; see also Rotation of Crops for Dogue Run, 1793.

4. On the new barn at Dogue Run farm, see GW to Anthony Whitting, 28 Oct. 1792, and enclosure.

5. GW's previous letter to Pearce was that of 20 April. On the planting of Tobias Lear's white thorn plants, see the farm reports for 25–31 May. On Lear's shipment of fruit trees, see Lear to GW, 12 February. John Christian Ehlers was the head gardener at Mount Vernon.

From Edmund Randolph

Sir   Philadelphia April 27. 1794.

I own, that if a loan could be completed to the amount of the whole fourteen millions, or if it could be even carried further, it would be adviseable, under the present situation of things, to go very great lengths, in obtaining money. But this is not the question; and as I think the step, which you may now take, will be much examined by the public, I will endeavour to present the case to you in a plain, simple view.[1]

You were authorized to borrow fourteen millions of dollars; that is two for the sinking fund and twelve for the foreign debt. You gave authority to borrow to the whole amount to Colo. Hamilton. In this sense his power is complete without any additional one; or in other words, a loan made under your first power would be binding upon the U.S.[2]

But in your instruction of 28th of August 1790, you prohibit him from borrowing more, than as much as will be necessary for completing the instalments or parts of the principal of the foreign debt, and the interest thereon to the end of the year 1791; unless the foreign debt can be changed to advantage. As no such charge could be made in the foreign debt, no more money was borrowed than what should be necessary to pay those instalments and the interest.

Hence Colo. Hamilton was under a necessity in August 1793 to obtain a relaxation of the instruction of the 28th of Aug: 1790, or he could not have borrowed one shilling more; as he did not, nor does now contemplate to change the foreign debt.

The instruction was accordingly relaxed by another on the 8th of Aug. 1793, in which you say, that the money to be borrowed shall be applied to purchases of the public debt.[3] The same thing had been said in your letter to Colo. Hamilton of the 27th of July. He was privy to the course, which the thing had taken in your mind: he made no objection—he drew the instruction in August 1793—the appropriation was demonstrably right at that time—nothing has occurred since to make it wrong—but the idea is, that the situation of public affairs requires that the money borrowed should be held ready for any other purpose.

I am persuaded, that this cannot be done *now* by the President; because he has shewn by his last instruction, that he would probably not have assented to the loan at all; if it had not been for the purpose of the sinking fund. He has once executed the power, which he had under the law; and he cannot execute it over again.

I shall not deny, however, that there may be great cases, in which appropriations must be diverted; nor yet, that the present may be one of them. But still the proper authority must do this. That proper authority is not the President, but congress and congress alone.

It is of real importance to consider, how far this change of appropriation may involve the President in past transactions. For it certainly will be said, that if the President could change his own appropriations, so might the Secretary of the treasury, to whom he gave such full powers—Indeed, I will not undertake to say, what would be the operation of this act, which is proposed to you.

I cannot see the full extent of the measure; but I see perfect safety, as well to yourself as to the public, by sending a letter, like this in substance to Colo. Hamilton.

"I cannot, under all the circumstances of the case, satisfy myself, that I am at liberty to go contrary to my last instructions; and that I have authority to direct the money, which I have expressly directed to be applied to the purchase of the public debt to be applied to any other object. Still however I am willing, that the embarrassments, which you consider as probable, shall be communicated to congress; and I have no objection to recommend to them to order the money to reserved for the exigencies, which you point out."[4] I have the honor, sir, to be with the highest respect Yr mo. ob. serv.

Edm: Randolph

ALS, DNA: RG 59, Miscellaneous Letters; LB, DNA: RG 59, GW's Correspondence with His Secretaries of State.

1. Randolph wrote this letter after examining a "bundle of papers" that he had requested from GW in a letter of 26 April. These documents concerned a recent Dutch loan for three million florins, which had occasioned a dispute between GW and Alexander Hamilton on the appropriate use of this money (Hamilton to GW, 21 April, 23 April [second letter], and 25 April [first letter], and GW to Hamilton, 22 April and 24 April [first letter]; see also Edmund Randolph to GW, 23 April).

2. Section 2 of "An Act making provision for the [payment of the] Debt of the United States," 4 Aug. 1790, authorized the president "to cause to be

borrowed on behalf of the United States, a sum or sums, not exceeding in the whole twelve million of dollars . . . to the paying off the whole of the said foreign debt" and "appropriated solely to those purposes." Section 4 of "An Act making Provision for the Reduction of the Public Debt," 12 Aug. 1790, authorized the president "to cause to be borrowed . . . a sum or sums not exceeding in the whole two millions of dollars" for the reduction of the public debt (*Stat.* 1:138–44, 186–87). For GW's giving Hamilton the authority to borrow $14 million, see GW's first letter to Hamilton of 28 Aug. 1790, and n.1 to that document.

3. See GW to Hamilton, 8 Aug. 1793 (first letter).

4. GW used Randolph's draft in his letter to Hamilton of this date.

From Edmund Randolph

Sunday Evening. [Philadelphia, 27 April 1794]

E. Randolph has the honor of inclosing to the President the draught of a nomination; and begs leave to suggest to him, whether it may not be adviseable to shew it to Colo. H., who will be with the President to morrow morning.[1]

E.R. has conversed with several gentlemen, who are of the same politics, with the *person* contemplated *as the successor.* Upon the whole, they think, that his appointment would be satisfactory; tho' they are not insensible of there being some objection. The particular individual, with whom the President wished E.R. to converse, concurs; but expresses himself thus. "I think, his deafness is an exception to him; but as no person, more acceptable to the Republicans here and France can be found, it would be adviseable to send him."

Colo. Fanisse, Aid de Camp to General Rochambeau, delivered me this morning a letter from him to E.R.; which will be shewn to the President to morrow.[2] Fanisse says, that Admiral Jervis, and General Gray told Rochambeau, that the English would force the U.S. to declare for, or against France without delay.

AL, DNA: RG 59, Miscellaneous Letters; LB, DNA: RG 59, GW's Correspondence with His Secretaries of State. The docket on the AL reads, "27. April 1794," and the letter-book copy is dated "27 April."

1. The draft, which has not been identified, probably is for GW's letter to Robert R. Livingston of 29 April, in which GW asks Livingston to succeed Gouverneur Morris as the U.S. minister plenipotentiary to France. For an alteration to the draft, see Randolph to GW, 28 April (first letter).

2. The letter from Donatien-Marie-Joseph de Vimeur, vicomte de Rocham-beau, to Randolph was written at Newport, R.I., on 18 April. After announcing his arrival in the United States and the circumstances leading to it, Rocham-beau wrote that he was waiting for instructions from the Executive Council of France. Anticipating that his health would soon be restored, Rochambeau wished to know the proper procedure for paying his respects to GW. His aide-de-camp, Lt. Col. Panisse, who has information about captured American vessels, is the bearer of this letter (in French, DNA: RG 59, Miscellaneous Let-ters). On the arrival of Rochambeau and his officers at Newport on 15 April, after surrendering the island of Martinique to British forces commanded by General Sir Charles Grey and Vice Admiral Sir John Jervis, see William Ellery to Alexander Hamilton, 22 April (*Hamilton Papers,* 16:309–12).

From Richard Dobbs Spaight

Sir N. Carolina New Bern 27th Apl 1794

Agreable to the request contained in the Secretary of Wars letter of the 24 of March last I have endeavoured to get informa-tion of the cannon of & above the calibre of eighteen pounds the property of this State.[1]

There are at Edenton 13 twenty four pounders 8 eighteen pounders also 6 twelve pounders there are likewise one or two twenty four pounders at Swansborough, of these last I have not received full information. none of those cannon have any appa-ratus whatever belonging to them.

I have as yet had no accounts whether there are any cannon at Wilmington or Beaufort as soon as I do I shall send on informa-tion of their number quality & condition.

In regards to the building the forts at Occacock & cape Fear your request of my superintending generally the business shall be complied with as far as is within my knowledge or abilities by paying every attention to it that is in my power. I have the honor to be with respect &c.

R.D. Spaight

LB, Nc-Ar: Governors' Letterbooks.

1. Knox's letter to Spaight of 24 March enclosed a copy of "An Act to pro-vide for the Defence of certain Ports and Harbors in the United States," 20 March (*Stat.* 1:345–46). GW, according to Knox, requested that Spaight assume responsibility for the "general direction of the business" in North Carolina. Knox wrote that an engineer would soon be appointed to plan and direct construction, and he asked Spaight to inform him of "any good cannon of and above the calibre of eighteen pounds and which could be ap-

propriated to the fortifications" in North Carolina (Nc-Ar: Governors' Letterbooks). Knox's letter to Spaight is nearly identical to the one sent to New Hampshire governor Josiah Bartlett on the same date (see n.3 of Knox to GW, 19 March). On the appointment of engineer Nicholas-Francis Martinon and the initial plans for fortifying the ports and harbors at Wilmington, which was on the Cape Fear River, and Ocracoke Inlet, N.C., see *ASP, Military Affairs,* 1:95–101.

From Bushrod Washington

Dear Uncle   Richmond [Va.] April 27th 1794
    I take the liberty of writing by Mr Maund who is going to Philadelphia, and of introducing him to you.[1] I wrote you some posts ago, respecting a suit of Hanchaw agt you in the High Court of Chancery, which I hope you have recieved.[2] with love to my Aunt I am most sincerely Your Affect. Nephew
                                                        Bushd Washington

ALS, ViMtvL. A notation on the cover indicates that this letter was sent in care of "J.J. Maund Esqr."
    1. Attorney John James Maund (d. 1802), an emigrant from Wales, served in the Virginia Senate, 1793–96. In September 1793, he received an appointment from the state of Virginia as superintendent for the Port of Yeocomico, including Kinsale, in Westmoreland County (*Virginia State Papers,* 6:538).
    2. For the previous letter on the legal suit filed against GW by John Henshaw, see Bushrod Washington to GW, 22 April. For GW's reply, see his letter to Bushrod Washington of 30 April.

Letter not found: from George Eimbeck, 28 April 1794. An entry in GW's executive journal for 15 May reads: "Received a letter from Geo. Eimbeck, Savanna 28 April 1794 on the subject of obtaining his pay &c. for services in the last war. Referred it to The Secy. of War" (*JPP,* 303).[1]

    1. For Eimbeck's earlier efforts to receive compensation, see his letter to GW of 12 May 1791, and n.2.

From Edmund Randolph

Sir   Philadelphia April 28. 1794
    With the change of the word "*embassy,*" which is a technical term for a particular diplomatic order, for "*mission,*" which is a general one; I cannot see the possible necessity for another alteration in the letter to Mr L—g—n.[1]

I sincerely believe, that Mr P——y would be agreeable to France; tho' not so agreeable as Mr L——n. The arrangement of Mr J—y, as resident in London, might be a fortunate circumstance, if he would assent to it. But I doubt this; because he has eye immediately on the government of N.Y.—and ultimately on the Presidency. Besides his present office is an abundance for his wants, and he can educate his children in their own country; which of itself is an immensity. However, if he could be consulted, without Mr L——n knowing it, I still repeat, that it would be a fortunate circumstance, should he remove the objection, which has been made to his nomination as envoy.[2] I have the honor, sir, to be with the highest respect yr mo. ob. serv.

Edm: Randolph

ALS, DLC:GW; LB, DLC:GW.

1. In his second letter to GW of 27 April, Randolph submitted a draft for GW's letter to Robert R. Livingston of 29 April, in which GW offered Livingston the post of U.S. minister plenipotentiary to France.

2. Thomas Pinckney was presently the U.S. minister plenipotentiary to Great Britain. John Jay was the current chief justice of the U.S. Supreme Court. He served as governor of New York State from 1795 until 1801. Although GW nominated Jay as an envoy extraordinary to Great Britain in his first letter to the U.S. Senate of 16 April, the nomination was not approved until 19 April (*U.S. Senate Executive Journal*, 1:150–52). For the offer of the British ministerial position to Jay, see GW to Jay, 29 April.

From Edmund Randolph

Sir   Philadelphia April 28. 1794.

I do myself the honor of submitting to your consideration the draught of a letter, intended as an answer to Mr Hammond's reply to Mr Pinckney's memorial on the instructions of the 6th of November 1793.[1]

The inclosed letter from Colo. Hamilton shews, that he has perused the draught; and upon the three first remarks contained in that letter I will either satisfy him, or abandon my own idea.[2]

The fourth observation speaks of a *tartness* of language; which, if it be more than the subject dictates, is more than I wished; and therefore I shall not hesitate to remove any improper asperity.

But the 5th observation requires me to know your pleasure, whether a *general* or *particular* answer shall be given. Before I began to write, I asked Mr Jay, whether he would prefer, that the subject should be left, as it is, or taken up by me in the way of refutation: He thought, that it was better to enter upon a refutation of Mr Hammond's memorial. Mr Jay will otherwise be obliged to do the same thing himself. And I cannot conceive, that a foreign minister ought to press upon the secretary of state doctrines, of great prejudice to the U.S.; and that the secretary should remain silent, as if he were afraid, or could not answer them.

However, I beg leave to assure you, that the sending of a general or particular letter is of no importance to any sensation of my own—I only wish for your directions; and let these be, what they may, they will be perfectly satisfactory to me.[3] I have the honor, sir, to be with the greatest respect yr. mo. ob. serv.

Edm: Randolph

ALS, DNA: RG 59, Miscellaneous Letters; LB, DNA: RG 59, GW's Correspondence with His Secretaries of State; LB, DNA: RG 59, Domestic Letters.

1. The draft of Randolph's letter to George Hammond, the British minister to the United States, of 1 May has not been identified. For the British order-in-council of 6 Nov. 1793, see n.1 of Randolph to GW, 3 April. Hammond's letter to Randolph of 11 April also refers to the order-in-council of 8 June 1793, which restricted the shipment of U.S. corn, flour, or meal to France or French colonies (DNA: RG 59, Notes from the British Legation). Pinckney's copy of his undated memorial to Lord Grenville, which objected to the British order-in-council of 8 June 1793, was enclosed in his letter to Randolph of 28 Jan. 1794 (both, DNA: Despatches from U.S. Ministers to Great Britain). The 8 June 1793 order-in-council, Pinckney's memorial, and Hammond's letter are in *ASP, Foreign Relations,* 1:240, 449–50.

2. For Alexander Hamilton's letter to Randolph of 27 April, which offers several suggestions for changes to Randolph's draft, see *Hamilton Papers,* 16:346–49.

3. For GW's reply, see his letter to Randolph of 29 April. For the final version of Randolph's letter to Hammond of 1 May, which was submitted to Congress with a cover letter of 12 May, see DNA: RG 59, Domestic Letters; see also *ASP, Foreign Relations,* 1:450–54.

From Saint Domingue Refugees at Norfolk, Va.

[Norfolk, Va., 28 April 1794]

Son Excellence le President des Etats unis de L'amérique

Dépouillés de leurs propriétés, chassés de leurs foyers, et par une série d'évènements dont il seroit inutile de retracer ici les horreurs, forcés de fuir leur patrie. Les malheureux colons de St Domingue se sont jettés dans les bras de leurs freres. Le Peuple généreux et hospitalier des Etats Unis de L'amérique; l'acceuil qu'ils en ont reçu a passé leurs espérances, et jamais ne s'effacera ni de leur souvenir ni de leurs cœurs. mais après un séjour de prés d'une année dont le malheur, le besoin et la perspective d'une pauvreté absolue aussi infaillible que prochaine, ont éternisé pour eux la durée accablante, les foibles ressources qu'ils avoient pu trouver dans les débris de leur ancienne fortune échappés avec tant de peine à tous les dangers qui les ont poursuivis jusques à la vue de ces paisibles rivages, se sont épuisées, et le moment est arrivé où ils vont devenir pour leurs hôtes bienfaisants une surcharge aussi affligeante que onéreuse. ils Croyaient du moins avec la belle saison voir arriver l'instant marqué par L'être qui seul dirige souverainement tous les èvénements, et déja la détermination de ceux résidents à Norfolk etoit bien prise de rentrer à quelque prix que ce soit sur leurs propriétes, lorsque l'embargo mis sur le Port de cette ville est venu les enchainer de nouveau sur ces bords.[1]

Sont-ils donc sans retour condamnés à y Périr de douleur et de misère: non, il leur reste encore un Espoir, et il est trop bien justifié pour ne pas y compter. L'impartialité et la Justice du très honnorable Congrés des états-unis est bien connue, ainsi que la Loyauté et la bonté de cœur de leur vertueux Président; c'est sur ces titres, aussi bien que sur la générosité éprouvée du peuple americain que les Colons de St Domingue résidents à Norfolk, se fondent pour réclamer de votre Excellence qu'elle veuille leur accorder; ou obtenir pour eux de l'honnorable Congrés des Etats-unis la faculté et les moyens de retourner a St Domingue leur patrie, avant l'expiration de L'Embargo et Sans tirer a conséquence, soit par une permission de Préter à leurs fraix un batiment qui ne se chargeroit d'aucune espèce de marchandises quelconques et n'emporteroit absolument que les passagers colons de St Domingue avec leurs effets et les seules provisions nécessaires pour leur traversée; soit plutôt en leur accordant un passage gratuit sur un batiment qui seroit expedié à cet effet aux frais des Etats Unis, ce qui seroit bien plus approprié à L'état de détresse et de denuement presque absolu où se trouvent ces Colons infortunés, et en meme tems plus digne de votre générosité et de votre bienfaisance.

tel est, Monsieur Le Président, l'objet de la petition que présentent à votre excellence les Colons de St Domingue soussignés; s'ils l'obtiennent de vous ou par votre compatissante intercession vous aurez mis le comble à leur reconnaissance, ils ne cesseront de faire des vœux pour la gloire et la prospérité des Etats-unis de L'amérique et béniront à jamais la mémoire de leur digne et vertueux Président.

Durand[2]

LS, DNA: RG 59, Miscellaneous Letters. This petition requested that GW or Congress permit the refugees at Norfolk to charter a vessel to take them to Saint Domingue before the expiration of the embargo or give them free passage on a ship sent by the United States for that purpose. It was enclosed with a letter to Edmund Randolph of this date, signed by eighteen French refugees at Norfolk, including most of the signers of the petition: "Nous avons l'honneur de vous adresser cy-joint une petition que nous vous prions d'avoir la bonté de mettre sous les yeux de son excellence le Président des Etats-unis" (DNA: RG 59, Miscellaneous Letters).

State Department clerk George Taylor, Jr., replied to the petitioners on 7 May that since the letter had arrived just as Randolph was departing for New Jersey "no definitive answer to it could be obtained from the President." He promised a further response after Randolph's return, adding, "I am apprehensive from what has hitherto been done on similar applications that the President will grant no further permissions to Vessels to depart during the continuance of the embargo" (DNA: RG 59, Domestic Letters). GW had granted a number of passports for ships to carry refugees to Saint Domingue (see Edmund Randolph to GW, 29 March, and n.2 to that document; Randolph to GW, 31 March [second letter], and n.1; Alexander Hamilton to GW, 22 April, and n.1; Hamilton to GW, 25 April [second letter], and n.1; and Hamilton to GW, 26 April, and n.1). However, on 1 May the cabinet advised that the practice be discontinued (see Hamilton to GW, 1 May, DLC:GW).

1. By a joint resolution of 26 March, Congress placed an embargo for thirty days on "all ships and vessels in the ports of the United States . . . bound to any foreign port or place." A resolution of 18 April extended the embargo until 25 May (*Stat.* 1:400–401).

2. Twenty-one additional persons signed this petition.

From Isaac Sherman

Sir,   Philadelphia 28th of April 1794.

By the advice of Mr Hamilton, I am induced to offer myself a candidate for Treasurer of the Mint; being informed that the present Treasurer intends soon to resign.[1]

I flatter myself upon experiment, that I should be found competent to the place; and should I be so happy as to obtain, I hope that my attention, fidelity and integrity would meet your entire approbation and that of the public.

I cannot but pressingly ask your attention to my request, which if granted, may be of more extensive utility than what regards myself.[2] I have the Honor to be, with the most perfect respect & Esteem, Your Most Obedt Servt

Isaac Sherman

ALS, DLC:GW.

Isaac Sherman (1753–1819) was a native of New Haven, Conn., and a veteran of the Revolutionary War, serving from 1775 until 1783. On his military career, see n.8 of GW to Jonathan Trumbull, Sr., 9–10 Oct. 1776 (*Papers, Revolutionary War Series*, 6:523). The Continental Congress appointed him an assistant surveyor for western lands in 1785 (*PCC*, 29:542).

1. On the resignation of Tristram Dalton as treasurer of the U.S. Mint, see his letter to GW of 24 April.

2. It was not Sherman but rather Nicholas Way who received the desired appointment (see GW to U.S. Senate, 19 May).

From John Vaughan

D. sir. 28. April 1794

Having mentioned to Mr Hamilton the Substance of a sentiment conveyed to me by D[r] Bancroft, He thought the communication would be agreeable to you I enclose the original & have made an extract.[1] I remain with the greatest esteem your st

Jn Vaughan

ALS, DNA: RG 59, Miscellaneous Letters.

1. Physician Edward Bancroft (1744–1821) was born in Westfield, Massachusetts. He settled in England in 1767 and in 1769 published *Remarks on the Review of the Controversy between Great Britain and her Colonies* (London), in which he defended the rights of the American colonists. During the Revolutionary War, however, he accepted payment from both sides for information. A noted chemist, specializing in the manufacture and use of dyes, he published *Experimental Researches Concerning the Philosophy of Permanent Colours* (London, 1794).

The original letter from Bancroft has not been identified. The following "Extract of a Letter from Dr Edward Bancroft. to Jn Vaughan dated 26 Feby 1794. London" appears at the top of the page, before Vaughan's note to GW. It reads: "We still flatter ourselves that no breach will take place between this country & the United States. Certainly this nation is very far from having any hostile dispositions towards yours & whatever Causes of Complaint may exist I am confident if time is allowed for discussion, & hasty rash measures avoided that all serious causes of discontent will be removed."

From Alexander Hamilton

[Philadelphia] April 29 1794

The Secretary of the Treasury presents his respects to the President of the United States & encloses the draft of a passport for a schooner called the Eliza of New York, for the President's signature. The application which accompanies it, comes from a number of French Emigrants now in New York. The Collector will be instructed to fill the blank with the name of the master which is not known.[1]

Alex. Hamilton

LB, DLC:GW.
    1. The enclosed passport and the application from the French emigrants from Saint Domingue have not been identified. Neither Hamilton's subsequent letter to John Lamb, the collector of customs at New York, nor the name of the schooner's master has been identified.

To John Jay

(Secret & confidential)
My dear Sir,   Philadelphia 29th April 1794
    Receive, I pray you, the suggestion I am going to impart with the friendship and caution the delicacy of it requires.[1]
    You are already informed that I am under the necessity of recalling Mr Gouvr. Morris from France—and you can readily conceive the difficulty which occurs in finding a successor that would be agreeable to that Nation, and who, at the same time, would meet the approbation of the friends of that Country in this.
    These considerations have induced me to ask you, if it could be mad⟨e⟩ to comport with your inclination, after you shall have finished your business as Envoy, and not before, to become the Resident Minister Plenipotentiary at London; that Mr Pinckney, by that mean⟨s⟩ might be sent to Paris?[2] I mean no more than

simply to ask the question, not intending (although the measure would remove the above difficulty) to press it in the smallest degree.

If you answer in the affirmative, be so good as to return the enclosed letter to me, and correspondent arrangements shall be made. If in the negative, I pray you to forward it, through the Penny Post or otherwise according to circumstances, to the Gentleman to whom it is directed, without delay—and in either case to let the transaction be confined entirely to ourselves.[3] With much truth & regard I am sincerely & affectionately Yours

Go: Washington

ALS, sold by Sotheby's (London), 1988, item 441; ADfS, DLC:GW; LB, DLC: GW. The text in angle brackets is from the draft.

1. On the subject of this letter, finding an appropriate replacement for Gouverneur Morris, the current U.S. minister to France, see Edmund Randolph to GW, 28 April (first letter).

2. For Jay's appointment as envoy extraordinary to Great Britain, see GW to U.S. Senate, 16 April (first letter). Thomas Pinckney was the U.S. minister to Great Britain.

3. For the enclosed letter, see GW to Robert R. Livingston, this date. For Jay's rejection of this suggestion, see his reply to GW of 30 April.

From Henry Knox

Sir,   War department April 29th 1794.

I have the honor to submit to your consideration a letter from Governor Moultrie of the 12th instant and a proposed answer thereto, intended to be sent by a Vessel sailing this day.[1]

The letter of the 2nd instant alluded to, is the letter I had the honor of reading to you yesterday and upon which I will obtain the Opinions of the heads of departments in order to be submitted to you.[2] I have the honor to be, Sir, with perfect respect, Your obedient Servant,

H. Knox

LS, DLC:GW; LB, DLC:GW.

1. The letter from South Carolina governor William Moultrie to Knox of 12 April, which has not been identified, was on the "subject of fortifying the harbor of Charleston" (*JPP*, 300). Knox's reply has not been identified.

2. Neither the letter of 2 April nor its subject matter has been identified.

To Robert R. Livingston

(Private)

Dear Sir,   Philadelphia 29th April 1794

Circumstances have rendered it expedient to recall Mr Gouvr Morris from his Mission to the Republic of France.[1]

Would it be convenient and agreeable to you to supply his place?

An affirmative answer, would induce an immediate nomination of you, for this appointment to the Senate, and the signification of your sentiments, relatively thereto, as soon as your determination is formed would oblige me; particularly as it is not expected that that body will remain much longer in Session.[2] With very great esteem & regard I am—Dear Sir Your Obedt Hble Servt

Go: Washington

ALS, NHi: Robert R. Livingston Papers; ADf[S], DNA: RG 59, Miscellaneous Letters; LB, DLC:GW. The cover is addressed to Livingston at "New York—or Clearmont." Clermont, the Livingston family estate, was situated on the east side of the Hudson River, and Clermont Manor, a New York State Historic Site, is located in Columbia County.

1. On the French government's dissatisfaction with Gouverneur Morris, see Thomas Jefferson's Report on Edmond Charles Genet and Gouverneur Morris, 11 Dec. 1793, *Jefferson Papers,* 27:504–6.

2. GW enclosed this letter in one he wrote to John Jay on this date. Livingston declined the appointment in a letter to GW of 10 May. For the nomination of James Monroe as Morris's successor, see GW to U.S. Senate, 27 May. The first session of the Third Congress ended on 9 June.

From the Magistrates of Montgomery County, Va.

April 29th 1794.

The Memorial of the undersigned Magistrates of the County of Montgomery, in the Commonwealth of Virginia, sheweth; That they conceive it essential to the existence of a Republican Government, that Elections of Representatives of the People, should be absolutely free; that if the Executive employ the force intrusted in their hands to destroy the rights of the People, or permit to be so employed, it will amount to a dissolution of the

Government; and that if any part of that force is so employed, it is evidence that such is the will of the Executive, until their disapprobation is evinced by the punishment of the offenders.

We therefore take this method to state to you a recent violation of that all important right of the People, the freedom of election; not doubting but this attempt, by a Military force, to prescribe to Freemen who they *shall* choose to represent them, will meet with the disapprobation of every department of the Federal Government.

We do therefore charge that Captain William Preston of the Troops of the United States, having command of a Company of Federal Soldiers at the Court House of Montgomery County, in the Commonwealth of Virginia, on the 18th day of March 1793, and an election being then and there held for a Representative, from the said Commonwealth of Virginia, to the Congress of the United States, did interfere in, and endeavour to influence the said election.[1]

That the said Captain Preston at the election aforesaid, insisted his Soldiers should be polled, and evinced a determination to enforce the receipt of their votes, and caused them to vote for Francis Preston, one of the Candidates at the said election.[2]

That during the time of taking the Poll, at the said Election, the said Captain Preston caused his Company of Soldiers, repeatedly to march to the Court House, and parade and manuvre before, and around the same, to the disturbance, displeasure, and terror of the Voters assembled there, and with intent to intimidate those, who were in favour of Abraham Trigg, a Candidate at the said Election.[3]

That the said Captain Preston drew up his Company of Soldiers before that door of the Court-house into which Voters usually pass'd, near to the door, and kept them there a long time; during which time they obstructed, and hindred sundry voters, who were going into the said Court-house, to give their votes for, and in favor of the said Abraham Trigg.

That while the said Captain Preston had his Company of Soldiers drawn up, as aforesaid, one of the Soldiers struck, and knocked down a Justice of the Peace, for the said County of Montgomery, in the presence, and by the approbation of him, the said Captain Preston, without any just provocation.

That the said Captain Preston permitted his Soldiers to mix

with the voters at the said Election, among whom they conducted themselves in an assuming, insolent, turbulent, and riotous manner; in which he the said Captain Preston encouraged them, by his presence and approbation.

That by approbation of him the said Captain Preston, the said Soldiers assaulted insulted, and threatned, to beat those Voters who were in favor of the said Abraham Trigg at the said election.

That during the election aforesaid, some of the said Soldiers assaulted, and abused a Magistrate of the said County, in the execution of his Office, by the approbation of the said Captain Preston.

That others of the said Soldiers, by approbation of him the said Captain Preston did place themselves before the door of the Court-house, into which Voters usually passed, at a time when the Company was not paraded there, and there used violence to prevent the Voters who were in favor of the said Abraham Trigg from going in, to give their votes.

That at some time during the continuance of the election aforesaid, the said Captain Preston placed himself in the Court-house, and caused a strong Fellow, whom he had there for the purpose, to throw out of the Court-house, such persons as rendered themselves obnoxious to him, by voting in favor of the said Abraham Trigg.

That the said Captain Preston caused some of his Soldiers to possess themselves of the door of the Court-house into which Voters usually passed, who while in possession thereof, forcibly kept out Voters, who attempted to pass into the said Court-house in order to give their votes.

That the said Captain Preston treated with contempt, the authority of a Magistrate, who ordered him to take the Soldiers, who were acting riotously, away from among the Voters.

That the said Captain Preston concerted with his Soldiers to raise an affray with the Country-men, who voted for the said Abraham Trigg.

That by the said illegal, and unwarrantable proceedings of the said Captain Preston, by preventing some, and intimidating others of the Voters, from giving their Votes for the said Abraham Trigg, he the said Captain Preston caused Francis Preston (Brother to the said Captain Preston) who was not the choice of a majority of the Electors, to be elected a Representative from the Commonwealth of Virginia, to the Congress of the United States, for the district whereof the said County of Montgomery is a part.[4]

That the said Captn Preston after the close of the Poll at the said Election, caused his Soldiers to raise a very dangerous affray with the Voters, who had given their Votes for the said Abraham Trigg, which affray he the said Captin Preston, began, encouraged, and abetted, making no endeavour to cea[se] the same, until the Soldiers were vanquished.

We rest ourselves assured, that the said Election will, by the House of Representatives, be declared void;[5] But we conceive that a Man, who by so many overt acts, hath discovered himself regardless of the rights of a free People, is unfit for a Command in their Armies.

We consider you, as Guardian of the Constitution of the United States, bound to preserve inviolate, the freedom of Election's, under that Constitution.

We consider you, as the fountain of Office, and Commander in Chief of the Army of the United States(.) responsible for those whom you have appointed, and command: and therefore we call to you, and demand, that the said Captain William Preston, for the before enumerated offences, be tryed by a Military Tribunal: We beg leave to observe, that we prefer this mode of trial, to a Civil prosecution, least the latter should only be treated with derision, and contempt, for what would give Francis Preston (Brother to the said Captain Preston) more satisfaction, than to have been elected by the influence of his Brother, and Soldiers, and to be able to justify the proceeding, by paying the amercement of a Jury, which if even considerable, would to his Estate be trifling. And your Memorialists is as in duty bound &c. &c.

> (signed) James McCorkle.
> (signed) Daniel Howe.
> (signed) James Craig.

The foregoing Memorial of the Magistrates of the County of Montgomery, is a true Copy from the Original remaining in the War-office of the United States.

April 29th 1794.   Jno. Stagg, Junr: chf clk

Copy, KyLoF.

1. Capt. William Preston of Virginia served in the U.S. Army, 1792–98. The court house for Montgomery County was in Christiansburg.

2. Francis Preston (1765–1836), brother of Capt. Preston and a 1783 graduate of William and Mary College, practiced law in Montgomery and Washington counties. He was a member of the Virginia House of Delegates, 1788–89 and 1812–14, and in the Virginia Senate, 1816–20. He served in the U.S. House of Representatives, 1793–97, after which he settled in Abingdon, Va., and resumed his law practice.

3. Abram (Abraham) Trigg (b. 1750) served in the Virginia militia during the Revolutionary War. He lived at Buchanan's Bottom, his estate on the New River, and practiced law in Montgomery County. He was a delegate to the Virginia ratification convention in 1788 and served in the U.S. House of Representatives, 1797–1809.

4. The fourth congressional district included the Virginia counties of Wythe, Greenbrier, Kanawha, Lee, Russell, Montgomery, Grayson and Washington.

5. On 17 April, the Standing Committee of Elections of the U.S. House of Representatives reported on Trigg's petition "complaining of an undue election and return." After considering evidence from other witnesses, including Francis Preston, and a lengthy discussion on 29 April, the House rejected the committee's recommendation to invalidate Preston's election (*Annals of Congress*, 3d Cong., 598–600, 607–14).

Letter not found: from William Pearce, 29 April 1794. GW wrote Pearce on 4 May that "Your letter of the 29th ulto, and the reports which were enclosed, came duly to hand."

To Edmund Randolph

Sir,   Philadelphia 29th April 1794

I have read the draught of yr letter, intended as an answer to the British Minister's reply to Mr Pinckneys Memorial, on the Instructions of the 8th of June 1793. Those of the 6th of Novr following stands unconnected with the subject.[1]

It is essential that all the cited cases should be correct; and that the general statement should be placed on incontrovertible ground; otherwise, the argument will recoil with redoubled force.

Close attention being given to these matters—and the ideas expressed without warmth or asperity, if upon a revision such should be found to have intermingled, I see no objection to the particular answer which is prepared.[2]

Go: Washington

ALS (letterpress copy), DNA: RG 59, Miscellaneous Letters; LB, DNA: RG 59, GW's Correspondence with His Secretaries of State.

1. On the draft of Randolph's letter of 1 May to British minister George Hammond, see Randolph to GW, 28 April (second letter), and notes 1 and 2.

2. For the final version of Randolph's letter, see DNA: RG 59, Domestic Letters; *ASP, Foreign Affairs,* 1:450–54.

From Edmund Randolph

[Philadelphia] April 29 1794

The Secretary of state has the honor of submitting to the President the inclosed rough draft of a letter to Mr G. Morris, *for the present only.*[1]

AL, DNA: RG 59, Miscellaneous Letters; LB, DNA: RG 59, GW's Correspondence with His Secretaries of State.

1. The enclosure was Randolph's letter of recall to Gouverneur Morris, U.S. minister to France, of this date. Neither the enclosed draft nor any final version has been identified. On Morris's receipt of this letter, see his letter to Randolph of 29 Aug. (DNA: RG 59, Despatches from U.S. Ministers to France).

From Alexander Hamilton

[Philadelphia] April 30 1794

The Secretary of the Treasury presents his respects to the President of the United States and encloses the draft of a Passport for the President's signature intended for the Ship Hope, now at Charleston, belonging to Mr Le Maigre of Philadelphia.[1] If the Passport is granted it will be transmitted to the Collector of Charleston to insert the name of the Captain, which is not known.[2]

A. Hamilton

There is an opportunity today for Charleton which mister Le Maigre is desirous of embracing.[3]

LB, DLC:GW.

1. The ship *Hope,* Capt. William Moodie, was at this time in Charleston, S.C., with a cargo of sugar, cotton, and coffee from the West Indies. By late June it had returned to Philadelphia with a cargo of rice, and by July, Philadelphia merchant Peter LeMaigre was advertising the ship for sale (*City Gazette and Daily Advertiser* [Charleston], 30 April and 31 May); *Philadelphia Gazette and Universal Daily Advertiser,* 30 June and 2 July).

2. Any letter from Hamilton to Isaac Holmes regarding this ship has not been identified.

3. The opportunity may have been the chance to send the passport to Charleston aboard the schooner *Industry,* whose anticipated sailing for Charleston on 1 May was advertised in the 25 April issue of the *Philadelphia Gazette and Universal Daily Advertiser.*

From Alexander Hamilton

Sir,   Treasy Departt April 30. 1794.

Inclosed I have the honor to send you the translation of a letter from Mr Fauchet, of the 21st instant.[1]

The arrangements of the Treasury have been taken so as to correspond with the epochs of promised payment. But I entertain no doubt that I can facilitate an arrangement between the Bank & Mr Fauchet which will accomplish in substance the object of his letter.[2] I did not think it proper, however, to take any definitive step without previously placing the subject under the eye of the President.

The Minister is desirous of securing an additional sum for satisfying two drafts of his predecessor, which he specifies. It will be within the compass of our means to perform this also. But it is not within the limit heretofore prescribed and it includes besides considerations which are proper only for the decision of the President.[3] With perfect respect &c.

                                    Alexandr Hamilton

LB, DLC:GW.

1. The enclosed translation of Jean-Antoine-Joseph Fauchet's letter to Hamilton of 21 April has not been identified. For the French version, see *Hamilton Papers,* 16:303–4. The French minister requested Hamilton to arrange the payment of 2.5 million livres due France according to an enclosed schedule that would coincide with the dates when Fauchet needed the money to meet his expenses. The schedule proposed a payment of $70,000 on 15 May and additional payments of between $30,000 and $38,000 on the first and fifteenth of each month until 1 Nov. (FrPMAE: Correspondance Politique, Etats-Unis, Supplement Volume 20). On the previous arrangement to pay this money on 3 Sept. and 5 Nov., see Cabinet Opinion, 11 March, and n.2 to that document, and Hamilton to GW, 18 March.

2. In his reply to Fauchet of 5 May, Hamilton suggested that the minister could obtain his desired "anticipation of the payments" through the Bank of the United States (*Hamilton Papers,* 16:377–78).

3. Fauchet asked for additional funds to pay for two debts incurred by

his predecessor, Edmond Genet, for $20,000 and $50,270. On the previous refusal of the Treasury Department to honor Genet's drafts, see Hamilton to GW, 4 January. For GW's approval of making the payments to Fauchet, see his letter to Hamilton of 2 May.

From John Jay

Dear Sir   New York 30 April 1794

I was this day honored with your's of yesterday. There is nothing I more ardently wish for than Retirement, and Liesure to attend to my Books and papers: but parental Duties not permitting it, I must acquiesce, & thank God for the many Blessings I enjoy. If the Judiciary was on its proper Footing, there is no public Station that I should prefer to the one in which you have placed me—it accords with my Turn of Mind, my Education & my Habits.[1]

I expect to sail in the Course of a Fortnight, and if my Prayers & Endeavours avail, my absence will not be of long Duration.[2]

The Gentleman to whom your Letter is addressed, is not in Town—To obviate Delay and accidents, I sent it to his Brother, who will doubtless forward it immediately, either by a direct Conveyance or by the Post.[3]

From the Confidence you repose in me I derive the most pleasing Emotions, and I thank you for them. Life is uncertain. whether I take your Letter with me or leave it here, it would in Case of my Death be inspected by others, who however virtuous, might be indiscreet. After much Reflection, I conclude it will be most prudent to commit it to you; without retaining any Copy or Memorandum except in my Memory, where the numerous proofs of your kind Attention to me are carefully preserved. with perfect Respect Esteem & Attachment I am Dear Sir Your oblidged and affectte Servt

John Jay

ALS, DLC:GW; ADf, Jay Papers.
    1. In his letter of 29 April, GW offered Jay, the chief justice of the Supreme Court, the position of U.S. minister plenipotentiary to Great Britain. John Jay and his wife, Sarah Van Brugh Livingston (1756–1802), had five children who survived infancy: Peter Augustus (1776–1843), Maria (1782–1856), Ann ("Nancy"; 1783–1856), William (1789–1858), and Sarah Louisa (1792–1818).
    2. On Jay's departure on 12 May for Great Britain, where he was to serve

as envoy extraordinary, see n.2 of Edmund Randolph's first letter to GW of 19 April.

3. GW's letter to Robert R. Livingston of 29 April may have been forwarded to his brother Edward Livingston (1764–1836), who at this time was an attorney in New York City. He represented New York State in the U.S. House of Representatives, 1795–1801, and was mayor of New York City, 1801–3, before moving to New Orleans in 1804. He represented Louisiana in the House of Representatives, 1823–29, and in the Senate, 1829–31, was Andrew Jackson's secretary of state, 1831–33, and served as U.S. minister to France, 1833–35.

From Henry Knox

Sir,   War Department. April 30th 1794

I have the honor to submit to your consideration a letter from the Governor of Georgia, and a Copy of a letter from me to which this is an answer.[1] I have the honor to be with perfect respect Your obedient servant

H. Knox

LS, DLC:GW; LB,DLC:GW

1. Knox probably enclosed the letter from Georgia Governor George Mathews to him of 1 April (G-Ar: Governors Letterbooks). Mathews acknowledged Knox's letters of 22 Feb. and 6 March and responded: "It is with astonishment, I am informed that the President of the United States entertains an Opinion, that more men are kept in service in this State, than what is necessary for the Protection of the frontiers, and states the number on duty to be from one thousand to twelve hundred. I cannot with precission ascertain what the numbers are, but am well assured they cannot exceed one half of what is suggested by you. and am confident any deminution of those in service will endanger the Safety of the state. for, whatever may be advanced to the Contrary, the Indians still continue their hostilities; and only a few weeks sence killed two Spies, and carried of[f] Horses to a considerable amount, thus Situated, in an almost constant state of Warfare I cannot refrain from remarking the injustice that appears to be, in denying the State of Georgia the protection of the general Government, whilst she so largely Contributes to its support."

Mathews enclosed a copy of his letter to Knox of 19 Feb., laying out his plan for the defense of Georgia's frontier (see G-Ar: Governors Letterbooks). He called this to "the particular attention of the President" with "a Confidence that he will on taking a serious review of the situation of our extended frontier, be of opinion with me, that the hundred Horse and foot in addition to the Federal troops (which does not exceed one hundred and thirty two privates, Seventy two of which will be discharged between this and the first of

July) will be inadequate to protection, and that nothing short of my requisitions can give security to the Settlers."

Matthews also discussed a problem with the pay of Georgia militia and explained the retention of prisoners taken from the town of the Creek chief White Lieutenant (on the latter, see Knox to GW, 13 Dec. 1793).

GW approved the draft of Knox's reply and returned it to Knox (*JPP*, 301). The draft has not been identified.

From John Leamy

Philadelphia April 30th 1794.

The Memorial of John Leamy, merchant and Citizen of the United States respectfully sheweth

That the said John Leamy has Property to the Amount of Sixty thousand Dollars now lying at the Havana, ariseing from shipments made from this Port, & only waiting proper conveyances to bring it hither, but that no Vessells are expected from that Port by which his said Property may be remitted to him.

That if the United States be forced into a War while so much of his Property remains out of his reach, your Memorialist's total ruin must be the inevitable consequence.

That he has a ship now lying in this Port, the Mary, Henry Stephens Master, burthen Two Hundred & nine Tons, which he wishes leave to send to Ballast to the Havana for the sole purpose of bringing home his said Property.[1]

Your Memorialist therefore prays that you will be pleased to take the foregoing circumstances into consideration & to grant him Permission to send out his said Vessell for the purpose aforesaid under such restrictions as you shall think proper to direct and your memorialist as in duty bound will for ever pray.[2]

John Leamy

ALS, DNA: RG 59, Petitions for Pardon.

1. According to the congressional resolve of 26 March, an embargo was placed on "all ships and vessels in the ports of the United States . . . bound to any foreign port" (*Stat.* 1:400). Leamy, therefore, could not send the *Mary* to Havana, Cuba, to retrieve his property.

2. GW forwarded this memorial to Edmund Randolph, who then wrote Alexander Hamilton and Henry Knox for their opinions (*Hamilton Papers,* 16:370).

From Nathaniel Skinner

Sir.   Boston 30th April 1794

I had this honor, while at Cadiz, informing your Excellency relative to the Algerines.[1] at last happily I am arrivd at my usual residence⟨,⟩ escaped from those pirates & feel tho it has been attended with a very heavy loss of property happy in being on that land of liberty oer which you preside.

The injury I suffer'd by being disposess'd of a freight of goods I had in the ship I own'd was great⟨,⟩ taken out without consent or recompense. this from Spaniards I did not feel so much, as they bear Americans little affection—But when on application to Wm Carmichael Esqr. at Madrid, to solicit for a permission (every day granted to the English) to reship some India goods I had with me for Gibralter, being originally destined for that market: I could not even hear from him after waiting two months I was more injur'd than by the Spaniards⟨,⟩ being finally obliged to run the risk of much property & what I held more dear the liberty of twelve persons. & I am not the only instance. there was another vessell situated as mine—& there are two more⟨,⟩ Ships Greenway & Rooksby ⟨*illegible*⟩d by the Spaniards that they do not chuse to adjudicate being now nine months in possession. months elapsed after their memorials were sent to Mr C. without a reply—& it is a well known thing each solicitation to him is treated with neglect.[2]

I do not attempt to injure Mr C. in the dark. I wrote to him that I should give notice of his conduct Even the British Consul at Cadiz, agent for us all ⟨four⟩ wrote pointing out the difficu[l]ties we suffer'd, but not a reply. No Consul then at Cadiz from America to aid in the large Commercial affairs of that place.[3]

Permit me to observe from the violent struggles in Morrocco for the Empire. there ports are all shut, which added to the effect the WISE measures adapted in this country will produce by & by the wish'd for Effect The ports of Sicilly are also Shut.[4] When I left that Quarter provisions of all kinds were very scarce.

Will your Excellency pardon me for suggesting a hint. A public character will be wanting at Morrocco as soon as the present dispute is settled[.] their freindship will cost little & should there be a navy to secure access to such a commanding port as Tangier—just in the straits mouth.[5]

The wife & several concubines of the hereditary candidate were drove to sea—put into St Michaels in distress were releiv'd & furnishd with an American vessell there by the American consul. & it has made a pleasing & grateful impression on the Moors.[6]

In the quarter of the world where I have been American property has sustaind much injury.

Unused to court or public life Your Excellency will pardon my direct address if improper. the apology a love for the country tempted me first to write from Spain. I am with the highest sentiments of respect with the warmest wishes for your every happiness with daily prayers that you may long continue to guide & direct us Your Excellencys Most Obedient Most Humble Servt

Nathl Skinner

ALS, DNA: RG 59, Miscellaneous Letters. The docket reads, "recd 14 May."

1. Skinner's letters to GW of 8 and 8–15 Oct. 1793, which he wrote at Cadiz, Spain, reported on the threat to American shipping from the Algerines and the detention of American vessels by Spanish authorities, including his own and the *Greenway* and *Rooksby*, mentioned below. For a list of American vessels detained at Spanish ports in October 1793, see "Ship News," *Dunlap and Claypoole's American Daily Advertiser* (Philadelphia), 20 Dec. 1793.

2. According to one newspaper report, as of 17 Nov. 1793, the *Rooksby, Greenway,* and a large number of other American vessels, "all lately arrived," were detained in Cadiz "and ordered to ride quarantine" because of the yellow fever epidemic in Philadelphia during the late summer and fall of 1793 (*Independent Gazetteer* [Philadelphia], 15 Feb. 1794). Another account reported that the *Rooksby, Greenway,* and five other American vessels departed Cadiz in November "with a Spanish 74, a frigate and a small convoy for the Havanna," Cuba. This report came from the captain of one of the vessels in this convoy (*Dunlap's American Daily Advertiser* [Philadelphia], 30 Jan.). For GW's own frustration with U.S. commissioner William Carmichael, see GW to Thomas Jefferson, 23 Aug. 1792.

3. James Duff was the British consul at Cadiz. Joseph Yznardi, Jr., was the designated American consul for Cadiz, but he did not arrive there until after Skinner's departure (GW to the U.S. Senate, 19 Feb. 1793, and Skinner to GW, 8 Oct. 1793, and n.1 to that document).

4. Skinner probably is referring to the thirty-day embargo of 26 March that was imposed on ships in U.S. ports and subsequently extended to 25 May (*Stat.* 1:400–401).

5. In 1796, James Simpson became the first U.S. consul assigned to Morocco (*U.S. Senate Executive Journal,* 1:209). The Strait of Gibraltar connects the Atlantic Ocean to the Mediterranean Sea and separates Spain from Morocco.

6. São Miguel, in the Atlantic Ocean, is the largest island in the Azores

and is 740 miles west of Cape Roca, Portugal. John D. Street was the U.S. vice-consul for the Azores (GW to U.S. Senate, 2 Aug. 1790).

To Bushrod Washington

Dear Bushrod   Philadelphia April 30th 1794.

Your letter of the 22d instt came to my hands yesterday afternoon. I thank you for the information contained in it, and for your kindness in offering to draw my answer to Henshaws Bill, now in the high Court of Chancery; before whom it seems, I am to appear.[1]

It is really hard that I am so often called before Courts in matters in which I have no interest; but am continually saddled with the expence of defence.

To the interrogatories of the Bill, I answer, from my best recollection, having no papers by me to resort to.

That John Tayloe, George Mason and myself were appointed Attornies by George Mercer & others, in England, to whom he had mortgaged his estate in Virginia, or part thereof, with directions to sell the same.[2]

That John Tayloe and myself accepted the trust—but Mason declined doing it.

That a dispute with respect to the priority of the Mortgage under which we were to sell, and one given by the former attorney of George Mercer in Virgina ensued—was carried into the high Court of Chancery in that State—and an Interlocutory decree obtained.

That pursuant to the said decretal order, Tayloe & myself (or rather myself alone for I had the whole trouble of it) sold the Mortgaged estate in November 1774, and to the best of my recollection, on the terms and in the manner set forth in the Bill. The money, when received to be subject to the future order of the Court.

That in the Month of May following, I attended the Congress which sat in Philadelphia; In June of the same year was appointed to the Command of the American Army, then assembled at Cambridge; and remained with it, in its different movements, for several years, before I returned to Virginia.

That finding, about the time the Bonds had become due,

there was no prospect of my returning to Virginia in any short time, or having it in my power to render any further service in discharge of the trust which had been committed to us. I informed Tayloe thereof; requested him to place the Bonds in the hands of a proper person to collect; and to take the whole matter upon himself; for, as I was unable to render any further assistance, I should no longer consider myself responsible for any thing which might happen thereafter.

Thus stood the matter about the period when the Bonds became due. After the death of Tayloe, & my continually refusing any agency in the business, further than to report what had been done by myself; and which no other was competent to, in a legal sense, It was, by a decree of the high Court of Chancery, in Virginia, put into the hands of John Francis Mercer, for purposes mentioned therein; & by him were the Bonds put into suit thereafter.

That Henshaw may have become a purchaser at the Sale in 1774 on the terms, and to the amount set forth in the Bill, is highly probable. But I have no recollection of his ever having made a tender of payment to me at Cambridge, or of the conversation which he has stated; and conceive, if application had been made to me for the purpose mentioned, he would have recd an answer to the effect I have here mentioned.

If I am not mistaken the Bill of Henshaw, which you have now sent, or one similar to it; has been before me once or twice already; & my answer obtained through Mr Jno. Mercer, to whom when served with the summons, I sent it; & by whom it was drawn.[3] I pray you if it be practicable in time, to enquire into the matter—There must be neglect somewhere if it is not to be produced. With much truth I am your sincere friend and Affectionate Uncle.

Go: Washington

ALS (letterpress copy), ViMtvL; LB, DLC:GW.

1. Besides his letter of 22 April, in which the bill of complaint was contained, Bushrod Washington also mentioned this suit by John Henshaw in a letter to GW of 27 April.

2. On George Mercer's assignment of power of attorney to GW, George Mason, and John Tayloe, the 1774 sale of Mercer's lands in Virginia, subsequent problems resulting from this sale, and the eventual assignment in 1782 of responsibility for the estate to Mercer's half-brother, John Francis Mercer, see GW's statement concerning George Mercer's estate, 1 Feb. 1789,

and Tobias Lear to John Rutherfurd, 18 April 1792. See also State of Money Collected by Lund Washington on Bonds Payable to the Honble John Tayloe Esqr. and George Washington Esqr. taken on the Sales of Colo. George Mercers Estate (Lund Washington's Account Book, 1761–85, MdAN).

3. On previous mention of Henshaw's complaint and GW's earlier receipt of this summons, see GW to John Francis Mercer of 23 July 1792 and 26 Oct. 1793, and Mercer's reply of 30 Nov. 1793.

From the Saint Domingue Refugees of Wilmington, Del.

[April 1794]

To The President of the United States, the Petition of Sundry Persons late of the Island of St Domingo, now residing at Wilmington in the Delaware State respectfully sheweth

That on the fourth day of October last, when Cape Francois was abandoned finally to the revolted Negroes, more than two hundred wretched French Inhabitants, of which number are your Petitioners, embarked for Wilmington in Delaware, where they arrived during the Month of November.

That after having escaped from the conflagration of the Cape, & the pillage of their slaves, they fell into the Hands of the Providence Privateers,[1] by whom they were entirely stript of the slender remains of their Fortunes.

That, being informed of the noble & generous resolution of Congress to grant fifteen thousand dollars for the relief of the wretched fugitives from St Domingo, the disposal of which sum they have confided to your Wisdom & Humanity,[2] We the Subscribers, being equally destitute with others, who have taken refuge on this Continent, beg leave, & most earnestly sollicit to be considered as proper objects of the publick Bounty.[3] Signed

La Bigne tans pour ma Seure Laurant que pour
mais deux neuveux Et mes deux niece
⟨Vve S⟩aurÿ
Madame Dulue et Ses Deux fille
Veve desCoin Bellair Et trois Enfants Et Sophie Pothiey
veuve Gué et huit enfan
DeLouville et sa fille
Ve. Baqué et ses deux fille
Borie pour son Epouse et Son fille

Ve. Souchay
Ve. Albre⟨pris⟩
Veve garés
Mad[am]e ⟨robin⟩ et son marÿe et sais sinque enfans
Couray
houard Desrochers
Mernier
Prion
Gervaize
Lehuédé et Son Epouse[4]
Marilouise et ces deux enfan⟨ts⟩
Nanons et ces quatre enf⟨ants⟩
Sophie et un anfant
adelaide et quatre enfan⟨ts⟩
Modeste et sa sœur
Reine et deux enfans
Sannitte et une enfan
jusethine et trois yinffant
Laurette & Ces deux Enfants
Marthonnc

LS, DNA: RG 59, Miscellaneous Letters. Filed with this petition at the end of 1794 is a certification signed by Charles Henry Wharton, Nicholas Way, George Bush, John Dickinson, and Gunning Bedford: "We whose names are underwritten have every reason to believe that the several Subscribers to the foregoing Petition are destitute of the means of present Subsistance, and are suffering accordingly." There are also three lists of "the French now destitute in Wilmington"—one in English and two in French. The English list tallies 53 "Whites" and 30 "Mulattos" or "Persons of Colour," and one French list agrees; the other French list records 54 whites and 30 mulattos. One of the French documents also gives the age of each individual. The lists consist mostly of the signatories and their families.

1. The petitioners were referring to British privateers sailing out of New Providence Island in the Bahamas.

2. The petitioners were referring to "An Act providing for the relief of such of the inhabitants of Saint Domingo, resident within the United States, as may be found in want of support," 12 Feb. (*Stat.* 6:13).

3. On 1 May, Secretary of State Edmund Randolph wrote to William Hemphill of Wilmington, who was supervising the distribution of relief money in Delaware, that "Mr John Dickinson and some other Gentlemen of your town have represented to the President of the United States, that there are many of the unfortunate inhabitants of St Domingo, now in great distress in Wilmington. Be so good as to inform me, whether they come within the description of the law. If any of them wish to return to that island, and they

can procure vessels without expense to the United States . . . passports will be furnished for them. I shall also give into the first safe hand going from hence an hundred dollars, for supplying of necessaries. You will oblige me by saying, whether a larger sum may be necessary for this object" (DNA: RG 59, Domestic Letters).

4. The remaining signatures were placed in a second column and belong, according to the lists of refugees, to persons of color.

Index